Vital Records of
Tamworth
and
Albany
New Hampshire

1887-2003

Richard P. Roberts

HERITAGE BOOKS
2006

HERITAGE BOOKS
AN IMPRINT OF HERITAGE BOOKS, INC.

Books, CDs, and more—Worldwide

For our listing of thousands of titles see our website
at
www.HeritageBooks.com

Published 2006 by
HERITAGE BOOKS, INC.
Publishing Division
65 East Main Street
Westminster, Maryland 21157-5026

Copyright © 2005 Richard P. Roberts

All rights reserved. No part of this book may be reproduced or transmitted in any form or by any means, electronic or mechanical, including photocopying, recording or by any information storage and retrieval system without written permission from the author, except for the inclusion of brief quotations in a review.

International Standard Book Number: 978-0-7884-3172-2

TABLE OF CONTENTS

Introduction 1

Tamworth Births 5

Tamworth Marriages 117

Tamworth Deaths 305

Albany Births 433

Albany Marriages 455

Albany Deaths 487

INTRODUCTION

Early vital records of many New Hampshire towns can be located either through the State's Vital Records Department or on microfilms made available through LDS Family History Centers. Some, however, have been lost or are inaccessible for various reasons. A valuable, but labor intensive, source of information for events occurring in 1887 and thereafter is the vital statistics which are provided in a section of the Annual Town Reports of many New Hampshire towns. Many of these town reports have been collected at the New Hampshire State Library in Concord, as well as more local repositories.

The amount of information published in these Annual Town Reports varies tremendously over time. Early records are far more detailed and comprehensive. Recent records are rather cursory, but issues of confidentiality and sensitivity to the privacy of those residents still living offsets the lack of information of genealogical value.

While the information provided is often very helpful, one must remember that it is not fool-proof or universally accurate, nor is it the primary source or the actual vital record itself. The fact that much of the data is self-reported suggests that it is reliable. However, errors in transcription, spelling (particularly with respect to French-Canadian and European families), and printing often are obvious. In addition, there may be, for example, two children listed as the third child of a particular couple, or the mother's maiden name, age or place of birth differs or is inconsistent from one entry to another. It is also important to note that a birth, marriage or death may have been reported in another town although the subject resided in Tamworth or Albany, or the entry may not have been made in the first place.

Despite these shortcomings, the information contained in the Annual Town Reports can be a valuable tool for the genealogist. Marriage and death records from the late 1800's often identify parents who were married nearly a century before. Finally, those families that have remained in Tamworth, Albany or adjacent towns for several generations can be traced and connected to the present.

Births - To the extent the information is available, the entries in the list of births are given as follows: child's name; date of birth; place of birth (where provided); the number of children in the family; father's name, place of birth, age and occupation; and the mother's maiden name, age and place of birth. As noted above, the amount of information in earlier records is substantially greater than in more recent years.

At times, the given names of many children are missing from the early reports. In this case, the sex of the child is given and they are listed chronologically at the beginning of the surname heading. On occasion, the child's name can be determined from marriage or death records, as well as secondary sources. These names are shown in brackets where available.

Marriages - To the extent the information is available, the entries in the list of marriages follow this format: groom's name; groom's residence; bride's name; brides residence; date of marriage; place of marriage (where provided); H, signifying husband's information, and W, signifying wife's information, each in the following order - age, occupation, number of the marriage (if other than first), father's name, father's place of birth, father's occupation, mother's name, mother's place of birth, and mother's occupation. The name of the official conducting the marriage has been omitted but is generally provided in the original document. A separate listing of brides in alphabetical order follows this section in order to allow for cross-referencing.

Deaths - To the extent available, the entries in the list of deaths contain the following information: name of decedent; place of death; date of death; age at death; cause of death; marital status; birthplace; father's name; father's place of birth; mother's name; and mother's place of birth. Most of the entries listing a cause of death are self-explanatory.

Missing Years - There are several years prior to 1893 during which Albany failed to publish the vital statistics as part of the annual report. In addition, the quality and completeness of the information in some years is questionable and, as always, an original source should be consulted.

543243.1(HS-FP)

TAMWORTH BIRTHS

ABBOTT,
stillborn son, b. 1/6/1911; fourth; Herbert E. Abbott (laborer, Sandwich) and Alice M. Gilman (Tamworth)
child, b. 11/5/1926; Herman Abbott and Edith Brown
George, b. 10/22/1945; sixth; Harry A. Abbott and Lois A. Copp
Maurice Garland, b. 10/17/1923; first; William D. Abbott (Jackson) and Alta C. Nickerson (Tamworth)
Ralph H., b. 1/19/1906; first; Herbert E. Abbott (laborer, Sandwich) and Alice M. Gilman (Tamworth)
Wanda L., b. 6/12/1950; first; Harry A. Abbott and Louise L. Hall

ACCARDI,
Lydia, b. 7/23/1996 in Rochester; Anthony R. Accardi and Marlene M. Pons

ADJUTANT,
Ruth Evelyn, b. 3/12/1920 in Tamworth; first; Roscoe Adjutant (farmer, Tuftonboro) and Blanche Perkins (Tamworth)

AILING,
Amelia, b. 9/12/1891; first; David F. Ailing (farmer, Barrington) and Sarah Govyons (Ireland)

AKER,
Marcia G., b. 10/7/1938; first; Welton G. Aker and Charlotte Hammond

ALAVOSIUS,
Sofia Estelle, b. 2/22/1991 in N. Conway; Mark P. Alavosius and Deborah Langevin

ALDRICH,
Wendy L., b. 2/19/1952; third; Lendal W. Aldrich and Eleanor L. Ellis

ALDRIDGE,
Linda Lee, b. 10/8/1941; first; Lendal W. Aldridge and Eleanor L. Ellis

ALWARD,
Crosby Bob, b. 8/18/1987 in Wolfeboro; David A. Alward and Deborah L. Buck

AMARAL,
Kyle Gregory, b. 9/3/1992 in N. Conway; Gregory Amaral and Kathryn A. Fogg

AMES,
daughter, b. 7/19/1902; first; John Ames (laborer, Tamworth) and Hattie D. Ames (Tamworth)
daughter, b. 12/29/1915 in Tamworth; fifth; John Ames (farmer, 36, Tamworth) and Harriet D. Ames (Tamworth)
child, b. 2/10/1929; Claud P. Ames and Ella Palmer
Allison Bailey, b. 6/27/1992 in Wolfeboro; Derek J. Ames and Karen M. LaRochelle
Angela Nannette, b. 3/18/1981 in N. Conway; Robin Ames and Joyce Blackler
Blanche Madeline, b. 9/9/1899 in Tamworth; Zimrie E. Ames and Ella J. Palmer (1963)
Bonnie Mae, b. 6/1/1953; first; Charles E. Ames and Evalena L. Nudd
Brian Joseph, b. 3/18/1965 in Laconia; seventh; Robert Joseph Ames and Beverly Ann Williams
Carle, b. 3/2/1923; seventh; Claude P. Ames (Tamworth) and Blanche E. Jeffers (Tamworth)
Carlotta D., b. 7/8/1941; Percy E. Ames and Beatrice Dalphond
Caroline, b. 4/18/1925; Claud Ames and Blanche Jeffers
Carollyn, b. 12/12/1959; third; Robert J. Ames and Beverly A. Williams
Carroll, b. 4/18/1925; Claud Ames and Blanche Jeffers
Casey Arron, b. 5/11/1993 in N. Conway; John P. Ames and Carrie A. Murphy
Charles E., Jr., b. 10/1/1958; second; Charles E. Ames and Elizabeth D. Nudd
Charles Ernest, b. 3/5/1932; Claud M. Ames and Emma Grace
Cindy Lee, b. 5/23/1962 in Laconia; fifth; Robert Joseph Ames and Beverly Ann Williams
Claude Milton, b. 9/14/1911; second; Claude P. Ames (laborer, Tamworth) and Blanche E. Jeffers (Tamworth)
Cory John Winfield, b. 6/7/1986 in Laconia; John P. Ames and Colleen Swan
Daniel M., b. 3/21/1980 in Wolfeboro; Robin Ames and Joyce Blackler
David C., b. 10/10/1956; second; Carl W. Tripp and Eleanor M.

Bickford
Debra A., b. 12/24/1956; first; Robert J. Ames and Beverly A. Williams (1957)
Derek W., b. 4/20/1980 in Laconia; Charles Ames, Jr. and Jeanne Warner
Dorothy E., b. 11/14/1902; seventh; Zimri Ames (farmer, Tamworth) and Ella J. Palmer (Sandwich)
Edith M., b. 7/14/1957; second; Ralph R. Ames and Ferne F. Hodge
Elizabeth J., b. 1/21/1958; second; Robert J. Ames and Beverly A. Williams
Elizabeth Marion, b. 11/19/1994 in N. Conway; Roy M. Ames, Jr. and Kathleen P. Foley
Ernest Edgar, b. 10/17/1909; first; Claude P. Ames (laborer, Tamworth) and Blanche E. Jeffers (Tamworth)
Esther Geraldine, b. 8/4/1926; Claud Ames and Blanche Jeffers
Ethel Irene, b. 3/10/1932; Claud Ames and Blanche Jeffers
Evan Ronald, b. 9/27/1990 in N. Conway; Ronald G. Ames and Cynthia L. Frye
Evelyn Audrey, b. 9/25/1930; Claude Ames and Blanche Jeffers
Gary Lee, b. 5/29/1970 in Laconia; Charles Ernest Ames and Evalena Lorraine Nudd
Gladys Marion, b. 8/15/1936; James P. Ames and Ada E. Eldridge
Hazel Georgiana, b. 11/7/1912; third; Claude Ames (laborer, Tamworth) and Blanche Jeffers (Warner)
Helen Abbie, b. 10/28/1915 in Tamworth; fourth; Claude P. Ames (teamster, 24, Tamworth) and Emmeline Jeffers (Tamworth)
Irene May, b. 12/20/1937; Claude M. Ames and Emma I. Grace
James R., b. 3/29/1905; second; John Ames (laborer, Tamworth) and Hattie Ames (Tamworth)
James Wesley, b. 3/3/1932; James R. Ames and Ada E. Eldridge
Jane Dolaries, b. 7/8/1930; James R. Ames and Ada E. Eldridge
John Philip, b. 4/12/1963 in Laconia; third; Charles Ernest Ames and Evalena Lorraine Nudd
Kaylee Nichole, b. 11/19/1992 in Laconia; Gary L. Ames and Nicole L. Hutchins
Luella C., b. 1/18/1908; third; John Ames (laborer, Tamworth) and Hattie D. Ames (Tamworth)
Maude Gillian, b. 5/1/1913; fourth; John Ames (farmer, Tamworth) and Harriet D. Ames (Tamworth)
Michael Scott, b. 10/30/1976 in Wolfeboro; Charles E. Ames, Jr. and Jeanne M. Warner

Perce Edward, b. 4/27/1918; fifth; Claud P. Ames (teamster, Tamworth) and Blanche E. Jeffers (Tamworth)
Peter E., b. 4/29/1954; first; Philip E. Ames and Helen C. Moulton
Philip Edward, b. 6/25/1934; C. Milton Ames and Emma Grace
Ralph Joseph, b. 10/23/1920 in Tamworth; Claud P. Ames (farm laborer, Tamworth) and Blanche E. Jeffers (Tamworth)
Richard Wayne, b. 6/20/1943; third; James R. Ames and Ada E. Eldridge
Robert C., b. 5/12/1961; fourth; Robert J. Ames and Beverly A. Williams
Robert Chester, b. 10/22/1936; Claude Milton Ames and Emma I. Grace
Ronald Gordon, b. 1/3/1934; James R. Ames and Ada Eldridge
Roy Milton, b. 9/5/1930; Claude Milton Ames and Emma I. Grace
Sarah Emily, b. 3/3/1992 in N. Conway; Roy M. Ames, Jr. and Kathleen P. Foley
Scott Allan, b. 4/4/1967 in Laconia; Charles Ernest Ames and Evalena Lorraine Nudd
Sherry M., b. 9/26/1954; first; Ralph R. Ames and Ferne F. Hodge
Susan M., b. 10/17/1951; second; Donald W. Ames and Reta M. Welch
Theresanne, b. 3/3/1965 in Laconia; second; Richard Wayne Ames and Barbara Marie Bushway
Valarie Jean, b. 10/9/1963; sixth; Robert Joseph Ames and Beverly Ann Williams

ANDERSON,
Everett G., b. 4/24/1908; second; H. S. Anderson (farmer, Tamworth) and Teresa Kelley (Boston, MA)
Matthew James, b. 8/24/1998 in Laconia; Brent A. Anderson and Kimberly A. Grimaldi

ANTHONY,
Amanda Heather, b. 6/11/1991 in N. Conway; Michael B. Anthony and Peggy A. Plummer
Angela May, b. 3/13/1970 in N. Conway; David Malcolm Anthony and Donna Lee Stewart
Bruce G., b. 9/15/1949; tenth; Arnold G. Anthony and Ruth F. Berry
Carol A., b. 3/11/1961; second; David A. Anthony and Arleen G. Harmon
Chester E., b. 3/14/1947; eighth; Arnold G. Anthony and Ruth F.

Berry
David A., b. 7/18/1939; fourth; Arnold G. Anthony and Ruth F. Berry
David Clyde, b. 3/16/1962 in N. Conway; third; David Arnold
  Anthony and Arleen Gertrude Harmon
David Malcolm, II, b. 11/18/1973 in N. Conway; David Malcolm
  Anthony and Donna Lee Stewart
Deborah A., b. 3/9/1960; first; David A. Anthony and Arlene G.
  Harmon
Donna L., b. 8/21/1949; sixth; Minard J. Anthony and Adelaide E.
  Ward
Elva E., b. 8/6/1944; seventh; Arnold G. Anthony and Ruth F. Berry
Erika Lynn, b. 3/14/1972 in N. Conway; David Malcolm Anthony and
  Donna Lee Stewart
Gladys R., b. 4/12/1938; third; Arnold Anthony and Ruth Berry
Hallie Lynn, b. 4/28/2000 in N. Conway; Michael Anthony and
  Jacqueline Anthony
Harry E., b. 3/12/1941; fifth; Arnold G. Anthony and Ruby F. Berry
Janeca Lucilla, b. 11/--/1934; Arnold G. Anthony and Ruth F. Berry
Jason Earle, b. 10/18/1968 in Laconia; Chester Earle Anthony and
  Judith W. Weare
Jennifer Jeanne, b. 6/16/1969 in N. Conway; Harry Edward Anthony
  and Joyce Carolyn Bradley
Richard A., b. 4/20/1953; fourth; William J. Anthony and Ethel M.
  Emerson
Robert Walter, b. 10/9/1963; fourth; David Arnold Anthony and
  Arleen Gertrude Harmon
Robin Elizabeth, b. 6/11/1977 in Laconia; Bruce G. Anthony and
  Brenda E. Knox
Shirley Ellen, b. 12/15/1942; sixth; Arnold G. Anthony and Ruth F.
  Berry
Stanley E., b. 6/19/1948; ninth; Arnold G. Anthony and Ruth F. Berry
Virginia J., b. 3/27/1949; third; William J. Anthony and Ethel M.
  Emerson
Warren Gilbert, b. 6/30/1936; Arnold G. Anthony and Ruth B. Berry
Wendy Elizabeth, b. 11/1/1974 in Laconia; Bruce Gordon Anthony
  and Brenda Elizabeth Knox
William J., Jr., b. 10/5/19156; fifth; William J. Anthony, Sr. and Ethel
  M. Emerson

ARMSTRONG,
Janice, b. 10/2/1944; fourth; John C. Armstrong and Lucille

MacDonald

ASPENWALL,
Charles Everett, b. 2/4/1926; William Aspenwall and Ethel Henderson

ASPINALL,
Charles S., b. 11/29/1953; first; Charles E. Aspinall and Jean A. Myers
Gregory J., b. 7/13/1955; second; Charles E. Aspinall and Jean A. Myers

ASPINWALL,
George Wallace, b. 12/22/1927; William Aspinwall and Ethel Henderson

ATWOOD,
Pamela J., b. 9/14/1951; first; Hubert L. Atwood and Priscilla N. Starey
Teresa Arlena, b. 8/1/1929; Gerald W. Atwood and Virginia A. Moody

AUSTIN,
Charles R., Jr., b. 7/25/1961; first; Charles R. Austin and Cheryl A. Dicey
Penney Marie, b. 2/16/1966 in Laconia; Charles Richard Austin and Cheryl Ann Dicey
Russell Allen, b. 1/10/1964 in Laconia; first; Charles Richard Austin and Cheryl Ann Dicey

BAKER,
Hazel L., b. 2/15/1952; first; Wallace H. Baker and Lorraine Bean
Jassmyn Lair, b. 1/10/2001 in Wolfeboro; Christopher Baker and Samantha Baker

BANFILL,
child, b. 4/18/1928; Benjamin B. Banfill and Lillian Allard
child, b. 5/28/1931; Benjamin D. Banfill and Lillian L. Allard
child, b. 4/23/1935; Herman Banfill and Elva Thompson
Benjamin Dale, b. 3/5/1973 in Laconia; Carroll Benjamin Banfill and Lois Carol Roberts

Carroll B., b. 11/8/1934; Benjamin Banfill and Lillian Allard
Daniel Charles, b. 1/14/1969 in Laconia; Carroll Benjamin Banfill and Lois Carol Roberts
Linda Marie, b. 8/30/1975 in Laconia; Carroll Benjamin Banfill and Lois Carol Roberts

BARTLETT,
daughter, b. 3/23/1891; third; Elroy G. Bartlett (millman, Moultonboro) and Imogene Evans (Moultonboro)
son, b. 11/9/1909; third; Leland C. Bartlett (manufacturer, Moultonboro) and Adelaide M. Mason (Tamworth)
son, b. 11/12/1914; fourth; Leland C. Bartlett (rake mfr., 32, Moultonboro) and Adelaide Mason (35, Tamworth)
Kimberly F., b. 6/2/1959; second; Robert C. Bartlett and Tobia Goodson
Lorenzo W., b. 3/28/1893; fourth; Elroy G. Bartlett (manufacturer, Meredith) and Imogene A. Evans (Moultonboro)
Marion M., b. 10/28/1908; second; Leland C. Bartlett (manufacturer, Moultonboro) and Adeline Mason (Tamworth)
Nellie M., b. 1/28/1907; first; L. C. Bartlett (manufacturer, Moultonboro) and A. M. Mason (Tamworth)
Robert E., b. 6/8/1938; first; Edson O. Bartlett and Nathalie H. Lord

BATES,
Mikayla Marie, b. 11/10/1998 in N. Conway; Joseph R. Bates and Laurie A. Thurston

BEAN,
child, b. 9/22/1923; third; Otis Bean (Charlestown, MA) and Elsie Brown (Tamworth)

BEATTIE,
Leanne Catherine, b. 10/30/1997 in New London; Scott Wayne Beattie and Patricia Ann McDermott

BECKWITH,
Stephanie Jean, b. 10/3/1972 in Laconia; George Frederic Beckwith and Ruth Inez Stokes

BEECHER,
Juliana Greenleaf, b. 5/22/1990 in N. Conway; Edward B. Beecher

and Christine A. Clyne

BEHR,
Ann, b. 2/16/1951; second; Charles E. Behr and Joan Kennedy
Brian Alexander, b. 3/8/1994 in N. Conway; Karl R. Behr and Sue E.
　Greb
Caitlin, b. 10/1/1986 in N. Conway; Karl Behr and Sue Greb
Edward A., b. 3/20/1953; third; Charles E. Behr and Joan Kennedy
Hillary, b. 3/8/1985 in N. Conway; Karl Behr and Sue Greb
Karl R., b. 10/21/1955; fourth; Charles E. Behr and Joan Kennedy
Robert L., b. 8/7/1961; fifth; Charles E. Behr and Joan Kennedy

BELCHER,
Andrew Whitely, b. 5/26/1982 in N. Conway; William Belcher and
　Shery Quint
Bradley Steves, b. 9/5/1984 in N. Conway; William Belcher and
　Sherry Quint

BELL,
Christopher James, b. 11/7/1990 in N. Conway; Mitchell S. Bell and
　Dodie A. Bolduc

BENNETT,
Benjamin Andrew, b. 1/21/1963 in N. Conway; fifth; James Willis
　Bennett and Patricia Elaine Hurd
Deni Rebecca, b. 5/9/1989 in N. Conway; Dennis W. Bennett and
　Lisa J. Sanborn
Erica Elizabeth, b. 7/15/1991 in N. Conway; Dennis H. Bennett and
　Lisa J. Sanborn
Kenneth J., b. 5/27/1955; first; James J. Bennett and Marie A.
　Hackett
William Michael, b. 4/11/1992 in N. Conway; Kenneth J. Bennett and
　Lisamarie Walker

BERGEN,
Cameron Francis, b. 4/1/1974 in Laconia; Dominic Nelson Bergen
　and Jeanne Louise English
Jason Paul, b. 11/13/1978 in Wolfeboro; Dominic Bergen and
　Jeanne English
Matthew James, b. 5/29/1983 in Wolfeboro; Dominic N. Bergen and
　Jeanne L. English

BERGERON,
Jesse James, b. 2/17/1983 in Hanover; Ronald C. Bergeron and Deborah Jean Burke

BERGEY,
Alicia S., b. 8/6/1955; first; Glenn A. Bergey and Patricia A. Selers
Stephen M., b. 2/4/1957; second; Glenn A. Bergey and Patricia A. Sellers

BERGSTROM,
Eric Michael, b. 3/9/1986 in N. Conway; Peter W. Bergstrom and Susan M. Remick
Kayla Lucille, b. 10/10/1987 in N. Conway; Peter W. Bergstrom and Susan M. Remick

BERRIER,
Wyatt Elias, b. 12/11/1992 in Plymouth; Thaddeus B. Berrier and Amy K. Berrier

BERRY,
son, b. 2/17/1891; seventh; Orrin S. Berry (farmer, Tamworth) and Lizzie M. Davis (Naples)
son, b. 2/17/1891; eighth; Orrin S. Berry (farmer, Tamworth) and Lizzie M. Davis (Naples)
daughter, b. 8/6/1896 in Tamworth; tenth; Orrin S. Berry (50, Tamworth) and Lizzie M. Davis (45)
son, b. 9/19/1907; fourth; Walter Berry (laborer, Tamworth) and G. Clough (Tamworth)
child, b. 12/2/1940; second; Ronald F. Berry and Eleanor A. Condon
Anita Anne, b. 7/12/1942; first; Howard E. Berry and Dorothea L. Moore
Audrey Grace, b. 4/14/1942; third; Ronald F. Berry and Eleanor A. Condon
Cynthia A., b. 1/29/1958; second; Ronald E. Berry and Norma P. Harmon
Edith Elizabeth, b. 10/14/1915 in Tamworth; seventh; Walter H. Berry (laborer, 42, Tamworth) and Grace L. Clough (Tamworth)
Edward R., b. 1/2/1957; first; Ronald E. Berry and Norma P. Harmon
Gladys, b. 5/24/1902; first; Walter H. Berry (laborer, Tamworth) and Grace L. Clough (Tamworth)
Judy M., b. 1/14/1951; first; Raymond A. Berry and Charlotte E.

Palmer
Lawrence, b. 5/25/1905; second; Walter H. Berry (laborer,
  Tamworth) and Grace Clough (Tamworth)
Madeline, b. 9/14/1903; second; Walter Berry (laborer, Tamworth)
  and Grace Clough (Tamworth)
Pauline E., b. 3/28/1938; first; Robert K. Berry and Edith M. Gilman
Raymond Elliott, b. 12/6/1909; fifth; Walter H. Berry (laborer,
  Tamworth) and Grace Clough (Tamworth)
Richard Gordon, b. 10/12/1918; sixth; Harry B. Berry (carpenter,
  Tamworth) and Elva Hope Murphy (Boston, MA)
Ronald Edward, b. 7/22/1930; Ronald Frank Berry and Elena A.
  Condon
Ruth Frances, b. 12/17/1915 in Tamworth; fifth; Harry B. Berry
  (carpenter, 36, Tamworth) and Elva Hope Murphy (Boston, MA)
Wayne Ellsworth, b. 11/29/1943; second; Howard E. Berry and
  Dorothea L. Moore

BICKFORD,
daughter, b. 3/31/1892; first; Wilber Bickford (farmer, Tamworth) and
  Sarah A. Bickford (Sandwich)
son, b. 2/28/1899; first; Fred J. Bickford (farmer, Tamworth) and
  Charlena Walker (Haleston, MA)
daughter, b. 10/25/1903; third; Frederick Bickford (farmer,
  Tamworth) and Charlina M. Walker (Holliston, MA)
son, b. 1/20/1913; sixth; Frederick J. Bickford (farmer, Tamworth)
  and Charlena M. Walker (Holliston, MA)
son, b. 6/16/1915 in Tamworth; first; Albert Bickford (farmer, 34,
  Conway) and Evelyn Moore (Tamworth)
Beatrice A., b. 5/31/1913; first; Beulah M. Bickford (Tamworth)
Carolyn Jennifer, b. 9/9/1973 in Wolfeboro; Carroll Frank Bickford
  and JoAnn Pearson
Carroll Simon, b. 4/19/1916; third; Wilbur J. Bickford (farmer,
  Tamworth) and Francis Hobbs (Boston, MA)
Charles, b. 8/2/1899; first; William Bickford (butcher, Albany) and
  Edith Parker (Boston)
Charles Frederick, b. 8/26/1909; fifth; Fred J. Bickford (farmer,
  Tamworth) and Charlina M. Walker (Holliston, MA)
Frank Wilbur, b. 2/4/1911; first; Wilbur J. Bickford (farmer,
  Tamworth) and Frances Hobbs (Boston, MA)
Janet L., b. 6/28/1952; second; Fred M. Bickford and Ingrid E.
  Engles

Joanna Karen, b. 6/20/1969 in Laconia; Fred Marsena Bickford and
    Ingrid Emma Ingles
Margaret L., b. 4/22/1906; fourth; Fred J. Bickford (farmer,
    Tamworth) and Charlina M. Walker (Holliston, MA)
Paul P., b. 9/9/1906; third; William Bickford (butcher, Albany) and
    Edith G. Parker (Boston, MA)
Roland Ernest, b. 7/19/1913; second; Wilbur J. Bickford (farmer,
    Tamworth) and Frances P. Hobbs (Boston, MA)
Sylvia M., b. 10/7/1905; second; John F. Bickford (laborer,
    Tamworth) and Mary Carrie Fifield (Sandwich)
Vera M., b. 2/26/1901; second; Fred J. Bickford (farmer, Tamworth)
    and Charlma Walker (Holliston, MA)
William Simon, b. 7/15/1909; third; John F. Bickford (laborer,
    Tamworth) and Mary C. Fifield (Sandwich)

BILLADON,
Leon A., b. 9/25/1894 in Tamworth; fifth; Leon Billadon (laborer, 28,
    Halifax, NS) and Harriet LaMontaign (27, Halifax, NS)

BIRMINGHAM,
Geoffrey Paul, b. 11/15/1990 in Wolfeboro; Paul J. Birmingham, Jr.
    and Judi L. Wilkinson

BIRTH,
Kasey Catherine, b. 12/7/1999 in N. Conway; Scott Birth and Diane
    Kistler-Birth

BLACK,
Beverly M., b. 1/12/1944; first; Richard J. Black and Ethel M. Elliott

BLACKEY,
Carrie G., b. 12/27/1901; first; Frank H. Blackey (laborer, Sandwich)
    and Gertrude Henderson (Tamworth)
Edwin A., b. 8/14/1904; second; Frank A. Blackey (laborer,
    Sandwich) and Gertrude Henderson (Tamworth)
Edwin Arthur, b. 10/19/1927; Edwin Blackey and Flora Whipple
Elizabeth E. L., b. 6/9/1942; second; Lloyd J. Blackey and Agnes
    Johnson
Frank Ellsworth, b. 8/21/1932; Edwin A. Blackey and Flora Whipple
Wilbur Emery, b. 5/31/1936; Edwin Arthur Blackey and Flora E.
    Whipple

BLACKIE,
Bernice Irene, b. 6/16/1909; first; John Blackie (laborer, Moultonboro) and Katharine Whiting (Tamworth); residence - Moultonboro

BLAISDELL,
son, b. 1/26/1890; second; Frank E. Blaisdell (farmer, Tamworth) and Annie Trepania (Clarenceville, Canada)

BLANCHARD,
Wayne Philip, Jr., b. 1/17/1985 in N. Conway; Wayne Blanchard and Beverly Commoss

BLEAKNEY,
Richard David, b. 11/8/1987 in Laconia; Richard R. Bleakney and Catharine A. Bray

BLISS,
Christiana Rose, b. 2/23/1992 in N. Conway; Derek Bliss and Christine Ann Fanaras
Derek Rudolph, b. 1/24/1995 in N. Conway; Derek Bliss and Christine Ann Fanaras
Myraih Rose, b. 2/23/1992 in N. Conway; Derek Bliss and Christine Ann Fanaras
Susan, b. 7/17/1947; first; Raymond W. Bliss and Mary K. Donovan

BOEWE,
Cassandra Lynn, b. 2/14/1989 in N. Conway; James L. Boewe and Brenda J. Eldridge
Ryan Thomas, b. 3/19/1987 in N. Conway; Ward A. Boewe and Gail A. Farrell

BONICA,
Andrew Joseph, b. 4/16/1992 in Lebanon; Dana R. Bonica and Laurie Shirley
Jennie Elizabeth, b. 9/19/1986 in Wolfeboro; Dana Bonica and Laurie Shirley

BOOKHOLDZ,
Marion E., b. 12/25/1893; second; Jacob Bookholdz (laborer, Baden, Germany) and Emma J. Caverly (Moultonboro)

BOOKHOLTZ,
Harold J., b. 1/27/1897; fifth; Jacob Bookholtz (laborer, Baden, Germany) and Emma J. Caverly (Tamworth)
Walter, b. 8/17/1900; seventh; Jacob Bookholtz (laborer, Baden, Germany) and Emma J. Caverly (Moultonboro)

BOOKHOLZ,
son, b. 11/15/1916; first; Leon W. Bookholz (laborer, Tamworth) and Ethel M. Sprague (Effingham)
Emma P., b. 8/17/1906; seventh; Jacob Bookholz (laborer, Braden, Germany) and Emma J. Caverly (Moultonboro)
Frances Pere, b. 2/17/1921 in Tamworth; first; Edward V. Bookholz (chauffeur, Tamworth) and Ellen Pere Whiting (Tamworth)
Teresa Louise, b. 6/19/1922; second; Edward V. Bookholz (Tamworth) and Ellen Pere Whiting (Tamworth)
Virginia Marie, b. 6/3/1923; third; Edward Bookholz (Tamworth) and Ellen Whiting (Tamworth)

BOOSKA,
Benjamin Emery, b. 5/29/1989 in Rochester; Paul M. Booska and Heather Pearson
Justin Seth, b. 12/21/1990 in Rochester; Paul M. Booska and Heather Pearson

BOOTHBY,
Autumn Ruth, b. 9/8/2001 in Lebanon; James Boothby and Heidi Boothby
Catherine D., b. 7/2/1954; third; James E. Boothby and Lois A. Foote
Edward J., b. 5/7/1957; fourth; James E. Boothby and Lois A. Foote
Gerald L., b. 5/29/1947; second; James E. Boothby and Lois A. Foote
John Allen, b. 9/14/1926; John Boothby and Mildred Rickards
Larry D., b. 8/7/1952; first; Lawrence D. Boothby and Frances E. Hobbs

BOTTING,
Lindsey Erwin, b. 7/30/1982 in Laconia; Calvin Botting and Sharon Locke
Mackenzie Laura Parlin, b. 10/3/1989 in Laconia; Calvin E. Botting and Sharon Locke

BOUCHER,
Lori Ellen, b. 1/26/1962 in N. Conway; fourth; Ernest John Boucher and Constance Margaret LeBlanc

BOUTIN,
Teresa Annette, b. 3/8/1963 in N. Conway; fifth; Harold Raymond Boutin and Marie Althea Hackett

BOWLES,
child, b. 1/26/1935; Roland R. Bowles and Lillian F. Walker
Bruce, b. 3/30/1937; Roland R. Bowles and Lillian F. Walker
James Carl, b. 2/6/1963 in Concord; second; David Arnold Bowles and Elizabeth May French
Kimberly Marie, b. 5/23/2000 in Laconia; James Bowles and Diane Bowles
Marsha Jean, b. 3/13/1970 in Laconia; David Arnold Bowles and Elizabeth May French
Michael Allen, b. 8/6/1998 in Laconia; James C. Bowles and Diane L. Kelsey

BOYD,
son, b. 11/6/1900; third; James L. Boyd (farmer, NB) and Elma R. Hill (PA)
Catherine E., b. 10/29/1895 in Tamworth; first; James W. Boyd (laborer, 28, NB) and Rose Hill (30, Tamworth)
Lutie, b. 9/5/1905; fifth; James T. Boyd (farmer, St. John, NB) and Elma R. Hill (Huntington, PA)
Mary Lillian, b. 11/2/1902; fourth; James T. Boyd (laborer, NB) and Alma Rose Hill (PA)

BOYLE,
Joshua James, b. 5/30/1982 in N. Conway; Michael Boyle, Sr. and Leona Dickinson
Michael H., Jr., b. 10/17/1980 in N. Conway; Michael Boyle and Leona Dickenson

BRACONNIER,
Jennifer Marie, b. 10/12/1989 in N. Conway; Richard H. Braconnier and Susan E. Serewicz

BRADBURY,
Thomas E., b. 9/23/1898; fourth; Ed. E. Bradbury (millman, Tamworth) and Mary A. Webster (Sandwich)

BRADY,
Mackenzie Marie, b. 1/7/2001 in Rochester; Philip Brady and Karrie Brady
Stephen Walter, b. 10/22/1998 in Rochester; Philip P. Brady and Karrie L. Smith

BRANDE,
Dorothea, b. 8/13/1949; first; Justin Brande and Susan Kennedy

BRENNAN,
David Ryan, b. 2/27/1987 in Wolfeboro; Charles A. Brennan and Lisa A. Elliott
Joshua, b. 5/25/2001 in N. Conway; Robert Brennan and Patricia Brennan
Michael Paul, b. 9/5/1984 in N. Conway; Charles Brennan and Lisa Elliott

BRETT,
Deborah J., b. 1/13/1949; fourth; Stanley L. Brett and Victoria L. Mason
Janice, b. 2/16/1943; second; Stanley L. Brett and Victoria L. Mason
Kenneth Arthur, b. 4/9/1917; first; Manley E. Brett (chauffeur, Otisfield, ME) and Helen H. Cole (Wolfeboro)
Patricia A., b. 12/1/1944; third; Stanley L. Brett and Victoria L. Mason
Stanley Larence, b. 9/1/1921 in Tamworth; second; Manley E. Brett (auto mechanic, Otisfield, ME) and Helen H. Cole (Tuftonboro)
Wayne, b. 4/16/1941; first; Stanley L. Brett and Victoria L. Mason

BROCKHOLTZ,
Sadie Louise, b. 7/1/1903; sixth; Jacob Brockholtz (laborer, Germany) and Emma J. Caverly (Moultonboro)

BROOKHOLZ,
Roland Earl, b. 9/21/1919; second; Leon W. Brookholz (Tamworth) and Esther May Sprague (Effingham)

BROOKS,
Donald M., b. 5/8/1958; sixth; Ambrose W. Brooks and Alice V. Smith

BROTHERS,
Cynthia L., b. 7/13/1950; second; Elmer W. Brothers and Esther G. Ames
Jamie Erin, b. 10/14/1979 in N. Conway; Jeffrey Brothers and Joyce Mondeau
Jared Aaron, b. 12/14/1983 in N. Conway; Jeffery A. Brothers and Joyce Elaine Mondeau
Kevin W., b. 11/4/1951; third; Elmer W. Brothers and Esther G. Ames
Samuel Alex, b. 8/19/1993 in Moultonborough; Michael B. Brothers and Margaret E. Weare
Seth Aaron, b. 8/14/1989 in Laconia; Michael B. Brothers and Margaret E. Weare
Skyla May, b. 4/26/1991 in Moultonborough; Michael B. Brothers and Margaret Weare
Stanley N., b. 9/2/1953; fifth; Elmer W. Brothers and Esther G. Ames
Stephen J., b. 9/2/1953; fourth; Elmer W. Brothers and Esther G. Ames
Susy Elizabeth, b. 1/4/1987 in Laconia; Michael B. Brothers and Margaret E. Weare

BROWN,
child, b. 12/26/1927; Carroll G. Brown and Eunice E. Whiting
Benjamin Pierce, b. 8/10/1989 in N. Conway; Timothy L. Brown and Kathi Susan Thompson
Charles W., Jr., b. 5/4/1950; seventh; Charles W. Brown and Doris L. Whiting
Charlotte Marie, b. 6/9/1926; Charles Brown and Doris Brown
Effie J., b. 1/5/1906; second; Alphonzo D. Brown (farmer, Albany) and Minnie E. Kenerson (Tamworth)
Ella Roberta, b. 2/19/1948; third; Robert W. Brown and Virginia E. Humphries
Elsie Ida, b. 8/8/1902; first; Alphonso Brown (farmer, Albany) and Minnie E. Keniston (Tamworth) (1905)
Helen Carolyn, b. 8/5/1923; first; Charles Brown (Ipswich, MA) and Doris Whiting (Tamworth)
Ida Evelyn, b. 7/12/1919; first; Charles W. Brown (Ipswich, MA) and

Evelyn Whiting (Tamworth)
Jennifer Lee, b. 12/29/1974 in N. Conway; Dennis Stanley Brown and Jan Ruth Thibodeau
Joshua Blake, b. 10/12/1990 in N. Conway; Timothy L. Brown and Kathi S. Thompson
Lucas James, b. 9/18/1995 in N. Conway; Timothy L. Brown and Kathi Susan Thompson
Priscilla May, b. 5/4/1931; Charles W. Brown and Doris Whiting
Robert William, b. 4/5/1910; third; Alphonso Brown (farmer, Albany) and Minnie E. Kenerson (Tamworth)
Shirley A., b. 9/26/1928; Charles W. Brown and Doris Whiting
Steven E., b. 7/25/1948; first; Robert E. Brown and Corinne S. Hersey

BRYANT,
stillborn son, b. 3/26/1890; second; George H. Bryant (millman, Tamworth) and Marion E. Sanford (Natick, MA)
Charles S., b. 9/1/1894 in Tamworth; second; John M. Bryant (machinist, 44, Tamworth) and Etta C. Carr (38, Effingham)

BRYER,
Ivan H., b. 12/25/1898; second; James T. Bryer (farmer, NB) and Elma R. Hill (PA)

BUCK,
Robbie John, b. 1/28/1997 in N. Conway; Robin Lee Buck and Johnna Lee Jordan

BUCKHOLY,
Frederick, b. 12/7/1891; first; Jacob Buckholy (laborer, Baden, Germany) and Emma J. Caverly (Moultonboro)

BUNKER,
daughter, b. 5/29/1889; sixth; Levi Bunker (farmer, Tamworth) and Hattie L. Webber (Hamilton, MA)
daughter, b. 7/29/1896 in Tamworth; seventh; Levi Bunker (49, Tamworth) and Hattie L. Webber (38, Hamilton, MA)
child, b. 1/17/1923; fourth; Frederick Bunker (Tamworth) and Elsie Davis (Tamworth)
Everett, b. 6/4/1903; first; Fred W. Bunker (laborer, Tamworth) and Elsie M. Davis (Tamworth)

Frank E., b. 12/6/1904; second; Fred W. Bunker (laborer, Tamworth) and Elsie Davis (Tamworth)
Richard Almond, b. 9/4/1917; third; Frederick Bunker (laborer, Tamworth) and Elsie M. Davis (Tamworth)

BURKE,
Alysha Brandi, b. 8/21/1989 in Wolfeboro; Kenneth T. Burke and Tammy S. Hammond
Eliza Grafton, b. 10/22/1995 in N. Conway; Geoffrey B. Burke and Andrea Greene
Leah Frances, b. 12/1/1992 in N. Conway; Geoffrey B. Burke and Andrea Greene

BUSHEY,
Charles E., b. 9/10/1947; second; Clarence J. Bushey and Audrey A. Parker

BUZZUTTO,
Evelyn Angelina, b. 10/17/1942; first; Nicholas D. Buzzutto and Ethel E. Young
Michael, b. 1/18/1945; first; Nicholas Buzzutto and Ethel E. Young

CABELL,
Hanna Grace, b. 9/15/1977 in Laconia; William D. Cabel and Susan M. Ackley
William Benjamin, b. 9/2/1986 in Laconia; William Cabell and Susan Ackley

CAMERON,
Jason Michial, b. 10/3/1985 in N. Conway; Brian Cameron and Lyn Williams

CANFIELD,
Adam Lysander, b. 12/30/1999 in N. Conway; Christian Canfield and Kelly Canfield
Gregory Lloyd, b. 8/28/1991 in N. Conway; Richard J. Canfield and Maryanne Iverson
Hannah Marie, b. 3/14/1988 in Tamworth; Brian E. Canfield and Candace A. Laing
Kimberly Lisa, b. 12/24/1973 in N. Conway; Richard Jesse Canfield and Maryanne Iverson

Melissa Lynne, b. 6/17/1981 in N. Conway; Richard Canfield, Jr. and Maryanne Iverson
Molly Juniper, b. 1/25/2000 in Lebanon; Christopher Canfield and Juniper Lamb
Willa Juniper, b. 1/25/2000 in Lebanon; Christopher Canfield and Juniper Lamb

CAPEN,
Robert E., Jr., b. 8/17/1948; third; Robert E. Capen and Marion L. Corbette

CARGILL,
Jordan Leigh, b. 9/25/1993 in N. Conway; Kenneth R. Cargill and Susannah Halpern

CARLETON,
Heather L., b. 11/25/1980 in N. Conway; Paul Carleton and Carla Particelli

CARLIN,
Jeffrey Alan, b. 8/10/1995 in Wolfeboro; James J. Carlin, Jr. and Susan Marie Libby

CARR,
Alice D., b. 9/30/1940; first; Robert T. Carr and Audrey F. Purdy
Arthur Warren, b. 8/25/1943; second; Robert T. Carr and Audrey F. Purdy
Patricia Ann, b. 6/17/1947; first; Charles M. Carr and Sylvia M. Chase

CARTER,
Heather Marie, b. 9/8/1983 in Laconia; Gordon W. Carter and Edith May Ames
Robert W., b. 4/14/1946; first; Robert W. Carter and Mary B. Welch
Sandra M., b. 7/15/1952; second; Robert W. Carter and Mary B. Welch
Sara May, b. 4/11/1978 in Laconia; Gordon Carter and Edith Ames

CASEY,
Eamon John, b. 10/5/1992 in N. Conway; John F. Casey and June Anderson

Lillian Delia, b. 2/8/1991 in N. Conway; John F. Casey and June Anderson

CATALANO,
Timothy Michael, b. 11/28/1990 in Tamworth; Bart Catalano and Kathryn Swan

CHABOT,
Joshua Paul, b. 1/1/1982 in Ware, MA; Jon Chabot and Patricia Maziarz

CHAMBERLAIN,
son, b. 4/16/1917; first; Ralph N. Chamberlain (farmer) and Florence B. Goodwin (Tamworth)
Elizabeth Idella, b. 11/2/1910; third; Charles Chamberlain (farmer, Wolfeboro) and Cora E. Hayford (Tamworth)
Margaret Julia, b. 11/13/1919; first; Milford W. Chamberlain (Boston, MA) and Lulu M. Lyman (Madison)
Raymond, b. 5/18/1900; second; C. W. Chamberlain (farmer, Wolfeboro) and Cora Hayford (Tamworth)
Sarah A., b. 2/7/1907; second; M. Chamberlain (draftsman, Boston, MA) and S. A. Edgerly (Ossipee)

CHANDLER,
son, b. 9/25/1900; first; Henry Chandler (farmer, Albany) and Winnifred Chick (Ossipee)
Inez, b. 9/2/1902; second; Henry M. Chandler (laborer, Albany) and Winnifred M. Chick (Ossipee)

CHASE,
son, b. 6/13/1889; first; Wilber F. Chase (salesman, Standish, ME) and Annie A. Patch (W. Newfield, ME); residence - Wolfeboro
son, b. 3/27/1893 in Tamworth; first; Augustus Chase (laborer, 24, Albany) and Annie D. Hobbs (23, Ossipee)
Annie M., b. 7/11/1908; third; A. A. Chase (laborer, Albany) and Ida E. Davis (Tamworth)
Bernice Louise, b. 7/10/1930; Flora E. Chase
Brian K., b. 9/9/1954; third; Preston N. Chase and Theresa A. Mason
Clifford Aquila, b. 9/14/1911; fifth; Augustus A. Chase (laborer, Albany) and Ida E. Davis (Tamworth)

Dean Elliott, b. 8/12/1941; first; Charles S. Chase and Abigail Elliott
Dewey R., b. 8/22/1898; first; Augustus Chase (laborer, Albany) and Alice Barnes (Hiram, ME)
Douglas Ande, b. 5/6/1953; second; Preston N. Chase and Teresa A. Mason
Earl A., b. 9/7/1906; second; Augustus A. Chase (laborer, Albany) and Ida E. Davis (Tamworth)
Flora, b. 1/15/1910; fourth; Augustus A. Chase (teamster, Albany) and Ida E. Davis (Tamworth)
Irene C., b. 7/3/1928; Flora Chase
Michelle Lynn, b. 12/10/1972 in Laconia; Kenneth Wayne Chase and Esther Susie Douglas
Silvia May, b. 5/10/1914; sixth; Augustus A. Chase (laborer, 45, Albany) and Ida E. Davis (35, Tamworth)
Vincent Forrest, b. 8/30/1965 in Laconia; second; Richard Preston Chase and Carol Jean Woodward
William H., b. 4/13/1901; first; Augustus Chase (laborer, Albany) and Ida E. Davis (Tamworth)

CHATTIN,
Rebecca Elizabeth, b. 2/28/1985 in N. Conway; William Chattin and Frances Stanley

CHENEY,
Gene Raymond, b. 7/6/1943; third; Albert M. Cheney and Elinor L. Lord

CHICK,
Carrie May, b. 6/22/1890; fourth; Charles F. Chick (ins. agent, Limington, ME) and Elvira L. Durrell (Tamworth)
Donna L., b. 7/13/1946; first; Robert M. Chick and Ruth E. Vittum

CHILD,
daughter, b. 4/11/1887; sixth; Herbert W. Child (farmer, Watertown, MA) and Hugaste A. (Tamworth)
Christopher Riddoch, b. 4/15/1968 in N. Conway; Robert Leslie Child and Floris Elizabeth Wright
David Livingstone, b. 4/8/1967 in N. Conway; Robert Leslie Child and Floris Elizabeth Wright
Douglas Colby, b. 4/15/1968 in N. Conway; Robert Leslie Child and Floris Elizabeth Wright

CHIPMAN,
Jessica Ann, b. 8/14/1985 in S. Tamworth; Peter Chipman and Lisa Perkins
Larissa June, b. 8/14/1985 in S. Tamworth; Peter Chipman and Lisa Perkins

CHUTE,
Christopher B., b. 6/6/1984 in Wolfeboro; Melvin Chute and Linda Krebs

CLAPP,
Priscilla, b. 10/25/1925; William Clapp and Eunice Hidden
Richard Irving, b. 5/20/1922; first; William Clapp (Lynn, MA) and Eunice Hidden (Tamworth)

CLARK[E],
Amy G., b. 8/28/1901; second; George E. Clark (farmer, Tamworth) and Hattie B. Dow (Tamworth)
Celia M., b. 3/9/1899; first; Edwin Clark (farmer, Tamworth) and Harriet Dow (Tamworth)
Earl J., b. 4/16/1904; first; A. Johnson Clark (blacksmith, PEI) and Flora M. Bunker (Tamworth)
Marion L., b. 11/23/1906; third; Edwin G. Clarke (farmer, Tamworth) and Hattie B. Dow (Tamworth)

CLEVELAND,
Aaron Maxwell, b. 1/2/1984 in Laconia; George Cleveland and Barbara Sauer
Jessie Ruth, b. 7/16/1987 in N. Conway; George M. Cleveland and Barbara C. Sauer

CLIFFORD,
Emma Nellie, b. 11/14/1909; second; Ernest L. Clifford (painter, Meredith) and Lenora B. Arling (Tamworth)
Roland E., b. 8/19/1911; third; Ernest L. Clifford (painter, Meredith) and Lenora B. Arling (Tamworth)

CLOUGH,
son, b. 6/28/1890; ninth; Herbert S. Clough (millman, Tamworth) and Hattie E. Mason (Tamworth)
daughter, b. 9/12/1892; fifth; Herbert S. Clough (laborer, Tamworth)

and Hattie B. Mason (Tamworth)
son, b. 2/17/1896 in Tamworth; fifth; Herbert S. Clough (40, Tamworth) and Harriet B. Mason (36, Tamworth)
child, b. 2/12/1898; seventh; Herbert Clough (farmer, Tamworth) and Hattie B. Mason (Tamworth)
Devon Lynne, b. 2/16/1991 in N. Conway; James R. Clough and Lynne Blackburn
Ida Louise, b. 9/24/1928; Edwin E. Clough and Louise D. Kimball
Jennie, b. 12/6/1891; first; Ira A. Clough (millman, Tamworth) and Mary A. Delaney (Salem, MA)
Lydia May, b. 4/21/1888; second; Herbert S. Clough (mechanic, Tamworth) and Hattie B. Clough (Tamworth)

COE,
David Marshall, b. 12/15/1936; Marshall Everett Coe and Grace E. Hough

COLE,
Florence Marion, b. 2/20/1911; fifth; Irving C. Cole (blacksmith, Somerville, MA) and Evelyn M. Wiggin (Tuftonboro)

CONLON,
Maria Theresa, b. 7/4/1998 in N. Conway; James V. Conlon and Caroline Cram

CONNER,
Kevin Michael, b. 8/6/1991 in Laconia; David R. Conner and Janet D. Streeter
Scott Charles, b. 11/12/1993 in Laconia; David R. Conner and Janet D. Streeter

COOK,
daughter, b. 11/8/1888; first; Clinton F. Cook (stage driver, Tamworth) and Lucy A. Cook (Hardwick, VT)
Colby Troy, b. 6/5/2003 in Laconia; Daniel Cook and Linda Cook
Cynthia M., b. 3/17/1958; fourth; John P. Cook and Patricia Forristall
Daniel Mark, b. 3/18/1962 in N. Conway; sixth; John Otis Cook and Patricia Forristall
Daniel Mark, Jr., b. 11/4/1988 in Laconia; Daniel M. Cook and Linda J. Hanson
Dylan Garret, b. 3/23/1994 in Laconia; Daniel M. Cook and Linda J.

Hanson
Isabel A. E., b. 2/17/1978 in N. Conway; Harold Cook and Alexandra Janiszyn
Lisa A., b. 12/19/1960; fifth; John O. Cook and Patricia Forristall
Timothy Edward, b. 12/22/1967 in N. Conway; Glenn Richard Cook and Joanne Harriet Welch
Vera E., b. 6/29/1961; third; Glen R. Cook and Joan H. Welch
Victoria M. R., b. 12/3/1982 in N. Conway; Harold Cook and Alexandra Janisyzn
Vincent P., b. 4/16/1955; third; John O. Cook and Patricia Forristall
William Howard, b. 2/23/1913; first; William H. Cook (foreman, Plymouth) and Mary L. Clough (Tamworth)
William Michael, b. 4/8/1977 in Hanover; Vincent P. Cook and Kathleen M. Ulitz
William R., Jr., b. 3/13/1956; first; William R. Cook and Betty A. Phelps

COOPERDOCK,
Sol Curtin, b. 6/23/1988 in Tamworth; Peter Cooperdock and Constance M. Curtin
Sydra Curtin, b. 1/30/1986 in Tamworth; Peter Cooperdock and Constance Marie Curtin

COPE,
Edwin, b. 11/11/1900; second; Charles Cope (farmer, England) and Annie Marston (Tamworth)

COSSETTE,
Abbigail Jean, b. 7/24/2000 in N. Conway; Thomas Cossette and Amanda Cossette

COTTRELL,
Miranda Leigh, b. 11/7/1997 in Wolfeboro; Robert C. Cottrell and Debra Jean Anderson

COUGHLAN,
Patricia Ann, b. 11/14/1978 in N. Conway; Arthur Coughlan, Jr. and Patricia Durkin

COVEY,
William U., b. 1/12/1955; fourth; Uradel P. Covey, Jr. and Charlotte

M. Brown

COVILLE,
Andrea M., b. 9/9/1958; first; Stanley B. Coville and Nancy Read
Edward R., b. 8/5/1960; second; Stanley B. Coville and Nancy Reed

COX,
Tristan Jeffrey, b. 4/1/2001 in Laconia; Allen Cox and Melissa Cox

COYLE,
Carolyn A., b. 10/8/1980 in Laconia; Joseph Coyle and Karen Lee

CRABTREE,
Jula May, b. 3/19/1914; second; Hollis E. Crabtree (laborer, 48, Franklin) and Alice V. Moody (19, Ossipee)

CRAFT,
Randy Noble, b. 12/18/1985 in Laconia; Robert Craft and Beth Eastman

CREPS,
Erik Joseph, b. 12/17/1978 in Wolfeboro; Lee Creps and Janet Wenant
Laurie Jo, b. 11/20/1963 in N. Conway; second; Joseph William Creps and Annice Lee Neal
Scott Joseph, b. 9/6/1964 in N. Conway; Joseph Creps and Annice Garland
Tyler Jamison, b. 10/16/1988 in Wolfeboro; Lee Creps and Janet L. Wenant
Zachary Allan, b. 12/24/1981 in Wolfeboro; Lee Creps and Janet Wenant

CROMLY,
daughter, b. 12/3/1892; third; Alexander Cromly (waiter, P. Medway, NS) and Bertha Abbott (Salem, MA); residence – Boston

CROSBY,
Arthur Edward, III, b. 5/15/1989 in N. Conway; Arthur E. Crosby, Jr. and Mary M. O'Connell

CROWELL,
Carolynn A., b. 7/9/1980 in N. Conway; John Crowell and Deborah Peaslee
Jonathan Adam, b. 4/18/1982 in N. Conway; John Crowell and Deborah Peaslee

CULLEN,
Timothy Doyle, b. 6/20/1979 in N. Conway; Robert Cullen and Donna Papillon

CUMMINGS,
Donald Edward, b. 4/16/1926; Harry Cummings and Maud Davis
Harry E., b. 4/22/1905; sixth; Ansel Cummings (farmer, Woburn, MA) and Rose B. Brown (Wellesley, MA)
Margaret, b. 6/27/1902; fifth; Ansel Cummings (farmer, Woburn, MA) and Rose B. Brown (Wellesley, MA)
Roger Harry, b. 1/14/1932; Harry E. Cummings and Maud Davis
Rose Carol, b. 3/15/1937; Harry E. Cummings and Maude S. Davis
Susan, b. 6/15/1949; first; Donald E. Cummings and Gladys J. Lawrence

CURRIER,
Richard David, b. 8/24/1964 in Wolfeboro; first; Stephen W. Currier and Joyce Marie Bickford
Roland E., b. 8/10/1900; first; Edwin F. Currier (mail carrier, Albany) and Florence Green (Tamworth)

CURTIN,
Rachael Noemie, b. 7/18/1984 in Tamworth; Thomas Curtin and Kerrie Trumble
Sean Trumble, b. 6/1/1988 in Tamworth; Thomas D. Curtin and Karrie Ann Trumble
Trevor Duffy, b. 8/5/1986 in Tamworth; Thomas Curtin and Kerrie Trumble

CURTIN-NOURSE,
Riston Brice, b. 11/19/1987 in Tamworth; Christopher F. Nourse and Kathleen C. Curtin
Tryson Reece, b. 11/2/1985 in Tamworth; Christopher Nourse and Kathleen Curtin

CURTIS,
Tina Marie, b. 7/14/1983 in N. Conway; Wesley M. Curtis and Raylene Marie Dennis

D'ONOFRIO,
Angela Karin, b. 9/18/1982 in Wolfeboro; John D'Onofrio and Sherrie Chase

DAMON,
child, b. 9/2/1949; third; Harry F. Damon, Jr. and Elizabeth S. Sherman
Christopher S., b. 8/31/1957; third; Steven F. Damon and Beverly M. Robinson

DANFORTH,
George, b. 6/6/1904; first; George C. Danforth (farmer, Sandwich) and Winnie Sanborn (Campton); residence – Sandwich

DANNIS [see Davis],
son, b. 9/20/1913; fourth; Joseph L. Dannis (laborer, Norway, ME) and Alice Smith (Stowe, ME)

DARLING,
son, b. 1/4/1895 in Tamworth; second; Henry M. Darling (laborer, 25, NB) and Nellie J. Dow (25, Tamworth)
daughter, b. 12/3/1903; fourth; Henry Darling (laborer, NB) and Nellie J. Dow (Tamworth)
Anna B., b. 3/16/1906; fourth; Henry Darling (laborer, NB) and Nellie J. Dow (Tamworth)

DASCOULIAS,
Joseph Robert, b. 8/2/1975 in Laconia; Robert Arthur Dascoulias and Gail Ruth Streeter

DAVERY,
child, b. 3/5/1923; first; Otis E. Davery (Tamworth) and Gladys E. Melanson (Grafton, MA)

DAVEY,
son, b. 7/31/1903; fifth; Henry Davey (laborer, NB) and Jennie Vittum (Sandwich)

DAVIS,
daughter, b. 3/6/1888; eleventh; William H. Davis (laborer, Effingham) and Mary M. Moody (Nashua)
daughter, b. 11/30/1907; third; J. L. Davis (laborer, Norway, ME) and Alice E. Smith (Stow, ME)
son, b. 4/6/1915 in Tamworth; ninth; Alvah Davis (farmer, 39, Ossipee) and Florence Wiggin (Ossipee)
son, b. 5/6/1916; tenth; Alva Davis (farmer, Ossipee) and Florence Wiggin (Ossipee)
son, b. 9/15/1916; sixth; John C. Davis (laborer, Tamworth) and Minnie A. Cameron (Campton)
son, b. 11/18/1917; eleventh; Alva Davis (farmer, Ossipee) and Florence B. Wiggin (Ossipee)
son, b. 1/22/1919; twelfth; Alvah Davis (Ossipee) and Florence B. Wiggin (Ossipee)
Christina Mia, b. 9/18/1966 in N. Conway; Everett Pitman Davis and Kathleen Christine Richler
Everett P., b. 8/4/1940; second; Chester Davis and Laura M. Pitman
Karen Jean, b. 7/4/1965 in Wolfeboro; first; Larry John Davis and Amy Pearl Whiting
Kay Ellen, b. 7/7/1966 in Wolfeboro; Larry John Davis and Amy Pearl Whiting
Larry John, b. 4/3/1941; third; Rodney C. Davis and Margaret C. Bower
Laura Carrie, b. 8/29/1893; first; Amos T. Davis (laborer, Tamworth) and Alice B. Berry (Tamworth)
Leland John, b. 5/1/1929; Lloyd Davis and Marion Philbrick
Linda D., b. 7/23/1947; fifth; Rodney C. Davis and Margaret C. Bowe
Lloyd, b. 6/24/1908; fifth; John C. Davis (laborer, Tamworth) and Annie Cameron (Lancaster)
Madison Marie, b. 10/11/1996 in N. Conway; David B. Davis and Carol A. Cole
Michael Richard, b. 10/29/1965 in Conway; second; Everett Pitman Davis and Kathleen Christine Richter
Neal K., b. 3/2/1949; sixth; Rodney C. Davis and Margaret C. Bower
Nellonie J., b. 6/18/1951; seventh; Rodney C. Davis and Margaret C. Bower
Patricia Ann, b. 11/29/1931; Lloyd Davis and Marion Philbrick
Ralph Angus, b. 6/22/1902; fourth; John C. Davis (laborer, Tamworth) and Minnie Cameron (Jefferson)
Rodney L., b. 6/22/1939; second; Rodney C. Davis and Margaret C.

Bower
Roseanna Barbara, b. 12/17/1943; fourth; Rodney C. Davis and Margaret C. Bower

DAVISON,
Kate Larrabee, b. 8/4/2000 in Laconia; Harry Davison and Susan Davison

DAY,
Bonnie Lee, b. 8/7/1956; fourth; Perley C. Day and Alice E. Anthony
Stacy Marie, b. 5/28/1972 in Wolfeboro; Percy Cleveland Day and Joyce Marie Morton
Warren L., b. 6/9/1946; second; Alfred W. Day and Jessie A. Richards

DEARBORN,
Jeffrey Allen, b. 5/15/1963 in Wolfeboro; first; Allen Earl Dearborn and Janice Lee Downs
Randall Lee, b. 11/25/1965 in Wolfeboro; second; Allen Earl Dearborn and Janice Lee Downs
Richard Earl, b. 11/25/1965 in Wolfeboro; third; Allen Earl Dearborn and Janice Lee Downs

DEATTE,
Clyde L., Jr., b. 4/9/1947; ninth; Clyde L. Deatte and Flora B. Jones
Rebecca E., b. 8/17/1951; seventh; Clyde L. Deatte and Flora B. Jones

DECHAPE-DFEWITT,
Saxon Michel, b. 3/6/1992 in N. Conway; Sherman H. Dewitt and Diane G. Dechape

DEDEUS,
Nicholas Paul, b. 8/13/1984 in Tamworth; Hilbert DeDeus and Elana Rascillo

DEERING,
Marjorie Louise, b. 12/12/1936; Elmer Deering and Frances Jackson

DESJARDINS,
Andrew Joseph, b. 11/8/1975 in N. Conway; Norman Hugh

Desjardins and Joan Mary Wiegers

DEVERY,
child, b. 4/16/1924; Otis Devery and Gladys Melanson

DEWITT,
Betty J., b. 10/18/1958; first; Jerome C. DeWitt and Bevrly J. Smith
Tobey Daniel, b. 10/7/1976 in Plymouth; Robert H. DeWitt and Cindy
   J. Smith

DICEY,
Cassandra Anne, b. 7/28/1966 in Laconia; Wendell Garfield Dicey
   and Julia Marion Leach
Cheryl A., b. 12/9/1944; second; Garfield W. Dicey and Helen B.
   Welch
Christine Anne, b. 1/5/1965 in Laconia; first; Wendell Garfield Dicey
   and Julia Marion Leach
Darrel Alan, b. 9/1/1979 in Laconia; Jeffrey Dicey and Sandra Bean
Dennis L., b. 1/20/1949; third; Garfield W. Dicey and Helen B. Welch
Jeffrey L., b. 10/10/1956; fourth; Garfield L. Dicey and Helen B.
   Welch
Tracy M., b. 3/16/1960; fifth; Garfield W. Dicey and Helen B. Welch
Trevor Andrew, b. 6/26/1973 in Wolfeboro; Dennis Lee Dicey and
   Florence Evelyn Nixon

DICKINSON,
Andrew Joseph, b. 8/24/1965 in Conway; fourth; Forrest Edward
   Dickinson and Leona Pearl Avery
Virginia Jean, b. 5/6/1969 in N. Conway; Forrest Edward Dickinson
   and Leona Pearl Avery

DIRIENZO,
Danny Paul, b. 7/30/1973 in Boston, MA; Joseph Michael DiRienzo
   and Harriet Ann Kukuruza

DISILVA,
Madison Lynn, b. 8/3/2001 in N. Conway; Albert Disilva and Kendra
   Disilva

DODGE,
Jordan Darcie, b. 8/23/1997 in N. Conway; David Dennis Dodge and

Shauna Lynn Woodward

DOE,
Philip Eveleth, b. 7/15/1914; second; Eugene C. Doe (laborer, 28, Maplewood, MA) and Anna Pearson (37, Beverly, MA)

DOUCETTE,
Aaron Michael, b. 9/25/1999 in Wolfeboro; Victor Doucette and Anna Doucette

DOUVILLE,
Ronald Leo, b. 12/25/1936; Romeo L. Douville and Dorothy Welch

DOW,
son, b. 2/27/1909; first; Charles L. Dow (laborer, Tamworth) and Nettie M. Barnes (Tamworth)
Cedric Clayton, Jr., b. 2/14/1953; eighth; Cedric C. Dow and Mary E. Buxton

DOWDING,
stillborn daughter, b. 10/27/1890; first; H. W. Dowding (clergyman, Bath, England) and Sarah Smeed (Littlehampton, England)

DOWNS,
daughter, b. 6/22/1889; first; Edward E. Downs (farmer, Tamworth) and Annie M. Spooner (Haverhill)
daughter, b. 1/24/1893; first; Henry L. Down (sic) (farmer, Tamworth) and Alice E. Smith (Greenville, MD)
son, b. 6/30/1894 in Tamworth; second; Joseph L. Douns (sic) (farmer, 22, Greenville, MD) and Alice E. Smith (Stowe, ME)
Albert E., b. 8/19/1901; third; Joseph L. Downs (laborer, Porter, ME) and Hattie B. Dow (Stow, ME)
Edna Caroline, b. 1/18/1921 in Tamworth; first; Elmer E. Downs (farmer, Tamworth) and Edna A. Blodgett (Brockton, MA)
Geraldine, b. 8/8/1905; first; Elias E. Downs (laborer, Porter, ME) and Mildred E. Page (Tamworth)
Jannice Lee, b. 12/24/1936; Clifford Downs and Winifred Weeks
John, b. 6/6/1925; Wilbur Downs and Hildagrade Schreater
Judith A., b. 10/20/1938; second; Clifford Downes and Winifred Weeks
Perley Eugene, b. 6/6/1919; first; Frank Downs (Milton) and Frances

Haley (Fryeburg, ME)

DREW,
Brittany Leigh-Elisabeth, b. 2/6/1998 in N. Conway; Frank Drew and Kimberly M. Pemberton
Cammy Lynn, b. 11/25/1965 in Conway; first; Frank Pearson Drew and Carolyn Janice Deatte
Cody Dillan, b. 5/7/1997 in Laconia; Fred A. Drew and Louise Marianne Lessard
Dale Alan, b. 6/15/1970 in N. Conway; Stephen Leonard Drew and Deborah Alice Tripp
Frank Pierson, b. 3/15/1967 in N. Conway; Frank Pierson Drew and Carolyn Janice Deatte
Frank Pierson-Nicholas, b. 10/9/1996 in N. Conway; Frank P. Drew, Jr. and Kimberly M. Pemberton
Fred A., b. 3/15/1967 in N. Conway; Frank Pierson Drew and Carolyn Janice Deatte
Kristal Louise, b. 1/7/1995 in Laconia; Fred A. Drew and Louise Marie-Ann Lessa
Nellie, b. 2/26/1900; first; William F. Drew (laborer, Tamworth) and Katie M. Hardy (Tamworth)
Sharon R., b. 11/25/1960; first; Arthur N. Drew and Marilyn J. Canney

DROUIN,
Eric Jon, b. 11/11/1959; third; Paul J. Drouin and Mildred J. Wilkinson

DUBE,
Andrew Ticehurst, b. 5/25/1988 in Tamworth; Mark Leonard Dube and Susan J. Ticehurst
Eric Ticehurst, b. 12/11/1990 in Tamworth; Mark L. Dube and Susan J. Ticehurst
Ryan John, b. 3/14/1991 in Concord; Tracey J. Dube and Kathleen B. Raymond

DUNLOP,
William J., b. 6/23/1941; first; William D. Dunlop and Hattie E. Sanborn

DUQUETTE,
Joshua Daniel, b. 4/16/1991 in N. Conway; Shawn Watts and Peggy L. Duquette

DYRENFORTH,
Thomas Andrew, b. 10/15/1983 in N. Conway; John C. Dyrenforth and Katherine Johnson

EASTMAN,
son, b. 10/15/1921 in Tamworth; first; Percy C. Eastman (carpenter, N. Conway) and Mildred G. Bickford (Sandwich)
Claud Percival, b. 8/4/1927; Percy Eastman and Mildred Bickford

EASTWICK,
Joy, b. 7/23/1937; Robert Eastwick and Mary E. Mason

EDGELL,
son, b. 8/4/1896 in Tamworth; first; William H. Edgell (28, Tamworth) and Emma F. Child (20, Tamworth)
son, b. 2/3/1899; third; William H. Edgell (laborer, Tamworth) and Emma Childs (Tamworth)

EDGERLY,
Herman D., b. 1/24/1908; second; S. C. Edgerly (farmer, Ossipee) and Maude E. Martin (Boston, MA)

EKLUND,
Caleb Kendell, b. 1/11/2000 in N. Conway; Erik Eklund and Kacey Eklund

ELDRIDGE,
Amanda Jean, b. 10/27/1978 in N. Conway; Ricky Eldridge and Pamela Comer
Brandan Matthew, b. 6/2/1999 in Laconia; Adam Eldridge and Sarah Eldridge
Brenda Jayne, b. 10/5/1963 in Wolfeboro; second; Hazen Andrew Eldridge and Shirley Joanne Roberts
Charles P., b. 4/27/1923; third; Raymond Eldridge (Ossipee) and Etta Eldridge (Ossipee)
David W., b. 6/1/1959; first; Hazen A. Eldridge and Shirley J. Roberts

Erica Lynn, b. 9/4/1991 in N. Conway; Scotty A. Eldridge and Terri L. Bates
Eva M., b. 3/4/1944; fourth; Lester Eldridge and Ida Judkins
Evelyn M., b. 11/17/1947; first; Roland R. Eldridge and Alfreda M. Drew
Frances J., b. 8/4/1923; fourth; Clifford D. Eldridge (Ossipee) and Etta Colby (Ossipee)
Hazen A., b. 5/31/1939; first; Hazen A. Eldridge and Ellen E. Plummer
Jacinta J., b. 2/11/1980 in N. Conway; David Eldridge and Doris Silva
James F., b. 6/25/1947; second; Andrew W. Eldridge and Marcia E. Gilman
Jonathan Andrew, b. 10/9/1975 in Wolfeboro; James P. Eldridge and Joan W. Welch
Joshua Russell, b. 3/21/1992 in N. Conway; Rodney H. Eldridge and Caroline J. Bickford
Logan John, b. 12/22/2000 in Laconia; Adam Eldridge and Sarah Eldridge
Mabel Mildred, b. 1/14/1920 in Tamworth; first; Raymond Eldridge (laborer, Ossipee) and Etta M. Eldridge (Ossipee)
Michelle Lynn, b. 7/29/1969 in Wolfeboro; James Franklin Eldridge and Kathleen Marie Hawes
Ricky L., b. 1/12/1957; third; Roland R. Eldridge and Alfreda M. Drew
Ricky Lester, Jr., b. 1/13/1977 in N. Conway; Ricky L. Eldridge and Pamela Comer
Robert Douglas, b. 12/15/1988 in N. Conway; Douglas E. Eldridge and Mary S. Dubois
Samuel Joseph, b. 7/20/1990 in N. Conway; Douglas E. Eldridge and Mary S. Dubois
Tony Jacob, b. 11/21/1988 in Laconia; Tony W. Eldridge and Linda G. Steadman
Tony Wayne, b. 9/10/1964 in N. Conway; fourth; Roland R. Eldridge and Alfreda May Drew
Vici Lynn, b. 11/27/1966 in N. Conway; Roland Robert Eldridge and Alfreda May Drew

ELIAS,
Thomas, b. 8/6/1905; first; Rogy Elias (merchant, Beyruth, Syria) and Nellie Turner (London, England)

ELLIOTT,
Eleanor, b. 2/14/1945; third; Albert S. Elliott and Gertrude Berry
Ethel May, b. 5/12/1911; fourth; Edwin J. Elliott (farmer, Taunton, MA) and Amanda Anderson (Gottenberg, Sweden)
Gertrude Eleanor, b. 5/28/1909; third; Edwin J. Elliott (farmer, Taunton, MA) and Amanda Anderson (Sweden)
Louise M., b. 11/28/1927; Harold Elliott and Evelyn Robarge
Marcia J., b. 7/26/1961; third; James T. Elliott and Dorothy J. Larrabee
Melanie A., b. 3/25/1960; second; James T. Elliott and Dorothy A. Larrabee
Melinda A., b. 2/22/1958; first; James T. Elliott and Dorothy A. Larrabee
Roger S., b. 6/6/1940; second; Albert S. Elliott and Gertrude L. Berry

EMERSON,
Dean Marvin, b. 3/31/1964 in Wolfeboro; first; Theodore W. Emerson and Eva Marie Emerson
Margaret, b. 9/14/1940; first; Levi W. Emerson and Margaret L. Pennell
Nancy, b. 4/24/1944; fourth; Levi W. Emerson and Margaret Pennell
Sandra Ann, b. 11/4/1942; third; Levi W. Emerson and Margaret L. Pennell
Tracy Evelyn, b. 3/25/1970 in Wolfeboro; Theodore Woodbury Emerson and Eva Marie Eldridge
Troy Woodbury, b. 3/25/1982 in Wolfeboro; Theodore Emerson and Eva Eldridge

EVANS,
daughter, b. 3/15/1898; fifth; Charles W. Evans (blacksmith, Moultonboro) and Esther L. Dade (Rockport, MA)
child, b. 5/29/1931; Almon G. Evans and Gladys F. Corbett
Almon G., b. 5/19/1903; second; Frank P. Evans (butcher, Moultonboro) and Idella E. Clough (Tamworth)
Almon Glenn, b. 11/15/1994 in Laconia; Frank C. Evans and Lynnemarie Schacht
Almon Grover, b. 5/23/1929; Almon G. Evans and Gladys F. Corbett
Barbara A., b. 1/7/1950; second; Leon A. Evans and Frances L. Panno
Catherine A., b. 5/16/1953; first; Almon G. Evans, Jr. and Shirley C. Webster

Cindy Ann, b. 2/14/1956; second; Gordon B. Evans and Marilyn A. Larrabee
Diana Marie, b. 5/20/1989 in Laconia; Frank C. Evans and Lynne M. Schacht
Frances C., b. 12/6/1948; first; Leon A. Evans and Frances L. Pairno
Frank C., b. 1/27/1957; first; Glenn P. Evans and Cora M. Grace
Frank Chandler, Jr., b. 6/17/1998 in Laconia; Frank C. Evans, Sr. and Lynne M. Schacht
Gloria Janica, b. 5/27/1932; Almon G. Evans and Gladys Corbett (1933)
Gordon Bruce, b. 7/12/1930; Almon G. Evans and Gladys F. Corbett
Hazel E., b. 6/11/1899; first; Frank P. Evans (butcher, Moultonboro) and Emma I. Clough (Tamworth)
Herberta, b. 5/4/1945; eighth; Almon G. Evans and Gladys Corbett
Jeffrey S., b. 12/19/1960; third; Gordon B. Evans and Marilyn A. Larrabee
Joan, b. 4/12/1959; second; Glenn P. Evans and Cora M. Grace
Lorrine Evelyn, b. 8/24/1927; Almon G. Evans and Gladys Corbett
Martha, b. 5/15/1938; seventh; Almon G. Evans and Gladys F. Corbett
Roger Gates, b. 9/8/1919; third; William Weston Evans (Townsend, MA) and Mary Esther Joslyn (Worcester, MA)
Wendy L., b. 4/21/1954; first; Gordon B. Evans and Marily A. Larrabee

EWING,
Mallory Jenny, b. 7/15/1984 in Portland, ME; Lawrence Ewing and Carol Cavalier

FARNUM,
Ann, b. 10/12/1952; second; Whipple W. Farnum and Jane A. Powell
Gregory Edward, b. 6/17/1993 in Laconia; William W. Farnum and Heidi J. Engman
Robert William, b. 6/14/1990 in Laconia; William W. Farnum and Heidi J. Engman
Walter W., b. 5/28/1954; fourth; Whipple W. Farnum and Jane A. Powell
William W., b. 5/28/1954; third; Whipple W. Farnum and Jane A. Powell

FAUNCE,
Dorothy H., b. 12/25/1908; first; Oliver J. Faunce (clergyman, Calais, VT) and Minnie E. Daying (Calais, VT)

FEDDERN,
Megan Lee, b. 4/22/1993 in Wolfeboro; Mark Feddern and Heather L. Glennon
Zachary Charles, b. 8/1/1990 in Wolfeboro; Mark H. Feddern and Heather L. Glennon

FEELEY,
Malcolm McC., b. 11/28/1942; third; John A. Feeley and Mildred McCollum

FENDERSON,
Heather Nicole, b. 6/2/1989 in N. Conway; Melvin C. Fenderson and Diane C. Carlson
Stephen Melvin, b. 10/7/1986 in N. Conway; Melvin Fenderson and Diane Carlson

FENNELL,
Lauretta, b. 11/18/1944; first; Edward R. Fennell and Frances Perrigo

FERGUSON,
Jennie May, b. 2/10/1893; fourth; James I. Ferguson (mechanic, Guysborough, NS) and Helen M. Balow (Barre, VT)
Kelsey Hope, b. 9/25/1990 in N. Conway; Earl L. Ferguson and Kimberly D. King

FERRARA,
Joseph Nicholas, b. 9/11/2002 in N. Conway; Jason Ferrara and Denise Ferrara

FEUERBORN,
Mark Wayne, b. 11/5/1976 in N. Conway; Wayne D. Feuerborn and Susan R. Ward

FLANAGAN,
Sandra K., b. 7/16/1948; first; Raymond Flanagan and Edna A. Andrews

FLOOD,
Marion, b. 10/5/1947; first; Robert A. Flood and Esther F. Steele

FLOYD,
son, b. 11/3/1889; second; A. Floyd (lumberman, Portland, ME) and Ida Mason (Tamworth)
son, b. --/--/1912; first; Perley E. Floyd (laborer, Tamworth) and Nettie A. Grant (Sandwich)
son, b. 8/12/1914; second; Perley E. Floyd (laborer, 24, Tamworth) and Nettie A. Grant (24, Sandwich)
Gary Perley, b. 9/9/1962 in Wolfeboro; second; Robert Perley Floyd and Joanne Reed
Randall R., b. 4/14/1960; first; Robert P. Floyd and Joanne Reed
Robert, b. 1/3/1934; Perley E. Floyd and Nettie A. Grant

FOLKINS,
Betsy J., b. 2/26/1951; first; Harry W. Folkins and Olive L. Puffer

FOLLET,
George H., b. 1/10/1890; first; Charles F. Follet (millman, Meredith) and Abbie S. Wallace (Tamworth)

FORNEY,
Shannon Elizabeth, b. 2/27/1978 in N. Conway; Micheal Forney and Sharon Goodyear

FOR[R]EST,
daughter, b. 9/5/1888; third; Jonathan A. Forrest (farmer, Newark, VT) and Emily F. Forrest (Conway)
son, b. 9/11/1891; fifth; Jonathan Forest (farmer, Westmore, VT) and Emily Bean (Conway)
John W., b. 5/4/1890; fourth; J. A. Forest (farmer, Newark, VT) and Emily F. Bean (Conway)

FORTIER,
son, b. 2/28/1914; fifth; Albert J. Fortier (laborer, 29, Ossipee) and Nellie W. Hobbs (23, Albany)
son, b. 3/21/1915 in Tamworth; sixth; Albert J. Fortier (farmer, 29, Ossipee) and Nellie J. Hobbs
son, b. 6/1/1917; seventh; Albert J. Fortier (laborer, Ossipee) and Nellie Hobbs (Albany)

Albert F., b. 9/7/1908; first; Albert J. Fortier (laborer, Ossipee) and
   Nellie W. Hobbs (Albany)
Carroll Weymouth, b. 1/13/1913; fourth; Albert J. Fortier (farmer,
   Ossipee) and Nellie W. Hobbs (Conway)
Doris Lavina, b. 5/6/1911; third; Albert J. Fortier (laborer, Ossipee)
   and Nellie W. Hobbs (Albany)
John Lane, b. 8/26/1926; Albert Fortier and Nellie Hobbs
Keith, b. 9/8/1920 in Tamworth; Albert J. Fortier (farmer, Ossipee)
   and Nellie Hobbs (Albany)
Martin, b. 8/26/1918; eighth; Albert J. Fortier (farmer, Ossipee) and
   Nellie W. Hobbs (Albany)
Merry A., b. 10/26/1952; second; Walter W. Fortier and Florence E.
   Welch
Norman Frank, b. 4/7/1934; Albert F. Fortier and Doris M. Bean
Ruth Eleanor, b. 11/3/1909; first; Albert J. Fortier (painter, Ossipee)
   and Nellie W. Hobbs (Albany)
Sally A., b. 6/29/1947; first; Walter W. Fortier and Florence E. Welch
Walter Wellman, b. 3/5/1922; tenth; Albert Fortier (Ossipee) and
   Nellie W. Hobbs (Albany)

FOSS,
Kareina Elizabeth, b. 8/3/2003 in N. Conway; Lance Foss and
   Chandra Foss

FOWLER,
Stewart, b. 2/9/1915 in Tamworth; first; James W. Robertson
   (farmer, 23, Tamworth) and Alys Fowler (Woodbury, CT)

FRENCH,
Lewis W., b. 8/15/1928; Ernest H. French and Mildred Newhall

FROST,
   daughter, b. 4/10/1888; first; Edwin M. Frost (farmer, Madison) and
      Addie Frost (Madison)
   child, b. 12/4/1944; second; Herbert E. Frost, Jr. and Ruth A. Walker
Alston Franklin, b. 8/29/1918; second; Arthur E. Frost (laborer,
      Madison) and Ethel Hobbs (Boston, MA)
Arthur E., b. 6/1/1894 in Tamworth; fifth; George F. Frost (farmer,
      34, Madison) and Jennie A. Story (35, Charlestown, MA)
Jane E., b. 2/5/1947; first; Norris W. Frost and Marion Frazee
Joan Muriel, b. 2/17/1953; second; Norris W. Frost and Marion M.

Frazier
Lawrence Edwin, b. 12/19/1916; first; Arthur E. Frost (laborer, Madison) and Ethel Hobbs (Boston, MA)
Norris William, b. 8/24/1920 in Tamworth; third; Arthur E. Frost (lumberman, Madison) and Ethel Hobbs (Forest Hills, MA)
Phyllis C., b. 6/4/1950; first; Lawrence E. Frost and Rita M. Lawson

FRYE,
Franklin P., b. 6/3/1903; third; Willard S. Frye (clergyman, Moultonboro) and Eva E. Bodwell (Manchester)

FURNBACH,
Tucker Daniel, b. 6/3/1996 in Laconia; Henry J. Furnbach and Cynthia J. Ullrich

GAGNE,
Angela Marie, b. 6/25/1973 in Wolfeboro; Peter Allan Gagne and Mary Louise Babb

GALE,
Matthew Daniel, b. 12/12/1976 in Laconia; Dennis H. Gale and Mary P. Molloy

GAMMON,
Jason Gerald, b. 3/12/1974 in N. Conway; John Stephen Gammon and Judy May Verrill
John Stephen, Jr., b. 3/4/1966 in N. Conway; John Stephen Gammon and Judy May Verrill

GARLAND,
son, b. 12/28/1888; third; George D. Garland (farmer, Conway) and Mary E. Garland (Effingham)
daughter, b. 8/4/1898; second; Ernest Garland (laborer, Tamworth) and Mary E. Grant (Sandwich)
child, b. 10/12/1938; fourth; Frank E. Garland and Muriel M. Clark
Annie May, b. 10/29/1902; fifth; George E. Garland (laborer, Tamworth) and Edna M. Grant (Moultonboro)
Donna M., b. 5/26/1940; fifth; Frank E. Garland and Muriel M. Clark
Frank E., b. 5/14/1906; seventh; George E. Garland (laborer, Tamworth) and Mary E. Grant (Sandwich)
Frederick G., b. 3/29/1897; first; George E. Garland (laborer,

Tamworth) and Edna M. Grant (Moultonboro)
Janet Beulah, b. 6/11/1930; Frank E. Garland and Muriel M. Clark
Jennie S., b. 1/20/1901; fourth; George E. Garland (laborer, Tamworth) and Mary E. Grant (Sandwich)
Louise Ethel, b. 6/2/1918; first; Frederick Grant Garland (farmer, Tamworth) and Rubie Eldora Stone (Guildhall, VT)
Mary F., b. 3/20/1904; sixth; George E. Garland (laborer, Tamworth) and Mary E. Grant (Sandwich)
Nancy Kay, b. 7/31/1936; Frank Ernest Garland and Muriel M. Clark
Osman Taft, b. 8/14/1909; eighth; George E. Garland (farmer, Tamworth) and Edna M. Grant (Moultonboro)

GERARD,
Aimee Loretta, b. 7/8/1994 in Laconia; Richard R. Gerard and Loralie Collins
Melissa Anne, b. 9/6/1995 in Laconia; Richard R. Gerard and Loralie Collins

GIBSON,
David C., b. 4/11/1940; first; George A. Gibson and Mary L. Vittum
Douglas Paul, b. 4/26/1942; first; George A. Gibson and Mary L. Vittum

GIDDINGS,
stillborn son, b. 6/21/1915 in Tamworth; third; Robert Giddings (laborer, 47, England) and Sarah Webster (Tamworth)
daughter, b. 10/11/1921 in Tamworth; third; Robert A. Giddings (farm Laborer, Erchfont, England) and Sadie M. Webster (Tamworth)

GILES,
Abram Jacob, b. 7/12/1997 in N. Conway; Todd Christopher Giles and Elaine Katharine Buzzell

GILMAN,
daughter, b. 4/12/1887; first; James W. Gilman (laborer, Tamworth) and Hattie B. (Tamworth)
daughter, b. 11/28/1888; second; James W. Gilman (farmer, Tamworth) and Hattie B. Davis (Tamworth)
daughter, b. 4/--/1895 in Tamworth; fifth; James Gilman (laborer, 33, Tamworth) and Harriet Davis (24, Tamworth)

son, b. 7/6/1898; first; Charles E. Gilman (motorman, Tamworth) and Florence Powers (Brownfield, ME)
daughter, b. 12/12/1898; seventh; James H. Gilman (laborer, Tamworth) and Hattie B. Davis (Tamworth)
stillborn daughter, b. 9/4/1906; tenth; James W. Gilman (laborer, Tamworth) and Hattie B. Davis (Tamworth)
stillborn son, b. 9/19/1907; eleventh; J. W. Gilman (laborer, Tamworth) and Hattie B. Davis (Tamworth)
Carol Nellie, b. 8/20/1923; fifth; Clifford Gilman (Sandwich) and Nellie Moore (Tamworth)
Dorothy K., b. 8/9/1942; fifth; Howard R. Gilman and Hazel M. Ellis
Edith May, b. 11/17/1906; second; Sumner H. Gilman (farmer, Tamworth) and Annie C. Remick (Tamworth)
Edwin F., b. 10/28/1910; second; Erwin A. Gilman (teamster, Wakefield) and Elsie M. Ross (Tamworth)
Elinor Lucille, b. 4/16/1918; second; Clifford J. Gilman (farmer, Sandwich) and Nellie M. D. Moore (Tamworth)
Elizabeth May, b. 6/17/1924; Clyde Gilman and Iva Perkins
Ellsworth Harold, b. 12/22/1922; first; Harold Gilman (Madison) and Margaret Nickerson (Tamworth)
Ernest W., b. 1/15/1901; eighth; James W. Gilman (laborer, Tamworth) and Harriet B. Davis (Tamworth)
Ethel May, b. 1/7/1909; first; Erwin A. Gilman (farmer, Union) and Elsie M. Ross (Tamworth)
Eva M., b. 11/15/1904; ninth; James W. Gilman (laborer, Tamworth) and Harriet B. Davis (Tamworth)
Grace Adella, b. 11/25/1920 in Tamworth; fourth; Clifford J. Gilman (farmer, Sandwich) and Nellie M. D. Moore (Tamworth)
Harold, b. 7/24/1896 in Tamworth; sixth; James Gilman (32, Tamworth) and Hattie B. Davis (28, Tamworth)
Helen, b. 6/16/1919; third; Reed B. Gilman (Fryeburg, ME) and Maud E. Thurston (Shapleigh, ME)
Howard R., b. 12/31/1902; first; Sumner H. Gilman (laborer, Tamworth) and Annie C. Remick (Tamworth)
John, b. 5/30/1925; Clifford Gilman and Nellie Moore
Judith E., b. 1/11/1939; fourth; Howard R. Gilman and Hazel M. Ellis
Laura Mary, b. 11/3/1915 in Tamworth; first; Clifford J. Gilman (laborer, 36, Sandwich) and Nellie M. I. Moore
Lizzie Ellen, b. 9/10/1893; fourth; James W. Gilman (laborer, Tamworth) and Hattie B. Davis (Tamworth)
Maria Evelyn, b. 8/11/1919; third; Clifford J. Gilman (Sandwich) and

Nellie M. D. Moore (Tamworth)
Reed Brackett, b. 12/18/1917; second; Reed Bracket Gilman (laborer, Fryeburg, ME) and Maud Thurston (Shapleigh, ME)
Samuel Howard, b. 1/30/1931; Howard R. Gilman and Hazel M. Ellis

GLIDDEN,
son, b. 7/25/1888; ninth; Frank O. Glidden (farmer, Calais, ME) and Maggie Woodman (Tamworth)
son, b. 6/11/1890; seventh; Frank O. Glidden (millman, ME) and M. A. Woodman (Tamworth)
son, b. 3/26/1899; first; William Glidden (laborer, Tamworth) and Eva Bodge (Moultonboro)

GLOVER,
daughter, b. 5/11/1888; third; Everett F. Glover (farmer, Deerfield, ME) and Laura A. Hutchins (Tamworth)

GOBELLE,
Norman R., b. 1/20/1938; first; Arthur Gobelle and Evelyn Wiggin

GONYO,
Cooper Wilfred, b. 6/1/1994 in Laconia; Wilfred Felix Gonyo and Kristie Thelma Roberts
Lincoln Emery, b. 9/17/1999 in Laconia; Wilfred Gonyo and Kristie Gonyo

GOODALL,
Anne Elizabeth, b. 12/26/1986 in N. Conway; Edwin Goodall and Cecilia Cox
Ellen Baker, b. 5/27/1988 in N. Conway; Edwin B. Goodall and Cecelia Cox
Justin Hollander, b. 2/28/1983 in Tamworth; Edwin B. Goodall and Olga Cecilia Cox

GOODHEART,
James Carr, b. 4/11/1977 in Laconia; Donald P. Goodheart and Ronnie S. Sagal

GOODSON,
David Ryan Chapman, b. 10/31/1992 in N. Conway; David C. Goodson and Lanette M. Langlois

Jennifer M., b. 7/5/1980 in Laconia; David Goodson and Ann McCarthy
Karly Margaret Bullen, b. 12/6/1991 in Franklin; Peter B. Goodson and Sarah M. Bullen
Kelly J., b. 11/1/1980 in Laconia; Peter Goodson and Janice Arnold
Mason Bernard, b. 11/9/1995 in Wolfeboro; David C. Goodson and Lanette M. Langlois
Peter B., b. 3/6/1952; third; Wilbur C. Goodson and Mildred E. Bickford
Sarah Alice, b. 1/14/1978 in Wolfeboro; Peter Goodson and Janice Arnold
Wilbur, b. 7/31/1934; Wilbur Goodson and Katherine Nairne

GOODWIN,
daughter, b. 5/–/1895 in Tamworth; third; Jeremiah C. Goodwin (farmer, 43, Tamworth) and Emma L. Bean (39, Penacook)

GORDON,
Haven Earl, Jr., b. 8/17/1962 in N. Conway; first; Haven Earl Gordon, Sr. and Rita Ann Crouse
Randall Scott, b. 10/29/1964 in Laconia; first; Haven Earl Gordon and Rita Ann Crouse
Sara Emily, b. 1/22/1987 in Wolfeboro; Mandall S. Gordon and Lorna L. Pearson
Trevor Earl, b. 6/1/1990 in Wolfeboro; Randall S. Gordon and Lorna L. Pearson

GOSNELL,
Vallie Raye, b. 10/18/2001 in Wolfeboro; Dane Gosnell and Angela Gosnell

GRACE,
son, b. 12/24/1888; sixth; Chandler P. Grace (farmer, Chatham) and Abbie E. Grace (Chatham)
son, b. 9/5/1890; ninth; Chandler P. Grace (farmer, Chatham) and Abbie E. Bean (Fryeburg, ME)
daughter, b. 5/1/1904; second; Joseph L. Grace (laborer, Chatham) and Lodena L. Cates (Stratford)
stillborn daughter, b. 8/26/1907; third; E. C. Grace (laborer, Albany) and Cora E. Smart (Tamworth)
son, b. 8/3/1914 in Tamworth; third; Perley C. Grace (laborer, 29,

Tamworth) and Nellie Berry (33, Tamworth)
son, b. 12/2/1916; fourth; Perley C. Grace (laborer, Tamworth) and Nellie M. Berry (Tamworth)
son, b. 5/24/1921 in Tamworth; sixth; Perley C. Grace (farm laborer, Tamworth) and Nellie M. Berry (Tamworth)
Barbara J., b. 3/31/1946; sixth; Roy E. Grace and Clara E. Moore
Charles E., b. 8/1/1906; second; Ernest C. Grace (laborer, Albany) and Cora E. Smart (Tamworth)
Christopher Spencer, b. 11/30/1998 in N. Conway; Bruce C. Grace and Carole M. Martin
Clayton M., b. 6/26/1902; first; Nelson D. Grace (farmer, Chatham) and Emma Marr (Limington, ME)
Cora Mae, b. 5/14/1934; Roy Ernest Grace and Clara E. Moore
Edith Irene, b. 1/12/1919; fourth; Perl C. Grace (Tamworth) and Nellie M. Berry (Tamworth)
Emma Irene, b. 3/25/1913; third; Ernest C. Grace (laborer, Albany) and Cora E. Smart (Tamworth)
Everett E., b. 5/29/1928; Guy S. Grace and Florence Eldridge
Ezra Kohl, b. 7/12/1999 in N. Conway; Roy Wesley Grace and Kimberly H. Grace
Guy Smart, b. 12/29/1903; first; Ernest C. Grace (laborer, Tamworth) and Cora Smart (Tamworth)
Janet E., b. 5/20/1937; third; Roy Grace and Clara Moore
Jere W., b. 8/13/1947; seventh; Roy E. Grace and Clara E. Moore
Larry L., b. 10/27/1940; fifth; Roy E. Grace and Clara E. Grace
Leah Elizabeth, b. 11/8/1911; second; Perley C. Grace (farmer, Tamworth) and Nellie Berry (Tamworth)
Leona M., b. 3/14/1913; fourth; Joseph Grace (laborer, Chatham) and Lodena Cates (Stratford)
Mary E., b. 3/8/1894 in Tamworth; first; F. Leslie Grace (farmer, 34, Chatham) and Lizzie B. Willey (24, Albany)
Myrtie, b. 5/2/1909; fourth; Ernest C. Grace (laborer, Albany) and Cora E. Smart (Tamworth)
Philip Chester, b. 6/29/1910; first; Perley C. Grace (farmer, Tamworth) and Nellie M. Berry (Tamworth)
Roy Ellsworth, b. 9/6/1936; Roy Ernest Grace and Clara E. Moore
Stanley E., b. 7/19/1938; first; Philip C. Grace and Harriet Murray

GRANT,
Evelyn O., b. 8/30/1907; second; E. A. Grant (laborer, Sandwich) and Lena M. Arling (Tamworth)

Orrie Belle, b. 9/12/1903; first; Ernest Grant (laborer, Sandwich) and
Lena M. Arling (Tamworth)

GRAY,
son, b. 12/8/1920 in Tamworth; first; Harold Gray (machinist, Old
Town, ME) and Beulah Bickford (Tamworth)
Erwin Nathaniel, b. 12/4/1917; second; Erwin N. Gray (laborer,
Madison) and Hattie Nickerson (Tamworth)

GREEN,
Clyde Franklin, b. 4/25/1929; Frank C. Green and Viola Vittum
Phyllis May, b. 6/25/1918; first; Frank Carter Green (laborer, Center
Harbor) and Viola D. Vittum (Sandwich)

GREGG,
Shawn Devaney, b. 4/16/1979 in N. Conway; Courtney Gregg and
Cathie Coan

GRIBBEL,
John Andrew, b. 6/6/1973 in Wolfeboro; John Gribbel, III and
Barbara Copeland Craig

GUECIA,
Aurora Elizabeth, b. 6/12/2003 in N. Conway; Philip Guecia and
Cecilia Guecia
Blythe Talmage, b. 3/11/2001 in Tamworth; Philip Guecia and
Cecilia Guecia

GUMPERT,
son, b. 5/27/1980 in Laconia; James Gumpert and Michelle Matthey

HADDOCK,
Karin Lynn, b. 11/27/1978 in Wolfeboro; Phillip Haddock and Glenda
Austin

HADFIELD,
Dawn Frances, b. 2/29/1972 in Wolfeboro; David Whitcomb Hadfield
and Eleanor Joyce Bunavicz

HALL,
daughter, b. 8/26/1948; sixth; Ernest F. Hall and Dorothy M. Foss

John E., b. 11/25/1947; second; Frank E. Hall and Dorothy E. Capen
Jonathan J., b. 2/10/1951; sixth; Ernest F. Hall and Dorothy M. Foss
Lynn Anne, b. 12/19/1975 in Laconia; Gerald Weston Hall and Mary Louise Green
Marjorie E., b. 9/9/1945; fifth; Ernest F. Hall and Dorothy M. Foss
Sandra E., b. 3/9/1949; third; Frank E. Hall and Dorothy E. Capen

HALSEY,
Darcy Larcom, b. 10/8/1976 in Meredith; Jonathan D. Halsey and Ainsley Bodman
Elizabeth Payson, b. 3/16/1981 in Concord; Jonathan Halsey and Ainsley Bodman
Gardner, b. 3/16/1981 in Concord; Jonathan Halsey and Ainsley Bodman

HAMEL,
Edward Bryant, b. 2/18/1982 in N. Conway; Gerard Hamel and Janis Stamps
Gerard Edward, Jr., b. 8/12/1979 in N. Conway; Gerard Hamel and Janis Stamps
Matthew Ryan, b. 5/13/1986 in N. Conway; Gerard E. Hamel and Janis Stamps
Nathaniel Edward, b. 8/14/1984 in N. Conway; Gerard Hamel and Janis Stamps

HAMILTON,
Kimberly Marie, b. 5/12/1995 in N. Conway; David Michael Hamilton and Ann Marjori Belisle

HAMMOND,
daughter, b. 4/17/1914; sixth; Edwin S. Hammond (farmer, 45, Ossipee) and Mary McGillivary (40, Antigonish, NS)
daughter, b. 2/19/1919; eighth; Edward S. Hammond (Ossipee) and Mary McGilliory (Antigonish, NS)
child, b. 2/18/1939; fourth; Edward Hammond and Charlotte L. Gill
Andrew, b. 11/20/1907; third; E. Hammond (farmer, Ossipee) and Mary McGillory (NS)
Carl W., b. 8/9/1901; second; Walter J. Hammond (mechanic, Cambridge, MA) and Blanche A. Hayford (Tamworth)
Celia, b. 10/18/1911; fifth; Edward Hammond (farmer, Ossipee) and Mary McGilliory (Antigonish, NS)

Charles, b. 10/3/1916; eighth; Edward S. Hammond (farmer, Ossipee) and Mary McGillivray (NS)
Dorothy Ann, b. 7/2/1937; Edward J. Hammond and Charlotte Gill
E. Joshua, b. 1/21/1975 in Laconia; Stanley Frank Hammond and Beverly Mae Black
Edward J., b. 10/15/1905; third; Edwin Hammond (farmer, Ossipee) and Mary McGilroy (Antigonish, NS)
Fred M., b. 1/28/1918; first; Fred M. Hammond (carpenter, Ossipee) and Gladys M. Harmon (Madison)
Howard, b. 8/8/1906; first; Fred L. Hammond (laborer, Albany) and Florence J. Moody (Watertown, MA)
J. Todd, b. 1/24/1973 in Laconia; Stanley Frank Hammond and Beverly Mae Black
Katherine M., b. 9/12/1903; first; Edward Hammond (farmer, Ossipee) and Mary McGillory (NS)
Mary, b. 5/18/1910; fifth; Edward S. Hammond (farmer, Ossipee) and Mary McGilliory (NS)
Patricia, b. 10/15/1945; fifth; Edward J. Hammond and Charlotte L. Gill
Robert William Edward, b. 7/4/1930; Edward J. Hammond and Charlotte Gill
Ruth M., b. 9/21/1897; Walter J. Hammond (laborer, Somerville, MA) and Blanche A. Hayford (Tamworth)

HANSON,
Rebecca King, b. 9/1/1978 in N. Conway; Robert Hanson, Jr. and Frances Ver Planck
Robert Winters, III, b. 3/13/1981 in N. Conway; Robert Hanson, Jr. and Frances Ver Planck

HARBISON,
Christina Marie, b. 4/16/1983 in Laconia; Cameron C. Harbison and Nancy Lee Bruning

HARDY,
Ethel, b. 9/4/1887; sixth; William H. Hardy (laborer, Tamworth) and Georgeana (Effingham)
Minnie E., b. 7/4/1890; seventh; William H. Hardy (farmer, Tamworth) and Georgiana Davis (Effingham)

HARMON,
Crystal Rose, b. 6/17/1991 in N. Conway; William J. Harmon and Rose A. Emerson
William James, b. 4/1/1964 in N. Conway; first; Harold Chester Harmon and Rosemary Hatch

HARRIS,
Lurlene Christabel, b. 1/3/1915 in Tamworth; first; Elsworth F. Harris (laborer, 21, Woburn, MA) and Mabel E. Cummings (Woburn, MA)

HARTLEY,
Daniel Wayne, b. 9/18/2001 in N. Conway; Erin Hartley and Amy Hartley
David Jewell, b. 5/13/2003 in N. Conway; Erin Hartley and Amy Hartley
Tara A., b. 9/1/1980 in N. Conway; John Hartley and Vicki Laclaire

HASKELL,
Margaret C., b. 11/16/1953; first; Nelson C. Haskell and Madeline C. Nichols

HATCH,
child, b. 8/2/1953; first; Leonard L. Hatch and Collen M. Field
Amanda Elizabeth, b. 6/6/1988 in Laconia; Fred Alden Hatch and Marcia Jane Elliott
Fred Nathaniel, b. 7/21/1994 in Laconia; Fred A. Hatch and Marcia J. Elliott

HAUSER,
Bradley Michael, b. 10/28/1989 in Laconia; Michael H. Hauser and Elizabeth Holt
Bryan Christopher, b. 5/19/1987 in Laconia; Michael H. Hauser and Elizabeth M. Holt

HAYES,
Susan E., b. 3/1/1944; third; Edward H. Hayes and Ruth B. Dixon

HAYFORD,
Arnold D., b. 5/6/1908; second; Durwood Hayford (laborer, Tamworth) and Joanna Dempsey (Ireland)

Arnold David, b. 2/21/1934; Arnold D. Hayford and Muriel Smalle
Daniel Albion, b. 5/22/1933; Arthur Hayford and Leona M. Herrick
Donald Bruce, b. 2/19/1934; Arnold D. Hayford and Muriel Smalle
Ernest A., Jr., b. 10/29/1957; fourth; Ernest A. Hayford and Elizabeth
   D. Nudd
Ernest Arthur, b. 8/20/1930; Arthur L. Hayford and Leona M. Herrick
Heather Lindsey, b. 10/31/1981 in Laconia; Randall Hayford and
   Susan Weare
J. Sumner, b. 6/22/1899; eighth; John Hayford (farmer, Tamworth)
   and Lenora Conners (Limerick, ME)
James E., b. 6/28/1953; second; Ernest E. Hayford and Elizabeth D.
   Nudd
James E., II, b. 3/4/1980 in Laconia; James Hayford and Judith
   Varney
Josephine Blanche, b. 2/12/1912; third; Durwood A. Hayford
   (laborer, Tamworth) and Johanna Dempsey (Ireland)
Katherine Ann, b. 2/23/1934; Lawrence Hayford and Katherine
   Desmond
Katherine M., b. 8/29/1929; Arthur L. Hayford and Leona M. Herrick
Kathleen, b. 4/22/1905; first; Durward Hayford (laborer, Tamworth)
   and Johanna Dempsey (Ireland)
Kathrine M., b. 9/27/1958; fifth; Ernest A. Hayford and Elizabeth D.
   Nudd
Lawrence David, b. 3/29/1931; Lawrence D. Hayford and -----
   Desmond
Lawrence David, b. 2/11/1937; Lawrence D. Hayford and Kathrine
   M. Desmond
Marie E., b. 5/30/1956; fourth; Ernest A. Hayford and Elizabeth D.
   Nudd
Paul Linwood, b. 3/31/1928; Arthur Hayford and Leona Herrick
Robert N., b. 2/16/1938; second; Arnold D. Hayford and Muriel E.
   Smalle
Timothy E., b. 10/24/1954; third; Earnest A. Hayford and Elizabeth
   D. Nudd

HAZELTINE,
Beth E., b. 8/13/1950; second; Malcolm F. Hazeltine and Myrtle E.
   Stacy
Malcolm F., Jr., b. 2/9/1952; third; Malcolm F. Hazeltine and Myrtle
   E. Stacy
Nathan E., b. 7/28/1948; first; Malcolm Hazeltine and Myrtle E. Stacy

HEATH,
Forrest Nathan, b. 10/28/1995 in N. Conway; Christopher R. Heath and Roberta Kohrs

HEIMLICH,
Abbey Elliott, b. 3/18/1989 in Laconia; Peter J. Heimlich and Melinda A. Elliott
Casey, b. 8/5/1982 in Laconia; Peter Heimlich and Melinda Elliott

HEMINGWAY,
Timothy Dennis, b. 7/16/1981 in Laconia; Kent Hemingway, Jr. and Barbara Chicco

HENDERSON,
Ethel Forrest, b. 5/2/1906; first; Harry S. Henderson (farmer, Tamworth) and Teresa C. Kelley (Boston, MA)

HENLE,
Elizabeth Forrest, b. 4/24/1991 in N. Conway; Paul J. Henle and Margaret A. Johnson

HERD,
stillborn child, b. 6/14/1887; first; Henry E. Herd (laborer, Berwick, ME) and Mary A. (Union)

HERGET,
Amanda Elliott, b. 7/28/1976 in N. Conway; Thomas K. Herget and Bonnie J. Kitchen
Tanner Ryan, b. 7/23/1982 in N. Conway; Thomas Herget and Bonnie Kitchen

HERLIHY,
Mackenzie Kathryn, b. 8/9/1998 in N. Conway; Thomas J. Herlihy and Alexandra Herlihy

HIDDEN,
daughter, b. --/--/1899; second; Samuel A. Hidden (farmer, Tamworth) and Elizabeth Fellows (Newcastle, DE)
Daniel William, b. 5/31/1973 in Wolfeboro; Samuel Bassett Hidden and Dorothy Janice Stein
David Michael, b. 10/6/1977 in Laconia; Samuel B. Hidden and

Dorothy J. Stein
Edwin William, b. 1/13/1937; William B. Hidden and Christine Johnson
Elizabeth Margurite, b. 3/23/1912; first; S. Harold Hidden (farmer, Tamworth) and Helen J. Bassett (Tamworth)
Frances Unice, b. 10/18/1919; fifth; Samuel Harold Hidden (Tamworth) and Helen Bassett (Tamworth)
Jackleen Helen, b. 11/4/1964 in Laconia; first; John Bray Hidden and Marilyn Dorr Nixon
James Samuel, b. 1/31/1972 in Laconia; Samuel Bassett Hidden and Dorothy Janice Stein
Joanna L., b. 2/15/1947; second; John B. Hidden and Mabel A. Bray
John B., b. 10/26/1940; first; John B. Hidden and Mabel A. Bray
Katharine Louise, b. 1/9/1918; fourth; Samuel Harold Hidden (farmer, Tamworth) and Helen Bassett (Tamworth)
Samuel, b. 11/21/1891; first; Samuel A. Hidden (farmer, Tamworth) and Elizabeth Bellows (Trenton, NJ)
Samuel B., b. 4/29/1939; second; William B. Hidden and Christine Johnson
Trisha Carleen, b. 5/18/1971 in Laconia; John Bray Hidden and Marilyn Dorr Nixon
William Bassett, b. 12/12/1913; second; Samuel H. Hidden (farmer, Tamworth) and Helen Bassett (Tamworth)

HILL,
daughter, b. 2/29/1896 in Tamworth; second; Carlton M. Hill (27, Tamworth) and Laura J. Tibbetts (24, Wolfeboro)
Adam James, b. 11/16/1991 in N. Conway; James W. Hill and Claire L. Rogers
William A., b. 12/2/1919; second; Charles A. Hill (Woburn, MA) and Grace Cowan (Chelsea, MA)

HILLARD,
Clarona Francis, b. 2/24/1926; Clarona Hillard and Doris Leach

HILLIER,
Molly Gay, b. 10/29/1972 in N. Conway; James David Hillier and Nancy Lee Clapp

HITCHCOCK,
Sandra Ellen, b. 9/19/1965 in Conway; second; Roy Clinton

Hitchcock, Jr. and Judith Ann Benoit

HOAG,
Roland Boyden, III, b. 8/8/1971 in Laconia; Roland Boyden Hoag, Jr. and Susan Adele Chappell

HOBBS,
son, b. 8/16/1900; fourth; Frank O. Hobbs (farmer, Ossipee) and Hattie Eastman (Albany)
son, b. 11/20/1901; fourth; Bert A. Hobbs (farmer, Tamworth) and Hattie E. Swain (Albany)
son, b. 7/14/1917; eighth; Albert W. Hobbs (farmer, Tamworth) and Harriet Swaine (Albany)
Ann, b. 10/10/1935; Leon Hobbs and Cecilia Hobbs
Brian P., b. 4/10/1955; second; Philip D. Hobbs and Mildred M. Williams
Celia E., b. 8/4/1908; sixth; Bert W. Hobbs (laborer, Tamworth) and Harriet E. Swaine (Albany)
Cora Louise, b. 2/25/1926; George Hobbs and Marjorie Frost (1933)
Dorothy, b. 9/11/1934; Leon Hobbs and Celia Hobbs
Elizabeth Frances, b. 5/28/1933; George Hobbs and Margery Frost
Ernest, b. 10/19/1905; fifth; Frank O. Hobbs (farmer, Ossipee) and Hattie F. Eastman (Albany)
Ernestine P., b. 7/28/1928; Ernest Hobbs and Christine Palmer
Frank W., b. 8/30/1940; fourth; Leon Hobbs and Celia E. Hobbs
Harry D., b. 7/5/1905; fourth; Bert W. Hobbs (farmer, Tamworth) and Hattie E. Swaine (Albany)
Helen M., b. 11/10/1938; first; Herbert Hobbs and Iva Mae Chenney
Henry W., b. 10/13/1908; sixth; Frank O. Hobbs (farmer, Ossipee) and Hattie F. Eastman (Albany)
Maurice, b. 5/15/1922; first; George W. Hobbs (Albany) and Marjorie Frost (Madison)
Natalie N., b. 10/14/1932; Henry W. Hobbs and Gertrude Emack
Patricia D., b. 10/8/1953; first; Philip D. Hobbs and Mildred M. Williams
Philip Duncan, b. 4/4/1930; Henry Hobbs and Gertrude Ennuck
Rose Marie, b. 1/1/6/1938; third; Leon Hobbs and Celia Hobbs
Sophronica, b. 3/29/1912; seventh; Bert W. Hobbs (farmer, Tamworth) and Hattie Swan (Albany)
Stanley H., b. 12/16/1934; Herbert Hobbs and Iva Cheney
Stella Ruth, b. 4/24/1924; George Hobbs and Marjorie Frost

HODGE,
Elwood N., II, b. 10/25/1959; eighth; Elwood N. Hodge and Doris M. Brooks

HODGKINS,
son, b. 12/21/1887; first; Henry T. Hodgkins (teacher, Tamworth) and Susan A. (Ossipee)

HOLLADAY,
Cacey Ryan, b. 7/6/1999 in N. Conway; Eric James Holladay and Rachel Ailene Holladay

HOLT,
Crystal Sue, b. 2/25/1984 in Laconia; Michael Holt and Suzanne Jacques

HOLZRICHTER,
James Edward, b. 3/25/1975 in Laconia; Bruce Henry Holzrichter and Susan Marie Tucker

HUGHES,
Abraham James, b. 12/2/1984 in Tamworth; David Hughes and Marilyn Cakars
Benjamin Zeno, b. 3/15/1979 in Laconia; David Hughes and Karen Selleck
Elizabeth A., b. 10/31/1987 in Chocorua; David Hughes and Marilynn Cakars

HURDER,
son, b. 7/17/1916; seventh; Benjamin Hurder (laborer, Queens Co., NB) and Inez A. Scribner (Kings Co., NB)

HUTCHINS,
son, b. 2/24/1888; second; Noah W. Hutchins (farmer, Albany) and Abbie A. Downs (Porter, ME)
son, b. 3/22/1890; third; Noah W. Hutchins (farmer, Albany) and Abbie A. Downs (Porter, ME)
son, b. 4/22/1892; fourth; William N. Hutchins (farmer, Albany) and Alice A. Downs (Porter, ME)
daughter, b. 9/17/1915 in Tamworth; third; Elias W. Hutchins (laborer, 42, Tamworth) and Isabel F. Osgood

son, b. 8/23/1917; fourth; Elias W. Hutchins (lfarmer, Tamworth) and Isabel F. Osgood (Tamworth)
son, b. 9/1/1917; second; Clarence E. Hutchins (laborer, Tamworth) and Ida B. Smith (Stowe, ME)
son, b. 8/2/1919; second; Walter Hutchins (Tamworth) and Grace E. Robarge (Tuftonboro)
daughter, b. 1/20/1920 in Tamworth; third; Clarence Hutchins (laborer, Tamworth) and Ida B. Smith (Stowe, ME)
daughter, b. 2/26/1920 in Tamworth; fifth; Elias W. Hutchins (caretaker, Tamworth) and Isabel F. Osgood (Tamworth)
son, b. 8/19/1921 in Tamworth; third; Walter C. Hutchins (carpenter, Tamworth) and Grace E. Robarge (Melvin Village)
Bruce E., b. 9/30/1950; fourth; Paul W. Hutchins and Leah C. Wentworth
Christina, b. 12/8/1925; Walter Hutchins and Georgia Roebarge
Donna L., b. 7/17/1947; second; Donald P. Hutchins and Helen L. Keen
Earl Emerson, b. 2/6/1918; first; Walter C. Hutchins (laborer, Tamworth) and Grace E. Robarge (Tuftonboro)
Edna, b. 2/21/1928; Walter C. Hutchins and Grace E. Robarge
Edward C., b. 1/25/1929; Clarence Hutchins and Marion Taylor
George, b. 10/6/1913; third; Elias W. Hutchins (laborer, Tamworth) and Isabelle Osgood (Tamworth)
Geraldine, b. 2/10/1921 in Tamworth; fourth; Clarence E. Hutchins (lumberman, Tamworth) and Ida Smith (Stow, ME)
Irene Bernice, b. 12/18/1915 in Tamworth; first; Clarence E. Hutchins (laborer, 24, Tamworth) and Ida B. Smith (Stowe, ME)
Linda, b. 10/24/1944; second; Paul W. Hutchins and Leah Wentworth
Paul W., Jr., b. 3/31/1947; third; Paul W. Hutchins and Leah C. Wentworth
Sandra Marie, b. 5/8/1942; first; Donald P. Hutchins and Helen L. Keen
William, b. 10/6/1913; second; Elias W. Hutchins (laborer, Tamworth) and Isabelle Osgood (Tamworth)

JACKSON,
daughter, b. 3/3/1888; second; Samuel H. Jackson (farmer, Tamworth) and Annie Purrington (Albany)
son, b. 10/7/1891; first; Charles N. Jackson (millman, Lowell, MA) and Lizzie A. Gardner (Tamworth)

Josephine L., b. 11/3/1907; fourth; S. H. Jackson (farmer, Tamworth) and A. B. Purrington (Albany)
Thelma, b. 11/18/1907; first; E. E. Jackson (laborer, Tamworth) and M. E. McNeal (Tamworth)

JAWORSKI,
Hilary Ann, b. 11/21/1985 in N. Conway; William Jaworski and Tammy Lunt

JEFFERS,
daughter, b. 9/13/1888; first; Milton W. Jeffers (farmer, Webster) and Abbie Downs (Porter, ME)
daughter, b. 8/27/1890; first; Fred L. Jeffers (millman, Boscawen) and G. M. Gilman (Stoneham, MA)
daughter, b. 6/24/1896 in Tamworth; fifth; Milton W. Jeffers (27, Webster) and Abbie B. Downs (27, Porter, ME)
son, b. 8/7/1897; sixth; Milton O. Jeffers (farmer, Webster) and Abbie B. Downs (Porter, ME)
daughter, b. 4/3/1899; seventh; Milton Jeffers (farmer, Webster) and Abbie B. Downs (Tamworth)
Charles M., Jr., b. 3/8/1950; fourth; Charles M. Jeffers and Madaline F. Jewett
Charles Milton, b. 7/15/1917; first; Gladys I. Jeffers (Tamworth)
Dorothy Louise, b. 12/13/1943; second; Charles M. Jeffers and Madaleine F. Jewett
Percey E., b. 4/24/1901; eighth; Milton Jeffers (laborer, Tamworth) and Abbie Downs (Porter, ME)
Robert, b. 3/30/1945; first; Charles M. Jeffers and Madaleine Jewett
Ryan Scott, b. 6/4/2002 in N. Conway; Dean Jeffers and Tricia Jeffers

JENKINS,
Dylan Franklin, b. 11/3/1992 in Laconia; Christopher F. Jenkins and Kelly M. Locke

JENNINGS,
Alan D., b. 1/11/1947; fourth; Bernard M. Jennings and Emily M. Hill
Beth Emily, b. 11/14/1968 in Laconia; Alan Douglas Jennings and Ann June Roberts
Gale M., b. 8/20/1949; fifth; Bernard M. Jennings and Emily M. Hill
Holly, b. 3/15/1967 in N. Conway; Alan Douglas Jennings and Ann

June Roberts
Keith, b. 5/9/1954; seventh; Bernard M. Jennings and Emily M. Hill
Keith Paul, b. 5/9/1972 in Laconia; Daniel Earl Jennings and Edith Carline Nixon

JOHNSON,
son, b. 3/16/1890; second; John W. Johnson (farmer, Tamworth) and Nellie Rogers (Porter, ME)
son, b. 6/30/1894 in Tamworth; third; Charles H. Johnson (laborer, 29, Lowell, MA) and Annie E. Gardiner (28, Tamworth)
son, b. 10/5/1896 in Tamworth; second; John W. Johnson (38, Tamworth) and Nellie Rogers (33, Porter, ME)
son, b. 6/10/1897; first; Newton N. Johnson (farmer, Tamworth) and Etta Moore
daughter, b. 5/30/1915 in Tamworth; second; Edwin R. Johnson (farmer, 30, NY) and Sylvia R. Elliott (Sandwich)
daughter, b. 3/12/1916; second; Harry S. Johnson (blacksmith, Brownfield, ME) and Alice E. Drake (Ossipee)
son, b. 7/31/1918; third; Harry S. Johnson (farmer, Brownfield, ME) and Alice E. Drake (Ossipee)
daughter, b. 1/12/1921 in Tamworth; fourth; Harry Johnson (farm laborer) and ----- Kelley
child, b. 10/17/1938; first; Forrest W. Johnson and Effie P. Bean
child, b. 5/20/1940; second; Forrest W. Johnson and Effie P. Bean
Adam Drue Mitchell, b. 2/7/1981 in N. Conway; Karl Johnson and Kathleen Mitchell
Benjamin, b. 11/25/1924; Harry S. Johnson and Alice E. Drake
Charlotte, b. 3/18/1927; Harry Johnson and Celie Drake
Christina, b. 11/24/1913; first; Edwin R. Johnson (farmer, NY) and Silvia R. Elliott (Sandwich)
Dale Wayne, b. 4/29/1969 in Laconia; Dennis Wayne Johnson and Rose Marie Hobbs
Dana Wayne, b. 4/29/1969 in Laconia; Dennis Wayne Johnson and Rose Marie Hobbs
Ethan Nathaniel, b. 8/4/1986 in N. Conway; Donald Johnson and Lisa Nickerson
Eunice, b. 8/24/1929; Harry S. Johnson and Alice Drake
Glenn E., Jr., b. 8/27/1980 in Wolfeboro; Glenn Johnson and Karren Mann
Grant Cody, b. 2/13/1991 in N. Conway; Todd Johnson and Michelle L. Bettencourt

Hannah Elizabeth, b. 8/27/1989 in N. Conway; Donald Johnson and Lisa A. Nickerson
Harry O., b. 12/4/1946; sixth; Forrest W. Johnson and Effie P. Bean
Jeffrey O., b. 10/16/1958; fourth; Marshall B. Johnson and Alice E. Williamson
Kim Terrie, b. 7/5/1978 in Wolfeboro; Glenn Johnson and Karren Mann
Marion Elizabeth, b. 3/21/1913; first; Harry S. Johnson (laborer, Brownfield, ME) and Alice E. Drake (Ossipee)
Olive D., b. 6/5/1893; second; Charles H. Johnson (millman, Lowell, MA) and Ann E. Gordon (Tamworth)
Paul William Mitchell, b. 12/6/1984 in Concord; K. Michael Johnson and Kathleen Mitchell
Rebecca May, b. 11/3/1966 in Wolfeboro; Forrest Westley Johnson and Effie Pauline Bean
Shirley J., b. 6/12/1953; third; Marshall B. Johnson and Alice E. Williamson
Tammy Lyn, b. 5/6/1971 in Wolfeboro; Glenn Edward Johnson and Karren Elaine Mann

JONES,
child, b. 3/12/1933; Frederick Jones and Jessie Brown
Adam H., b. 2/26/1980 in N. Conway; David Jones and Debra Plummer
Chester David, b. 4/28/1975 in N. Conway; David Henry Jones and Debra Ann Plummer
Daniel P., b. 9/23/1957; first; Joseph E. Jones and Judith E. Gilman
Denise E., b. 10/27/1958; second; Joseph E. Jones and Judith E. Gilman
Douglas P., b. 10/6/1947; first; James M. Jones and Virginia Bookholz
Jamie Marie, b. 7/30/1976 in N. Conway; David H. Jones and Debra A. Plummer
Melissa Eleanor, b. 6/2/1978 in N. Conway; Robert Jones and Cynthia Berry
Timothy S., b. 6/2/1960; third; Joseph E. Jones and Judith E. Gilman
William Franklin, b. 2/23/1932; Harry F. Jones and Ruth E. Fortier

JORDON,
Mitchell Dean, b. 10/10/1963 in Wolfeboro; second; Haven E. Gordon and Rita A. Crouse

KALLED,
Christian Pierce, b. 10/6/1982 in Hanover; John Kalled and Barbara Kalled

KAYSER,
Megan Clark, b. 4/8/1976 in Laconia; Paul Kayser and Judith R. Weare

KELLY,
Benjamin Thomas, b. 2/27/2001 in Wolfeboro; Steve Kelly and Barbara Kelly

KEMP,
Barbara Elaine, b. 5/15/1937; Harry E. Kemp and Lela Jayne LeGro
Phyllis E., b. 5/31/1940; second; Harry E. Kemp and Lela J. LeGro

KENDRICK,
Tory Nathan, b. 7/17/1975 in N. Conway; Gregg Albert Kendrick and Verlene Jane Ohlson

KIERSTEAD,
child, b. 10/6/1928; Thomas Kierstead and Lillian M. Brown
Flora May, b. 8/14/1937; Thomas E. Kierstead and Lillian M. Brown
Ina Gertrude, b. 6/16/1932; Thomas Kierstead and Lillian Brown
Marjorie True, b. 10/15/1930; Thomas E. Kierstead and Lillian Brown

KIMBALL,
daughter, b. 12/19/1893; fourth; Orrin S. Kimball (tailor, Tamworth) and Cora F. Bickford (Somersworth)
Anita L., b. 9/1/1946; third; Charles Kimball and Christine M. Bean
Louise, b. 7/24/1893; second; Samuel O. Kimball (merchant, Tamworth) and Sarah F. Gilman (Tamworth)
Marion R., b. 3/26/1888; third; Orrin S. Kimball (merchant, Tamworth) and Cora F. Bickford (Great Falls)
Philip A., b. 10/8/1889; first; Samuel O. Kimball (merchant, Tamworth) and Sarah F. Gilman (Tamworth)

KING,
Brady William, b. 8/26/2002 in N. Conway; Christopher King and Heidi King
Judith H., b. 3/14/1940; first; Arthur C. King and Edith C. Walker

Kathleen, b. 5/31/1944; second; Arthur C. King and Edith K. Walker

KNOWLTON,
son, b. 12/2/1893; first; Calvin C. Knowlton (laborer, Tamworth) and Ella M. Peasley (Sandwich)
son, b. 4/15/1917; first; Haven C. Knowlton (carpenter, Tamworth) and Ida M. Downs (Tamworth)
Joanne P., b. 7/5/1947; first; Kenneth H. Knowlton and Marjorie E. Griffin

KNOX,
Susan Carey, b. 3/9/1977 in Laconia; Brent E. Knox and Catherine D. Boothby

KOCH,
Ezra Bartlett, b. 7/30/1981 in Laconia; Eugene Koch and Deborah Chappell

KOHUT,
Carl Tomsen, b. 1/2/1991 in Laconia; Carl D. Kohut and Patricia A. Gray
Katherine Barnard, b. 5/16/1989 in Laconia; Carl D. Kohut and Patricia A. Gray

KYPRIDES,
Demetra Christine, b. 8/13/1975 in Wolfeboro; Peter Emanuel Kyprides and Patricia Munro Lockwood

LACHANCE,
Roger Allen, b. 9/13/1937; Raymond LaChance and Irene Wheeler

LALIBERTE,
David Earle, b. 1/8/1982 in N. Conway; David Laliberte and Diane McNally

LAMOUNTAGNE,
daughter, b. 11/30/1919; third; Joseph Exyard Lamountagne (Ossipee) and Lenora Bell Arling (Tamworth)
Eunice A., b. 4/25/1917; second; Joseph E. Lamountagne (laborer, Ossipee) and Lenora B. Arling (Tamworth)

LAMY,
Cayleen Amann, b. 2/28/1991 in N. Conway; Michael A. Lamy and
    Christine R. Amann
Corbyn Michael, b. 2/15/1993 in N. Conway; Michael A. Lamy and
    Christine R. Amann

LANCIAUX,
Alain Maurice, Jr., b. 4/2/1991 in N. Conway; Alain M. Lanciaux and
    Lorraine P. Pelletier

LANE,
Edward H., b. 10/3/1914; second; Albert M. Lane (laborer, 37, Troy,
    NY) and Alice Gilligan (31, Portsmouth)
Henry J. E., Jr., b. 8/22/1939; first; Henry J. E. Lane and Ethel M.
    Pennell
Henry James, b. 5/25/1916; first; James Martin Lane (laborer,
    Madison) and Clara A. Fickett (Madison)
Meredith Donna, b. 10/4/1941; second; Henry J. Lane and Ethel M.
    Pennell
Rita Elizabeth, b. 1/26/1918; second; James M. Lane (miner,
    Albany) and Clara E. Fickett (Silver Lake)

LANGLEY,
Gail Lee, b. 6/20/1941; second; Donald A. Langley and Eva M.
    Thomas

LAPETE,
Michael Tyler, b. 5/24/1985 in N. Conway; Stephen LaPete and Beth
    Scogin

LARKIN,
Constantina Jasmine, b. 2/4/1991 in N. Conway; Steven R. Larkin
    and Stavroula Christodoulou

LARRABEE,
Allan Bruce, b. 8/20/1937; Raymond E. Larrabee and Thelma Vittum
Andrew Herbert, b. 9/27/1963 in Laconia; first; Arnold Herbert
    Larrabee and Juidth Rose Weare
Arnold H., b. 1/4/1939; seventh; Raymond Larrabee and Dorothy T.
    Vittum
Donald Edwin, b. 2/27/1930; Raymond Larrabee and Dorothy T.

Vittum
Doratha A., b. 7/12/1934; Raymond Larrabee and Thelma D. Vittum
Elizabeth M., b. 7/19/1927; Raymond Larrabee and Dorothy T. Vittum
Julie Lynn, b. 6/6/1968 in Wolfeboro; Alan Douglas Larrabee and Sandra Marie Hutchins
Keith Arnold, b. 10/13/1968 in Wolfeboro; Arnold Herbert Larrabee and Donna Lee Hutchins
Marilyn Alice, b. 10/8/1933; Raymond Larrabee and Thelma Vittum
Raymond L., b. 8/21/1928; Raymond Larrabee and Dorothy T. Vittum
Susan Marie, b. 5/10/1966 in Wolfeboro; Alan Bruce Larrabee and Sandra Marie Hutchins
Timothy Sean, b. 2/22/1966 in Laconia; Arnold Herbert Larrabee and Judith Rose Weare

LAUZON,
Jacob Francis, b. 4/19/1993 in N. Conway; Peter D. Lauzon and Linda A. Webster

LAVOIE,
Andrew Roger, b. 8/14/1998 in N. Conway; Michael D. Lavoie and Jill E. Babcock
Robert Michael, b. 6/7/1996 in N. Conway; Michael D. Lavoie and Jill E. Babcock

LEACH,
son, b. 6/29/1916; fifth; William Leach (laborer, NY) and Alma Jeffers (Tamworth)
son, b. 3/15/1920 in Tamworth; eighth; William F. Leach (farmer, NY) and Alma C. Jeffers (Tamworth)
Bernice Abbie, b. 3/21/1910; third; William F. Leach (laborer, NY) and Alma Jeffers (Tamworth)
Doris A., b. 9/7/1907; second; W. F. Leach (laborer, NY) and Elma C. Jeffers (Tamworth)
Edward Murray, b. 3/25/1918; seventh; William F. Leach (laborer, New York City) and Alma C. Jeffers (Tamworth)
Georgia Louise, b. 5/22/1926; William Leach and Elinor Jeffers
Ida May, b. 9/26/1914 in Tamworth; fourth; William Leach (laborer, 30, NY) and Alma Jeffers (26, Tamworth)
John Milton, b. 4/6/1913; fourth; William F. Leach (laborer, NY) and

Alma C. Jeffies (Tamworth)
Marjorie Louise, b. 4/18/1923; tenth; William E. Leach (NY) and
  Anna L. Jaffers (Tamworth)
Richard Clyde, b. 2/11/1922; ninth; William Leach (NY City) and
  Alma C. Jeffers (Tamworth)
Rintha L., b. 4/19/1906; second; William F. Leach (laborer, NY) and
  Alma C. Jeffers (Tamworth)

LEAVITT,
son, b. 8/23/1888; second; John A. Leavitt (farmer, New Milford, IL)
  and Nellie J. Gilman (Sandwich)
Joshua Morton, b. 6/13/1983 in N. Conway; Scott M. Leavitt and
  Cynthia M. Cochrane

LEIGHTON,
Beverly J., b. 7/9/1941; first; Charles Leighton, Jr. and Louise I.
  Stacy
Bonnie M., b. 10/28/1948; fourth; Charles A. Leighton and Louise I.
  Stacy
Tina Marie, b. 8/23/1972 in Wolfeboro; Charles Larry Leighton and
  Sally Ann Covey
Wendell, b. 12/25/1943; second; Charles A. Leighton and Louise I.
  Stacy

LESSARD,
Kenneth Cody, b. 10/27/1995 in Wolfeboro; Mark E. Lessard and
  Stacey M. Mansfield

LIBBY,
Brandy Lynn, b. 9/27/1993 in N. Conway; Paul G. Libby and Donna
  M. Lucente
Christopher Scott, b. 5/16/1985 in N. Conway; Paul Libby and April
  Ryder

LIONETTA,
Nicholas Scott, b. 6/26/1997 in N. Conway; Scott Michael Lionetta
  and Susan Lynne Lefevre
Shannon Noel, b. 8/13/2000 in N. Conway; Scott Lionetta and Susan
  Lionetta

LITTLEFIELD,
son, b. 4/28/1888; sixth; George F. Littlefield (farmer, Madison) and Carrie Whitaker (Conway)
Megan Mary, b. 3/15/1999 in Wolfeboro; Norman Littlefield and Tricia Littlefield

LLOYD,
Brandon Dean, b. 10/14/1974 in Portsmouth; Wayne Stephen Lloyd and Betty Ruth Shindledecker
Daniel Isac, b. 3/2/2002 in Dover; Jeffrey Lloyd and Cheryl Lloyd
Scott Paul, b. 7/23/1979 in Exeter; Gary Lloyd and Denise Perry
Sonya Marie, b. 3/22/1988 in N. Conway; Jeffrey R. Lloyd and Cheryl Rhines

LONG,
daughter, b. 7/31/1904; first; Almon Long (carpenter, Eaton) and Lena M. Ross (Tamworth); residence – Conway
daughter, b. 12/1/1908; second; Almon E. Long (mechanic, Eaton) and Lena M. Ross (Tamworth)
daughter, b. 2/7/1914; fourth; Elmer E. Long (carpenter, 41, Eaton) and Lena M. Ross (27, Tamworth)

LOUGHRAN,
Wesley Jefferson, b. 7/12/2003 in Tamworth; Dennis Quinn and Margaret Loughran

LOVERING,
H. Hamblin, b. 9/17/1896 in Tamworth; second; Jonas J. Lovering (33, Freedom) and Annie F. Morris (33, Yarmouth, NS)

LOWD,
Patricia Alice, b. 1/20/1941; second; Burton W. Lowd and Florence E. Perkins

LYNCH,
Timothy Joseph, b. 1/18/1989 in N. Conway; Mark E. Lynch and Rebecca A. Metivier

LYNDES,
Jillian Elizabeth, b. 4/14/1983 in Laconia; Rodney R. Lyndes and Susan Marie Ames

MACDONALD,
Dennis L., b. 12/27/1958; fourth; Forrest G. MacDonald and Barbara M. Hobbs
Jennifer Jean, b. 4/27/1974 in Wolfeboro; Forrest George MacDonald and Pamela Jane Atwood
Kathy May, b. 8/19/1962 in Laconia; sixth; Forrest George MacDonald and Barbara May Hobbs

MADUSKUIE,
Eric Roy, b. 5/9/1976 in Wolfeboro; Edward S. Maduskuie and Christine F. Bennett
Tarndra Rachel, b. 6/9/1979 in Wolfeboro; Edward Maduskuie and Christine Bennett

MAHER-COVILLE,
Mackenzie Gay, b. 7/1/1986 in N. Conway; Edward Coville and Nicole E. Maher

MALLAR,
daughter, b. 9/28/1997 in N. Conway; Mark Christopher Evans and Margo Lee Mallar
Alana K. S., b. 5/6/1994 in N. Conway; Mark C. Evans and Margo L. Mallar

MARKS,
Michael John, b. 1/22/1989 in Laconia; Michael J. Marks and Lisa Marie Perry

MARRONE,
Anthony Thomas, b. 12/1/1987 in N. Conway; Anthony Marrone and Gail G. Farrell
Nicholas John, b. 9/2/1991 in N. Conway; Anthony Marrone and Gail G. Farrell

MARSH,
son, b. 12/24/1898; first; Frank Marsh (laborer, Portugal) and Mary Sileo (Portugal)
Michael Scott, b. 1/19/1967 in Laconia; Raymond Royal Marsh and Jean Constance Plette

MARSHALL,
son, b. 3/5/1972 in N. Conway; John Lee Marshall and Cynthia Lou Frye
Jody Lee, b. 4/10/1971 in Laconia; John Lee Marshall and Cynthia Lou Frye

MARSTON,
son, b. 2/8/1897; second; John F. Marston (farmer, Tamworth) and Clara E. Remick (Tamworth)

MARTEL,
Benjamin Francis, b. 1/13/2000 in Laconia; James Martel and Jennifer Leiblein-Martel
Deborah L., b. 9/23/1959; fifth; Morton C. Martel and Violet D. Eldridge
Mary A., b. 5/7/1957; fourth; Morton C. Martel and Violet D. Eldridge

MARTIN,
Charles, b. 4/1/1944; first; Louville K. Martin and Helen Weed
Lynne M., b. 10/23/1951; second; Louville K. Martin and Helen Weede
Margaret, b. 2/10/1900; first; Lyman L. Martin (carpenter, Lovell, ME) and Ida M. Kennison (Tamworth)
William G., b. 8/18/1912; third; Lyman L. Martin (farmer, Lovell, ME) and Ida M. Kumiston (Tamworth)

MARTINEZ,
Charlene, b. 10/15/1946; first; Alexander Martinez and Shirley M. Wright

MASON,
daughter, b. 7/31/1891; first; Wilmer N. Mason (mechanic, Tamworth) and Joanna W. Folsom (Tamworth)
son, b. 12/28/1895 in Tamworth; first; Ernest S. Mason (farmer, 18, Winchester, MA) and Mabel C. Henderson (18, Madison)
son, b. 11/14/1896 in Tamworth; second; Earnest L. Mason (20, Tamworth) and Leafy Downs (20, Tamworth)
son, b. 2/7/194; fourth; Clinton C. Mason (carpenter, 31, Tamworth) and Flora V. McPhearson (31, Somerville, MA)
child, b. 6/28/1925; A. H. Mason and Blanche Ames
child, b. 6/28/1928; A. Horace Mason and Blanche M. Ames

Arthur H., b. 2/28/1901; first; Arthur L. Mason (student, Tamworth) and Elizabeth C. Chick (Tamworth)
Camila A., b. 2/5/1916; fifth; Chester L. Mason (farmer, Tamworth) and Mabel G. McPherson (Milton, MA)
Charles Bernard, b. 12/30/1911; second; Clinton C. Mason (blacksmith, Tamworth) and Flora D. McPherson (Somerville, MA)
Charlotte, b. 1/8/1910; third; Arthur L. Mason (teamster, Tamworth) and Elizabeth C. Chick (Tamworth)
Danielle Sandra, b. 7/16/1993 in N. Conway; Preston H. Mason and Julie L. Larrabee
Dorothea Loraine, b. 1/20/1913; third; Clinton C. Mason (carpenter, Tamworth) and Flora O. McPherson (Somerville, MA)
Ethel Rose, b. 5/23/1910; first; Clinton S. Mason (blacksmith, Tamworth) and Flora McPherson (Somerville, MA)
Harold L., b. 2/18/1918; second; Chester L. Mason (carpenter, Tamworth) and Mabel G. McPherson (Milton, MA)
Joyce Ann, b. 7/18/1933; Hi. Mason and Edna A. Cummings
Mary Etta, b. 1/28/1917; fifth; Clinton C. Mason (carpenter, Tamworth) and Flora V. McPherson (Somerville, MA)
Michael Alan, b. 3/15/1995 in N. Conway; Preston Haralan Mason and Julie Lynn Larrabee
Nicole Elizabeth, b. 7/16/1976 in Laconia; Arthur Mason III and Bonnie B. Conway
Pauline L., b. 7/8/1907; second; A. L. Mason (teamster, Tamworth) and E. C. Chick (Tamworth)
Perley, b. 12/4/1894 in Tamworth; first; Ernest L. Mason (laborer, 24, Tamworth) and Leafy Downs (18, Tamworth)
Teresa Arlene, b. 9/30/1921 in Tamworth; first; Hiram E. Mason (auto mechanic, Tamworth) and Edna Cummings (Woburn, MA)
Victoria, b. 8/14/1923; second; Horace A. Mason (Tamworth) and Blanche M. Ames (Tamworth)
Wendy G., b. 1/10/1954; second; Arthur H. Mason and Ruth E. Philbrick

MASTON,
daughter, b. 12/2/1887; first; John F. Maston (farmer, Tamworth) and Carrie E. (Tamworth)

MATHER,
John Sutton, b. 8/28/1953; third; Sydney C. Mather and Marjorie Mayers

MATTROSS,
Ruth, b. 10/16/1894 in Tamworth; seventh; Gilbert Mattross (laborer, 37, Montreal, Canada) and Susan M. Williams (33, Ossipee)

McCABE,
Barry David, b. 8/10/1985 in N. Conway; David McCabe and Patricia Keefe
Marlene Taryn, b. 2/6/1998 in Portland, ME; David McCabe and Patricia McCabe

McCARTHY,
Declan Sean, b. 2/16/1991 in Portsmouth; Sean M. McCarthy and Paula J. Schaffer
Ian Perry, b. 1/1/1988 in N. Conway; William J. McCarthy and Ruth M. Asselin
Jordan Christine, b. 10/19/1989 in N. Conway; William J. McCarthy, III and Ruth M. Asselin
Kevin Joseph, b. 8/11/1975 in Laconia; Kevin Joseph McCarthy and Angela Joan Boewe

McCREARY,
Christopher Paul, b. 12/26/1973 in N. Conway; Dann Paul McCreary and Pamela Alene Pierce

McDANIELS,
Lisa Shirley, b. 11/28/1962 in N. Conway; first; Wallace Andrew McDaniels and Shirley Ellen Anthony

McGILL,
Ashley Julia, b. 8/31/1995 in N. Conway; Robert T. McGill and Karen L. Bergeron
Stacey Elizabeth, b. 12/18/1992 in N. Conway; Robert T. McGill and Karen L. Bergeron

McKAY,
Matthew Bryan, b. 3/7/1989 in N. Conway; William S. McKay and Brenda M. Lundberg

McKEY,
Ellen B., b. 8/29/1958; first; Richard H. McKey and Marie L. Linder

McMANUS,
Jesse Daniel, b. 6/9/1989 in N. Conway; Peter T. McManus and Lisa M. Bongette

McNEAL,
daughter, b. 4/14/1888; first; Harry McNeal (farmer, St. Johns, NB) and Martha E. Perkins (Tamworth)
Uriah, b. 5/7/1890; second; Harry McNeal (farmer, St. Johns, NB) and Martha E. Perkins (Tamworth)

MELOON,
Helen Elizabeth, b. 6/27/1933; Howard M. Meloon and Edith A. Moore

MERRILL,
Donna J., b. 9/25/1939; second; Maurice E. Merrill and Annette S. Prescott
Richard Bradbury, b. 10/26/1936; Maurice Merrill and Annette Prescott

MIRACLE,
Chelsea Lynn, b. 7/2/1992 in N. Conway; Lee R. Miracle, Jr. and Rhonda A. Divitto

MITCHELL,
Jacob Richard, b. 3/27/1982 in Wolfeboro; Richard Mitchell and Leah Gammons

MOCK,
Rachel Starr, b. 9/2/1979 in Concord; Wayne Mock and Anne Spaulding
Tobias Walker, b. 10/31/1981 in Concord; Wayne Mock and Anne Spaulding

MONEYPENNY,
Madeline Damon, b. 2/20/2000 in N. Conway; Christopher Moneypenny and Lianne Prentice

MOODY,
stillborn daughter, b. 3/20/1895 in Tamworth; first; William H. Moody (laborer, 28, Tamworth) and Lora E. Davis (22, Tamworth)
daughter, b. 2/11/1904; second; Nathaniel E. Moody (laborer, Tamworth) and Nancy L. Pascoe (Freedom)
Alfred H., b. 9/29/1908; first; Joseph A. Moody (laborer, Tamworth) and Nettie Williams (Ossipee)
Anna Clara, b. 7/15/1914; third; Lester E. Moody (farmer, 31, Ossipee) and Mary E. Cochran (41, Portland, ME)
Cora Nettie, b. 4/30/1923; sixth; Joseph Moody (Boston, MA) and Nettie Williams (Ossipee)
Dawn S., b. 7/22/1957; second; Roger Moody and Virginia C. Haney
Edward Lester, b. 2/17/1911; second; Lester E. Moody (farmer, Ossipee) and Mary E. Corcoran (Portland, ME)
Florence Elizabeth, b. 4/2/1910; second; Joseph A. Moody (laborer, Tamworth) and Nettie N. Williams (Tamworth)
Fred Ellsworth, b. 2/3/1935; Myron Moody and Katherine Smith
Gertrude Maud, b. 4/12/1921 in Tamworth; seventh; Joseph Moody (farm laborer, Boston, MA) and Nettie Williams (Tamworth) (see following entry)
Gertwood Maud, b. 4/12/1922; seventh; Joseph Moody (Boston, MA) and Nettie Williams (Tamworth) (see preceding entry)
Gladys Mendora, b. 2/13/1913; third; Joseph A. Moody (laborer, Boston, MA) and Nettie Williams (Ossipee)
Katherine M., b. 3/30/1915 in Tamworth; fourth; Joseph A. Moody (laborer, 25, Boston, MA) and Nettie Williams (Ossipee)
Mary, b. 1/19/1909; first; Lester E. Moody (farmer, Ossipee) and Mary E. Corcoran (Portland)
Nancy, b. 4/28/1942; first; Merton Moody and Evelyn R. Mudgett
Robert James, b. 5/16/1997 in Laconia; Robert Paul Moody and Helen Arlene Slade
Rosalind H., b. 5/22/1949; first; Edward L. Moody and Dorothy King
Theodore Joseph, b. 7/7/1919; sixth; Joseph Moody (Boston, MA) and Nettie Williams (Tamworth)
Walter Lang, b. 7/3/1917; Joseph A. Moody (laborer, Boston, MA) and Nettie Williams (Ossipee)

MOON,
Roland Samuel, b. 7/30/1912; second; Samuel J. Moon (laborer, Conway) and Minnie Marston (Tamworth)

MOORE,
son, b. 3/16/1888; second; Edwin Moore (farmer) and Mary
   Kennerson (Tamworth)
son, b, 3/24/1906; seventh; Edgar H. Moore (farmer, S. Berwick,
   ME) and Mary A. Kenerson (Tamworth)
child, b. 1/18/1929; Richard D. Moore and Eva Shedd
Albert Richard, b. 6/29/1922; second; Richard Moore (Tamworth)
   and Eva Ella Shedd (Grantham)
Clara Elizabeth, b. 8/20/1913; third; Samuel J. Moore (laborer,
   Conway) and Minnie A. Marston (Tamworth)
Donald Ross, b. 3/14/1920 in Tamworth; second; William E. Moore
   (farmer, Tamworth) and Alice M. Ross (Tamworth)
Emma May, b. 10/22/1923; third; William E. Moore (Tamworth) and
   Alice M. Ross (Tamworth)
Herbert Franklin, b. 8/10/1918; first; William Edgar Moore (farmer,
   Tamworth) and Alice May Ross (Tamworth)
Roland Samuel, b. 7/30/1915 in Tamworth; third; Samuel J. Moore
   (laborer, 34, Conway) and Minnie Marston (24, Tamworth)

MOSHER,
Michael David, b. 7/19/1995 in Laconia; James R. Mosher and
   Deborah Arleen Anthony
Tonya Marie, b. 8/30/1991 in Laconia; James R. Mosher and
   Deborah A. Anthony

MOULTON,
daughter, b. 5/29/1888; first; Luman I. Moulton (mechanic, Albany)
   and Carrie Davis (Tamworth)
daughter, b. 8/23/1889; second; L. I. Moulton (mechanic, Albany)
   and Carrie E. Davis (Tamworth)
daughter, b. 3/20/1891; third; Cyrus A. Moulton (laborer) and Lizzie
   B. Foss (Tamworth)
son, b. 3/8/1895 in Tamworth; fifth; Cyrus A. Moulton (laborer, 34,
   Moultonboro) and Lizzie B. Foss (24, Tamworth)
child, b. 7/6/1927; Harley E. Moulton and Gladys Hitchcock
child, b. 4/13/1928; Harley E. Moulton and Gladys Hitchcock
Bernard Drahan, b. 8/29/1909; first; Chester A. Moulton (laborer,
   Tamworth) and Katherine F. Drahan (Cambridge, MA)
Franklin A., b. 3/31/1903; second; Willis Moulton (farmer, Sandwich)
   and Lydia E. Allard (Newark, VT)
R. S., Jr., b. 8/24/1948; second; Robert S. Moulton and Maxine C.

Tagart
Sharlene D., b. 1/8/1951; third; Richard S. Moulton and Maxine C. Tagart

MUDGETT,
Alexander James, b. 6/30/1999 in N. Conway; Jamie Roger Mudgett and Amanda Lee Dunn
Gretchen, b. 3/26/1982 in N. Conway; James Mudgett and Ann Roberts
Jamie Roger, b. 5/26/1975 in Laconia; James Roger Mudgett and Ann June Roberts
Robert E., b. 3/6/1956; first; Eugene R. Mudgett and Joan J. Sarni
Scott Gary, b. 4/21/1977 in N. Conway; James R. Mudgett, Jr. and Ann June Roberts

NASAF,
Mike, b. 5/27/1905; first; Mike Nasaf (pedler, Mt. Lebanon, Syria) and Mary Carry (Mt. Lebanon, Syria)

NASON,
Harold E., b. 9/13/1952; fourth; Walter A. Nason and Yvonne T. Petitpas
Kevin Charles, b. 6/28/1979 in Laconia; Allen Nason and Rebecca Whiting
Mary E., b. 5/2/1950; second; Walter A. Nason and Yvonne T. Petitpas
Sally J., b. 9/8/1951; third; Walter A. Nason and Yvonne T. Petitpas
Tommy R., b. 8/26/1980 in N. Conway; Allen Nason and Rebecca Whiting

NELSON,
Barbara, b. 6/25/1930; John R. Nelson and Lillian Walker
Christopher Todd, b. 9/26/1983 in Laconia; Peter A. Nelson and Deborah Jean Stewart
Gene Ramon, b. 4/14/1936; Lawrence Elyn Nelson and Lahlia Lovering
Joshua James, b. 4/14/1982 in Laconia; Peter Nelson and Deborah Stewart
Rebecca A., b. 6/5/1949; second; Maurice L. Nelson and Elizabeth Kapka
Rebekkah Joy, b. 10/15/1990 in Plymouth; Peter A. Nelson and

Deborah J. Stewart

NEWALL,
Jamison Patrick, b. 10/1/1985 in N. Conway; Jacob Newall and Judie Swanberry

NEWCOMB,
Andrew N., b. 1/15/1979 in Laconia; Robert N. Newcomb and Kristina Grondal
David Thomas, b. 11/7/1981 in Laconia; Robert Newcomb and Kristina Grondal

NEWSOM,
Laven Coates, b. 9/10/1990 in N. Conway; Samuel B. Newsom and Damon Herkness
Riley Herkness, b. 7/8/1992 in N. Conway; Samuel B. Newsom and Damon Herkness

NICKERSON,
son, b. 11/15/1894 in Tamworth; third; Jerome C. Nickerson (laborer, 30, NS) and Atheria Wentgel (28, NS)
Alta C., b. 6/13/1895 in Tamworth; first; George E. Nickerson (farmer, 26, Tamworth) and Carrie B. White (23, Madison)
Etta M., b. 8/12/1900; fourth; Jerome Nickerson (laborer, NS) and Eltheria Wentzel (NS)
Evelyn, b. 6/10/1903; second; George E. Nickerson (farmer, Tamworth) and Carrie White (Madison)
Hattie E., b. 12/25/1896 in Tamworth; third; Ezra Nickerson (2-, Tamworth) and Emma Perkins (26, Tamworth)
Lawrence G., b. 5/9/1955; second; Lawrence Nickerson and Helen C. Carney
Lisa, b. 3/9/1953; first; Lawrence Nickerson and Helen E. Carney (1956)
Margaret Putnam, b. 10/28/1903 in Tamworth; Ezra Nickerson and Emma M. Perkins (1965)
Sarah M., b. 5/23/1908; sixth; Ezra Nickerson (farmer, Tamworth) and Emma M. Perkins (Tamworth)
Valarie M., b. 6/3/1957; third; Lawrence E. Nickerson and Helen E. Carney
Winfield, b. 1/23/1891; first; Ezra Nickerson (mechanic, Tamworth) and Emma Perkins (Tamworth)

NOLET,
Jacqueline Jeanne, b. 7/9/1990 in N. Conway; Mark A. Nolet and Kimberely L. Waterman

NORCROSS,
Amber Lynn, b. 6/3/1988 in N. Conway; Thomas E. Norcross and Patricia L. Sheppard
Andria Lee, b. 3/19/1991 in N. Conway; Andy L. Norcross and Ann Marie Cash
Andy Lee, b. 9/4/1971 in Laconia; Arthur Zebulon Norcross and Irene May Ames
Barry Lee, b. 8/18/1966 in Wolfeboro; Charles Dennis Norcross and Faye Valerie Mudgett
Brian Charles, b. 9/9/1963 in Wolfeboro; second; Charles Dennis Norcross and Faye Valerie Mudgett
Gardner Lloyd, b. 7/24/1962 in Wolfeboro; first; Charles Dennis Norcross and Faye Valerie Mudgett
Haley Kate, b. 5/26/1996 in N. Conway; Gardner L. Norcross and Susan M. Davidson
Justin Milton, b. 4/24/1981 in Laconia; Milton Norcross and Regina Swan
Kyle Severance, b. 2/21/1984 in Laconia; Milton Norcross and Regina Swan
Lucas Tanner, b. 7/14/1992 in N. Conway; Gardner L. Norcross and Susan M. Davidson
Milton A., b. 3/4/1957; first; Arthur Z. Norcross and Irene M. Ames
Thomas Elmer, b. 11/16/1966 in Laconia; Arthur Zublon Norcross and Irene May Ames

NOYES,
Jarred Wayne, b. 10/16/1989 in N. Conway; Wendell W. Noyes and Kim E. Cote
Jessica Lynn, b. 6/25/2002 in N. Conway; Judson Noyes and Tracey Noyes
Kenneth James, b. 2/24/1988 in Hanover; Wendell W. Noyes and Kim E. Cote

NYLAND,
Hannah Grace, b. 6/1/1996 in N. Conway; James S. Nyland and Mirian D. Sayler

O'KEEFE,
Courtney Ana, b. 8/15/1996 in N. Conway; James R. O'Keefe and Tammy L. Barnes
Kyle Leeland, b. 2/6/1998 in N. Conway; James R. O'Keefe and Tammy L. Barnes
Liam Asher, b. 1/13/2000 in N. Conway; James O'Keefe and Tammy O'Keefe
Willow Adelaide, b. 8/22/2003 in N. Conway; James O'Keefe and Tammy O'Keefe

OKTAVEC,
Christopher Michael, b. 4/22/1992 in Laconia; Michael J. Oktavec and Justine E. Pitula

OSGOOD,
Fannie J., b. 1/19/1893; first; Herman L. Osgood (painter, Tamworth) and Ellen I. Freeman (Worcester, MA)
George Addison, b. 12/9/1896 in Tamworth; third; Herman L. Osgood (30, Tamworth) and Ellen I. Freeman (35, Worcester, MA)
Laura Isabel, b. 7/28/1924; Lillian Osgood
Lilian, b. 5/17/1894 in Tamworth; second; Herman L. Osgood (painter, 25, Tamworth) and Ellen I. Freeman (34, Worcester, MA)

OWENS,
Leona Lee, b. 1/28/1962 in N. Conway; first; Edward Jay Owens and Marie Esther Bickford

PAGE,
son, b. 7/3/1891; fourth; Moses F. Page (farmer, Tamworth) and Lizzie E. Robinson (Gorham)
daughter, b. 11/4/1898; first; Arthur C. Page (blacksmith, Gilmanton) and Mary A. Remick (Tamworth)
daughter, b. 12/30/1898; first; Edgar Page (laborer, Lynn) and Grace Davis (Tamworth)
daughter, b. 6/20/1914; sixth; Arthur C. Page (blacksmith, 45, Gilmanton) and Mary Abbie Remick (34, Tamworth)
son, b. 1/26/1916; eighth; Arthur C. Page (blacksmith, Gilmanton) and Mary Abbie Remick (Tamworth)
Benjamin W., b. 9/4/1908; fourth; Arthur C. Page (blacksmith,

Gilmanton) and Abbie E. Remick (Tamworth)
Bertha Mary, b. 6/20/1912; sixth; Arthur C. Page (blacksmith, Gilmanton) and Mary Abbie Remick (Tamworth)
Dixie C., b. 1/19/1910; fifth; Arthur C. Page (blacksmith, Gilmanton) and Abbie Remick (Tamworth)
Doris Irene, b. 9/16/1906; second; Edgar P. Page (laborer, Lynn, MA) and Grace A. Davis (Tamworth)
Esther, b. 4/14/1905; third; Arthur C. Page (blacksmith, Gilmanton) and Mary A. Remick (Tamworth)
Eva Serena, b. 12/13/1902; second; Arthur C. Page (blacksmith, Gilmanton) and Mary A. Remick (Tamworth)
Howard F., b. 5/29/1889; first; Horace A. Page (farmer, Tamworth) and Bertha C. Howard (Brockton, MA)
Mary E., b. 7/20/1950; first; Oliver E. Page and Winona H. Clemons

PALMER,
Ariel Adriana, b. 9/29/1991 in Laconia; Daniel R. Palmer and Sacha M. Eldridge
Charlotte E., b. 10/12/1930; Herbert Palmer and Addie M. Grace
Clarence Edward, b. 8/16/1933; Herbert E. Palmer and Addie M. Grace
Jeffrey Richard, b. 12/27/2000 in N. Conway; Daniel Palmer and Lori Palmer
Joan L., b. 9/26/1960; second; Clarence E. Palmer and Dorothy L. Jordan
Mariah Danielle, b. 3/17/1990 in Laconia; Daniel R. Palmer and Sacha Miai Eldridge
Patsy Marie, b. 12/28/1942; first; Harland C. Palmer and June E. Holbrook
Robert C., b. 1/21/1958; first; Clarence E. Palmer and Dorothy L. Jordan
Virginia Pearl, b. 4/10/1924; Herbert E. Palmer and Gladys May Eldridge

PARKER,
Montana James, b. 5/20/1990 in N. Conway; Ran
Robert L., b. 9/3/1946; first; Gerald H. Parker and Elizabeth L. Bushey

PARSONS,
Angela P., b. 1/16/1947; third; Michael F. Parsons and Theresa

Reddy
Richard, b. 3/11/1945; first; Michael F. Parsons and Jean T. Reddy

PASCOE,
stillborn daughter, b. 7/24/1909; first; William J. Pascoe (merchant, Freedom) and Josie L. Moulton (Freedom)
Eulalie, b. 12/30/1911; second; William J. Pascoe (merchant, Freedom) and Josie L. Moulton (Eaton)

PEARL,
Harold Franklin, b. 9/22/1917; second; Harry W. Pearl (farmer, Porter, ME) and Sadie E. Whiting (Tamworth)

PEARSON,
Scott Charles, b. 9/5/1986 in Wolfeboro; Charles Pearson and Karen Sennett

PEASLEE,
Caitlynn Dorothy, b. 9/1/1998 in Laconia; Philip E. Peaslee and Patricia I. Merrithew
Christina Louise, b. 8/5/1977 in Hanover; Charles H. Peaslee and Dorothy A. Roberts

PENNELL,
son, b. 5/16/1894 in Tamworth; third; Charles H. Pennell (laborer, 35, Buxton, ME) and Addie M. Brown (21, Somersworth)
Dwight Robert, b. 6/2/1933; Edd. Pennell and Dora Williams
Edith Mildred, b. 1/10/1916; second; Edwin Pennell (laborer, Tamworth) and Dora L. Williams (Tamworth)
Edwin C., b. 12/22/1924; Edwin A. Pennell and Dora L. Williams
Ethel May, b. 11/6/1912; first; Edwin Pennell (laborer, Tamworth) and Dora Williams (Tamworth)
Lilla M., b. 4/8/1900; third; Charles H. Pennell (laborer, Buxton, ME) and Addie M. Brown (Somersworth)
Reginald E., b. 12/14/1939; first; Reginald E. Pennell and Helen J. Remick

PERKINS,
daughter, b. 1/6/1891; second; William Perkins (farmer, Jackson) and Lizzie C. Grover (Sandwich)
daughter, b. 2/18/1892; third; William H. Perkins (farmer, Jackson)

and Lizzie C. Graves (Sandwich)
son, b. 4/23/1892; seventh; Frank H. Perkins (clergyman,
 Manchester) and Fanny F. Sanborn (Orange)
son, b. 4/13/1895 in Tamworth; fourth; William H. Perkins (farmer,
 34, Jackson) and Elizabeth C. Graves (34, Sandwich)
son, b. 10/28/1913; second; Charles W. Perkins (butcher,
 Tamworth) and Katherine O'Donohue (Lowell, MA)
son, b. 8/23/1915 in Tamworth; first; Pike G. Perkins (farmer, 20,
 Tamworth) and Stella A. Bickford (Sandwich)
Arthur C., b. 7/2/1898; fifth; William H. Perkins (farmer, Jackson) and
 Elizabeth Graves (Sandwich)
Arthur Robert, b. 5/15/1912; first; Charles W. Perkins (butcher,
 Tamworth) and Katherine O'Donahue (Lowell, MA)
Blanche E., b. 3/26/1901; third; Hiram L. Perkins (laborer, Ossipee)
 and Harriet Clough (Effingham)
Charles W., b. 7/30/1887; first; William W. Perkins (farmer, Jackson)
 and Lizzie C. (Sandwich)
Claude H., b. 11/28/1900; stillborn; second; Alston W. Perkins
 (farmer, Jackson) and Ella M. Bryer (Sandwich)
Dorothy, b. 7/5/1916; third; Charles W. Perkins (farmer, Tamworth)
 and Katherine E. O'Donahue (Lowell, MA)
Etta M., b. 5/1/1897; second; Hiram L. Perkins (laborer, Ossipee)
 and Etta Clough (Epping)
Kurt William, b. 7/10/1962 in Wolfeboro; fourth; Pike Gordon
 Perkins, Jr. and Emily Erma Nickerson
Lawrence, b. 9/14/1909; first; Oscar Perkins (laborer, Meredith) and
 Edith J. Davis (Ossipee); residence – Meredith
Patricia A., b. 6/20/1953; third; Pike G. Perkins, Jr. and Emily E.
 Nickerson
Paul T., b. 1/23/1945; second; Theodore G. Perkins and Marguerite
 Buck
Peter Warren, b. 1/12/1942; first; Theodore G. Perkins and
 Marguerite E. Buck
Philip E., b. 6/25/1948; fourth; Theodore G. Perkins and Marguerite
 E. Buck
Pike G., Jr., b. 3/23/1930; Pike G. Perkins and Estella A. Bickford
Pike Gordon, III, b. 2/25/1970 in Wolfeboro; Pike Gordon Perkins, Jr.
 and Shirley G. Sherman
Robert H., b, 2/5/1951; second; Pike G. Perkins and Emily E.
 Nickerson

PERRY,
Courtney Elizabeth, b. 8/11/1996 in N. Conway; Dean P. Perry and Charlotte E. Sullivan
Desiree Lynn, b. 12/2/1982 in Wolfeboro; Allen Perry and Barbara Berry
Erica Rose, b. 5/31/1991 in N. Conway; Sheldon P. Perry and Nina Sawicki
Sheldon Reid, b. 5/11/1988 in N. Conway; Sheldon P. Perry and Nina Sawicki

PERRYMAN,
Michael R., b. 12/4/1954; second; Herbert R. Perryman, Jr. and Genevieve D. Ruch

PHELAN,
Rede Joseph, b. 11/26/1978 in N. Conway; Edward Phelan and Roberta Wagner

PHENIX,
Matthew Alan, b. 8/26/1986 in Tamworth; Alan Phenix and Carol Emery

PHILLIPPI,
Evan Robertson, b. 10/31/1981 in Concord; Karl Phillippi and Elizabeth O'Dell

PHILLIPS,
daughter, b. 5/29/1915 in Tamworth; first; Thomas F. Phillips (electrician, 32, Dorchester, MA) and Margaret Johnston (NS)
Paula Lee, b. 7/26/1969 in N. Conway; Thomas William Phillips and Ann Marie Moore
Terry Marie, b. 2/10/1971 in N. Conway; Thomas William Phillips and Ann Marie Moore

PIKE,
Heather Scott, b. 11/14/2000 in Wolfeboro; Harold Pike and Laura Pike

PIPER,
Jason P., b. 6/7/1980 in N. Conway; Bruce Piper and Patricia Nadeau

Jennifer Marjorie, b. 8/15/1987 in N. Conway; Bruce Piper and
  Patricia A. Nadeau
Kyle Arthur, b. 10/16/1993 in N. Conway; Bruce M. Piper and
  Patricia A. Nadeau

PIXTON,
Chance William, b. 6/7/2003 in N. Conway; Felix Pixton and Ellen
  Pixton

PLANT,
daughter, b. 5/22/1890; eighth; Joseph Plant (laborer, Quebec,
  Canada) and Ellen Morrell (Old Town, ME)
son, b. 2/6/1903; eleventh; Joseph Plant (farmer, Quebec) and Ellen
  Morrill (Oldtown, ME)

PLUMMER,
Betty J., b. 4/17/1951; first; Charles F. Plummer and Doris M.
  Palmer
Debra A., b. 4/15/1955; second; Clarence R. Plummer, Jr. and
  Louise M. Underhill
Frank J., b. 1/4/1955; third; Raymond E. Plummer and Bernice L.
  Chase
George R., b. 12/26/1953; first; Clarence R. Plummer, Jr. and Louise
  M. Underhill
Jane E., b. 8/26/1958; fourth; Charles F. Plummer and Doris M.
  Palmer
Linda M., b. 9/26/1951; first; Raymond E. Plummer and Bernice L.
  Chase
Peggy Ann, b. 6/14/1964 in Laconia; fourth; Raymond E. Plummer
  and Bernice L. Chase
Richard C., b. 8/12/1955; third; Charles F. Plummer and Doris M.
  Palmer
Rosemary E., b. 6/20/1956; third; Clarence R. Plummer and Louise
  M. Underhill
Sandra M., b. 1/18/1954; second; Charles F. Plummer and Doris M.
  Palmer
Susan M., b. 9/26/1957; fourth; Clarence R. Plummer and Louise M.
  Underhill

POLEN,
Rowan Leroy, b. 5/19/1995 in Chocorua; Dale Ray Polen, Jr. and

Suzanne McCollum

PONT,
Hilary Laurel, b. 11/14/1979 in N. Conway; William Pont and Laurel Glidden

POWERS,
Bruce Allen, b. 7/31/1934; Grover O. Powers and Ada May Leach

PRAY,
Julian E., b. 6/24/1902; fourth; Joseph Pray (blacksmith, Salmon Falls) and Harriet Montague (Halifax)
Julius P., b. 6/24/1902; fifth; Joseph Pray (blacksmith, Salmon Falls) and Harriet Montague (Halifax)
Roland, b. 6/26/1901; third; Joseph Pray (blacksmith, Salmon Falls) and Harriet LaMontain (Halifax, NS)

PRESCOTT,
Lee Stillman, b. 10/20/1941; first; John P. Prescott and Laura T. Wheaton

PUGH,
Alison Staples, b. 12/17/1991 in N. Conway; Charles L. Pugh and Rebekah Staples

PURRINGTON,
Eva, b. 4/15/1891; first; Daniel Purrington (laborer, Albany) and Flora Davis (Tamworth)
Marion E., b. 8/27/1905; first; Ralph C. Purrington (farmer, Albany) and Elsie M. Sawyer (Lynn, MA)
Raymond Albert, b. 10/24/1893; second; Daniel C. Purrington (laborer, Albany) and Flora M. Davis (Tamworth)
Viola M., b. 12/16/1894 in Tamworth; third; Daniel C. Purington (laborer, 21, Albany) and Flora M. Davis (21, Tamworth)

QUIMBY,
son, b. 3/28/1892; fourth; Preston Quimby (painter, Sandwich) and Dell A. Banks (Boston)

RAMSEY,
Janice, b. 4/23/1938; first; Louis L. Ramsey and Charlotte

Thibadeau

RANGER,
daughter, b. 6/25/1889; first; John T. Ranger (carpenter, Irasburg, VT) and Annie L. Bryant (Tamworth); residence - Lake Village

RAYMOND,
Charles Herbert, b. 12/4/1941; second; Joseph E. Raymond and A. F. Berthiaume

READ,
Ellen, b. 7/29/1952; first; Thomas Read and Joan A. Cooke

REED,
Helen, b. 7/25/1945; fifth; Richard W. Reed and Clara Enebuske

REESE,
Robert P., b. 8/29/1939; second; Richard C. Reese and Velma V. Ellis

REINHOLD,
Nathan Allen, b. 6/10/1985 in Laconia; Robert Reinhold and Patricia Krebe

REMICK,
son, b. 2/15/1895 in Tamworth; fourth; Frank P. Remick (farmer, 44, Sandwich) and Florence E. Durrell (31, Tamworth)
son, b. 5/1/1899; second; Frank Remick (farmer, Tamworth) and Elizabeth Downs (Tamworth)
Alexandra Jude, b. 5/24/1994 in Laconia; Randall J. Remick and Kristen A. Gesmundo
Alpheus Dexter, b. 3/23/1910; first; Fred Remick (laborer, Tamworth) and Winnifred J. Dooley (Ireland)
Betty J., b. 9/9/1938; second; Charles W. Remick and Elizabeth A. Davis
David, b. 6/16/1938; first; Dexter A. Remick and Dorothy A. Graves
Earl H., b. 5/30/1900; second; Haywood Remick (merchant, Tamworth) and Annie M. Johnson (Brooklyn, NY)
Edwin Crofts, b. 9/18/1903; first; Edwin Remick (physician, Tamworth) and Emily Alice Crofts (Roxbury, MA)
Harry E., b. 8/23/1951; first; Charles W. Remick and Charlotte D.

Seavey
Jacob Charles, b. 4/29/1996 in Laconia; Ronald C. Remick, Jr. and Lisa Anne Binsack
Levi W., b. 6/3/1895 in Tamworth; second; E. Haywood Remick (merchant, 34, Tamworth) and Annie M. Johnson (34, Brooklyn, NY)
Lincoln, b. 8/17/1900; third; Frank Remick (carpenter, Tamworth) and Elizabeth Davis (Tamworth)
Mary Winnifred, b. --/--/1912; second; Frederick Remick (laborer, Tamworth) and Winnifred Dooley (Ireland)
Randall J., b. 11/11/1961; second; Ronald C. Remick and Doris L. Brown
Ronald Charles, b. 12/20/1935; Charles W. Remick and Elizabeth Davis
Serena F., b. 6/14/1897; first; Frank Remick (farmer, Tamworth) and Elizabeth Davis (Tamworth)
Stuart Newell, b. 8/22/1942; third; Charles W. Remick and Elizabeth A. Davis
Susan M., b. 8/14/1961; second; David Remick and Helen M. Hobbs
Zachary Joseph, b. 9/23/1994 in Laconia; Ronald C. Remick and Lisa A. Binsack

REMY,
Elizabeth Mica, b. 10/27/1981 in N. Conway; Michael Remy and Susan Manship

RHODES,
Christopher Allan, b. 1/7/1978 in Wolfeboro; Kenneth Rhodes and Jane Baisley
Douglas Burton, b. 10/14/1976 in Wolfeboro; Kenneth C. Rhodes and Jane E. Baisley

RICHARDSON,
Ariel, b. 1/1/1889; third; C. S. Richardson (minister, Newbury, VT) and Selina Richardson (Newbury, VT)

RICKER,
Aaron William, b. 1/15/1991 in N. Conway; George A. Ricker and Susan A. Turcotte
Alex Christopher, b. 11/15/1998 in Wolfeboro; George A. Ricker and Susan A. Turcotte

Lottie E., b. 3/11/1896 in Tamworth; first; William W. Ricker (26, Springvale, ME) and Edith C. Ross (19, Tamworth)

RINES,
Jerildine M., b. 3/30/1952; first; Stanley J. Rines and Marilyn J. Davis
Steven Edward, b. 11/28/2003 in Wolfeboro; Thomas Rines and Kelly Rines

ROBACKER,
Leigh Nichole, b. 10/17/1986 in N. Conway; Paul Robacker and Kristin Bombardier

ROBARGE,
daughter, b. 6/27/1915 in Tamworth; eighth; Lewis E. Robarge (lumber man, 39, Peabody, MA) and Bessie A. Elliott (Plymouth)
daughter, b. 9/18/1919; ninth; Lewis Robarge (Peabody, MA) and Bessie A. Elliott (Plymouth)
Irene Perl, b. 11/15/1920 in Tamworth; tenth; Lewis Robarge (lumberman, Peabody, MA) and Bessie A. Elliott (Plymouth)

ROBBINS,
Daniel Robiller, b. 4/15/1990 in N. Conway; James D. Robbins and Sabina E. Robiller
Katherine Elsie, b. 9/7/1994 in N. Conway; James D. Robbins and Sabina Robiller

ROBERGE,
Ernest LeRoy, b. 11/14/1936; Ernest LeRoy Roberge and Cleora Clough

ROBERTS,
son, b. 4/14/1914; first; Harry Roberts (farmer, 35, Tamworth) and Alice M. Perkins (23, Tamworth)
Aloha Lee, b. 12/25/1946; fourth; Harry G. Roberts and June M. Quincy
Ann June, b. 3/9/1948; second; Emery R. Roberts and Fayrlyn O. Leso
Barbara L., b. 4/20/1951; fourth; Charles E. Roberts and Gertrude C. Ripley

Benjamin John, b. 9/21/1999 in Laconia; Richard Roberts and
    Sharon Roberts
Brenda J., b. 12/11/1952; fifth; Emery R. Roberts and Faye O. Leso
Carolyn G., b. 12/8/1940; first; Harry G. Roberts and June M. Quincy
Emery George, b. 3/11/2000 in Laconia; Whipple Roberts and
    Jackleen Roberts
Faye Thelma, b. 4/15/1994 in Laconia; Whipple G. Roberts and
    Jackleen L. Hidden
Gabriel Lynne, b. 10/20/1992 in Laconia; Richard R. Roberts and
    Sharon L. Richards
Harry P., b. 9/4/1959; ninth; Emery G. Roberts and Faye O. Leso
Jennifer Alice, b. 10/27/1968 in N. Conway; Emery Roy Roberts and
    Fayralyn Olga Leso
Joan D., b. 11/3/1950; fourth; Emery R. Roberts and Fayralyn O.
    Leso
John E., b. 1/30/1956; seventh; Emery R. Roberts and Faye O. Leso
Kerry F., b. 3/30/1954; sixth; Emery R. Roberts and Faye O. Leso
Kristie Thelma, b. 10/3/1965 in Conway; eleventh; Emery Roy
    Roberts and Fayralyn Onga Leso
Linda C., b. 10/21/1949; third; Emery R. Roberts and Fayralyn O.
    Leso
Lois C., b. 5/23/1944; third; Charles E. Roberts and Gertrude C.
    Ripley
Philip C., b. 9/16/1949; fifth; Harry G. Roberts and June M. Quincy
Richard R., b. 10/9/1960; tenth; Emery R. Roberts and Faye O. Leso
Roy Emery, b. 4/23/1922; second; Harry Roberts (Tamworth) and
    Alice Perkins (Tamworth)
Virginia E., b. 5/1/1946; first; Emery R. Roberts and Fayralyn O.
    Leso
Whipple, b. 12/22/1997 in Laconia; Whipple George Roberts and
    Jackleen Helen Hidden
Whipple G., b. 12/15/1957; eighth; Emery R. Roberts and Faye O.
    Leso
Whitney Page, b. 1/22/1993 in Laconia; Whipple G. Roberts and
    Jackleen H. Hidden

ROBERTSON,
daughter, b. 10/11/1889; first; M. E. Robertson (expressman, Eaton)
    and Carrie A. Woodman (Portsmouth)
son, b. 10/28/1894 in Tamworth; fourth; Mark E. Robertson (hotel
    proprietor, 28, Eaton) and Carrie Woodman (29, Portsmouth)

daughter, b. 7/9/1915 in Tamworth; second; Elmer R. Robertson (25, Haverhill, MA) and Ruth Sawyer
Anna T., b. 7/8/1901; fifth; Mark E. Robertson (hotel proprietor, Eaton) and Carrie A. Woodman (Portsmouth)
Charles W., b. 12/7/1920 in Tamworth; first; Charles W. Robertson (merchant, Tamworth) and Marion E. Bookholz (Tamworth)
Philip A., b. 7/8/1901; sixth; Mark E. Robertson (hotel proprietor, Eaton) and Carrie A. Woodman (Portsmouth)

ROBILLER,
Jordan Oliver, b. 1/19/1994 in N. Conway; Oliver G. Robiller and Christy Lee Daly

ROBINSON,
daughter, b. 11/23/1899; first; Henry Robinson (carpenter, Tamworth) and Laura M. Gilman (Boston)
stillborn son, b. 11/21/1900; second; Henry Robinson (carpenter, Tamworth) and Laura M. Gilman (Boston, MA)
Adam Elliott, b. 5/14/1986 in Laconia; Bruce E. Robinson and Diane M. Lord
Andrea, b. 12/20/1952; third; Harold C. Robinson and Barbara L. Smith
Bertha Mable, b. 7/10/1922; second; Chester A. Robinson (Tamworth) and Grace Nancy Moody (Madison)
Beverly M., b. 7/2/1929; Chester A. Robinson and Grace Moody
Bruce E., b. 6/12/1950; second; Henry E. A. Robinson and Ann J. Webster
Chester A., b. 2/3/1900; first; John G. Robinson (painter, Tamworth) and Bertha Bunker (Tamworth)
Cynthia S., d. 2/23/1952; third; Henry E. Robinson and Ann J. Webster
Donald L., b. 10/6/1946; first; Henry E. Robinson and Annie J. Webster
Dorothy Dawn, b. 4/15/1931; Henry W. Robinson and Evelyn C. W. Smalle
Edward Daniel, b. 11/26/1981 in Laconia; John Robinson and Brenda Roberts
Fred W., b. 5/24/1895 in Tamworth; second; Henry B. Robinson (carpenter, 28, Tamworth) and Mary L. Wiggin (23, Tamworth)
Harold C., b. 7/30/1921 in Tamworth; first; Chester A. Robinson (farm laborer, Tamworth) and Grace M. Moody (Madison)

Henry Weeks, b. 1/20/1893; first; Henry B. Robinson (carpenter, Tamworth) and Mary L. Wiggin (Tamworth)
Karen Alice, b. 5/28/1979 in Laconia; John Robinson and Brenda Roberts
Katherine E., b. 2/28/1980 in Wolfeboro; Bruce Robinson and Diane Lord
Leslie J., b. 7/15/1915 in Tamworth; first; Henry W. Robinson (carpenter, 21, Tamworth) and Irene Edna Alley (18, Haverhill, MA)
Mary B., b. 5/31/1958; fourth; Henry E. A. Robinson and Ann J. Webster
Megan Leigh, b. 1/10/1984 in Laconia; Bruce Robinson and Diane Lord
Sarah Joan, b. 8/21/1976 in Laconia; John E. Robinson and Brenda J. Roberts
Timothy John, b. 12/4/1973 in Laconia; John Edward Robinson and Brenda Joyce Roberts

ROGERS,
Arlene, b. 8/12/1938; sixth; Irving W. Rogers and Addie M. Grace
Jean M., b. 5/10/1945; seventh; Irving Rogers and Addie Grace
Mary Ann, b. 8/4/1937; Irving Rogers and Addie Grace

ROSS,
daughter, b. 4/21/1887; second; John Ross (farmer, Albany) and Hattie E. (Tamworth)
son, b. 7/2/1890; first; Onslow S. Ross (laborer, Albany) and Hattie Moody (Tamworth)
son, b. 1/14/1892; seventh; John W. Ross (farmer, Albany) and Hattie E. Knox (Tamworth)
daughter, b. 5/5/1892; first; Mark S. Ross (farmer, Albany) and Emma Harriman (Albany)
son, b. 2/14/1896 in Tamworth; second; Mark S. Ross (36, Tamworth) and Emma Harriman (29, Albany)
son, b. 4/16/1899; fourth; Onslow S. Ross (laborer, Albany) and Harriet Moody (Tamworth)
daughter, b. 7/14/1918; second; Harold E. Ross (Tamworth) and Grace Kennett (Effingham)
son, b. 1/6/1921 in Tamworth; third; Harold E. Ross (chauffeur, Tamworth) and Grace Kennett (Effingham)

Abby May, b. 12/12/1893; second; Onslow S. Ross (laborer, Albany) and Hattie A. Moody (Tamworth)
Harold Edward, b. 9/22/1932; Harold E. Ross and Grace E. Kennett
Pamela, b. 8/11/1948; first; Ernest J. Ross and Betty Thigpen

ROWE,
Allan E., b. 10/31/1951; second; Ivan E. Rowe and Barbara M. Schoolcraft
Angela Jean, b. 11/15/1968 in Berlin; Linda Lee Rowe
Linda L., b. 8/30/1949; first; Ivan Rowe and Barbara M. Schoolcraft

ROWLAND,
Ashley Elizabeth, b. 4/14/1987 in Laconia; Steven F. Rowland and Annette E. Giampino

RUO,
Nicholas Agostino, b. 3/28/1995 in Laconia; Robert Michael Ruo and Diane Natalie Labelle

RUSSELL,
Maya Allyson, b. 5/29/2003 in Lebanon; Brian Russell and Kiera Russell

RYDER,
Jodi A., b. 9/25/1959; second; Alton E. Ryder and Sally A. Clark
Judy M., b. 6/8/1961; third; Alton E. Ryder and Sally A. Clark
Michael B., b. 10/30/1957; first; Alton E. Ryder and Sally A. Clark
Nellie Elizabeth, b. 8/21/1942; fourth; Perley A. Ryder and Gertrude Kingston

SALVAGE,
stillborn daughter, b. 6/12/1894 in Tamworth; first; John E. Salvage (merchant, 27, Tamworth) and Abbie F. Fullerton (25, Laconia)

SANBORN,
son, b. 10/7/1890; first; John F. Sanborn (farmer, Tamworth) and Addie M. Green (Tamworth)
Ellis R., b. 9/10/1893; second; John F. Sanborn (farmer, Saco, ME) and Addie M. Green (Tamworth)
Kenneth Oliver, b. 4/30/1913; first; Albert J. Sanborn (laborer, Tamworth) and Carrie J. Putnam (Charlestown)

Lisa Joy, b. 8/1/1964 in Laconia; first; Raymond F. Sanborn and Janet E. Woodward
Robert Clifford, b. 11/8/1922; first; Clifford H. Sanborn (Tamworth) and Inez Welch (Dover)

SANDOZ,
Charles Setter, b. 12/15/1972 in Wolfeboro; Charles Edouard Sandoz and Margaret Anne Johnson
Edouard Stuart, b. 9/28/1970 in Wolfeboro; Charles Edouard Sandoz and Margaret A. Johnson
Katherine Denise, b. 4/5/1969 in Wolfeboro; Charles Edouard Sandoz and Margaret Ann Johnson

SANPHY,
Autumn Lynn, b. 10/26/2002 in N. Conway; Tamen Sanphy and Kimberly Sanphy

SAUJON,
Stephanie Joan, b. 1/6/1964 in N. Conway; first; Royce A. Saujon and Joann J. Pearson

SCEGGELL,
Harvey L., b. 4/24/1907; first; A. B. Sceggell (engineer, Springvale, ME) and Belle Gilman (Tamworth)

SCHNEIDER,
April Margarete, b. 9/16/1987 in Rochester; Arthur F. Schneider and Sabine M. Schneider

SCHNUR,
Paul Leo, b. 2/15/1936; Leo Schnur, M.D. and Alien Miller

SCHOOLCRAFT,
Alice May, b. 5/29/1896 in Tamworth; second; Walter B. Schoolcraft (26, Boston, MA) and Edith M. Moulton (17, Albany)
Gladys Edith, b. 8/21/1909; sixth; Walter Schoolcraft (carpenter, Boston, MA) and Edith M. Moulton (Albany)
Philip A., b. 4/12/1907; sixth; W. B. Schoolcraft (carpenter, Boston, MA) and E. M. Moulton (Albany)

SCOLARO,
Ian Nathan, b. 6/24/1979 in N. Conway; Ricky Scolaro and Rose Ricker
Mathew Adam, b. 5/30/1978 in N. Conway; Ricky Scolaro and Rose Ricker

SCOTINA,
Dylan Robert, b. 8/27/1992 in N. Conway; Antonio Scotina and Christine Patch

SEKENSKI,
Haven James, b. 4/24/2001 in N. Conway; Paul Sekenski and Rebecca Meserve-Sekenski

SELLER,
Bjorn Victor, b. 12/9/1982 in Wolfeboro; Richard Seller and Eve Henrickson

SEVERANCE,
Fred Allen, b. 5/13/1936; LeRoy Severance and Harriet J. Wiggin

SEVERY,
Alan W., b. 9/12/1944; first; Merle E. Severy and Teresa Bookholz

SHACKFORD,
Tony James, b. 8/28/1971 in Laconia; Loren Albert Shackford, Jr. and Sherry Marie Ames

SHANNON,
Penelope, b. 2/2/1945; first; Charles Shannon and Evelyn M. Welch

SHARP,
John Douglas, b. 8/24/1995 in Wolfeboro; Douglas J. Sharp and Donna V. Seamans

SHAUGHNESSY,
Susan, b. 8/26/1905; fifth; Charles Shaughnessy (coachman, Limerick, Ireland) and Mary Shaaeen (Limerick, Ireland); residence – Boston, MA

SHAW,
Allan Buckley, b. 4/26/1975 in N. Conway; Robert B. Shaw and
   Diane D. Hall

SHEEHAN,
David Michael, b. 3/2/2002 in Wolfeboro; David Sheehan and Tina
   Sheehan
Kathlina Mae, b. 4/10/1989 in N. Conway; Daniel T. Sheehan and
   Lisa A. Taylor
Lillian Margaret, b. 8/5/1999 in Wolfeboro; David Sheehan and Tina
   Sheehan

SHEPARD,
Christopher Scott, b. 3/5/1984 in Laconia; John Shepard and Linda
   Chadbourne
Leah Melinda, b. 5/14/1991 in N. Conway; John G. Shepard and
   Linda A. Chadbourne

SHEPPARD,
Sarah Lynn, b. 7/3/1986 in N. Conway; Stewart Sheppard and
   Denise Smith

SHIRLEY,
Thomas S., b. 10/30/1957; fourth; Thomas J. Shirley and Mary C.
   Phryaw

SIMMS,
Clifton, Jr., b. 7/12/1928; Clifton Simms and Elsie E. Banfill

SIMONS,
Samantha Jo, b. 9/6/1994 in N. Conway; Scott C. Simons and
   Penelope Brooks

SLATTERY,
Megan Ann, b. 10/17/1986 in N. Conway; Timothy Slattery and
   Jeanne Muise

SMALLE,
Virginia A., b. 6/28/1949; first; Theodore B. Smalle and Alice R.
   Zakarian

SMITH,
stillborn daughter, b. 11/12/1889; Rolfe L. Smith (Sandwich) and Carrie E. Smith (Laconia)
son, b. 4/27/1892; second; Jacob G. Smith (farmer, Tamworth) and Eliza A. Adams (Haverhill)
son, b. 8/19/1906; third; Clarence J. Smith (laborer, Tamworth) and Cora M. Forrest (Sandwich)
Christine Edna, d. 1/29/1970 in Laconia; Richard Edward Smith and Linda Lee Covey
Curtis Everett, b. 7/21/1910; fourth; Clarence Smith (laborer, Tamworth) and Cora Forrest (Tamworth)
Ethel, b. 4/18/1887; first; Rolfe L. Smith (millman, Sandwich) and Carrie E. (Laconia)
Gladys E., b. 11/18/1903; first; Clarence J. Smith (laborer, Tamworth) and Cora M. Forrest (Sandwich)
Gloria J., b. 2/3/1955; first; George F. Smith and Gladys M. Ames
Hanna Rose, b. 5/8/1982 in Tamworth; Samuel Smith and Geraldine Graham
Harold E., b. 9/23/1910; second; Frank H. Smith (laborer, Cornish, ME) and Ada A. Marston (Tamworth)
Harold G., b. 5/27/1903; first; Elmore Smith (laborer, Tamworth) and Grace Smith (Burke, VT); residence – VT
Joseph Michael, b. 11/6/1986 in N. Conway; Michael Smith and Andrea Burnell
Karl Johan, b. 3/5/1975 in Boston, MA; Karl Arnold Smith and Mihaela Nora Georgescu
Kate E., b. 3/9/1980 in Laconia; James Smith, Jr. and Mary Carpenter
Marion Carrie, b. 1/21/1905; second; Clarence Smith (laborer, Tamworth) and Cora M. Forrest (Sandwich)
Marston, b. 12/21/1904; first; Frank H. Smith (farmer, Cornish, ME) and Ada A. Marston (Tamworth)
Molly Jennifer, b. 10/18/1988 in Hanover; Michael J. Smith and Jay E. Acas
Nicholas Palmer, b. 8/21/1987 in N. Conway; Denise M. Pomeroy
Sherilee D., b. 5/3/1952; second; Kenneth E. Smith and Eleanor G. Rogers

SMOOT,
Wayne W., b. 12/27/1951; second; Jack R. Smoot and Stella R. Hobbs

SOLAR,
Harry Matthew, b. 10/3/1977 in Laconia; Robert L. Solar and June M. Alston

SOUZA,
Jennette Coryn, b. 8/23/1986 in N. Conway; John Souza and Debra Merritt

SPAULDING,
Evelyn Martha, b. 10/28/1909; first; Robert C. Spaulding (farmer, Tamworth) and Eunice M. Hoag (Tamworth)
Marion I., b. 7/2/1908; first; R. C. Spaulding (farmer, Tamworth) and Eunice M. Hoag (Tamworth)

SPECKMAN,
Boyd H., b. 10/15/1953; third; Robert E. Speckman and Violet D. Eldridge

SPINNEY,
Amber D., b. 6/18/1980 in Concord; Philip Spinney and Susan MacIver
Joel Steven, b. 11/1/1978 in Laconia; Philip Spinney and Susan MacIver
Michael Erik, b. 4/2/1977 in Laconia; Philip C. Spinney and Susan D. MacIver

STACY,
Christobel I., b. 6/18/1928; Nathan J. Stacy and Gladys M. Ames
Louise Irene, b. 1/5/1923; first; Nathan Stacy (Madison) and Gladys Ames (Tamworth)
Myrtle Edna, b. 2/2/1924; Nathan Stacy and Gladys Annis

STAFFORD,
Georgianna Welles, b. 3/31/2001 in N. Conway; Hansel Stafford and Isabelle Stafford

STALEY,
Sarah E., b. 7/3/1980 in Laconia; Victor Staley and Margaret Weare

STAPLES,
Diane E., b. 11/17/1953; eighth; Walter S. Staples and Mildred E. Goodwin
Mark A., b. 3/2/1957; ninth; Walter S. Staples and Mildred E. Goodwin
Sky Tomica, b. 11/30/1981 in Tamworth; Mark Staples and Yvonne Jones

STEARNS,
Aldo M., b. 10/11/1898; first; Andrew J. Stearns (farmer, Mt. Vernon) and Cora E. Mason (Albany)

STEELE,
Elizabeth Allen, b. 7/25/1913; second; Frederick L. Steele (farmer, Cincinnati, OH) and Margaret W. Twitchell (Boston, MA)
Esther Freeman, b. 8/3/1919; third; F. Lincoln Steele (Cincinnati, OH) and Margaret W. Twitchell (Dorchester, MA)
Frederick Lincoln, b. 5/15/1912; first; Frederick Z. Steele, Jr. (farmer, Cincinnati, OH) and Margaret Twitchell (Boston, MA)
Henry Lincoln, b. 12/18/1978 in Laconia; Nathaniel Steele and Helen Read

STEVENS,
Linda M., b. 1/9/1950; second; Willard E. Stevens and Adelaide M. Fischer

STEWART,
Linda Nelson, b. 6/21/1972 in Laconia; Kenneth Millet Stewart and Kathryn Chalmers Dale

STOCKER,
Korinne Janelle, b. 5/12/1979 in N. Conway; Jeffrey Stocker and Kathleen Gallagher

STOKES,
child, b. 3/20/1924; Arthur P. Stokes and Harriet M. Hutchins
Eleanor Frances, b. 8/12/1921 in Tamworth; fourth; Arthur P. Stokes (farm laborer, Harrison, ME) and Harriet Hutchins (Tamworth)
Kenneth P., d. 2/28/1923; fifth; Arthur P. Stokes (Harrison, ME) and Harriet M. Hutchins (Tamworth)

Oris Arthur, b. 11/10/1913; first; Arthur P. Stokes (laborer, Harris, ME) and Hattie M. Hutchins (Tamworth)
Roland Arthur, b. 5/8/1927; Arthur P. Stokes and Hattie M. Hutchins

STONE,
Cynthia Ann, b. 12/5/1952; third; Philip W. Stone and Irene L. Leso
Dale Whitman, b. 12/27/1963 in Laconia; third; Lothrop Bruce Stone and Ruth Williams Staples
Dawn M., b. 8/12/1961; second; Lothrop B. Stone and Ruth W. Staples
Philip William, II, b. 11/20/1962 in N. Conway; sixth; Philip William Stone and Irene Louise Leso
Vicki D., b. 9/24/1954; fourth; Philip W. Stone and Irene L. Leso

STREETER,
Bradley Earl, b. 10/28/1977 in Laconia; Robert Streeter and Rae Ann Dyer
Brian Almon, b. 7/19/1974 in N. Conway; Robert Streeter and Rae Ann Dyer
Gail R., b. 9/13/1952; second; Joseph A. Streeter and Mildred D. Marshall
Hunter Richard, b. 4/18/1999 in Wolfeboro; Brian A. Streeter and Angela Mae Streeter
Janet D., b. 1/15/1961; fifth; Joseph A. Streeter and Mildred D. Marshall
Joel F., b. 8/18/1950; first; Joseph A. Streeter and Mildred D. Marshall
Julie Heather, b. 8/30/1987 in Laconia; Mark D. Streeter and Melanie A. Elliott
Kate Michelle, b. 7/27/1984 in Laconia; Joel Streeter and Minda Mason
Laurie Jo, b. 3/12/1955; third; Joseph A. Streeter and Mildred D. Marshall
Mark D., b. 6/27/1957; fourth; Joseph A. Streeter and Mildred D. Marshall
Rayetta, b. 4/26/1952; fourth; Clifford R. Streeter and Lorraine E. Evans
Raymond, b. 4/26/1952; fifth; Clifford Streeter and Lorraine E. Evans
Richard L., b. 2/1/1950; first; Clifford L. Streeter and Lorraine E. Evans
Robert, b. 1/31/1951; first; Clifford R. Streeter and Lorraine E. Evans

Ronald, b. 1/31/1951; first; Clifford R. Streeter and Lorraine E. Evans

Rono, b. 9/11/1956; sixth; Clifford R. Streeter and Lorraine E. Evans

William Douglas, b. 10/2/1997 in Tamworth; Robert B. Streeter and Amy Beth Carter

William Joel, b. 2/14/1981 in Laconia; Joel Streeter and Minda Nason

SULLIVAN,
Charlotte Elizabeth, b. 9/2/1971 in Wolfeboro; Forrest Sullivan and Beverly Marie Arendt

SULZER,
Glen K., b. 11/18/1955; third; William J. Sulzer and Gloria J. Evans

SUPPES,
Morgan McKinnon, b. 7/28/1981 in N. Conway; Bruce Suppes and Nancy Glidden

SUTHERLAND,
Dorothy Eleanor, b. 1/13/1943; fourth; Donald M. Sutherland and Elizabeth M. Hidden

SWAN,
Amanda Marie Michelle, b. 3/4/1985 in S. Tamworth; Allen Swan and Linda Colt

Chelsea Marie, b. 8/29/1989 in N. Conway; Christopher H. Swan and Deborah A. Whiting

Cheyenne Dorothy-Ruth, b. 8/15/1996 in N. Conway; Christopher H. Swan and Stephanie A. Anthony

Christopher Lee, b. 10/20/1984 in N. Conway; Christopher Swan and Deborah Whiting

Savannah Lynn, b. 2/13/1986 in N. Conway; Christopher H. Swan and Deborah A. Whiting

SWEARINGEN,
Matthew James, b. 5/25/2000 in Wolfeboro; James Swearingen and Carrie Swearingen

SWEET,
Lois Francis, b. 6/17/1926; Melvin Sweet and Olive Southick

Melvin, T., Jr., b. 5/19/1929; Melvin T. Sweet and Olive Southwick

SWENSON,
Amanda Leigh, b. 10/10/1978 in Laconia; Neil Swenson and Tammy Hoch
Jeremy D., b. 1/15/1980 in Laconia; Neil Swenson and Tammy Hoch
Mathew Jarod, b. 1/5/1982 in Laconia; Neil Swenson and Tammy Hoch

SWITAJ,
Matthew David, b. 4/28/1988 in Laconia; David D. Switaj and Donna F. Hodge
Zachary John, b. 6/27/1992 in Laconia; David D. Switaj and Donna F. Hodge

TAGGETT,
C. W., Jr., b. 2/7/1940; first; Charles W. Taggett and Mildred G. Harris
Cynthia L., b. 7/11/1946; third; Charles W. Taggett and Mildred G. Harris
William Henry, b. 1/31/1943; second; Charles W. Taggett and Mildred G. Harris

TAPPAN,
Stephen Henry, b. 1/24/1941; first; Hanry R. Tappan and Margaret I. Vittum

TATARCZUK,
Acre Colvin, b. 1/12/2003 in N. Conway; Scott Tatarczuk and Sarah Tatarczuk

TAYLOR,
Caitlin Peers, b. 8/28/1976 in Laconia; Donald L. Taylor and Peggy S. McClanahan
Collin Anthony Edward, b. 6/7/2003 in N. Conway; Shawn Taylor and Eileen Taylor
Elizabeth Jean, b. 4/12/1965 in Laconia; first; William Henry Taylor and Jean Marie Rogers
Myron E., b. 2/15/1958; second; Paul I. Taylor and Eleanor B. LaBonte

Stanley P., b. 12/14/1955; first; Paul I. Taylor and Eleanor B. LaBonte

TEWKSBURY,
son, b. 3/22/1903; first; Isaac Tewksbury (laborer, Tamworth) and Eva M. Swain (Meredith)
Clayton B., b. 8/17/1903; second; Wesley Tewksbury (farmer, Sandwich) and Nettie Barnes (Tamworth)

THELEMARCK,
Hannah Kristina, b. 2/26/2001 in N. Conway; Claes Thelemarck and Vikki Thelemarck
Lea Rose, b. 11/11/1999 in N. Conway; Claes Thelemarck and Vikki Thelemarck

THOMPSON,
Brenna Kay, b. 5/30/1989 in N. Conway; Andrew B. Thompson and Jacalyn M. Anacker
Kathi S., b. 7/23/1957; fifth; Leslie E. Thompson and Marie C. King
Kelly Jean, b. 4/16/1984 in N. Conway; Robert Thompson and Patricia Terwillinger
Sara Helen, b. 9/15/1972 in N. Conway; James Lionel Thompson and Mary Roberta Tasker

THURSTON,
Betty S., b. 3/17/1960; third; Daniel C. Thurston and Ellen D. Smith

TICE,
Karen Lye, b. 8/1/1976 in Wolfeboro; Roger B. Tice and Shirley M. Ames
William Stuart, b. 10/24/1972 in Wolfeboro; Roger Bruce Tice and Shirley May Ames

TILTON,
son, b. 8/17/1896 in Tamworth; first; Ira B. Tilton (29, Tamworth) and Alice L. Meader (30, Tamworth)
son, b. 8/21/1898; third; Ira B. Tilton (farmer, Tamworth) and Alice Marston (Tamworth)
son, b. 6/20/1903; fourth; Ira B. Tilton (farmer, Tamworth) and Alice L. Meader (Tamworth)

Andrew Lee, b. 10/23/1983 in N. Conway; Leslie H. Tilton and
    Nancy Lee Hoag
Caroline, b. 4/30/1900; third; Ira D. Tilton (farmer, Tamworth) and
    Alice M. Meade (Tamworth)

TIMS,
Hugh M., b. 6/14/1980 in N. Conway; Robert Tims and Ellen Tenney

TODD,
Alaina Marie, b. 5/6/1998 in Portland, ME; Jeffrey Todd and Carolyn
    Todd
Colleen Patricia, b. 5/6/1998 in Portland, ME; Jeffrey Todd and
    Carolyn Todd

TOWNSEND,
Grace M., b. 5/24/1995 in N. Conway; Charles G. Townsend and
    Debora L. Maille

TRAMMELL,
William Ross Aldor, b. 12/8/1986 in Wolfeboro; William Trammell
    and Sandra MacGregor

TRASK,
Beverly Anne, b. 2/20/1942; first; Robert H. Trask and Dorothy E.
    Moore
Frank Wesley, b. 6/28/1933; Harold B. Trask and Emma L. Moulton
Howard R., b. 9/12/1952; first; Robert H. Trask and Priscilla A.
    Myers
Marion Louise, b. 9/28/1910; second; Frank Trask (laborer,
    Sandwich) and Elizabeth B. Bennett (Tamworth)
Robert Harold, b. 3/7/1922; second; Harold B. Trask (Sandwich) and
    Emma L. Moulton (Tamworth)
Ruth, b. 4/2/1925; Harold Trask and Emma Moulton
Stanley Moulton, b. 10/4/1919; first; Harold B. Trask (Sandwich) and
    Emma L. Moulton (Tamworth)

TREMBLAY,
Joshua Bradley, b. 10/18/1979 in Wolfeboro; Dennis Tremblay and
    Mary Trena

TRENT,
Marissa Lynn, b. 10/21/1996 in Wolfeboro; Francis S. Trent and
  Donna M. Breen
Micaela Marie, b. 10/1/1994 in Wolfeboro; Francis S. Trent and
  Donna M. Breen

TRIPP,
Alan E., b. 11/29/1956; second; Dale F. Tripp and Eleanor M.
  Bickford

TRUDEAU,
Justin Evan, b. 1/2/1999 in N. Conway; Randy Joseph Trudeau and
  Tara Kristina Burdette

TUCKER,
Jacob David, b. 7/8/2000 in N. Conway; Glenn Tucker and Lisa
  Tucker

ULITZ,
James Michael, b. 3/5/1988 in N. Conway; Michael B. Ulitz and
  Stephanie L. Chase

URQUHART,
Rebecca Mae, b. 6/27/1975 in Laconia; Kenneth Nelson Urquhart
  and Mary Ann Stockman
Scott Willard, b. 7/27/1978 in Laconia; Kenneth Urquhart and Mary
  Stockman

VACHON,
Sean Michael, b. 3/13/1998 in N. Conway; Ronald F. Vachon and
  Cynthia L. Tibbetts
Stephen Ronald, b. 7/6/2000 in N. Conway; Ronald Vachon and
  Cynthia Vachon

VARNEY,
daughter, b. 6/28/1890; second; George O. Varney (farmer,
  Ossipee) and Clara A. Bryer (Lake Village)
daughter, b. 12/8/1898; third; George O. Varney (farmer, Tamworth)
  and Clara E. Bryer (Sandwich)
Amber May, b. 11/10/1983 in N. Conway; Joseph R. Varney and
  Michele Sue Bugbee

Arthur, b. 1/6/1889; first; George O. Varney (farmer, Ossipee) and Clara E. Bryer (Lake Village)
Maurice Earle, b. 3/8/1942; first; Harold M. Varney and Viola A. Eldridge

VENO,
Matthew Craig, b. 3/18/1979 in N. Conway; Steven Veno and Christina Birch

VER PLANCK,
Katherine Browne, b. 5/13/1979 in N. Conway; Edward Ver Planck and Rebecca Riley

VITTUM,
stillborn daughter, b. 12/24/1911; first; Leonard C. Vittum (farmer, Sandwich) and Laura I. Hutchinson (S. Hanson, MA)
stillborn child, b. 11/21/1912; Herbert A. Vittum (laborer, Sandwich) and Alice E. Clark (PEI)
daughter, b. 12/1/1914 in Tamworth; fourth; Herbert A. Vittum (laborer, 31, Sandwich) and Alice Clark (33, NS)
Adam Q., b. 6/21/1980 in Laconia; Allan Vittum and Sally Hunt
Alezander Hunt, b. 1/29/1978 in Laconia; Alan Vittum and Sally Hunt
Brewster D., b. 9/30/1953; second; Kenneth F. Vittum and Frances V. Lord
Dorothy T., b. 1/18/1907; first; H. A. Vittum (laborer, Sandwich) and Alice H. Clark (PEI)
Kenneth F., Jr., b. 8/4/1952; first; Kenneth F. Vittum and Frances V. Lord
Mary Louise, b. 5/17/1920 in Tamworth; fourth; Herbert Vittum (farm laborer, Sandwich) and Agnes Ames (Tamworth)
Merton C., b. 11/4/1908; second; Herbert A. Vittum (laborer, Sandwich) and Alice H. Clarke (PEI)
Neil A., b. 6/21/1980 in Laconia; Allan Vittum and Sally Hunt
Norman Earl, b. 5/18/1931; Merton C. Vittum and Rachel Merrow
Reba Annette, b. 4/21/1923; sixth; Herbert A. Vittum (Sandwich) and Alice H. Clark (PEI)

VIVEIROS,
Nicholas James, b. 11/21/1997 in N. Conway; Ernest Paul Viveiros and Lynn Hathaway

WALKER,
son, b. 8/28/1952; seventh; W. Edward Walker and Myrtle L. Page
Barbara A., b. 4/21/1951; sixth; Walter E. Walker and Myrtle L. Page
Clifford, b. 4/9/1944; second; William E. Walker and Hazel V. Frost
Daniel Richard, b. 7/21/1979 in Laconia; Richard Walker and Barbara Gaudette
Emily Brooke, b. 11/20/2003 in N. Conway; Steven Walker and Amanda Walker
Jack, b. 6/--/1955; ninth; Walter E. Walker and Myrtle E. Walker
James A., b. 8/9/1945; fourth; Walter E. Walker and Myrtle L. Page
Jason Earl, b. 6/25/1977 in N. Conway; Steven S. Walker and Deborah J. Beckwith
Jeremy A., b. 3/15/1980 in Wolfeboro; Stephen Walker and Gail Masterman
Lilian Frances, b. 3/8/1911; third; Walter C. Walker (mail carrier, Holliston, MA) and Hattie B. Bickford (Tamworth)
Nancy J., b. 8/5/1947; fifth; Walter E. Walker and Myrtle L. Page
Richard, b. 6/22/1944; third; Walter E. Walker and Myrtle L. Page
Robert H., b. 10/6/1953; eighth; Walter E. Walker and Myrtle L. Page
Sandra Lee, b. 2/22/1941; first; W. Edward Walker and Myrtle Lucy Page
Sherri Marie, b. 3/5/1983 in Laconia; Richard E. Walker and Barbara A. Gaudette
Stephen Scott, Jr., b. 4/20/1976 in N. Conway; Stephen S. Walker and Deborah J. Beckwith
Walter Edward, b. 7/28/1902; first; Walter C. Walker (laborer, Holliston, MA) and Hattie B. Bickford (Tamworth)
Walter Edward, b. 10/25/1942; second; Walter E. Walker and Myrtle L. Page

WALLACE,
daughter, b. 6/19/1888; sixth; Henry Wallace (farmer, Saccarappa, ME) and Fannie J. Glidden (Sandwich)
son, b. 7/2/1890; seventh; Henry Wallace (farmer, Sacarappa, ME) and Fannie Glidden (Sandwich)

WALTON,
Daniel Howard, b. 10/13/1996 in Wolfeboro; Harold E. Walton and Kelly L. Given

WARLICK,
Ashley Molander, b. 2/1/1979 in N. Conway; Louis Warlick and Patricia Akley

WARREN,
Beverly P., b. 1/21/1959; fourth; Clifton W. Warren and Beatrice E. Frost
Bruce E., b. 8/5/1956; third; Clifton W. Warren and Beatrice E. Frost

WASON,
Sarah Frances, b. 1/28/1983 in N. Conway; Erle B. Wason and Mary Jane Robinson

WASSON,
Carole Marion, b. 5/4/1937; Leslie C. Wasson and Marion Johnson
Eric Vincent, b. 5/25/1967 in Laconia; Dannie Edward Wasson and Elizabeth Jane Chase
Joyce A., b. 1/6/1939; third; Leslie Wasson and Marion Johnson
Mark C., b. 9/22/1958; first; Dannie E. Wasson and Elizabeth J. Chase
Paul Henry, b. 3/20/1943; fifth; Leslie Wasson and Marion Johnson
Priscilla J., b. 3/9/1934; Leslie Wasson and Marion Johnson
Robert L., b. 2/17/1940; fourth; Leslie C. Wasson and Marion Johnson
Ryan Mitchell, b. 6/26/1973 in Laconia; Dannie Edward Wasson and Elizabeth Jane Chase
Vicki B., b. 6/22/1960; second; Dannie E. Wasson and Elizabeth J. Chase

WATSON,
Mary Elizabeth, b. 10/13/1979 in Laconia; Roger Watson and Sandra Schull
Pamelia L., b. 7/24/1959; third; Myles E. Watson, Jr. and Joan A. Leveille

WEARE,
Gabriel Erich, b. 5/5/1978 in Laconia; Thomas Weare and Patricia Perkins
Joshua Edmund, b. 1/25/1975 in Laconia; Thomas Edmund Weare and Patricia Ann Perkins
Margaret E., b. 1/3/1959; fifth; Donald E. Weare and Reta M. Welch

Michael E., b. 1/3/1959; fourth; Donald E. Weare and Reta M. Welch
Susan M., b. 10/17/1951; third; Donald E. Weare and Reta M. Welch
Thomas E., b. 3/27/1949; second; Donald E. Weare and Reta M. Welch

WEBSTER,
Hattie M., b. 6/7/1888; third; Alpheus Webster (farmer, Albany) and Francena Perkins (Tamworth)
Julia Larsson, b. 4/23/1971 in Laconia; Wayne Chester Webster and Janet Louise Bickford
Linda Jean, b. 12/26/1941; second; Chester W. Webster and Hazel G. Ames
Marcella Ruth, b. 12/24/1969 in Laconia; Wayne Chester Webster and Janet Louise Bickford
Rose M., b. 5/3/1950; third; William F. Webster and Nola H. Frie
Ruth C., b. 6/18/1938; first; Chester W. Webster and Hazel G. Ames
Wayne, b. 12/11/1944; third; Chester W. Webster and Hazel G. Ames

WEEKS,
son, b. 3/12/1887; third; William Weeks (farmer, Tamworth) and Mary E. (Tamworth)
daughter, b. 5/14/1891; fourth; William Weeks (farmer, Tamworth) and Mary Blaisdell (Tamworth)
son, b. 1/18/1892; first; Charles A. Weeks (farmer, Wakefield) and Mamie S. Hayford (Tamworth)
Andrew Warren, b. 4/1/1981 in N. Conway; Nathan Weeks and Sandra Jones
Betty Lou Gale, b. 11/1/1941; second; Carroll R. Weeks and Arlene Bruno
Ida May, b. 3/18/1894 in Tamworth; second; Charles A. Weeks (farmer, 43, Wakefield) and Mamie S. Hayford (24, Tamworth)

WEISSMAN,
Mark James, b. 5/1/1991 in N. Conway; Michael J. Weissman and Melodie A. Sylvester

WELCH,
son, b. 1/9/1916; third; James Welch (mill operator, Ossipee) and Gertrude Eldridge (Ossipee)

daughter, b. 5/23/1921 in Tamworth; fifth; James Welch (mill operator, Ossipee) and Gertrude Eldridge (Ossipee)

Austin Eldridge, b. 1/27/1918; fourth; James Welch (farmer, Ossipee) and Gertrude M. Eldridge (Ossipee)

Beatrice T., b. 10/28/1923; fourth; Russell Welch (Ossipee) and Hester Clark (Alton)

Brenda D., b. 11/2/1955; second; Edwin P. Welch and Pricilla M. Brown

Christopher James, b. 3/1/1973 in N. Conway; Frederick Russell Welch and Martha Lucille Alward

Curtis John, b. 3/1/1973 in N. Conway; Frederick Russell Welch and Martha Lucille Allard

Edwin Preston, b. 4/4/1931; James Welch and Gertrude Eldridge

Emily L., b. 12/18/1939; first; Francis J. Welch and Emma M. Loud

Evelyn Margaret, b. 5/23/1923; sixth; James Welch (Ossipee) and Gertrude Eldridge (Ossipee)

Florence Ethel, b. 4/10/1920 in Tamworth; second; Russell Welch (fireman Port. mill, Ossipee) and Hester Clark (Alton)

Francella J., b. 8/25/1954; second; Francis J. Welch and Emma M. Loud

Frank Allen, b. 2/2/1964 at N. Conway; first; Frederick R. Welch and Martha L. Alward

Frederic Russell, b. 6/9/1942; eighth; Russell A. Welch and Hester R. Clark

Helen Barbara, b. 3/29/1922; third; Russell Welch (Ossipee) and Hester Rose Clark (Alton)

Kelley Marie, b. 7/6/1969 in N. Conway; Frederick Russell Welch and Martha Lucille Alward

Kimberly Lynn, b. 1/5/1972 in N. Conway; Douglas Alan Welch and Virginia Ellen Roberts

Peter A., b. 9/10/1939; first; Austin E. Welch and Dorothy L. French

Richard D., b. 8/6/1945; second; Austin E. Welch and Dorothy French

Russell, b. 12/8/1928; Russell Welch and Hester R. Clark

Sherilyn A., b. 6/7/1954; first; Edwin P. Welch and Priscilla M. Brown

Stephanie Faye, b. 7/17/1966 in N. Conway; Douglas Alan Welch and Virginia Ellen Roberts

Suzan J., b. 8/27/1957; third; Edwin P. Welch and Priscilla M. Brown

Tammy Lynn, b. 10/15/1964 in Wolfeboro; first; Richard David Welch and Betty E. Watson

Wendy Lee, b. 5/18/1968 in Wolfeboro; Richard David Welch and Betty Ethel Watson

WENDELL,
Christine Ann, b. 12/14/1963 in Wolfeboro; third; George Almus Wendell and Beatrice Christine Palmer

WHIPPLE,
Benjamin Ford, b. 6/24/1974 in N. Conway; Parker Cushman Whipple and Donna Louise Ford
Cynthia Jane, b. 7/8/1936; Frank Preston Whipple and Augusta May Doe
Diane, b. 7/15/1945; third; Frank P. Whipple and Augusta M. Doe
Marilyn June, b. 7/17/1933; Frank P. Whipple and Augusta M. Doe
Peter R., b. 3/1/1957; first; Parker C. Whipple and Joan Phenix
Sarah Katherine, b. 8/16/1971 in N. Conway; Parker Cushman Whipple and Donna Louise Ford

WHITE,
John David, Jr., b. 10/18/1983 in N. Conway; John D. White and Robyn Jackson
Marie E., b. 11/12/1928; Walter G. White and Estella Wiggin
Raecene Elizabeth, b. 10/8/1996 in N. Conway; Rusy E. White, Sr. and Wendy S. Lariviere
Walter G., b. 4/9/1899; third; L. L. White (freight agt., Haverhill, MA) and Elizabeth Pascoe (Freedom) (1900 – "reported as Ossipee last year by mistake")

WHITING,
son, b. 3/22/1890; sixth; George F. Whiting (laborer, Ossipee) and Anna H. Choate (Sandwich)
daughter, b. 8/15/1892; seventh; George F. Whiting (laborer, Ossipee) and Anna H. Choate (Sandwich)
daughter, b. 7/2/1896 in Tamworth; fifth; Frank Whiting (42, Ossipee) and Annie H. Chute (40, Moultonboro)
daughter, b. 4/21/1919; second; Fred H. Whiting (Boston, MA) and Ethel E. Jeffers (Tamworth)
Alice Reid, b. 1/23/1911; second; Almon J. Whiting (butcher, Tamworth) and Elizabeth Palmer (Sandwich)
Almon Reid, b. 1/22/1902; first; Almon J. Whiting (farmer, Tamworth) and Elizabeth R. Palmer (Sandwich)

Anita Mae, b. 4/26/1966 in Laconia; Raymond Victor Whiting and Geraldine Suzie Nudd

Anne, b. 12/31/1935; Roland G. Whiting and Hazel McKenzie

Beatrice A., b. 9/16/1902; stillborn; third; Charles E. Whiting (laborer, Moultonboro) and Jennie B. Wade (Moultonboro)

Brenda Lee, b. 1/6/1962 in Laconia; fifth; Raymond Victor Whiting and Geraldine Susie Nudd

Bryce R., b. 7/8/1954; second; George R. Whiting and Rona A. Simonds

Cain I., b. 3/18/1980 in Laconia; Lewis Whiting and Darlene Whiting

Carroll, b. 11/17/1925; Roland Whiting and Hazel MacKenzie

Chester F., b. 5/20/1903; first; Arthur C. Whiting (laborer, Tamworth) and Fannie E. Forrest (Tamworth)

Clayton H., b. 3/9/1905; second; Arthur C. Whiting (laborer, Tamworth) and Fannie E. Forrest (Tamworth)

David Lyle, b. 3/24/1938; fifth; Roland G. Whiting and Hazel M. Mackenzie (1942)

Deborah Ann, b. 1/23/1964 in Laconia; fifth; Raymond V. Whiting and Geraldine S. Nudd

Doris L., b. 10/9/1905; fourth; William H. Whiting (farmer, Ossipee) and Lulu A. Floyd (Tamworth)

Doris Thelma, b. 1/19/1910; stillborn; fifth; Charles E. Whiting (laborer, Tamworth) and Jennie B. Wade (Moultonboro)

Eleanor Ruth, b. 7/30/1918; first; Frederick H. Whiting (farmer, Boston, MA) and Ethel Jeffers (Tamworth)

Elizabeth, b. 8/5/1945; eighth; Roland G. Whiting and Hazel Mackenzie

Ellen P., b. 9/26/1903; third; William H. Whiting (farmer, Tamworth) and Lulu A. Floyd (Tamworth)

Eunice Etta, b. 8/23/1910; first; Fred M. Whiting (laborer, Tamworth) and Georgia Jeffers (Warner)

Florence, b. 11/28/1900; second; Charles Whiting (laborer, Moultonboro) and Jennie B. Wade (Moultonboro)

Garfield, b. 12/28/1957; second; Raymond V. Whiting and Geraldine S. Nudd

George Richard, b. 6/4/1931; George R. Whiting and Hazel M. McKenzie

Gregory Thomas, b. 3/19/1962 in Laconia; first; David Lyle Whiting and Phylis Diane Clark

Holly, b. 3/4/1959; fifth; George R. Whiting and Rona A. Simonds

Howard W., b. 9/7/1902; second; William H. Whiting (farmer, Ossipee) and Lulu A. Floyd (Tamworth)
Ida E., b. 7/17/1901; first; William H. Whiting (farmer, Ossipee) and Lulu A. Floyd (Tamworth)
Jeffrey Lee, b. 3/19/1962 in Laconia; second; David Lyle Whiting and Phylis Diane Clark
John Gilman, b.4/12/1922; third; Frederick H. Whiting (Boston, MA) and Ethel Jeffers (Tamworth)
Kayla Elizabeth Cory, b. 9/15/1994 in Laconia; Richard E. Whiting and Colleen M. Swan
Kevin Duane, b. 9/24/1965 in Laconia; second; Russell Ford Whiting, Jr. and Herberta Ann Evans
Lawrence W., b. 1/14/1905; first; Claude D. Whiting (laborer, Tamworth) and Edith L. Ames (Tamworth)
Leland Floyd, b. 6/29/1933; Roland Whiting and Hazel MacKenzie
Lena, b. 7/6/1904; fourth; Charles E. Whiting (laborer, Tamworth) and Jennie B. Wade (Moultonboro)
Lewis V., b. 4/1/1899; first; Charles E. Whiting (laborer, Tamworth) and Jennie B. Wade (Sandwich)
Mabel E., b. 8/4/1907; third; A. C. Whiting (laborer, Tamworth) and Fanny E. Forrest (Tamworth)
Patricia, b. 8/1/1944; seventh; Roland G. Whiting and Hazel MacKenzie
Patricia, b. 10/17/1955; third; George R. Whiting and Rona A. Simonds
Pauline, b. 1/7/1943; sixth; Roland G. Whiting and Hazel M. MacKenzie
Raymond V., b. 9/5/1928; Louis V. Whiting and Mamie Bennett
Rebecca, b. 1/1/1957; fourth; George R. Whiting and Rona A. Simonds
Rebecca J., b. 12/17/1959; fourth; Raymond V. Whiting and Geraldine S. Nudd
Richard E., b. 1/7/1959; third; Raymond V. Whiting and Geraldine S. Nudd
Roland G., b. 8/25/1907; fifth; W. H. Whiting (farmer, Ossipee) and Lulu A. Floyd (Tamworth)
Vivian Marie, b. 3/14/1910; fourth; Arthur C. Whiting (laborer, Tamworth) and Fannie Forrest (Tamworth)
Winslow, b. 3/25/1931; Howard W. Whiting and Madeline Eastwick

WHITMAN,
William, 3rd, b. 8/1/1900; second; William Whitman, Jr. (com. merchant, Andover, MA) and Ruth Loring (Prides Crossing, MA) (1916)

WIGGIN,
son, b. 2/17/1890; first; James H. Wiggin (laborer, Tamworth) and Capitola S. Nute (Milton)
son, b. 7/14/1921 in Tamworth; third; Roscoe A. Wiggin (auto mechanic, Union) and Nellie F. Drew (Tamworth)
Gary William, b. 1/23/1949; third; Kenneth E. Wiggin and Lillian I. Demers
Harold Hardy, b. 4/18/1928; Roscoe A. Wiggin and Nellie F. Drew
Jerry Bruce, II, b. 4/17/1965 in Wolfeboro; second; Jerry Bruce Wiggin and Linda Lee Dore
Kenneth, b. 4/28/1944; second; Kenneth A. Wiggin and Lillian I. Demers
Linda L., b. 3/6/1959; fourth; Kenneth E. Wiggin and Lillian I. Demers
Lorraine Elizabeth, b. 3/21/1924; Maurice E. Wiggin and Mary Elizabeth Cook
Mabel F., b. 9/1/1896 in Tamworth; second; James H. Wiggin (30, Tamworth) and Capitola S. Nute (30, Milton)
Nellie S., b. 6/7/1888; first; Hardy L. Wiggin (farmer, Tamworth) and Emma R. Floyd (Effingham)
Neurine Elaine, b. 4/1/1942; first; Kenneth E. Wiggin and Lillian I. Demers
Travis Jason, b. 4/30/1973 in Wolfeboro; Gary William Wiggin and Sharron Louise Herbold

WILKESMAN,
Keith Richard, b. 9/2/1976 in Laconia; Charles R. Wilkesman and Donna M. Quimby

WILKINSON,
Alan Trask, b. 9/4/1932; Clinton Wilkinson and Marion L. Trask
Andrew Seth, b. 3/1/2000 in Wolfeboro; Kraig Wilkinson and Lisa Wilkinson
Grace Elizabeth, b. 4/3/2003 in Wolfeboro; Kraig Wilkinson and Lisa Wilkinson

Kraig Alan, b. 12/6/1973 in N. Conway; Norman Clinton Wilkinson and Rochelle Patricia Feuerborn
Kristin Nichelle, b. 12/11/1974 in N. Conway; Norman Clinton Wilkinson and Rochelle Patricia Feuerborn
Norman Clinton, b. 4/29/1930; Robert C. Wilkinson and Marion L. Trask
Sophie Victoria, b. 11/14/1998 in Wolfeboro; Kraig A. Wilkinson and Lisa R. Giasson

WILLIAMS,
stillborn son, b. 12/20/1904; fourth; Justus W. Williams (sawyer, Ossipee) and Myrtie Smart (Tamworth)
stillborn child, b. 9/14/1906; fifth; Justus W. Williams (sawyer, Ossipee) and Myrtle Smart (Tamworth)
stillborn son, b. 8/6/1909; ninth; William H. Williams (laborer, Ossipee) and Susan Welch (Ossipee)
child, b. 5/21/1926; Charles Williams and Lilla Pennell
child, b. 5/31/1930; Charles Williams and Lilla Pennell
child, b. 9/11/1934; Charles Williams and Lillay Pennell
Beverly A., b. 5/25/1938; seventh; Charles Williams and Lilla Pennell
Brian Charles, b. 6/23/1965 in Laconia; second; Robert Alston Williams and Cynthia Ann Chamberlain
Charles J., b. 8/4/1896 in Tamworth; third; Justin M. Williams (40, Ossipee) and Mertie E. Smart (22, Tamworth)
Edith M., b. 7/23/1906; seventh; William H. Williams (laborer, Ossipee) and Susie Welch (Ossipee)
Henry A., b. 12/20/1903; sixth; William H. Williams (laborer, Ossipee) and Susie Welch (Ossipee)
Holly J., b. 12/18/1961; second; Paul E. Williams and Martha Evans
Irving Nute, b. 8/9/1910; William H. Williams (laborer, Ossipee) and Susie Welch (Ossipee)
Kyleigh Jean, b. 3/13/1992 in Laconia; Michael D. Williams and Janice M. Burke
Michael D., b. 8/23/1958; first; Paul E. Williams and Martha Evans
Mildred May, b. 1/14/1928; Charles Williams and Lilla Pennell
Myrtle, b. 6/30/1900; fourth; Justus Williams (sawyer, Ossipee) and Myrtie Smart (Tamworth)
Paul Edward, b. 7/10/1936; Charles Williams and Lilla Pennell
Ralph J., b. 5/1/1901; fifth; William H. Williams (laborer, Ossipee) and Susie Welch (Ossipee)
Robert A., b. 8/11/1941; eighth; C. J. Williams and Lilla Pennell

Tammy Lynn, b. 8/9/1963 in Laconia; first; Robert Alston Williams and Cynthia Ann Chamberlain

Walter S., b. 4/8/1910; first; Dora Williams (Ossipee)

WOODES,
Robert Clifton, b. 6/16/1942; first; Robert C. Woodes and Carol N. Gilman

WOODWARD,
Andrea May, b. 5/8/1966 in Laconia; Freeman Earl Woodward and Jacqueline Lorraine Tibbetts

Austin James, b. 6/28/1970 in Laconia; Robert Carl Woodward and Sheila Rae Dall

Carol Jean, b. 3/16/1943; fifth; Forrest G. Woodward and Mary E. Leavitt

Cody Austin, b. 12/8/1990 in N. Conway; Austin J. Woodward and Shanna C. Barbour

Duane Calvin, b. 12/30/1967 in Laconia; Freeman Earl Woodward and Jacqueline Lorraine Tibbetts

Freeman Earle, b. 3/5/1942; third; Forrest G. Woodward and Mary E. Leavitt

Howard Forrest, b. 11/12/1936; Forrest George Woodward and Mary E. Leavitt

Janet E., b. 9/26/1940; third; F. G. Woodward and Mary E. Leavitt

Jeremy Shurman, b. 10/2/1981 in Laconia; John Woodward and Theresa Boewe

Melvin R., b. 2/20/1949; seventh; Forrest G. Woodward and Mary E. Leavitt

Robert, b. 4/14/1945; sixth; Forrest Woodward and Mary E. Leavitt

Shauna Lynn, b. 8/3/1978 in N. Conway; Robert Woodward and Sheila Dall

Theresa Lynn, b. 4/15/1964 in Laconia; first; Freeman E. Woodward and Jacquelyn L. Tibbits

WRIGHT,
Adam Monroe, b. 3/26/1997 in N. Conway; Scott Monroe Wright and Sarah Gray

WROBLESKI,
Seth Gabriel, b. 4/13/1981 in N. Conway; William Wrobleski and Louise Bienvenue

YORK,
Kathleen A., b. 11/19/1947; first; Richard A. York and Catherine Pregent

YOUNG,
Chester F., b. 8/11/1900; first; Chester F. Young (contractor, Cambridge, MA) and Florence Rogers (Brookline, MA); residence – Brighton
Howard, Jr., b. 3/7/1925; Howard Young and Evelyn Ellis
Mary Evelyn, b. 12/20/1922; second; Howard E. Young (Eaton) and Evelyn Virgie Ellis (Eaton)
Virginia Mae, b. 8/26/1924; Howard Young and Evelyn Ellis

ZIMMERMANN,
Chad Westcott, b. 4/8/1987 in N. Conway; Robert Zimmermann and Cheryl A. Vernon

TAMWORTH
MARRIAGES

ABBOTT,
George Thompson of Falmouth, ME m. Penelope Gillian **Wheeler** of Falmouth, ME 7/26/1997
Harry A., Jr. of Madison m. Lillian L. **Bell** of Tamworth 1/24/1950 in Meredith; H – 20, truck driver; W – 19, at home
Herbert E. of Sandwich m. Alice May **Gilman** of Tamworth 5/30/1905 in Tamworth; H – 22, laborer, b. Sandwich, s/o R. Freeman Abbott (Tamworth) and Abbie A. Tappan (Sandwich); W – 18, housework, b. Tamworth, d/o James W. Gilman (Tamworth) and Harriet Davis (Tamworth)
William D. m. Alta **Nickerson** 10/20/1920 in N. Conway; H – 20, laborer, b. Jackson, s/o Asa Abbott and Marantha Grant; W – 25, teacher, b. Tamworth, d/o George E. Nickerson and Carrie White

ACKER,
J. Bruce of Tamworth m. Linda Jean **Thorp** of Conway 1/1/1989

ACTON,
Lloyd Phelps of Boston, MA m. Susan McMillen **Beall** of Decator, IL 3/5/1966; H – 27, arch. dsgn.; W – 22, int. dsgn.

ADJUTANT,
Christopher A. of Tamworth m. Laura E. **Moore** of Tamworth 6/20/1987
Roscoe m. Blanche **Perkins** 10/18/1919 in Warner; H – 21, laborer, s/o Willey Adjutant and Eliza J. Piper; W – 18, housework, d/o Hiram Perkins and Etta Clough

AGUIRRE,
Julio R. of MA m. Maria **Welch** of Tamworth 11/13/1988

ALBERS,
Frederick W. of Chocorua m. Hallie M. **Schneider** of Chocorua 8/19/1982

ALDEN,
Elton D. m. Ruth E. **Jackins** 3/31/1956 in Tamworth; H – 40, mechanic; W – 42, teacher

ALDRIDGE,
Lendal W. of Bartlett m. Eleanor L. **Ellis** of Tamworth 9/17/1938 in N. Conway; H – 27, auto mechanic; W – 19, housework

ALLAN,
Michael S. of Essex Jct., VT m. Christina A. **Prause** of Essex Jct., VT 6/12/1994

ALLEN,
Charles B. of Chocorua m. Valerie M. **Nickerson** of Chocorua 8/9/1986

ALT,
Christopher B. of Tamworth m. Barbara A. **Divitto** of Providence, RI 9/15/1979

ALTMAN,
Micah of Pasadena, CA m. Kylie K. **Mills** of Pasadena, CA 8/26/1995

AMADOR,
Franz G. of Seattle, WA m. Dorothy I. **Neville** of Seattle, WA 8/17/1991

AMBROSE,
L. Ramond m. Mabel R. **Long** 4/25/1931 in Tamworth
Langdon J. m. Gladys R. **Anthony** 6/18/1955 in Sandwich; H – 35, welder; W – 17, at home

AMES,
Alan A. of Tamworth m. Jo-Ann **Thompson** of Effingham 8/8/1969; H – 19; W - 18
Carl W. of Tamworth m. Jean A. **Wheeler** of Sandwich 2/29/1952 in Sandwich; H – 28, lumbering; W – 18, at home
Charles E. of Tamworth m. Evalena L. **Nudd** of Sandwich 9/14/1951 in Moultonboro; H – 19, woodsman; W – 18, at home
Charles E. of Tamworth m. Laura M. **Levesque** of Tamworth 9/15/2001
Charles E., Jr. of Tamworth m. Jeanne M. **Warner** of Tamworth 4/23/1976; H – 18; W – 17

Claud P. of Tamworth m. Blanche E. **Jeffers** of Tamworth 1/15/1909 in Tamworth; H – 21, laborer, b. Tamworth, s/o Zimri Ames (Tamworth, farmer) and Ella Palmer (Sandwich, housewife); W – 18, housework, b. Tamworth, d/o Milton W. Jeffers (Webster, farmer) and Abbie Downs (Tamworth, housewife)

Claude Milton m. Emma **Grace** 3/29/1930 in Tamworth

Ernest E. m. Bertha L. **Frost** 4/12/1928 in Madison

Gary L. of Tamworth m. Nicole L. **Hutchins** of Tamworth 5/11/1991

James R. m. Ada E. **Eldredge** 1/18/1930 in Tamworth

James W. of Tamworth m. Joanne **Stoddard** of Ossipee 7/1/1950 in Tamworth; H – 18, lumbering; W – 17, at home

John of Tamworth m. Hattie **Ames** of Tamworth 12/29/1900 in Tamworth; H – 23, laborer, s/o George H. Ames (Tamworth) and Mary Woodman (Tamworth); W – 17, housework, d/o Z. Ames (Tamworth) and Ella Palmer (Sandwich)

John Harmon m. Marion Cleveland **Doe** 7/25/1926 in Tamworth

John P. of Tamworth m. Colleen M. **Swan** of N. Sandwich 7/7/1984

John Philip of S. Tamworth m. Carrie Ann **Murphy** of Moultonboro 7/22/1989

Joseph, Jr. of Tamworth m. Elizabeth C. F. **Miller** of Tamworth 6/24/1893 in Tamworth; H - 55, farmer, b. Tamworth, s/o Joseph Ames (Tamworth) and Abigail Glidden (Tamworth); W - 50, housekeeping, d/o Robert Steele (Yorkshire, England) and Mary Steele (England)

Peter E. of Tamworth m. Joan M. **Lowd** of Conway 8/19/1978; H – 24; W – 24

Philip E. of Tamworth m. Helen C. **Moulton** of Tamworth 9/14/1952 in Tamworth; H – 18, farmer; W – 18, at home

Richard Wayne of Tamworth m. Barbara Marie **Bushman** of Ctr. Tuftonboro 3/3/1964 in Conway; H – 22, woodsman; W – 19, at home

Robert J. m. Beverly A. **Williams** 5/30/1956 in Tamworth; H – 35, farmer; W – 18, at home

Robin M. of S. Tamworth m. Joyce N. **Blackler** of S. Tamworth 5/23/1979

Ronald G. of Tamworth m. Cynthia L. **Marshall** of Tamworth 5/16/1987

Roy M. of Tamworth m. Lois A. **Conner** of Ctr. Ossipee 4/14/1951 in Moultonboro; H – 20, lumbering; W – 18, at home

Roy M. of Tamworth m. Kathleen **Foley** of Tamworth 8/31/1991

Roy M., Jr. of Tamworth m. Sheila J. **Corhran** of Sandwich
5/23/1973; H – 20; W – 20
Roy M., Jr. of Tamworth m. Pamela A. **Beeler** of Conway 2/7/1981

ANADOR,
John A. of UT m. Katherine P. **Loring** of UT 5/29/1982

ANAIR,
Richard M. of Meredith m. Diane M. **Stoneman** of Chocorua
1/16/1982

ANAND,
Sanjay Kumar of Galveston, Texas m. Laurie Anne **McKinnon** of
Galveston, Texas 9/20/1997

ANDERSON,
John E. of S. Yarmouth, MA m. Valma O. **Hill** of W. Yarmouth, MA
10/6/1973; H – 68; W – 63
John N. of Tamworth m. Cathleen G. **Martin** of Moultonboro
8/5/1972; H – 24; W – 27

ANDUJAR,
Wilfredo of Tamworth m. Francella **Aries** of Tamworth 12/13/1985

ANSLEY,
Charles of New York City, NY m. Patricia **Palmer** of Long Island, NY
7/12/1939 in Tamworth; H – 31, actor; W – 24, actress

ANTHONY,
Bruce Gordon of Tamworth m. Brenda Elizabeth **Knox** of Tamworth
6/24/1972; H – 22; W – 18
Chester Earle of Tamworth m. Judith Weare **Larrabee** of Tamworth
7/2/1967; H – 20, forestry; W – 20, waitress
David A. m. Arleen G. **Harmon** 9/4/1959 in Tamworth; H – 20,
furniture factory; W – 18, at home
David C. of Tamworth m. Deborah J. **Alexander** of Tamworth
10/2/1993
David M. of Tamworth m. Donna L. **Stewart** of Tamworth 6/8/1969;
H – 21; W – 20
Francis William of Tamworth m. Emily Erma **Perkins** of Tamworth
9/28/1968; H - 41; W – 39

Gerald Edward of Tamworth m. Shirley **Bennett** of Tamworth 5/2/1998

Gregory Alan of Tamworth m. Linda Lee **Fulcher** of Center Harbor 4/24/1971; H – 22; W – 19

Robert of Tamworth m. Susan **Emerson** of Tamworth 9/26/1981

Robert W. of Tamworth m. Valerie A. **Hartford** of Center Ossipee 7/2/1985

Warren G. m. Janette E. **Grace** 4/20/1957 in Tamworth; H – 20, mechanic; W – 18, tel. clerk

ARGENTO,

Nicholas of MA m. Ruth Anne **Bacon** of MA 2/20/1981

ARLING,

James G. m. Sara B. **Schenck** 10/14/1910 in Tamworth; H – 58, farmer, b. Barrington, s/o David Arling; W – 70, teacher, b. NJ, d/o Peter Schenck (NJ) and Rebecca Haruiss (NJ)

Roy E. of Tamworth m. Lulu M. **Gilman** of Tamworth 12/27/1903; H – 22, laborer, b. Tamworth, s/o James G. Arling (Barrington) and Emma M. Bickford (Tamworth); W – 20, housework, b. Tamworth, d/o Erwin A. Gilman (Tamworth) and Martha A. Drew (Wolfeboro)

ARMSTRONG,

Daryl V. of Houston, Texas m. Jo Anne **White** of Houston, Texas 9/8/1998

ARREOLA,

Bernardino of Benton, PA m. Kathy May **Sholley** of Benton, PA 7/8/1995

ARTIS,

Gene P. of Tamworth m. Constance M. **Wastell** of Tamworth 12/31/1994

ASPINALL,

Charles E. of Tamworth m. Jean **Myers** of Brooklyn, NY 11/2/1947 in Tamworth; H – 21, woodsman; W – 20, comptometer operator

Gregory J. of Tamworth m. Vanessa C. **Shepard** of Tamworth 8/20/1977; H – 22; W – 21

Gregory J. of Cazenovia, NY m. Brenda M. **Moneypenny** of Cazenovia, NY 8/25/1984

ASPINWALL,
William m. Ethel **Henderson** 4/8/1929 in Ossipee

ATWOOD,
Thompson S. of Standish, ME m. Cynthia T. **Browne** of Standish, ME 8/24/1996

AUSTIN,
Charles R. m. Cheryl A. **Dicey** 8/27/1960 in Tamworth; H – 19, Highway Dept.; W – 15, at home
Joseph F. m. Mildred D. **Yeaton** 11/1/1930 in Conway

AUTIO,
Thomas Peter of Wellesley, MA m. Barbara Ann **Clem** of W. Newton, MA 10/26/1968; H – 32; W - 30

AVERILL,
Gerald A. m. Arlene M. **Barry** 2/22/1953 in Tamworth; H – 21, florist; W – 18, at home

AVERY,
Lyndon Edward of Moultonboro m. Penney Marie **Austin** of Tamworth 6/3/1989

AYER,
Bruce A. of Tamworth m. Robbin L. **Nelson** of Nutting Lake, MA 6/27/1992
Forrest D. m. Doris **Elliott** 8/10/1927 in Laconia

BAIN,
Frederick W. of Tamworth m. Luella B. **McIntyre** of Ctr. Tuftonboro 4/8/1944 in Center Harbor; W – 46, woodsman; W – 34, housework

BAKER,
Christopher E. of W. Ossipee m. Samantha L. **Emerson** of W. Ossipee 9/11/1999

David Leon of Derry m. Laurrie Ann **Hinckley** of Tamworth 3/28/1975; H – 19; W - 18

Wallace H. of Tamworth m. Lorraine **Bean** of Ctr. Ossipee 3/4/1950 in Tamworth; H – 28, lumberjack; W – 16, housework

BALLARD,
Hollis B. of Tamworth m. Mary E. **Bartlett** of Tamworth 2/12/1888 in Tamworth; H - 32, blacksmith, b. Tamworth, s/o William W. Ballard (Tamworth); W - 22, housework, b. Tamworth, d/o Lorenzo D. Bartlett (Tamworth)

BALLO,
Michael Sandor of Durham, NC m. Joanna Laura **Pi-Sunyer** of Durham, NC 8/26/2000

BANCROFT,
Harold R. m. Alice **Elliott** 7/7/1934 in Wakefield

BANFILL,
Carroll Benjamin of Tamworth m. Lois Carol **Roberts** of Tamworth 12/24/1967; H – 33, farmer; W – 23, factory

Herman F. m. Edner M. **Butterfield** 10/21/1933 in Conway

BARIL,
Arthur F., Jr. m. Dorothy **Lavoie** 3/15/1958 in Tamworth; H – 23, shoe worker; W – 23, at home

BARNA,
Czeslaw J. of Franklin m. Dorothy M. **Trask** of Tamworth 5/5/1951 in Tamworth; H – 32, salesman; W – 30, clerk

BARNARD,
Allan F. of Woburn, MA m. Karen M. **Dipaolo** of Tamworth 11/21/1992

BARNES,
Fred E. m. Florence **Whiting** 12/30/1929 in Tamworth

BAROCCI,
Thomas A. of Newton, MA m. Monica M. **Radvany** of Newton, MA 6/25/1983

BARTLETT,
Leland C. of Tamworth m. Nellie A. **Mason** of Tamworth 9/28/1904 in Tamworth; H – 22, manufacturer, b. Moultonboro, s/o Elory G. Bartlett (Meredith) and Imogene Evans (Moultonboro); W – 24, b. Tamworth, d/o John L. Mason (Tamworth) and Nellie Varney (Dover)
Robert C. m. Tobia **Goodson** 9/24/1955 in Tamworth; H – 20, farmer; W – 20, at home

BASLEY,
Elmer Wayne m. Elizabeth M. **Colby** 6/12/1925 in Tamworth

BASSETT,
James C. of Tamworth m. Fannie A. **Tilton** of Portsmouth 2/13/1892 in Tamworth; H - 58, physician, b. Jackson, s/o David Bassett and Ann Burnham (Newfield, ME); W - 34, housework, b. Portsmouth, d/o Jefferson C. Tilton (Coliair, ME) and F. Hatch (Freeport, ME)

BAXTER,
Francis of Marshfield, MA m. Cynthia **Duprey** of Marshfield, MA 12/6/1975; H – 27; W - 26

BEAN,
Fred Roland m. Sarah M. **Nickerson** 7/16/1927 in N. Conway
Otis m. Elsia Ida **Brown** 6/11/1919 in Conway; H – 28, teamster, s/o Otis Bean and Mary A. McDearmont; W – 17, housework, d/o Alphonso D. Brown and Minnie Ella Kennerson

BEARD,
Gary Lee of Mercer Island, WA m. Jane **Farnum** of Tamworth 10/6/1974; H – 28; W – 26
John Ross of Cleveland, OH m. Nancy Lee **Wickersham** of Tamworth 6/18/1965 in Tamworth; H – 22, student; W – 21, student

BEAUCHESNE,
Laurier W. of Bethel, ME m. Holly M. **Walega** of Bethel, ME 8/15/1998

BEAUDET,
Michael R. of Conway m. Shirley Jean **Johnson** of Tamworth
12/30/1972; H – 21; W – 19

BECKER,
Robert A. of Boston, MA m. Nannette **Pritchard** of Boston, MA
9/24/1971; H – 33; W – 24

BEDFORD,
Bruce Walton of Tamworth m. Brenda Doris **Welch** of Tamworth
8/5/1973; H – 27; W – 18

BEHR,
Charles E. of Tamworth m. Joan **Kennedy** of Madison 2/26/1949 in
N. Conway; H – 36, farmer; W – 24, at home
Karl R. of Tamworth m. Sue E. **Greg** of Tamworth 7/14/1984

BELDNER,
Raymond Edward of San Francisco, CA m. Catharine Elizabeth
Clark of San Francisco, CA 8/23/1997

BENNETT,
Dennis W. of Tamworth m. Susan B. **Stewart** of Tamworth
5/30/1982
Dennis W. of Tamworth m. Lisa J. **Sanborn** of Tamworth 4/8/1987
Donald K. of Rochester m. Elaine E. **Knox** of Tamworth 12/6/1969;
H – 42; W – 42
Kenneth J. of Tamworth m. Denise A. **Higgins** of Tamworth
6/28/2003
Lawrence E. of Tamworth m. Marjorie **Hobbs** of Tamworth
10/7/1945 in Conway; H – 32, farmer; W – 43, cook
Lawrence Edward of Tamworth m. Hester Rose **Welch** of Tamworth
7/6/1963 in Center Ossipee; H – 50, laborer; W – 61, mill
worker

BERGEN,
Dominic N. of Tamworth m. Jeanne L. **English** of Effingham
6/24/1972; H – 23; W – 22

BERGERON,
Grant S. of Manchester m. Jane E. **Frost** of Tamworth 10/26/1974; H – 27; W – 27
Ronald C. of Tamworth m. Deborah J. **Burke** of Tamworth 12/24/1982

BERGSTROM,
Peter W. of Tamworth m. Susan M. **Remick** of Tamworth 7/29/1984

BERRY,
Albert C. of Tamworth m. Bertha S. **Davis** of Cambridge, MA 11/26/1942 in Conway; H – 40, mason; W – 46, state investigator
Edward Ronald of Tamworth m. Lori Ann Madeline **Juhasz** of Tamworth 7/16/1988
Everett W. m. Thelma L. **Graffam** 5/2/1925 in Tamworth
Everett W. m. Ethel L. **Gilman** 6/5/1932 in Ctr. Sandwich
Frank m. Eleanor **Condon** 6/29/1929 in Conway
Howard E. of Tamworth m. Dorothea L. **Moore** of Albany 7/12/1941 in Rochester; H – 19, laborer; W – 19, stenographer
Raymond A. of W. Ossipee m. Charlotte E. **Eldridge** of Tamworth 6/3/1950 in Moultonville; H – 20, painter; W – 19, at home
Raymond E. of Tamworth m. Gladys M. **Palmer** of Tamworth 4/5/1942 in Wolfeboro; H – 31, woodsman; W – 35, housework
Robert K. m. Edith M. **Gilman** 9/12/1932 in Tamworth
Ronald E. m. Norma P. **Harmon** 10/27/1956 in Tamworth; H – 26, carpenter; W – 17, waitress
Walter H. of Tamworth m. Grace E. **Clough** of Tamworth 6/24/1901 in Tamworth; H – 28, laborer, b. Tamworth, s/o Orrin S. Berry (Tamworth) and Lizzie Davis (Biddeford, ME); W – 19, housework, b. Tamworth, d/o Herbert Clough (Tamworth) and Hattie Mason (Tamworth)
William Daniel of New Bedford, MA m. Lisa Ann **Lariviere** of New Bedford, MA 6/11/1997

BICKFORD,
Benjamin of Tamworth m. Addie **Tibbetts** of Tamworth 9/17/1892 in Tamworth; H - 60, farmer, b. Madison, s/o Benjamin Bickford (Parsonsfield, ME) and Hannah Clain (Parsonsfield, ME); W - 48, housework, b. Limerick, ME, d/o Roswell Torrey and Sarah Hardy

Carl O. m. Elva L. **Floyd** 4/17/1937 in Plymouth
Carroll of Tamworth m. Joan **Eldridge** of Tamworth 2/14/1981
Carroll Frank of Eaton m. JoAnn P. **Saujon** of Tamworth 12/31/1971; H – 29; W – 34
Chester J. of Sandwich m. Alice M. **Cooper** of Newark, NJ 6/6/1923 in Tamworth; H – 29; W - 25
George H. of Tamworth m. Edith **Cook** of Tamworth 8/3/1894 in Tamworth; H - 23, laborer, b. Lowell, MA, s/o George Bickford (Tamworth, laborer) and Jennie Benjin (Lowell, MA, housework); W - 18, housework, b. Wolfeboro, d/o James R. Cook (Bartlett, farmer) and Mary A. Bunker (Tamworth, housework)
James B. of Sandwich m. Eva E. **Bickford** of Tamworth 11/24/1892 in Tamworth; H - 23, laborer, b. Sandwich, s/o Noah W. Bickford (Rochester) and Ursula Bryer (Sandwich); W - 22, housework, b. Tamworth, d/o Simon Bickford (Tamworth) and Mary Folsom (Tamworth)
James H. of Tamworth m. Clara E. **Blackburn** of Tamworth 1/1/1890 in Wolfeboro Jct.; H - 25, farmer, b. Tamworth, s/o Enoch Bickford (Eaton); W - 24, teacher, b. Gaysville, VT, d/o John H. Blackburn (Salem, MA)
John F. of Tamworth m. M. Carrie **Fifield** of Sandwich 10/31/1903; H – 26, laborer, b. Tamworth, s/o Simon Bickford (Barrington) and Mary Folsom (Tamworth); W – 21, housework, b. Sandwich, d/o William Fifield (Tamworth) and Abbie Knox (Ossipee)
Paul P. m. Marion **Lyman** 6/24/1933 in Madison
Wilbur J. of Tamworth m. Sarah A. **Bickford** of Sandwich 8/3/1889 in Sandwich; H - 22, farmer, b. Tamworth, s/o Simon Bickford (Tamworth); W - 17, housework, b. Sandwich, d/o Noah Bickford (Sandwich)
Wilbur J. m. Frances **Hobbs** 5/12/1910 in Tamworth; H – 43, farmer, b. Tamworth, s/o Simon Bickford (Barrington) and Mary Falsome (Tamworth); W – 20, dressmaker, b. Boston, MA, d/o Frank O. Hobbs (Ossipee) and Hattie F. Eastman (Albany)
Wyatt T. of Tamworth m. Lizzie **Beede** of Sandwich 2/12/1888 in Tamworth; H - 44, farmer, b. Sandwich, s/o Freeman Bickford (Boothbay, ME); W - 52, housework, b. Sandwich, d/o Hugh Beede (Sandwich)

BILLINGS,
Peter D. of Center Ossipee m. Joanne M. **Clark** of Tamworth 12/28/1979
Peter D. of Ctr. Ossipee m. Ruth Ann **Primus** of Ctr. Ossipee 7/3/2003

BILODEAU,
Wayne Louis of ME m. Anne Marie **Brooks** of ME 10/8/1988

BIRMINGHAM,
Paul J., Jr. of Tamworth m. Judi L. **Wilkinson** of Tamworth 5/20/1989

BISHOP,
Noel E. of Tamworth m. Jennifer J. **Kovach** of Tamworth 5/6/2001

BLACK,
James m. Clara B. **Knight** 5/15/1921 in Chocorua; H – 54, teamster, b. Lancaster, s/o John Black and Margaret McMann; W – 47, at home, 2nd, b. Tamworth, d/o Isaac N. Kimball and Emely A. Sanborn

BLACKEY,
Edwin A. m. Flora E. **Whipple** 7/27/1927 in Conway
Frank A. of Tamworth m. Gertrude **Henderson** of Tamworth 1/10/1901 in Tamworth; H – 28, laborer, b. Sandwich, s/o Elijah S. Blackey (Sandwich) and Carrie E. Blanchard (Sandwich); W – 22, housekeeper, b. Tamworth, d/o Edwin D. Henderson (Sandwich) and Ada Forest (Madison)

BLAISDELL,
Charles A. m. Lena **Wyman** 12/31/1917 in Chocorua; H – 27, U. S. Navy, b. Tamworth, s/o Frank E. Blaisdell and Annie E. Trepania; W – 20, b. Balasore, India, d/o Herbert E. Wyman and Gertrude M. Kneeland
Victor Julien of Tamworth m. Margaret A. **Casey** of Hingham, MA 9/10/1912 in Conway; H – 30, chauffeur, b. Concord, s/o Henri G. Blaisdell (Dorchester) and Lilla Dale Leonard (Passumpsic, VT); W – 22, b. Hingham, MA, d/o George Casey (Hingham, MA) and Margaret MacDonald (NS)

BLANCHARD,
Gerald R. of Ashland, MA m. Evelyn M. **Wedge** of Ashland, MA 5/12/1984
William S. of Tamworth m. Cheryl E. **Brooks** of Tamworth 3/31/1984

BLEAKNEY,
Richard R. of Tamworth m. Catharine A. **Newcomb** of Tamworth 8/10/1985

BLISS,
Eli C. W. of Chelsea, MA m. Hannah C. **Ham** of Tamworth 9/6/1887 in Tamworth; H - 39, merchant, b. Chelsea, MA, s/o Eli C. Bliss and Adeline; W - 21, school teacher, b. Tamworth, d/o Lowell Ham
William P. of La Cienega, NM m. Lucinda F. **Williams** of La Cienega, NM 9/7/1991

BLODGETT,
August L. m. Nettie **Wadley** 12/6/1922 in Tamworth; H – 30, b. Dedham, MA; W – 40, b. Gilmanton

BLUE,
John A. of Somerville, MA m. Elizabeth M. **Alt** of Cambridge, MA 8/20/1972; H – 29; W – 30

BODGE,
Charles F. of Tamworth m. Leona J. **Warner** of Westfield, VT 9/2/1905 in Westfield, VT; H – 28, mechanic, b. Moultonboro, s/o Joseph F. Bodge (Strafford) and Jennie B. Nichols (Chatham); W – 26, none, b. Lowell, VT, d/o William H. Warner (Georgia, VT) and Mary Wakefield (Lowell, VT)
Harry E. of Moultonboro m. Annie M. **Glidden** of Tamworth 4/2/1898 in Tamworth; H – 19, farmer, b. Moultonboro, s/o Daniel M. Bodge (Moultonboro) and Ellen Bodge (Tuftonboro); W – 18, b. Tamworth, d/o Frank A. Glidden (Calais, ME) and Maggie Woodman (Tamworth)

BOEWE,
Christopher C. of Tamworth m. Joyce E. **Sherwood** of Silver Lake 4/26/1980

James L. of Tamworth m. Brenda J. **Eldridge** of Tamworth 6/12/1982
Nicholas A. of Chocorua m. Renee S. **Boucher** of Chocorua 5/5/2002
Walter M. of Tamworth m. Denise M. **Miller** of Madison 3/18/1978; H – 19; W – 18
Ward A. of Tamworth m. Gail A. **Farrell** of Tamworth 6/21/1980

BOHL,
Jesse Pieter of VA m. Mei Leng **Lau** of VA 8/12/1988

BOHMILLER,
Stephen A. of Chocorua m. Lorie J. **Watson** of Chocorua 11/3/1991

BONTAITES,
Alan J. of Tamworth m. Kristine M. **Klein** of Tamworth 7/6/1991

BOOKHOLZ,
Edward V. m. Ellen P. **Whiting** 9/26/1920 in Moultonboro; H – 25, farmer, b. Tamworth, s/o Jacon Bookholz and Emma J. Caverly; W – 16, b. Tamworth, d/o William H. Whiting and Lulu Floyd
Frederick F. m. Ethel V. **Wiggin** 10/3/1918 in Bartlett; H – 26, carpenter, b. Tamworth, s/o Jacob Bookholz and Emma J. Caverley; W – 24, b. SD, d/o Everett D. Wiggin and Elizabeth A. Libby
Harold m. Rita L. **Lovering** 5/15/1926 in Rochester
Leon W. m. Esther **Sprague** 4/25/1915 in Effingham; H – 24, laborer, b. Tamworth, s/o Jacob Bookholz and Emma Caverley; W – 18, housework, b. Effingham, d/o Charles Sprague and Annie Furnald
Walter B. m. Isabelle **Walker** 11/12/1930 in Wakefield

BOONE,
Percival A. m. Hazel **Roebarge** 6/15/1922 in Manchester; H – 33, b. Manchester; W – 16, b. Tuftonboro

BOOTHBY,
James Edward, III of Tamworth m. Heidi Ann **Parks** of Tamworth 10/1/1989

Lawrence D. of Tamworth m. Elizabeth F. **Hobbs** of Tamworth 3/21/1952 in Milford; H – 23, hospital attendant; W – 18, student

BORGAULT,
Henry J. of Laconia m. Katherine L. **Hidden** of Tamworth 8/2/1941 in Laconia; H – 21, machinist; W – 23, school teacher

BOSSE,
William H. of Kitchener, ON m. Julia M. **Jean-Marie** of Kitchener, ON 8/2/1993

BOTTING,
Calvin E. of Tamworth m. Sharon G. **Locke** of Tamworth 10/11/1975; H – 24; W - 24

BOUTIN,
Harold Raymond of Ossipee m. Patricia Elaine **Boyd** of Tamworth 12/17/1962 in Tamworth; H – 35, waiter; W – 32, housewife

BOUVE,
Howard Allston, III of Malden, MA m. Kristin **Loud** of Malden, MA 10/21/1989

BOWLES,
David A. m. Elizabeth M. **French** 9/16/1961 in Concord; H – 26, civil engineer; W – 24, stenographer
James C. of Tamworth m. Diane L. **Kelsey** of Lee 7/20/1985
Roland R. m. Lillian W. **Nelson** 6/2/1933 in Plymouth

BOWLEY,
Roland G. of Tamworth m. Lora M. **Baker** of Tamworth 1/19/1951 in Sandwich; H – 21, auto maint.; W – 17, at home

BOWMAN,
Michael R. of Tamworth m. Caroline P. **Lafavore** of Dover 7/30/1993

BOYLAN,
Stephen P. of Somerville, MA m. Lynne **Farnum** of Somerville, MA 6/27/1992

BRADBURY,
Duane Lee of Tamworth m. Catherine Susan **Beane** of Tamworth 2/18/1995

BRADLEY,
John Francis of Chocorua m. Mary Peaco **Todd** of Arlington, MA 9/9/1989

BRANDE,
Justin of Tamworth m. Susan **Kennedy** of Madison 10/9/1948 in Tamworth; H – 31, farming; W – 23, at home

BRASWELL,
Emory H. of New York m. Rita M. **Collins** of New York 10/5/1952 in Tamworth; H – 20, student; W – 22, bank clerk

BRENNAN,
Charles A. of Tamworth m. Lisa A. **Elliott** of Tamworth 5/26/1984
Charles A. of Tamworth m. Kimberly Lee **Nolet** of Tamworth 7/8/2000
Christopher J. of Tamworth m. Darlene E. **Nason** of Tamworth 9/11/1982

BRESETTE,
Glen D. of Tamworth m. Sharon R. **Drew** of Tamworth 7/19/1987
Timothy A. of Tamworth m. Laurie D. **Irish** of Yarmouth, ME 9/7/1991

BRETT,
Stanley L. of Tamworth m. Victoria **Mason** of Tamworth 11/2/1940 in Center Harbor; H – 19, laborer; W – 17, at home
Wayne of Tamworth m. Judith Ann **Brubeck** of Madison 8/8/1962 in N. Conway; H – 21, salesman; W – 19, tele. operator

BREWER,
Alexander R. of Lynn, MA m. Joan M. **Fontaine** of Lynn, MA 8/10/1963 in Tamworth; H – 21, shoe worker; W – 18, shoe worker

BRIDGES,
Wilbur M. of ME m. Barbara K. **Johnson** of Tamworth 6/18/1977; H − 38; W − 36

BROCK,
David Hackett of Marblehead, MA m. Caroline R. **MacDougall** of Marblehead, MA 10/29/1965 in Tamworth; H − 28, teacher; W − 26, teacher

BRODIE,
E. W. m. Ella M. **Quimby** 7/3/1915 in Manchester; H − 45, shoemaker, 2nd, b. Pittsburg, MA, s/o Campbell Brodie and Florinda Baxter; W − 39, lodging house, 2nd, b. Lowell, MA

BROOKS,
Gordon H. of Cherry Valley, MA m. Margaret L. **Ackley** of Rockdale, MA 8/3/1946 in Tamworth; H − 25, student; W − 23, social worker

BROSS,
Shawn M. of Tamworth m. Tammy L. **White** of Tamworth 12/5/1998

BROTHERS,
Elmer W. of W. Ossipee m. Esther G. **Ames** of Tamworth 1/29/1949 in Ctr. Ossipee; H − 20, millworker; W − 22, stenographer

Jeffrey A. of Tamworth m. Joyce E. **Mondeau** of Tamworth 10/30/1977; H − 25; W − 21

Kevin Wayne of Tamworth m. Patricia Ruth **Calder** of Ossipee 710/31/1970; H − 18; W − 22

Michael B. of Tamworth m. Marcia **Noyes** of Jackson 6/29/1968; H − 19; W − 17

Michael B. of Tamworth m. Margaret E. **Staley** of Tamworth 12/22/1984

Stephen J. of Tamworth m. Jean J. **Craft** of ME 10/22/1977; H − 24; W − 18

BROWN,
Albert F. of Tamworth m. Clara **Craven** of Lynn, MA 8/31/1912 in Tamworth; H − 37, laborer, b. Tamworth, s/o Alonzo Brown (Albany) and Rachel Hurd (Acton, ME); W − 41, housework, b. England, d/o John Leach (England) and Elizabeth Leach

Alonzo m. Eliza **Willey** 9/30/1910 in Tamworth; H – 72, farmer, b. Albany, s/o Asa Brown (Conway) and Abigail Head (Albany); W – 64, housewife, b. Tamworth, d/o Reuben D. Hobbs (Ossipee) and Elmira Nickerson (Tamworth)

Charles W. m. Evelyn I. **Whiting** 1/4/1918 in Tamworth; H – 23, farmer, b. Ipswich, MA, s/o David Brown and Rose A. Smith; W – 16, b. Tamworth, d/o William Whiting and Lulu Floyd

Charles W. m. Dorris L. **Whiting** 10/8/1922 in Tamworth; H – 28, b. Ipswich, MA; W – 17, b. Tamworth

Charles W., Jr. of Tamworth m. Susan M. **Oliveira** of Tamworth 10/5/1985

David N. of Tamworth m. Jean C. **Solbes** of Tamworth 10/2/1985

Edwin J. of Ossipee m. Inzie A. **Bickford** of Tamworth 6/22/1889 in S. Tamworth; H - 34, laborer, b. Northwood, s/o H. Brown (Northwood); W - 33, housework, b. Nashua, d/o Mark Ranger (Hollis)

Ellsworth C. of Tamworth m. Doralyn A. **Currier** of Tamworth 1/15/1951 in Sandwich; H – 23, lumbering; W – 20, at home

Elmer m. Grace E. **McKerom** 7/29/1928 in Tamworth

Franklin J. m. Phyllis A. **Frost** 2/14/1959 in Tamworth; H – 20, Army; W – 27, tel. opr.

Gordon L. m. Alice M. **Cotton** 7/19/1930 in Tamworth

James of Waterford, ME m. Martha E. **McNeil** of Tamworth 9/4/1904 in Waterford, ME; H – 57, farmer, b. Albany, ME, s/o Samuel Brown (Albany, ME) and Myra Estes (Bethel, ME); W – 44, housework, b. Tamworth, d/o Lorenzo D. Perkins (Tamworth) and Sarah H. Kennerson (Albany)

Joseph E., Jr. of Andover, MA m. Deborah J. **Christie** of Andover, MA 9/3/1994

Robert E. of Tamworth m. Corrine S. **Hersey** of Wolfeboro 6/16/1946 in Wolfeboro; H – 21, dragline operator; W – 20, tel. operator

Timothy of Tamworth m. Kathi **Thompson** of Tamworth 9/20/1981

BROWNE,
Dale M. of Tamworth m. Isabel A. **Caranci** of Tamworth 10/15/1975; H – 30; W - 24

BROWNELL,
Lawrence M. m. Frances L. **Williams** 4/18/1953 in Conway; H – 32, meterman; W – 22, clerk

BRYANT,
Edward E. of Tamworth m. Nettie E. **Sherwood** of Portsmouth 5/22/1893 in Tamworth; H - 34, farmer, b. Tamworth, s/o John Bryant (Tamworth) and Susan E. Gilman (Tamworth); W - 24, housekeeping, b. Barnesville, NB, d/o Daniel Sherwood (Barnesville, NB) and Eliza A. Case (Barnesville, NB)

BUCK,
Ormsby J. m. Carolyn E. **Hall** 6/12/1954 in Nashua; H – 28, student; W – 21, student
Tracy L. of Dudley, MA m. Sarah L. **Terrill** of Dudley, MA 8/12/1989

BUCKHOLY,
Jacob of Tamworth m. Emma J. **Brown** of Tamworth 7/3/1891 in Tamworth; H - 21, farmer, b. Baden, Germany, s/o Benjamin Buckholy (Baden, Germany) and Marion Buckholy (Baden, Germany); W - 28, housework, b. Moultonboro, d/o Benjamin Caverly and Hannah Caverly

BUDROE,
Edward H. of Tamworth m. Barbara J. **Eldridge** of W. Ossipee 10/2/1948 in Center Ossipee; H – 18, truck driver; W – 19, at home

BUNKER,
Alan Damon of Tamworth m. Kathleen Elaine **Cloran** of Tamworth 9/21/1997
Fred W. of Tamworth m. Elsie M. **Davis** of Tamworth 3/29/1903; H – 19, laborer, b. Tamworth, s/o Levi W. Bunker (Tamworth) and Hattie R. Webber (Wenham, MA); W – 15, b. Tamworth, d/o William H. Davis (Effingham) and Mary M. Mooney (Nashua)

BURDICK,
Glenn of Tamworth m. Kim M. **Newton** of Tamworth 8/26/1989

BURKE,
Frank Weston of Tamworth m. Virginia Arlene **Chesley** of Gilford 6/11/1968; H – 27; W – 30
Geoffrey B. of Chocorua m. Andrea P. **Greene** of Chocorua 9/21/1991

Thomas William of N. Conway m. Jacqwelyn Lee **Allen** of Chocorua 6/30/1974; H – 19; W – 19

BURNELL,
Alton E. of N. Conway m. Laurie J. **Streeter** of Tamworth 4/24/1982 Harvey F. m. Collen L. **Parent** 7/4/1959 in Tamworth; H – 24, farmer; W – 29, housewife

BURRAGE,
Robert E. of Westbrook, ME m. Kathryn I. **Grey** of Westbrook, ME 9/8/1990

BURRER,
Phillip Farrell of Wayland, MA m. Cheri Antoinette **Ventura** of Jefferson, MA 2/1/1997

BURROWS,
Jon Lester of Ctr. Sandwich m. Wendy Lee **Evans** of Tamworth 11/3/1973; H – 23; W – 19

BUSHEY,
Timothy A. of Freedom m. Krystal A. **Demars** of Freedom 10/4/2003

BUSWELL,
Robert R. of Center Ossipee m. Cora L. **Hobbs** of Tamworth 7/12/1947 in Conway; H – 21, laborer; W – 21, waitress

BUTTERFIELD,
Fernan R. m. Clare E. **Smith** 9/25/1954 in Jackson; H – 24, radio operator; W – 20, at home

BUTTRICK,
Clifton R. of Loudon m. Virginia P. **Palmer** of Tamworth 8/25/1966; H– 46, construction; W – 42, housewife

BUXTON,
Charles A. of Tamworth m. Nettie **Daw** of Tamworth 12/12/1912 in Tamworth; H – 24, laborer, b. Providence, RI, s/o Charles H. Buxton (Hartford, CT) and Isador Brann (Woodville, RI); W – 29, housework, b. Tamworth, d/o Samuel W. Barnes (Hiram, ME) and Emma Bean (Stowe, ME)

BUZZELL,
Charles P. of Tamworth m. Ida M. **Gilman** of Tamworth 9/27/1894 in Tamworth; H -26, physician, b. Nottingham, s/o Andrew E. Buzzell (Barrington, farmer) and Eliza Tuttle (Strafford, housekeeping); W - 32, housekeeping, b. Tamworth, d/o David Gilman (Eaton, farmer) and M. J. Gilman (Devonshire, England, housekeeping)

BUZZUTTO,
Nick D. of Tamworth m. Ethel E. **Young** of Tamworth 8/9/1941 in Tamworth; H – 29, truck driver; W – 21, maid

BYERS,
Brent M. of Newburyport, MA m. Marnie L. **Cutrone** of Newburyport, MA 9/7/1991

BYRNE,
James D. of Jamaica Plain, MA m. Barbara J. **Schwer** of Natick, MA 7/14/1974; H – 45; W – 33

CABELL,
William D. of Tamworth m. Susan M. **Ackley** of Tamworth 6/11/1977; H – 30; W – 32

CAHILL,
Edward J., Jr. of Tamworth m. Kris E. **Magee** of Tamworth 6/6/1994

CAMERON,
Bruce H. of W. Ossipee m. Anita M. **Nudd** of Tamworth 7/17/1993
Herb J. of Tamworth m. Andrea L. **Jaques** of Tamworth 8/8/1993

CANFIELD,
Christopher R. of Tamworth m. Juniper D. **Lamb** of Tamworth 3/31/1996

CANNEY,
Haven E. m. Donna J. **White** 9/25/1954 in Wolfeboro; H – 20, laborer; W – 18, at home
Haven E. m. Donna J. **Foss** 5/17/1958 in Sandwich; H – 24, furniture factory; W – 21, factory worker

CARLSON,
Dana Francis of Tamworth m. Deborah Ann **Swan** of Tamworth 6/20/1998
Richard H. of Tamworth m. Candy L. **White** of Tamworth 9/27/1996

CARNEY,
Alan of Brighton, MA m. Andrea M. **Coville** of Brighton, MA 8/25/1990

CAROLAN,
Brian Patrick of Wellesley, MA m. Nadine Michelle **Hanna** of Wellesley, MA 9/30/1995

CARPENTER,
Allen R. of Tamworth m. Patricia J. **Walker** of Tamworth 11/15/1996

CARR,
Charles M. of Tamworth m. Sylvia M. **Chase** of Tamworth 12/24/1941 in Tamworth; H – 27, truck driver; W – 27, nursemaid
Kenneth C. m. Collen M. **Hatch** 10/2/1954 in Tamworth; H – 22, lumber; W – 19, at home
Richard E. m. Evelyn M. **Lewis** 1/8/1958 in Stratham; H – 21, tree surgeon; W – 18, at home

CARTER,
Gordon Winslow of Tamworth m. Edith May **Ames** of Tamworth 8/28/1976; H – 20; W - 19
Lisle W. of Tamworth m. Elsie M. **Gilman** of Tamworth 6/10/1944 in Conway; H – 51, factory supt.; W – 53, own home
Lisle W. m. Katheryn A. **Kenney** 11/19/1960 in Wolfeboro; H – 68, retired; W – 64, nurses aid
Robert W. of Tamworth m. Marybelle **Welch** of Tamworth 4/6/1944 in Tamworth; H – 20, US Navy; W – 22, US Navy

CARUSO,
James V. of Los Angeles, CA m. Emilie E. **Smith** of Los Angeles, CA 6/20/1992

CASWELL,
William A. m. Bertha G. **Flint** 7/14/1931 in Tamworth

CATE,
William R. of Florida m. Veronica **DuBois** 4/26/1949 in Tamworth; H – 38, machinist; W – 26, waitress

CAVE,
Edwin F. of Brookline, MA m. Joan **Lincoln** of Newton, MA 9/26/1970; H – 73; W – 49

CAVERLY,
Leonard W. of Tamworth m. Nellie E. **Day** of Tamworth 8/19/1888 in Tamworth; H - 23, farmer, b. Meredith, s/o Benjamin F. Caverly; W - 21, housework, b. Sandwich, d/o John Day

CAYER,
James J. of Tamworth m. Susan E. **Winters** of Tamworth 9/13/1998

CHADBOURN,
Herbert m. Harriett **Ross** 4/2/1921 in Conway; H – 54, fireman, 2nd, b. Ossipee, s/o Isaac Chadbourn and Hannah Leighton; W – 58, housekeeper, 3rd, b. Tamworth, d/o Edward F. Knox and Abigail Mason

CHADWICK,
Rufus Herbert of Seattle, WA m. Elizabeth Michaud **Lanou** of Seattle, WA 7/22/1995

CHAMBERLAIN,
Ralph W. m. Florence B. **Andrews** 6/18/1916 in Tamworth; H – 23, electrician, b. Wolfeboro, s/o Jeremiah C. Goodwin and Emma Bean; W – 32, housework, 2nd, b. Tamworth, d/o Charles W. Chamberlain and Cora Hayford
Raymond m. Marjorie **Gay** 5/20/1934 in Conway

CHARLEBOS,
Paul F. of Felts Mills, NY m. Vern F. **Burdick** of Felts Mills, NY 7/29/1984

CHASE,
Augustus of Tamworth m. Annie D. **Hobbs** of Tamworth 4/12/1893 in Tamworth; H - 23, teamster, b. Albany, s/o Alonzo Chase (Conway) and Annie Littlefield (Albany); W - 22, housekeeping,

b. Tamworth, d/o Joseph W. Hobbs (Ossipee) and Patience Connor (Madison)

Augustus of Tamworth m. Ida E. **Davis** of Tamworth 5/20/1900 in Tamworth; H – 29, laborer, s/o Alonzo Chase (Conway) and Annie Littlefield (Albany, ME); W – 22, housework, d/o William H. Davis (Effingham) and Mary Mooney (Nashua)

Brian of Tamworth m. Mary Beth **Robinson** of Tamworth 9/26/1981

Brian K. of Tamworth m. Mary F. **Dunn** of Tamworth 6/21/1996

Charles S. m. Abbie **Elliott** 11/8/1916 in Tamworth; H – 22, farmer, b. Tamworth, s/o Augustus Chase and Annie Hobbs; W – 21, b. England, d/o Dicey Elliott

Leslie O. m. Doris **Fortier** 5/9/1934 in Sanbornville

Preston N. of Conway m. Teresa A. **Mason** of Tamworth 2/7/1942 in Conway; H – 25, defense work; W – 20, at home

Richard Preston of Tamworth m. Carol Jean **Woodward** of Tamworth 10/9/1963 in Tamworth; H – 20, armed forces; W – 20, at home

Vincent F. of Tamworth m. Michele A. **McDavitt** of Tamworth 9/26/1999

CHENEY,

Albert M. of Tamworth m. Elinor L. **Lord** of Tamworth 7/1/1939 in Tamworth; H – 20, laborer; W – 16, at home

Alfred M. of Tamworth m. Shirley A. **Pay** of Somersworth 7/30/1966; H – 34, truck driver; W – 21, shoe shop

Edward H. of Enfield m. Mildred E. **Daley** of Tamworth 8/18/1979

Ralph B. of Tuftonboro m. Pearl E. **Dodge** of Tuftonboro 9/23/1945 in Tamworth; H – 23, jet mechanic; W – 18, at home

Raymond E. of Tuftonboro m. Hattie W. **Jones** of Madison 2/2/1946 in Tamworth; H – 19, US Army; W – 17, at home

CHESLEY,

Joshua E. of Ossipee m. Minnie C. **Clark** of Tamworth 4/29/1893 in Tamworth; H - 24, laborer, b. Eaton, s/o George W. Chesley (Effingham) and Anna H. Elliot (Tamworth); W - 21, housekeeping, b. Tamworth, d/o Gilman Clarke (Gilmanton) and Laura Newton (Sandwich)

CHICK,

Robert M. of Madison m. Ruth E. **Vittum** of Tamworth 10/20/1943 in Ctr. Sandwich; H – 25, US Navy; W – 23, teacher

William C., Jr. of Madison m. Michelle M. **Boothby** of Tamworth 9/5/1992

CHICO,
Jesus Maria, Jr. of Ridgefield, CT m. Rebecca Lynne **Dennis** of Ridgefield, CT 9/30/1989

CHRISTIAN,
Percy Lee, Jr. of Victoria, Texas m. Ruth Ann **Aldrich** of Tamworth 5/27/1967; H – 29, US Navy; W – 23, secretary

CHURCH,
Phillips D. of MA m. Lillian L. **Theriault** of MA 4/2/1977; H – 41; W – 29

CHUTE,
Paul E. of Tamworth m. Kathleen E. **Hayford** of Tamworth 9/18/1938 in N. Conway; H – 27, laborer; W – 31, waitress

CICCHETTI,
George Joseph of Littleton, CO m. Carol Rita **Urquhart** of Littleton, CO 7/7/1972; H – 24; W – 25

CIRACO,
Michael of N. Conway m. Patricia **Shannon** of Tamworth 5/24/1981

CLANCY,
Dana T. of Tamworth m. Mary R. **Knapp** of Tamworth 12/19/1973; H – 25; W – 21

CLAPP,
Ian W. of Tamworth m. Judith A. **Valerio** of Tamworth 9/7/1985
Ian W. of Tamworth m. Theresa L. **Boewe** of Tamworth 8/27/1994
William Irving m. Eunice Angelina **Hidden** 2/19/1922 in Tamworth; H – 27, b. Lynn, MA; W – 23, b. Tamworth

CLARK[E],
A. Johnson of Tamworth m. Flora M. **Bunker** of Tamworth 6/24/1903; H – 37, mechanic, b. PEI, s/o Joseph Clarke (sic) (PEI) and Isabelle Muttart (PEI); W – 24, housework, b.

Tamworth, d/o Levi Bunker (Tamworth) and Hattie Webber (Wenham, MA)
Edwin G. of Tamworth m. Addie B. **Dow** of Tamworth 12/28/1897 in Tamworth; H – 23, farmer, b. Tamworth, s/o Gilman Clark (Meredith) and Laura A. Newton (Sanbornton); W – 23, b. Tamworth, d/o Daniel Dow (Tamworth) and Ruth Brown (Tamworth)
Lucian G. of Tamworth m. Susan C. **Granville** of Tamworth 6/20/1895 in Madison; H - 54, clergyman, b. Thetford, VT, s/o Eli Clark (Strafford, VT) and Sophronia Clark (Strafford, VT); W - 57, housewife, b. Tamworth, d/o Alfred Hatch (Tamworth) and Charlotte Hatch (Jackson)
Lucian G. of Tamworth m. Josephine **Parker** of Boston 12/15/1898 in Tamworth; H – 57, clergyman, b. Thetford, VT, s/o Eli Clark (Strafford, VT) and Saphronia Tyler (Strafford, VT); W – 44, nurse, b. Boston, d/o John C. Baker (England) and Margaret Bradford (Boston)
Lucian G. of Tamworth m. Jennie Holmes **Mooney** of S. Hanson, MA 6/12/1912 in Rochester; H – 71, clergyman, b. Thetford, VT, s/o Eli Clarke (Strafford, VT) and Sophronia Tyler (Strafford, VT); W – 41, housewife, b. Patterson, NJ, d/o Thomas Holmes (Glassco, Scotland) and Rose Dorr (Brooklyn, NY)

CLAYTON,
Kenneth Wayne of Tamworth m. Kathleen M. **Bolger** of Tamworth 5/17/1997

CLEVELAND,
George of Tamworth m. Barbara **Donovan** of Tamworth 6/27/1981
Thomas G. of Tamworth m. Ruth E. **Taylor** of Milton, MA 7/6/1996

CLIFFORD,
Ernest E. of Moultonboro m. Ethel W. **Carter** of Tamworth 8/17/1986
Ernest I. of Tamworth m. Leonora B. **Arling** of Tamworth 12/25/1905 in Conway; H – 21, painter, b. Meredith, s/o James A. Clifford (Walden, VT) and Clara Bixby (Meredith); W – 19, housework, b. Tamworth, d/o James G. Arling (Bennington) and Emma M. Bickford (Tamworth)
George W. of Tamworth m. Rose E. **Plant** of Tamworth 12/25/1905 in Conway; H – 33, painter, b. Walden, VT, s/o William Clifford

(Walden, VT) and Celia Lam (Walden, VT); W – 19, housework, b. Tamworth, d/o Joseph Plant (St. Lambert, Canada) and Ellen Morrill (Bangor, ME)

CLOUGH,
Edwin E. m. Louise D. **Kimball** 11/3/1927 in Tamworth
George W. of Tamworth m. Sarah A. **Bickford** of Tamworth 12/2/1908 in Tamworth; H – 50, teamster, b. Tamworth, s/o W. W. Clough (Tamworth) and M. A. Whitney (Tamworth); W – 34, laundress, b. Sandwich, d/o Noah Bickford (Biddeford, ME) and Ursula Bryar (Sandwich)

CLOUTIER,
Robert L. of Burlington, VT m. Nicola S. **Rotberg** of Burlington, VT 6/20/1993

COBB,
William H. of Milford, CT m. Margaret A. **Sandoz** of Wonalancet 5/27/1979

COCHRANE,
Bruce E., Jr. of Tamworth m. Marianne **Shannon** of Tamworth 10/19/1991

COHEN,
Alfred of Rome m. Marion **Cleveland** of Tamworth 3/10/968; H – 49; W – 42

COLBY,
Robert E. of Ossipee m. Lisa J. **Chipman** of S. Tamworth 11/4/1990
Royal P. m. Louise B. **White** 6/11/1955 in Ctr. Ossipee; H – 41, laborer; W – 44, housekeeper

CONDINO,
David A. of MA m. Martha E. **Ondras** of MA 10/30/1982

CONLEY,
Martin J. of Revere, MA m. Ann Marie **Ciccone** of Revere, MA 6/21/1985

CONNELLY,
Dennis M. of Milton, MA m. Phyllis C. **Frost** of Milton, MA 10/27/1978; H – 35; W – 28

CONNER,
David R. of Tamworth m. Janes **Streeter** of Tamworth 8/18/1984

CONRAD,
David W. of NJ m. Karen M. **Hoogerhyde** of NJ 5/27/1977; H – 26; W – 25
George A. m. Gladys R. **Marston** 11/21/1937 in Tamworth

COOK,
Daniel Mark of Tamworth m. Linda Jean **Hanson** of Tamworth 8/2/1988
John O., Jr. of Tamworth m. Nancy Irene **Nudd** of Moultonboro 6/26/1971; H – 19; W – 18
Kevin Glenn of Tamworth m. Cindy Lynn **Eldridge** of Tamworth 10/14/1989
Vincent Perry of Tamworth m. Kathleen M. **Ulitz** of Tamworth 6/28/1975; H – 20; W – 19
William H. of Tamworth m. Mary L. **Wade** of Tamworth 4/16/1912 in Nashua; H – 50, foreman, b. Campton, s/o George Cook (Woodstock) and Mary E. Glover (Woodstock); W – 25, housekeeping, b. Tamworth, d/o Herbert S. Clough and Hattie Mason (Tamworth)

COOKE,
Carl Leverette of Conway m. Lena Pauline **Alden** of Stoughton, MA 5/31/1963 in Tamworth; H – 44, salesman; W – 34, clerk

COOLIDGE,
Frederic S. of Greensboro, VT m. Janine D. **Brierre** of Tamworth 7/13/1974; H – 56; W – 49

COOPER,
Theodore H. m. Margaret **Cummings** 4/13/1922 in Tamworth; H – 25, b. Newark, NJ; W – 19, b. Tamworth

CORBETT,
Harris G. m. Marion M. **Judd** 9/8/1931 in Conway

Welby W. of Tamworth m. Ellen **Careau** of Whitefield 11/25/1939 in Fryeburg, ME; H – 62, carpenter; W – 52, laundress

CORCORAN,
Frederick J. of Wellesley Hills, MA m. Frances Black **Cleveland** of Baltimore, MD 5/3/1969; H – 25; W – 23

CORSON,
George E. of Tamworth m. Edna C. **Vasey** of Tamworth 6/26/1940 in Moultonboro; H – 21, furniture work; W – 19, at home

CORT,
Henry R., Jr. of Bellport, NY m. Ann **Spicer** of Tamworth 6/19/1948 in Tamworth; H – 20, student; W – 20, student

COSLETT,
John Scott of Tamworth m. Leeann Louise **Colbath** of Wakefield 9/25/1976; H – 18; W – 18

COSSETTE,
Thomas Paul of Tamworth m. Amanda Jean **Eldridge** of Tamworth 5/20/1999

COSTER,
John Gerard of MA m. Susannah Bacon **Keith** of MA 9/24/1988

COUCH,
Walter O. of Tamworth m. Janice L. **Anthony** of Tamworth 6/25/1989

COULOMBE,
Louis D. m. Imogene B. **Coulombe** 5/10/1957 in Tamworth; H – 23, construction; W – 24, at home

COURCHAINE,
Russell A. of Tamworth m. Emma L. **Hartford** of Tamworth 12/7/2002

COURTEMANCHE,
Jeffrey P. of Woburn, MA m. Deborah C. **Croto** of Woburn, MA 10/19/1985

COVILLE,
Edward R. of Tamworth m. Nicole E. **Maher** of Tamworth 9/27/1980
Stanley B. of W. Ossipee m. Nancy **Read** of Tamworth 8/25/1951 in Tamworth; H – 25, forestry; W – 19, at home

COX,
Allen Jeffrey of Tamworth m. Melissa Jean **Cook** of Tamworth 9/11/1999
Michael J. of Tamworth m. Mary B. **Fowler** of Tamworth 6/27/1992

CRANE,
James P. of Japan m. Peggy A. **Koble** of Japan 9/27/1985

CREPS,
Lee of Chocorua m. Janet Lynne **Wenant** of Center Ossipee 11/30/1974; H – 26; W – 21

CRESSEY,
Dean M. of Windham, ME m. Theresa E. **Cady** of Portland, ME 12/7/1991

CROCE,
Nickolas A. of Canton, MA m. Jacqueline A. **Powers** of Canton, MA 2/26/1994

CROCHERON,
Wesley H. of Chocorua m. Frances E. **Crocheron** of Chocorua 3/7/1997

CROWLEY,
William F. m. Abbie F. **Reed** 9/5/1936 in N. Conway

CUMMINGS,
Elmer A. of Tamworth m. Arlene N. **Carr** of Fryeburg, ME 7/7/1943 in Conway; H – 47, farmer; W – 31, maid
Harry E. m. Maud **Davis** 8/15/1925 in Tamworth

CURRIER,
Edwin F. of Tamworth m. Laura M. **Gilman** of Tamworth 9/26/1892 in Tamworth; H - 21, teamster, b. Albany, s/o Hiram S. Currier (Albany) and Harriett A. Hobbs (Ossipee); W - 19, table girl, b.

Boston, d/o George E. Gilman (Tamworth) and Orissa Seavey (Great Falls)
Edwin F. of Tamworth m. Flora E. **Green** of Tamworth 10/29/1898 in Tamworth; H – 26, teamster, b. Albany, s/o Hiram S. Currier (Albany) and Harriet A. Hobbs (Ossipee); W – 23, housework, b. Tamworth, d/o Roscoe Green (Madison) and Abbie Hardy (Tamworth)
Jesse A., Jr. m. June M. **Lee** 4/23/1959 in Madison; H – 31, mill worker; W – 31, clerk
Roland E. m. Hazel E. **Evans** 10/20/1926 in Tamworth

CURTIS,
Tony of Ipswich, MA m. Heather Mary **Mulley** of Ipswich, MA 11/1/1997
Wesley M. of Chocorua m. Raylene M. **Dennis** of Chocorua 5/21/1983

CUTTER,
Brian K. of Tamworth m. Andrea A. **Bryan** of Tamworth 6/14/1993

DAIGLE,
Louis P. of Tamworth m. Suzanne M. **Ziballo** of Tamworth 4/28/1984

DAILEY,
Timothy D. of Bergenfield, NJ m. Ann Marie **Toussaint** of Tyngsboro, MA 4/28/1990

DAMON,
Christopher S. of Tamworth m. Donna M. **McCarthy** of Tamworth 8/23/1986
Herbert S. of Tamworth m. Margaret **Neilson** of Wilmington, MA 10/12/1946 in Tamworth; H – 28, student; W – 30, nurse
Stephen F. of Tamworth m. Virginia Wheeler **White** of Bartlett 2/14/1970; H – 47; W – 47

DARLING,
Henry M. of Sandwich m. Nellie J. **Dow** of Tamworth 12/22/1892 in Tamworth; H - 22, laborer, b. NS, s/o John Darling (NB) and Catherine Darling (NB); W - 23, housework, b. Tamworth, d/o Daniel Dow (Tamworth) and Ruth Brown (Tamworth)

DASCOULIAS,
Joseph R. of Madison m. Kristine E. **Willey** of Madison 10/10/1998
Robert A. of Tilton m. Gail R. **Streeter** of Tamworth 7/3/1971; H – 20; W – 18

DAVIDSON,
Gaston H. m. Emma I. **Edgerley** 10/3/1935 in Ossipee
Nestor Michael of Washington, DC m. Clare **Huntington** of Washington, DC 8/21/1999

DAVIS,
Alan J. of Chocorua m. Arlene **Leclerc** of Somersworth 3/13/1982
Amos T. of Tamworth m. Alice B. **Berry** of Tamworth 10/15/1892 in Tamworth; H – 29, expressman, b. Tamworth, s/o Hiram T. Davis (Effingham) and Sarah Hodsdon (Effingham); W – 24, housework, b. Tamworth, d/o Nathaniel Berry (Tamworth) and Abbie Blake (Tamworth)
Amos T. of Tamworth m. Cora E. **Stearns** of Tamworth 3/22/1911 in Tamworth; H – 48, undertaker, b. Tamworth, s/o Hiram T. Davis (Effingham) and Sarah Hodgdon (Effingham); W – 45, housework, b. Albany, d/o Hiram Mason (Albany) and Angelina Head (Tamworth)
Chester m. Laura Maud **Pitman** 12/14/1929 in Pittsfield
Chester of Tamworth m. Hazle E. **Brooks** of Conway 2/6/1943 in Jackson; H – 36, farm laborer; W – cook
Clifford K. m. Carrie May **Chick** 1/1/1917 in Chocorua; H – 24, plumber, b. Ossipee, s/o John C. Davis and Minnie A. Nason; W – 26, b. Tamworth, d/o Charles F. Chick and Elvira Durrell
David L. of Laconia m. Barbara Jean **Hilton** of Tamworth 3/17/1967; H – 24, electrician; W – 20, housewife
Everett Pitman of Tamworth m. Kathleen Christine **Richter** of Germany 1/21/1963 in Center Ossipee; H – 22, laborer; W – 21, druggist
Franklin W. of Tamworth m. Mabel A. **Bennett** of Portsmouth 9/19/1893 in Tamworth; H - 26, reporter, b. Newington, s/o Franklin Davis (Bangor, ME) and Amanda M. Ware (Norfolk, MA); W - 25, teacher, b. Bucksport, ME, d/o John S. Bennett (Bucksport, ME) and Albertina Hatch (N. Berwick, ME)
Jeffrey A. m. Patricia V. A. **Provencal** 9/5/1959 in Somersworth; H – 19, wood turner; W – 17, shoe factory

John C. of Ossipee m. Annie **Cameson** of Tamworth 6/22/1887 in Tamworth; H - 21, laborer, b. Tamworth, s/o Joseph M. Davis (Ossipee, farmer); W - 16, housework

Larry John of Tamworth m. Amy Pearl **Whiting** of Wolfeboro 5/9/1964 in Water Village; H – 23, logger; W – 20, factory

Robert E. of Tamworth m. Alice M. **Chandler** of Bartlett 12/20/1941 in Laconia; H – 30, truck driver; W – 32, school teacher

Robert M. of Tamworth m. Debra L. **Priest** of Tamworth 1/1/2000

Rodney C. of Tamworth m. Margaret B. **Mayott** of Effingham Falls 9/29/1938 in Effingham; H – 22, laborer; W – 18, housework

Roy W. m. Frances A. **Lord** 9/5/1935 in Rochester

Sidney of Tamworth m. Ruth E. **Tyler** of Madison 12/14/1946 in Rochester; H – 29, laborer; W – 27, school teacher

DAVISON,
Harry J. of Center Ossipee m. Edith C. **Jennings** of Tamworth 9/23/1978; H – 23; W – 25

Harry J. of Tamworth m. Susan M. **Larrabee** of S. Tamworth 11/12/1994

Harry James of Tamworth m. Janice Arnold **Goodson** of Tamworth 8/27/1988

DAY,
Percy Cleveland of Tamworth m. Joyce Marie **Morton** of Tamworth 8/28/1971; H – 22; W – 19

Warren Levon of Tamworth m. Judith May **Garland** of Ctr. Barnstead 12/4/1976; H – 30; W – 31

DEARBORN,
Allan E. m. Janice L. **Downs** 5/31/1956 in Tamworth; H – 22, machine operator; W – 19, cashier

Kenneth A. m. Sarah B. **Davis** 10/19/1932 in Moultonboro

DEDEUS,
Hilbert of Tamworth m. Elana A. **Roscilla** of Tamworth 5/20/1984

DELUDE,
Robert L. of Tamworth m. Myrtle L. **Walker** of Tamworth 11/11/1991

DEMAINE,
David K. of Chocorua m. Lisa M. **Marks** of Chocorua 11/23/2003

DEROSIER,
David Edward of Tamworth m. Joan Diane **Costello** of Tamworth 3/12/1999

DEVORE,
Andrew C. of New York, NY m. Olivia A. **Pi-Sunyer** of New York, NY 7/24/1993

DICEY,
Garfield W., Pvt. of Danbury m. Helen B. **Welch** of Tamworth 12/25/1942 in Chocorua; H – 21, soldier; W – 20, at home
Jeffrey L. of Tamworth m. Sandra A. **Bean** of Albany 6/15/1974; H – 18; W - 18
Wendell Garfield of Tamworth m. Barbara Ann **Hickey** of Ctr. Ossipee 12/26/1963 in Center Ossipee; H – 20, construction; W – 19, housekeeper
Wendell Garfield of Tamworth m. Julia Marion **Leach** of Center Sandwich 10/19/1964 in Tamworth; H – 20, millwork; W – 20, at home

DICKINSON,
Andrew J. of Tamworth m. Tammy L. **Chick** of Conway 8/29/1987

DIEFENBACH,
Philip Joseph of Tamworth m. Patricia Ann **Albino** of Tamworth 12/9/1995

DIMITA,
Vito of Tamworth m. Kathleen **Brownlee** of Tamworth 10/22/1949 in N. Conway; H – 52, artist; W – 47, innkeeper

DISILVA,
Albert Joseph of Tamworth m. Kendra **Dentino** of Tamworth 5/15/1999

DODGE,
Fred C. of Beverly, MA m. Clara L. **Remmonds** of Beverly, MA 11/15/1900 in Tamworth; H – 37, accountant, s/o Amos A. Dodge and Elizabeth A. Cole; W – 38, teacher, d/o John Remmonds and Clarisa A. Lovett

DOE,
Eugene C. of Parsonsfield, ME m. Anna P. **Wood** of Beverly, MA 10/1/1911 in Tamworth; H – 26, laborer, b. Parsonsfield, ME, s/o Eugene M. Doe (Parsonsfield, ME) and Myra Lord (Limerick, ME); W – 29, nurse, b. Beverly, MA, d/o George B. Pearson (Beverly, MA) and Mary Wallace (Beverly, MA)
Eugene M. of Parsonsfield, ME m. Mary S. **Weeks** of Tamworth 11/7/1908 in Tamworth; H – 54, farmer, b. Parsonsfield, ME, s/o Amasa Doe (Parsonsfield, ME) and Mary J. Pease (Parsonsfield, ME); W – 39, housekeeper, b. Tamworth, d/o W. W. Hayford (Tamworth) and Mary M. Ellis (Carthage, ME)

DONOVAN,
Brendan Joseph of Upper Marlboro, MD m. Nicole Barbara **Lehner** of Upper Marlboro, MD 10/11/1997
Brian Scott of Tamworth m. Tracey Lynne **Mitchell** of Tamworth 9/2/1995
Timothy G. of Tamworth m. Roberta C. **Ward** of Tamworth 6/18/1983

DORHEIM,
Malcolm A. of W. Lynn, MA m. Virginia E. **Howell** of Saugus, MA 12/31/1979

DOUCETTE,
Victor C. of Wolfeboro m. Ann Louise **Bourbeau** of Tamworth 6/13/1998

DOUGLAS,
Warren L. m. Addie M. **Smith** 1/1/1955 in Sandwich; H – 68, laborer; W – 64, at home

DOUVILLE,
Romeo Leo m. Dorothy E. **Welch** 6/6/1936 in Freedom

DOW,
Charles L. of Tamworth m. Nettie M. **Tewksbury** of Tamworth 7/21/1908 in Tamworth; H – 45, farmer, b. Tamworth, s/o John C. Dow (Tamworth) and Augusta Smith (Tamworth); W – 23, housework, b. Tamworth, d/o Samuel Barnes (Hiram, ME) and Emma Bean

Ralph P. of Gray, ME m. Evelyn B. **Bartlett** of Tamworth 7/19/1911 in Tamworth; H – 22, teacher, b. Gray, ME, s/o William H. Dow (Lewiston, ME) and Clara W. Pennell (Gray, ME); W – 20, at home, b. Tamworth, d/o Elroy G. Bartlett (Meredith) and Imogene Evans (Moultonboro)

DOWNS,
Clifford F. m. Winifred **Weeks** 8/21/1934 in Tamworth
Clifford F., Jr. of Tamworth m. Bonita Marie **Swan** of Sandwich 2/3/1962 in Conway; H – 17, student; W – 16, student
Clifford F., Jr. of Tamworth m. Sally A. **French** of Meredith 9/3/1971; H – 26; W – 29
Edward F. of Tamworth m. Annie **Mack** of Sandwich 9/1/1888 in Tamworth; H - 23, farmer, b. Tamworth, s/o Daniel Downs; W - 20, housework, b. Haverhill, d/o Thomas Spooner (Haverhill)
Elias E. of Tamworth m. Mildred E. **Page** of Tamworth 12/25/1899 in Chocorua; H – 28, farmer, b. Porter, ME, s/o Joseph Downs (Brownfield, ME) and Sarah F. Downs (Tamworth); W – 17, b. Tamworth, d/o Moses P. Page (Tamworth) and Lizzie Robinson (Tamworth)
Elmer E. m. Ada Anne **Blodgett** 6/26/1918 in Tamworth; H – 24, chauffeur, b. Tamworth, s/o Joseph L. Downs and Alice C. Smith; W – 24, b. Brockton, MA, d/o Edward S. Blodgett and Martha A. E. McDonald
Harry J. m. Rose A. **Smith** 12/27/1937 in Tilton
Joseph of Tamworth m. Mary H. **Potter** of Tamworth 6/16/1895 in Sandwich; H - 51, farmer, 2nd, b. Brownfield, s/o Daniel Downs (Lyman, ME, farmer) and Elmira Downs (Hiram, ME, housewife); W - 41, housewife, 2nd, b. Lake Village, d/o John M. Potter (Gilford) and Olive M. Potter (Gilmanton, housewife)
Joseph L. of Tamworth m. Alice **Smith** of Tamworth 2/28/1892 in Tamworth; H - 19, farmer, b. Tamworth; W - 16, housework, b. Stowe, ME
Wilbur R. of Tamworth m. Grace Adella **Blackmer** of Madbury 7/26/1913 in Dover; H – 20, laborer, b. Tamworth, s/o John Downs and Mary Kenerson; W – 23, teacher, b. Madbury, d/o Charles Blackmer and Hannah S. Nute

DRAKE,
Albert of Millbury, MA m. Pauline M. **Stinchfield** of Worcester, MA 6/7/1950 in Tamworth; H – 24, salvage dealer; W – 18, at home

Arthur R. C. m. Nellie B. **Phillips** 7/4/1936 in Chocorua
Samuel T. of Tamworth m. Eunice A. **Burleigh** of Pittsfield
12/5/1892 in Pittsfield; H - 65, mechanic, b. Hampton, s/o Daniel Drake and Zilah Taylor (Hampton); W - 60, housework, b. Strafford, d/o Joseph Roberts (Strafford) and Mary Daniels (Strafford)

DRAPER,
Donald Richard of Tamworth m. Tina Marie **Leighton** of Tamworth 10/15/1995

DREW,
Arthur N. m. Marilyn J. **Canney** 1/31/1953 in Tamworth; H – 20, lumbering; W – 20, telephone operator
Elden W. m. Gladys F. **Clark** 5/24/1916 in Tamworth; H – 22, laborer, b. Dexter, ME, s/o Thomas Drew and Gertrude Folsom; W – 18, b. Center Harbor, d/o William Clark and Lizzie Wade
Frank P., Jr. of Tamworth m. Kimberly M. **Pemberton** of Tamworth 7/16/1994
Frank Pearson of Tamworth m. Carolyn Janice **Deatte** of Tamworth 5/15/1962 in Conway; H – 35, L. E. O.; W – 20, shop inspec.
Fred A. of Tamworth m. Louise M. **Lessard** of Tamworth 6/12/1993
Harry H. m. Gladys **Jeffers** 1/30/1919 in Laconia; H – 38, lumberman, s/o Charles F. Drew and Fannie Carr; W – 22, waitress, d/o Milton Jeffers and Abbie Downs
John D. of Tamworth m. Hannah J. **Varney** of Tamworth 12/25/1887 in Somersworth; H - 53, laborer, 2nd, b. Tamworth, s/o Thomas Drew (Tamworth, farmer) and Martha; W - 40, housework, 2nd, b. Tamworth, d/o William Hutchins (Tamworth, farmer) and Lusinda
John N. of Tamworth m. Cora E. **White** of Ossipee 1/30/1890 in Tamworth; H - 28, farmer, b. Tamworth, s/o John D. Drew (Tamworth); W - 29, housework, b. Ossipee, d/o Josiah White (Ossipee)
Tony P. of Tamworth m. April P. **Libby** of Tamworth 4/28/1990
William F. of Tamworth m. Katie B. **Hardy** of Tamworth 12/22/1898 in Tamworth; H – 22, teamster, b. Tamworth, s/o John D. Drew (Tamworth) and Hannah Huckins (Tamworth); W – 18, housework, b. Tamworth, d/o William F. Hardy (Tamworth) and Georgiana Davis (Ossipee)

DROUIN,
Christopher Lee of Tamworth m. Abigail Margaret **Preece** of Tamworth 6/10/1999

DROWNS,
Kenneth W. m. Janice L. **Anthony** 11/13/1955 in Tamworth; H – 28, lumber; W – 21, at home

DRUGG,
Charles Howard of Tamworth m. Louise Adria **Tandy** of Franklin 6/27/1965 in Center Ossipee; H – 49, construction; W – 53, stitcher

DUBE,
Mark L. of Tamworth m. Susan J. **Ticehurst** of Tamworth 8/22/1987
Tracey John of Tamworth m. Kathleen Barbara **Raymond** of Canterbury 7/15/1989

DUFAULT,
Armand of Laconia m. Katherine M. **Hayford** 9/18/1948 in Laconia; H – 20, laborer; W – 19, at home

DUNCOMBE,
Richard A. of PA m. Irene M. F. **Curran** of PA 8/9/1988

DUNHAM,
Theodore, III of Tamworth m. Linda M. **Bunten** of Tamworth 6/20/1978; H – 32; W – 34

DUPONT,
Peter Andrew of Sanford, ME m. Dawn Marie **Howarth** of N. Berwick, ME 7/15/1995

DWINNELLS,
Alton E. of Hartford, CT m. Carolyn E. **Hammond** of Tamworth 5/15/1943 in Durham; H – 28, machine operator; W – 20, college student

DWYER,
Elmer W. m. Gertrude **Harrington** 10/17/1927 in Tamworth

DYER,
Charles N. of Tamworth m. Patricia R. **Pickering** of Campton 7/11/1970; H – 24; W – 18
Keith R. m. Arlene V. **Ryder** 11/1/1958 in Tamworth; H – 21, mill worker; W – 20, furniture factory
Stanley A., Jr. of Tamworth m. Sharon Kay **Jenneke** of Tamworth 6/11/1999

EASTWICK,
John of Tamworth m. Dorothea L. **Mason** of Tamworth 7/2/1938 in Tamworth; H – 27, civil engineer; W – 25, clerk
Robert m. Mary E. **Mason** 1/25/1936 in Tamworth
Robert of Tamworth m. Bertha M. **Robinson** of Tamworth 12/1/1947 in Meredith; H – 35, carpenter; W – 25, clerical work

ECKSTROM,
Paul of Bristol, CT m. Ann Marie **Burke** of Lawrence, MA 9/6/1986

EDGAR,
David U. of Chocorua m. Edith H. **Edgar** of Chocorua 8/15/1982

EDGELL,
William H. of Tamworth m. Emma F. **Childs** of Tamworth 8/11/1894 in Tamworth; H - 26, laborer, b. Tamworth, s/o Charles H. Edgell (Tamworth, farmer) and Mary F. Page (Hillsboro, housekeeping); W - 19, housework, b. Tamworth, d/o Herbert W. Childs (Stoneham, MA, farmer) and Augusta A. Bickford (Tamworth, housekeeping)

EDGERLY,
Satchel C. of Tamworth m. Maude E. **Martin** of Cambridge, MA 1/1/1905 in Cambridge, MA; H – 39, farmer, b. Ossipee, s/o John Edgerly (Tamworth) and Abby A. Dore (Ossipee); W – 26, housework, b. Boston, MA, d/o George K. Martin and Mary J. Heannia

EGAN,
Thomas F. of Tamworth m. Pamela **Shepardson** of Tamworth 11/22/1986
William A. of Floral City, FL m. Sandra A. **Place** of Ctr. Ossipee 11/8/2002

ELARDO,
Larry W. of Groveland, MA m. Dianne L. **Plantamura** of Groveland, MA 3/16/1991

ELDRIDGE,
Adam G. of Chocorua m. Sarah J. **Robinson** of Chocorua 10/5/1996
Andrew W. m. Marcia E. **Gilman** 9/25/1937 in Tamworth
Clyde A. of Ossipee m. Eleanor L. **Gilman** of Tamworth 8/24/1939 in Tamworth; H – 28, woodsman; W – 21, at home
David W. of Tamworth m. Dori M. **Silva** of Tamworth 5/19/1979
David W. of Tamworth m. Stacie A. **Whitty** of Tamworth 6/19/1993
Harry P., Jr. of Ossipee m. Christabel I. **Stacy** of Tamworth 1/18/1946 in Tamworth; H – 18, millhand; W – 18, at home
Harry Plummer of W. Ossipee m. Shirley Jean **Beaudet** of Tamworth 12/22/1976; H – 48; W – 23
Hazen A. of Tamworth m. Ellen E. **Plummer** of Sandwich 11/12/1938 in Tamworth; H – 18, laborer; W – 18, at home
Hazen A. m. Shirley J. **Roberts** 7/10/1958 in Tamworth; H – 19, White Lake Park; W – 19, stenographer
James F. of Tamworth m. Joanne W. **Cook** of Tamworth 12/12/1973; H – 26; W – 36
Jeffrey A. of W. Ossipee m. Jennifer L. **Morgan** of Tamworth 3/17/2001
John of Ossipee m. Alice **Chase** of Tamworth 8/7/1900 in Ossipee; H – 27, laborer, s/o Daniel Eldridge (Ossipee) and Elsie Nichols (Ossipee); W – 22, housework, d/o Samuel Barnes (Hiram, ME) and Emma A. Bean (Hiram, ME)
John of Ossipee m. Josephine **Brown** of RI 11/13/1923 in Tamworth; H – 47; W – 42
Kenneth William of Tamworth m. Charlene Louise **Hawes** of N. Sandwich 6/28/1964 in N. Sandwich; H – 20, mechanic; W – 18, at home
Perley L. of Ossipee m. Charlotte **Palmer** of Tamworth 9/27/1947 in Tamworth; H – 16, furniture worker; W – 16, at home
Ricky L. of Chocorua m. Abigail K. **Sparks** of Eaton 4/7/2001
Ricky Lester of Tamworth m. Pamela Jean **Comer** of Conway 7/31/1976; H – 19; W - 18
Ritchie of Center Ossipee m. Virginia P. **Eldridge** of Tamworth 4/10/1947 in Tamworth; H – 25, saw mill; W – 23, at home
Ritchie of Ctr. Ossipee m. Christobell Stacy **Elliott** of S. Tamworth 7/18/1964 in Ctr. Ossipee; H – 42, millwork; W – 36, millwork

Roland R. of Tamworth m. Alfreda M. **Drew** of Tamworth 11/18/1946 in Tamworth; H – 17, sawmill worker; W – 16, at home
Scotty Allen of Tamworth m. Terri Lynn **Bates** of N. Conway 9/9/1989
Scotty Clifton of Tamworth m. Sandra Ann **Emerson** of Tamworth 6/16/1962 in Tamworth; H – 23, laborer; W – 19, at home
Tony W. of Tamworth m. Linda G. **LeBlanc** of Tamworth 4/27/1985
Walter Clyde of Ossipee m. Peggy Ann **Anthony** of Tamworth 10/30/1999

ELIAS,

Rogy of Tamworth m. Nellie **Turner** of Tamworth 9/12/1904 in Tamworth; H – 34, merchant, b. Syria, s/o Joseph Elias (Syria) and Mary Andenoose (Syria); W – 30, housekeeper, b. Loudon, d/o George Turner (Loudon) and Jossephine Macha (Wresbordun)

ELLIOTT,

Albert m. Gertrude **Berry** 8/5/1931 in Tamworth
James T. m. Dorothy A. **Larrabee** 6/25/1955 in Tamworth; H – 23, auto mechanic; W – 20, packer
Richard J. m. Christobell S. **Eldridge** 8/2/1958 in W. Ossipee; H – 41, truck driver; W – 30, at home
Roger S. of Chocorua m. Joyce B. **Hutchinson** of Madison 9/14/1986

ELLIS,

Scott Lawrence of Hotchkiss, CO m. Lydia More **Thompson** of Vincetown, NJ 6/12/1971; H – 22; W – 22

EMERSON,

Theodore Woodbury of Tamworth m. Eva Marie **Eldridge** of Tamworth 6/22/1963 in Chocorua; H – 21, boss helper; W – 19, sander

EMERY,

J. Wesley of Tamworth m. Lizzie M. **Whiting** of Tamworth 7/7/1894 in Sandwich; H - 21, laborer, b. Tamworth, s/o Daniel S. Emery (Gilmanton, millman) and Abbie M. Clough (Tamworth, housekeeping); W - 15, at home, b. Tamworth, d/o Levi T.

Whiting (Tamworth, farmer) and Mary E. Sanborn (Quincy, MA, housekeeping)

EMPEY,
Winston Basil of S. Portland, ME m. Carolyn Frances **Bray** of S. Portland, ME 5/31/1997

ENGELMANN,
Earl G., Jr. of Ketchum, IA m. Susan D. **Twitchell** of Ketchum, IA 6/5/1993

ERICKSON,
Robert D. of Tamworth m. Pamela J. **Clemons** of Tamworth 11/19/1977; H – 31; W – 24
Robert Dennis of Tamworth m. Katheryn G. **Armstrong** of Tamworth 10/18/1986

EVAGASH,
Joseph J. of Naugatuck, CT m. Charrington S. **Miller** of Naugatuck, CT 7/12/1985

EVANS,
Almon G. m. Gladys F. **Corbett** 6/14/1926 in Laconia
Almon G., Jr. of Tamworth m. Shirley C. **Webster** of Madison 4/13/1952 in Effingham Falls; H – 22, truck operator; W – 20, clerk
Alton B. m. Nancy P. **Breed** 8/6/1955 in Sandwich; H – 24, construction; W – 18, at home
Alton Brooks of Tamworth m. Patricia Ann **Fox** of Porter, ME 1/24/1970; H – 38; W – 25
Ansel, Jr. of rx m. Sharon A. **Bell** of Tamworth 2/14/1981
Frank C. of Tamworth m. Lynne M. **Schacht** of Effingham 6/28/1980
Frank Chandler of Tamworth m. Lynne Marie **Schacht** of Effingham 4/15/1989
Frank P. of Moultonboro m. Idella E. **Moody** of Tamworth 7/23/1893 in Tamworth; H - 30, butcher, b. Moultonboro, s/o Daniel B. Evans (Moultonboro) and Susan O. Potter (Moultonboro); W - 21, housekeeping, b. Tamworth, d/o William Clough (Tamworth) and Martha A. Whiting (Tamworth)
Glenn P. m. Cora M. **Grace** 8/18/1956 in Center Ossipee; H – 21, trucker; W – 22, clerk

Leon A. of Tamworth m. Frances L. **Panno** of N. Conway 9/24/1947 in Tamworth; H – 17, farmer; W – 19, ward maid

Walter B. m. Mabel J. **Lambee** 5/4/1918 in Tamworth; H – 48, farmer, b. Tamworth, s/o George W. Evans and Emely A. Hodgdon; W – 40, teacher, b. Washington, DC, d/o Edward Lambee and Joanna Mason

EWING,
Lawrence Willard of PA m. Carol Ann **Cavalier** of PA 10/23/1976; H – 28; W – 25

FAIRBANKS,
Douglas R. of Lynn, MA m. Merlene E. **Richard** of Lynn, MA 9/12/1987

FALLON,
Lawrence m. Ethel O. **Savard** 6/6/1953 in Tamworth; H – 36, attorney; W – 27, medical secretary

FARNHAM,
Arthur E. of Acton, ME m. Eva F. **Hobbs** of Tamworth 7/4/1898 in Tamworth; H – 20, farmer, b. Acton, ME, s/o Joseph Farnham (Acton, ME) and Sarah N. Snow (Marblehead); W – 22, housework, b. Tamworth, d/o William H. Hardy (Tamworth) and Georgiana Davis (Effingham)

FARNUM,
Walter W. of Erie, CO m. Pamela J. **Wentworth** of Erie, CO 6/17/1978; H – 24; W – 24

Whipple W. of Tamworth m. Jane Arlene **Powell** of Harrison, NE 3/12/1947 in Tamworth; H – 35, farmer; W – 23, stenographer

William W. of Tamworth m. Margaret B. **Wiesner** of Tamworth 4/19/1976; H – 22; W - 21

William W. of Tamworth m. Heidi J. **Engman** of Tamworth 10/1/1988

FARRELL,
Dennis J. of Tamworth m. Charlene A. **Taylor** of Tamworth 10/26/1991

FEDDERN,
Mark H. of Chocorua m. Heather L. **Glennon** of Chocorua 2/24/1990

FELLOWS,
Henry M. of Fryeburg, ME m. Carrie C. **Tewksbury** of Tamworth 8/20/1887 in Tamworth; H - 40, farmer, b. Fryeburg, ME; W - 21, housework, b. Tamworth, d/o William Tewksbury and Adeline

FENDERSON,
Robert E. m. Elizabeth **Eldridge** 2/1/1961 in Ctr. Ossipee; H – 21, millwork; W – 23, millwork

FERGUSON,
Edward M. of Laconia m. Doris L. **Herrick** of Tamworth 3/30/1945 in Laconia; H – 23, soldier; W – 21, machinist

FERLAND,
Paul Eugene of Pawtucket, RI m. Laura Jean **Beaulieu** of Pawtucket, RI 11/25/1989

FERNANDEZ,
Domingo J. of Hollywood, FL m. Karen L. **Condon** of Hollywood, FL 10/15/1986

FERRARA,
Jason Anthony of Chocorua m. Denice Alice **Santosuosso** of Somerville, MA 8/30/1997

FEUERBORN,
Wayne D. of Chocorua m. Sandra L. **Brown** of Chocorua 1/16/1998

FINLEY,
Alexander of Cambridge, MA m. Jane E. **O'Brien** of Wellesley, MA 8/3/1992

FISHER,
Russell S. m. Margaret N. **Fisher** 8/21/1954 in Tamworth; H – 39, draftsman; W – 40, nurse

FISKE,
Donald W. of Dedham, MA m. Barbara P. **Wolf** of Cambridge, MA 9/10/1938 in Tamworth; H – 22, student; W – 20, student

FLETCHER,
Allen E. m. Mary W. **Remick** 11/7/1936 in N. Conway
Robert George of Tamworth m. Karen Ruth **Hill** of Tamworth 7/2/1988

FLEXNER,
James T. of New York m. Agnes D. **Halsey** of New York 8/31/1938 in Tamworth; H – 30, author; W – 24, singer

FLOOD,
David J. of Middlefield, CT m. Casey L. **Clemons** of Middlefield, CT 6/7/2002

FLOYD,
Grant A. of Tamworth m. Regina M. **Deming** of Sandwich 12/20/1939 in Durham; H – 25, auto mechanic; W – 26, telephone op.
Perley of Tamworth m. Nettie **Grant** of Sandwich 5/8/1911 in Sandwich; H – 21, merchant, b. Tamworth, s/o Almon Floyd (Parsonsfield, ME) and Ida Mason (Tamworth); W – 20, at home, b. Sandwich, d/o Aristus W. Grant (Sandwich) and Elizabeth Bennett (Sandwich)

FOCHT,
Glenn D. of Grafton, MA m. Barbara A. **Rugo** of Northbridge, MA 9/28/2002

FOGG,
Almon Hall of Center Ossipee m. Barbara L. **Roberts** of S. Tamworth 2/19/1972; H – 23; W - 20
George S. m. Bernice L. **Cox** 11/7/1928 in Freedom

FOGLEY,
Peter F. of Newburyport, MA m. Joan M. **Czajkowski** of Newburyport, MA 10/19/1985

FOLEY,
Cyril J. m. Nella M. **Farina** 10/18/1959 in Tamworth; H – 49, wine clerk; W – 52, beauty parlor owner

FOLKINS,
Harry W. of Tamworth m. Olive L. **Puffer** of Burlington, VT 7/4/1942 in N. Conway; H – 36, NH Forest Service; W – 28, teacher

FOLLANSBEE,
Joseph Andrew of W. Ossipee m. Sarah Grace **Elliott** of W. Ossipee 7/4/1999
Somerby C. m. Eva M. G. **Gould** 11/1/1917 in Chocorua; H – 32, leather dealer, 2nd, b. W. Newbury, MA, s/o Frank M. Follansbee and Lizzie A. Colby; W – 32, 2nd, b. Birmingham, England, d/o Thomas Hawkins and Hannah Tomay

FOLLETT,
Charles F. of Tamworth m. Abbie S. **Wallace** of Tamworth 4/4/1887 in Tamworth; H - 30, laborer, b. Meredith, s/o George H. Follett and Maria; W - 19, b. Tamworth, d/o Henry Wallace and Fannie Wallace

FONSECA,
Paul R. of Vernon, CT m. Susan M. **Hale** of Vernon, CT 8/24/1996

FORD,
Edmund M. of Tamworth m. Grace **Smith** of Tamworth 8/5/1911 in Tamworth; H – 47, scale maker, b. Morgan, VT, s/o Hobart B. Ford (Hamden, VT) and Lucy A. Morse (Groton, VT); W – 27, at home, b. Burke, VT, d/o Frank P. Smith (Tamworth) and Alice Humphry (Burke, VT)
Walter J. of PA m. Constance H. **Libby** of Tamworth 10/28/1952 in Bristol, CT; H – 28, office manager; W – 27, store clerk

FORSYTHE,
Edwin B., Jr. of W. Ossipee m. Vicki **Stone** of Tamworth 5/31/1975; H – 25; W - 20

FORTIER,
Albert F. m. Doris M. **Bean** 5/27/1933 in Tamworth
Carroll m. Phyllis M. **Greene** 9/19/1937 in Tamworth
John L. m. Rita M. **Shea** 5/16/1954 in Conway; H – 27, purchasing agent; W – 23, secretary
Walter W. of Tamworth m. Florence E. **Welch** of Tamworth 7/3/1943 in Tamworth; H – 21, soldier; W – 23, tel. operator

FOSS,
Lance F. of Tamworth m. Chandra L. **O'Brien** of Tamworth 10/13/2001

FOURNIER,
Michael A. of W. Ossipee m. Pamela J. **Miller** of W. Ossipee 10/24/1998

FRASE,
Kimberly K. of Sandwich m. Lauren A. **Ulitz** of Tamworth 5/18/1985

FRECHETTE,
Maurice Edward of N. Conway m. Patricia Jane **Hammond** of Tamworth 5/6/1967; H – 22, coal & oil; W – 21, waitress

FREDRICKSON,
Paul E. of Tamworth m. Virginia M. **Wing** of Conway 5/9/1991

FREETO,
Robert P. of S. Tamworth m. Janet T. **Davis** of S. Tamworth 2/1/2003

FRENCH,
David Vestal of Wonalancet m. Donna Read **Miller** of Wonalancet 6/10/1995

FROMM,
William A. m. Beulah M. **Gray** 11/5/1961 in Wentworth; H – 77, retired; W – 69, housework

FROST,
Arthur E. m. Ethel **Hobbs** 4/30/1916 in Conway; H – 22, chauffeur, b. Tamworth, s/o George F. Frost and Jennie Storey; W – 22, waitress, b. Boston, MA, d/o Frank O. Hobbs and Hattie Eastman

Bernard Elwin of Porter, ME m. Shirley Ellen **Anthony** of Tamworth 4/20/1964 in Tamworth; H – 32, woodsman; W – 21, factory worker

Edwin M. m. Mary A. **Moore** 3/10/1921 in Tamworth; H – 55, farmer, 2nd, b. Madison, s/o George W. Frost and Eliza A. Mason; W –

58, housekeeper, 2nd, b. Tamworth, d/o William Kenerson and Sophia Drew

Lawrence E. of Tamworth m. Rita M. **Lawson** of Tamworth 7/4/1948 in Tamworth; H – 31, RR mail clerk; W – 28, telephone operator

Norris W. of Tamworth m. Patricia J. **Barton** of E. Andover 11/22/1985

Wayne Cecil of Dover m. Marie Esther **Bickford** of Madbury 9/14/1963 in Tamworth; H – 25, foundry; W – 18, Capital Windows

FRY,

Edward F. of Gladwyne, PA m. Alexandra M. **Erickson** of Gladwyne, PA 8/19/1984

FRYE,

Randolph C. of Moultonboro m. Cynthia M. **Cook** of S. Tamworth 7/23/1977; H – 20; W – 19

FULCHER,

Charles E. of Tamworth m. Cheryl L. **Skillings** of Tamworth 10/24/1987

FULLER,

Richard F. of MA m. Carolyn D. **Gray** of MA 6/16/1988

William E. of Tamworth m. Gladys L. **Brewer** of Tamworth 9/13/1947 in Bradford; H – 39, bulldozer operator; W – 35, housework

FURNBACH,

Henry James of Tamworth m. Cynthia Joan **Ullrich** of Tamworth 9/24/1988

FUSELIER,

Christopher J. of Woodbridge, NJ m. Elizabeth A. **Cooper** of Woodbridge, NJ 9/14/1991

GAGNE,

Gerald William of Tamworth m. Judith Ann **Thompson** of Tamworth 10/21/2000

GALLANT,
David Allen of Tamworth m. Lynn Marie **Marcoux** of Tamworth 2/17/1997

GALLUP,
George W. of Tamworth m. Carrie A. **Osgood** of Tamworth 10/11/1939 in Meredith; H – 66, farmer; W – 69, housework

GANEM,
George A. of Wollaston, MA m. Suzanne **White** of Wollaston, MA 5/16/1979

GARBOWICZ,
Edward M. m. Betty J. **Remick** 6/11/1960 in Ossipee; H – 28, accountant; W – 21, secretary

GARDNER,
Mark S. of Freedom m. Stephanie F. **Welch** of Tamworth 8/29/1987

GARDON,
Stefan G. of Germany m. Cacilia T. **Schutter** of Germany 10/2/1992

GARLAND,
Frank E. m. Meriue M. **Clark** 9/9/1928 in Strafford
George E. of Tamworth m. Mary E. **Grant** of Sandwich 5/17/1896 in Tamworth; H - 21, farmer, b. Tamworth, s/o George D. Garland (Conway, farmer) and Jenny C. Ross (Albany, deceased); W - 20, teacher, b. Moultonboro, d/o Francis H. Grant (Sandwich, farmer) and Huldah B. Abbott (Tamworth, housewife)
George Ernest m. Edna M. **King** 7/10/1914 in Tamworth; H – 40, laborer, 2nd, b. Tamworth, s/o George D. Garland and Jennie C. Ross; W – 38, housework, 3rd, b. Moultonborough, d/o Frank Grant and Hulda Abbott

GARTRELL,
Christopher D. of MA m. Penelope B. **Hocking** of MA 10/9/1977; H – 24; W – 32

GATTEY,
Devin M. of Lexington, MA m. Rebecca T. **Rotberg** of Lexington, MA 6/30/1990

GAUDET,
James Richard of Tamworth m. Pamela Jean **Kasper** of Lee 8/6/1988

GEIGER,
Christopher James of Belmont, MA m. Laurie Jane **Foster** of Belmont, MA 11/11/1995

GEORGE,
Mark S. of Boulder, CO m. Donna A. **Luedke** of Charleston, SC 7/27/1996

GERVAIS,
Albert J. of Ashland m. Hazel I. **McGuire** of Tamworth 8/20/1945 in Ashland; H – 47, lumber operator; W – 28, at home

GIBBONS,
John A. of Tamworth m. Barbara J. **Ferber** of Yonkers, NY 5/5/1984

GIBSON,
David C. m. E. Paige **Norcross** 3/3/1961 in Ctr. Ossipee; H – 20, Navy; W – 19, secretary
Douglas P. of Tamworth m. Patricia A. **Freeman** of Barrington 2/4/1978; H – 36; W – 29
George A. of Tamworth m. Mary L. **Vittum** of Tamworth 7/22/1939 in Conway; H – 25, auto mechanic; W – 19, at home

GIGUERE,
Albert D. of Chocorua m. Marti **Dietrich** of Chocorua 7/20/1979

GILLIS,
Allen M. m. Lottie M. **Ellis** 12/27/1926 in Conway
Allen W. of Tamworth m. Alma R. **Chadbourne** of Bartlett 7/12/1942 in N. Conway; H – 41, road maintenance; W – 21, at home
Derek W. of ME m. Jennifer S. **Caldwell** of ME 9/6/2003
Eugene M. of Brockton, MA m. Eveleth May **Grey** of Pembroke, MA 7/5/1975; H – 26; W – 28

GILMAN,
Bert E. of Tamworth m. Ethel M. **Johnson** of Tamworth 3/8/1903; H – 20, laborer, b. Amherst, s/o George T. Gilman (Merrimack)

and Abbie Butterfield (Amherst); W – 17, b. Tamworth, d/o John W. Johnson (Tamworth) and Nellie Rogers (Porter, ME)

Charles A. of Tamworth m. Adaline R. **Folsom** of Tamworth 5/20/1891 in Tamworth; H - 36, laborer, b. Tamworth, s/o George W. Gilman (Newmarket) and Ellen J. Bickford (Tamworth); W - 49, housework, b. Albany, d/o William Rose (Tamworth) and Sally Rilley (Albany)

Clifford J. of Tamworth m. Nellie M. D. **Moore** of Tamworth 11/24/1913 in Tamworth; H – 24, laborer, b. Sandwich, s/o John F. Gilman and Laura E. Bennett; W – 18, housework, b. Tamworth, d/o Edgar H. Moore and Mary A. Kenerson

Edmund T. of Tamworth m. Mary C. **Foss** of Hopkinton 8/18/1903; H – 59, colporter, b. Tamworth, s/o Ezra Gilman (Tamworth) and Patience Tibbetts (Farmington); W – 49, teacher, b. Hopkinton, d/o J. G. M. Foss and Alvira Connor

Edwin F. of Tamworth m. Arlene **Littlefield** of Ossipee 7/10/1943 in Ctr. Ossipee; H – 33, railroad; W – 24, at home

Erwin A. of Tamworth m. Elsie M. **Ross** of Tamworth 7/3/1906 in Tamworth; H – 45, farmer, b. Wakefield, s/o Benjamin P. Gilman (Brookfield) and Mary A. Pike (Wolfeboro); W – 17, housekeeping, b. Tamworth, d/o Onslow S. Ross (Albany) and Hattie Moody (Tamworth)

Harold E. m. Margaret **Nickerson** 5/27/1922 in N. Conway; H – 27, b. Madison; W – 18, b. Tamworth

Herbert M. of Tamworth m. Ada L. **Clarke** of Lawrence, MA 5/6/1893 in Tamworth; H - 24, farmer, b. Tamworth, s/o William P. Gilman (Tamworth) and Mary A. Bryant (Tamworth); W - 24, dry goods clerk, b. Lawrence, MA, d/o William Clarke and Ruth Chick (Tamworth)

Howard R. m. Hazel M. **Lawrence** 10/23/1930 in Ctr. Ossipee

John C. of Tamworth m. Minnie E. **Parker** of Madison 7/24/1943 in Madison; H – 18, farmer; W – 18, maid

Reed B. m. Maud **Thurston** 11/13/1915 in Tamworth; H – 20, laborer, b. Fryeburg, ME, s/o Randolph Gilman and Alma Austin; W – 17, housework, b. Silver Lake, d/o Isaac Thurston and Lizzie Foss

Sumner H. of Tamworth m. Annie C. **Remick** of Tamworth 4/2/1902; H – 41, farmer, b. Charlestown, MA, s/o David H. Gilman (Madison) and Mary J. Hutchins (England); W – 27, housework, b. Tamworth, d/o Alpheus D. Remick (Tamworth) and Ann J. Hurd (Exeter, ME)

Wilber J. m. Lena May **Brown** 8/25/1918 in Sandwich; H – 31, machinist, 2nd, b. Fryeburg, ME, s/o John F. Gilman and Laura E. Bennett; W – 24, housekeeper, b. Sandwich, d/o Daniel O. Brown and Elizabeth Fogg

GLAWS,
J. Peter of Chocorua m. Sylvia M. **Lund** of Rochelle, IL 6/1/1972; H – 22; W – 25

GLENN,
David D. of Stamford, CT m. Victoria L. **Furth** of Stamford, CT 3/22/1986

GLENNCROSS,
Stephen M. of Tamworth m. Deborah P. **Calnan** of Tamworth 6/12/1998

GLIDDEN,
Carl S. of Wolfeboro m. Bernice A. **Ames** of Tamworth 11/23/1938 in Tamworth; H – 28, mechanic; W – 22, at home
William C. of Tamworth m. Evvie M. **Bodge** of Moultonborough 5/8/1897 in Tamworth; H – 20, farmer, b. Sandwich, s/o Frank O. Glidden (Calais, ME) and Maggie Woodman (Tamworth); W – 21, b. Tuftonboro, d/o Daniel Bodge (Moultonboro) and Ellen Bodge (Tuftonboro)

GLOADE,
Kenneth David of Kennebunk, ME m. Joanna Lee **Hidden** of Tamworth 6/15/1968; H – 20; W – 21

GOBELLE,
Arthur J. m. Evelyn E. **Wiggin** 8/14/1936 in Tamworth
Norman R. m. Ruth C. **Webster** 1025/1956 in Tamworth; H – 18, engineer; W – 18, secretary

GOODNO,
Ralph Holmes of Durham m. Pauline E. **Hayford** of Tamworth 6/14/1947 in Tamworth; H – 24, student; W – 22, student

GOODSON,
David C. of Tamworth m. Lanette M. **Langlois** of Tamworth 5/16/1992

David Chester of Tamworth m. Wynetta Elaine **Eldridge** of Tamworth 9/9/1967; H – 18, forestry; W – 19, student

Peter B. of Chocorua m. Janice M. **Arnold** of Silver Lake 10/11/1975; H – 23; W – 19

Peter B. of Chocorua m. Charlotte F. **Goodreau** of Madison 9/21/2002

Peter Blake of Chocorua m. Sarah Margaret **Bullen** of Chocorua 4/30/1988

Timothy Steddom of Tamworth m. Jody Louise **Papointe** of Tamworth 7/31/1976; H – 26; W - 20

Wilbur C. of Tamworth m. Mildred E. **Bickford** of Tamworth 6/15/1947 in Tamworth; H – 37, grocer; W – 22, at home

GORDON,
Haven E. m. Jacquelyn **Young** 9/13/1956 in Tamworth; H – 19, wood heeler; W – 16, at home

Haven E. m. Rita A. **Crouse** 12/13/1961 in Tamworth; H – 24, laborer; W – 18, at home

Ralph S. of Mt. Vernon, ME m. Grace A. **Haughton** of Tamworth 3/1/1908 in Tamworth; H – 29, farmer, b. Mt. Vernon, ME, s/o Lorenzo Gordon (Mt. Vernon, ME) and Ida Norton (Mt. Vernon, ME); W – 22, housewife, b. Newbury, MA, d/o J. Wheelwright (Newbury, MA) and Alice R. Upton (Salem, MA)

Randall S. of S. Tamworth m. Lorna L. **Pearson** of Watertown, MA 6/28/1986

Timothy of Centre Harbor m. M. Abbie **Berry** of Tamworth 5/21/1894 in Tamworth; H - 63, station agent, 2nd, b. Tuftonboro, s/o Timothy Gordon (farmer) and Mehitable Morrison (housekeeping); W - 49, dressmaker, 3rd, b. Tamworth, d/o Benjamin Moulton (Tamworth, farmer) and Nancy Moulton (Tamworth, housekeeping)

William H. m. Celia **Martin** 4/16/1927 in Winchester

GOSS,
Lewis J. of Meredith m. Flora E. **Chase** of Tamworth 12/3/1945 in Tamworth; H – 34, laborer; W – 34, furniture worker

GOTJEN,
John C. of Chocorua m. Barbara J. **Drake** of Chocorua 5/8/1982

GOURLEY,
Kirkland S. of Tamworth m. Carolyn Ann **Greenamyer** of Alton 2/5/1977; H – 50; W – 35

GRACE,
Carroll O. of Tamworth m. Eleanor F. **Merritt** of Norwell, MA 1/10/1941 in Center Harbor; H – 26, woodsman; W – 29, teacher
Ernest C. of Tamworth m. Cora E. **Smart** of Tamworth 8/25/1902; H – 21, laborer, b. Albany, s/o Chandler P. Grace (Chatham) and Abby E. Bean (Conway); W – 18, b. Tamworth, d/o Charles E. Smart (Tamworth) and Addie E. Berry (Tamworth)
Everett E. of Tamworth m. Shirley A. **Brown** of Tamworth 7/2/1950 in Tamworth; H – 22, furniture factory; W – 21, clerk
Guy S. m. Florence **Eldridge** 6/8/1924 in Tamworth
Jeffrey of Tamworth m. Risa **Stevens** of ME 4/10/1981
Jere Wayne of Tamworth m. Gail Frances **Sweithelm** of Conway 3/3/1972; H – 24; W – 24
John Francis of Gill, MA m. Leslie Ann **Wheeler** of Gill, MA 6/24/1995
Perley C. of Tamworth m. Nellie M. **Berry** of Tamworth 12/23/1909 in Tamworth; H – 24, farmer, b. Tamworth, s/o Chandler P. Grace (Chatham, farmer) and Abbie E. Bean (Stowe, ME, housewife); W – 28, housework, d/o Orren S. Berry (Tamworth, laborer) and Elizabeth Davis (Biddeford, ME, housewife)
Philip C. of Tamworth m. Harriet L. **Murray** of Penacook 1/1/1938 in Penacook; H – 27, laborer; W – 22, b. nursemaid
Robert E. m. Janet K. **Hill** 12/6/1958 in Tamworth; H – 19, Air Force; W – 18, tel. operator
Roy E. m. Clara **Moore** 1/1/1934 in Tamworth
Roy W. of Laconia m. Kimberly H. **Seamans** of Tamworth 10/16/1993

GRAFFAM,
Robert of Tamworth m. Debra **Boutilier** of Tamworth 7/15/1981

GRANT,
Alexander G. of Boston, MA m. Carol E. **Sawyer** of Boston, MA 6/23/1990

Joseph m. Sue **Russell** 4/14/1956 in Tamworth; H – 21, trucker; W – 18, shoe factory

Lyle L. m. Marguerite **Fall** 1/18/1936 in Tamworth

Richard E. of Tamworth m. Charlene **Severance** of Suncook 9/22/1978; H – 18; W – 18

GRAVES,
Clifford R. of E. Fryeburg, ME m. Wendy F. **Dirubbo** of E. Fryeburg, ME 5/15/1993

GRAY,
Harold M. m. Bulah M. **Bickford** 10/28/1919 in Tamworth; H – 27, machinist, s/o Granville M. Gray and Lucy M. White; W – 27, housework, d/o Wilber J. Bickford and Abbie Bickford

Lloyd E., Jr. of Uxbridge, MA m. Patricia G. **Naylor** of Uxbridge, MA 7/4/1986

Warren of Manchester m. Ernestine Mae **DesRosier** of S. Tamworth 12/27/1963 in Manchester; H – 29, stock clerk; W – 27, at home

GREEN,
Frank C. m. Viola D. **Vittum** 6/3/1916 in Tamworth; H – 22, electrician, b. Cemter Harbor, s/o G. W. Green and Mary Carter; W – 17, housework, b. Sandwich, d/o Otis H. Vittum and Albertha Danforth

GREENE,
George C. of CA m. Jean W. **Hoag** of CA 6/25/1977; H – 43; W – 39

GREGORY,
John of Jamaica Plain, MA m. Beth M. **Maury** of Jamaica Plain, MA 7/17/2001

GRIFFIN,
Matthew D. of Boston, MA m. Elizabeth M. **Sandeman** of Boston, MA 6/26/1992

Scott Robert of Chocorua m. Kendra Michelle **Hubbard** of Steep Falls, ME 9/2/2000

GRUE,
Daniel F. of Tamworth m. Tammy S. **Quinlan** of Tamworth 6/28/2002

GUAY,
Raymond R. of Laconia m. Mary T. **Hayford** of Tamworth 11/23/1950 in Tamworth; H – 25, accountant; W – 23, at home

GUCKER,
Alexander L. of Billerica, MA m. Alice M. **Kenney** of Lincoln, MA 10/9/1972; H – 33; W – 35

GUECIA,
Philip John of Chocorua m. Cecilia Talmage **Johnson** of Chocorua 9/16/2000

GUILBAULT,
Anthony J. of Tamworth m. Alyssa L. **Davis** of Tamworth 7/7/2001

GUMPERT,
James S. of Tamworth m. Michelle M. **Matthey** of Tamworth 7/30/1977; H – 27; W – 25

GUNNILL,
John F. of Anchorage, AK m. Maryann **Rowe** of Anchorage, AK 6/20/1986

GUPTILL,
Irving Elmer of Glen m. Kerry Faye **Roberts** of Conway 5/25/1974; H – 20; W – 20

GURICK,
George Ray, Jr. of Boston, MA m. Sandra Kathryn **Flanagan** of Tamworth 6/21/1969; H – 21; W – 21

GUSTAFSON,
Frederic B. of Hampton, VA m. Eleanor **Twitchell** of Concord, MA 6/28/1940 in Tamworth; H – 26, teacher; W – 26, teacher

GUTBERLET,
James Michael of San Jose, CA m. Mary Kathryn **Haine** of Santa Clara, CA 6/29/1985

GUYER,
Alec J. of Tamworth m. Tonya M. **Martin** of Tamworth 3/28/2001

HADDEN,
Christopher of Concord, MA m. Nan **Kenney** of Concord, MA 5/18/1974; H – 25; W - 23

HADDON,
Arthur L. of Havana, Cuba m. Katherine P. **Loring** of Tamworth 8/9/1941 in Tamworth; H – 24, Int. Tel. Co.; W – 21, at home

HADINGHAM,
Evan W. of Cambridge, MA m. Janet L. **Johnson** of Cambridge, MA 9/17/1983

HAFFORD,
Ronald Reginald of Presque Isle, ME m. Marilyn Esther **Pullen** of Lewiston, ME 5/17/1964 in Tamworth; H – 29, horse trainer; W – 41, at home

HAGERTY,
Shawn Michael of Tamworth m. Jennifer Anne **Howell** of Tamworth 7/11/1997

HALE,
Roger W. of Eaton m. Donna L. **Bachle** of Tamworth 5/10/1986

HALL,
Anthony C. of Brooktondale, NY m. Una M. **Moneypenny** of Brooktondale, NY 6/30/1990
Frederick W. of NY m. Sarah **Lloyd** of Chocorua 10/4/1980
Gerald W. of Tamworth m. Mary L. **Green** of Natick, MA 5/31/1975; H – 41; W – 27

HAMEL,
Gerard E. of N. Conway m. Janis **Stamps** of Tamworth 10/8/1977; H – 40; W – 26

HAMMOND,
Edward of Tamworth m. Mary **McGilliory** of Boston 11/30/1901 in Boston; H – 30, laborer, b. Ossipee, s/o Silas Hammond (Saco, ME) and Mehitable Williams (Ossipee); W – 28, housekeeper, b. Antigonish, NS, d/o Hugh McGilliory (Antigonish, NS) and Jennie Smith (Antigonish, NS)
Edward J. m. Charlotte Lydia **Gill** 10/30/1930 in Conway
Fred L. of Tamworth m. Florence J. **Moody** of Tamworth 11/4/1903; H – 26, laborer, b. Albany, s/o Ichabod Hammond (Tamworth) and Sarah Ross (Albany); W – 22, housework, b. Watertown, MA, d/o Levi W. Moody (Tamworth) and Mary J. Davis (Ossipee)
Fred M. of Tamworth m. Sadie M. **Garland** of Tamworth 4/26/1891 in Tamworth; H - 18, farmer, b. Ossipee, s/o D. W. Hammond (Effingham) and Mary N. Marston (Ossipee); W - 20, housework, b. Tamworth, d/o George P. Garland (Conway) and Jane C. Rose (Albany)
Fred M. m. Ethel M. **Lane** 4/21/1915 in Hollis, ME; H – 42, mill man, 2nd, b. Ossipee, s/o D. Waymouth Hammond and Mary Marston; W – 36, teacher, 2nd, b. Portland, ME, d/o William H. Parker and Lenora Paine
Fred M. m. Bertha M. **Goodwin** 4/16/1919 in Manchester; H – 45, mill man, 4th, s/o D. Weymouth Hammond and Mary Marston; W – 38, stenographer, d/o Joseph S. Goodwin and Fannie S. Smith
George R. m. Frances M. **Thurston** 10/1/1955 in Ossipee; H – 23, truck driver; W – 18, at home
George R. of Tamworth m. Barbara H. **Nolen** of Tamworth 9/27/1994
Stanley Frank of Tamworth m. Beverly Mae **Black** of Tamworth 7/12/1969; H – 30; W – 25
Walter J. of Tamworth m. Blanch A. **Hayford** of Tamworth 10/4/1892 in Tamworth; H - 21, plumber, b. Somerville, MA, s/o D. W. Hammond (Tamworth) and Mary A. Marston (Ossipee); W - 19, housework, b. Tamworth, d/o David Hayford (Tamworth) and Elizabeth Ames (Tamworth)

HANLON,
Samuel O. of Bridgton, ME m. Mae A. **Minnehan** of Lewiston, ME 4/6/1941 in Tamworth; H – 24, radio man; W – 22, waitress

HANSCOM,
Walter H. of Rochester m. Esther F. **Page** of Tamworth 10/24/1942 in Berwick, ME; H – 73, contractor; W – 39, housekeeper

HANSEN,
Neil Malcolm of Tamworth m. Linda Jean **Mills** of Tamworth 6/7/1968; H – 25; W - 27
Richard Dalrymple of Conway m. Ann **Thurston** of Tamworth 8/30/1963 in Bedford; H – 24, milkman; W – 18, secretary

HANSON,
Peter R. of Chocorua m. Vicki B. **Wasson** of Chocorua 10/21/1979
Robert W., Jr. of Tamworth m. Frances K. **VerPlanck** of Tamworth 4/12/1975; H – 27; W – 25

HAPGOOD,
Guy F. m. Abbie **Grace** 11/2/1918 in Tamworth; H – 34, farmer, b. Stratford, s/o Calvin Hapgood and Lizzie Barnett; W – 15, b. Tamworth, d/o Joseph Grace and Lodema L. Cates

HARGENS,
Roger S. of Elk Grove, IL m. Yvonne A. **Kolman** of Elk Grove, IL 8/25/1990
William Garman of Philadelphia, PA m. Amy Lou **Raesler** of Manchester, CT 7/17/1965 in Tamworth; H – 22, banking; W – 21, student

HARKNESS,
Frank E. m. Marjory **Gane** 1/5/1918 in Wonalancet; H – 43, lawyer, 2nd, b. Chicago, IL, s/o Edson J. Harkness and Marianna Bates; W – 37, b. Yonkers, NY

HARMON,
Harold Chester of Tamworth m. Rosemary **Hatch** of Conway 8/30/1963 in Bedford; H – 18, laborer; W – 17, chambermaid
Robert H. of Tamworth m. Linda C. **Roberts** of Chocorua 3/23/1971; H – 24; W – 21
Robert Henry of Tamworth m. Marlee Ilean **Moulton** of Tamworth 9/4/1965 in Tamworth; H – 18, laborer; W – 19, clerk
William James of Tamworth m. Rose **Emerson** of Tamworth 9/23/1989

HARMSEN,
Douglas Jan of New York, NY m. Christina Elizabeth **Rouner** of New York, NY 9/16/1995

HARRINGTON,
Ernest A. S. m. Flora I. **Galucia** 7/13/1919 in Tamworth; H – 27, machinist, s/o Clarence F. Harrington and Mabel E. Grant; W – 27, at home, d/o Charles E. Galucia and Harriett E. Holmes
Pres. T. m. Bertha M. **Rogers** 9/5/1931 in Wakefield

HARRIS,
Edward H. of Magnolia, MA m. Ruth C. **Boyd** of Danvers, MA 8/18/1966; H – 69, retired; W – 61, secretary
V. Steven, Jr. of Tamworth m. Virginia R. **Lane** of N. Reading, MA 12/23/1984

HARTFORD,
Perley Gordon of Tamworth m. Rachael Blanch **Dow** of Tamworth 6/29/1963 in Center Ossipee; H – 30, self employed; W – 40, factory
Wayne L. m. Cynthia **Twombly** 10/28/1959 in N. Conway; H – 25, sheet metal; W – 21, bank teller

HARTLEY,
Erin Spencer of New Port Richey, FL m. Amy Elizabeth **Hamlin** of Center Harbor 10/23/1999

HASKELL,
Nelson Cary of Tamworth m. Ruth H. **Ahern** of Tamworth 3/17/1973; H – 67; W – 58

HASTIE,
George B. m. Dorothy B. **Blevens** 5/23/1937 in Tamworth

HATCH,
Fred A. of Tamworth m. Marcia J. **Elliott** of Tamworth 5/15/1982
George A. m. Ida M. **Gove** 10/19/1910 in Tamworth; H – 63, laborer, b. Charlestown, s/o Abijah Hatch (Medford, MA) and Elizabeth E. Battles (Hingham, MA); W – 45, nurse, b. Tamworth, d/o Frank A. Gove and Sarah M. Evans (Tamworth)
Osman P. m. Katherene B. **Hatch** 8/19/1932 in Lebanon

Wilbur Clifford, Jr. of Tamworth m. Darlene Roxanne **Swanson** of Tamworth 6/3/1995

HAYFORD,
A. David of Tamworth m. Gloria B. **Aspinall** of Madison 1/12/1983
A. David of Chocorua m. Marsha G. **Williamson** of Chocorua 4/17/1993
Abner W. of Tamworth m. Katherine **Marx** of Tamworth 1/13/1904 in Tamworth; H – 34, laborer, b. Tamworth, s/o David Hayford and Ann Ames; W – 29, housework, b. Germany, d/o Adam Marx (Germany)
Arnold D. m. Muriel **Smalle** 12/3/1933 in Tamworth
Arnold D. of Chocorua m. Ashana R. **Michaels** of Chocorua 9/22/2001
Arthur L. m. Leona **Herrick** 11/19/1927 in Tamworth
Daniel A. of Tamworth m. Patricia A. **Jack** of Ctr. Ossipee 1/20/1951 in Laconia; H – 17, laborer; W – 17, student
Durwood of Tamworth m. Joanna **Dempsy** of Tamworth 11/5/1903; H – 26, laborer, b. Tamworth, s/o David Hayford (Tamworth) and Ann E. Ames (Tamworth); W – 25, housework, b. Cambridge, MA, d/o Michel Dempsy (Ireland)
Ernest A. m. Elizabeth D. **Nudd** 5/9/1953 in Tamworth; H – 22, retired; W – 25, housework
Lawrence E. m. Katherine **Desmond** 4/28/1924 in Chocorua
Paul L. of Tamworth m. Caroline F. **Demeritt** of Ctr. Ossipee 5/28/1950 in Moultonville
Randall Everett of Center Ossipee m. Susan May **Weare** of Tamworth 8/23/1969; H – 18; W – 18

HAYNES,
Charlie O. of Amesbury, MA m. Helen L. **Bassani** of Amesbury, MA 6/1/1991

HAYS,
George C. of Boston, MA m. Lizzie I. **Hayford** of Tamworth 8/26/1890 in Tamworth; H - 31, mechanic, b. Boston, MA, s/o William Hays (Boston, MA); W - 25, housework, b. Tamworth, d/o David Hayford (Tamworth)

HAZEN,
John W. of Newburyport, MA m. Robin D. **Ricker** of Newburyport, MA 10/26/1990

HEFFERNAN,
Michael J. of Branford, CT m. Holly J. **Foley** of Branford, CT 2/6/1993

HEILFERTY,
Robert J. of Alexandria, VA m. Marianne G. **Mayer** of Alexandria, VA 9/2/1990

HEIMLICH,
Peter J. of Tamworth m. Melinda A. **Elliott** of Tamworth 8/17/1980

HENDERSON,
Everett G. m. Margaret **Blake** 9/17/1932 in Concord

HENRY,
Gerald J. of Aurora, CO m. Patricia Ann **Brett** of Aurora, CO 11/19/1966; H – 23, station agent; W – 21, stewardess

HENSON,
William H. of Cumberland, RI m. Nancy L. **Cardoso** of Cumberland, RI 6/22/1996

HERLIHY,
Thomas J. Michael of Tamworth m. Alexandra Hydee **Bradford** of Tamworth 2/14/1998

HERSEY,
Leonard of Vernal, UT m. Katharine **Page** of Brookline, MA 10/14/1923 in Tamworth; H – 24; W – 27

HIEBERT,
John Clement of Cambridge, MA m. Rebecca Baldwin **Tipton** of Cambridge, MA 6/10/2000

HIDDEN,
John B. of Tamworth m. Mabel A. **Bray** of Buffalo, NY 9/29/1938 in Tamworth; H – 23, laborer; W – 18, beauty culture

John Bray of Tamworth m. Marilyn Dorr **Nixon** of Tamworth 5/9/1964 in Chocorua; H – 23, carpenter; W – 17, at home
S. Harold of Tamworth m. Helen J. **Bassett** of Tamworth 1/1/1912 in Tamworth; H – 20, farmer, b. Tamworth, s/o Samuel A. Hidden (Tamworth) and Elizabeth J. Bellows (Trenton, NJ); W – 18, teacher, b. Tamworth, d/o James C. Bassett (Bartlett) and Fannie A. Tilton (Raymond)
Samuel A. of Tamworth m. Elizabeth **Bellows** of Tamworth 11/7/1889 in Tamworth; H - 23, farmer, b. Tamworth, s/o John D. Hidden (Tamworth); W - 22, housework, b. Trenton, NJ, d/o Alonzo J. Bellows (Boston, MA)
William B. m. Christine **Johnson** 11/1/1932 in Ctr. Sandwich

HILL,
David A. of Tamworth m. Annie L. **Forest** of Tamworth 12/28/1891 in Tamworth; H - 27, farmer, b. Dayton, ME, s/o William W. Hill (Dayton, ME) and Sarah S. Jellerson (Waterborough, ME); W - 27, housework, d/o Timothy Bean (Stow, ME)
Lorne M. of Tamworth m. Angela M. **Salmon** of Tamworth 5/17/2003
William A. m. Cordelia P. **Johnson** 12/13/1914 in Tamworth; H – 44, mason, 2nd, b. Woburn, MA, s/o John T. Hill and Adelia White; W – 67, boarding house, 3rd, b. Tamworth, d/o John Chick and Sarah Clark
William A. m. Fannie E. **Whiting** 4/12/1922 in Tamworth; H – 50, b. Woburn, MA; W – 38, b. Tamworth

HOAGLAND,
Edward B. m. Marion J. **Corbett** 5/8/1953 in Tilton; H – 52, hotel owner; W – 44, agent, N.E.T.&T.

HOBBS,
Bert W. of Tamworth m. Eva F. **Hardy** of Tamworth 10/8/1892 in Tamworth; H - 17, farmer, b. Tamworth, s/o Josiah Hobbs (Tamworth) and Sophrona Johnson (Tamworth); W - 17, housework, b. Tamworth, d/o William H. Hardy (Tamworth) and Georgiana Davis
Bert W. of Tamworth m. Hattie **Swain** of Conway 9/14/1895 in Chocorua; H - 20, farmer, 2nd, b. Tamworth, s/o Josiah Hobbs (Albany, mason) and Sophronia Hobbs (Tamworth, housewife); W - 19, housewife, b. Conway, d/o Annette Swain (Albany, housewife)

Charles W. m. Caroline R. **Fownes** 6/18/1921 in Chocorua; H – 47, state official, 2nd, b. Salem, MA, s/o Charles A. Hobbs and Bertha Howard; W – 47, at home, b. Swampscott, MA, d/o George Fownes and Caroline F. Roberts

Ernest m. Cristine L. **Palmer** 10/20/1927 in Tamworth

Frank Wilson of Tamworth m. Sandra Clara **Watson** of Tamworth 7/13/1963 in S. Tamworth; H – 22, tree climber; W – 19, at home

George m. Marjie **Frost** 12/25/1919 in Tamworth; H – 23, mill man, s/o Bert W. Hobbs abd Hattie M. Swain; W – 17, d/o Elibeous Frost and Minnie Troman

Henry W. m. Gertrude M. **Emack** 10/25/1927 in Conway

Herbert m. Ethel **Moody** 2/14/1921 in Tamworth; H – 19, machinist, b. Tamworth, s/o Bert W. Hobbs and Hattie Swaine; W – 17, none, b. Tamworth, d/o Thorn E. Moody and Nancy Pascoe

Joseph W. of Tamworth m. Maria **Towle** of Freedom 7/5/1893 in Tamworth; H - 61, farmer, b. Ossipee, s/o Samuel D. Hobbs (Ossipee) and Louisa Moody (Ossipee); W - 51, housekeeping

Josiah of Tamworth m. Amanda **Eastman** of Albany 4/30/1889 in Tamworth; H - 48, farmer, b. Tamworth, s/o R. D. Hobbs (Ossipee); W - 50, housework, b. Albany, d/o Theophilas Brown (Tamworth)

Josiah m. Ruth **Darling** 6/23/1918 in Tamworth; H – 19, forest work, b. Tamworth, s/o Bert W. Hobbs and Hattie A. Swaine; W – 18, b. Tamworth, d/o Henry Darling and Nellie Dow

Leon m. Celia **Hobbs** 11/27/1924 in Conway

Philip D. of Tamworth m. Mildred M. **Williams** of Tamworth 11/12/1949 in Ctr. Ossipee; H – 19, woodworker; W – 21, at home

Thomas of Tamworth m. Beatrice **Drinkwater** of Ossipee 3/19/1945 in Ctr. Ossipee; H – 27, US Army; W – 26, at home

Wilbur of Tamworth m. Catherine M. **Boland** of NY 9/21/1912 in Tamworth; H – 23, teamster, b. Boston, MA, s/o Frank O. Hobbs (Ossipee) and Hattie F. Eastman (Albany); W – 27, waitress, b. London, England, d/o William E. Boland (Limerick, Ireland) and Frances E. Collins (London, England)

HOCH,
George A. of Chocorua m. Sandra L. **Scammon** of Rye 7/6/1982

HODGE,
Dennis F. of Tamworth m. Deborah Page **Bullard** of Tamworth 11/13/1999
Elwood N. m. Doris M. **Tallman** 2/28/1957 in Tamworth; H – 52, millworker; W – 40, furniture factory

HOFHEINZ,
Roy Mark, Jr. of Houston, Texas m. Harriet Felton **Parker** of Cambridge, MA 6/15/1963 in Chocorua; H – 27, student; W – 24, student

HOLBROOK,
Chester D. m. Eulalie E. **Pascoe** 4/28/1956 in Tamworth; H – 70, retired; W – 44, at home
Peter R. of Tamworth m. Lisa J. **Bennett** of Tamworth 10/1/2003

HOLDEN,
William M. of Tamworth m. Mary A. **Glidden** of Tamworth 9/8/1892 in Tamworth; H - 58, carpenter, b. Lunenburg, MA, s/o William W. Holden (Shirley, ME) and Sophia E. Adams (Lunenburg, MA); W - 69, housework, b. Tamworth, d/o Aaron Head (Tamworth) and Rhoda Webster

HOLLADAY,
Ronald James of Ohio m. Mary Joan **Staples** of Laconia 8/17/1968; H – 24; W – 24

HOLLAND,
James A. of Framingham, MA m. Jeanne M. **Credit** of Framingham, MA 6/27/1992

HOLLIDAY,
Paul H. of New York, NY m. Ruth **Nairne** of Tamworth 2/23/1946 in Tamworth; H – 26, dentist; W – 23, chemist

HOLT,
Andrew James, Jr. of Salem, MA m. Heidi Sue **Heusner** of Salem, MA 10/2/1999
George T. of Greenfield m. Annie H. **Whiting** of Tamworth 9/20/1902; H – 36, optician, b. Greenfield, s/o Horace E. Holt

(Greenfield) and Maria Stewart; W – 35, b. Wiscasset, ME, d/o Jabez H. Hobson and Olive R. Goodell (Limington, ME)

HORTON,
Peter R. of Ocean Park, ME m. Helen G. **Breasted** of Ocean Park, ME 7/19/1987

HOWARD,
Walter Palmer, Sr. of Manchester m. Dorothy Graves **Remick** of Tamworth 7/21/1976; H – 68; W – 60

HOWELL,
John A., Jr. of New York, NY m. Laura E. **Weymouth** of Tamworth 9/27/1985

HOWIE,
Colin A. of Norwood, MA m. Marilyn **Allen** of Tamworth 9/22/1973; H – 46; W – 33

HUCKINS,
Charles F. of Tamworth m. Sadie V. **Burleigh** of Bristol 1/26/1898 in Bristol; H – 29, farmer, b. Tamworth, s/o James H. Huckins (Tamworth) and Laura Pettingill (Sandwich); W – 28, teacher, b. Bristol, d/o James A. Burleigh (Stratham) and Jane B. Ham (Strafford)
Ferdinand A. of Tamworth m. Nancy A. **Forbush** of Charlestown, MA 10/4/1897 in Tamworth; H – 76, farmer, b. Effingham, s/o Stephen Huckins (Gilmanton) and Pauline Webb (Portland, ME); W – 60, nurse, b. Holderness, d/o Samuel Jenness and Hannah Huckins (Effingham)

HUDDLESTON,
Carl David of Chocorua m. Janet Leigh **Bergeron** of Chocorua 6/10/1989

HUGHES,
David of Tamworth m. Marilyn **Cakars** of Center Harbor 5/12/1984

HUNTINGTON,
Henry P. of Barrow, AK m. Kathleen A. **Burek** of Davis, CA 10/2/1993

HUNTOON,
Wayne Alan of Chocorua m. Jean L. **Dionne** of Chocorua 9/10/1989

HURD,
Alton m. Helen E. **Gilman** 9/22/1934 in Ashland

HURST,
James W. of Hanover m. Susan B. **Damon** of Tamworth 6/7/1986

HURTUBISE,
Hilary J. of Auburn, ME m. Elizabeth M. **Orpin** of Lewiston, ME 8/25/1966; H – 41, social worker; W – 29, social worker

HUTCHINS,
Clarence E. m. Ida B. **Smith** 10/4/1915 in Tamworth; H – 24, farmer, b. Tamworth, s/o William N. Hutchins and Augusta Downs; W – 18, b. Stowe, d/o Walter C. Smith and Hattie Downs
Conrad Paul of Tamworth m. Judith Ann **Clark** of Gorham 9/22/1962 in Gorham; H – 21, autobody rep.; W – 18, T. B. M. oper.
Donald P. of Tamworth m. Helen L. **Keen** of Tamworth 11/8/1941 in Conway; H – 18, woodsman; W – 16, at home
Elias W. m. Isabel F. **Osgood** 9/2/1910 in Tamworth; H – 23, laborer, b. Tamworth, s/o Noah W. Hutchins (Albany) and Augusta A. Downs (Porter, ME); W – 18, nurse, b. Tamworth, d/o Herman L. Osgood (Tamworth) and Ellen I. Freeman (Worcester, MA)
Paul W. of Tamworth m. Leah C. **Wentworth** of Fryeburg, ME 6/14/1941 in Fryeburg, ME; H – 21, mechanic; W – 18, housework
Walter C. m. Grace **Robarge** 1/25/1917 in Moultonboro; H – 19, farmer, b. Tamworth, s/o William N. Hutchins and Agusta Downs; W – 16, b. Melvin, d/o Lewis Robarge and Bessie Elliott

IRELAND,
John F. of Scotch Plains, NJ m. Doreen **Hoffay** of Scotch Plains, NJ 10/30/1993

IRISH,
Charles D. m. Joyce R. **Nystedt** 8/12/1955 in Tamworth; H – 27, upholsterer; W – 23, nurse

ISGUR,
David C. of Wolfeboro m. Linda **Wiggin** of Tamworth 5/20/1984

JACKSON,
Enoch E. of Tamworth m. Madeline E. **McNeal** of Tamworth 3/31/1907 in Tamworth; H – 20, laborer, b. Tamworth, s/o S. H. Jackson (Tamworth) and A. B. Purrington (Albany); W – 18, housework, b. Tamworth, d/o Harry McNeal (St. Johns, NB) and Martha Perkins (Tamworth)
George N. of Tamworth m. Barbara K. **Johnson** of Tamworth 11/14/1983

JACOB,
Thomas m. Una **Ritchie** 9/16/1934 in Tamworth

JACOBS,
Steven A. of Tamworth m. Tammy L. **Jaworski** of Tamworth 4/19/1996

JACOBSON,
Marty G. of Tamworth m. Elizabeth A. **Wilcox** of Tamworth 8/1/1992

JAKOBS,
Karl Kenneth of Ely, MN m. Melissa **Wells** of Ely, MN 7/5/1997

JAMIESON,
William S. of Tamworth m. Juidth A. **Champagne** of Tamworth 6/23/1984

JARDINE,
Kent I. of S. Tamworth m. Brenda L. **Whiting** of Tamworth 12/25/1995

JARNAGIN,
Eric N. of Amesbury, MA m. Antonea V. **Evans** of Amesbury, MA 5/27/2001

JEAN,
Thomas Michael of Winchester, MA m. Robin **Wheeler** of Cambridge, MA 6/27/1970; H – 25; W – 26

JEFFERS,
Charles M. of Tamworth m. Madeline F. **Holman** of Tamworth 3/2/1943 in Tamworth; H – 25, furniture worker; W – 27, furniture worker
Dean Alan of Chocorua m. Tricia Mia **Saucier** of Chocorua 6/26/1999
Fred L. of Tamworth m. Gertie M. **Gilman** of Tamworth 4/4/1888 in Tamworth; H - 28, farmer, b. Webster, s/o Edward F. Jeffers (Webster); W - 15, housework, d/o John Gilman (Tamworth)
Milton W. of Tamworth m. Abbie T. **Downs** of Tamworth 9/24/1887 in Tamworth; H - 21, farmer, b. Webster, s/o Edward F. Jeffers (Tamworth) and Emerlain; W - 18, housework, b. Tamworth, d/o Joseph Downs (Tamworth)
Percy E. of Tamworth m. Estella A. **Berry** of Moultonboro 12/14/1952 in Tamworth; H – 51, lumbering; W – 37, at home

JENKENS,
Alton L., Jr. of Chocorua m. Catherine J. **Drake** of Italy 8/29/1992
J. Anthony of Cambridge, MA m. Joy E. **Hoskins** of Newton Highlands, MA 8/9/1997

JENKINS,
Christopher F. of Old Orchard, ME m. Kelly M. **Locke** of Tamworth 10/26/1991
Clarence H. m. Luella **Ames** 6/19/1927 in Moultonboro
Laurence m. Mary W. **Coombs** 4/9/1925 in Tamworth

JENNINGS,
Alan Douglass of Tamworth m. Ann June **Roberts** of Tamworth 10/30/1965 in Tamworth; H – 18, laborer; W – 17, student
Daniel E. of Tamworth m. Edith C. **Nixon** of Tamworth 9/8/1970; H – 26; W – 17
Keith Paul of Tamworth m. Erin J. **Sharp** of Tamworth 1/8/1995
Paul B. of N. Conway m. Cynthia M. **Boewe** of Tamworth 9/26/1977; H – 35; W – 21

JESKE,
Vernon Edward of Angwin, CA m. Holly Jean **Sutherland** of Napa, CA 6/25/1995

JESSUP,
John A. of Cleveland Heights, OH m. Ellen D. **Cleveland** of Cleveland Heights, OH 8/4/1984

JOBE,
Nathaniel Abraham, Jr. of St. Paul, VA m. Wistar Laird **Rochelle** of Lynchburg, VA 12/22/1963 in Tamworth; H – 22, student; W – 22, student

JOHNSON,
Albert F. of Tamworth m. Effie A. **Poland** of Gloucester, MA 1/4/1905 in Gloucester, MA; H – 46, carpenter, b. NY, s/o Charles Johnson (Sweden) and Frederica Nelson (Germany); W – 27, teacher, b. Gloucester, MA, d/o William H. Poland and Emma C. Pulsifer

Arthur W. m. Judith O. **Austin** 9/10/1960 in Tamworth; H – 20, hosp. maintenance; W – 20, secretary

Charles H. of Tamworth m. Lizzie A. **Gardner** of Tamworth 3/12/1888 in Tamworth; H - 24, laborer, b. Lowell, MA, s/o Henry H. Johnson (Jackson, ME); W - 22, housework, b. Tamworth, d/o Joseph A. Gardner (Wakefield)

Charles H. of Tamworth m. Abbie **Ericson** of Tamworth 10/12/1901 in Tamworth; H – 37, laborer, b. Lowell, MA, s/o Henry H. Johnson (Jackson) and Drusilla Goodwin (Monmouth, ME); W – 43, housework, b. Nashua, d/o Joseph Butterfield (Manchester) and Elmira Truell (Manchester)

Dennis Wayne of Tamworth m. Rose Marie **Hobbs** of Tamworth 5/10/1965 in Center Ossipee; H – 23, Milt. service; W – 27, at home

Donald of Tamworth m. Lisa A. **Nickerson** of Tamworth 9/8/1984

Edwin N. m. Florence **Merryfield** 8/25/1910 in Tamworth; H – 20, laborer, b. Tamworth, s/o John W. Johnson (Tamworth) and Nellie Rogers (Porter, ME); W – 20, housewife, b. Porter, ME, d/o Charles H. Merryfield (Porter, ME) and Martha McDonald (Porter, ME)

Edwin N. of Weare m. Gladys I. **Drew** of rx 8/8/1945 in Weare; H – 55, trucking; W – 46, housekeeper

Edwin R. of Tamworth m. Sylvia R. **Elliott** of Sandwich 1/30/1913 in Tamworth; H – 28, farmer, b. Brooklyn, NY, s/o William R. Johnson and Annie N. Johnson; W – 20, housewife, b. Sandwich, d/o John Elliott and Ida E. Roe

Forrest R. of Tamworth m. Christine A. **Buchanan** of Tamworth 6/29/1996

Forrest W. of Tamworth m. Effie P. **Bean** of Tamworth 7/11/1938 in Moultonboro; H – 19, laborer; W – 14, at school

Glenn E. of Tamworth m. Karen E. **Mann** of N. Reading, MA 8/15/1970; H – 21; W – 23

Harry of Brownfield, ME m. Alice **Drake** of Tamworth 11/12/1912 in Tamworth; H – 24, blacksmith, b. Brownfield, ME, s/o George Johnson (Brownfield, ME) and Jane Day (Porter, ME); W – 19, housework, b. Tamworth, d/o Benjamin Drake (Ossipee) and Lizzie Farnham (Ossipee)

Harry Otis of Tamworth m. Ruth Ann **Hallett** of Conway 9/4/1971; H – 24; W – 28

Jack of Tamworth m. Cathie **Pirone** of ME 7/24/1981

John W. of Tamworth m. Julia **Galloway** of Albany 8/11/1908 in Tamworth; H – 51, farmer, b. Tamworth, s/o Nathaniel Johnson (Tamworth) and Sarah Sanborn (Acton, ME); W – 41, housekeeper, b. Bath, d/o Ezra Smith (Bath) and Elizabeth Bishop (Landaff)

Keith L. of Tamworth m. Carolyn D. **Jones** of Tamworth 4/2/2003

Larry Alan of Effingham m. Mary Leona **Lind** of Effingham 8/25/1972; H – 24; W – 37

Richard D. of CO m. Merry Lee **Eldridge** of Tamworth 11/16/1977; H – 20; W - 22

Theodore of Tamworth m. Katherine B. **MacMillan** of Cambridge, MA 12/12/1943 in Tamworth; H – 52, publisher; W – 46, teacher

JONES,

Carl W. of Wayzata, MN m. Susan C. **Lincoln** of Newton, MA 7/15/1978; H – 26; W – 24

Charles of Tamworth m. Marilyn **Howie** of Tamworth 10/5/1981

Chester D. of Albany m. Erin J. **Jennings** of Albany 8/15/1998

Frederick W. m. E. Jessie **Brown** 5/2/1926 in Silver Lake

James M. of Nubieber, CA m. Virginia M. **Bookholz** of Tamworth 12/15/1946 in Tamworth; H – 23, US Navy; W – 23, Nurse, RN

Joseph E. m. Judith E. **Gilman** 5/18/1956 in Wolfeboro; H – 23, laborer; W – 17, at home

Robert George of Madison m. Cynthia A. **Berry** of Tamworth 1/15/1977; H – 23; W – 19

William L. of Tamworth m. Linda M. **Kelley** of Tamworth 5/9/2003

JORDICE,
Mark A. of Arlington, MA m. Amy R. **Bouve** of Arlington, MA 8/12/1995

KALOGAROPOULOS,
Peter of Tamworth m. Cindy Ann **Mirabito** of Tamworth 6/3/1995

KAMERLING,
Samuel W. m. Helen F. **Haurs** 7/9/1932 in Tamworth

KANE,
Carl F. of Tamworth m. Alice G. **Armstrong** of Dunbarton 11/4/1946 in Grasmere; H – 30, farmer; W – 21, at home
John Dandridge Henley, III of Sandy Spring, MD m. Martha C. **Damon** of Tamworth 10/4/1975; H – 30; W – 26

KARP,
Allan of MA m. Lisa **Keith** of Gilford 8/9/1981

KAUFMAN,
Peter Stanley of Houston, Texas m. Megan Cole **Jamison** of Houston, Texas 11/18/1995

KAYSER,
Paul of Tamworth m. Judith W. **Anthony** of Tamworth 11/1/1975; H – 26; W – 28

KELLEY,
Harry V. of Sandown m. Evelyn A. **Banfill** of Tamworth 1/14/1939 in Tamworth; H – 34, laborer; W – 35, cook
Henry B. of Tamworth m. Lizzie **Drake** of Ossipee 6/19/1897 in Tamworth; H – 44, carpenter, b. Centre Harbor, s/o Thomas Kelley (Moultonboro) and Sally Bickford (Moultonboro); W – 24, housekeeper, b. Ossipee, d/o E. C. Farnham (Wakefield) and Eunice Moody (Tamworth)

KELLY,
John J. of Chocorua m. Marilyn D. **Hidden** of Tamworth 9/29/1990

KENNARD,
John H. m. Lydia M. **Lund** 3/30/1935 in Chocorua

KENNEDY,
Thomas A. of Cambridge, MA m. Felice M. **Apter** of Cambridge, MA 9/2/1990

KENNETT,
A. Crosby, III of S. Portland, ME m. Andrea **Johnson** of S. Portland, ME 12/28/2002
Edson C. m. Marion L. **Kent** 10/5/1935 in Madison

KENNEY,
Ronald Douglas of Tamworth m. Suzanne Marie **Alie** of Tamworth 5/5/2000

KEOUGH,
Gary H. of Salem, MA m. Kendal A. **Britt** of Peabody, MA 4/6/1991

KERN,
Frank A. of Watertown, MA m. Janet E. **Mersfelder** of Watertown, MA 9/5/1987

KERSTEN,
Martin W. of Westford, MA m. Kristin L. **Nelson** of Westford, MA 9/12/1992

KEYSER,
Kevin Wayne of Tamworth m. Rachel Mann **Parady** of Tamworth 10/2/1999

KIERSTEAD,
Thomas J. m. Laura A. **Weeks** 6/7/1930 in Parsonsfield, ME

KILEY,
John G. m. Harriet W. **Smith** 4/23/1955 in Tamworth; H – 65, writer; W – 51, secretary

KILHAM,
Peter H. m. Frances P. **Breese** 12/31/1934 in Tamworth

KILLEEN,
Jameson A. of Melrose, MA m. Michele L. **Cutrone** of Tamworth 10/16/1992

KIMBALL,
Melvin N. of Tamworth m. Susan **Martin** of Boston 6/21/1899 in Boston; H – 28, laborer, b. Tamworth, s/o I. N. Kimball (Tamworth) and Emily Sanborn (Tamworth); W – 34, dressmaker, b. England, d/o Joseph Martin (England) and Elizabeth Fields (England)

Robert Erwin of Tamworth m. Mary Elaine **Page** of Tamworth 10/10/1971; H – 31; W – 21

Samuel O. of Tamworth m. Sarah F. **Gilman** of Tamworth 5/15/1889 in Dover; H - 36, merchant, b. Tamworth, s/o Isaac Kimball (Parsonsfield, ME); W - 30, housework, b. Tamworth, d/o Joseph Gilman (Effingham)

Winslow B. of Tamworth m. Mary M. **Tilton** of Tamworth 3/8/1898 in Tamworth; H – 22, farmer, b. Tamworth, s/o Isaac N. Kimball (Madison) and Emily A. Sanborn (Tamworth); W – 29, b. Tamworth, d/o Daniel Q. Tilton (Tamworth) and Caroline Blake (Wakefield)

Winslow B. of Tamworth m. Edith M. **Hewitt** of Laconia 8/3/1942 in Belmont; H – 66, contractor; W – 51, at home

KING,
Christopher W. of Tamworth m. Heidi A. **Williams** of Tamworth 7/21/2001

Christopher William of Chocorua m. Trisha Carleen **Hidden** of Chocorua 6/10/1995

Jerry D. of MA m. Rebecca A. **Lord** of MA 5/29/1977; H – 28; W – 26

John W. of Tamworth m. Sadie A. **Nickerson** of Tamworth 12/31/1902; H – 40, laborer, b. Hansford, NS, s/o Oliver King (Mt. Pleasant, NS) and Rebecca Peel (Hansford, NS); W – 42, housework, b. Tamworth, d/o Robert Nickerson (Albany) and Sarah A. Wentworth (Lebanon, ME)

John W. m. Anna M. **Fernald** 10/22/1931 in Intervale

John W. of Tamworth m. Gertrude M. **Merry** 11/4/1939 in Tamworth; H – 76, gardener; W – 68, housekeeper

Oliver M. m. Edna M. **Garland** 9/14/1910 in Meredith; H – 18, laborer, b. Albany, s/o John King (NS) and Luella Cheney (Wells Beach, ME); W – 34, housewife, b. Moultonboro, d/o Frank Grant (Sandwich) and Huldah B. Abbott (Tamworth)

Oliver M. m. Helen S. **French** 8/20/1914 in Tamworth; H – 21, chauffeur, 2nd, b. Albany, s/o John W. King and Leuella Mason;

W – 24, designer, 2nd, b. Tamworth, d/o Harold French and Louise Ramberger
Roland N. of Laconia m. Denise L. **Repassy** of Laconia 12/23/1977; H – 28; W – 26

KINGHAM,
Thomas B. of New York, NY m. Charlotte A. **Kelley** of New York, NY 9/18/1993

KLIEN,
Paul M. of MA m. Kristin N. **Wilkinson** of ME 6/28/2003

KNAPP,
Herbert C. of Laconia m. Josephine J. **Strong** of Tamworth 12/1/1945 in Conway; H – 32, laborer; W – 36, attendant

KNIGHT,
W. D. of Tamworth m. Clara B. **Kimball** of rx 9/12/1897 in Tamworth; H – 21, laborer, b. Tamworth, s/o James P. Knight (Moultonboro) and Juliette L. Clough (Tamworth); W – 23, b. Tamworth, d/o Isaac N. Kimball (Madison) and Emily A. Sanborn (Tamworth)

KNOWLTON,
Calvin C. m. Sarah R. **Blaisdell** 5/30/1920 in Moultonboro; H – 63, carpenter, 2nd, b. Tamworth, s/o Weston Knowlton and Anna Cooley; W – 64, housekeeper, 2nd, b. Tamworth, d/o Albert Eastman and Mary Remick
Haven C. of Tamworth m. Ida M. **Downs** of Tamworth 12/5/1911 in Tamworth; H – 18, carpenter, b. Tamworth, s/o Calvin C. Knowlton (Tamworth) and Etta M. Prosely (Sandwich); W – 21, waitress, b. Tamworth, d/o Charles Downs (Tamworth) and Ella Smith (Porter, ME)
Kenneth m. Marjorie E. **Griffin** 2/10/1937 in Wolfeboro

KNOX,
Brent E. of Tamworth m. Catherine D. **Boothby** of Tamworth 7/17/1972; H – 18; W – 18
Bruce R. m. Marie A. **Ryder** 8/18/1958 in Conway; H – 19, gas station; W – 18, tel. operator

Charles E. of Sandwich m. Emily E. **Nickerson** of Tamworth
9/4/1946 in Tamworth; H – 21, student; W – 17, student
Herbert E. of Ossipee m. Emma N. **Tewksbury** of Tamworth
11/5/1889 in Madison; H - 31, farmer, b. Ossipee, s/o Ephran K.
Knox (Ossipee); W - 21, housework, b. Tamworth, d/o William
Tewksbury (Tamworth)

KOCH,
Eugene B. of Wonalancet m. Deborah L. **Chappell** of Wonalancet
6/28/1980

KORPI,
Roger E. of Tamworth m. Susan A. **Alosa** of Tamworth 9/18/1982

KORSON,
Jay Henry of Chocorua m. Sabra Rogers **MacLeod** of Amherst
7/23/1988

KREBS,
Ernest A. of New Bedford, MA m. Susan E. **Sylvia** of New Bedford,
MA 7/6/1991

KRUPULA,
Arnie E. of Tamworth m. Shirley **Hattenburg** of Tamworth 3/31/1995

KUKURUZA,
Wayne R. of Tamworth m. Stephanie Joanne **James** of N. Conway
1/15/1977; H – 22; W – 18

KUMM,
Frederick Guinness of Tamworth m. Gillian **Galvin** of Melbourne,
Australia 7/25/1964 in Tamworth; H – 28, product. manager; W
– 27, secretary

LADD,
Joshua F. of Oceanside, CA m. Sky T. **Staples** of Tamworth
11/10/2001

LAFFIN,
Donald Roy of Tamworth m. Marie Vesta **Bryan** of Sweden, ME
2/22/1971; H – 62; W – 54

LALIBERTE,
David of Tamworth m. Diane **McNally** of Tamworth 7/15/1981

LAMBERT,
Arthur Alfred of Tamworth m. Ann **Farnum** of Tamworth 6/24/1972; H – 22; W – 19

LAMONT,
Corliss of New York, NY m. Beth **Fennell** of New York, NY 7/24/1986

LANDESMAN,
Jeffrey S. of Altadena, CA m. Laura E. **Wheeler** of Altadena, CA 7/17/1993

LANOU,
Gregory Peter of Portland, ME m. Tracy Elizabeth **Skillin** of Portland, ME 8/23/1997

LAPORTE,
David Earl of Brooklyn, NY m. Sharon Lee **Baybutt** of Brooklyn, NY 7/2/1995
Roc Lyne Emile of Troy m. Neurine Elaine **Wiggin** of Tamworth 6/8/1963 in Chocorua; H – 23, student; W – 21, student

LAROSE,
Joseph m. Mary **Stenson** 9/15/1933 in Tamworth

LARRABEE,
Alan Bruce of Tamworth m. Sandra Marie **Hutchins** of Tamworth 4/10/1965 in Center Ossipee; H – 27, mach. oper.; W – 22, secretary
Arnold Herbert of Tamworth m. Judith Rose **Weare** of Tamworth 11/3/1962 in Ctr. Ossipee; H – 23, assembly; W – 15, at home
Arnold Herbert of Tamworth m. Donna Lee **Hutchins** of Tamworth 10/1/1966; H – 27, caretaker; W – 19, housewife
Donald E. m. Joyce B. **Eldridge** 6/15/1954 in Ctr. Ossipee; H – 24, mill; W – 24, clerk
Keith A. of S. Tamworth m. Melanie **Palmer** of S. Tamworth 7/11/1992
Raymond m. Dorothy **Vittum** 6/13/1927 in Tamworth

LAUZON,
Peter D. of Chocorua m. Linda A. **Webster** of Chocorua 7/10/1993

LAVOIE,
Richard H. of Tamworth m. Angela L. **Clark** of Tamworth 8/14/1996

LAWRENCE,
George W. m. Velma L. **Cayes** 9/5/1953 in Laconia; H – 26, asst. mgr., Woolworth's; W – 22, office clerk

LEACH,
Lyle D. m. Eileen B. **Hutchins** 11/21/1936 in Conway
Thomas J. of Fryeburg, ME m. Jennifer L. **Tibbetts** of Fryeburg, ME 10/27/2001
William F. of Tamworth m. Alma C. **Jeffers** of Tamworth 12/25/1905 in Tamworth; H – 22, laborer, b. NY State, s/o Charles F. Leach and Fanny James; W – 19, at home, b. Warner, d/o Milton Jeffers (Webster) and Abbie Downs (Porter, ME)

LEBROKE,
Charles F., III of Jackson m. Gretchen **Behr** of Tamworth 10/16/1993

LEE,
Gordon J. of Cambridge, MA m. Susan M. **Fisher** of Cambridge, MA 6/16/1996

LEFEBVRE,
Jeffery J. of Denver, CO m. Alexandra J. **Bates** of Denver, CO 6/23/1998

LEMAY,
Michael R. of Tamworth m. Heather A. **Green** of Tamworth 10/10/1987

LEMIEUX,
Paul David of Medford, MA m. Lyn-Anne Marie **Barker** of Salem, MA 7/23/1995

LEP,
John A. of Tamworth m. Linda R. **Davis** of Tamworth 12/22/1982

LESSARD,
Pierre L. of Tamworth m. Julie L. **Larrabee** of Tamworth 2/23/1991

LESSER,
Edward R. of PA m. Emily J. **Bliss** of PA 9/4/1982

LEVESQUE,
Eric M. of Accomac, VA m. Alisa **Ordway** of Tamworth 8/15/1992

LEVINSON,
Mark A. of Tamworth m. Lorraine C. **Jacques** of Tamworth 7/11/1986

LEWIS,
Sheldon W. m. Helen R. **Thompson** 8/15/1931 in Center Harbor

LEWRY,
Willard H. of W. Baldwin, ME m. Audrey V. **Snow** of Portland, ME 8/17/1945 in Tamworth; H – 45, accountant; W – 34, at home

LIBBY,
Elson of Ossipee m. Lois F. **Sweet** of Tamworth 10/31/1942 in S. Tamworth; H – 20, shipfitter; W – 16, at home
Lawrence E. m. Mildred V. **Bower** 9/26/1953 in Ossipee; H – 28, mechanic; W – 19, at home
Lawrence H. m. Ardella M. **Keen** 3/2/1958 in Tamworth; H – 29, merchant; W – 26, at home
Paul G. of Tamworth m. April P. **Ryder** of W. Ossipee 7/26/1975; H – 21; W – 19
Paul G. of Tamworth m. Donna M. **Gallear** of Tamworth 8/23/1991
Paul Gordon of Tamworth m. Sharon L. **Buswell** of Tamworth 2/29/1972; H – 17; W – 19
Truman of Conway m. Constance M. **Hammond** of Tamworth 6/14/1941 in Tamworth; H – 21, carpenter; W – 16, student

LIBERTY,
James of Tamworth m. Maria **Bryer** of Sandwich 1/29/1896 in Tamworth; H - 58, farmer, b. Quebec, Canada, s/o Mitchel Liberty (Quebec, Canada, deceased) and Mary Liberty (Quebec, Canada, deceased); W - 50, housekeeper, b.

Rochester, d/o Charles Hartford (Rochester, deceased) and Ruth Trickey (Rochester, housekeeping)

LINTON,
Ralph B. of Tamworth m. Dorothy E. **Hoitt** of Manchester 8/15/1945 in Manchester; H – 44, principle (sic); W – 39, school teacher

LIONETTA,
Scott Michael of S. Tamworth m. Susan Lynne **Lefevre** of S. Tamworth 5/20/1995

LIPMEN,
Philip A. of Cambridge, MA m. Pamela K. **Sutherland** of Cambridge, MA 9/19/1987

LITTLEFIELD,
Dana O. of Tamworth m. Joy Abigail **Hamlin** of Tamworth 8/21/1999
Eugene H. m. Gladys F. **Drew** 8/2/1920 in Bartlett; H – 21, laborer, b. Jackson, s/o Fred E. Littlefield and Emma P. Hodge; W – 21, housekeeper, 2nd, b. Moultonboro, d/o William J. Clark and Lizzie A. Wade
Norman F. H., Jr. of Tamworth m. Tricia B. **Bailey** of Moultonboro 9/5/1998
Orace R. m. Beatrice M. **Johnson** 12/17/1936 in Moultonboro
Paul A. m. Marjorie **Cook** 11/2/1957 in Tamworth; H – 29, lumber; W – 15, at home

LLOYD,
Bruce of Tamworth m. Dale **Bragdon** of Tamworth 10/14/1989
Jeffrey R. of Tamworth m. Cheryl L. **Rhines** of Center Ossipee 6/16/1984

LOCK,
Frank m. Etta **Perkins** 7/28/1928 in Tamworth

LOIKA,
Fred of Maynard, MA m. Delphine **Campbell** of Maynard, MA 9/20/1964 in Tamworth; H – 45, funeral director; W – 42, funeral director

LORD,
John G. of Wolfeboro m. Kay E. **Davis** of Chocorua 6/28/1986
Merton G. m. Dorothy M. **Pike** 1/9/1937 in Tamworth

LORING,
David H. of Chocorua m. Kathlyn L. **Van Frost** of Chocorua 6/28/1986
Stephen G. of Columbia, SC m. Joan M. **Gero** of Columbia, SC 10/26/1985

LOUD,
Clarence B. m. Marilyn J. **Whipple** 12/29/1956 in Ossipee; H – 27, mill worker; W – 23, nurse
Edward D. of Ctr. Ossipee m. Ruth G. **Hilton** of Tamworth 4/17/1943 in Moultonboro; H – 27, journalist; W – 20, housework

LOVELL,
David Eric of Hampton m. Shirley Lorraine **Swale** of Tamworth 12/12/1972; H – 27; W – 33

LOVETT,
Paul M. of VA m. Katherine E. **Mayer** of VA 10/8/1977; H – 28; W – 22

LOWD,
Bernard m. Marion **Elliott** 7/3/1930 in Ossipee
Lindel F. m. Stella R. **Lowd** 10/1/1953 in Tamworth; H – 35, laborer; W – 29, at home

LOWRIE,
John P. of New York, NY m. Ellen L. **McLain** of New York, NY 12/21/1986

LOZEAU,
Roger P. of Chocorua m. Charlotte E. **Perry** of Chocorua 10/12/2002

LUKINGHAMMER,
Dale A. of Englewood, CO m. Jo A. **Jughes** of Englewood, CO 7/28/1985

LURIE,
Michael D. of Cambridge, MA m. Anne G. **Lloyd** of Cambridge, MA 8/24/1985

LYMAN,
Brian Patrick of Madison m. Eleanor Amanda **Elliott** of Chocorua 6/14/1964 in Madison; H – 23, plumber; W – 19, secretary

LYSCARS,
Alan Stanley of MA m. Margaret Folsom **Cleveland** of MA 8/27/1988

MACCURTAIN,
Gerald T. of Roslindale, MA m. Catherine A. **Fallon** of Roslindale, MA 10/8/1983

MACDONALD,
Forrest G. of Tamworth m. Barbara H. **MacDonald** of Tamworth 12/28/1980
Forrest G., Jr. of Tamworth m. Pamela Jane **Atwood** of S. Tamworth 7/20/1973; H – 19; W – 21

MACK,
Jeffrey R. of IL m. Candy L. **Gee** of IL 6/21/1980

MACKWELL,
Stephen J. of State College, PA m. Christine A. **White** of State College, PA 1/29/1990

MACOMBER,
Harry T. of Tamworth m. Marie B. **Varney** of Tamworth 5/14/1994
Harvey W. m. Audrey F. **Carr** 11/2/1959 in N. Conway; H – 27, salesman; W – 38, housewife
Harvey W. of Tamworth m. Alice D. **Carr** of Concord 6/22/1962 in Bartlett; H – 30, carpenter; W – 21, secretary

MACY,
Donald R. m. A. Edith **Albrecht** 7/20/1955 in Tamworth; H – 33, salesman; W – 34, telephone operator

MADUSKUIE,
Edward S. of Tamworth m. Christine F. **Bennett** of Wrentham, MA 7/13/1975; H – 19; W – 28
Edward S. of Chocorua m. Marletta D. **Benoit** of Chocorua 8/25/2001

MALENFANT,
Jeffrey John of Chocorua m. Sharon Ann **Sapar** of Chocorua 12/10/1988

MALLAR,
John L. m. Dorothy A. **Hammond** 7/29/1961 in Tamworth; H – 24, student; W – 23, statistical analysis

MANN,
William W., Jr. of N. Reading, MA m. Susan R. **Maurer** of Stoneham, MA 5/21/1983

MANNA,
Charles Robert of Beacon, NY m. Elizabeth Quincy **Weisner** of Tamworth 8/20/1974; H – 29; W - 22

MARION,
Jon G. of Portland, ME m. Patricia E. **Grace** of Tamworth 10/21/1972; H – 29; W - 21

MARSH,
Michael S. of Tamworth m. Michelle L. **Naylor** of Tamworth 7/19/1986
Stephen Winthrop of Tamworth m. Dorothy L. **Hall** of Belmont, MA 3/23/1968; H – 73; W – 59

MARSHALL,
George L., Jr. m. Ruth D. **Page** 12/27/1916 in Tamworth; H – 24, carpenter, b. Somerville, MA, s/o George L. Marshall and Annie L. Whitman; W – 22, b. Tamworth, d/o Horace A. Page and Bertha E. Howard
John Lee of S. Tamworth m. Cynthia Lou **Frye** of Moultonboro 6/23/1972; H – 24; W – 20

MARTEL,
Morton C. m. Violet D. **Speckman** 10/6/1956 in Moultonboro; H – 28, mechanic; W – 24, nurse

MARTIN,
David L. of PA m. Katherine E. **Mills** of Tamworth 4/24/1982
Louville K. of Tamworth m. Helen **Weed** of Sandwich 9/12/1940 in Moultonboro; H – 37, caretaker; W – 27, teacher

MARTINEAU,
Jason A. N. of Tamworth m. Elizabeth E. **Willis** of Tamworth 9/29/1979

MASON,
Arthur H. of Tamworth m. Ruth E. **Philbrick** of Laconia 10/26/1946 in Laconia; H – 18, machine operator; W – 19, clerk
Arthur Horace, III of S. Tamworth m. Bonnie Bea **Conway** of Lincoln 10/27/1973; H – 26; W – 22
Arthur L. of Tamworth m. Lizzie C. **Chick** of Tamworth 11/17/1900 in Madison; H – 16, laborer, s/o Alphonzo Mason (Tamworth) and Emma J. Floyd (Porter, ME); W – 17, housework, d/o Charles F. Chick (Lewiston, ME) and Elvira Durrell (Tamworth)
Chester L. m. Mabel G. **McPhearson** 1/9/1915 in Sandwich; H – 20, carpenter, b. Tamworth, s/o Luwellen G. Mason and Minnie M. Kenney; W – 22, housework, b. Milton, MA, d/o Roderic J. McPhearson
Ernest of Tamworth m. Leafy **Downs** of Tamworth 11/11/1893 in Tamworth; H - 23, millman, b. Tamworth, s/o John G. Mason (Tamworth) and Lucetta Hayford (Tamworth); W - 18, housekeeping, b. Tamworth, d/o Joseph Downs (Brownfield, ME) and Shua Rounds (Brownfield, ME)
Ernest S. of Tamworth m. Clara M. **Frost** of Tamworth 11/27/1902; H – 34, laborer, b. Winchester, MA, s/o Hiram Mason (Albany) and Angie Head (Madison); W – 32, housework, b. Madison, d/o George Frost and Mary Mason
George W. of Albany m. Louise **Locklin** of Tamworth 3/25/1900 in Tamworth; H – 21, laborer, s/o Elijah Mason (Albany) and Lizzie Frost (Albany); W – 20, housework, d/o Roscoe Green (Madison) and Abbie Hardy (Tamworth)
Harry O. of Tamworth m. Clara E. **Downs** of Tamworth 9/9/1893 in Tamworth; H - 22, laborer, b. Tamworth, s/o William Mason

(Tamworth) and Emily J. Osgood (Tamworth); W - 16, housekeeping, b. Tamworth, d/o Elias Downs (Porter, ME) and Sabra Rounds (Porter, ME)

Hiram E. m. Edna A. **Cummings** 6/14/1921 in Ossipee; H – 25, chauffeur, b. Tamworth, s/o Ernest S. Mason and Mabel Henderson; W – 25, post mistress, b. Woburn, MA, d/o Ansel Cummings and Blanche Brown

Horace m. Blanche **Ames** 1/31/1919 in Rochester; H – 18, box fitter, s/o Arthur Mason and Elizabeth Chick; W – 19, housework, d/o Zimri Ames and Ella Palmer

Llewellyn G. of Tamworth m. Minnie M. **Canney** of Sandwich 4/8/1893 in Tamworth; H - 24, millman, b. Tamworth, s/o William Mason (Tamworth) and Emily J. Osgood (Tamworth); W - 19, housekeeping, b. Sandwich, d/o John Canney (Tuftonboro) and Alice McPenniman (Sandwich)

Preston H. of Tamworth m. Julie L. **Larrabee** of Tamworth 11/26/1994

Richard R. of Tamworth m. Pauline V. **Hutchins** of Wolfeboro 4/15/1946 in Wolfeboro; H – 20, laborer; W – 18, at home

MASSE,
Wayne N. of Damvers, MA m. Marcia M. **Wilins** of Danvers, MA 6/20/1987

MATE,
John E. of New York, NY m. Linda J. **Pearson** of Philadelphia, PA 9/30/1978; H – 55; W – 31

MATHER,
Anthony C. of Tamworth m. Beverley A. **Clark** of Tamworth 2/16/1962 in Tamworth; H – 22, Navy; W – 19, clerk

MATSUO,
Akira Christoph of Zushi-shi, Japan m. Sarai E. **Lyon** of Tamworth 12/27/2000

MAUCH,
Matthew Eric of Sandwich m. Alison Marie **Bernard** of Tamworth 6/25/1988

MAURA,
Edward L. of Tamworth m. Teresa L. **Welch** of Tamworth 8/25/1990

MAURAN,
William L., Jr. m. Grace E. **Amundson** 8/18/1956 in Tamworth; H – 45, physician; W – 39, writer

MAYBERRY,
Conrad of Maynard, MA m. Irene F. **Malcolm** of Maynard, MA 8/10/1969; H – 55; W – 51

MAYER,
Richard A. of Hadley, MA m. Joan A. **Spalding** of Hadley, MA 6/30/1984
William S. of New York m. Elizabeth G. **Pratt** of Tamworth 7/17/1950 in Tamworth; H – 25, US Navy; W – 25, at home

McAULIFFE,
William P., Jr. of Norwood, MA m. Deborah Joy **Brett** of Brookline, MA 8/17/1974; H – 32; W – 25

McBEE,
William Hunter of MD m. Julia Marie **Newcomb** of MD 8/27/1988

McCARTHY,
Francis of W. Springfield, MA m. Barbara **Belanger** of W. Springfield, MA 4/5/1975; H – 28; W – 19
Kevin Joseph of Tamworth m. Angela Joan **Boewe** of Tamworth 3/15/1975; H – 21; W – 17
Sean M. of Tamworth m. Paula J. **Schaffer** of Tamworth 9/12/1987
Thomas Mark of Locust Valley, NY m. Lori Marie **Tapfar** of Locust Valley, NY 7/22/1995
William J. of Tamworth m. Ruth M. **Asselin** of Tamworth 6/6/1987
William J., III of Tamworth m. Margaret L. **Loughran** of Tamworth 9/24/1994

McCONARTY,
Stephen R. of Ctr. Ossipee m. Marie D. **Bisenti** of Ctr. Ossipee 6/18/2002

McCORMACK,
George Edwin of N. Sandwich m. Jean Marie **Taylor** of Tamworth
6/27/1975; H – 29; W – 30

McDONALD,
Forrest G. of Ctr. Ossipee m. Barbara M. **Hobbs** of Tamworth
4/7/1951 in Tamworth; H – 19, agriculture; W – 18,
housekeeper
John m. Blanche Evelyn **Bunker** 1/1/1920 in Ossipee; H – 28,
teamster, b. NS, s/o John McDonald and Mary Short; W – 23,
housework, b. Tamworth, d/o Levi Bunker and Hattie Webber
Peter Franklin of Chocorua m. Valerie **Nickerson-Allen** of Chocorua
6/5/1999

McGILL,
Robert T. of Tamworth m. Karen L. **Bergeron** of Tamworth
3/14/1987

McGRATH,
Brian J., Jr. of Fryeburg, ME m. Denise M. **DuBois** of Tamworth
6/29/1996

McHOSE,
Robert E. of Hiram, ME m. Cecilia R. **Betzen** of Hiram, ME
9/21/1985

McLENDON,
Eric of Tamworth m. Stephanie J. **Dahl** of Tamworth 10/5/1996

McNULTY,
Michael C. of Tamworth m. Diane J. **Lawrence** of Tamworth
7/27/1985

McNEAL,
Harry of Tamworth m. Martha E. **Perkins** of Tamworth 4/18/1887 in
Tamworth; H - 27, farmer, b. St. John, NB; W - 27, b.
Tamworth, d/o Lorenzo Perkins and Sarah

McQUERRIE,
David A. of Salem, MA m. Wendy L. **Saunders** of Salem, MA
8/11/1992

MEADER,
Donald Norman of Center Ossipee m. Barbara Gladys **Staples** of Tamworth 8/24/1963 in Tamworth; H – 21, salesman; W – 19, student

MELANSON,
Joseph I. m. Cynthia J. **Whipple** 10/20/1956 in Tamworth; H – 21, builder; W – 20, beautician
Roy m. Lena **Arsenault** 10/24/1934 in Tamworth
Wayne A. of Tamworth m. Rosemary E. **Woolsey** of Tamworth 7/13/1991

MERCHANT,
Michael J. of Salisbury m. Rene **Streeter** of Tamworth 5/5/1984

MERCIER,
George R. of MA m. Carol A. **Mercier** of MA 12/2/1988

MERRIAM,
Harry A. m. Nellie **Wiggin** of Tamworth 10/10/1905 in Lawrence, MA; H – 23, machinist, b. Lawrence, MA, s/o Fred O. Merriam and Caroline O. Merriam; W – 17, none, b. Tamworth, d/o Hardress L. Wiggin (Tamworth) and Emma R. Floyd (Eaton)

MERRILL,
Richard Forest of S. Tamworth m. Rhonda Lee **Varney** of Ctr. Ossipee 5/1/1988

MERRITHEW,
Scott Edward of Tamworth m. Margaret Ellen **Brothers** of Tamworth 2/20/1999

MERRITT,
Stephen F. of Tamworth m. Debra A. **Doane** of Wilmington, MA 11/11/1984

MERROW,
Lyford Ambrose of Chocorua m. Judith Wyman **Polley** of Loudon 9/22/1974; H – 45; W - 44

MESSER,
Clinton F. of Peabody, MA m. Emma E. **Finerty** of Hamilton, MA 10/17/1908 in Tamworth; H – 27, salesman, b. Peabody, MA, s/o George C. Messer (Peabody, MA) and Margaret E. Pierce (Peabody, MA); W – 25, b. Hamilton, MA, d/o Otis Ingalls (Lynn, MA) and Laura E. Tucker (Concord)

METZGER,
John J. of Penfield, NY m. Rebecca W. **Hall** of Penfield, NY 5/12/1973; H – 24; W – 25

MICHAUD,
Alfred W. of Manchester m. Doris M. **Plummer** of Tamworth 5/27/1966; H – 33, truck driver; W – 34, packer

MICHIE,
Alan K. of Tamworth m. Carol E. **Ochs** of Tamworth 9/8/1990

MILLETTE,
David E. of Tamworth m. Deanna L. **Smith** of Tamworth 5/2/1986

MILLS,
Ernest M. of Tamworth m. Greta A. **Salathe** of S. Sutton 4/28/1990
Gerald of New Durham m. Lois Elaine **Barnes** of Farmington 7/17/1964 in Tamworth; H – 29, shoe cutter; W – 23, at home
Henry of Tamworth m. Rena **Richards** of Swansea 5/3/1952 in Swansea; H – 67, builder; W – 63, housekeeper

MILNE,
Alan C. of Tamworth m. Mary H. **Hunham** of Tamworth 9/10/1985

MOCK,
Wayne Kenneth of Tamworth m. Anne Margaret **Spalding** of Tamworth 10/10/1975; H – 31; W – 30

MOLLOY,
Michael Karl of CA m. Nano **Bliss** of Tamworth 9/4/1977; H – 28; W – 26

MONAHAN,
Daniel G. of Medford, MA m. Heather G. **Woodcock** of Medford, MA 5/29/1993

MONFET,
Michael Edward of Ctr. Ossipee m. Melissa Lee **Woodward** of Ctr. Ossipee 8/21/1999

MOODY,
Charles A. m. Gloria J. **Macus** 9/18/1955 in Tamworth; H – 20, USAF; W – 19, auditor

Elmer P. m. Margaret **McBride** 11/8/1921 in Meredith; H – 24, mill man, b. Albany, NY, s/o William N. Moody and Mabel G. Moore; W – 18, none, b. Boston, MA, d/o Mary A. McBride

Ernest A. m. Vivian **Hobbs** 11/14/1914 in Tamworth; H – 27, teamster, b. Tamworth, s/o Edwin Moody and Isibel Smith; W – 18, housework, b. Ossipee, d/o Wentworth Hobbs

George m. Elizabeth S. **Hobbs** 1/22/1931 in Tamworth

Joseph A. of Tamworth m. Nettie **Williams** of Tamworth 9/2/1908 in Tamworth; H – 20, laborer, b. Tamworth, s/o Levi W. Moody (Tamworth) and Mary J. Davis; W – 17, waitress, b. Ossipee, d/o W. H. Williams (Ossipee) and Susie Welch (Ossipee)

Lester E. of Tamworth m. Mary E. **Corcoran** of Boston, MA 12/3/1907 in Brookline, MA; H – 24, farmer, b. Ossipee, s/o Irene Moody (Ossipee); W – 34, cook, b. Portland, ME, d/o James Corcoran (PEI) and Mary E. Sheehan (PEI)

Merton E. m. Evelyn R. **Mudgett** 6/29/1929 in Moultonboro

Nathaniel E. of Tamworth m. Nancy M. **Pascoe** of Freedom 8/17/1900 in Tamworth; H – 21, laborer, s/o George H. Moody (Tamworth) and Mary Hobbs (Ossipee); W – 18, housework, d/o Harry Pascoe

Robert Paul of Tamworth m. Helen A. **Thorner** of Tamworth 8/26/1995

William Brooks Blaisdell of Newport. RI m. Susan **Bowditch** of Boston, MA 9/17/1966; H – 29, US Navy; W – 28, teacher

William H. of Tamworth m. Idella E. **Clough** of Tamworth 6/8/1889 in Tamworth I.W.; H - 23, farmer, b. Tamworth, s/o George H. Moody (Tamworth); W – 17, housework, b. Tamworth, d/o William B. Clough (Tamworth)

William H. of Tamworth m. Mattie D. **Eldridge** of Tamworth 8/15/1909 in Tamworth; H – 43, farmer, b. Tamworth, s/o

George H. Moody (Tamworth, farmer) and Mary Hobbs (Ossipee, housewife); W – 33, housework, b. Ossipee, d/o Isaac Buzwell (Ossipee, farmer) and Mary J. Gilman (Ossipee, housewife)

MOONEY,
Edward F., Jr. of Salem, MA m. Laurie A. **Baker** of Salem, MA 5/5/1979
Paul W. of Chocorua m. Marie A. **Guerrera** of Seabrook Beach 4/12/1979
Paul W. of Danvers, MA m. Brenda Susan **Stoney** of Danvers, MA 8/12/1989

MOORE,
Frank F. m. Minnie E. **Allard** 5/29/1918 in Tamworth; H – 28, RR trackman, b. Tamworth, s/o Edgar Moore and Mary Kenerson; W – 18, b. Eaton, d/o Lorenzo Allard and Annie C. Smith
Fred L. of Tamworth m. Edith R. **Gilman** of Tamworth 1/19/1903; H – 42, merchant, b. ME, s/o William H. Moore (Meriden, ME) and Katherine Campbell (Princeton, ME); W – 33, b. Tamworth, d/o David H. Gilman (Madison) and Mary J. Hutchins (England)
George A. m. Annie **Bennett** 6/24/1933 in Tamworth
Kenneth K. m. Mildred **Nutt** 12/2/1933 in Tamworth
Richard D. m. Eva Ella **Shedd** 12/25/1919 in Tamworth; H – 26, laborer, s/o Edgar H. Moore and Mary Kenerson; W – 23, d/o Albert L. Shedd and Ella Chase
Robert F. of Tamworth m. Ella M. **DeWitt** of Conway 10/1/1967; H – 38, road work; W – 45, store clerk
Ronald K. of Tamworth m. Julie A. **Leach** of Conway 9/26/1982
Ronald Kenneth of Tamworth m. Heidi J. **Cote** of Tamworth 8/20/2000
Samuel J. of Tamworth m. Minnie A. **Marston** of Tamworth 12/9/1905 in Tamworth; H – 27, laborer, b. Conway, s/o John H. Moore (Springvale, ME) and Anna Littlefield (Albany); W – 18, housekeeping, b. Tamworth, d/o John F. Marston (Tamworth) and Carrie E. Remick (Tamworth)
William E. of Tamworth m. Alice M. **Ross** of Tamworth 6/4/1913; in Tamworth; H – 25, laborer, b. Tamworth, s/o Edgar H. Moore and Mary A. Kenerson; W – 21, housework, b. Tamworth, d/o Mark S. Ross and Emma A. Harriman

MOOT,
Alexander W. of Cambridge, MA m. Nancy E. **Roosa** of Cambridge, MA 9/7/1991

MORGAN,
Christopher of Tamworth m. Suzanne V. **Balomenos** of Tamworth 6/28/1980
Donald G. of Hartford, CT m. Margaret E. **Prince** of Lake Forest, IL 8/29/1942 in Tamworth; H – 31, college teacher; W – 29, social worker
Edward Prince of PA m. Mary Lou **Hatcher** of PA 10/15/1988
Shawn Kerry of Sussex, WI m. Mary Ann **Lemke** of Sussex, WI 10/7/1995

MORRILL,
Arthur E. of Rochester m. Olive M. **Sweet** of Tamworth 3/27/1943 in Tamworth; H – 22, factory worker; W – 21, factory worker
Richard A. of Lynn, MA m. Kathleen R. **Davis** of Tamworth 10/30/1983
Timothy W. of Tamworth m. Cynthia A. **Stone** of Tamworth 11/26/1977; H – 28; W – 24

MORSE,
Stephen of Tamworth m. Gina M. **DiMaio** of Tamworth 10/5/2002

MORTON,
Edmund J. of S. Tamworth m. Donna L. **Foisy** of S. Tamworth 6/28/1980

MOSHER,
James R. of Tamworth m. Deborah A. **Anthony** of Tamworth 5/30/1979
Myles W. of RI m. Marcelle M. **Hamelin** of Canada 7/5/1988

MOULTON,
Burleigh I. m. Helen A. **Ames** 2/28/1953 in Center Harbor; H – 34, lumbering; W – 37, at home
Chester A. of Tamworth m. Katie F. **Drohan** of Cambridge, MA 10/4/1908 in Conway; H – 26, laborer, b. Tamworth, s/o Alonzo Moulton (Albany) and L. B. Kennerson (Albany); W – 27,

housework, b. MA, d/o David Drohan (Ireland) and Katherine Doohan (Ireland)
James E. of Ossipee m. Maude L. **Adjutant** of Tamworth 11/10/1941 in Ossipee; H – 22, woodsman; W – 28, housework
Luman J. of Tamworth m. Carrie **Davis** of Tamworth 10/27/1887 in Lovell, ME; H - 24, laborer, b. Madison, s/o Alonzo Moulton (Tamworth, farmer); W - 16, housework, b. Tamworth, d/o William Davis (Tamworth, laborer) and Mary
Robert E. of Tamworth m. Muriel E. **Canney** of Tamworth 7/27/1947 in Tamworth; H – 22, machinist; W – 19, stenographer
Willis of Tamworth m. Lydia E. **Allard** of Tamworth 7/19/1897 in Tamworth; H – 28, farmer, b. Sandwich, s/o Frank P. Moulton (Sandwich) and Annette Quimby (Sandwich); W – 31, dressmaker, b. Newark, VT, d/o Benjamin H. Allard (Albany) and Eliza Allard (Brownfield, ME)

MUDGETT,
James R. of Tamworth m. Cynthia A. **Jones** of Tamworth 3/7/1987
James Roger, Jr. of Moultonboro m. Ann J. **Jennings** of Tamworth 9/28/1974; H – 24; W - 26

MURDOCK,
David W. of Greenwich, CT m. Mary P. **Foster** of New York City, NY 8/17/1940 in Tamworth; H – 28, chef; W – 19, chambermaid

MURPHY,
Ryan P. of Tamworth m. Heidi L. **Fortier** of Tamworth 8/9/2002

NARODE,
Ronald B. of S. Deerfield, MA m. Sarah G. **Cleveland** of S. Deerfield, MA 7/5/1986

NARWICZ,
Charles, Jr. of Arnold, MD m. Lee P. **Glaws** of Betheda, MD 8/18/1979

NASIF,
Harry M. of W. Roxbury, MA m. Easter A. **Dugan** of Brookline, MA 5/10/1939 in Whittier; H – 33, insurance; W – 24, nurse

NATION,
Barry Lee of Center Barnstead m. Rosalind H. **Moody** of Rochester 5/23/1970; H – 26; W – 21

NEDEAU,
Frank E. of New Sharon, ME m. Edith C. **Russell** of New Sharon, ME 10/26/1940 in Tamworth; H – 22, laborer; W – 18, at home

NELSON,
John m. Lillian **Walker** 3/14/1930 in Tamworth
Peter of Ossipee m. Deborah **Stewart** of Tamworth 9/19/1981
Robert W. of Chocorua m. Kelly A. **Maiato** of Chocorua 10/3/1992

NESPECA,
Mark P. of Washington, DC m. Danielle L. **Weymouth** of Wonalancet 6/8/1974

NEVELLS,
Stanley Richard of Bridgeton, ME m. Virginia Jean **Anthony** of Tamworth 9/1/1968; H – 26; W – 19

NEVINS,
Richard P. of Simsbury, CT m. Nancy G. **Avallone** of Bristol, CT 8/9/1997

NEWCOMB,
Andrew N. of Chocorua m. Veranika Y. **Rainik** of MA 8/7/2003

NEWSOM,
Samuel, Jr. of California m. Sylvia C. **Bowditch** of California 7/19/1949 in Tamworth; H – 50, landscape artist; W – 38, technician
Samuel B. of Tamworth m. Rebecca L. **Colcord** of Tamworth 7/8/1978; H – 23; W – 22

NICHOLS,
John E. of W. Ossipee m. Beverly L. **Olson** of W. Ossipee 8/2/1969; H – 39; W – 33
Stephen P. of Tamworth m. Kim **Klitgaard** of Tamworth 5/18/1996

NICKERSON,
Archie of Tamworth m. Irma J. **White** of Ossipee 8/27/1896 in Tamworth; H - 31, farmer, b. Tamworth, s/o Alonzo Nickerson (Tamworth, clergyman) and Melina Ham (Albany, housekeeping); W - 33, teacher, b. Ossipee, d/o Josiah G. White (Tamworth, deceased) and Hannah M. Devnell (Dover, housekeeping)

David W. of Tamworth m. Nancy J. **Bean** of Tamworth 7/3/1983

Ezra of Tamworth m. Emma M. **Perkins** of Tamworth 4/20/1890 in Tamworth; H - 20, millman, b. Tamworth, s/o Alonzo Nickerson (Tamworth); W - 20, teacher, b. Tamworth, d/o Lorenzo Perkins (Tamworth)

George E. of Tamworth m. Carrie B. **White** of Madison 6/20/1894 in Tamworth; H - 25, farmer, b. Tamworth, s/o Joseph R. Nickerson (Albany, farmer) and Sarah P. Marston (Sandwich, housekeeping); W - 22, at home, b. Madison, d/o David White (Madison, farmer) and Maria Gannett (Tamworth, housekeeping)

George R., Pfc., of Tamworth m. Lorena L. **Higgins** of Madison 9/1/1944 in Madison; H – 27, US Army; W – 27, at home

Lawrence E. of Tamworth m. Geraldine **Pascoe** of Ossipee 9/5/1943 in Tamworth; H – 24, shipbuilder; W – 18, clerk

Lawrence G. of Chocorua m. Susan **Mitchko** of Chocorua 9/24/1983

Wendell A. of Tamworth m. Blanche L. **Templeton** of Ossipee 10/5/1940 in Wolfeboro; H – 28, wood worker; W – 22, nurse

NIGHTINGALE,
Charles m. Ethel A. **Parmelee** 8/6/1921 in Chocorua; H – 45, salesman, b. NY, s/o Jerome Nightingale and Louise Whitney; W – 36, stenographer, b. NY, d/o Elias Redfield and ----- Parmelle

NISWANDER,
G. Donald of Boston, MA m. Patricia **Damon** of Tamworth 5/31/1952 in Tamworth; H – 27, medical doctor; W – 26, occupational therapy

NIXON,
Dean W. of Tamworth m. Norrine L. **Tefft** of Concord 9/10/1977; H – 28; W – 30

Michael J. of Tamworth m. Lee-Anne **McCue** of Tamworth 6/14/2003

William D. of Sandwich m. Bertha L. **Marshall** of Tamworth 6/22/1941 in Tamworth; H – 22, machinist; W – 22, bookkeeper

NORCROSS,

Andy L. of S. Tamworth m. Ann Marie **Cash** of S. Tamworth 2/10/1991

Arthur Z. m. Irene M. **Ames** 7/15/1956 in Center Ossipee; H – 19, millman; W – 18, clerk

Barry Lee of Tamworth m. Dorian Mary **LaPlante** of W. Ossipee 4/1/1989

Charles D. of Tamworth m. Faye V. **Mudgett** of Sandwich 1/27/1962 in Center Ossipee; H – 18, lumber mill; W – 17, student

Gardner L. of Tamworth m. Susan M. **Davidson** of Conway 10/6/1984

Justin M. of Richfield, MN m. Jennifer A. **Marton** of Richfield, MN 10/5/2001

Peter Frederick of Tamworth m. Solange Frances **Dubois** of Jefferson 5/29/1965 in Lancaster; H – 19, tow motor oper.; W – 18, stitcher

Thomas E. of Tamworth m. Patricia L. **Sheppard** of Tamworth 6/15/1985

NOURSE,

Christopher F. of Tamworth m. Kathleen C. **Curtin** of Tamworth 5/18/1985

NOYES,

Judson A. of Tamworth m. Tracey L. **Anthony** of Tamworth 5/8/1993

Wendell W. of Tamworth m. Kim E. **Cote** of Tamworth 10/12/1985

NUTTER,

John B. of Sandwich m. Gladys **Bickford** of Tamworth 6/3/1912 in Tamworth; H – 21, chauffeur, b. Sandwich, s/o Benjamin Nutter (Sandwich) and Effie Abbott (Holderness); W – 19, waitress, b. Tamworth, d/o Silas Bickford (Sandwich) and Nellie Brown (Sandwich)

NYSTEDT,
Paul A. m. Nema T. **Hill** 9/28/1957 in Tamworth; H – 56, minister; W – 49, secretary

O'KEEFE,
James Robert of Tamworth m. Tammy Lin **Barnes** of Tamworth 7/4/1997

O'LEARY,
Joseph M. of Holbrook, MA m. Lorraine M. **Weeks** of Rockland, MA 8/28/1993
Paul J. of Beverly, MA m. Kelly A. **Donahue-Berns** of Peabody, MA 8/7/1995

O'NEIL,
John H., Jr. of NY m. Nina **Gomes** of NY 8/23/1980

O'SHAUGNESSY,
James J. of Tamworth m. Marjorie M. **Richardson** of Center Harbor 2/15/1969; H – 35; W – 25

OBERTING,
Paul Mark of Chocorua m. Jennifer Leigh **Bergeron** of Chocorua 11/11/1995

OKTAVEC,
Michael John of Tamworth m. Justine E. **Pitula** of Manchester 10/1/1988

OLKKOLA,
Justin P. of Tamworth m. Sarah J. **Knox** of Tamworth 7/28/2001
Robert Patrick of Chicago, IL m. Susanne Charlotte **Fritzsche** of Chicago, IL 6/24/1989

OLSON,
David Carl of Tamworth m. Sally Ann **Fortier** of Tamworth 3/26/1966; H – 25, grocer; W – 18, student

OSBORN,
Frank E. of Franklin, MA m. Gertrude E. **Meader** of Tamworth 9/12/1908 in Tamworth; H – 36, merchant, b. Upton, MA, s/o J.

A. P. Osborn (Gorham, ME) and Abbie Whiting (Buxton, ME); W – 38, teacher, b. Tamworth, d/o Otis Meader (Sandwich) and Elizabeth G. Hoag (Sandwich)

OSGOOD,
Herman L. of Tamworth m. Ellen I. **Freeman** of Tamworth 2/13/1892 in Tamworth; H - 25, painter, b. Tamworth, s/o Samuel A. Osgood (Tamworth) and Lydia D. Welch; W - 30, housework, b. Worcester, MA, d/o George E. Freeman (Portland, ME) and Lucetta D. Hatch (Puttson, ME)

OUELLETTE,
Robert C. of Tamworth m. Karen L. **Wilson** of Tamworth 4/24/1993

OWENS,
Edward J. m. Marie E. **Bickford** 7/22/1961 in Tamworth; H – 20, woodheel mill; W – 16, student

PAGE,
Arthur C. of Gilmanton m. Mary A. **Remick** of Tamworth 10/17/1897 in Tamworth; H – 30, blacksmith, b. Gilmanton, s/o Dixie C. Page (Gilmanton) and Cyrena Webster (Gilmanton); W – 19, b. Tamworth, d/o A. D. Remick (Tamworth) and Ann J. Hurd (Gilmanton)

Edgar P. of Tamworth m. Grace A. **Davis** of Tamworth 8/30/1898 in Tamworth; H – 18, laborer, b. Lynn, s/o Moses A. Page (Tamworth) and Elizabeth Robinson; W – 18, housework, b. Tamworth, d/o William H. Davis (Effingham) and Mary Mooney (Nashua)

Edgar Perry m. Agnes May **Goodwin** 5/24/1914 in Tamworth; H – 34, milkman, 2nd, b. Lynn, MA, s/o Moses P. Page and Elizabeth Robinson; W – 28, housework, b. Tamworth, d/o J. C. Goodwin and Emma Bean

Howard Franklin m. Eva L. **Pollard** 5/18/1918 in Ossipee; H – 28, clerk, b. Tamworth, s/o Horace A. Page and Bertha Howard; W – 53, merchant, 2nd, b. New Albany, NS, d/o Asaph Whitman and Jane Payson

Oliver E. of Tamworth m. Winona H. **Clemons** of Bartlett 4/24/1948 in Tamworth; H – 49, mason; W – 40, peg mill worker

PALMA,
John m. Evelyn **Francis** 5/25/1957 in Tamworth; H – 40, auto mechanic; W – 28, shoe stitcher

PALMER,
Clarence E. m. Dorothy L. **Jordan** 5/21/1954 in Ctr. Ossipee; H – 20, sprayer; W – 21, sprayer
Daniel Richard of S. Tamworth m. Sacha Miai **Eldridge** of S. Tamworth 9/16/1989
Daniel Richard of Tamworth m. Lori Lynn **Wickham** of Tamworth 6/27/1998
Harland C. of Tamworth m. June E. **Holbrook** of Ctr. Ossipee 6/27/1942 in Tamworth; H – 19, woodsman; W – 16, at home
Herbert m. Gladys **Eldridge** 5/7/1921 in W. Ossipee; H – 20, farmer, b. Sandwich, s/o Herbert Palmer and Annie Tappin; W – 17, at home, b. Ossipee, d/o Plummer Eldridge and Emma Welch
Herbert E. m. Addia **Grace** 10/28/1930 in Tamworth
Michael J. of Tamworth m. Heidi **Clarke** of Tamworth 9/12/1998
Richard W. of Tamworth m. Evelyn G. **Hill** of Tamworth 10/20/1985

PARKER,
Bruce Wesley of Madison m. Sandra Lee **Walker** of Tamworth 6/19/1962 in Madison; H – 19, student; W – 21, housewife

PARKIN,
George P. m. Arlene M. **Davis** 8/22/1954 in Tamworth; H – 23, US Air Force; W – 19, at home

PARKS,
Edward Lee of Methuen, MA m. Elva E. **Anthony** of Tamworth 7/6/1968; H – 26; W – 24
Jeffrey C. of Meredith m. Alesia J. **Saujon** of Tamworth 7/27/1985
Robert L. of VA m. Pamela I. **Homeyer** of Chocorua 6/26/1982

PARRIS,
LeRoy A. of Sandwich m. Myrtle G. **McPherson** of Tamworth 5/16/1947 in Tamworth; H – 51, woodsman; W – 36, hairdresser

PARSONS,
Jeffrey C. of VT m. Allison J. **Taylor** of VT 9/12/1982

PATTEN,
James Charles of Manchester m. Pamela Joyce **Taylor** of S. Tamworth 2/7/1964 in Concord; H – 19, hospital attendant; W – 18, at home

PAUL,
Ronald M. of Tamworth m. Nano **Bliss** of Tamworth 9/25/1971; H – 25; W - 20

PAULA,
Arthur of Worcester, MA m. Marion **Stinchfield** of Worcester, MA 10/7/1950 in Tamworth; H – 23, foundry; W – 24, at home

PEARL,
Harry W. of Porter, ME m. Sadie E. **Whiting** of Tamworth 3/6/1911 in Tamworth; H – 24, farmer, b. Porter, ME, s/o Frank Pearl (Porter, ME) and Caroline Rounds (Porter, ME); W – 16, housekeeper, b. Tamworth, d/o George F. Whiting (Ossipee) and Annie Choate (Moultonboro)

PEARSONS,
John m. Cora B. **Williams** 12/13/1914 in Tamworth; H – 27, mill man, 2nd, b. Wakefield, MA, s/o John H. Pearsons and Carrie L. Davis; W – 19, housework, b. Ossipee, d/o William Williams and Sadie Welch

PEASE,
Benjamin F. of Tamworth m. Lucinda **Whitaker** of rx 4/7/1897 in Tamworth; H – 68, teamster, b. Meredith, s/o John M. Pease (Meredith) and Betsy Whitaker (Meredith); W – 59, housekeeper, b. Tamworth, d/o Simon Blake (Wakefield) and Caroline ----- (Canada East)

PEASLEE,
Charles H. m. Dorothy A. **Roberts** 2/3/1957 in Center Sandwich; H – 31, millwork; W – 20, at home
Philip E. of Tamworth m. Patricia **Merrithew** of Tamworth 8/1/1998

PEDATO,
Frank m. Marguerite **Hutchins** 9/23/1934 in Freedom

PELOQUIN,
Thomas M. of Steamboat Springs, CO m. Jennifer L. **Johnson** of Steamboat Springs, CO 6/14/1996

PENNELL,
Charles H. of Buxton, ME m. Addie M. **Brown** of Tamworth 10/25/1889 in Tamworth I.W.; H - 30, laborer, b. Buxton, ME, s/o A. H. Pennell (Buxton, ME); W - 17, housework, b. Tamworth, d/o Alonzo Brown (Tamworth)
Dwight R. m. Lillian B. **Allard** 6/30/1956 in Milton; H – 23, machine operator; W – 18, at home
Edwin of Tamworth m. Dora **Williams** of Tamworth 11/4/1912 in Tamworth; H – 18, laborer, b. Tamworth, s/o Charles Pennell (Buxton, ME) and Addie Brann (Tamworth); W – 22, housework, b. Tamworth, d/o William H. Williams (Ossipee) and Susie Welch (Ossipee)
Edwin C. m. Betty J. **Drew** 1/21/1955 in Milton; H – 30, railroad; W – 20, tel. operator
Guy m. Jessie M. **Brown** 6/23/1920 in N. Conway; H – 24, general mechanic, b. Tamworth, s/o Charles Pennell and Addie Brown; W – 17, housework, b. Albany, d/o Mark Brown and Eva M. Mason
Guy, Jr. of Tamworth m. Charlene L. **Harris** of Tamworth 10/26/1985
Reginald E. of Tamworth m. Helen J. **Remick** of Tamworth 6/18/1939 in Lebanon, ME; H – 21, furniture work; W – 16, at home

PERKINS,
Alston of Tamworth m. Ella M. **Bryer** of Tamworth 12/12/1893 in Tamworth; H - 23, farmer, b. Jackson, s/o Pike G. Perkins (Jackson) and Mary A. Eastman (Jackson); W - 20, housework, b. Sandwich, d/o James R. Bryer (Sandwich) and Rhoda E. Bennett (Sandwich)
Bert A. of Tamworth m. Marion A. **Smith** of Center Harbor 6/22/1912 in Tamworth; H – 20, laborer, b. Ossipee, s/o Hiram L. Perkins (Moultonboro) and Etta Clough (Effingham); W – 22, b. Brattleboro, VT, d/o Albert A. Smith (Westfield, MA) and Anna Barrett (Hinsdale)
Everett S. of Tamworth m. Annie L. **Hill** of Tamworth 1/1/1911 in Sandwich; H – 56, farmer, b. Sandwich, s/o George Perkins

(Wells, ME) and S. M. Blackey (Randolph, VT); W – 45, housekeeper, b. Stowe, ME, d/o Timothy Bean (Stowe, ME) and Mary A. Heath (Fryeburg, ME)

Philip Earl of Westbrook, ME m. Karen Anne **Cobb** of Alexandria, VA 8/28/1971; H – 23; W – 22

Pike G. m. Estella **Bickford** 12/9/1914 in Tamworth; H – 19, farmer, b. Tamworth, s/o William H. Perkins and Lizzie Gray; W – 19, waitress, b. Sandwich, d/o Silas Bickford

Pike G., Jr. of Tamworth m. Emily E. **Knox** of Tamworth 7/23/1950 in Tamworth; H – 20, Marine; W – 21, at home

Quincy G. m. Alice A. **Pascoe** 5/29/1918 in Boston, MA; H – 44, chauffeur, 2nd, b. Tamworth, s/o John N. Perkins and Mary A. Tibbitts; W – 38, b. Freedom, d/o Henry Pascoe and Philomen Dorr

Robert Hilton of Tamworth m. Barbara May **Hill** of Tamworth 1/7/1972; H – 20; W – 17

Terrance Kenny of Tamworth m. Yvonne **Baumenn** of Tamworth 7/31/1999

PERRY,
Samuel G. of Seattle, WA m. Lisa A. **Olson** of Euless, Texas 9/26/1992

PETERSON,
Hugo P. of Salem, MA m. Lucy S. **Hodgkins** of Tamworth 10/25/1952 in Tamworth; H – 72, retired; W – 58, at home

Osler L. of Roxbury, MA m. Sandra A. **Freeto** of Newton, MA 1/2/1971; H – 24; W - 23

PETRIE,
Russell C. of Freedom m. Cynthia M. **Lawton** of Freedom 5/18/2002

PHAIR,
Jeremy R. of Tamworth m. Johelen J. **Grimsley-Chubbuck** of Tamworth 12/24/2002

PHANEUF,
Mark Fitzgerald of Nashville, TN m. Lee Ann **Remick** of Tamworth 1/2/1999

PHENIX,
George Spencer m. Evelyn **Bolles** 9/1/1916 in Chocorua; H – 25, secretary, b. New Britain, CT, s/o George P. Phenix and Maria E. Stevens; W – 27, b. Cambridge, MA, d/o Frank Bolles and Elizabeth Q. Swan

Richard of Tamworth m. Priscilla M. **Richards** of Durham 10/18/1947 in Durham; H – 21, author; W – 27, secretary

PHILIBERT,
Kevin D. of Tamworth m. Tammy M. **Legault** of Tamworth 6/14/1997

PHILLIPPI,
Karl Evan of Hamden, CT m. Joan Helen **Urquhart** of Hamden, CT 7/25/1970; H – 20; W – 18

PHILLIPS,
Charles E. m. Nellie B. **Whittier** 5/8/1910 in Tamworth; H – 44, laborer, b. Swampscott, s/o James E. Phillips (Swampscott, MA) and Belinda Weeks (Tamworth); W – 45, dressmaker, b. Madison, d/o Benjamin Bickford (Madison) and Mary Robertson (Conway)

Thomas William of Tamworth m. Ann Marie **Moore** of Tamworth 12/21/1968; H – 18; W – 15

PI-SUNYER,
Francis X. m. Penelope **Wheeler** 6/24/1961 in Tamworth; H – 27, M.D.; W – 25, student

PICKERING,
Ellsworth Everette, Jr. of Tamworth m. Catherine Comer **Harris** of Tamworth 12/13/1963 in Center Ossipee; H – 20, mill worker; W – 40, mill worker

PICKMAN,
Anthony P. of Bedford, MA m. Alice P. **Loring** of Tamworth 9/27/1941 in Tamworth; H – 25, radio engineer; W – 23, architect

PIERCE,
Maurice A. m. Alice R. **Whiting** 8/22/1936 in Sandwich

PIKE,
Fred W. of N. Conway m. Minnie A. **Young** of Tamworth 1/22/1890 in Madison; H - 25, bookkeeper, b. Wolfeboro, s/o Ezra B. Pike (ME); W - 18, housework, b. Manchester, d/o Lorenzo J. Young (Manchester)

J. Edison, Jr. of Chocorua m. Beverly G. **Haley** of N. Conway 9/4/1988

PIXTON,
Felix M. of Tamworth m. Ellen M. **Blanchard** of Tamworth 8/11/2001

PLACE,
Arthur Johnson of Wonalancet m. Sally Worthington Smith **Gray** of Wonalancet 10/12/1997

Dale E. of Somerville, MA m. Karen J. **Perlow** of Somerville, MA 9/5/1993

PLANT,
George E. of Tamworth m. Ida M. **Tuttle** of dx 10/5/1901 in Dover; H – 26, laborer, b. Monson, ME, s/o Joseph Plant (St. Lambert, Canada) and Ellen Morrill (Bangor, ME); W – 22, mill operator, b. Newmarket, d/o Hazen Tuttle (Wakefield) and Mary A. Stevens (Littlefield, ME)

PLUMMER,
Charles F. of Tamworth m. Doris M. **Palmer** of Tamworth 6/24/1950 in Tamworth; H – 26, lumbering; W – 18, student

Charles Franklin of Tamworth m. Margaret Louise **Emerson** of Milton 9/22/1968; H – 46; W - 26

Clarence R., Jr. m. Louise M. **Underhill** 5/30/1953 in Laconia; H – 31, farmer; W – 18, student

Frank James of Tamworth m. Cynthia Rae **Swenson** of Tamworth 8/18/1973; H – 18; W – 19

Raymond E. of Tamworth m. Bernice L. **Chase** of Tamworth 10/17/1948 in Conway; H – 23, truck driver; W – 18, at home

POHJU,
Victor A. of Tamworth m. Karen M. **MacDonald** of Tamworth 9/11/1992

POLLARD,
Edward S. of Tamworth m. Eva L. **Whitman** of Somerville, MA 10/4/1897 in Somerville, MA; H – 42, merchant, b. Tamworth, s/o Jonathan Pollard (Kingston) and Mary R. Moulton (Moultonboro); W – 33, dressmaker, b. New Albany, NS, d/o Asaph Whitman (New Albany) and Jane Paysen (Annapolis, NS)

POTTER,
Arthur Langdon of Conway m. Hazel Helen Evans **Currier** of Tamworth 5/4/1963 in Ossipee; H – 72, retired; W – 63, retired
Harold I. m. Carol A. **Chase** 6/22/1957 in N. Conway; H – 18, painter; W – 17, student

POULES,
Robert Allan, III of E. Templeton, MA m. Sylvia Anita **Dyer** of Tamworth 5/8/1965 in Wolfeboro; H – 26, hosp. attend.; W – 20, stud. nurse

POWERS,
Bernard L. m. Doris A. **Leach** 4/21/1934 in Meredith
Philip of Salem, MA m. Marjorie **Doliber** of Salem, MA 9/12/1970; H – 48; W – 47

PRATT,
Robert G. of New York, NY m. Alix Elizabeth **Paschen** of Framingham Center, MA 7/31/1965 in Tamworth; H – 28, credit ana.; W – 23 – teacher

PRICE,
Richard of Kezar Falls, ME m. Beth Lorraine **Millett** of Chocorua 7/1/1973; H – 29; W – 29

PRINCE,
Edward P. of Tamworth m. Dorothy E. **Kennedy** of Manchester 10/28/1946 in Manchester; H – 29, foreign service officer; W – 30, foreign service clerk

PRIVE,
Philip E. of Effingham m. Marilyn D. **Kelly** of Effingham 6/20/1998

PROCTOR,
Gerald E. m. Mary L. **Lake** 5/30/1953 in Nashua; H – 27, lineman; W – 24, telephone operator

PROVOST,
George Lewis m. Edith Frances **Bryant** 10/5/1920 in Moultonboro; H – 50, clerk, 2nd, b. New Canaan, CT, s/o Lewis Provost and Mary Avery; W – 26, b. Wells, ME, d/o George H. Bryant and Marion E. Sandford

PRUSSMAN,
Erik C. of Rowley, MA m. Kathleen L. **Winslow** of Rowley, MA 6/18/1998

PUGH,
Thomas J. of Tamworth m. Carrie M. **Mauhs** of Tamworth 9/28/1985

PULSIFER,
Frederick J. m. Carolyn E. **Gove** 9/2/1955 in Laconia; H – 32, mechanic; W – 35, teacher

PURRINGTON,
Daniel of Albany m. Flora **Davis** of Tamworth 5/29/1891 in Tamworth; H - 18, laborer, b. Albany, s/o G. M. Purrington (Sandwich) and Susan Moody (Madison); W - 18, housework, b. Tamworth, d/o William Davis (Effingham) and Mary Mooney (Nashua)

Daniel C. m. Vivian I. **Moody** 8/7/1919 in Tamworth; H – 45, laborer, 2nd, s/o George W. Purrington and Susan Moody; W – 2nd, d/o Wentworth B. Hobbs and Myra K. Knox

Ralph H. of Tamworth m. Elsie M. **Sawyer** of Tamworth 1/5/1904 in Tamworth; H – 25, laborer, b. Albany, s/o George W. Purrington (Alton) and Susan Moody (Eaton); W – 19, b. Lynn, MA, d/o Francis A. Sawyer (Limerick, ME) and Mary D. Colton (Troy, ME)

PURVES,
Theodore Rehn of Oakland, CA m. Suzanne Elizabeth **Cockrell** of Oakland, CA 7/10/1999

QUIMBY,
Benjamin C. of Wenham, MA m. Annie L. **Robinson** of Tamworth 1/8/1896 in Tamworth; H - 23, plumber, b. Somerville, MA, s/o Ivory Quimby (Sandwich, plumber) and Susan C. Quimby (Salem); W - 21, dressmaker, b. Tamworth, d/o Addison R. Robinson (Meredith, postmaster) and Mary E. Swasey (Meredith, deceased)

RACINE,
Wendell S. m. Evelyn **Gobelle** 7/11/1953 in Tamworth; H – 24, US Army; W – 36, at home

RAND,
Clinton LeShore of W. Ossipee m. Carolyn Jean **Hunt** of W. Ossipee 7/25/1976; H – 35; W – 28

RANDALL,
John Lear of Philadelphia, PA m. Walden Katherine **Semmes** of Tamworth 8/17/1963 in Chocorua; H – 24 – student; W – 22, student

RANGER,
John of Tamworth m. Edith **Lank** of Moultonboro 8/19/1901 in Tamworth; H – 39, laborer, b. Tamworth, s/o Mark Ranger (Plymouth) and Hannah Colby (Tamworth); W – 32, housekeeper, b. Moultonboro, d/o Lon Colby (Moultonboro) and Nancy J. Knox (Ossipee)

RATLIFF,
Daniel L. of Tamworth m. Marcella J. **LeGendre** of Tamworth 10/12/1991

READ,
Richard W. m. Clara F. **Enebuske** 9/17/1927 in Tamworth
William G. of Wonalancet m. Patricia A. **Sorlien** of S. Tamworth 9/20/1980

READING,
Michael G. of CA m. Natanya **Pearlman** of CA 8/16/2003

REARDON,
William R. of E. Hampton, CT m. Irene H. **Smith** of E. Hampton, CT 5/19/1990

RECORD,
Charles W. of Cazenovia, NY m. Jean M. **Aspinall** of Tamworth 1/1/1990

RECTOR,
James S. of Vienna, Austria m. Phyllis Ann **Schroeder** of Moscow, USSR 11/1/1975; H – 24; W – 24

REECE,
Richard m. Velma **Ellis** 9/26/1936 in Chocorua

REINGOLD,
Robert of Tamworth m. Pamela **Langlois** of Tamworth 11/7/1981

REINHOLD,
Robert V. of Tamworth m. Patricia A. **Krebs** of Tamworth 2/26/1984

REMICK,
A. Dexter m. Dorothy A. **Graves** 12/12/1936 in N. Conway
Charles W. m. Elizabeth A. **Davis** 1/1/1934 in Tamworth
David m. Helen M. **Hobbs** 12/1/1958 in Wolfeboro; H – 20, Air Force; W – 20, at home
Edwin of Tamworth m. Emily A. **Crafts** of Roxbury, MA 11/8/1900 in Boston, MA; H – 34, physician, s/o Levi E. Remick (Tamworth) and Harriet Bedee (Tamworth); W – at home, d/o William A. Crafts (Roxbury, MA) and Emily Doggett (Roxbury, MA)
Edwin C. m. Marion E. **Miles** 10/25/1930 in Wolfeboro
Frank of Tamworth m. Elizabeth F. **Davis** of Tamworth 5/26/1895 in Tamworth; H - 44, carpenter, b. Tamworth, s/o Samuel E. Remick (Tamworth, farmer) and Hannah Remick (Tamworth, housewife); W - 20, housewife, b. Tamworth, d/o William N. Davis (Effingham, laborer) and Mary M. Davis (Nashua, housewife)
Fred of Tamworth m. Winifred **Dooley** of St. Louis, MO 4/--/1909 in Conway; H – 40, farmer, b. Tamworth, s/o Alpheus D. Remick (Tamworth, farmer) and Ann J. Hurd (Exeter, housewife); W –

31, housekeeping, b. Ireland, d/o Patrick Dooley (Ireland, farmer) and Mary McCook (Ireland, housewife)

H. Haywood of Tamworth m. Annie May **Johnson** of Tamworth 10/25/1891 in Tamworth; H - 30, merchant, b. Tamworth, s/o Levi E. Remick (Tamworth) and Harriett Beede (Tamworth); W - 30, housework, b. Brooklyn, NY, d/o Charles Johnson (Sweden) and Friedericka Nilson (Germany)

Harry H. of Tamworth m. Helen A. **Wheeler** of Lowell, MA 1/8/1908 in Nashua; H – 43, merchant, b. Tamworth, s/o Charles H. Remick (Tamworth) and A. M. Tarlton (Piermont); W – 34, b. Lowell, MA, d/o Joseph A. Wheeler (Concord, MA) and Julia A. Kingsbury (Francestown)

James H. of Tamworth m. Cora M. **Atwood** of Sandwich 7/4/1894 in Tamworth; H - 21, clerk, b. Tamworth, s/o Francis P. Remick (Tamworth, farmer) and Fanny J. Norton (Buxton, ME, housekeeping); W - 20, at home, b. Sandwich, d/o John G. Atwood (Sandwich, blacksmith) and Sarah J. Atwood (Sandwich, housekeeping)

Levi W. of Tamworth m. Margaret **Cooper** of Tamworth 10/7/1943 in Tamworth; H – 48, grocer; W – 41, at home

Levi Wadsworth of Tamworth m. Marjorie Evelyn **Ayer** of Haverhill, MA 11/24/1923 in Tamworth; H – 28; W – 19

Michael D. of Tamworth m. Doreen L. **Jeffers** of Tamworth 7/3/1991

Ronald C. m. Doris L. **Brown** 7/8/1956 in Center Ossipee; H – 20, mechanic; W – 20, secretary

Willie M. of Tamworth m. Lucy A. **Bradbury** of Tamworth 11/20/1888 in Tamworth; H - 31, farmer, b. Tamworth, s/o Henry H. Remick (Tamworth); W - 28, housework, b. Tamworth, d/o Edward Bradbury (Tamworth)

RESCHKE,
Thomas C. of Lynn, MA m. Diana L. **Russell** of Lynn, MA 12/31/1975; H – 21; W – 25

REYNOLDS,
Paul W. of E. Stoneham, ME m. Leslie J. **Waltzer** of Tamworth 5/12/1990

RHINES,
Irving K. m. Eleanor M. **Eldridge** 6/16/1955 in Sandwich; H – 29, machine operator; W – 24, nurses' aid

RICH,
Michael O. of MA m. Lydia A. **Shrier** of MA 8/23/2003
William Augustus of Westford, VT m. Emily Ann **Rinkema** of Westford, VT 7/19/1997

RICHARDS,
Justin L. of Tamworth m. Flavelle **Hills** of Tamworth 2/25/1984

RICHARDSON,
Stephen A. of Argyll, Scotland m. Margaret P. **Black** of Cambridge, MA 5/27/1945 in Tamworth; H – 24, mariner; W – 23, student

RICKARDS,
Hanford E. of Tamworth m. Helen F. **Gillis** of Tamworth 4/1/1947 in Tamworth; H – 42, farmer; W – 18, housework
Hanford E. of Tamworth m. Helen F. **Gillis** of Tamworth 8/24/1949 in Tamworth; H – 44, farmer; W – 20, housework

RICKER,
Charles A. of Tamworth m. Melissa L. **Reid** of Tamworth 8/7/1993
George Arron of Tamworth m. Susan Anne **Turcotte** of Tamworth 8/12/1989
Moses E. of Tamworth m. Sharon A. **Bell** of Tamworth 9/23/1984
William W. of Springvale, ME m. Edith C. **Ross** of Tamworth 7/4/1894 in Tamworth; H - 24, expressman, b. Saco, ME, s/o Daniel Ricker (Somersworth, shoemaker) and Lucinda F. Welch (Shapleigh, ME, housekeeping); W - 18, housekeeping, b. Tamworth, d/o Henry Ross (Albany, farmer) and Hattie E. Knox (Tamworth, housekeeping)

RIGBY,
George E. m. Charlotte A. **Seavy** 12/5/1936 in Conway

ROBERTS,
Arthur S. of Tamworth m. Ada E. **Curtis** of Kezar Falls 3/25/1898 in Effingham; H – 29, farmer, b. Tamworth, s/o Charles C. Roberts (Tamworth) and Hannah J. Neil (Meredith); W – 30, teacher, b. Parsonsfield, d/o Eleazer Whiting (Parsonsfield) and Mary A. Watson (Parsonsfield)
Brian D. of Effingham m. Nellie E. **McLendon** of Effingham 9/29/2002

Charles H. of Tamworth m. Bertha M. **Whiting** of Lake Village 1/3/1890 in Tamworth; H - 29, farmer, b. Tamworth, s/o Charles C. Roberts; W - 17, housework, b. Tamworth, d/o George Whiting (Meredith)
David Brian of MA m. Susan Linda **Christiansen** of Tamworth 9/11/1988
Edgar J. of Tamworth m. Eva M. **Berry** 2/19/1913 in Tamworth; H – 41, farmer, b. Tamworth, s/o George W. Roberts and Hannah Emery; W – 43, housework, b. Tamworth, d/o Nathaniel Berry and Abbie Blake
Emery R. of Tamworth m. Fayralyn O. **Leso** of W. Ossipee 7/29/1945 in Ctr. Ossipee; H – 23, truck driver; W – 18, furniture factory
George W. m. Thelma E. **Harvey** 9/18/1935 in Belmont
Harry C. of Tamworth m. Alice M. **Perkins** of Tamworth 11/10/1913 in Tamworth; H – 35, farmer, b. Tamworth, s/o George W. Roberts and Hannah Emery; W – 25, housework, b. Tamworth, d/o William H. Perkins and Lizzie C. Graves
John E. of Chocorua m. Dawn M. **Mason** of Ctr. Ossipee 12/7/1980
Lynn P. of Intervale m. Marguerite E. **Sanborn** of Tamworth 9/1/1979
Richard N. of Springfield, VT m. Frances E. **Hidden** of Springfield, VT 8/16/1941 in Tamworth; H – 24, office clerk; W – 21, stenographer

ROBERTSON,
Elmer R. of Tamworth m. Ruth W. **Sargent** of Tamworth 6/23/1913 in Madison; H – 23, steward, b. Tamworth, s/o Mark E. Robertson and Carrie A. Woodman; W – 23, none, b. Haverhill, MA, d/o Harry C. Sargent and Mary Gould
James W. of Tamworth m. Alys **Fowler** of Woodbury, CT 6/4/1913 in Woodbury, CT; H – 22, farmer, b. Tamworth, s/o Mark E. Robertson and Carrie A. Woodman; W – 28, stenographer, b. Woodbury, CT, d/o William Fowler and Martha E. Galpin
Mark E. m. Isibel B. **Stanwood** 12/5/1914 in Bartlett; H – 48, hotel keeper, 2nd, b. Eaton, s/o Charles Robertson and Jane Snow; W – 35, stenographer, 2nd, b. Newburyport, MA, d/o Charles Stanwood and Louise Wilson

ROBILLER,
Oliver G. of Tamworth m. Christy L. **Daly** of Tamworth 3/28/1992

ROBINSON,
Addison R. of Tamworth m. Margaret H. **Elwell** of Tamworth 4/24/1895 in Tamworth; H - 46, postmaster, 2nd, b. Meredith, s/o John G. Robinson (Meredith, hotel proprietor) and Lucinda H. Robinson (New Hampton, housewife); W - 27, housewife, b. Kennebunkport, d/o John Elwell (Kennebunkport, teamster) and Esther M. Elwell (Kennebunkport, housewife)

Andrew Jordt of Hartford, CT m. Louise Albro **Barker** of Baltimore, MD 6/23/1963 in Wonalancet; H – 21, student; W – 20, student

Bruce E. of Tamworth m. Diane M. **Lord** of W. Ossipee 11/29/1975; H – 25; W – 22

Chester A. m. Grace **Moody** 5/21/1921 in Conway; H – 21, laborer, b. Tamworth, s/o John G. Robinson and Bertha L. Bunker; W – 18, none, b. Madison, d/o William Moody and Mabel Moore

Harold C. of Tamworth m. Barbara L. **Smith** of Tamworth 9/27/1947 in Conway; H – 26, truck driver; W – 18, stenographer

Henry B. of Tamworth m. Mary L. **Wiggin** of Tamworth 12/26/1892 in Tamworth; H - 25, mechanic, b. Tamworth, s/o Addison Robinson (Meredith) and Nellie M. Swasey (Moultonboro); W - 21, housework, b. Tamworth, d/o Arthur L. Wiggin (Tamworth) and Mary L. Drowns (Newington)

Henry B. of Tamworth m. Laura M. **Gilman** of Tamworth 6/28/1899 in Chocorua; H – 32, contractor, b. Tamworth, s/o A. R. Robinson (Tamworth) and Nellie M. Swasey (Sandwich); W – 25, b. Boston, d/o George E. Gilman (Tamworth) and Orissa J. Seavey (Tamworth)

Henry W. of Tamworth m. Irene E. **Alley** 12/24/1913 in Tamworth; H – 20, carpenter, b. Tamworth, s/o Henry B. Robertson and Mary L. Wiggin; W – 18, at home, b. Haverhill, MA, d/o Daniel B. Alley and Alice A. Gray

Henry W. m. Gertrude M. **Emack** 10/25/1927 in Conway

John Edward of Conway m. Brenda Joyce **Roberts** of Tamworth 8/7/1971; H – 19; W – 18

John G. of Tamworth m. Bertha L. **Bunker** of Tamworth 12/2/1899 in Chocorua; H – 25, painter, b. Tamworth, s/o A. R. Robinson (Tamworth) and Nellie M. Swasey (Sandwich); W – 20, housework, b. Tamworth, d/o Levi W. Bunker (Tamworth) and Hattie B. Webber (Tamworth)

ROGER,
Earl Theodore of Whitefield m. Linda Mae **Phillips** of Tamworth 12/13/1970; H – 28; W – 20

ROGERS,
Adam Blaine of FL m. Marie Antonia **Caruso** of FL 9/30/1988
George B. of Durham m. Gertrude M. **Bickford** of Tamworth 8/16/1941 in Tamworth; H – 22, laborer; W – 20, at home
Michael Frederick of Long Beach, CA m. Amy Elizabeth **Cutrone** of Long Beach, CA 6/26/1999

ROLLO,
David Timothy of Williamsport, PA m. Erinn Heather **Wright** of Williamsport, PA 10/4/1997

ROMEL,
John Vincent of Union, NJ m. Gael Elizabeth **Moran** of Tamworth 6/27/1970; H – 23; W – 22

ROSS,
Ernest J. of Tamworth m. Mary E. **Knox** of Ossipee 4/6/1940 in Ctr. Ossipee; H – 19, laborer; W – 18, at home
Harland of Tamworth m. Mariette **Martin** of Tamworth 4/30/1964 in Tamworth; H – 31, laborer; W – 31, secretary
Harold E. m. Grace **Kennett** 4/12/1915 in Tamworth; H – 23, chauffeur, b. Tamworth, s/o John W. Ross and Harriet Knox; W – 18, housework, b. Effingham, d/o Frank Kennett and Emma Sanborn
Kenneth m. Hilda **Johnson** 4/1/1934 in Madison

ROSSBACH,
David C. of Essex, MA m. Daren J. **Davis** of Chocorua 5/16/1986

ROWE,
C. Daniel of Atlanta, GA m. Elizabeth A. **Robertson** of Smyrna, GA 8/29/1986
Ernest J. G. of Tamworth m. Grace Aurelia **Morey** of Franklin 6/9/1973; H – 83; W – 77

ROWELL,
Frank of Tamworth m. Patricia A. **Harding** of Tamworth 11/3/1973; H – 29; W – 22

ROY,
Dwaine P. of Tamworth m. Kelly M. **Bodnar** of Rochester 10/28/1995

RUDD,
Roland of Brooklyn, NY m. Katherine B. **McDonald** of Brookline, MA 12/9/1941 in Tamworth; H – 24, piano teacher; W – 25, at home

RUNNELL,
John C. of Ossipee m. Abbie D. **Brown** of Tamworth 10/3/1903; H – 39, laborer, b. Buxton, ME, s/o Alexander Runnell (Buxton) and Sarah G. Berry (Buxton); W – 24, housework, b. Tamworth, d/o Alonzo Brown (Albany) and Rachel Hurd (Milton)

RUSSELL,
Lewis H. of Johnson m. Alice **Crabtree** of Tamworth 11/8/1923 in Tamworth; H – 40; W – 28
Michael of Wells, ME m. Miriam **Knight** of Wells, ME 12/28/1973; H – 31; W – 27

RYAN,
Thomas R., Jr. of IL m. Patricia M. **Thompson** of IL 8/6/1977; H – 25; W – 27

RYDER,
Alton E. m. Sally Ann **Clark** 9/29/1956 in N. Conway; H – 18, teamster; W – 18, at home
Lloyd W. of Tamworth m. Ruth J. **Welch** of Ctr. Ossipee 8/22/1952 in Ctr. Ossipee; H – 17, lumbering; W – 18, housework
Lynwood P. m. Winifred G. **White** 6/25/1955 in Tamworth; H – 18, woodsman; W – 17, none

SAGONA,
Charles L. of Tamworth m. Mary K. **MacKinnon** of Watertown, MA 2/23/1974; H – 55; W – 58

SAILOR,
George R., Jr. m. Jean A. **Devenport** 9/9/1935 in Tamworth

SALLET,
Herbert W. of Lincoln, MA m. Kittredge E. **Henchman** of Weston, MA 1/4/1986

SALOIS,
Dean B. of E. Greenwich, RI m. Marion L. **Lloyd** of E. Greenwich, RI 8/7/1983

SALVATI,
Domenic A. of Medford, MA m. Rachel M. **Davis** of Danvers, MA 6/2/1990

SAMPSON,
Wayne of Tamworth m. Frances W. **Saujon** of Effingham 8/15/1992

SANBORN,
Frederick A. of San Diego, CA m. Jannette G. **Horan** of San Diego, CA 9/6/1984

John F. of Tamworth m. Addie M. **Green** of Tamworth 4/4/1887 in Tamworth; H - 23, laborer, b. Saco, ME, s/o Freeman Sanborn (Tamworth, farmer); W - 17, b. Tamworth, d/o Rosco Green

Raymond F. m. Janet E. **Woodward** 6/27/1959 in Tamworth; H – 25, truck driver; W – 18, at home

Sidney W. of Stowe, ME m. Alice F. **Thompson** of Tamworth 9/22/1945 in Chocorua; H – 43, mason; W – 35, teacher

SANPHY,
Tanen D. of N. Conway m. Kimberly J. **Whitaker** of Tamworth 9/30/2001

SARGENT,
David W. of Tuftonboro m. Margaret B. **Wiesner** of Tamworth 10/27/2001

Raymond W. of Fryeburg, ME m. Nancy C. **Taylor** of Fryeburg, ME 12/23/1978; H – 42; W – 42

SAULNIER,
John of Tamworth m. Emma **Barnes** of Tamworth 10/15/1898 in Tamworth; H – 33, farmer, b. NS, s/o R. Saulnier (NS) and Charlotte (NS); W – 34, housework, b. Hiram, ME, d/o Timothy Bean (Hiram, ME) and Victoria Bean

SAUNDERS,
Harry A. of Winthrop, MA m. Helen R. **Malone** of Winthrop, MA 5/26/1973; H – 76; W – 69

SAVARD,
Albert J. of Canada m. Mildred **Hayford** of Tamworth 5/7/1923 in Conway; H – 34; W – 28
Albert J. of Tamworth m. Esther **Freeman** of Brighton, MA 1/8/1949 in N. Conway; H – 60, caretaker; W – 43, office manager
Emile H. of York, PA m. Patricia **Alfred** of Tamworth 9/22/1951 in Conway; H – 22, lineman; W – 20, at home

SAVARY,
Zantford L. of Somerville, MA m. Effie J. **Kenerson** of Tamworth 12/24/1888 in Tamworth; H - 23, carpenter, b. Digby, NS, s/o William H. Savary; W - 17, teacher, b. Tamworth, d/o William Kenerson

SAVINI,
Donald Edward, Sr. of Tamworth m. Tammie Lynn **Seatten** of Tamworth 8/10/2000

SAYERS,
David S. of MI m. Tamara J. **Idsinga** of MI 10/4/2003

SCARINGI,
Gene of Providence, RI m. Dorothea R. **Ward** of Pawtucket, RI 9/4/1948 in Tamworth; H – 40, clergyman; W – 36, teacher

SCEGGEL,
Arthur B. of Ossipee m. Belle **Gilman** of Tamworth 2/18/1907 in Tamworth; H – 22, engineer, b. Springvale, ME, s/o C. B. Sceggell (Haverhill, MA) and Maggie Londo (Springvale, ME); W – 18, housework, b. Tamworth, d/o James W. Gilman (Tamworth) and Hattie B. Davis (Tamworth)

SCHARF,
David L. of Sparkill, NY m. Katharine T. **Stehli** of Sparkill, NY 9/19/1992

SCHILLER,
Matthias Johannes of London, United Kingdom m. Tara Ann **Moriarty** of Wellesley, MA 8/23/1997

SCHMOLL,
Brand E. of Boston, MA m. Carol **Chase** of Boston, MA 6/2/1973; H – 23; W – 20

SCHNEIDER,
Arthur F. of Chocorua m. Sabine M. **Kelley** of Rochester 5/17/1987

SCHOFIELD,
Richard Garry of Derry m. Sally-Ann **Stoddard** of Lexington, MA 9/30/1973; H – 24; W – 20

SCHOOLCRAFT,
Walter B. of Tamworth m. Edith M. **Moulton** of Tamworth 11/10/1894 in Tamworth; H - 24, carpenter, b. Boston, MA, s/o Herman G. Schoolcraft (Canada, carpenter) and Nellie Ross (Albany, housekeeping); W - 16, at home, b. Albany, d/o Alonzo W. Moulton (Albany, farmer) and Belinda Kennerson (Albany, housekeeping)

SCHOPF,
James William of Columbus, OH m. Julie **Morgan** of S. Hadley, MA 8/7/1965 in Tamworth; H – 23, student; W – 21, student

SCHULTZE,
Andrew Kyle of Tamworth m. Toni-Ann **Whitman** of Hampton Bays, NY 8/19/1989
William C. of Tamworth m. Barbara M. **Varney** of Tamworth 11/15/2003

SCOLARO,
Ricky A. of Ossipee m. Rose Ann **Ricker** of Tamworth 5/19/1976; H – 23; W - 19

Ricky Anthony of Tamworth m. Kara Holly **Caisse** of Tamworth 8/16/1997

SCOTT,
Arthur Burton of Tamworth m. Emma Adams **Johnson** of Tamworth 3/13/1965 in Conway; H – 69, retired; W – 65, nurse
Douglas J. of VT m. Roberta A. **Willis** of VT 3/1/1980
Jefferson MacDonald of Starks, ME m. Hilda **Chase** of Belmont 1/8/2000

SCRUTON,
Joseph O. of Holderness m. Lucy M. **Wallace** of Tamworth 11/29/1892 in Tamworth; H - 22, farmer, b. Holderness, s/o Edward Scruton (Centre Harbor) and Amy A. Tate (Tuftonboro); W - 17, housework, b. Tamworth, d/o Henry Wallace (Sacarappa, ME) and Fannie Glidden (Madison)

SEARS,
William M. of Tamworth m. Patricia A. **Ormond** of Tamworth 10/19/1991

SEVERY,
Merle E. of Sandwich m. Teresa L. **Bookholz** of Tamworth 9/19/1942 in Chocorua; H – 20, student; W – 20, student

SHACKFORD,
Loren Albert of Madison m. Sherry Marie **Ames** of Tamworth 1/16/1971; H – 18; W – 16

SHAMBAUGH,
Benjamin Dibble of Tamworth m. Ellen Peabody **Keith** of Tamworth 12/2/1972; H – 21; W – 18

SHAMBOUGH,
Benjamin D. of Chocorua m. Lisa M. **Scott** of Chocorua 3/3/1979

SHANNON,
Charles of Wolfeboro m. Evelyn M. **Welch** of Tamworth 2/15/1941 in Laconia; H – 21, clerk; W – 18, at home
Edwin S. of Tamworth m. Ellen R. **Coffey** of Tamworth 7/24/1998

Mathew W. of Tamworth m. Diana E. **Ugo** of Stoughton, MA 6/24/1978; H – 19; W – 19

SHARP,
Douglas J. of Tamworth m. Donna V. **Seamans** of Tamworth 4/2/1994
Irwin S. of Tamworth m. Lisa L. **Whittemore** of Tamworth 8/25/1990

SHATTUCK,
Lawrence A. of Tamworth m. Frances D. **Coderre** of Tamworth 7/25/2003

SHAUGHNESSY,
Michael of Manchester m. Susan **Chase** of Silver Lake 9/1/1973; H – 25; W – 23

SHEAN,
Hayden W. of Lynn, MA m. Elizabeth L. **Oneill** of Lynn, MA 4/2/1995

SHEAR,
G. Scott of MA m. Katharine Ann **Kilbourn** of MA 9/10/1988
William A. of VA m. Noelle M. **Prince** of Tamworth 8/10/1980

SHEPPERD,
Robert Allan of Conway m. Violet Dorothy **Martel** of Tamworth 7/3/1965 in Center Ossipee; H – 22, foreman; W – 31, laborer

SHERMAN,
Robert F. of Woodbridge, CT m. Lynne E. **Jakubauskas** of Woodbridge, CT 7/10/1993

SHIELDS,
Lawrence R. m. Camilla E. **Prior** 7/19/1936 in Tamworth

SIDWELL,
James S. of Boxborough, MA m. Darcy S. **Goguen** of Cambridge, MA 10/26/1991

SILVAN,
Emanuel J. of Tamworth m. Fannie A. **Bassett** of Tamworth 4/2/1900 in Tamworth H – 34, shoemaker, s/o Frank Silvan

(Portugal) and Rosa Silvan (Portugal); W – 42, housework, d/o Jefferson C. Hilton (Calais, ME) and Submit Hatch (Freeport, ME)

SIMMERS,
Nyal B., Pvt. of Wilmington, DE m. Rita T. **Richards** of Fitchburg, MA 10/26/1942 in Tamworth; H – 20, soldier; W – 16, assembler

SIMON,
Gregory R. of Wonalancet m. Heidi K. **Locke** of Clifton Park, NY 8/14/1993

SIMONDS,
Carl Everett of Tamworth m. Evelyn Leanard **Lent** of Lower Bartlett 5/23/1964 in Whitefield; H – 19, landscaper; W – 18, cashier

SIMONEAU,
Jean A. m. Barbara **Bowles** 9/5/1955 in Laconia; H – 25, student; W – 25, X-ray technician

SIMONETTI,
Dennis G. of Providence, RI m. Karen M. **Curtin** of Providence, RI 12/7/1986

SIMONS,
Scott C. of Tamworth m. Penelope J. **Brooks** of Tamworth 8/2/1992

SIMPSON,
George Adam, Jr. of E. Orange, NJ m. Kit Nordbo **Therkildsen** of New York, NY 12/27/1969; H – 48; W – 24

SINCLAIR,
Craig M. of S. Tamworth m. Tenny O. **Doyle** of S. Tamworth 12/24/1992

SLOCUM,
James E. m. Ann A. **Rubel** 9/6/1954 in Tamworth; H – 24, student; W – 21, student

SMACH,
Kent D. of Cambridge, MA m. Amy P. **Wettergreen** of Cambridge, MA 9/8/2001

SMALLE,
Theodore B. of Tamworth m. Alice N. **Zakarian** of Tamworth 6/21/1947 in Tamworth; H – 24, insulator; W – 22, secretary

SMALLEY,
Robert F. of MA m. Barbara S. **Franklin** of MA 4/17/1988

SMITH,
Albert W. of Tamworth m. Alice J. **Emery** of Tamworth 8/20/1891 in Tamworth; H - 21, millman, b. Stowe, ME, s/o Salman Smith (Stowe, ME) and Betsey Nickerson (Jackson); W - 21, housework, b. Tamworth, d/o David Emery (Gilmanton) and Abbie Clough (Tamworth)
Albert W. m. Minnie A. **Fennell** 11/17/1934 in Boston, MA
Clarence S. of Tamworth m. Cora M. **Forrest** of Tamworth 4/16/1903; H – 22, laborer, b. Tamworth, s/o Levi Smith (Tamworth) and Hattie B. Mason (Tamworth); W – 18, b. Sandwich, d/o Hiram Forrest and Annie L. Bean
David V. of Somerville, MA m. Helena J. **Goldstein** of Somerville, MA 6/27/1987
Elaine R. of Peabody, MA m. Tricia G. **McPherson** of Peabody, MA 7/16/1994
Frank H. of Tamworth m. Ada A. **Marston** of Tamworth 12/26/1901 in Tamworth; H – 38, laborer, b. Cornish, ME, s/o John Smith (Cornish, ME) and Ann Johnson (Parsonsfield, ME); W – 26, housekeeper, b. Tamworth, d/o John F. Marston (Tamworth) and Ida A. Huckins (Tamworth)
Gerald Earl Young on Monkton, Canada m. Edna Marie **Hanna** of Monkton, Canada 7/10/1997
Gilman A. of New Hampton m. Blanche M. **Mason** of Tamworth 1/17/1948 in Tamworth; H – 50, foreman; W – 29, cook
Henry B. of Tamworth m. Sarah L. **Ralston** of Tamworth 6/18/1894 in Tamworth; H - 45, farmer, 2nd, b. Tamworth, s/o Jacob B. Smith (Tamworth, farmer) and Abigail Price (Tamworth, housework); W - 50, housekeeping, b. Granville, NS, d/o Joseph Ralston (Scotland, farmer) and Jane Walker (Scotland, housekeeping)

Jacob G. of Tamworth m. Eliza A. **Mason** of Tamworth 4/19/1892 in Tamworth; H - 41, farmer, b. Tamworth, s/o Jacob B. Smith (Tamworth) and Abigail B. Price (Tamworth); W - 36, housework, b. Haverhill, d/o Philip Adams and Rosa A. Adams

James, Jr. of Tamworth m. Mary **Westover** of Tamworth 9/22/1979

Kenneth H. of Cambridge, MA m. Anne Marie **Biernacki** of Cambridge, MA 10/18/1997

Marshall E. of Fryeburg, ME m. Nellie E. **Hayford** of Tamworth 9/1/1904 in Tamworth; H – 27, mechanic, b. Stow, ME, s/o Marshall Smith (Stow, ME) and Jennie Brown (Cornish, ME); W – 28, housework, b. Tamworth, d/o Albion Hayford (Tamworth) and Ella Whiting (Tamworth)

Michael Jeffrey of Chocorua m. Jay Eileen **Acas** of Chocorua 6/12/1988

Michael W. of Chocorua m. Ola C. **Gagne** of Berlin 11/9/2002

Noel Raymond of Montrose, PA m. Linda Drew **Newton** of Easthampton, MA 6/24/1989

Ralph B. of Tamworth m. Alice K. **Pettrie** of Bartlett 7/27/1907 in Tamworth; H – 24, teamster, b. Tamworth, s/o Charles C. Smith (Tamworth) and Lizzie F. Weeks (Somersworth); W – 21, waitress, b. Attica, NY, d/o William Pettrie (England) and Alice Cutts (England)

Thaddeus B. of Tamworth m. Amy K. **Berrier** of Tamworth 8/8/1987

Wade Q. of Tamworth m. Teena L. **Blake** of Tamworth 6/7/2003

Walter C. of Tamworth m. Hattie M. **Downs** of Tamworth 2/2/1889 in Tamworth; H - 22, farmer, b. Stow, ME; W - 15, housework, b. Tamworth, d/o Elias Downs

Walter C. m. Addie M. **Littlefield** 7/18/1932 in Conway

SOLAR,
Robert Louis of Tamworth m. Jane Meredith **Alston** of Hampton Falls 6/23/1974; H – 28; W – 23

SOMMER,
Roger A. of Morton, IL m. Carol A. **Morrisey** of Morton, IL 7/26/1971; H – 27; W – 28

SOROFF,
Daniel A. of Boston, MA m. Elizabeth H. **Johnson** of Boston, MA 8/8/1998

SOUCEY,
James Louis of Tamworth m. Candi Ann **Chevrette** of Amesbury, MA 8/27/1970; H – 21; W – 19

SOULIA,
Chad W. of Chocorua m. Amy M. **Harte** of Chocorua 7/7/2001

SOUTHALL,
William Henry m. Ruth Marie **Bickford** 6/9/1920 in Chocorua; H – 32, telephone, b. England, s/o Samuel Southall and Elizabeth Hanley; W – 18, at home, b. Tamworth, d/o William Bickford and Edith Parker

SOUZA,
John P. of Tamworth m. Debra C. **Merritt** of Tamworth 2/2/1986

SPA[U]LDING,
Ralph H. of Tamworth m. Essie I. **Hanson** of Sandwich 4/21/1903; H – 32, farmer, b. Tamworth, s/o Addison Spaulding (Canada) and Ida M. Felch (Tamworth); W – 26, housework, b. Sandwich, d/o R. Hanson (Moultonboro) and V. Bean (Somersworth)

Robert C. A. of Tamworth m. Eunice M. **Hoag** of Sandwich 6/27/1907 in Sandwich; H – 26, foreman, b. Tamworth, s/o A. C. Spaulding (Quebec) and Ida M. Felch (Tamworth); W – 22, teacher, b. Tamworth, d/o Thomas W. Hoag (Sandwich) and M. E. Cartland (Parsonsfield, ME)

Rufus W. of Shelburne m. Florence **Spaulding** of Tamworth 11/30/1905 in Tamworth; H – 29, farmer, b. Bellows Falls, VT, s/o Charles H. Spalding (Campton, PQ) and Addie M. Swan (Canaan, VT); W – 27, at home, b. Tamworth, d/o Addison Spaulding (Campton, PQ) and Ida D. Felch (Tamworth)

SPEAR,
David S. of Seattle, WA m. Stephanie A. **Wenckus** of Seattle, WA 6/20/1992

SPECKMAN,
Robert E. of Tamworth m. Violet D. **Eldridge** of Ossipee 9/8/1951 in Ossipee; H – 23, logger; W – 18, at home

SPENGLER,
Silas L. of Manhattan, NY m. Christine M. **Peters** of Manhattan, NY 8/7/1993

SPIEGEL,
Mark R. of MA m. Faith B. **Rafkind** of MA 1/3/1981

SPINDLE,
Henry M. of Meredith m. Lilla M. **Farnham** of Tamworth 10/30/1951 in Laconia; H – 73, retired; W – cook

STACY,
Nathan John m. Gladys M. **Ames** 4/12/1922 in Tamworth; H – 20, b. Madison; W – 20, b. Tamworth

STAFFORD,
Hans Burke of Tamworth m. Isabelle Oakes **Hunnewell** of Tamworth 8/19/1995

STALEY,
Victor E. of Tamworth m. Margaret E. **Weare** of Tamworth 12/1/1979

STALL,
Thomas G. of Reading, OH m. Edna M. **Nickerson** of Tamworth 11/10/1945 in Chocorua; H – 24, dry cleaning; W – 21, at home

STAPLES,
Daniel Victor of Tamworth m. Susan Marie **Willey** of Conway 8/17/1963 in N. Conway; H – 21, shipper; W – 20, secretary
Mark A. of Tamworth m. Yvonne N. **Harris** of Tamworth 8/30/1980
Ralph of Saco, ME m. Flora B. **Howard** of Tamworth 12/25/1907 in Tamworth; H – 26, mechanic, b. Newfield, ME, s/o W. H. Staples (Newfield, ME) and Mary I. Miles (Limerick, ME); W – 28, housekeeper, b. Harrison, ME, d/o Henry Howard (Harrison, ME) and C. Kenniston (Lovell, ME)
Stephen Walter of Tamworth m. Yvonne Nancy **Jones** of Conway 3/4/1972; H – 24; W – 18
Walter S. of Tamworth m. Virginia B. **Barnard** of Eliot, ME 8/10/1968; H – 55; W - 48

Winslow of Tamworth m. Clara M. **Liberty** of Tamworth 12/8/1890 in Tamworth; H - 25, laborer, b. Tamworth, s/o Charles Staples; W - 18, housework, b. VT, d/o James Liberty (Canada)

STARK,
Robert Theodore of Tamworth m. Marjorie L. **Richardson** of Conway 11/26/1964 in Conway; H – 25, student; W – 21, student

STEELE,
Dana Allen, Jr. of Tamworth m. Helen **Read** of Tamworth 6/21/1969; H – 26; W – 24
Edward T. of Cleveland, OH m. Heidi E. **Hunt** of Cleveland, OH 8/8/1987
James Emerson, II of Kennebunkport, ME m. Lynn Mae **Martin** of Kennebunkport, ME 4/6/1974; H – 21; W – 22
Nathaniel A. of Tamworth m. Helen R. **Steele** of Tamworth 7/22/1978; H – 28; W – 33

STEHLI,
Henry H. of S. Tamworth m. Diane E. **Casey** of Greenwich, CT 10/12/1994

STEVENS,
Ralph John of N. Harwich, MA m. Roberta J. **Perkins** of Tamworth 8/3/1985
Roland m. Esther F. **Hanscom** 12/13/1958 in Center Ossipee; H – 69, retired; W – 53, at home

STEVENSON,
Charles of Tamworth m. Francis A. **Perkins** of Tamworth 5/11/1887 in Tamworth; H - 32, laborer, b. Tamworth, s/o Lorenzo Stevenson (Tamworth) and Lucy B.; W - 21, b. Jackson, d/o Pike G. Perkins

STEWART,
Albert Alexander of Tamworth m. Joyce Annie **Chassie** of Berlin 12/3/1967; H – 20, student; W – 17, at home

STINCHFIELD,
Philip A. of Worcester, MA m. Ann E. **Fitzpatrick** of Worcester, MA 1/26/1951 in Tamworth; H – 23, metal dealer; W – 18, housework

STODDARD,
Clark M. m. Eleanor M. **Davis** 10/22/1960 in N. Haverhill; H – 20, truck driver; W – 24, furniture factory
Donald T. of Ossipee m. Maude A. **Gordon** of Tamworth 7/23/1950 in Tamworth; H – 16, at home; W – 16, at home

STOKES,
Arthur P. of Tamworth m. Hattie M. **Hutchins** of Tamworth 4/25/1913 in Tamworth; H – 20, laborer, b. Harrison, ME, s/o Horace P. Stokes and Annie P. Pike; W - 15, at home, b. Tamworth, d/o William N. Hutchins and Augusta Dame

STONE,
Bruce L. m. Ruth W. **Staples** 1/9/1960 in Tamworth; H – 17, student; W – 18, waitress

STRAIN,
Noel T. of Beaufort, SC m. Katlyn M. **Hamalainen** of Tamworth 12/27/2002

STREETER,
Bradley E. of Sandwich m. Karen A. **Robinson** of Sandwich 8/17/2002
Brian A. of Tamworth m. Laurie Anne **Mee** of ME 7/12/2003
Brian Almon of Tamworth m. Angela Mae **Eldridge** of Tamworth 6/7/1997
Clifford R. of Tamworth m. Lorraine E. **Evans** of Tamworth 9/19/1947 in Gorham; H – 23, truck driver; W – 20, clerk
Joel F. of Tamworth m. Minda M. **Mason** of Tamworth 5/30/1979
Joel Franklin of Tamworth m. Lorraine Loretta **Steele** of Tamworth 10/25/1997
Joseph A. of Tamworth m. Mildred D. **Marshall** of Tamworth 2/3/1950 in Bartlett; H – 29, truck driver; W – 17, at home
Mark D. of Tamworth m. Melanie A. **Elliott** of Chocorua 5/24/1980

STRONG,
Robert S. m. Josephine L. **Jackson** 4/30/1927 in Ctr. Ossipee
William J. of Revere, MA m. Patricia **Reilly** of Revere, MA 8/17/1985

STRUHL,
Kevin of Boston, MA m. Marjorie Ann **Oettinger** of Boston, MA 6/4/1989

SULLIVAN,
Brian George of Tamworth m. Jennifer Louise **Snow** of Tamworth 8/19/2000
George Edward, III of MA m. Tammy Lynn **Welch** of Tamworth 4/30/1988
L. Kevin of Forrest Hills, NY m. Harriet M. **Richards** of New York, NY 10/8/1983

SUPPES,
Bruce D. of Tamworth m. Nancy A. **Melanson** of ME 7/13/1980

SWAN,
Christopher of Tamworth m. Deborah A. **Whiting** of Tamworth 7/12/1984

SWAYNE,
William Wager of New York, NY m. Elizabeth C. **Snow** of New York, NY 12/18/1965 in Tamworth; H – 27, field rep.; W – 25, editorial ass.

SWEET,
George W. of Melrose, MA m. Gayle I. **Nelson** of Melrose, MA 9/12/1992

SWENSON,
Neil E. of Tamworth m. Tammy L. **Hoch** of Tamworth 12/10/1977; H – 21; W – 19

SWIRZEWSKI,
Stanley J. of New Britain, CT m. Lynn J. **Allen** of New Britain, CT 9/17/1983

SYLVAIN,
Roy C. of Tamworth m. Lynn M. **Watson** of Tamworth 6/27/1992

TAIT,
Stanley J. of Tamworth m. Rebecca A. **Burns** of Tamworth 2/3/2003

TALAVERA,
Gilbert of Salem, MA m. Virginia L. **Drew** of Marblehead, MA 5/15/1987

TALBOT,
Timothy J. of Tamworth m. Lynne H. **MacDonald** of Tamworth 6/29/1996

TAPPAN,
Fred W. m. Barbara **Eastwick** 6/29/1929 in Whittier
Henry m. Margaret **Vittum** 12/18/1937 in Conway

TASKER,
Mark F. of Madison m. Lillian E. **Moulton** of Tamworth 1/4/1890 in Madison; H - 23, farmer, b. Madison, s/o Mark F. Tasker (Sandwich); W - 21, housework, b. Albany, d/o A. W. Moulton (Albany)

TATARCZUK,
Scott B. of S. Tamworth m. Sarah C. **Burnett** of S. Tamworth 6/16/2001

TAYLOR,
Franklin B. of Hanover m. Alice B. **Remick** of Tamworth 6/27/1906 in Tamworth; H – teacher, b. Central Falls, RI, s/o Frederick C. Taylor (Nantucket, MA) and Parmelia C. Chase (Nantucket, MA); W – teacher, b. Tamworth, d/o Levi Remick (Tamworth) and Harriet Bedee (Tamworth)
George A. of Conway m. Nellie A. **Jackson** of Tamworth 5/1/1913 in Tamworth; H – 26, farmer, b. Bridgeton, ME, s/o Burleigh M. Taylor and Mary E. Thurston; W – 25, stenographer, b. Tamworth, d/o Samuel H. Jackson and Annie B. Purrington
James D. of Winthrop, MA m. Mary A. **Jordon** of Brighton, MA 3/15/1975; H – 37; W – 26

Keith R. m. Eleanor F. **Palmer** 8/11/1954 in Tamworth; H – 20, US Army; W – 18, waitress

Shawn C. of Tamworth m. Eileen M. **Cannon** of Tamworth 7/22/2000

William Henry of Sandwich m. Jean Marie **Rogers** of Tamworth 4/30/1964 in Sandwich; H – 18, mechanic; W – 18, mill worker

TEASDALE,
John m. Nellie **Nystedt** 6/29/1957 in Meredith; H – 23, brick layer; W – 20, student

TEE,
David Fowler of Dallas, Texas m. Carol J. **Sleight** of Milford, ME 10/4/1975; H – 28; W – 22

TERRY,
Ernest of Billerica, MA m. Catherine F. **Mills** of Billerica, MA 5/28/1938 in Tamworth; H – 46, die cutter; W – 45, bookbinder

TERYEK,
Daniel Sidney of Tamworth m. Xann Louise **French** of Tamworth 7/1/2000

TEW,
Peter Arthur of Phoenix, AZ m. Marina **Hansen** of Phoenix, AZ 6/24/1972; H – 32; W – 26

TEWKSBURY,
Isaac A. of Tamworth m. Eva M. **Swain** of Albany 8/13/1902; H – 26, laborer, b. Tamworth, s/o William M. Tewksbury (Tamworth) and Adeline Mack (Madison); W – 22, housework, b. Meredith, d/o Henry Swain and Annuth Brown

THOMAS,
Dannie L. of Tamworth m. Caryn D. **Troutman** of Tamworth 12/15/1978; H – 18; W – 17

Frank F. m. Elfreda J. **Connor** 2/19/1955 in Manchester; H – 44, minister; W – 50, P. O. clerk

Scott of Lynn, MA m. Rachel **Bourdages** of Lynn, MA 10/25/1999

THOMPSON,
Charles G. m. Alice **Bemis** 6/17/1933 in Tamworth

THOMSON,
Scott J. of Lynn, MA m. Patricia A. **Reardon** of Tamworth 11/9/1993

THURSTON,
Alan W. of Tamworth m. Mary F. **Marro** of Andrews AFB, MD 4/19/1986
Christopher Jon of Silverthorne, CO m. Karen Margaret **Davis** of Silverthorne, CO 8/9/1997
Daniel C. m. Ellen D. **Smith** 2/18/1961 in Ctr. Ossipee; H – 21, tractor driver; W – 20, millwork
Larry C. of Ossipee m. Denice M. **Capalbo** of W. Ossipee 3/10/1973; H – 22; W – 19
Paris W. m. Hansine Elizabeth **Peterson** 9/23/1914 in Chocorua; H – 39, carpenter, b. Madison, s/o Jerome S. Thurston and Agnes Ellis; W – 36, housework, b. Denmark, d/o Jenz Peterson and Katherine Obec

TICE,
Roger Bruce of Ossipee m. Shirley May **Ames** of Tamworth 9/17/1971; H – 22; W – 19

TIEDMAN,
George of Newport, VT m. Maude C. **Corliss** of Tamworth 7/13/1940 in Newport; H – 68, retired; W – 65, housekeeper

TILTON,
Frank E. of Sandwich m. Clara B. **Tilton** of Sandwich 11/3/1897 in Tamworth; H – 29, butcher, b. Sandwich, s/o Albert Tilton (Sandwich) and Sarah Hoyt (Sandwich); W – 25, housekeeper, b. Sandwich, d/o Jonathan Tappan (Sandwich) and Julia Nute (Sandwich)

TISDALE,
Robert A. m. Mildred T. **Richards** 4/1/1934 in Madison

TOLMAN,
Gerald C. of Concord, MA m. Barbara A. **Sinsabaugh** of Concord, MA 8/8/1992

TONE,
Walter J., Jr. m. Jacquelyn L. **Abbott** 12/27/1958 in Tamworth; H – 27, gas – electric; W – 30, office manager

TONINO,
Richard P. of Burlington, VT m. Ellen M. **Postlewaite** of Burlington, VT 7/14/1979

TORNROSE,
William F. m. Marcia L. **Sadler** 8/11/1957 in Tamworth; H – 20, student; W – 18, secretary

TRACY,
John Patrick of Texas m. Kelly Marie **Locke** of Tamworth 2/22/1988

TRASK,
Frank W. of Tamworth m. Joyce L. **Howe** of N. Conway 7/27/1952 in N. Conway; H – 19, student; W – 19, student
Harold B. m. Emma L. **Moulton** 8/5/1918 in Moultonboro; H – 21, b. Sandwich, s/o Frank W. Trask and Belle E. Bennett; W – 19, b. Tamworth, d/o Willis Moulton and Ella Allard
Howard R. of Tamworth m. Mary E. **Labrie** of Tamworth 6/8/1985
Howard R. of Tamworth m. Laura J. **Campbell** of Tamworth 9/7/2002
Robert H. of Tamworth m. Dorothy E. **Moore** of Tamworth 6/21/1941 in Sanbornville; H – 19, electrician; W – 20, asst. postmistress
Robert H. of Tamworth m. Priscilla A. **Myers** of Brooklyn, NY 10/6/1951 in Tamworth; H – 29, electrician; W – 28, clerical
Stanley of Tamworth m. Lena **Cyr** of Tamworth 10/4/1940 in N. Conway; H – 20, carpenter; W – 27, cook

TREFRY,
Wayne A. of Tamworth m. Melissa **Robinson** of Tamworth 8/4/2001

TRENT,
Frank S. of Tamworth m. Donna M. **Breen** of Tamworth 7/4/1994

TRIPP,
Dale F. of Tamworth m. Eleanor M. **Bickford** of Tamworth 8/7/1948 in Tamworth; H – 23, doctor of chiropractic; W – 21, music

TRUOG,
Robert David of Newton, MA m. Amy **Wittet** of Newton, MA 10/7/1989

TUCKER,
Glenn Cushing of Chocorua m. Lisa Beth **Langlois** of Chocorua 6/29/1999

TUFF,
Alfred P. of NH m. Letitia M. **Weymouth** of Tamworth 2/14/1980

TUFTS,
Charles F. of Waltham, MA m. Madeline T. **Gosseline** of Waltham, MA 6/25/1993

TUPPER,
Charles Warren, III of Chocorua m. Barbara Jane **Olsen** of Attleboro, MA 12/21/1963 in Attleboro, MA; H – 22, student; W – 22, teacher

TURCOTTE,
Harry Howard m. Katherine **Boyd** 11/10/1918 in Concord; H – 29, laborer, b. Concord, s/o William H. Turcotte and Emma Saltmarsh; W – 20, teacher, b. Tamworth, d/o Thompson Boyd and Rose Hill

TUTT,
Allen C. m. Elizabeth **Edgerly** 5/26/1934 in Wakefield

TWITCHELL,
Roger Thayer, Jr. of York, PA m. Sandra Madison **Norcross** of Boston, MA 8/3/1963 in Chocorua; H – 34, teacher; W – 26, counselor

TYE,
Richard J. of Brunswick, ME m. Henrietta S. **McBee** of Brunswick, ME 10/6/1984

ULITZ,
Michael B. of Tamworth m. Stephanie L. **Chase** of Tamworth 9/24/1983

Michael Bernard of Tamworth m. Donna F. **Switaj** of Tamworth 8/2/1997

URQUHART,
Kenneth N. of Tamworth m. Lori J. **Chase** of Tamworth 12/24/1992

VALENTINE,
Malcom W. of Tamworth m. Gwendolyn C. **Marcotte** of Tamworth 9/21/1983

VANDER CLUTE,
Norman R. m. Faith E. **Bowlitch** 8/16/1958 in Tamworth; H – 25, lawyer; W – 22, student

VANDERLAAN,
Peter Wilson of NM m. Mary Beth **Bliss** 12/29/1976; H – 26; W – 24

VARNEY,
George O. of Tamworth m. Clara E. **Bryer** of Tamworth 6/18/1887 in Tamworth; H - 24, laborer, b. Ossipee, s/o Clark T. Varney (Berwick, ME, farmer) and Hannah J.; W - 25, housekeeper, b. Sandwich, d/o John F. Bryer (Sandwich, farmer) and Sarah
Harold M. of Tamworth m. Viola A. **Eldridge** of Tamworth 8/23/1941 in Ossipee; H – 27, woodsman; W – 19, at home
Joseph R. of Chocorua m. Michele S. **Bugbee** of Chocorua 5/21/1983
Joseph R. of Chocorua m. Diane **Baker** of Newburyport, MA 1/1/1994
Ronald E. of Concord m. Barbara M. **Buck** 6/17/1978; H – 33; W – 41

VASEY,
Earle F. m. Edna C. **Downs** 2/14/1935 in Chocorua

VELEZ,
Damaso Ray of Rutland, VT m. Lisa Marie **Nelson** of Rutland, VT 7/29/1995

VENEZIALE,
Paul J. of PA m. Claire L. **Mooney** of PA 7/31/1977; H – 26; W – 28

VIERCZHALEK,
Kenneth J. of Arlington, MA m. Alice B. **Pugh** of Arlington, MA 9/22/1990

VILBIG,
Mark P. of Tamworth m. Joisse S. **Rumary** of Tamworth 7/19/2001

VINCENT,
Frank W., Jr. of Baguio, PI m. Mary L. **Boyden** of Winchester, MA 9/7/1938 in Tamworth; H – 25, teacher; W – 21, at home

VITTUM,
Alfred O. m. Dorothy **Dearborn** 3/2/1925 in Tamworth
Alfred Otis m. Mildred C. **Brown** 2/3/1935 in Portsmouth
Brewster Dale of Tamworth m. Kathleen Ellen **McCormack** of Moultonboro 10/17/1971; H – 18; W – 18
Kenneth F. m. Frances Viola **Lord** 10/27/1934 in Fryeburg, ME
Kenneth F. m. Rita M. **Leblanc** 2/28/1959 in Plymouth; H – 45, auto salesman; W – 36, machine opr.
Leonard H. of Tamworth m. Laura I. **Hutchinson** of Whitman, MA 4/28/1908 in Whitman, MA; H – 31, clerk, b. Sandwich, s/o Cyrus B. Vittum (Sandwich) and Lizzie C. Dodge (Sandwich); W – 32, teacher, b. S. Hanson, MA, d/o A. D. Hutchinson (Whitman, MA) and E. P. L. Woodward (England)
Merton C. m. Rachel **Hodge** 12/13/1929 in Wolfeboro

VLASS,
Michael R. of Medfield, MA m. Kristin J. **Ohnemus** of Medfield, MA 4/21/1990

VOEGTLIN,
Kenneth P. of Tamworth m. Sonia **Berry** of Tamworth 9/10/1994

WAITE,
John A. of Somerville, MA m. Amy G. **Semmes** of Somerville, MA 6/27/1987

WAKEFIELD,
Arthur D. m. Anne **Whiting** 8/1/1953 in Center Harbor; H – 19, truckman; W – 17, at home

WAKEMAN,
Russell J. of MI m. Winifred R. **Swope** of MU 8/13/1977; H – 22; W – 21

WALDON,
Arthur T. of Tamworth m. Katherine **Sleeper** of Tamworth 12/9/1902; H – 31, farmer, b. Indianapolis, IN, s/o Treadwell Waldron (sic) (Waldon, NY); W – boarding house

WALKER,
Richard Earl of Tamworth m. June Rachel **Sawin** of Littleton, MA 9/16/1966; H – 22, US Army; W – 17, assembler
Robert H. of Tamworth m. Grace E. **Stoe** of Tamworth 3/29/1980
Stephen S. of Tamworth m. Amanda J. **Miller** of Ctr. Conway 9/15/2001
Walter C. of Melrose, MA m. Hattie B. **Bickford** of Tamworth 10/1/1901 in Tamworth; H – 26, engineer, b. Holliston, MA, s/o Charles H. Walker (Holliston, MA) and Margaret E. Annetts (Holliston, MA); W – 20, housework, b. Tamworth, d/o Gilman Bickford (Tamworth) and Annie Remick (Sandwich)
Walter Edward of Tamworth m. Myrtle L. **Page** of Tamworth 7/28/1940 in Fryeburg, ME; H – 37, truckman; W – 19, waitress

WALLACE,
Donald W. m. Evelyn M. **Spaulding** 1/1/1934 in Sandwich
Jeffrey Michael of Salem, OR m. Cathie Jean **Perkins** of Wasco, OR 12/21/1974; H – 25; W – 30

WALTER,
Ralph of Tamworth m. Jeanne F. **Kurinskas** of Tamworth 3/29/1985

WALTZ,
Arnold William of S. Windham, ME m. Pamela Jean **Burdin** of Lisbon, ME 5/24/1964 in Tamworth; H – 32, psychiatric aid; W – 20, at home

WARD,
Harold M. m. June P. **McCaughin** 7/4/1953 in N. Conway; H – 24, field engineer; W – 25, at home

WARING,
Timothy K. of Ashburn, VA m. Constance J. **Harrington** of Ashburn, VA 6/22/2002

WARREN,
Gary W. of Bridgton, ME m. Lisa J. **Allen** of Chocorua 6/4/1983

WASON,
Grant M. of Bradford, MA m. Tarry L. **Maltman** of Bradford, MA 8/28/1983

WASSON,
Ryan M. of Del Mar, CA m. Kimberly Ann **Johnson** of Del Mar, CA 4/17/1999

WATKINS,
Robert Mason of Southwick, MA m. Sandra Frances **Sweeney** of Southwick, MA 9/23/1989

WATSON,
Conrad C. m. Eleanor F. **Bock** 6/5/1960 in Tamworth; H – 20, paper mill; W – 18, secretary
Donald Richard of Tamworth m. Kathy Lynn **Baker** of Derry 7/9/1974; H – 20; W – 16

WEARE,
Michael E. of Tamworth m. Jacqueline A. **Bailey** of Tamworth 8/13/1994
Thomas Edmund of Tamworth m. Linda Lee **Rowe** of Tamworth 5/27/1971; H – 22; W – 21
Thomas Edmund of Tamworth m. Patricia Ann **Eldridge** of Tamworth 6/14/1975; H – 25; W – 22

WEBSTER,
Alfred L. m. Minnie F. **Welch** 5/4/1919 in Tamworth; H – 31, laborer, 2nd, s/o George Webster and Christina Burr; W – 18, housework, d/o James Welch and Mabel Schuter
Chester W. of Tamworth m. Hazel G. **Ames** of Tamworth 10/26/1942 in Moultonboro; H – 30, woodsman; W – 29, housework

Ray P. of Barton, VT m. Melba P. **Smith** of Tamworth 4/21/1940 in Exeter; H – 23, garage prop.; W – 22, stenographer

WEDGE,
Dennis Anthony of Conway m. Evelyn Mae **Eldridge** of Tamworth 6/25/1966; H – 23, laborer; W – 18, tel. operator

WELCH,
Austin E. of Tamworth m. Dorothy E. **French** of Tamworth 3/1/1939 in Tamworth; H – 21, laborer; W – 20, waitress
Edwin P. of Tamworth m. Priscilla M. **Brown** of Tamworth 10/5/1952 in Tamworth; H – 21, farmer; W – 21, tel. operator
Francis J. m. Josie **Nickerson** 9/18/1937 in Conway
Harry E. m. Vera I. **Bodge** 1/25/1930 in S. Tamworth
Marlon E. of Gorham, ME m. Jennifer K. **McEvoy** of Gorham, ME 7/2/2001
Richard David of Tamworth m. Betty Ethel **Watson** of Tamworth 2/27/1964 in Tamworth; H – 18, logger; W – 18, clerk
Russell m. Hester **Clark** 6/2/1917 in Tamworth; H – 20, woodsman, b. Ossipee, s/o Peter Welch and Cora Kimball; W – 17, d/o William Clark and Elizabeth Wade

WENTWORTH,
Harold, III of ME m. Sharon **Drew** of Tamworth 4/18/1981

WESTON,
Miles G. of Bristol, VT m. Julia B. **Randall** of Middlebury, VT 10/12/1991

WHEATON,
Edward Fry Sexton of San Diego, CA m. Celine Ann **Perreault** of San Diego, CA 8/5/2000

WHIPPLE,
Frank P. m. Augusta May **Doe** 4/29/1932 in Wakefield
Frank P. of Tamworth m. Doris E. **Rock** of Groton, VT 7/5/1951 in Saco, ME; H – 43, lumber op.; W – 38, housewife
Frank P. m. Marguerite H. **Leavitt** 3/8/1953 in Center Ossipee; H – 44, contractor; W – 43, at home
Parker C. m. Joan **Phenix** 1/14/1956 in Tamworth; H – 32, forester; W – 28, teacher

Parker C. of Tamworth m. Donna L. **Ford** of Franconia 8/23/1969; H – 45; W – 27

WHITE,
Alfred P. of Tamworth m. Candy L. **Fallen** of Tamworth 1/29/1994
John D. of Tamworth m. Valerie M. **Emerson** of Tamworth 11/15/1992
John O. of Tamworth m. Robyn K. **Jackson** of Tamworth 4/9/1983
T. William of Merrimack m. Joy C. **Bleakney** of Tamworth 11/1/1980

WHITEING,
Carroll W. of Grafton, MA m. Rita M. **Wooten** of Grafton, MA 2/14/1985

WHITESIDE,
Taylor F. of Wakefield, MA m. Nicole E. **Maher** of Wonalancet 12/29/2001

WHITESIDES,
George M. of Cambridge, MA m. Barbara **Breasted** of Cambridge, MA 6/28/1969; H – 30; W – 28

WHITING,
Almon J. of Tamworth m. Lizzie E. **McClosky** of Laconia 2/9/1901 in Laconia; H – 40, farmer, b. Tamworth, John Whiting (Limerick, ME) and Ellen Allen (Cornish, ME); W – 32, mill operator, b. Sandwich, d/o Ambrose Palmer (Sandwich) and Carrie Moulton (Moultonboro)
Arthur C. of Tamworth m. Fanney E. **Forrest** of Tamworth 10/4/1902; H – 21, laborer, b. Tamworth, s/o George F. Whiting (Ossipee) and Annie Choate (Sandwich); W – 20, housework, b. Tamworth, d/o Hiram Forrest and Annie L. Bean (Conway)
Charles E. of Tamworth m. Jennie B. **Gale** of Moultonboro 9/1/1898 in Sandwich; H – 22, laborer, b. Moultonboro, s/o George Whiting (Ossipee) and Annie E. Choat (Sandwich); W – 23, housework, b. Moultonboro, d/o Lyman Wade (Centre Harbor) and Martha Blackey (Centre Harbor)
Clude D. of Tamworth m. Edith L. **Ames** of Tamworth 12/25/1903; H – 22, laborer, b. Tamworth, s/o Almon J. Whiting (Tamworth) and Lucy Smith (Tamworth); W – 18, housework, b. Tamworth, d/o Zimri Ames (Tamworth) and Ella J. Palmer (Sandwich)

Frank A. of Tamworth m. Mary Annette **Carr** of Tamworth 1/1/1923 in Tamworth; H – 65; W - 57

Fred M. of Tamworth m. Georgia E. **Jeffers** of Tamworth 9/16/1909 in Tamworth; H – 19, laborer, b. Tamworth, s/o George F. Whiting (Ossipee, farmer) and Annie Choate (Moultonboro, housewife); W – 16, housework, b. Warner, d/o Milton W. Jeffers (Webster, farmer) and Abbie Downs (Tamworth, housewife)

Frederick H. m. Ethel E. **Jeffers** 12/2/1917 in Tamworth; H – 22, farmer, b. Boston, MA, s/o Frank A. Whiting and Abbie C. Hobson; W – 28, b. Tamworth, d/o Fred L. Jeffers and Gertrude M. Gilman

George R. of Tamworth m. Rona A. **Simonds** of Tamworth 7/14/1951 in Sandwich; H – 20, woodsman; W – 18, at home

Howard W. m. Madeline **Eastwick** 5/11/1928 in Wolfeboro

Jeffrey L. of Tamworth m. Theresa **Woodward** of Tamworth 7/8/1984

Leland F. m. Edith A. **Horne** 6/22/1957 in Meredith; H – 24, truck driver; W – 19, secretary

Lewis R. of Tamworth m. Deborah J. **Fryman** of Tamworth 6/15/1996

Richard E. of Tamworth m. Martha S. **Simpson** of Mebane, NC 12/14/1978; H – 19; W – 27

Richard E. of Tamworth m. Colleen M. **Ames** of Tamworth 1/15/1990

Robert P. m. Jessie E. **Boothby** 7/17/1929 in Sanbornville

Roland G. m. Hazel **MacKenzie** 12/2/1925 in Tamworth

Steven D. of S. Tamworth m. Cheryl A. **Kusala** of S. Tamworth 10/5/1996

Victor L. m. Madeline **Clough** 9/7/1920 in Moultonboro; H – 21, laborer, b. Tamworth, s/o Charles Whiting and Jennie Gale; W – 21, housework, 2nd, b. Sandwich, d/o Elmer Elliott and Maud Mitchell

Victor L. m. Mamie E. **Bennett** 2/14/1928 in Sandwich

William H. of Tamworth m. Lulu A. **Floyd** of Tamworth 10/3/1900 in Moultonboro; H – 41, farmer, s/o George C. Whiting (Limerick, ME) and Ellen J. Johnson (Beverly, MA); W – 19, housework, d/o A. Floyd (Brownfield, ME) and Ida Mason (Tamworth)

WHITNEY,
Charles m. Elizabeth D. **Lincoln** 9/2/1914 in Tamworth; H – 55, teacher of art, 2nd, b. Pittston, ME, s/o Isaac S. Whitney and Mary E. Mitchell; W – 55, Chris. Sci. prac., b. Roxbury, MA, d/o Charles D. Lincoln and Maria L. Prowty

WHITTAKER,
Scott C. of Fryeburg, ME m. Joy E. **MacDonald** of Tamworth 4/27/1973; H – 18; W – 18

WHITTIER,
Charles P. of Boston, MA m. Nellie M. **Bickford** of Tamworth 6/26/1890 in Tamworth; H - 25, carpenter, b. Webster, s/o Charles C. Whittier (Webster); W - 25, dressmaker, b. Madison, d/o Benjamin F. Bickford (Madison)
Stephen M. of Chocorua m. Gayle A. **Sullo** of Chocorua 8/18/2001

WHYTE,
Peter H. of Haverhill, MA m. Jacqueline R. **Kirvan** of Haverhill, MA 6/22/1996

WIGGIN,
Arthur E. of Tamworth m. Anna M. **Tewksbury** of Sandwich 8/5/1897 in Sandwich; H – 20, laborer, b. Tamworth, s/o Joseph A. Wiggin (Tamworth) and Frances Hutchins (Damascotta); W – 17, b. Sandwich, d/o James Tewksbury (Sandwich) and Sarah F. Hurley (Salem, MA)
Gary W. of Tamworth m. Sharron **Herbold** of Ossipee 1/2/1971; H – 21; W – 21
Harold H. m. Marilyn J. **Mudgett** 9/11/1954 in Center Sandwich; H – 26, laborer; W – 20, stenographer
Kenneth Alfred of Tamworth m. Lea Irna **Bushway** of Claremont 9/11/1965 in Claremont; H – 21, student; W – 18, student
Kenneth E. of Tamworth m. Lillian I. **Demers** of Tamworth 8/27/1941 in Conway; H – 20, mechanic; W – 21, waitress
Leander T. m. Katie **Drew** 12/11/1924 in Tamworth
Richard A. of Tamworth m. Katharine F. **Tuttle** of Wakefield 6/15/1942 in Wakefield; H – 23, US Army; W – 20, at home
Roscoe A. of Wakefield m. Minnie E. **Hardy** of Tamworth 3/6/1909 in Tamworth; H – 24, shoemaker, b. Acton, ME, s/o John W. Wiggin (Acton, ME, farmer) and Mary E. Elliott (Tuftonboro,

housewife); W – 18, at home, b. Tamworth, d/o William H. Hardy (Tamworth, farmer) and Georgiana Davis (Effingham, housewife)

Sylvester of Tamworth m. Mrs. Annie **Williams** of Arlington, MA 6/2/1888 in Tamworth; H - 34, mechanic, b. Tamworth, s/o Henry Wiggin, Jr.; W - 37, housework, b. Arlington, MA, d/o Daniel Wilson

WILDER,
Norman E. m. Kate E. **Read** 6/21/1936 in Lyme

WILES,
Robert H. of Winslow, ME m. Sally L. **McCue** of Winslow, ME 8/6/1985

WILKINSON,
Alan T. of Tamworth m. Norma J. **Bugbee** of Claremont 12/5/1998
Kraig Alan of Tamworth m. Lisa Renea **Giasson** of Moultonboro 10/24/1997

WILLEY,
Ralph W. m. Lillian E. **Bickford** of Tamworth 2/17/1913 in Portland, ME; H – 36, carpenter, b. Fryeburg, ME, s/o Amri Luther Willey and Mary J. Walker; W – 35, housework, b. Tamworth, d/o Gilman Bickford and Annie L. Remick

WILLIAMS,
Charles J. m. Lilla May **Pennell** 10/30/1920 in Tamworth; H – 24, fireman, b. Tamworth, s/o Justus Williams and Mertie Smart; W – 20, clerk, b. Tamworth, d/o Charles Pennell and Addie Brown

Charles J., Jr. of Tamworth m. Hope N. **Jackson** of Ctr. Ossipee 2/10/1945 in E. Rochester; W – 20, furniture worker; W – 18, waitress

Gary R. of Madison m. Jo Ann **Wilkinson** of Tamworth 2/16/1991

Gregory John of Newtown, PA m. Carolyn Davis **Watt** of Newtown, PA 6/27/1998

Henry B. of Philadelphia, PA m. Rebecca **Gallagher** of Montpelier, VT 9/6/1943 in Tamworth; H – 35, com. officer, US Army; W – 38, VT. State Dept. of Education

Justin W. of Tamworth m. Clara A. **Perkins** of Tamworth 6/8/1911 in Acton, ME; H – 55, sawyer, b. Ossipee, s/o Shaba Williams

(Ossipee) and Lydia Welch (Ossipee); W – 53, housekeeper, b. New Durham, d/o Benjamin Perkins (New Durham) and Olive Deland (New Durham)

Justus W. of Tamworth m. Mertey E. **Smart** of Tamworth 5/14/1888 in Conway; H - 32, mill-man, b. Ossipee, s/o Shaber Williams (Ossipee); W - 16, housework, b. Tamworth, d/o Charles Smart

Michael Dean of Chapel Hill, NC m. Lucinda Lee **Edlund** of Chapel Hill, NC 8/30/1997

Paul E. m. Martha **Evans** 6/29/1957 in Center Ossipee; H – 20, truck driver; W – 19, at home

Richard W. of Tamworth m. Margie L. **Williams** of Tamworth 6/21/1952 in Moultonville; H – 28, farmer; W – 18, at home

Richard W. of Tamworth m. Dorothy **Crozier** of N. Conway 7/15/1980

Robert Alston of Tamworth m. Cynthia Ann **Chamberlain** of Tamworth 10/13/1962 in Tamworth; H – 21, carpenter help; W – 18, student

Ward B. m. Judith A. **Downs** 4/27/1957 in Ossipee; H – 24, draftsman; W – 18, at home

WINTERS,
Jesse I. of ME m. Catherine L. **Hanson** of Tamworth 6/14/2003

WITTE,
Nicholas H. of Portland, ME m. Anne **Lloyd** of Portland, ME 6/1/1991

WITZEL,
Erich A. m. Jane M. **Thompson** 3/4/1961 in Tamworth; H – 29, dentist; W – 20, student nurse

WLASSICH,
John James of Dover, MA m. Amey Dexter **Moot** of Dover, MA 9/18/1999

WOOD,
Adams J. of Black Mountain, NC m. Francine M. **Cavanaugh** of Black Mountain, NC 8/8/2002

Jason A. of ME m. Melissa M. **Smith** of ME 8/9/2003

WOODES,
Robert C. of Madison m. Carol N. **Gilman** of Tamworth 10/25/1941 in Tamworth; H – 23, furniture worker; W – 18, at home

WOODSIDE,
Bruce E. of Holliston, MA m. Patricia A. **Carr** of Tamworth 5/11/1974; H – 34; W - 25

WOODWARD,
Freeman Earl of Tamworth m. Jacquelyne Lorraine **Tibbetts** of Center Ossipee 8/29/1963 in Tamworth; H – 21, carpenter; W – 18, student
John Shurman of S. Tamworth m. Barbara Jean **Spaulding** of Tamworth 5/20/1995
Robert C. of Tamworth m. Sheila R. **Dall** of Kezar Falls, ME 2/14/1970; H – 24; W – 23

WORCESTER,
Edward D. of Brighton, MA m. Susan P. **McKeefrey** of Brighton, MA 9/22/1985

WORMWOOD,
Herbert E. of Ossipee m. Minnie **Tibbetts** of Tamworth 1/27/1894 in Effingham; H - 20, mechanic, b. Ossipee, s/o Charles Wormwood (Kennebunk, ME, farmer) and Huldah Eldridge (housework); W - 19, housework, b. Madison, d/o Stephen Tibbetts (laborer) and Mary Richards

WRIGHT,
Howard H. of Avon, CT m. Elizabeth H. **Nichols** of Simsbury, CT 8/21/1986

WYNNE,
William Ernest of Oklahoma m. Elizabeth **Whiting** of Tamworth 11/27/1964 in Tamworth; H – 21, armed forces; W – 19, office mgr.

YARNELL,
Stephen of PA m. Barbara **Porter** of PA 8/29/1981

YEATON,
Fred m. Rosie Blanche **Cummings** 8/4/1915 in Concord; H – 28, baggageman, b. Pittsfield, s/o Joseph Yeaton and Olive Collins; W – 24, housework, b. Woburn, MA, d/o Ansel Cummings and Rosie Blanch Brown

YONTS,
Stewart H. of Houston, Texas m. Becky L. **Little** of Houston, Texas 10/6/1987

YOUNG,
Stanley L. m. Ethel **Hirsch** 9/9/1918 in Tamworth; H – 33, patrolman, state road, b. Rochester, s/o John Young and Emma L. Lord; W – 37, housekeeper, 3rd, b. Templeton, MA, d/o George H. Crocker

ZACK,
James M. of Collingswood, NJ m. Terri A. **McIlvried** of Collingswood, NJ 10/22/1994

ZOWASKY,
Robert K. of Tamworth m. Theresa M. **Thurston** of Tamworth 8/24/2002

Abbott, Jacquelyn L. – Tone, Walter J., Jr.
Acas, Jay Eileen - Smith, Michael Jeffrey
Ackley, Margaret L. – Brooks, Gordon H.
Ackley, Susan M. – Cabell, William D.
Adjutant, Maude L. – Moulton, James E.
Ahern, Ruth H. – Haskell, Nelson Cary
Albino, Patricia Ann - Diefenbach, Philip Joseph
Albrecht, A. Edith – Macy, Donald R.
Alden, Lena Pauline – Cooke, Carl Leverette
Aldrich, Ruth Ann – Christian, Percy Lee, Jr.
Alexander, Deborah J. - Anthony, David C.
Alfred, Patricia – Savard, Emile H.
Allard, Lillian B. – Pennell, Dwight R.
Allard, Lydia E. – Moulton, Willis
Allard, Minnie E. – Moore, Frank F.
Allen, Jacqwelyn Lee – Burke, Thomas William
Allen, Lisa J. – Warren, Gary W.
Allen, Lynn J. – Swirzweski, Stanley J.
Allen, Marilyn – Howie, Colin A.
Alley, Irene E. – Robinson, Henry W.
Alosa, Susan A. – Korpi, Roger E.
Alston, Jane Meredith – Solar, Robert Louis
Alt, Elizabeth M. – Blue, John A.
Ames, Bernice A. – Glidden, Carl S.
Ames, Blanche – Mason, Horace
Ames, Colleen M. - Whiting, Richard E.
Ames, Edith L. – Whiting, Clude D.
Ames, Edith May – Carter, Gordon Winslow
Ames, Esther G. – Brothers, Elmer W.
Ames, Gladys M. – Stacy, Nathan John
Ames, Hattie – Ames, John
Ames, Hazel G. – Webster, Chester W.
Ames, Helen A. – Moulton, Burleigh I.
Ames, Irene M. – Norcross, Arthur Z.
Ames, Luella – Jenkins, Clarence H.
Ames, Sherry Marie – Shackford, Loren Albert
Ames, Shirley May – Tice, Roger Bruce
Amundson, Grace E. – Mauran, William L., Jr.
Andrews, Florence B. – Chamberlain, Ralph W.
Anthony, Deborah A. – Mosher, James R.
Anthony, Elva E. – Parks, Edward Lee

Anthony, Gladys R. – Ambrose, Langdon J.
Anthony, Janice L. – Drowns, Kenneth W.
Anthony, Janice L. - Couch, Walter O.
Anthony, Judith W. – Kayser, Paul
Anthony, Peggy Ann - Eldridge, Walter Clyde
Anthony, Shirley Ellen – Frost, Bernard Elwin
Anthony, Tracey L. - Noyes, Judson A.
Anthony, Virginia Jean – Nevells, Stanley Richard
Apter, Felice M. - Kennedy, Thomas A.
Aries, Francella – Andujar, Wilfredo
Arling, Leonora B. – Clifford, Ernest L.
Armstrong, Alice G. – Kane, Carl F.
Armstrong, Katheryn G. – Erickson, Robert Dennis
Arnold, Janice M. – Goodson, Peter B.
Arsenault, Lena – Melanson, Roy
Aspinall, Gloria B. – Hayford, A. David
Aspinall, Jean M. - Record, Charles W.
Asselin, Ruth M. – McCarthy, William J.
Atwood, Cora M. - Remick, James H.
Atwood, Pamela Jane – MacDonald, Forrest G., Jr.
Austin, Judith O. – Johnson, Arthur W.
Austin, Penney Marie - Avery, Lyndon Edward
Avallone, Nancy G. - Nevins, Richard P.
Ayer, Marjorie Evelyn – Remick, Levi Wadsworth

Bachle, Donna L. – Hale, Roger W.
Bacon, Ruth Anne – Argento, Nicholas
Bailey, Jacqueline A. - Weare, Michael E.
Bailey, Tricia B. - Littlefield, Norman F. H., Jr.
Baker, Diane - Varney, Joseph R.
Baker, Kathy Lynn – Watson, Donald Richard
Baker, Laurie A. – Mooney, Edward F., Jr.
Baker, Lora M. – Bowley, Roland G.
Balomenos, Suzanne V. – Morgan, Christopher
Banfill, Evelyn A. – Kelley, Harry V.
Barker, Louise Albro – Robinson, Andrew Jordt
Barker, Lyn-Anne Marie - Lemieux, Paul David
Barnard, Virginia B. – Staples, Walter S.
Barnes, Emma – Saulnier, John
Barnes, Lois Elaine – Mills, Gerald
Barnes, Tammy Lin - O'Keefe, James Robert

Barry, Arlene M. – Averill, Gerald A.
Bartlett, Evelyn B. – Dow, Ralph P.
Bartlett, Mary E. - Ballard, Hollis B.
Barton, Patricia J. – Frost, Norris W.
Bassani, Helen L. - Haynes, Charlie O.
Bassett, Fannie A. – Silvan, Emanuel J.
Bassett, Helen J. – Hidden, S. Harold
Bates, Alexandra J. - Lefebvre, Jeffery J.
Bates, Terri Lynn - Eldridge, Scotty Allen
Baumenn, Yvonne - Perkins, Terrance Kenny
Baybutt, Sharon Lee - LaPorte, David Earl
Beall, Susan McMillen – Acton, Lloyd Phelps
Bean, Doris M. – Fortier, Albert F.
Bean, Effie P. – Johnson, Forrest W.
Bean, Lorraine – Baker, Wallace H.
Bean, Nancy J. – Nickerson, David W.
Bean, Sanrda A. – Dicey, Jeffrey L.
Beane, Catherine Susan - Bradbury, Duane Lee
Beaudet, Shirley Jean – Eldridge, Harry Plummer
Beaulieu, Laura Jean - Ferland, Paul Eugene
Beede, Lizzie - Bickford, Wyatt T.
Beeler, Pamela A. – Ames, Roy M., Jr.
Behr, Gretchen - Lebroke, Charles F., III
Belanger, Barbara – McCarthy, Francis
Bell, Sharon A. – Evans, Ansel, Jr.
Bell, Sharon A. – Ricker, Moses E.
Bellows, Elizabeth - Hidden, Samuel A.
Bemis, Alice – Thompson, Charles G.
Bennett, Annie – Moore, George A.
Bennett, Christine F. – Maduskie, Edward S.
Bennett, Lisa J. - Holbrook, Peter R.
Bennett, Mabel A. - Davis, Franklin W.
Bennett, Mamie E. – Whiting, Victor L.
Bennett, Shirley - Anthony, Gerald Edward
Benoit, Marletta D. - Maduskuie, Edward S.
Bergeron, Janet Leigh - Huddleston, Carl David
Bergeron, Jennifer Leigh - Oberting, Paul Mark
Bergeron, Karen L. – McGill, Robert T.
Bernard, Alison Marie - Mauch, Matthew Eric
Berrier, Amy K. – Smith, Thaddeus B.
Berry, Alice B. - Davis, Amos T.

Berry, Cynthia A. – Jones, Robert George
Berry, Estella A. – Jeffers, Percy E.
Berry, Eva M. – Roberts, Edgar J.
Berry, Gertrude – Elliott, Albert
Berry, M. Abbie - Gordon, Timothy
Berry, Nellie M. – Grace, Perley C.
Berry, Sonia - Voegtlin, Kenneth P.
Betzen, Cecilia R. – McHose, Robert E.
Bickford, Bulah M. – Gray, Harold M.
Bickford, Eleanor M. – Tripp, Dale F.
Bickford, Estella – Perkins, Pike H.
Bickford, Eva E. - Bickford, James B.
Bickford, Gertrude M. – Rogers, George B.
Bickford, Gladys – Nutter, John B.
Bickford, Hattie B. – Walker, Walter C.
Bickford, Inzie A. - Brown, Edwin J.
Bickford, Lillian E. – Willey, Ralph W.
Bickford, Marie E. – Owens, Edward J.
Bickford, Marie Esther – Frost, Wayne Cecil
Bickford, Mildred E. – Goodson, Wilbur C.
Bickford, Nellie M. - Whittier, Charles P.
Bickford, Ruth Marie – Southall, William Henry
Bickford, Sarah A. - Bickford, Wilbur J.
Bickford, Sarah A. – Clough, Eugene W.
Biernacki, Anne Marie - Smith, Kenneth H.
Bisenti, Marie D. - McConarty, Stephen R.
Black, Beverly Mae – Hammond, Stanley Frank
Black, Margaret P. – Richardson, Stephen A.
Blackburn, Clara E. - Bickford, James H.
Blackler, Joyce N. – Ames, Robin M.
Blackmer, Grace Adelia – Downs, Wilbur R.
Blaisdell, Sarah R. – Knowlton, Calvin C.
Blake, Margaret – Henderson, Everett G.
Blake, Teena L. - Smith, Wade Q.
Blanchard, Ellen M. - Pixton, Felix M.
Bleakney, Joy C. – White, T. William
Blevens, Dorothy B. – Hastie, George B.
Bliss, Emily J. – Lesser, Edward R.
Bliss, Mary Beth – Vanderlaan, Peter Wilson
Bliss, Nano – Paul, Ronald M.
Bliss, Nano – Molloy, Michael Karl

Blodgett, Ada Anne – Downs, Elmer E.
Bock, Eleanor F. – Watson, Conrad C.
Bodge, Evvie M. – Glidden, William C.
Bodge, Vera I. – Welch, Harry E.
Bodnar, Kelly M. - Roy, Dwaine P.
Boewe, Angela Joan – McCarthy, Kevin Joseph
Boewe, Cynthia M. – Jennings, Paul B.
Boewe, Theresa L. - Clapp, Ian W.
Boland, Catherine M. – Hobbs, Wilbur
Bolger, Kathleen M. - Clayton, Kenneth Wayne
Bolles, Evelyn – Phenix, George Spencer
Bookholz, Teresa L. – Severy, Merle E.
Bookholz, Virginia M. – Jones, James M.
Boothby, Catherine D. – Knox, Brent E.
Boothby, Jessie E. – Whiting, Robert P.
Boothby, Michelle M. - Chick, William C., Jr.
Boucher, Renee S. - Boewe, Nicholas A.
Bourbeau, Ann Louise - Doucette, Victor C.
Bourdages, Rachel - Thomas, Scott
Boutilier, Debra – Graffam, Robert
Bouve, Amy R. - Jordice, Mark A.
Bowditch, Susan – Moody, William Brooks Blaisdell
Bowditch, Sylvia C. – Newsom, Samuel, Jr.
Bower, Mildred V. – Libby, Lawrence E.
Bowles, Barbara – Simoneau, Jean A.
Bowlitch, Faith E. – Vander Clute, Norman R.
Boyd, Katherine – Turcotte, Harry Howard
Boyd, Patricia Elaine – Boutin, Harold Raymond
Boyd, Ruth C. – Harris, Edward H.
Boyden, Mary L. – Vincent, Frank W., Jr.
Bradbury, Lucy A. - Remick, Willie M.
Bradford, Alexandra Hydee - Herlihy, Thomas J. Michael
Bragdon, Dale - Lloyd, Bruce
Bray, Carolyn Frances - Empey, Winston Basil
Bray, Mabel A. – Hidden, John B.
Breasted, Barbara – Whitesides, George M.
Breasted, Helen G. – Horton, Peter R.
Breed, Nancy P. – Evans, Alton B.
Breen, Donna M. - Trent, Frank S.
Breese, Frances P. – Kilham, Peter H.
Brett, Deborah Joy – McAuliffe, William P., Jr.

Brett, Patricia Ann – Henry, Gerald J.
Brewer, Gladys L. – Fuller, William E.
Brickbeck, Judith Ann – Brett, Wayne
Brierre, Janine D. – Coolidge, Frederic S.
Britt, Kendal A. - Keough, Gary H.
Brooks, Anne Marie - Bilodeau, Wayne Louis
Brooks, Cheryl E. – Blanchard, William S.
Brooks, Hazle E. – Davis, Chester
Brooks, Penelope J. - Simons, Scott C.
Brothers, Margaret Ellen - Merrithew, Scott Edward
Brown, Abbie D. – Runnell, John C.
Brown, Addie M. - Pennell, Charles H.
Brown, Doris L. – Remick, Ronald C.
Brown, E. Jessie – Jones, Frederick W.
Brown, Elsia Ida – Bean, Otis
Brown, Emma J. - Buckholy, Jacob
Brown, Jessie M. – Pennell, Guy
Brown, Josephine – Eldridge, John
Brown, Lena May – Gilman, Wilber J.
Brown, Mildred C. – Vittum, Alfred Otis
Brown, Priscilla M. – Welch, Edwin P.
Brown, Sandra L. - Feuerborn, Wayne D.
Brown, Shirley A. – Grace, Everett E.
Browne, Cynthia T. - Atwood, Thompson S.
Brownlee, Kathleen – Dimita, Vito
Bryan, Andrea A. - Cutter, Brian K.
Bryan, Marie Vesta – Laffin, Donald Roy
Bryant, Edith Frances – Provost, George Lewis
Bryer, Clara E. - Varney, George O.
Bryer, Ella M. - Perkins, Alston
Bryer, Maria - Liberty, James
Buchanan, Christine A. - Johnson, Forrest R.
Buck, Barbara M. – Varney, Ronald E.
Bugbee, Michele S. – Varney, Joseph R.
Bugbee, Norma J. - Wilkinson, Alan T.
Bullard, Deborah Page - Hodge, Dennis F.
Bullen, Sarah Margaret - Goodson, Peter Blake
Bunker, Bertha L. – Robinson, John G.
Bunker, Blanche Evelyn – McDonald, John
Bunker, Flora M. – Clark, A. Johnson
Bunten, Linda M. – Dunham, Theodore, III

Burdick, Vern F. – Charlebos, Paul F.
Burdin, Pamela Jean – Waltz, Arnold William
Burek, Kathleen A. - Huntington, Henry P.
Burke, Ann Marie – Eckstrom, Paul
Burke, Deborah J. – Bergeron, Ronald C.
Burleigh, Eunice A. - Drake, Samuel T.
Burleigh, Sadie V. – Huckins, Charles F.
Burnett, Sarah C. - Tatarczuk, Scott B.
Burns, Rebecca A. - Tait, Stanley J.
Bushman, Barbara Marie – Ames, Richard Wayne
Bushway, Lea Irna – Wiggin, Kenneth Alfred
Buswell, Sharon L. – Libby, Paul Gordon
Butterfield, Edner M. – Banfill, Herman F.

Cady, Theresa E. - Cressey, Dean M.
Caisse, Kara Holly - Scolaro, Ricky Anthony
Cakars, Marilyn – Hughes, David
Calder, Patricia Ruth – Brothers, Kevin Wayne
Caldwell, Jennifer S. - Gillis, Derek W.
Calnan, Deborah P. - Glencross, Stephen M.
Cameson, Annie - Davis, John C.
Campbell, Delphine – Loika, Fred
Campbell, Laura J. - Trask, Howard R.
Canney, Marilyn J. – Drew, Arthur N.
Canney, Minnie M. - Mason, Llewellyn G.
Canney, Muriel E. – Moulton, Robert E.
Capalbo, Denice M. – Thurston, Larry C.
Caranci, Isabel A. – Browne, Dale M.
Cardoso, Nancy L. - Henson, William H.
Careau, Ellen – Corbett, Welby W.
Carr, Alice D. – Macomber, Harvey W.
Carr, Arlene N. – Cummings, Elmer A.
Carr, Audrey F. – Macomber, Harvey W.
Carr, Mary Annette – Whiting, Frank A.
Carr, Patricia A. – Woodside, Bruce E.
Carter, Ethel W. – Clifford, Ernest E.
Caruso, Marie Antonia - Rogers, Adam Blaine
Casey, Diane E. - Stehli, Henry H.
Casey, Margaret A. – Blaisdell, Victor Julien
Cash, Ann Marie - Norcross, Andy L.
Cavalier, Carol Ann – Ewing, Lawrence Willard

Cavanaugh, Francine M. - Wood, Adams J.
Cayes, Velma L. – Lawrence, George W.
Chadbourne, Alma R. – Gillis, Allen W.
Chamberlain, Cynthia Ann – Williams, Robert Alston
Champagne, Judith A. – Jamieson, William S.
Chandler, Alice M. – Davis, Robert E.
Chappell, Deborah L. – Koch, Eugene B.
Chase, Alice – Eldridge, John
Chase, Bernice L. – Plummer, Raymond E.
Chase, Carol – Schmoll, Brand E.
Chase, Carol A. – Potter, Harold I.
Chase, Flora E. – Goss, Lewis J.
Chase, Lori J. - Urquhart, Kenneth N.
Chase, Stephanie L. – Ulitz, Michael B.
Chase, Susan – Shaughnessy, Michael
Chase, Sylvia M. – Carr, Charles M.
Chassie, Joyce Annie – Stewart, Albert Alexander
Chesley, Virginia Arlene – Burke, Frank Weston
Chevrette, Candi Ann – Soucey, James Louis
Chick, Carrie May – Davis, Clifford K.
Chick, Lizzie C. – Mason, Arthur L.
Chick, Tammy L. – Dickinson, Andrew J.
Childs, Emma F. - Edgell, William H.
Chipman, Lisa J. - Colby, Robert E.
Christiansen, Susan Linda - Roberts, David Brian
Christie, Deborah J. - Brown, Joseph E., Jr.
Ciccone, Ann Marie – Conley, Martin J.
Clark, Angela L. - Lavoie, Richard H.
Clark, Catharine Elizabeth - Beldner, Raymond Edward
Clark, Gladys F. – Drew, Elden W.
Clark, Hester – Welch, Russell
Clark, Joanne M. – Billings, Peter D.
Clark, Judith Ann – Hutchins, Conrad Paul
Clark, Meriue M. – Garland, Frank E.
Clark, Minnie C. - Chesley, Joshua E.
Clark, Sally Ann – Ryder, Alton E.
Clarke, Ada L. - Gilman, Herbert M.
Clarke, Heidi - Palmer, Michael J.
Clem, Barbara Ann – Autio, Thomas Peter
Clemons, Casey L. - Flood, David J.
Clemons, Pamela J. – Erickson, Robert D.

Clemons, Winona H. – Page, Oliver E.
Cleveland, Ellen D. – Jessup, John A.
Cleveland, Frances Black – Corcoran, Frederick J.
Cleveland, Margaret Folsom - Lyscars, Alan Stanley
Cleveland, Marion – Cohen, Alfred
Cleveland, Sarah G. – Narode, Ronald B.
Cloran, Kathleen Elaine - Bunker, Alan Damon
Clough, Grace E. – Berry, Walter H.
Clough, Idella E. - Moody, William H.
Clough, Madeline – Whiting, Victor L.
Cobb, Karen Anne – Perkins, Philip Earl
Cockrell, Suzanne Elizabeth - Purves, Theodore Rehn
Coderre, Frances D. - Shattuck, Lawrence A.
Coffey, Ellen R. - Shannon, Edwin S.
Cohrhan, Sheila J. – Ames, Roy M., Jr.
Colbath, Leeann Louise – Coslett, John Scott
Colby, Elizabeth M. – Basley, Elmer Wayne
Colcord, Rebecca L. – Newsom, Samuel B.
Collins, Rita M. – Braswell, Emery H.
Comer, Pamela Jean – Eldridge, Ricky Lester
Condon, Eleanor – Berry, Frank
Condon, Karen L. – Fernandez, Domingo J.
Conner, Lois A. – Ames, Roy M.
Connor, Elfreda J. – Thomas, Frank F.
Conway, Bonnie Bea – Mason, Arthur Horace, III
Cook, Cynthia M. – Frye, Randolph C.
Cook, Edith - Bickford, George H.
Cook, Joanne W. – Eldridge, James F.
Cook, Marjorie – Littlefield, Paul A.
Cook, Melissa Jean - Cox, Allen Jeffrey
Coombs, Mary W. – Jenkins, Laurence
Cooper, Alice M. – Bickford, Chester J.
Cooper, Elizabeth A. - Fuselier, Christopher J.
Cooper, Margaret – Remick, Levi W.
Corbett, Gladys F. – Evans, Almon G.
Corbett, Marion J. – Hoagland, Edward B.
Corcoran, Mary E. – Moody, Lester E.
Corliss, Maude C. – Tiedman, George
Costello, Joan Diane - Derosier, David Edward
Cote, Kim E. – Noyes, Wendell W.
Cotton, Alice M. – Brown, Gordon L.

Coulombe, Imogene B. – Coulombe, Louis D.
Coville, Andrea M. - Carney, Alan
Cox, Bernice L. – Fogg, George S.
Crabtree, Alice – Russell, Lewis H.
Craft, Jean J. – Brothers, Stephen J.
Crafts, Emily A. – Remick, Edwin
Craven, Clara – Brown, Albert F.
Credit, Jeanne M. - Holland, James A.
Crocheron, Frances E. - Crocheron, Wesley H.
Croto, Deborah C. – Courtemanche, Jeffrey P.
Crouse, Rita A. – Gordon, Haven E.
Crozier, Dorothy – Williams, Richard W.
Cummings, Edna A. – Mason, Hiram E.
Cummings, Margaret – Cooper, Theodore H.
Cummings, Rosie Blanche – Yeaton, Fred
Curran, Irene M. F. - Duncombe, Richard A.
Currier, Doralyn A. – Brown, Ellsworth C.
Currier, Hazel Helen Evans – Potter, Harold Langdon
Curtin, Karen M. – Simonetti, Dennis G.
Curtin, Kathleen C. – Nourse, Christopher F.
Curtis, Ada E. – Roberts, Arthur S.
Cutrone, Amy Elizabeth - Rogers, Michael Frederick
Cutrone, Marnie L. - Byers, Brent M.
Cutrone, Michele L. - Killeen, Jameson A.
Cyr, Lena – Trask, Stanley
Czajkowski, Joan M. – Fogley, Peter F.

Dahl, Stephanie J. - McLendon, Eric
Daley, Mildred E. – Cheney, Edward H.
Dall, Sheila R. – Woodward, Robert C.
Daly, Christy L. - Robiller, Oliver G.
Damon, Martha C. – Kane, John Dandridge Henley, III
Damon, Patricia – Niswander, G. Donald
Damon, Susan B. – Hurst, James W.
Darling, Ruth – Hobbs, Josiah
Davidson, Susan M. – Norcross, Gardner L.
Davis, Alyssa L. - Guilbault, Anthony J.
Davis, Arlene M. – Parkin, George P.
Davis, Bertha S. – Berry, Albert C.
Davis, Carrie - Moulton, Luman J.
Davis, Daren J. – Rossbach, David C.

Davis, Eleanor M. – Stoddard, Clark M.
Davis, Elizabeth A. – Remick, Charles W.
Davis, Elizabeth F. - Remick, Frank
Davis, Elsie M. – Bunker, Fred W.
Davis, Flora - Purrington, Daniel
Davis, Grace A. – Page, Edgar P.
Davis, Ida E. – Chase, Augustus
Davis, Janet T. - Freeto, Robert P.
Davis, Karen Margaret - Thurston, Christopher Jon
Davis, Kathleen R. – Morrill, Richard A.
Davis, Kay E. – Lord, John G.
Davis, Linda R. – Lep, John A.
Davis, Maud – Cummings, Harry E.
Davis, Rachel M. - Salvati, Domenic A.
Davis, Sarah B. – Dearborn, Kenneth A.
Daw, Nettie – Buxton, Charles A.
Day, Nellie E. - Caverly, Leonard W.
Dearborn, Dorothy – Vittum, Alfred O.
Deatte, Carolyn Janice – Drew, Frank Pearson
Demars, Krystal A. - Bushey, Timothy A.
Demeritt, Caroline F. – Hayford, Paul L.
Demers, Lillian I. – Wiggin, Kenneth E.
Deming, Regina M. – Floyd, Grant A.
Dempsy, Joanna – Hayford, Durwood
Dennis, Raylene M. – Curtis, Wesley M.
Dennis, Rebecca Lynne - Chico, Jesus Maria, Jr.
Dentino, Kendra - Disilva, Albert Joseph
Desmond, Katherine – Hayford, Lawrence E.
DesRosier, Ernestine Mae – Gray, Warren
Devenport, Jean A. – Sailor, George R., Jr.
DeWitt, Ella M. – Moore, Robert F.
Dicey, Cheryl A. – Austin, Charles R.
Dietrich, Marti – Giguere, Albert D.
DiMaio, Gina M. - Morse, Stephen
Dionne, Jean L. - Huntoon, Wayne Alan
Dipaolo, Karen M. - Barnard, Allan F.
Dirubbo, Wendy F. - Graves, Clifford R.
Divitto, Barbara A. – Alt, Christopher B.
Doane, Debra A. – Merritt, Stephen F.
Dodge, Pearl E. – Cheney, Ralph B.
Doe, Augusta Mae – Whipple, Frank P.

Doe, Marion Cleveland – Ames, John Harmon
Doliber, Marjorie – Powers, Philip
Donahue-Berns, Kelly A. - O'Leary, Paul J.
Donovan, Barbara – Cleveland, George
Dooley, Winifred – Remick, Fred
Dow, Addie B. – Clark, Edwin G.
Dow, Nellie J. - Darling, Henry M.
Dow, Rachael Blanch – Hartford, Perley Gordon
Downs, Abbie T. - Jeffers, Milton W.
Downs, Clara E. - Mason, Harry O.
Downs, Edna C. – Vasey, Earle F.
Downs, Hattie M. - Smith, Walter C.
Downs, Ida M. – Knowlton, Haven C.
Downs, Janice L. – Dearborn, Allan E.
Downs, Judith A. – Williams, Ward B.
Downs, Leafy - Mason, Ernest
Doyle, Tenny O. - Sinclair, Craig M.
Drake, Alice – Johnson, Harry
Drake, Barbara J. – Gotjen, John C.
Drake, Catherine J. - Jenkens, Alton L., Jr.
Drake, Lizzie – Kelley, Henry B.
Drew, Alfreda M. – Eldridge, Roland R.
Drew, Betty J. – Pennell, Edwin C.
Drew, Gladys F. – Littlefield, Eugene H.
Drew, Gladys I. – Johnson, Edwin N.
Drew, Katie – Wiggin, Leander T.
Drew, Sharon – Wentworth, Harold, III
Drew, Sharon R. – Bresette, Glen D.
Drew, Virginia L. – Talavera, Gilbert
Drinkwater, Beatrice – Hobbs, Thomas
Drohan, Katie F. – Moulton, Chester A.
Dubois, Solange Frances – Norcross, Peter Frederick
DuBois, Denise M. - McGrath, Brian J., Jr.
DuBois, Veronica – Cate, William R.
Dugan, Easter A. – Nasif, Harry M.
Dunn, Mary F. - Chase, Brian K.
Duprey, Cynthia – Baxter, Francis
Dyer, Sylvia Anita – Poules, Robert Allan, III

Eastman, Amanda - Hobbs, Josiah
Eastwick, Barbara – Tappan, Fred W.

Eastwick, Madeline – Whiting, Howard W.
Edgar, Edith H. – Edgar, David U.
Edgerley, Emma I. – Davidson, Gaston H.
Edgerly, Elizabeth – Tutt, Allen C.
Edlund, Lucinda Lee - Williams, Michael Dean
Eldredge, Ada E. – Ames, James R.
Eldridge, Amanda Jean - Cossette, Thomas Paul
Eldridge, Angela Mae - Streeter, Brian Almon
Eldridge, Brenda J. – Boewe, James L.
Eldridge, Charlotte E. – Berry, Raymond A.
Eldridge, Christobell S. – Elliott, Richard J.
Eldridge, Cindy Lynn - Cook, Kevin Glenn
Eldridge, Eleanor M. – Rhines, Irving K.
Eldridge, Elizabeth – Fenderson, Robert E.
Eldridge, Eva Marie – Emerson, Theodore Woodbury
Eldridge, Evelyn Mae – Wedge, Dennis Anthony
Eldridge, Florence – Grace, Guy S.
Eldridge, Gladys – Palmer, Herbert
Eldridge, Joan – Bickford, Carroll
Eldridge, Joyce B. – Larrabee, Donald E.
Eldridge, Mattie D. – Moody, William H.
Eldridge, Merry Lee – Johnson, Richard D.
Eldridge, Patricia Ann – Weare, Thomas Edmund
Eldridge, Sacha Miai - Palmer, Daniel Richard
Eldridge, Viola A. – Varney, Harold M.
Eldridge, Violet D. – Speckman, Robert E.
Eldridge, Wynetta Elaine – Goodson, David Chester
Elliott, Abbie – Chase, Charles S.
Elliott, Alice – Bancroft, Harold R.
Elliott, Christobell Stacy – Eldridge, Ritchie
Elliott, Doris – Ayer, Forrest D.
Elliott, Eleanor Amanda – Lyman, Brian Patrick
Elliott, Lisa A. – Brennan, Charles A.
Elliott, Marcia J. – Hatch, Fred A.
Elliott, Marion – Lowd, Bernard
Elliott, Melanie A. – Streeter, Mark D.
Elliott, Melinda A. – Heimlich, Peter J.
Elliott, Sarah Grace - Follansbee, Joseph Andrew
Elliott, Sylvia R. – Johnson, Edwin R.
Ellis, Eleanor L. – Aldridge, Lendal W.
Ellis, Lottie M. – Gillis, Allen M.

Ellis, Velma – Reece, Richard
Elwell, Margaret H. - Robinson, Addison R.
Emack, Gertrude M. – Hobbs, Henry W.
Emerson, Margaret Louise – Plummer, Charles Franklin
Emerson, Rose - Harmon, William James
Emerson, Samantha L. - Baker, Christopher E.
Emerson, Sandra Ann – Eldridge, Scotty Clifton
Emerson, Susan – Anthony, Robert
Emerson, Valerie M. - White, John D.
Emery, Alice J. - Smith, Albert W.
Enebuske, Clara F. – Read, Richard W.
English, Jeanne L. – Bergen, Dominic N.
Engman, Heidi J. - Farnum, William W.
Erickson, Alexandra M. – Fry, Edward F.
Ericson, Abbie – Johnson, Charles H.
Evans, Antonea V. - Jarnagin, Eric N.
Evans, Hazel E. – Currier, Roland E.
Evans, Lorraine E. – Streeter, Clifford R.
Evans, Martha – Williams, Paul E.
Evans, Wendy Lee – Burrows, Jon Lester

Fall, Marguerite – Grant, Lyle L.
Fallen, Candy L. - White, Alfred P.
Fallon, Catherine A. – MacCurtain, Gerald T.
Farina, Nella M. – Foley, Cyril J.
Farnham, Lilla M. – Spindle, Henry M.
Farnum, Ann – Lambert, Arthur Alfred
Farnum, Jane – Beard, Gary Lee
Farnum, Lynne - Boylan, Stephen P.
Farrell, Gail A. – Boewe, Ward A.
Fennell, Beth – Lamont, Corliss
Fennell, Minnie A. – Smith, Albert W.
Ferber, Barbara J. – Gibbons, John A.
Fernald, Anna M. – King, John W.
Fifield, M. Carrie – Bickford, John F.
Finerty, Emma E. – Messer, Clinton F.
Fisher, Margaret N. – Fisher, Russell S.
Fisher, Susan M. - Lee, Gordon J.
Fitzpatrick, Ann E. – Stinchfield, Philip A.
Flanagan, Sandra Kathryn – Gurick, George Ray, Jr.
Flint, Bertha G. – Caswell, William A.

Floyd, Elva L. – Bickford, Carl O.
Floyd, Lulu A. – Whiting, William H.
Foisy, Donna L. – Morton, Edmund J.
Foley, Holly J. - Heffernan, Michael J.
Foley, Kathleen - Ames, Roy M.
Folsom, Adaline R. - Gilman, Charles A.
Fontaine, Joan M. – Brewer, Alexander R.
Forbush, Nancy H. – Huckins, Ferdinand A.
Ford, Donna L. – Whipple, Parker C.
Forest, Annie L. - Hill, David A.
Forrest, Cora M. – Smith, Clarence S.
Forrest, Fanney E. – Whiting, Arthur C.
Fortier, Doris – Chase, Leslie O.
Fortier, Heidi L. - Murphy, Ryan P.
Fortier, Sally Ann – Olson, David Carl
Foss, Donna J. – Canney, Haven E.
Foss, Mary C. – Gilman, Edmund T.
Foster, Laurie Jane - Geiger, Christopher James
Foster, Mary P. – Murdock, David W.
Fowler, Alys – Robertson, James W.
Fowler, Mary B. - Cox, Michael J.
Fownes, Caroline R. – Hobbs, Charles W.
Fox, Patricia Ann – Evans, Alton Brooks
Francis, Evelyn – Palma, John
Franklin, Barbara S. - Smalley, Robert F.
Freeman, Ellen I. - Osgood, Herman L.
Freeman, Esther – Savard, Albert J.
Freeman, Patricia A. – Gibson, Douglas P.
Freeto, Sandra A. – Peterson, Osler L.
French, Dorothy L. – Welch, Austin E.
French, Elizabeth M. – Bowles, David A.
French, Helen S. – King, Oliver M.
French, Sally A. – Downs, Clifford F., Jr.
Fritzsche, Susanne Charlotte - Olkkola, Robert Patrick
Frost, Bertha L. – Ames, Ernest E.
Frost, Clara M. – Mason, Ernest S.
Frost, Jane E. – Bergeron, Grant S.
Frost, Marjie – Hobbs, George
Frost, Phyllis A. – Brown, Franklin J.
Frost, Phyllis C. – Connelly, Dennis M.
Frye, Cynthia Lou – Marshall, John Lee

Fryman, Deborah J. - Whiting, Lewis R.
Fulcher, Linda Lee – Anthony, Gregory Alan
Furth, Victoria L. – Glenn, David D.

Gagne, Ola C. - Smith, Michael W.
Gale, Jennie B. – Whiting, Charles E.
Gallagher, Rebecca – Williams, Henry B.
Gallear, Donna M. - Libby, Paul G.
Galloway, Julia – Johnson, John W.
Galucia, Flora I. – Harrington, Ernest A. S.
Gane, Marjorie – Harkness, Frank E.
Galvin, Gillian – Kumm, Frederick Guinness
Gardner, Lizzie A. - Johnson, Charles H.
Garland, Edna M. – King, Oliver M.
Garland, Judith May – Day, Warren Levon
Garland, Sadie M. - Hammond, Fred M.
Gay, Marjorie – Chamberlain, Raymond
Gee, Candy L. – Mack, Jeffrey R.
Gero, Joan M. – Loring, Stephen G.
Giasson, Lisa Renea - Wilkinson, Kraig Alan
Gill, Charlotte Lydia – Hammond, Edward J.
Gillis, Helen F. – Rickards, Hanford E.
Gilman, Alice May – Abbott, Herbert E.
Gilman, Belle – Sceggel, Arthur B.
Gilman, Carol N. – Woodes, Robert C.
Gilman, Edith M. – Berry, Robert K.
Gilman, Edith R. – Moore, Fred L.
Gilman, Eleanor L. – Eldridge, Clyde A.
Gilman, Elsie M. – Carter, Lisle W.
Gilman, Ethel L. – Berry, Everett W.
Gilman, Gertie M. - Jeffers, Fred L.
Gilman, Helen E. – Hurd, Alton
Gilman, Ida M. - Buzzell, Charles P.
Gilman, Judith E. – Jones, Joseph E.
Gilman, Laura M. - Currier, Edwin F.
Gilman, Laura M. – Robinson, Henry B.
Gilman, Lulu M. – Arling, Roy E.
Gilman, Marcia E. – Eldridge, Andrew W.
Gilman, Sarah F. - Kimball, Samuel O.
Glaws, Lee P. – Narwicz, Charles, Jr.
Glennon, Heather L. - Feddern, Mark H.

Glidden, Annie M. – Bodge, Harry E.
Glidden, Mary A. - Holden, William M.
Gobelle, Evelyn – Racine, Wendell S.
Goguen, Darcy S. - Sidwell, James S.
Goldstein, Helena J. – Smith, David W.
Gomes, Nina – O'Neil, John H., Jr.
Goodson, Janice Arnold - Davison, Harry James
Goodson, Tobia – Bartlett, Robert C.
Goodwin, Agnes May – Page, Edgar Perry
Goodwin, Bertha M. – Hammond, Fred M.
Gordon, Maude A. – Stoddard, Donald T.
Gosseline, Madeline T. - Tufts, Charles F.
Goudreau, Charlotte F. - Goodson, Peter B.
Gould, Eva M. G. – Follansbee, Somerby C.
Gove, Carolyn E. – Pulsifer, Frederick J.
Gove, Ida M. – Hatch, George A.
Grace, Abbie – Hapgood, Guy F.
Grace, Addia – Palmer, Herbert E.
Grace, Cora M. – Evans, Glenn P.
Grace, Emma – Ames, Claude Milton
Grace, Janette E. – Anthony, Warren G.
Grace, Patricia E. – Marion, Jon G.
Graffam, Thelma L. – Berry, Everett W.
Grant, Mary E. - Garland, George E.
Grant, Nettie – Floyd, Perley
Granville, Susan C. - Clark, Lucian G.
Graves, Dorothy A. – Remick, A. Dexter
Gray, Beulah M. – Fromm, William A.
Gray, Carolyn D. - Fuller, Richard F.
Gray, Sally Worthington Smith - Place, Arthur Johnson
Green, Addie M. - Sanborn, John F.
Green, Flora E. – Currier, Edwin F.
Green, Heather A. – Lemay, Michael R.
Green, Mary L. – Hall, Gerald W.
Greenamyer, Carolyn Ann – Gourley, Kirkland S.
Greene, Andrea P. - Burke, Geoffrey B.
Greene, Phyllis M. – Fortier, Carroll
Greg, Sue E. – Behr, Karl R.
Grey, Eveleth May – Gillis, Eugene M.
Grey, Kathryn I. - Burrage, Robert E.
Griffin, Marjorie E. – Knowlton, Kenneth

Grimsley-Chubbuck, Johelen J. - Phair, Jeremy R.
Guerrera, Maria A. – Mooney, Paul W.

Haine, Mary Kathryn – Gutberlet, James Michael
Hale, Susan M. - Fonseca, Paul R.
Haley, Beverly G. - Pike, J. Edison, Jr.
Hall, Carolyn E. – Buck, Ormsby J.
Hall, Dorothy L. – Marsh, Stephen Winthrop
Hall, Lillian M. – Abbott, Harry A., Jr.
Hall, Rebecca W. – Metzger, John
Hallett, Ruth Ann – Johnson, Harry Otis
Halsey, Agnes D. – Flexner, James T.
Ham, Hannah C. - Bliss, Eli C. W.
Hamalainen, Katlyn M. - Strain, Noel T.
Hamelin, Marcelle M. - Mosher, Myles W.
Hamlin, Amy Elizabeth - Hartley, Erin Spencer
Hamlin, Joy Abigail - Littlefield, Dana O.
Hammond, Carolyn E. – Dwinnells, Alton E.
Hammond, Constance M. – Libby, Truman
Hammond, Dorothy A. – Mallar, John L.
Hammond, Patricia Jane – Frechette, Maurice Edward
Hanna, Edna Marie - Smith, Gerald Earl Young
Hanna, Nadine Michelle - Carolan, Brian Patrick
Hanscom, Esther F. – Stevens, Roland
Hansen, Marina – Tew, Peter Arthur
Hanson, Catherine L. - Winters, Jesse I.
Hanson, Essie I. – Spaulding, Ralph H.
Hanson, Linda Jean - Cook, Daniel Mark
Harding, Patricia A. – Rowell, Frank
Hardy, Eva F. - Hobbs, Bert W.
Hardy, Katie B. – Drew, William F.
Hardy, Minnie E. – Wiggin, Roscoe A.
Harmon, Arleen G. – Anthony, David A.
Harmon, Norma P. – Berry, Ronald E.
Harrington, Constance J. - Waring, Timothy K.
Harrington, Gertrude – Dwyer, Elmer E.
Harris, Catherine Comer – Pickering, Ellsworth Everette, Jr.
Harris, Charlene L. – Pennell, Guy, Jr.
Harris, Yvonne N. – Staples, Mark A.
Harte, Amy M. - Soulia, Chad W.
Hartford, Emma L. - Courchaine, Russell A.

Hartford, Valerie A. – Anthony, Robert W.
Harvey, Thelma E. – Roberts, George W.
Hatch, Collen M. – Carr, Kenneth C.
Hatch, Katherene B. – Hatch, Osman P.
Hatch, Rosemary – Harmon, Harold Chester
Hatcher, Mary Lou - Morgan, Edward Prince
Hattenburg, Shirley - Krupula, Arnie E.
Haughton, Grace A. – Gordon, Ralph S.
Haurs, Helen F. – Kamerling, Samuel W.
Hawes, Charlene Louise – Eldridge, Kenneth William
Hayford, Blanch A. - Hammond, Walter J.
Hayford, Katherine M. – Budroe, Edward H.
Hayford, Kathleen E. – Chute, Paul E.
Hayford, Lizzie I. - Hays, George C.
Hayford, Mary T. – Guay, Raymond R.
Hayford, Mildred – Savard, Albert J.
Hayford, Nellie E. – Smith, Marshall E.
Hayford, Pauline E. – Goodno, Ralph Holmes
Henchman, Kittredge E. – Sallet, Herbert W.
Henderson, Ethel – Aspinwall, William
Henderson, Gertrude – Blackey, Frank A.
Herbold, Sharron – Wiggin, Gary W.
Herrick, Doris L. – Ferguson, Edward M.
Herrick, Leona – Hayford, Arthur L.
Hersey, Corinne S. – Brown, Robert E.
Heusner, Heidi Sue - Holt, Andrew James, Jr.
Hewitt, Edith M. – Kimball, Winslow B.
Hickey, Barbara Ann – Dicey, Wendell Garfield
Hidden, Eunice Angelina – Clapp, William Irving
Hidden, Frances E. – Roberts, Richard N.
Hidden, Joanna Lee – Gloade, Kenneth David
Hidden, Katherine L. – Bourgault, Henry J.
Hidden, Marilyn D. - Kelly, John J.
Hidden, Trisha Carleen - King, Christopher William
Higgins, Denise A. - Bennett, Kenneth J.
Higgins, Lorena L. – Nickerson, George R.
Hill, Annie L. – Perkins, Everett S.
Hill, Barbara May – Perkins, Robert Hilton
Hill, Evelyn G. – Palmer, Richard W.
Hill, Janet K. – Grace, Robert E.
Hill, Karen Ruth - Fletcher, Robert George

Hill, Nema T. – Nystedt, Paul A.
Hill, Valma O. – Anderson, John E.
Hills, Flavelle – Richards, Justin L.
Hilton, Barbara Jean – Davis, David L.
Hilton, Ruth G. – Loud, Edward D.
Hinckley, Laurrie Anne – Baker, David Leon
Hirsch, Ethel – Young, Stanley L.
Hoag, Eunice M. – Spaulding, Robert C. A.
Hoag, Jean W. – Greene, George C.
Hobbs, Annie D. - Chase, Augustus
Hobbs, Barbara M. – McDonald, Forrest G.
Hobbs, Celia – Hobbs, Leon
Hobbs, Cora L. – Buswell, Robert R.
Hobbs, Elizabeth F. – Boothby, Lawrence D.
Hobbs, Elizabeth S. – Moody, George
Hobbs, Ethel – Frost, Arthur E.
Hobbs, Eva F. – Farnham, Arthur E.
Hobbs, Frances – Bickford, Wilbur J.
Hobbs, Helen M. – Remick, David
Hobbs, Marjorie – Bennett, Lawrence E.
Hobbs, Rose Marie – Johnson, Dennis Wayne
Hobbs, Vivian – Moody, Ernest A.
Hoch, Tammy L. – Swenson, Neil E.
Hocking, Penelope B. – Gartrell, Christopher D.
Hodge, Rachel – Vittum, Merton C.
Hodgkins, Lucy S. – Peterson, Hugo P.
Hoffay, Doreen - Ireland, John F.
Hoitt, Dorothy E. – Linton, Ralph B.
Holbrook, June E. – Palmer, Harland C.
Holman, Madeline F. – Jeffers, Charles M.
Homeyer, Pamela I. – Parks, Robert L.
Hoogerhyde, Karen M. – Conrad, David W.
Horan, Jannette G. – Sanborn, Frederick A.
Horne, Edith A. – Whiting, Leland F.
Hoskins, Joy E. - Jenkens, J. Anthony
Howard, Flora B. – Staples, Ralph
Howarth, Dawn Marie - Dupont, Peter Andrew
Howe, Joyce L. – Trask, Frank W.
Howell, Jennifer Anne - Hagerty, Shawn Michael
Howell, Virginia E. – Dorheim, Malcolm A.
Howie, Marilyn – Jones, Charles

Hughes, Jo A. – Lukinghammer, Dale A.
Hunham, Mary H. – Milne, Alan C.
Hunnewell, Isabelle Oakes - Stafford, Hans Burke
Hunt, Carolyn Jean – Rand, Clinton LeShore
Hunt, Heidi E. – Steele, Edward T.
Huntington, Clare - Davidson, Nestor Michael
Hutchins, Donna Lee – Larrabee, Arnold Herbert
Hutchins, Eileen B. – Leach, Lyle D.
Hutchins, Hattie M. – Stokes, Arthur P.
Hutchins, Marguerite – Pedato, Frank
Hutchins, Nicole L. - Ames, Gary L.
Hutchins, Pauline V. – Mason, Richard R.
Hutchins, Sandra Marie – Larrabee, Alan Bruce
Hutchinson, Joyce B. – Elliott, Roger S.
Hutchinson, Laura I. – Vittum, Leonard H.

Idsinga, Tamara J. - Sayers, David S.
Irish, Laurie D. - Bresette, Timothy A.

Jack, Patricia A. – Hayford, Daniel A.
Jackins, Ruth E. – Alden, Elton D.
Jackson, Hope N. – Williams, Charles J., Jr.
Jackson, Josephine L. – Strong, Robert S.
Jackson, Nellie A. – Taylor, George A.
Jackson, Robyn K. – White, John O.
Jacques, Lorraine C. – Levinson, Mark A.
Jakubauskas, Lynne E. - Sherman, Robert F.
James, Stephanie Joanne – Kukuruza, Wayne R.
Jamison, Megan Cole - Kaufman, Peter Stanley
Jaques, Andrea L. - Cameron, Herb J.
Jaworski, Tammy L. - Jacobs, Steven A.
Jean-Marie, Julia M. - Bosse, William H.
Jeffers, Alma C. – Leach, William F.
Jeffers, Blanche E. – Ames, Claud P.
Jeffers, Doreen L. - Remick, Michael D.
Jeffers, Ethel E. – Whiting, Frederick H.
Jeffers, Georgia E. – Whiting, Fred M.
Jeffers, Gladys – Drew, Harry H.
Jenneke, Sharon Kay - Dyer, Stanley A., Jr.
Jennings, Ann J. – Mudgett, James Roger, Jr.
Jennings, Edith C. – Davison, Harry J.

Jennings, Erin J. - Jones, Chester D.
Johnson, Andrea - Kennett, A. Crosby, III
Johnson, Annie May - Remick, H. Haywood
Johnson, Barbara K. – Bridges, Wilbur M.
Johnson, Barbara K. – Jackson, George N.
Johnson, Beatrice M. – Littlefield, Orace R.
Johnson, Christine – Hidden, William B.
Johnson, Cordelia P. – Hill, William A.
Johnson, Elizabeth H. - Soroff, Daniel A.
Johnson, Emma Adams – Scott, Arthur Burton
Johnson, Ethel M. – Gilman, Bert E.
Johnson, Hilda – Ross, Kenneth
Johnson, Janet L. – Hadingham, Evan W.
Johnson, Jennifer J. - Peloquin, Thomas M.
Johnson, Kimberly Ann - Wasson, Ryan M.
Johnson, Shirley Jean – Beaudet, Michael R.
Jones, Carolyn D. - Johnson, Keith L.
Jones, Cynthia A. – Mudgett, James R.
Jones, Hattie W. – Cheney, Raymond E.
Jones, Yvonne Nancy – Staples, Stephen Walter
Jordan, Dorothy L. – Palmer, Clarence E.
Jordon, Mary A. – Taylor, James D.
Judd, Marion M. – Corbett, Harris G.
Juhasz, Lori Ann Madeline - Berry, Edward Ronald

Kasper, Pamela Jean - Gaudet, James Richard
Keen, Ardella M. – Libby, Lawrence H.
Keen, Helen L. – Hutchins, Donald P.
Keith, Ellen Peabody – Shambaugh, Benjamin Dibble
Keith, Lisa – Karp, Allan
Keith, Susannah Bacon - Coster, John Gerard
Kelley, Charlotte A. - Kingham, Thomas B.
Kelley, Linda M. - Jones, William L.
Kelley, Sabine M. – Schneider, Arthur F.
Kelly, Marilyn D. - Prive, Philip E.
Kelsey, Diane L. – Bowles, James C.
Kenerson, Effie J. - Savary, Zantford L.
Kennedy, Dorothy E. – Prince, Edward P.
Kennedy, Joan – Behr, Charles E.
Kennedy, Susan – Brande, Justin
Kennett, Grace – Ross, Harold E.

Kenney, Alice M. – Gucker, Alexander L.
Kenney, Katheryn A. – Carter, Lisle W.
Kenney, Nan – Hadden, Christopher
Kent, Marion L. – Kennett, Edson C.
Kilbourn, Katharine Ann - Shear, G. Scott
Kimball, Clara B. – Knight, W. D.
Kimball, Louise D. – Clough, Edwin E.
King, Edna M. – Garland, George Ernest
Kirvan, Jacqueline R. - Whyte, Peter H.
Klein, Kristine M. - Bontaites, Alan J.
Klitgaard, Kim - Nichols, Stephen P.
Knapp, Mary R. – Clancy, Dana T.
Knight, Clara B. – Black, James
Knight, Miriam – Russell, Michael
Knox, Brenda Elaine – Anthony, Bruce Gordon
Knox, Elaine E. – Bennett, Donald K.
Knox, Emily E. – Mayer, William S.
Knox, Mary E. – Ross, Ernest J.
Knox, Sarah J. - Olkkola, Justin P.
Koble, Peggy A. – Crane, James P.
Kolman, Yvonne A. - Hargens, Roger S.
Kovach, Jennifer J. - Bishop, Noel E.
Krebs, Patricia A. – Reinhold, Robert V.
Kurinskas, Jeanne F. – Walter, Ralph
Kusala, Cheryl A. - Whiting, Steven D.

Labrie, Mary E. – Trask, Howard R.
Lafavore, Caroline P. - Bowman, Michael R.
Lake, Mary L. – Proctor, Gerald E.
Lamb, Juniper D. - Canfield, Christopher R.
Lambee, Mabel J. – Evans, Walter B.
Lane, Ethel M. – Hammond, Fred M.
Lane, Virginia R. – Harris, V. Steven, Jr.
Langlois, Lanette M. - Goodson, David C.
Langlois, Lisa Beth - Tucker, Glenn Cushing
Langlois, Pamela – Reingold, Robert
Lank, Edith – Ranger, John
Lanou, Elizabeth Michaud - Chadwick, Rufus Herbert
LaPlante, Dorian Mary - Norcross, Barry Lee
Lariviere, Lisa Ann - Berry, William Daniel
Larrabee, Dorothy A. – Elliott, James T.

Larrabee, Judith Weare – Anthony, Chester Earle
Larrabee, Julie L. - Lessard, Pierre L.
Larrabee, Julie L. - Mason, Preston H.
Larrabee, Susan M. - Davison, Harry J.
Lau, Mei Leng - Bohl, Jesse Pieter
Lavoie, Dorothy – Baril, Arthur F., Jr.
Lawrence, Diane J. – McNulty, Michael C.
Lawrence, Hazel M. – Gilman, Howard R.
Lawson, Rita M. – Frost, Lawrence E.
Lawton, Cynthia M. - Petrie, Russell C.
Leach, Doris A. – Powers, Bernard L.
Leach, Julie A. – Moore, Ronald K.
Leach, Julia Marion – Dicey, Wendell Garfield
Leavitt, Marguerite H. – Whipple, Frank P.
LeBlanc, Linda G. – Eldridge, Tony W.
Leblanc, Rita M. – Vittum, Kenneth F.
Leclerc, Arlene – Davis, Alan J.
Lee, June M. – Currier, Jesse A., Jr.
Lefevre, Susan Lynne - Lionetta, Scott Michael
Legault, Tammy M. - Philibert, Kevin D.
LeGendre, Marcella J. - Ratliff, Daniel L.
Lehner, Nicole Barbara - Donovan, Brendan Joseph
Leighton, Tina Marie - Draper, Donald Richard
Lemke, Mary Ann - Morgan, Shawn Kerry
Lent, Evelyn Leanard – Simonds, Carl Everett
Leso, Fayralyn O. – Roberts, Emery R.
Lessard, Louise M. - Drew, Fred A.
Levesque, Laura M. - Ames, Charles E.
Lewis, Evelyn M. – Carr, Richard E.
Libby, April P. - Drew, Tony P.
Libby, Constance H. – Ford, Walter J.
Liberty, Clara M. - Staples, Winslow
Lincoln, Elizabeth D. – Whitney, Charles
Lincoln, Joan – Cave, Edwin F.
Lincoln, Susan C. – Jones, Carl W.
Lind, Mary Leona – Johnson, Larry Alan
Little, Becky L. – Yonts, Stewart H.
Littlefield, Addie M. – Smith, Walter C.
Littlefield, Arlene – Gilman, Edwin F.
Lloyd, Anne - Witte, Nicholas H.
Lloyd, Anne G. – Lurie, Michael D.

Lloyd, Marion L. – Salois, Dean B.
Lloyd, Sarah – Hall, Frederic W.
Locke, Heidi K. - Simon, Gregory R.
Locke, Kelly M. - Jenkins, Christopher F.
Locke, Kelly Marie - Tracy, John Patrick
Locke, Sharon G. – Botting, Calvin E.
Locklin, Louise – Mason, George W.
Long, Mabel R. – Ambrose, L. Ramond
Lord, Diane M. – Robinson, Bruce E.
Lord, Elinor L. – Cheney, Albert M.
Lord, Frances A. – Davis, Roy W.
Lord, Frances Viola – Vittum, Kenneth F.
Lord, Rebecca A. – King, Jerry D.
Loring, Alice P. – Pickman, Anthony P.
Loring, Katherine P. – Haddon, Arthur L.
Loring, Katherine P. – Anador, John A.
Loud, Kristin - Bouve, Howard Allison, III
Loughran, Margaret L. - McCarthy, William J., III
Lovering, Rita L. – Bookholz, Harold
Lowd, Joan M. – Ames, Peter E.
Lowd, Stella R. – Lowd, Lindel F.
Luedke, Donna A. - George, Mark S.
Lund, Lydia M. – Kennard, John H.
Lund, Sylvia M. – Glaws, J. Peter, III
Lyman, Marion – Bickford, Paul P.

MacDonald, Barbara H. – MacDonald, Forrest G.
MacDonald, Joy E. – Whittaker, Scott C.
MacDonald, Karen M. - Pohju, Victor A.
MacDonald, Katherine B. – Rudd, Roland
MacDonald, Lynne H. - Talbot, Timothy J.
MacDougall, Caroline R. – Brock, David Hackett
Mack, Annie - Downs, Edward F.
MacKenzie, Hazel – Whiting, Roland G.
MacKinnon, Mary K. – Sagona, Charles L.
MacLeod, Sabra Rogers - Korson, Jay Henry
MacMillan, Katherine B. – Johnson, Theodore
Macus, Gloria J. – Moody, Charles A.
Magee, Kris E. - Cahill, Edward J., Jr.
Maher, Nicole E. – Coville, Edward R.
Maher, Nicole E. - Whiteside, Taylor F.

Maiato, Kelly A. - Nelson, Robert W.
Malcolm, Irene F. – Mayberry, Conrad
Malone, Helen R. – Saunders, Harry A.
Maltman, Tarry L. – Wason, Grant M.
Mann, Karen E. – Johnson, Glenn E.
Marcotte, Gwendolyn C. – Valentine, Malcom W.
Marcoux, Lynn Marie - Gallant, David Allen
Marks, Lisa M. - Demaine, David K.
Marro, Mary F. – Thurston, Alan W.
Marshall, Bertha L. – Nixon, William D.
Marshall, Cynthia L. – Ames, Ronald G.
Marshall, Mildred D. – Streeter, Joseph A.
Marston, Ada A. – Smith, Frank H.
Marston, Gladys R. – Conrad, George A.
Marston, Minnie A. – Moore, Samuel J.
Martel, Violet Dorothy – Shepperd, Robert Allan
Martin, Cathleen G. – Anderson, John N.
Martin, Celia – Gordon, William H.
Martin, Lynn Mae – Steele, James Emerson, II
Martin, Mariette – Ross, Harland
Martin, Maude E. – Edgerly, Satchel C.
Martin, Susan – Kimball, Melvin N.
Martin, Tonya M. - Guyer, Alec J.
Marton, Jennifer A. - Norcross, Justin M.
Marx, Katherine – Hayford, Abner W.
Mason, Blanche M. – Smith, Gilman A.
Mason, Dawn M. – Roberts, John E.
Mason, Dorothea L. – Eastwick, John
Mason, Eliza A. - Smith, Jacob G.
Mason, Mary E. – Eastwick, Robert
Mason, Minda M. – Streeter, Joel F.
Mason, Nellie A. – Bartlett, Leland C.
Mason, Teresa A. – Chase, Preston N.
Mason, Victoria – Brett, Stanley L.
Matthey, Michelle M. – Gumpert, James S.
Mauhs, Carrie M. – Pugh, Thomas J.
Maurer, Susan R. – Mann, William W., Jr.
Maury, Beth M. - Gregory, John
Mayer, Katherine E. – Lovett, Paul M.
Mayer, Marianne G. - Heilferty, Robert J.
Mayott, Margaret B. – Davis, Rodney C.

McBee, Henrieta S. – Tye, Richard J.
McBride, Margaret – Moody, Elmer P.
McCarthy, Donna M. – Damon, Christopher S.
McCaughin, June P. – Ward, Harold M.
McClosky, Lizzie E. – Whiting, Almon J.
McCormack, Kathleen Eleen – Vittum, Brewster Dale
McCue, Lee-Anne - Nixon, Michael J.
McCue, Sally L. – Wiles, Robert H.
McDavitt, Michele A. - Chase, Vincent F.
McEvoy, Jennifer K. - Welch, Marlon E.
McGilliory, Mary – Hammond, Edward
McGuire, Hazel L. – Gervais, Albert J.
McIlvried, Terri A. - Zack, James M.
McIntyre, Luella B. – Bain, Frederick W.
McKeefrey, Susan P. – Worcester, Edward D.
McKerom, Grace E. – Brown, Elmer
McKinnon, Laurie Anne - Anand, Sanjay Kumar
McLain, Ellen L. – Lowrie, John P.
McLendon, Nellie E. - Roberts, Brian D.
McNally, Diane – Laliberte, David
McNeal, Madeline E. – Jackson, Enoch E.
McNeil, Martha E. – Hayford, Abner W.
McPhearson, Mabel G. – Mason, Chester L.
McPherson, Myrtle G. – Parris, LeRoy A.
McPherson, Tricia G. - Smith, Elaine R.
Meader, Gertrude E. – Osborn, Frank E.
Mee, Laurie Anne - Streeter, Brian A.
Melanson, Nancy A. – Suppes, Bruce D.
Mercier, Carol A. - Mercier, George R.
Merrithew, Patricia - Peaslee, Philip E.
Merritt, Debra C. – Souza, John P.
Merritt, Eleanor F. – Grace, Carroll O.
Merry, Gertrude M. – King, John W.
Merryfield, Florence – Johnson, Edwin N.
Mersfelder, Janet E. – Kern, Frank A.
Michaels, Ashana R. - Hayford, Arnold D.
Miles, Marion E. – Remick, Edwin C.
Miller, Amanda J. - Walker, Steven S.
Miller, Charrington S. – Evagash, Joseph J., Jr.
Miller, Denise M. – Boewe, Walter M.
Miller, Donna Read - French, David Vestal

Miller, Elizabeth C. F. - Ames, Joseph, Jr.
Miller, Pamela J. - Fournier, Michael A.
Millett, Beth Lorraine – Price, Richard
Mills, Catherine F. – Terry, Ernest
Mills, Katherine E. – Martin, David L.
Mills, Kylie K. - Altman, Micah
Mills, Linda Jean – Hansen, Neal Malcolm
Minnehan, Mae A. – Hanlon, Samuel O.
Mirabito, Cindy Ann - Kalogaropoulos, Peter
Mitchell, Tracey Lynne - Donovan, Brian Scott
Mitchko, Susan – Nickerson, Lawrence G.
Mondeau, Joyce E. – Brothers, Jeffrey A.
Moneypenny, Brenda M. – Aspinall, Gregory J.
Moneypenny, Una M. - Hall, Anthony C.
Moody, Ethel – Hobbs, Herbert
Moody, Florence J. – Hammond, Fred L.
Moody, Grace – Robinson, Chester A.
Moody, Idella - Evans, Frank P.
Moody, Rosalind H. – Nation, Barry Lee
Moody, Vivian I. – Purrington, Daniel C.
Mooney, Claire L. – Veneziale, Paul J.
Mooney, Jennie Holmes – Clarke, Lucien G.
Moore, Ann Marie – Phillips, Thomas William
Moore, Clara – Grace, Roy E.
Moore, Dorothea L. – Berry, Howard E.
Moore, Dorothy E. – Trask, Robert H.
Moore, Laura E. – Adjutant, Christopher A.
Moore, Mary A. – Frost, Edwin M.
Moore, Nellie M. D. – Gilman, Clifford J.
Moot, Amey Dexter - Wlassich, John James
Moran, Gael Elizabeth – Romel, John Vincent
Morey, Grace Aurelia – Rowe, Ernest J. G.
Morgan, Jennifer L. - Eldridge, Jeffrey A.
Morgan, Julie – Schopf, James William
Moriarty, Tara Ann - Schiller, Matthias Johannes
Morrisey, Carol A. – Sommer, Roger A.
Morton, Joyce Marie – Day, Percy Cleveland
Moulton, Edith M. - Schoolcraft, Walter B.
Moulton, Emma L. – Trask, Harold B.
Moulton, Helen C. – Ames, Philip E.
Moulton, Lillian E. - Tasker, Mark F.

Moulton, Marlee Ilean – Harmon, Robert Henry
Mudgett, Evelyn R. – Moody, Merton E.
Mudgett, Faye V. – Norcross, Charles D.
Mudgett, Marilyn J. – Wiggin, Harold H.
Mulley, Heather Mary - Curtis, Tony
Murphy, Carrie Ann - Ames, John Phillip
Murray, Harriet L. – Grace, Philip C.
Myers, Jean – Aspinall, Charles E.
Myers, Priscilla A. – Trask, Robert H.

Nairne, Ruth – Holliday, Paul H.
Nason, Darlene E. – Brennan, Christopher J.
Naylor, Michelle L. – Marsh, Michael S.
Naylor, Patricia G. – Gray, Lloyd E., Jr.
Neilson, Margaret – Damon, Herbert S.
Nelson, Gayle I. - Sweet, George W.
Nelson, Kristin L. - Kersten, Martin W.
Nelson, Lillian W. – Bowles, Roland R.
Nelson, Lisa Marie - Velez, Damaso Ray
Nelson, Robbin L. - Ayer, Bruce A.
Neville, Dorothy I. - Amador, Franz G.
Newcomb, Catharine A. – Bleakney, Richard R.
Newcomb, Julia Marie - McBee, William Hunter
Newton, Kim M. - Burdick, Glenn
Newton, Linda Drew - Smith, Noel Raymond
Nichols, Elizabeth – Wright, Howard H.
Nickerson, Alta – Abbott, William D.
Nickerson, Edna M. – Stall, Thomas G.
Nickerson, Emily E. – Knox, Charles E.
Nickerson, Josie – Welch, Francis J.
Nickerson, Lisa A. – Johnson, Donald
Nickerson, Margaret – Gilman, Harold E.
Nickerson, Sadie A. – King, John W.
Nickerson, Sarah M. – Bean, Fred Roland
Nickerson, Valerie M. – Allen, Charles B.
Nickerson-Allen, Valerie - McDonald, Peter Franklin
Nixon, Edith C. – Jennings, Daniel E.
Nixon, Marilyn Dorr – Hidden, John Bray
Nolen, Barbara H. - Hammond, George R.
Norcross, E. Paige – Gibson, David C.
Norcross, Sandra Madison – Twitchell, Roger Thayer, Jr.

Noyes, Marcia – Brothers, Michael B.
Nudd, Anita M. - Cameron, Bruce H.
Nudd, Elizabeth D. – Hayford, Ernest A.
Nudd, Evalena L. – Ames, Charles E.
Nudd, Nancy Irene – Cook, John O., Jr.
Nutt, Mildred – Moore, Kenneth K.
Nystedt, Joyce R. – Irish, Charles D.
Nystedt, Nellie – Teasdale, John

O'Brien, Chandra L. - Foss, Lance F.
O'Brien, Jane E. - Finley, Alexander
Ochs, Carol E. - Michie, Alan K.
Oettinger, Marjorie Ann - Struhl, Kevin
Ohnemus, Kristin J. - Vlass, Michael R.
Oliveira, Susan M. – Brown, Charles W., Jr.
Olsen, Barbara Jane – Tupper, Charles William, III
Olson, Beverly L. – Nichols, John E.
Olson, Lisa A. - Perry, Samuel G.
Ondras, Martha E. – Condino, David A.
Oneill, Elizabeth L. - Shean, Hayden W.
Ordway, Alisa - Levesque, Eric M.
Ormond, Patricia A. - Sears, William M.
Orpin, Elizabeth M. – Hurtubise, Hilary J.
Osgood, Carrie A. – Gallup, George W.
Osgood, Isabel F. – Hutchins, Elias W.

Page, Esther F. – Hanscom, Walter H.
Page, Katharine – Hersey, Leonard
Page, Mary Elaine – Kimball, Robert Erwin
Page, Mildred E. – Downs, Elias E.
Page, Myrtle L. – Walker, Walter Edward
Page, Ruth D. – Marshall, George L., Jr.
Palmer, Charlotte – Eldridge, Perley E.
Palmer, Cristine L. – Hobbs, Ernest
Palmer, Doris M. – Plummer, Charles F.
Palmer, Eleanor F. – Taylor, Keith R.
Palmer, Gladys M. – Berry, Raymond E.
Palmer, Melanie - Larrabee, Keith A.
Palmer, Patricia – Ansley, Charles
Palmer, Virginia P. – Buttrick, Clifton R.
Panno, Frances L. – Evans, Leon A.

Papointe, Jody Louise – Goodson, Timothy Steddom
Parady, Rachel Mann - Keyser, Kevin Wayne
Parent, Collen L. – Burnell, Harvey F.
Parker, Harriet Felton – Hofheinz, Roy Mark, Jr.
Parker, Josephine – Clark, Lucian G.
Parker, Minnie E. – Gilman, John C.
Parks, Heidi Ann - Boothby, James Edward, III
Parmelee, Ethel A. – Nightingale, Charles
Paschen, Alix Elizabeth – Pratt, Robert G.
Pascoe, Alice A. – Perkins, Quincy G.
Pascoe, Eulalie E. – Holbrook, Chester D.
Pascoe, Geraldine – Nickerson, Lawrence E.
Pascoe, Nancy M. – Moody, Nathaniel E.
Pay, Shirley A. – Cheney, Alfred M.
Pearlman, Natanya - Reading, Michael G.
Pearson, Linda J. – Mate, John E.
Pearson, Lorna L. – Gordon, Randall S.
Pemberton, Kimberly M. - Drew, Frank P., Jr.
Pennell, Lilla May – Williams, Charles J.
Perkins, Alice M. – Roberts, Harry C.
Perkins, Blanche – Adjutant, Roscoe
Perkins, Cathie Jean – Wallace, Jeffrey Michael
Perkins, Clara A. – Williams, Justin W.
Perkins, Emily Erma – Anthony, Francis William
Perkins, Emma M. - Nickerson, Ezra
Perkins, Etta – Lock, Frank
Perkins, Francis A. - Stevenson, Charles
Perkins, Martha E. - McNeal, Harry
Perkins, Roberta J. – Stevens, Ralph John
Perlow, Karen J. - Place, Dale E.
Perry, Charlotte E. - Lozeau, Roger P.
Peters, Christine M. - Spengler, Silas L.
Peterson, Hansine Elizabeth – Thurston, Paris W.
Pettrie, Alice K. – Smith, Ralph B.
Phenix, Joan – Whipple, Parker C.
Philbrick, Ruth E. – Mason, Arthur H.
Phillips, Linda Mae – Roger, Earl Theodore
Phillips, Nellie B. – Drake, Arthur R. C.
Pi-Sunyer, Olivia A. - DeVore, Andrew C.
Pickering, Patricia R. – Dyer, Charles N.
Pike, Dorothy M. – Lord, Merton G.

Pirone, Cathie – Johnson, Jack
Pitman, Laura Maud – Davis, Chester
Pitula, Justine E. - Oktavec, Michael John
Place, Sandra A. - Egan, William A.
Plant, Rose E. – Clifford, George W.
Plantamura, Dianne L. - Elardo, Larry W.
Plummer, Doris M. – Michaud, Alfred W.
Plummer, Ellen E. – Eldridge, Hazen A.
Poland, Effie A. – Johnson, Albert F.
Pollard, Eva L. – Page, Howard Franklin
Polley, Judith Wyman – Merrow, Lyford Ambrose
Porter, Barbara – Yarnell, Stephen
Postlewaite, Ellen M. – Tonino, Richard P.
Potter, Mary H. - Downs, Joseph
Powell, Jane Arlene – Farnum, Whipple W.
Powers, Jacqueline A. - Croce, Nickolas A.
Pratt, Elizabeth G. – Mayer, William S.
Prause, Christina A. - Allan, Michael S.
Preece, Abigail Margaret - Drouin, Christopher Lee
Primus, Ruth Ann - Billings, Peter D.
Prince, Margaret E. – Morgan, Donald G.
Prince, Noelle M. – Shear, William A.
Prior, Camilla E. – Shields, Lawrence R.
Pritchard, Nannette – Becker, Robert A.
Provencal, Patricia V. A. – Davis, Jeffrey A.
Puffer, Olive L. – Folkins, Harry W.
Pugh, Alice B. - Vierczhalek, Kenneth J.
Pullen, Marilyn Esther – Hafford, Ronald Reginald

Quimby, Ella M. – Brodie, E. W.
Quinlan, Tammy S. - Grue, Daniel F.

Radvany, Monica M. – Barocci, Thomas A.
Raesler, Amy Lou – Hargens, William Garman
Rafkind, Faith B. – Spiegel, Mark R.
Rainik, Veranika Y. - Newcomb, Andrew N.
Ralston, Sarah L. - Smith, Henry B.
Randall, Julia B. - Weston, Miles G.
Raymond, Kathleen Barbara - Dube, Tracey John
Read, Helen – Steele, Dana Allen, Jr.
Read, Kate E. – Wilder, Norman E.

Read, Nancy – Coville, Stanley B.
Reardon, Patricia A. - Thomson, Scott J.
Reed, Abbie F. – Crowley, William F.
Reid, Melissa L. - Ricker, Charles A.
Reilly, Patricia – Strong, William J.
Remick, Alice B. – Taylor, Franklin B.
Remick, Annie C. – Gilman, Sumner H.
Remick, Betty J. – Garbowicz, Edward M.
Remick, Dorothy Graves – Howard, Walter Palmer, Sr.
Remick, Helen J. – Pennell, Reginald E.
Remick, Lee Ann - Phaneuf, Mark Fitzgerald
Remick, Mary A. – Page, Arthur C.
Remick, Mary W. – Fletcher, Allen E.
Remick, Susan M. – Bergstrom, Peter W.
Remmonds, Clara L. – Dodge, Fred C.
Repasy, Denise L. – King, Roland N.
Rhines, Cheryl L. – Lloyd, Jeffrey R.
Richard, Merlene E. – Fairbanks, Douglas R.
Richards, Harriet M. – Sullivan, L. Kevin
Richards, Mildred T. – Tisdale, Robert A.
Richards, Priscilla M. – Phenix, Richard
Richards, Rena – Mills, Henry
Richards, Rita T. – Simmers, Nyal B., Pvt.
Richardson, Marjorie L. – Stark, Robert Theodore
Richardson, Marjorie M. – O'Shaughnessy, James J.
Richter, Kathleen Christine – Davis, Everett Pitman
Ricker, Robin D. - Hazen, John W.
Ricker, Rose Anne – Scolaro, Ricky A.
Rinkema, Emily Ann - Rich, William Augustus
Ritchie, Una – Jacob, Thomas
Robarge, Grace – Hutchins, Walter C.
Roberts, Ann June – Jennings, Alan Douglass
Roberts, Barbara L. – Fogg, Almon Hall
Roberts, Brenda Joyce – Robinson, John Edward
Roberts, Dorothy A. – Peaslee, Charles H.
Roberts, Kerry Faye – Guptill, Irving Elmer
Roberts, Linda C. – Harmon, Robert H.
Roberts, Lois Carol – Banfill, Carroll Benjamin
Roberts, Shirley J. – Eldridge, Hazen A.
Robertson, Elizabeth A. – Rowe, C. Daniel
Robinson, Annie L. - Quimby, Benjamin C.

Robinson, Bertha M. – Eastwick, Robert
Robinson, Karen A. - Streeter, Bradley E.
Robinson, Mary Beth – Chase, Brian
Robinson, Melissa - Trefry, Wayne A.
Robinson, Sarah J. - Eldridge, Adam G.
Rochelle, Wistar Laird – Jobe, Nathaniel Abraham, Jr.
Rock, Doris E. – Whipple, Frank P.
Roebarge, Hazel – Boone, Percival A.
Rogers, Bertha M. – Harrington, Pres. T.
Rogers, Jean Marie – Taylor, William Henry
Roosa, Nancy E. - Moot, Alexander W.
Roscilla, Elena A. – DeDeus, Hilbert
Ross, Alice M. – Moore, William E.
Ross, Edith C. - Ricker, William W.
Ross, Elsie M. – Gilman, Erwin A.
Ross, Harriett – Chadbourn, Herbert
Rotberg, Nicola S. - Cloutier, Robert L.
Rotberg, Rebecca T. - Gattey, Devin M.
Rouner, Christina Elizabeth - Harmsen, Douglas Jan
Rowe, Linda Lee – Weare, Thomas Edmund
Rowe, Maryann – Gunnill, John F.
Rubel, Ann A. – Slocum, James E.
Rugo, Barbara A. - Focht, Glenn D.
Rumary, Joisse S. - Vilbig, Mark P.
Russell, Diana L. – Reschke, Thomas C.
Russell, Edith C. – Nedeau, Frank E.
Russell, Sue – Grant, Joseph
Ryder, April P. – Libby, Paul G.
Ryder, Marie A. – Knox, Bruce R.

Sadler, Martha L. – Tornrose, William F.
Salathe, Greta A. - Mills, Ernest M.
Salmon, Angela M. - Hill, Lorne M.
Sanborn, Lida J. – Bennett, Dennis W.
Sanborn, Marguerite E. – Roberts, Lynn P.
Sandeman, Elizabeth M. - Griffin, Matthew D.
Sandoz, Margaret A. – Cobb, William H.
Santosuosso, Denice Alice - Ferrara, Jason Anthony
Sapar, Sharon Ann - Malenfant, Jeffrey John
Sargent, Ruth W. – Robertson, Elmer R.
Saucier, Tricia Mia - Jeffers, Dean Alan

Saujon, Alesia J. – Parks, Jeffrey C.
Saujon, Frances W. - Sampson, Wayne
Saujon, JoAnn P. – Bickford, Carroll Frank
Saunders, Wendy L. - McQuerrie, David A.
Savard, Ethel O. – Fallon, Lawrence
Sawin, June Rachel – Walker, Richard Earl
Sawyer, Carol E. - Grant, Alexander G.
Sawyer, Elsie M. – Purrington, Ralph H.
Scammon, Sandra L. – Hoch, George A.
Schacht, Lynne M. – Evans, Frank C.
Schacht, Lynne Marie - Evans, Frank Chandler
Schaffer, Paula J. – McCarthy, Sean M.
Schenck, Sara B. – Arling, James G.
Schneider, Hallie M. – Albers, Frederick W.
Schroeder, Phyllis Anne – Rector, James S.
Schutter, Cacilia T. - Gardon, Stefan G.
Schwer, Barbara J. – Byrne, James D.
Scott, Lisa M. – Shambough, Benjamin D.
Seamans, Donna V. - Sharp, Douglas J.
Seamans, Kimberly H. - Grace, Roy W.
Seavy, Charlotte A. – Rigby, George E.
Semmes, Amy G. – Waite, John A.
Semmes, Walden Katherine – Randall, John Lear
Severance, Charlene – Grant, Richard E.
Shannon, Marianne - Cochrane, Bruce E., Jr.
Shannon, Patricia – Ciraco, Michael
Sharp, Erin J. - Jennings, Keith Paul
Shea, Rita M. – Fortier, John L.
Shedd, Eva Ella – Moore, Richard D.
Shepardson, Pamela – Egan, Thomas F.
Shepherd, Vanessa C. – Aspinall, Gregory J.
Sheppard, Patricia L. – Norcross, Thomas E.
Sherwood, Joyce E. – Boewe, Christopher C.
Sherwood, Nettie E. - Bryant, Edward E.
Sholley, Kathy May - Arreola, Bernardino
Shrier, Lydia A. - Rich, Michael O.
Silva, Dori M. – Eldridge, David W.
Simonds, Rona A. – Whiting, George R.
Simpson, Martha S. – Whiting, Richard E.
Sinsabaugh, Barbara A. - Tolman, Gerald C.
Skillin, Tracy Elizabeth - Lanou, Gregory Peter

Skillings, Cheryl L. – Fulcher, Charles E.
Sleeper, Katherine – Waldon, Arthur T.
Sleight, Carol J. – Tee, David Fowler
Smalle, Muriel – Hayford, Arnold D.
Smalley, Evelyn C. – Robinson, Henry W.
Smart, Cora E. – Grace, Ernest C.
Smart, Mertey E. - Williams, Justus W.
Smith, Addie M. – Douglas, Warren L.
Smith, Alice - Downs, Joseph L.
Smith, Barbara L. – Robinson, Harold C.
Smith, Clare E. – Butterfield, Fernan R.
Smith, Deanna L. – Millette, David E.
Smith, Ellen D. – Thurston, Daniel C.
Smith, Emilie E. - Caruso, James V.
Smith, Grace – Ford, Edmund M.
Smith, Harriet W. – Kiley, John G.
Smith, Ida B. – Hutchins, Clarence E.
Smith, Irene H. - Reardon, William H.
Smith, Marion A. – Perkins, Bert A.
Smith, Melba P. – Webster, Ray P.
Smith, Melissa M. - Wood, Jason A.
Smith, Rose A. – Downs, Harry J.
Snow, Audrey V. – Lewry, Willard H.
Snow, Elizabeth C. – Swayne, William Wager
Solbes, Jean C. – Brown, David N.
Sorlien, Patricia A. – Read, William G.
Spalding, Anne Margaret – Mock, Wayne Kenneth
Spalding, Joan A. – Mayer, Richard A.
Sparks, Abigail K. - Eldridge, Ricky L.
Spaulding, Barbara Jean - Woodward, John Shurman
Spaulding, Evelyn M. – Wallace, Donald W.
Spaulding, Florence – Spalding, Rufus W.
Speckman, Violet D. – Martel, Morton C.
Spicer, Ann – Cort, Henry R., Jr.
Sprague, Esther – Bookholz, Leon W.
Stacy, Christabel I. – Eldridge, Harry P., Jr.
Staley, Margaret E. – Brothers, Michael B.
Stamps, Jankis – Hamel, Gerard E.
Stanwood, Isibel B. – Robertson, Mark E.
Staples, Barbara Gladys – Meader, Donald Norman
Staples, Mary Joan – Holladay, Ronald James

Staples, Ruth W. – Stone, Bruce L.
Staples, Sky T. - Ladd, Joshua F.
Stearns, Cora E. – Davis, Amos T.
Steele, Helen R. – Steele, Nathaniel A.
Steele, Lorraine Loretta - Streeter, Joel Franklin
Stehli, Katharine T. - Scharf, David L.
Stenson, Mary – LaRose, Joseph
Stevens, Risa – Grace, Jeffrey
Stewart, Deborah – Nelson, Peter
Stewart, Donna L. – Anthony, David M.
Stewart, Susan B. – Bennett, Dennis W.
Stinchfield, Marion – Paula, Arthur
Stinchfield, Pauline M. – Drake, Albert
Stoddard, Joanne – Ames, James W.
Stoddard, Sally-Ann – Schofield, Richard Garry
Stoe, Grace E. – Walker, Robert H.
Stone, Cynthia A. – Morrill, Timothy W.
Stone, Vicki – Forsythe, Edwin B., Jr.
Stoneman, Diane M. – Anair, Richard M.
Stoney, Brenda Susan - Mooney, Paul W.
Streeter, Gail R. – Dascoulias, Robert A.
Streeter, Janes – Conner, David R.
Streeter, Laurie J. – Burnell, Alton E.
Streeter, Rene – Merchant, Michael J.
Strong, Josephine J. – Knapp, Herbert C.
Sullo, Gayle A. - Whittier, Stephen M.
Sutherland, Holly Jean - Jeske, Vernon Edward
Sutherland, Pamela K. – Lipmen, Philip A.
Swain, Eva M. – Tewksbury, Isaac A.
Swain, Hattie - Hobbs, Bert W.
Swale, Shirley Lorraine – Lovell, David Eric
Swan, Bonita Marie – Downs, Clifford F., Jr.
Swan, Colleen M. – Ames, John P.
Swan, Deborah Ann - Carlson, Dana Francis
Swanson, Darlene Roxanne - Hatch, Wilbur Clifford, Jr.
Sweeney, Sandra Frances - Watkins, Robert Mason
Sweet, Lois F. – Libby, Elson
Sweet, Olive M. – Morrill, Arthur E.
Sweithelm, Gail Frances – Grace, Jere Wayne
Swenson, Cynthia Rae – Plummer, Frank James
Switaj, Donna F. - Ulitz, Michael Bernard

Swope, Winifred R. – Wakeman, Russell J.
Sylvia, Susan E. - Krebs, Ernest A.

Tallman, Doris M. – Hodge, Elwood N.
Tandy, Louise Adria – Drugg, Charles Howard
Tapfar, Lori Marie - McCarthy, Thomas Mark
Taylor, Allison J. – Parsons, Jeffrey C.
Taylor, Charlene A. - Farrell, Dennis J.
Taylor, Jean Marie – McCormack, George Edward
Taylor, Nancy C. – Sargent, Raymond W.
Taylor, Pamela Joyce – Patten, James Charles
Taylor, Ruth E. - Cleveland, Thomas G.
Tefft, Norrine L. – Nixon, Dean W.
Templeton, Blanche L. – Nickerson, Wendell A.
Terrill, Sarah L. - Buck, Tracy L.
Tewksbury, Anna M. – Wiggin, Arthur E.
Tewksbury, Carrie C. - Fellows, Henry M.
Tewksbury, Emma N. - Knox, Herbert E.
Tewksbury, Nettie M. – Dow, Charles L.
Theriault, Lillian L. – Church, Phillips D.
Therkildsen, Kit Nordbo – Simpson, George Adam, Jr.
Thompson, Alice F. – Sanborn, Sidney W.
Thompson, Helen R. – Lewis, Sheldon W.
Thompson, Jane M. – Witzel, Erich A.
Thompson, Jo-Ann – Ames, Alan A.
Thompson, Kathi – Brown, Timothy
Thompson, Lydia More – Ellis, Scott Lawrence
Thompson, Patricia M. – Ryan, Thomas R., Jr.
Thorner, Helen A. - Moody, Robert Paul
Thorp, Linda Jean - Acker, J. Bruce
Thurston, Ann – Hansen, Richard Dalrymple
Thurston, Frances L. – Hammond, George R.
Thurston, Maud – Gilman, Reed B.
Thurston, Theresa M. - Zowasky, Robert K.
Tibbetts, Addie - Bickford, Benjamin
Tibbetts, Jacquelyne Lorraine – Woodward, Freeman Earl
Tibbetts, Jennifer L. - Leach, Thomas J.
Tibbetts, Minnie - Wormwood, Herbert E.
Ticehurst, Susan J. – Dube, Mark L.
Tilton, Clara B. – Tilton, Frank E.
Tilton, Fannie A. - Bassett, James C.

Tilton, Mary M. – Kimball, Winslow B.
Todd, Mary Peaco - Bradley, John Francis
Toussaint, Ann Marie - Dailey, Timothy D.
Towle, Maria - Hobbs, Joseph W.
Trask, Beverley A. – Mather, Anthony C.
Trask, Dorothy M. – Barna, Czeslaw J.
Troutman, Caryn D. – Thomas, Dannie L.
Turcotte, Susan Anne - Ricker, George Arron
Turner, Nellie – Elias, Rogy
Tuttle, Ida M. – Plant, George E.
Tuttle, Katharine F. – Wiggin, Richard A.
Twitchell, Eleanor – Gustafson, Frederic B.
Twitchell, Susan D. - Engelmann, Earl G., Jr.
Twombly, Cynthia – Hartford, Wayne L.
Tyler, Ruth E. – Davis, Sidney

Ugo, Diana E. – Shannon, Mathew W.
Ulitz, Kathleen M. – Cook, Vincent Perry
Ulitz, Lauren A. – Frase, Kimberly K.
Ullrich, Cynthia Joan - Furnbach, Henry James
Underhill, Louise M. – Plummer, Clarence R., Jr.
Urquhart, Carol Rita – Cicchetti, George Joseph
Urquhart, Joan Helen – Phillippi, Karl Evan

Valerio, Judith A. – Clapp, Ian W.
Van Frost, Kathlyn L. – Loring, David H.
Varney, Barbara M. - Schultze, William C.
Varney, Hannah J. - Drew, John D.
Varney, Marie B. - Macomber, Harry T.
Varney, Rhonda Lee - Merrill, Richard Forest
Vasey, Edna C. – Corson, George E.
Ventura, Cheri Antoinette - Burrer, Phillip Farrell
Ver Planck, Frances K. – Hanson, Robert W., Jr.
Vittum, Dorothy – Larrabee, Raymond
Vittum, Margaret – Tappan, Henry
Vittum, Mary L. – Gibson, George A.
Vittum, Ruth E. – Chick, Robert M.
Vittum, Viola D. – Green, Frank C.

Wade, Mary L. – Cook, William H.
Wadley, Nettie – Blodgett, August L.

Walega, Holly M. - Beauchesne, Laurier W.
Walker, Edith C. – King, Arthur C.
Walker, Isabelle – Bookholz, Walter B.
Walker, Lillian – Nelson, John
Walker, Myrtle L. - Delude, Robert L.
Walker, Patricia J. - Carpenter, Allen R.
Walker, Sandra Lee – Parker, Bruce Wesley
Wallace, Abbie S. - Follett, Charles M.
Wallace, Lucy M. - Scruton, Joseph O.
Waltzer, Leslie J. - Reynolds, Paul W.
Ward, Dorothea R. – Scaringi, Gene
Ward, Roberta C. – Donovan, Timothy G.
Warner, Jeanne M. – Ames, Charles E., Jr.
Warner, Leona J. – Bodge, Charles F.
Wasson, Vicki B. – Hanson, Peter R.
Wastell, Constance M. - Artis, Gene P.
Watson, Betty Ethel – Welch, Richard David
Watson, Lorie J. - Bohmiller, Stephen A.
Watson, Lynn M. - Sylvain, Roy C.
Watson, Sarah Clara – Hobbs, Frank Wilson
Watt, Carolyn Davis - Williams, Gregory John
Weare, Judith Rose – Larrabee, Arnold Herbert
Weare, Margaret E. – Staley, Victor E.
Weare, Susan May – Hayford, Randall Everett
Webster, Linda A. - Lauzon, Peter D.
Webster, Ruth C. – Gobelle, Norman R.
Webster, Shirley C. – Evans, Almon G., Jr.
Wedge, Evelyn M. – Blanchard, Gerald R.
Weed, Helen – Martin, Louville K.
Weeks, Laura A. – Kierstead, Thomas J.
Weeks, Lorraine M. - O'Leary, Joseph M.
Weeks, Mary S. – Doe, Eugene M.
Weeks, Winifred – Downs, Clifford F.
Welch, Brenda Doris – Bedford, Bruce Walton
Welch, Dorothy E. – Douville, Romeo Leo
Welch, Evelyn M. – Shannon, Charles
Welch, Florence E. – Fortier, Walter W.
Welch, Helen B. – Dicey, Garfield W., Pvt.
Welch, Hester Rose – Bennett, Lawrence Edward
Welch, Maria - Aguirre, Julio R.
Welch, Marybelle – Carter, Robert W.

Welch, Minnie F. – Webster, Alfred L.
Welch, Ruth J. – Ryder, Lloyd W.
Welch, Stephanie F. – Gardner, Mark S.
Welch, Tammy Lynn - Sullivan, George Edward, III
Welch, Teresa L. - Maura, Edward L.
Wells, Melissa - Jakobs, Karl Kenneth
Wenant, Janet Lynne – Creps, Lee
Wenckus, Stephanie A. - Spear, David S.
Wentworth, Leah C. – Hutchins, Paul W.
Wentworth, Pamela J. – Farnum, Walter W.
Westover, Mary – Smith, James, Jr.
Wettergreen, Amy P. - Smach, Kent D.
Weymouth, Danielle L. – Nespaca, Mark P.
Weymouth, Laura E. – Howell, John A., Jr.
Weymouth, Letitia M. – Tuff, Alfred R.
Wheeler, Helen A. – Remick, Harry H.
Wheeler, Jean A. – Ames, Carl W.
Wheeler, Laura E. - Landesman, Jeffrey S.
Wheeler, Leslie Ann - Grace, John Francis
Wheeler, Penelope – Pi-Sunyer, Francis X.
Wheeler, Penelope Gillan - Abbott, George Thompson
Wheeler, Robin – Jean, Thomas Michael
Whipple, Cynthia J. – Melanson, Joseph I.
Whipple, Flora E. – Blackey, Edwin A.
Whipple, Marilyn J. – Loud, Clarence B.
Whitaker, Kimberly J. - Sanphy, Tanen D.
Whitaker, Lucinda – Pease, Benjamin F.
White, Candy L. - Carlson, Richard H.
White, Carrie B. - Nickerson, George E.
White, Christine A. - Mackwell, Stephen J.
White, Cora E. - Drew, John N.
White, Donna J. – Canney, Haven E.
White, Irma J. - Nickerson, Archie
White, Jo Anne - Armstrong, Daryl V.
White, Louise B. – Colby, Royal P.
White, Suzanne – Ganem, George A.
White, Tammy L. - Bross, Shawn M.
White, Virginia Wheeler – Damon, Stephen F.
White, Winifred G. – Ryder, Lynnwood P.
Whiting, Alice R. – Pierce, Maurice A.
Whiting, Amy Pearl – Davis, Larry John

Whiting, Anne – Wakefield, Arthur D.
Whiting, Annie H. – Holt, George T.
Whiting, Bertha M. - Roberts, Charles H.
Whiting, Brenda L. - Jardine, Kent I.
Whiting, Deborah A. – Swan, Christopher
Whiting, Dorris L. – Brown, Charles W.
Whiting, Elizabeth – Wynne, William Ernest
Whiting, Ellen P. – Bookholz, Edward V.
Whiting, Evelyn I. – Brown, Charles W.
Whiting, Fannie E. – Hill, William A.
Whiting, Florence – Barnes, Fred E.
Whiting, Lizzie M. - Emery, J. Wesley
Whiting, Sadie E. – Pearl, Harry W.
Whitman, Eva L. – Pollard, Edward S.
Whitman, Toni-Ann - Schultze, Andrew Kyle
Whittemore, Lisa L. - Sharp, Irwin S.
Whittier, Nellie B. – Phillips, Charles E.
Whitty, Stacie A. - Eldridge, David W.
Wickersham, Nancy Lee – Beard, John Ross
Wickman, Lori Lynn - Palmer, Daniel Richard
Wiesner, Elizabeth Quincy – Manna, Charles Robert
Wiesner, Margaret B. – Farnum, William W.
Wiesner, Margaret B. - Sargent, David W.
Wiggin, Ethel V. – Bookholz, Frederick F.
Wiggin, Evelyn E. – Gobelle, Arthur J.
Wiggin, Linda – Isgur, David C.
Wiggin, Mary L. - Robinson, Henry B.
Wiggin, Neurine Elaine – LaPorte, Roc Lyne Emile
Wilcox, Elizabeth A. - Jacobson, Marty G.
Wilins, Marcia M. – Masse, Wayne N.
Wilkinson, Jo Ann - Williams, Gary R.
Wilkinson, Judi L. - Birmingham, Paul J., Jr.
Wilkinson, Kristin N. - Klien, Paul M.
Willye, Kristine E. - Dascoulias, Joseph R.
Willey, Eliza – Brown, Alonzo
Willey, Susan Marie – Staples, Daniel Victor
Williams, Annie, Mrs. - Wiggin, Sylvester
Williams, Beverly A. – Ames, Robert J.
Wiliams, Cora B. – Pearsons, John
Williams, Dora – Pennell, Edwin
Williams, Frances L. – Brownell, Lawrence M.

Williams, Heidi A. - King, Christopher W.
Williams, Lucinda F. - Bliss, William P.
Williams, Margie L. – Williams, Richard W.
Williams, Mildred M. – Hobbs, Philip D.
Williams, Nettie – Moody, Joseph A.
Williamson, Marsha G. - Hayford, A. David
Willis, Elizabeth E. – Martineau, Jason A. N.
Wills, Roberta A. – Scott, Douglas J.
Wilson, Karen L. - Ouellette, Robert C.
Wing, Virginia M. - Fredrickson, Paul E.
Winslow, Kathleen L. - Prussman, Erik C.
Winters, Susan E. - Cayer, James J.
Wittet, Amy - Truog, Robert David
Wolf, Barbara P. – Fiske, Donald W.
Wood, Anna P. – Doe, Eugene C.
Woodcock, Heather G. - Monahan, Daniel G.
Woodward, Carol Jean – Chase, Richard Preston
Woodward, Janet E. – Sanborn, Raymond F.
Woodward, Melissa Lee - Monfet, Michael Edward
Woodward, Theresa – Whiting, Jeffrey L.
Woolsey, Rosemary E. - Melanson, Wayne A.
Wooten, Rita M. – Whiteing, Carroll M.
Wright, Erinn Heather - Rollo, David Timothy
Wyman, Lena – Blaisdell, Charles A.

Yeaton, Mildred D. – Austin, Joseph F.
Young, Ethel E. – Buzzutto, Nick D.
Young, Jacquelyn – Gordon, Haven E.
Young, Minnie A. - Pike, Fred W.

Zakarian, Alice N. – Smalle, Theodore B.
Zibailo, Suzanne M. – Daigle, Louis P.

Tamworth Deaths

ABBEY,
Mildred E., d. 10/14/1994 in N. Conway; Elmer Abbey and Sarah Smith

ABBOTT,
infant son, d. 1/6/1911 at – in Tamworth; b. Tamworth; Herbert E. Abbott (Sandwich) and Alice M. Gilman (Tamworth)
Alta C., d. 2/14/1986 in Ossipee; George Nickerson and Carrie White
William Daniel, d. 10/15/1974 at 74 in Wolfeboro; b. NH; residence – Chocorua

ABBRUZZI,
James B., d. 7/16/1986 in Tamworth; James Abbruzzi and Grace Kenney

ACKER,
Jennie P., d. 12/17/1986 in N. Conway; Carl Andreassen and Martha -----
Marion Taylor, d. 11/7/1976 at 84 in Plymouth; b. NH; residence - Dorchester

ADRIANCE,
Samuel R., d. 8/25/1921 at --; cerebral apoplexy; mill manager; single; b. NY

ALBEE,
Helen R., d. 10/14/1939 at 75

ALEXANDER,
Winifred, d. 10/--/1947 at 73/4/13 in Guilford, CT

ALLARD,
Elmira Wilson, d. 8/19/1919 at 89/5/7; housewife; widow; b. Newport, ME; Oliver Rollins and Hannah Clark

ALT,
Martha B., d. 11/21/1995 in ME; Augustus Boyden and Frances Waggener
Richard M., d. 8/14/1995 in N. Conway; Emile C. Alt and Ida M. Myers

AMES,
stillborn child, d. 2/10/1929 at –
Ada, d. 7/16/1994 in Laconia; Wilbur Eldridge and Myrtle Templeton
Bertha L., d. 1/18/1979 in N. Conway; John Frost and Bertha Hammond
Blanche E., d. 5/30/1974 at 83 in Laconia; b. NH; residence - Tamworth
Caroline Loraine, d. 9/21/1925 at 0/5/3
Carolyn Louise, d. 2/22/1935 at 9/10/2
Charles J., d. 11/14/1913 at 75/5/29 in Tamworth; lumber dealer, married; b. Tamworth; James Ames and Joanna Hayford
Charles J., Jr., d. 1/21/1912 at 48/7/17 in Tamworth; clerk; married; b. Tamworth; Charles J. Ames (Tamworth) and Mary H. Flood (Tamworth)
Claude Milton, d. 1/12/1993 in Tamworth; Claude P. Ames and Blanche Jeffers
Claude P., d. 1/2/1956 at 67/11/18 in Tamworth
Dorothy E., d. 1/8/1903 at 0/1/23 in Tamworth; b. Tamworth; Zimri E. Ames (Tamworth) and Ella Palmer (Sandwich)
Ella J., d. 4/15/1933 at 70/4/18
Emman Irene, d. 2/5/1993 in Laconia; Ernest Grace and Cora Smart
Evelyn A., d. 3/3/1931 at 0/5/28
Florence A., d. 12/13/1994 in N. Conway; William E. Frost and Florence E. Thurston
George, d. 11/15/1985 in Wolfeboro; Ernest Ames and Louise Frost
George H., d. 2/18/1910 at 64/8/28 in Tamworth; farmer; widower; b. Tamworth; Joseph Ames (Tamworth) and Abigail Glidden (Calais, ME)
Hattie D., d. 12/31/1958 at 75 in Tamworth
James Roland, d. 9/29/1971 at 66 in Laconia; b. NH; residence - Tamworth
Jane Dolaries, d. 7/9/1930 at 0/0/1
John N., d. 11/10/1950 at 71/2/16 in S. Tamworth
Joseph, Jr., d. 3/11/1913 at 79/4/27 in Tamworth; farmer; widower; b. Tamworth; Joseph Ames and Abigail Glidden
Mary A., d. 11/7/1899 at 50/7/14 in Tamworth; housewife; married; b. Tamworth; William Woodman (Tamworth) and F. Woodman
Mary H., d. 7/9/1925 at 81/7/3
Melissa A., d. 9/8/1952 at 80/0/7 in Portland, ME
Paul T., d. 11/9/1954 at 0/0/2 in Wolfeboro
Robert C., d. 8/16/1937 at 0/8/24

Sarah, d. 12/22/1895 at 91 in Tamworth; housekeeper; single; b. Tamworth; John Ames and Sarah Glidden

Susan, d. 6/7/1892 at 54/4 in Tamworth; housework; b. Tamworth; Lorenzo Stevens and Lucy Morse

Zinnie E., d. 1/19/1927 at 68/11/1

AMIDON,
Frances Eleene, d. 10/17/1989 in Wolfeboro; Orman R. Howard and Mebelle Horne

Herbert Maxwell, d. 11/27/1989 in Wolfeboro; Herbert W. Amidon and Gertrude Hayden

AMSDEN,
Edwin, d. 7/11/1953 at 89 in Wolfeboro

ANDERSON,
Martha, d. 9/11/1948 at 72/4/3 in Laconia

Richard C., d. 1/7/2000 in Tamworth; John Anderson and Sigrid Edmund

Rutherford B., d. 12/1/1971 at 68 in Tamworth; b. MA; residence - Tamworth

ANDREWS,
James, d. 2/21/1904 at 76/1/21 in Tamworth; farmer; widower; b. RI; Isaac Andrews and Mary Tucker

Viola M., d. 5/7/1970 at 71 in Tamworth; b. ME; residence – Lynn, MA

ANTHONY,
Harry E., d. 1/26/1974 at 32 in Rochester; b. NH; residence - Sanbornville

Richard L., d. 1/15/1951 at 0/3/26 in Wolfeboro

Ruth F., d. 9/11/1994 in Wolfeboro; Harry Berry and Elva Murphy

William John, d. 2/24/1974 at 50 in Manchester; b. ME; residence - Tamworth

APPLEBY,
Everett S., d. 6/16/2000 in Wolfeboro; Everett Appleby and Leeta Dennis

AREY,
George T., d. 8/20/1915 at 33/1/13; pulmonary tuberculosis; accountant; married; b. Lowell, MA; Richard H. Arey and Rose Parazina

ARLAND,
James G., d. 11/5/1926 at 74/4

ARLING,
David F., d. 11/20/1940 at 79; b. Tamworth
David W., d. --/--/1896 at 72/8 in Tamworth; farmer; married
Emma M., d. 1/14/1909 at 47/2/29 in Tamworth; housewife; married; b. Sandwich; Alonzo Bickford (Barrington) and Mary A. Moulton (Tamworth)
Lulu M., d. 8/22/1977 at 93 in Meredith; b. NH; residence - Tamworth
Roy E., d. 6/21/1960 at 78 in Tamworth
Sarah, d. 11/5/1939 at 77; b. Ireland
Sarah B., d. 9/9/1912 at 67 in Tamworth; housewife; married; b. New Germantown, NJ; Peter Schenck and Rebecca Harris

ARMSTRONG,
Robert, d. 11/12/1943 at 70/11/2 in Tamworth

ARSENAULT,
Joseph Gerard, d. 9/18/1999 in Tamworth; Aequile Arsenault and Delima Leblanc

ARTIS,
Gene P., d. 6/7/2000 in Wolfeboro; John Artis and Ezzie Ganons

ASPINALL,
Charles E., d. 10/22/1994 in Rochester; William Aspinall and Ethel Lord

ATKINS,
Abbie, d. 3/25/1928 at 89/9/10
Charles H., d. 8/1/1939 at 79/5; b. Lynn, MA
Jennie M., d. 6/23/1947 at 86/0/29 in Tamworth

ATKINSON,
Emma P., d. 2/6/1925 at 70/3/27
Langdon M., d. 3/25/1916 at 58/7/5; pulmonary tuberculosis; pullman con.; married; b. Madison; John M. Atkinson and Ann Odell

ATWELL,
Dorothy, d. 5/14/1980 in Meredith; William Nelson and Marjorie Campbell

ATWOOD,
Grace Luvie, d. 9/7/1963 at 85 in Laconia; b. Stark; residence - Tamworth
Harriet W., d. 4/30/2002 in N. Conway; Albert Atwood and Grace Wade

AYER,
Celon E., d. 9/9/1936 at 58/4/14
Forrest D., d. 8/28/1967 in Laconia; b. Haverhill, MA; residence - Tamworth

BAGLEY,
Rexford E., d. 10/18/1918 at 16/2/1; lobar pneumonia; laborer; single; b. Tamworth; Elno Bagley and Sadie E. Sargent

BAGNALL,
Arnold, d. 7/26/1934 at 27/9/7

BALLARD,
Mary Ella, d. 5/7/1888 at 23/2; housekeeper; married; b. Tamworth; Lorenzo D. Bartlett (Meredith) and Mary E. Brown (Sandwich)

BANFILL,
infant, d. 4/18/1928 at –
Benjamin D., d. 7/7/1990 in Laconia; Willard Banfill and Harriet Bickford
Lillian A., d. 5/1/1982 in Laconia; Mayhew Allard and Julia Sawyer
Willie, d. 1/28/1954 at 81 in Moultonboro

BANKS,
Mary E., d. 11/29/1914 at 80/11/1; pneumonia; widow

BANNISTER,
Beatrice G., d. 9/14/1983 in Wolfeboro; Harry Barrett and Eleanor York

BARTLETT,
infant son, d. 11/10/1909 at 0/0/1 in Tamworth; b. Tamworth; Leland C. Bartlett (Moultonboro) and Adelaide Mason (Tamworth)
Adelaide M., d. 12/13/1923 at 44/1/25; b. Tamworth; John L. Mason and Ellen S. Varney
Drusilla, d. 10/14/1897 at 61/11/8 in Tamworth; housewife; married
Elroy G., d. 8/26/1911 at 54/7/28 in Tamworth; manufacturer; married; b. Meredith; Lorenzo D. Bartlett (Meredith) and Ellen Brown
Imogene A., d. 5/27/1911 at 54/8/7 in Tamworth; housewife; married; b. Moultonboro; Clark Evans and Esther Robinson
Leland C., d. 11/27/1918 at 35; broncho pneumonia; manufacturer; married; b. Boston, MA; Elroy C. Bartlett and Imogene Evans
Lorenzo D., d. 7/14/1897 at 74 in Tamworth; mechanic; widower; b. Meredith; Joseph Bartlett and Betsy Leavitt
Lorenzo W., d. 8/31/1900 at 7/5/3 in Tamworth; b. Conway; Elroy G. Bartlett (Meredith) and Imogene Evans (Moultonboro)
Marian, d. 12/13/1887 at 1/6/23 in Tamworth; b. Tamworth; E. G. Bartlett (Meredith) and ----- Evans (Moultonboro)
Marion M., d. 5/8/1909 at 0/6/10 in Tamworth; b. Tamworth; Leland C. Bartlett (Moultonboro) and Adelaide Mason (Tamworth)
Mary A., d. --/--/1896 at 65 in Tamworth; housewife; married; b. Sandwich; Larkin D. Brown and Susan Severance
Nellie M., d. 1/28/1907 at 0/0/1 in Tamworth; b. Tamworth; L. C. Bartlett (Moultonboro) and A. M. Mason (Tamworth)

BASSETT,
J. C., d. 2/9/1897 at 64/4/22 in Tamworth; physician; married; b. Jackson; David Bassett and Ann Burnham
Lydia A., d. 6/28/1891 at 59/4/18 in Tamworth; housewife; married; b. Exeter; Joseph Tilton and Susan F. Stickney
Timothy D., d. 2/10/1887 at 55/8/14 in Lake Village; machinist; married

BATCHELDER,
George F., d. 8/21/1913 at 67/5/21 in Tamworth; retired; married; b. Concord; George H. Bachelder and Sarah A. Clough

George M., d. 9/29/1941 at 59/2/8 in Tamworth

BEAN,
Elizabeth A., d. 1/1/1903 at 77/3 in Tamworth; housewife; widow; b. Loudon; Eliphalet Bean and Alice Willey
Otis, d. 6/29/1969 at 79 in Wolfeboro; residence - Tamworth
Timothy, d. 3/19/1905 at 79/10/30 in Tamworth; farmer; widower; b. Brownfield, ME; Nathan Bean and Rhoda Dutch

BEAUCHESNE,
Laurier Wilfred, d. 10/5/1996 in Chocorua; Albert Beauchesne and Germaine Roy

BECK,
Charles, d. 4/15/1931 at 83/6/10
Lillie S., d. 4/29/1946 at 88/9/11 in Tamworth

BEDFORD,
Martha T., d. 7/8/1986 in N. Conway; Mavo Tolman and Ruth Dunbar

BEEDE,
Achsa, d. 4/17/1903 at 69 in Tamworth; housewife; widow; David James
Rufus L., d. 4/2/1901 at 72/7/27 in Tamworth; laborer; married; b. Gilmanton; Eli Beede and Betsey Judkins
William H., d. 8/20/1913 at 76/2/16 in Tamworth; broker; married; b. Tamworth; Samuel S. Beede and Nancy Boyden

BEHM,
John, d. 12/6/1985 in Tamworth; John Behm and Constance Trapoulanis

BEHR,
Charles E., d. 3/7/1987 in Tamworth; Gustave E. Behr, Jr. and Gertrude Fox
Gertrude F., d. 7/8/1979 in Tamworth; Jebez Fox and Susan Thayer

BELIVEAU,
Henry J., d. 2/14/2001 in Tamworth; Donat Beliveau and Mary Robideaux

BENNER,
Eva M., d. 11/24/1956 at 82 in Tamworth

BENNETT,
Arthur R., d. 4/21/1958 at 84 in Center Harbor
Charles, d. 2/24/1969 at 97 in Ossipee; b. NH; residence - Tamworth
Cora M., d. 2/27/1905 at 30/3/1 in Tamworth; housekeeping; married; b. Samdwich; Wyatt F. Bennett (Sandwich) and Mary A. Hancock (Cornwall, England)
Edward W., d. 12/29/1924 at 46
Wyatt F., d. 7/13/1904 at 76/9/2 in Tamworth; farmer; widower; b. Sandwich; John Bennett and Lucinda Fogg

BERNARD,
Joseph S., d. 9/24/1945 at 65/0/0 in Tamworth

BERRY,
Abby J., d. 4/18/1934 at 88/2/18
Alice E., d. 7/6/1970 at 77 in Ossipee; b. NH; residence – Tamworth
Chester C., d. 4/16/1983 in Londonderry; Orrin Berry and Mary Davis
Daniel, d. 3/8/1903 at 9 in Tamworth; b. Tamworth; Orren S. Berry (Tamworth) and Lizzie M. Davis
David J., d. 4/24/1889 at 61/9/20; farmer; married; b. Tamworth
Eleanor A., d. 1/7/1978 at 66 in Tamworth; b. NH; residence - Tamworth
Ellen, d. 6/12/1889 at 44/9; single; b. Tamworth; Samuel Berry (Barnstead) and Susan Chick (Barnstead)
Elva H., d. 3/3/1959 at 75 in Wolfeboro
Emma F., d. 4/28/1890 at 37/3 in Tamworth; housework; single; b. Tamworth; David Berry (Ossipee) and Insie Hyde (Ossipee)
Ethel M., d. 9/24/1959 at 50/8/17 in Portland, ME
Everett, d. 5/19/1965 at 68 in Wolfeboro; b. Tamworth; residence - Tamworth
Frank, d. 9/10/1899 at 23/10/1 in Tamworth; farmer; single; b. Tamworth; Nathaniel Berry (Tamworth) and Abbie Blake (Tamworth)
Frank Ronald, d. 5/7/1989 in Raton, NM; Walter E. Berry and Grace A. Clough
George A., d. 3/3/1961 at 79 in Wolfeboro
Gladys, d. 5/25/1902 at 0/0/1 in Tamworth; b. Tamworth; Walter H.

Berry (Tamworth) and Grace L. Clough (Tamworth)
Harry D., d. 6/15/1966 at 86 in Center Harbor; b. Tamworth; residence - Tamworth
Herman D., d. 8/9/1941 at 64/10/16 in Conway
Hollis S., d. 2/18/1889 at 56/0/16; married; b. Tamworth
Howard Ellsworth, d. 2/10/1989 in Tamworth; Walter Henry Berry and Grace Lillian Clough
Ida A., d. 1/15/1922 at 66/1/14; b. Tamworth; Daniel Berry and Irene Hyde
Ida M., d. 3/24/1960 at 79 in Wolfeboro
Irene, d. 4/28/1895 at -- in Tamworth; widow; b. Wolfeboro; Samuel Hyde and Mary Taylor
Lawrence W., d. 8/15/1979 in Tamworth; Walter Berry and Grace Clough
Lester L., d. 9/11/1973 at 82 in Tamworth; b. NH; residence - Tamworth
Madeline M., d. 5/5/1904 at 0/7/20 in Tamworth; b. Tamworth; Walter H. Berry (Tamworth) and Grace L. Clough (Tamworth)
Martin Edward, d. 4/9/1970 at – in Conway; b. N. Conway
Martin F., d. 4/18/1941 at 0/4/16 in Conway
Mary A., d. 9/20/1889 at 76/5; housewife; married
Mary E., d. 11/5/1939 at 87/4/14; b. Naples, ME
Nathaniel, d. 12/1/1930 at 87/3/13
Orrin S., d. 4/3/1923 at 76; b. Tamworth; Daniel Berry and Irene Hyde
Robert K., d. 6/10/1985 in Wolfeboro; Harry Berry and Edith Gilman
Roland, d. 2/3/1983 in Manchester; Walter Berry and Grace Clough
Ronald E., d. 5/30/2002 in Laconia; Frank Berry and Eleanor Condon
Samuel, d. 3/11/1891 at 92 in Tamworth; farmer; widower; Nathaniel Berry
Samuel, d. 10/18/1899 at 75 in Tamworth; farmer; b. Tamworth; Joseph Berry
Thelma, d. 11/11/1928 at 21/7/24
Walter H., d. 12/22/1950 at 76 in Moultonboro

BEXSON,
Sydney G., d. 9/23/1971 at 75 in Tamworth; b. England; residence - Tamworth

BICKFORD,
infant son, d. 1/22/1913 at 0/0/2 in Tamworth; b. Tamworth; Frederick H. Bickford and Charlina M. Walker
Addie, d. 11/27/1910 at 66 in Tamworth; housewife; married; b. Limerick, ME; Roswell Torrey and Sarah Hardy (Portland, ME)
Alice, d. 3/27/1969 at 71 in Tamworth; b. Newark, NJ; residence - Tamworth
Alonzo, d. 5/10/1930 at 52/6/5
Ann, d. 4/20/1890 at 84/7/11 in Tamworth; housekeeper; widow; b. Barrington; James Arling (Strafford) and Ellen ----- (Strafford)
Benjamin, d. 6/22/1914 at 87/0/3; arteriosclerosis; farmer; widower; b. Parsonsfield, ME; Benjamin Bickford and Lydia Cram
Carl O., d. 8/5/1994 in Laconia; Roy Bickford and Lenora Brown
Charlene M. Walker, d. 7/13/1968 at 91 in Melrose, MA; residence – Melrose, MA
Charles F., d. 1/17/1910 at 0/4/22 in Tamworth; b. Tamworth; Frederick J. Bickford (Tamworth) and Charlina Walker (Holliston, MA)
Chester J., d. 11/30/1964 at 71 in Tamworth; b. Sandwich; residence - Tamworth
Enoch, d. 2/4/1895 at 68/2/23 in Tamworth; carpenter; married; b. Madison; Benjamin Bickford (Parsonsfield) and Lydia Cram (Parsonsfield)
Eva E., d. 5/26/1938 at 68/8/29; b. Tamworth
Evelyn J., d. 4/18/1955 at 74 in Tamworth
Frederick J., d. 12/7/1928 at 60/11/24
Hannah, d. 9/30/1912 at 75/11/19 in Tamworth; widow; b. Hallowell, ME; Washington Rollins (Damariscotta, ME) and Hannah Little (Whitefield, ME)
Irene H., d. 2/28/1935 at 84/9/12
J. H., d. 3/2/1908 at 43/10/11 in Tamworth; laborer; divorced; b. Tamworth; Enoch Bickford (Eaton) and Susan Lord (Eaton)
James B., d. 12/1/1946 at 77/11/22 in Tamworth
James W., d. 10/11/1902 at 78/11/23 in Tamworth; farmer; widower; b. Madbury; James Bickford (Strafford) and Ann Arling (Barrington)
Joan W., d. 6/17/1983 in Tamworth; Harry Welch and Vera Bodge
John F., d. 5/8/1888 at 29/3/17; merchant; single; b. Tamworth; Enoch Bickford (Eaton) and Susan Lord (Eaton)
Lenora, d. 3/20/1966 at 88 in Wolfeboro; b. Gilford; residence - Tamworth

Mary, d. 2/6/1888 at 70/3/4; housekeeper; married; b. Sandwich; ----
Tasker
Mary, d. 10/2/1891 at 60/6/3 in Tamworth; housewife; married; b.
Eaton; Enoch Robertson and Hephzibath Bean
Mary, d. 10/4/1895 at 58/1/3 in Tamworth; housekeeper; widow; b.
Tamworth
Nellie E., d. 9/11/1958 at 86 in Wolfeboro
Sarah, d. 6/5/1895 at 70 in Tamworth; widow; b. Lebanon, ME;
Moses Wentworth (Berwick) and Sally Jackson (Eaton)
Sarah J., d. 8/13/1898 at 67/0/23 in Tamworth; married; b. Tamworth
Silas H., d. 3/18/1934 at 67/3/21
Simon, d. 7/23/1893 at 65/1/24 in Tamworth; farmer; married; b.
Barrington; James Bickford and Annie Arlin
Sumner, d. 7/11/1911 at 53/6/22 in Tamworth; hotel clerk; divorced;
b. Madison; Benjamin Bickford and Olive Lawrence
William N., d. 8/24/1920 at 52/2/14 in Tamworth; chronic
myocarditis; farmer; married; Benjamin Bickford and Mary
Robertson

BINGEL,
Walter J., d. 9/14/2000 in Chocorua

BLACK,
Ethel E., d. 12/23/1991 in Tamworth; Edwin Elliott and Amanda
Anderson
James, d. 4/29/1940 at 73/5/18; b. Lancaster
Richard, d. 5/30/1966 at 68 in Wolfeboro; b. Marlboro, VT; residence
- Tamworth

BLACKBURN,
John H., d. 6/13/1901 at 66/4/7 in Tamworth; manufacturer; married;
b. Salem; Henry Blackburn (England) and Selma Woodbury

BLACKEY,
Edwin, d. 3/13/1980 in Laconia; Frank Blackey and Gertrude
Henderson
Flora E., d. 1/20/1987 in Wolfeboro; Clarence O. Whipple and
Minnie Hibbard
Frank A., d. 1/4/1954 at 81 in Milton
Gertrude C., d. 12/15/1972 at 93 in Rochester; b. NH; residence -
Milton

BLAISDELL,
Abigail, d. 5/3/1897 at 86/11/11 in Tamworth; housekeeper; widow
Abner C., d. 3/15/1977 at 87 in Rochester; b. NH; residence - Rochester
Albion, d. 3/25/1918 at 69/7/2; peritonitis; farmer; married; b. Tamworth; Stetson Blaisdell and Sally Emery
Frank E., d. 10/18/1913 at 59/0/10 in Tamworth; farmer; married; b. Tamworth; Zenas Blaisdell and Martha Hubbard
John W., d. 2/19/1925 at 86/4/20
Winnifred E., d. 7/15/1955 at 75 in Nashua

BLAKE,
Frank S., d. 6/14/1914 at 65/1/14; pneumonia; married; b. Tamworth; Simon Blake and Caroline Whitney
Lucy Dean, d. 10/1/1927 at 93/4/29
Harry, d. 3/7/1938 at 76/11; b. Tamworth
Mary Ruth, d. 10/5/1942 at 48/7/18 in Tamworth
Simon, d. 8/14/1889 at 84/11/6; farmer; widower; b. Wakefield; John Blake (Wakefield) and Marion Sanborn

BLAKELEY,
Harry W., Sr., d. 9/19/1964 at 48 in Tamworth; b. Boston, MA; residence – S. Wellfleet, MA

BLEAKLY,
Howard G., d. 7/31/1954 at 86 in Tamworth

BLISS,
Derek, d. 8/9/2003 in Tamworth; Ernest Rumph and Valeska Bliss

BLOCHER,
Stephen L., d. 5/10/1973 at 30 in S. Tamworth; b. PA; residence - Madison

BLODGETT,
Nellie M., d. 9/25/1926 at 44/11/20

BODGE,
Charles F., d. 11/20/1961 at 84 in Laconia
James J., d. 6/4/1936 at 76/4/21
Jennie, d. 6/18/1918 at 67/7/14; angina pectoris; housewife; married;

b. Tamworth; James A. Nichols and Mary D. Lord

BODUCH,
Barbara Helen, d. 11/24/1999 in Tamworth; Edward Bowers and Helen Nash

BODWELL,
Clarence H., d. 6/18/1949 at 19 in Tamworth

BOEWE,
Daniel Edward, d. 3/31/1998 in Tamworth; Ward A. Boewe and Gail Ann Farrell

BOGART,
Margaret, d. 5/26/1964 at 75 in Tamworth; b. Franklin, PA; residence - Tamworth

BOLAND,
William, d. 4/14/1930 at 74/8/29

BOOKHOLTZ,
Sadie, d. 9/11/1903 at 0/2/10 in Tamworth; b. Tamworth; Jacob Bookholtz (Germany) and Emma J. Caverly (Moultonboro)

BOOKHOLZ,
Edward V., d. 3/4/1964 at 69 in Laconia; b. Tamworth; residence – Tamworth
Ellen Whiting, d. 5/16/1968 at 64 in Melbourne, FL; residence - Tamworth
Emma J., d. 8/22/1930 at 68/3/19
Frances P., d. 9/22/1934 at 13/7/5
Isabelle W., d. 5/23/1986 in Tamworth; Walter C. Walker and Hattie B. Bickford
Jacob, d. 3/7/1926 at 55/10/22
Walter, d. 2/21/1980 in Laconia; Jacob Bookholz and Emma Caverly

BOOMER,
George Dupont, d. 7/1/1999 in Chocorua; Lucius Boomer and Jorgine Slettede

BOOTHBY,
John A., d. 1/31/1970 at 68 in Laconia; b. NH; residence - Tamworth
John Allen, d. 11/25/1926 at 0/2/7
Raymond A., d. 7/2/1986 in Wolfeboro; Charles Boothby and Irene Hayford

BOSANQUET,
Esther, d. 6/25/1980 in Laconia; Grover Cleveland and Frances Folsom

BOSSIE,
Tresia, d. 6/16/1914 at 1/11/29; shock, congestion; b. Dover; Paul Bossie and Rena Drew

BOUCHARD,
Hector J., d. 12/15/1988 in Wolfeboro; Eli Bouchard and Amelia -----

BOUDREAU,
Harriett E., d. 5/24/1974 at 66 in Tamworth; b. ME; residence – Tamworth

BOWLES,
Lillian Walker, d. 1/5/1998 in Wolfeboro; Walter C. Walker and Hattie Bickford

BOYDEN,
Roland, d. 10/4/1981 in Tamworth; Walter Boyden and Elizabeth Beale

BRADBURY,
Beatrice, d. 10/15/1905 at 0/2/27 in Laconia; b. Weirs; Edward E. Bradbury (Tamworth) and Mary A. Webster (Sandwich)
Esther A. M., d. 9/2/1898 at 61/3/14 in Tamworth; housework; widow; b. Tamworth; Reuben Yeaton and Lucy Knight

BRADFORD,
William H., d. 12/1/1968 at 58 in Wolfeboro; b. MA; residence – Chocorua

BRADY,
Edwina A., d. 2/14/1983 in Wolfeboro; Nathaniel Andrew and

Edwina Dobbins

BRAY,
Pearl S., d. 3/26/1988 in Laconia; Levi Snyder and Emma McAndrews

BREASTED,
Helen E., d. 8/20/2000 in Tamworth; Charles Ewing and Mary Everts
James H., Jr., d. 5/4/1983 in Laconia; James Breasted and Francis Hart

BRENNAN,
Mark, d. 2/21/1981 in Wolfeboro; George Brennan and Mary Ward

BRETT,
Manley E., d. 12/27/1954 at 61/5/5 in Pembroke

BRIGGS,
Emily Elizabeth, d. 5/29/1963 at 94 in Laconia; b. Chicago, IL; residence - Tamworth
Harold L., d. 10/19/1988 in Wolfeboro; William Briggs and Florence Gunther

BROMAN,
Elizabeth A., d. 6/21/1951 at 54 in Laconia

BROSS,
Rose, d. 5/7/2003 in Tamworth; Joseph Gjuresko and Theresa Nagy

BROTHERS,
Elmer Wayne, d. 8/23/1994 in Wolfeboro; Lawrence Brothers and Beatrice Palmer
Esther Ames, d. 5/22/1995 in Tamworth; Claude Ames and Blanche Jeffers

BROWN,
Alonzo, d. 8/6/1914 at 75/5/11; ascitis; farmer; married; b. Albany; Asa C. Brown and Abbie Head
Alphonzo D., d. 9/17/1979 in Wolfeboro; Jeremiah Brown and Jane Smith
Andrew J., d. 10/17/1910 at 81/9/2 in Tamworth; farmer; married; b.

Hampton Falls; Jeremiah Brown (Deerfield) and Sarah Williams (Hampton Falls)

Carlos J., d. 5/24/1975 at 56 in Chocorua; b. VT; residence - Madison

Carroll Grant, d. 11/13/1990 in Ossipee; George Brown and Myrtle Grant

Charles, d. 2/20/1918 at 79/8/10; old age; retired; widower; b. Tamworth; Charles Brown and Sereph Marshall

Charles W., d. 6/7/1985 in Ossipee; David Brown and Rose Smith

Doris L., d. 12/7/2003 in Tamworth; William Whiting and Lula A. Floyd

Elizabeth, d. 10/14/1935 at 46/2/24

Elmer, d. 3/4/1974 at 85 in Ossipee; b. NH; residence - Tamworth

Emma Mae, d. 4/24/1999 in N. Conway; William Edgar Moore and Alice Mae Ross

Eunice E., d. 4/21/1973 at 62 in Tamworth; b. NH; residence - Tamworth

Evelyn Ida, d. 7/12/1919 at 17/11/25; housewife; married; b. Tamworth; William Whiting and Lulu Floyd

Hiram C., d. 5/31/1943 at 74/11/6 in Tamworth

Lizi R., d. 2/13/1988 in N. Conway; Alex Rasmussen and Anna Johansen

Mary A., d. 1/19/1911 at 72/10/23 in Tamworth; housewife; widow; William C. Hurd (Acton, ME) and Caroline Blaisdell (Acton, ME)

Mary A. E., d. 8/24/1913 at 78/5/6 in Tamworth; housewife; married; b. NS; John Bennett and Abigail Spring

Mary S., d. 11/26/1911 at 79/5/20 in Tamworth; widow; b. Brentwood; Stephen Dudley (Brentwood) and Mary P. Twombly (Somersworth)

Rachel, d. 3/21/1900 at 53/9/5 in Tamworth; housewife; married; b. Acton, ME; William Hurd (Acton, ME) and Carrie Blaisdell (Lebanon, ME)

Robert, d. 10/22/1981 in Franconia; Alphonzo Brown and Minnie Kenneson

Sarah, d. 7/26/1895 at 70/4/25 in Tamworth; single

Stephen, d. 7/22/1893 at 91 in Tamworth; laborer; widower

Susan, d. 10/16/1932 at 67/5/13

Virginia E., d. 8/3/1951 at 37 in Laconia

BROWNE,
Percy C., d. 4/1/1992 in N. Conway; Percy Browne and Mary Faxon

BRUCE,
Elizabeth, d. 5/29/1920 at 88/8/21 in Concord; myocarditia; farmer; widow; Josiah Folsom and Hulda Downs

BRYANT,
child, d. 3/26/1890 at -- in Tamworth; b. Tamworth; George H. Bryant and Marion Sanford

Albertine H. C., d. 12/1/1935 at 79/11/24

Charles S., d. 8/31/1887 at 28/2/25 in Tamworth; watchmaker; single; b. Tamworth; Jeremiah G. Bryant (Tamworth) and Nancy Meader (Tamworth)

George H., d. 5/19/1922 at 66/6/7; b. Tamworth; Wyatt Bryant and Hannah Chick

Hannah C., d. 4/22/1901 at 67/6/27 in Tamworth; housewife; married; b. Tamworth; John Chick (Limington, ME) and Lucy Bryant (Tamworth)

Jerry S., d. --/--/1896 at 85/9 in Tamworth; farmer; married; b. Tamworth; Walter Bryant (Newmarket) and Ruth Gilman (Haverhill)

John, d. 1/29/1892 at 66/5/3 in Tamworth; farmer; widower; b. Tamworth; John Bryant and Mary Chick

John M., d. 10/29/1940 at 90/3/4; b. Tamworth

Leander, d. 5/5/1902 at 68/1/10 in Moultonboro; merchant; married; b. Tamworth; John Bryant (Tamworth) and Mary Chick (Effingham)

Lizzie E., d. 8/13/1940 at 80/7/17; b. Tamworth

Marion, d. 1/8/1922 at 65/3/1; b. Natick, MA; Alphonso Sandford and Evelyn Morse

Nancy, d. 12/19/1901 at 84/1/17 in Tamworth; housewife; widow; b. Tamworth; Isaac Meader (Tamworth) and Thankful Whiting (Machias, ME)

Wyatt, d. 1/24/1902 at 69/5/20 in Tamworth; farmer; widower; b. Tamworth; John Bryant (Tamworth) and Mary Chick (Effingham)

BUCK,
Warren F., d. 4/12/1960 at 68 in Tamworth

BUCKMINSTER,
William R., d. 10/14/1939 at 67/8/27; b. Melrose, MA

BUNKER,
child, d. 1/17/1923 at --; b. Tamworth; Frederick Bunker and Elsie Davis
Elsie M., d. 11/23/1957 at 68 in Rochester
Fred W., d. 6/26/1954 at 70 in Laconia
Hattie L., d. 9/25/1934 at 80/1/14
Levi, d. 7/3/1914 at 66/10/25; disease of heart; laborer; married; b. Tamworth; Nathaniel W. Bunker and Emeline Kenison
Nathaniel, d. 10/22/1897 at 77/7/5 in Tamworth; shoemaker; widower

BURGESS,
James S., d. 7/30/2002 in Ossipee

BURKE,
Eleanor Marie, d. 5/10/1996 in Wolfeboro; Robert Fay and Ellen Burlton
John L., d. 5/23/1989 in N. Conway; William Burke and Agnes Maguire

BURLEIGH,
Francis N., d. 4/1/1893 at 70/10 in Tamworth; shoemaker; widower; b. Sandwich; William Burleigh (Lee) and Dolly W. Kennison (Sandwich)

BUTLER,
Agnes A., d. 7/13/1960 at 72 in Laconia

BUTTERFIELD,
C. W. (female), d. --/--/1896 at 49/0/30 in Tamworth; single; b. Concord; George Butterfield (MA) and Matr'sa Burbank

BUZZELL,
Julia H., d. 1/3/1975 at 79 in Laconia; b. NH; residence - Tamworth

CAIN,
Wilson Frank, d. 4/30/1999 in Tamworth; Frank Cain and Viola Mae
-----

CALHOUN,
Ada A., d. 12/4/1951 at 81 in Laconia

CAMERON,
Joseph, d. 12/6/1985 in Tamworth; Washington Cameron and Mary Peters

CAMPBELL,
Frances M., d. 10/26/1991 in N. Conway; Henry Paulsen and Anna New

CANNEY,
Forrest, d. 5/15/1976 at 81 in Laconia; b. NH; residence - Tamworth
John P., d. 12/11/1902 at 68/4/4 in Tamworth; farmer; married; b. Tuftonboro; Ira Canney (Tuftonboro) and Betsey Thompson

CANNIFF,
Maud, d. 7/25/1953 at 82 in Tamworth

CANNON,
Legrand, III, d. 1/24/1999 in Chocorua; Legrand Cannon, Jr. and Jeannette Peabody

CARDINALE,
Ralph J., d. 4/4/1979 in N. Conway; Jerome Cardinale and Phillemina Depeople
Susie, d. 11/28/1986 in N. Conway; ----- and Carmela Citerella

CARLE,
Edna T., d. 6/4/1908 at 21/9/9 in Tamworth; single; b. Newfield, ME; F. L. Tibbetts (Manchester) and ----- (Limington, ME)
Florence E., b. 2/9/1942 at 80/3/12 in Tamworth
Frank H., d. 7/4/1940 at 82/1/18; b. Portland, ME

CARLETON,
Myrtie A., d. 3/17/1918 at 56/4/6; b. Groveland, MA

CARLTON,
Clara B., d. 6/7/1916 at 30/4/6; peritonitis

CARPENTER,
Aileen Wood, d. 7/21/1999 in Tamworth; Frederick J. Carpenter and Nellie Roberts

CARR,
Charles M., d. 10/24/1986 in Wolfeboro; Charles A. Carr and Elsie Smith
Robert T., d. 4/9/1959 at 43/8/26 in Portland, ME

CARTER,
Elsie M., d. 11/3/1957 at 67 in Tamworth
Gordon W., d. 1/20/2002 in Wolfeboro; James Carter and Ethel Wallace
Katheryn, d. 11/25/1980 in Wolfeboro; Percy Jelleson and Grace Smart

CARTLAND,
Eunice E., d. 4/4/1950 at 49/4/20 in Tamworth
Harriet E., d. 12/23/1962 at 87 in Laconia; b. Lynn, MA; residence − Tamworth
Joseph J., d. 1/18/1956 at 91/3/1 in Tamworth

CAVERL[E]Y,
Benjamin F., d. 6/22/1889 at 59/6; farmer; married; b. VT; Samuel Caverley and Martha Daniels
Hannah E., d. --/--/1894 at 69 in Tamworth; housekeeper; widow

CHADBOURN,
Harriett E., d. 6/15/1938 at 82/11/5; b. Tamworth

CHADWICK,
James R., d. 9/24/1905 at 62 in Tamworth; physician; widower; b. Boston, MA; Chris C. Chadwick and Louisa Read

CHAMBERLAIN,
Charles, d. 11/3/1921 at 59/5/14; gun shot wound; farmer; divorced; b. Wolfeboro; John R. Chamberlain and Hannah Chamberlain
Florence B., d. 2/4/1970 at 86 in Laconia; b. NH; residence − Tamworth
Lula M., d. 9/28/1982 in N. Conway; Frank Lyman and Margaret Kennerson
Ralph Nelson, d. 2/11/1962 at 69 in Laconia; b. Wolfeboro; residence − Tamworth
Raymond Edwin, d. 11/12/1970 at 70 in Laconia; residence − Laconia; buried in Tamworth

Sarah, d. 4/21/1911 at 34/8/6 in Tamworth; housewife; married; b. Ossipee; John Edgerly (Tamworth) and Abigail Dorr (Ossipee)

CHANDLER,
Sylvanius, d. 7/11/1925 at 70

CHAPMAN,
Alexander H., d. 8/1/1975 at 73 in N. Conway; b. NY; residence - Tamworth
Frances E., d. 11/25/2000 in Wolfeboro; Frederick Moore and Charlotte Young
Simeon W., d. 9/28/1891 at 67/0/28 in Tamworth; farmer; single; b. Tamworth; Joseph Chapman and Hulda Howard

CHASE,
Abigail Elliott, d. 11/30/1969 at 64 in Ossipee; residence – Rochester; buried in Tamworth
Augustus A., d. 6/16/1932 at 18/8/20
Charles S., d. 3/16/1968 at 73 in Rochester; residence - Rochester
Clifford A., d. 6/10/1956 at 43 in Tamworth
Earl A., d. 10/23/1909 at 3/1/16 in Tamworth; b. Tamworth; Augustus A. Chase (Albany) and Ida E. Davis (Tamworth)
Everett Russell, d. 6/30/1997 in N. Conway; Arthur Chase and Lillian Peterson
Ida M., d. 4/17/1942 at 64/4/4 in Tamworth
Linda Jean, d. 5/2/1963 at 21 in Tamworth; b. Laconia; residence – Tamworth
Marie, d. 4/2/1980 in Laconia; Peter Sharon and Alice Jandran
Preston Newton, d. 10/16/1998 in Tamworth; Frank Chase and Leona Newton
Ruth Abigail, d. 7/29/1969 at 79 in Laconia; b. NH; residence - Tamworth
William H., d. 12/30/1931 at 25

CHESLEY,
Eliza F., d. 12/6/1902 at 90/8 in Tamworth; farmer; married; b. Tamworth; Samuel Chapman (Greenland) and Betsey Folsom (Tamworth)
Emma, d. 3/12/1940 at 90/6/9; b. Tamworth
James J., d. 2/26/1908 at 94/8/11 in Tamworth; farmer; widower; b. New Durham; Miles Chesley (Durham) and Mary Furber

(Farmington)
Sarah H., d. --/--/1894 at 88/10/17 in Tamworth; housekeeper; widow; b. Tamworth; William Clark (Beverly, MA) and Eunice Hidden (Tamworth)

CHESTLY,
Minnie C., d. 2/2/1946 at 74/9/11 in Laconia

CHICK,
Abbie I., d. 11/27/1922 at 82/8/29
Charles F., d. 9/11/1919 at 82/1/18; seaman; married; b. Limington, ME
Walter B., d. 4/11/1888 at 62/2; farmer; widower; b. Tamworth; John Chick (Limington, ME) and Lucy Bryant (Tamworth)

CHILD,
Nettie L., d. 2/26/1898 at 17/7/20 in Tamworth; single; b. Tamworth; Herbert Child (Stoneham) and Augusta Bickford (Tamworth)

CLARK,
Asa C., d. 1/14/1897 at 81/6 in Tamworth; mechanic; married; b. Sandwich; Robert Clark and Sally Davis
Flora M., d. 1/26/1961 at 82 in Laconia
Gilman, d. 3/24/1908 at 87/0/19 in Tamworth; farmer; married; b. Meredith; Stephen Clark (Scotland)
Idella F., d. 5/20/1888 at 17/4/4; housework; single; b. Tamworth; Gilman Clark (Meredith) and Laura A. Newton (Sanbornton)
Laura A., d. 10/25/1931 at 94/1/22
Leona A., d. 4/8/2000 in Wolfeboro; Kenneth Woodman and Faye Saunders
Meredith, d. 1/21/1944 at 56/6/20 in Tamworth
Ruth B., d. 3/19/1909 at 72/11/19 in Tamworth; housewife; widow; b. Tamworth; John Chick (Limington, ME) and Lucy Ann Bryant
Susan G., d. 1/29/1898 at 60/2/5 in Tamworth; housewife; married; b. Tamworth; Weldon Hatch
William J., d. 9/28/1931 at 62/11/9

CLARKE,
Isabella, d. 3/14/1912 at 6/1/0 in Tamworth (sic); housewife; married; b. PEI; Adam Muttart (PEI) and Martha Rose (PEI)
Johnson, d. 4/24/1951 at 85/7/13 in Laconia

Joseph E., d. 8/7/1912 at 76 in Tamworth; laborer; widower; b. PEI; Johnson Clark and Emma Fisher

CLEVELAND,
Alice E., d. 6/12/1992 in Wolfeboro; Charles R. Erdman and Estelle Pardee
Francis Grover, d. 11/8/1995 in Wolfeboro; Stephen G. Cleveland and Frances Folsom

CLIFFORD,
James M., d. 11/10/1903 at 87/5/10 in Tamworth; farmer; b. NY; Jonathan Clifford and Susan Sanborn
Nancy A., d. 12/19/1911 at 95/3/6 in Tamworth; housework; widow; b. Barnet, VT; ----- Haughton (Scotland)

CLOUGH,
Beatrice, d. 9/7/1943 at 30/3/7 in Tamworth
Charles W., d. 5/20/1926 at 73/9/20
Edwin E., d. 3/6/1952 at 61/5/8 in Tamworth
George, d. 5/22/1923 at 66/0/21; b. Tamworth; William Clough and Martha Whiting
Harriet, d. 10/13/1928 at 73/8/16
Herbert S., d. 2/9/1917 at 62; acute dilitation of heart; farmer; married; b. Tamworth; Thomas Clough and Mary Stockdale
Ida Louise, d. 5/27/2001 in N. Conway; Edwin Clough and Louise Kimball
Louise K., d. 7/27/1982 in N. Conway; Samuel Kimball and Sarah Gilman
Martha A., d. 7/28/1921 at 87/9/20; senility dementia; at home; widow; b. Tamworth; John Whiting and Martha Rankins
Mary H., d. 10/18/1889 at 80/11/8; widow; b. Albany; Thomas Clough and Mary Hawkins
Sarah A., d. 3/27/1950 at 75 in Moultonboro
William B., d. 7/27/1905 at 77/3/25 in Tamworth; farmer; married; b. Tamworth; Samuel Clough (Tamworth) and Mary Hawkins (Tamworth)

COBB,
Almedia C., d. 4/8/1920 at 78/3/5 in Tamworth; lobar pneumonia; farmer; widow; Samuel Brown and Olive Webster

CODERRE,
Edgar N., d. 7/19/1999 in Manchester; Roland Coderre and Noella Chaput

COFFIN,
Albert B., d. 10/17/1938 at 52/10/20; b. Washburn, ME

COGSWELL,
Amanda F., d. 11/11/1905 at 89/6/18 in Tamworth; housekeeping; widow; b. Stanford, Canada; Jabez Page (Gilmanton) and Susan Osgood
Joseph, d. 12/27/1895 at 87/8/26 in Tamworth; farmer; married; b. Tamworth; Joseph Cogswell (Atkinson) and Judith Colby (Atkinson)
Susan M., d. 8/11/1911 at 73/10/15 in Tamworth; single; b. Tamworth; Joseph Cogswell and Amanda F. Page (Stanstead, Quebec)

COIT,
Robert, d. 8/11/1942 at 81/1/22 in Tamworth

COLE,
Evelyn M., d. 12/31/1915 at 38/0/25; peritonitis; married; b. Tuftonboro; Leander F. Wiggin and Nancy Horn
James B., d. 8/11/1903 at 65 in Tamworth; laborer

COLLINS,
John, d. 9/9/1932 at 83
Seward B., d. 12/7/1952 at 53/7/15 in Laconia

COLPITTS,
Julia, d. 10/11/1943 at 75/8/23 in Wolfeboro

COLTON,
Eliza, d. 4/--/1895 at 80/4/27 in Tamworth; housekeeper; married; b. Unity, ME; Frederick Stexenf (sic) and Betsey Gilkey (Gorham)

CONNER,
John, d. 2/22/1981 in Wolfeboro; Edwin Conner and Mary Blake

COOK,
Charles P., d. 12/21/1891 at 71/8/5 in Tamworth; merchant; married; b. Tamworth; Timothy Cook and Mary F. Price
Clinton S., d. 9/2/1915 at 71/1/29; pulmonary oedema; retired; married; b. Tamworth; Charles P. Cook and Susan B. Staples
John Otis, Sr., d. 4/25/1996 in Lebanon; Wilbur A. Cook, Sr. and Edna Adams
Lucy A., d. 11/13/1929 at 78/8/6
Rebecca D., d. 1/23/1914 at 91/2/20; cerebral embolism; widow; b. Porter, ME; True Guptal
Sarah E., d. 3/6/1942 at 54/3/22 in Laconia
Susan B., d. 5/11/1910 at 86/6/22 in Tamworth; housewife; widow; b. Lebanon, ME; Nicholas Staples and Olive Ricker (Lebanon, ME)
William H., d. 10/9/1921 at 60; cirrhosis of liver; farm manager; divorced; b. Campton; Charles Cook

COOLEY,
William S., d. 8/23/1906 at 41/0/26 in Tamworth; carpenter; married; b. Ossipee; Alfred C. Cooley (Ossipee) and Abby Felch (Tamworth)

COPP,
Cordelia P., d. 4/12/1887 at 47 in New Gloucester, ME; housekeeper; married

CORBETT,
Flossie G., d. 2/9/1937 at 53/10/23

CORKUM,
Marion R., d. 4/27/1986 in Wolfeboro; Harold L. Bartlett and Leoner M. Crush

COTE,
James J., d. 4/25/2002 in Manchester; George Cote and Agnes Sullivan
Kenneth, d. 10/4/1969 at 18 in Tamworth; b. NH; residence - Meredith

COTTON,
Annie A., d. 3/28/1919 at 63/11; housekeeper; widow; b. Tamworth;

George W. Evans and Emily A. Hodgdon

COWIE,
Gladys E., d. 6/20/1987 in Wolfeboro; Elias Babbin and Josephine Nadau

COYNE,
Francis W., d. 1/8/1962 at 57 in Tamworth; b. Manchester; residence - Manchester

CRABTREE,
Julia M., d. 12/13/1915 at 1/9/7; pneumonia; b. Tamworth; Hollis E. Crabtree and Alice Moody

CRAM,
Mary Ann, d. 12/19/1959 at 43 in Tamworth

CRANE,
Harriet S., d. 4/3/1932 at 76/5/18

CRAWFORD,
Reginold B., d. 6/23/1979 in Tamworth; Bertram Crawford and Rotha -----

CROFT,
Jeffrey S., d. 8/7/2001 in Tamworth; Brian Croft and Mary Hederson

CUMMINGS,
Ansel, d. 1/1/1924 at 66
Elmer A., d. 1/14/1986 in Tamworth; Ansel Cummings and Blanche Brown
Harry E., d. 11/21/1967 at 62 in Tamworth; b. Tamworth; residence - Tamworth
Rosie B., d. 9/9/1952 at 83 in Moultonboro

CUMMISKY,
Charles, d. 1/27/1947 at 51/6/7 in Laconia

CURRIER,
Edwin F., d. 4/7/1924 at 51
Emily V., d. 12/15/1963 at 88 in Sandwich; b. Sandwich; residence -

Sandwich
Flora E., d. 10/18/1956 at 81 in Tamworth
Hiram S., d. 12/31/1910 at 78/0/8 in Tamworth; farmer; widower; b. Sandwich; Benjamin Currier (Sandwich) and Ruhannah Jewell (Sandwich)
Roland E., d. 4/14/1961 at 60 in Ctr. Ossipee

CUSHING,
Lucia M., d. 10/23/1893 at 63/3 in Tamworth; housekeeper; married; b. Boston, MA; H. B. Elsworth and Lucia Wood

CUTRONE,
Norma K., d. 3/20/2002 in Bennington, VT; Charles Drake and Olive Cook

DALTON,
Thomas, d. 9/28/1959 at 58 in Tamworth

DAMON,
Cindy, d. 10/25/1968 at 20 in Hanover; b. MA; residence – Tamworth
Florence E., d. 7/21/2001 in N. Conway; Earl Carpenter and Alice Reynolds
Frances Shove, d. 8/14/1989 in N. Conway; Agustus Shove and Rebecca Tozier
Harry F., d. 1/11/1969 at 82 in Tamworth; b. MA; residence - Tamworth

DANFORTH,
Lottie Mae, d. 9/5/1966 at 40 in N. Conway; b. Norway, ME; residence – Tamworth

DANIELS,
Ruth Elaine, d. 11/7/1972 at 92 in Concord; b. NS; residence – Concord

DAUDON,
Rene, d. 1/28/1981 in Wolfeboro; Lucien Daudon and Josaphene Neveux

DAVEY,
Harriet A., d. 12/12/1951 at 80/3/9 in Tamworth

DAVIDSON,
Gaston H., d. 2/7/1975 at 74 in Franklin; b. MA; residence – Northfield

DAVIE,
Arlene M., d. 6/30/1979 in Wolfeboro; Otis Davie and Gladys Melanson

DAVIS,
Ada M., d. 3/28/1887 at 9/3 in Tamworth; b. Tamworth; William H. Davis (Tamworth) and Mary M. Mooney (Nashua)
Alice B., d. 12/10/1917 at 48/9/22; typhoid tuberculosis; divorced; b. Tamworth; Nathaniel Berry and Abbie J. Blake
Alva, d. 12/19/1972 at 96 in Tamworth; b. Ossipee; residence - Tamworth
Amos Tuck, d. 6/15/1916 at 53/6/6; cerebral embolism; undertaker; married; b. Tamworth; Hiram T. Davis and Sarah Hodgsdon
Bessie A., d. 5/3/1887 at 1/10/18 in Tamworth; b. Tamworth; Amasa H. Davis (Effingham) and Carrie F. Hardy (Tamworth)
Caroline A., d. 5/13/1977 at 71 in Wolfeboro; b. ME; residence - Effingham
Chester, d. 4/4/1991 in Tamworth; Alva Davis and Florence Wiggin
Deland John, b. 3/20/1930 at 0/10/4
Florence B., d. 5/23/1943 at 64/8/16 in Tamworth
Guy V., d. 6/21/1923 at 15/2/15; b. Ossipee; Alva Davis and Florence Wiggin
Hattie P., d. 12/26/1925 at 74/9/5
Hazel Estelle, d. 2/16/1995 in N. Conway; Asa Abbott and Marantha -----
Hiram T., d. 12/20/1906 at 71/6/11 in Tamworth; undertaker; married; b. Effingham; Joseph Davis (Durham) and Mary Tuttle (Lee)
Howard George, d. 5/10/1974 at 79 in Rochester; b. ME; residence - Somersworth
John C., d. 8/18/1947 at 80/7/17 in S. Portland, ME
Joseph M., d. 3/5/1915 at 66/2/4; heart disease with dropsy; laborer; married; b. Effingham; George Davis and Mehitable Champion
Laura B., d. 4/5/1890 at 10/1/25 in Tamworth; b. Tamworth; Amasa

H. Davis (Tamworth) and Carrie F. Hardy (Tamworth)
Laura C., d. 8/3/1897 at 3/11/5 in Tamworth; b. Tamworth; Amos T. Davis (Tamworth) and Alice Berry (Tamworth)
Laura M., d. 4/11/1941 at 32 in N. Conway
Mary A., d. 1/6/1922 at 73/7; b. Nashua; George Mooney
Minnie A., d. 5/21/1929 at 56/11/3
Nancy T., d. 2/28/1902 at 90/1/18 in Tamworth; widow; b. Parsonsfield; Simon Whitten
Otis Earl, d. 6/14/1976 at 72 in Tamworth; b. NH; residence - Tamworth
Raymond Alvah, d. 7/26/1995 in Wolfeboro; Alvah Davis and Florence Wiggin
Sarah, d. 11/4/1926 at 91/6/28
Valentine, d. 2/10/1919 at 67/5/11; farmer; widower; b. Jackson; Jonathan Davis
Wallace W., d. 7/17/1964 at 60 in Tamworth; b. Lynn, MA; residence – Lynn, MA
William H., d. 10/11/1918 at --; lobar pneumonia; farm laborer; married; b. Tamworth; George Davis and Mehitable Bickford

DAWE,
John Shepard, Jr., d. 10/13/1990 in Manchester; John S. Dawe, Sr. and Josephine Gross
Ruth M., d. 1/2/1987 in N. Conway; William P. Taylor and Halloween Vars

DAWES,
Zita H., d. 2/26/1977 at 68 in Tamworth; b. PA; residence - Tamworth

DAY,
Alfred Warren, d. 10/22/1990 in Wolfeboro; Perley Day, Sr. and Edna Emerson
Emily, d. 8/24/1941 at 88/3/9 in Tamworth

DE LARA,
Robert Malcolm, d. 6/19/1975 at 54 in Conway; b. MA; residence – Tamworth

DE SAINT PHALLE,
Andre, d. 8/16/1967 at 60 in Chocorua; b. Paris, France; residence –

New York City

DEARBORN,
Sarah Davis, d. 7/24/1993 in Wolfeboro; Alva Davis and Florence Wiggin

DEATTE,
Clyde L., d. 9/19/1973 at 68 in N. Conway; b. VT; residence - Tamworth
Flora B., d. 8/1/1971 at 59 in N. Conway; b. NH; residence - Tamworth

DELARUE,
John A., d. 6/14/1949 at 60/2/1 in Rochester

DELLAWAY,
N., d. 1/7/1908 at 75/6/2 in Tamworth; carpenter; married; b. Belfast, ME; Silas Dellaway and C. Brackett

DESMOND,
Walter J., d. 8/22/1977 at 60 in Tamworth; b. MA; residence - Tamworth

DEVLIN,
Florence E., d. 5/28/1962 at 89 in Concord; b. Toronto, Canada; residence - Tamworth

DINSMORE,
Grace Agnes, b. 10/9/1918 at --; lobar pneumonia; housewife; married; b. Tamworth; William H. Davis and Mary M. Mooney

DODGE,
Ezra P., d. --/--/1900 at 63 in Tamworth; farmer; divorced; b. Windham; Theodon Dodge and Eliza Andrews
Fred C., d. 5/18/1912 at 48/10/24 in Tamworth; clerk; married; b. Beverly, MA; Amos A. Dodge (Beverly, MA) and Elizabeth Cole

DOLE,
Elizabeth E., d. 9/20/1941 at 75/0/13 in Tamworth

DONOVAN,
Bertha H., d. 2/28/1975 at 56 in Boston, MA; residence – Boston, MA

DORE,
Ernest G., d. 5/14/1986 in N. Conway; Walter G. Dore and Rose M. Stanley

DORMAN,
Richworth, d. 10/5/1895 at 98/7/5 in Tamworth; carpenter; married; b. Newfield, ME; Charles Dorman and ----- Boothby

DOUGLAS,
Addie M., d. 12/28/1957 at 67 in Laconia

DOW,
infant son, d. 3/2/1909 at 0/0/3 in Tamworth; b. Tamworth; Charles L. Dow (Tamworth) and Nettie M. Barnes (Tamworth)
Abbie, d. 3/31/1928 at 67/10/24
Annie Stearns, d. 12/28/1916 at 73/10/8; abdominal tumor; widow; b. Boston, MA; George Butterfield and Matrassa P. Lull
Charles E., d. 3/19/1928 at 63/4
Charles H., d. 4/9/1914 at 88/2/26; cancer of stomach; retired; married; b. Tamworth; David Dow and Deborah Gilman
Daniel M., d. --/--/1896 at 70/5/23 in Tamworth; laborer; married; b. Tamworth; Jonathan Dow and Katherine Chesley
Franklin G., d. 10/7/1914 at 75/0/0; cerebral apoplexy; laborer; married; b. Tamworth; Jonathan Dow and Lavina Cushing
John C., d. 12/17/1916 at 78/6/19; anaemia; widower; b. Tamworth; John Dow and Lavina Cushing
Phoebe, d. 5/4/1922 at 84; b. Tamworth; Stephen Brown
Ruth, d. 8/18/1902 at 63/11 in Tamworth; widow; b. Tamworth; Stephen Brown (Tamworth) and Mary Bryer

DOWDING,
son, d. 10/27/1890 at -- in Tamworth; b. Tamworth; H. W. Dowding (Littlehampton) and Sarah Smeed (Littlehampton, England)

DOWNS,
Ada B., d. 12/29/1952 at 58/4/23 in Tamworth
Alice, d. 8/14/1936 at 61/3/28

Belle A., d. 1/23/1904 at 24/3/23 in Tamworth; housekeeper; single; b. Tamworth; Charles Downs (Tamworth) and Ella F. Smith (Cornish, ME)

Charles P., d. 12/4/1929 at 73/7/5

Clifford, d. 4/9/1981 in Tamworth; Joseph Downs and Alice Smith

Daniel, d. 6/2/1905 at 89/4/10 in Sandwich; farmer; widower; b. Fryeburg, ME; Uriah Downs (Alfred, ME)

Elias, d. 11/24/1920 at 79/8/5 in Tamworth; cerebral embolism; farmer; widower; Daniel Downs and Susan Johnson

Ella F., d. 6/6/1922 at 62/9; b. Cornish, ME; John Smith and Ann Johnson

Elmer Elias, d. 1/14/1962 at 67 in Manchester; b. Tamworth; residence - Tamworth

George W., d. 7/22/1959 at 80 in Laconia

Geraldine, d. 8/8/1905 at – in Tamworth; b. Tamworth; Elias E. Downs (Porter, ME) and Mildred E. Page (Tamworth)

Gertrude A., d. 2/6/1962 at 80 in Laconia; b. Tamworth; residence - Tamworth

Joseph L., d. 7/11/1947 at 74/10/27 in Tamworth

Mrs. Elias, d. 8/25/1919 at 73/8; housewife; married; b. Porter, ME; Nathaniel Rowns and Harriet Porter

Susan, d. 2/8/1905 at 78/10/23 in Sandwich; housewife; single; b. Tamworth; Phineas Johnson (Tamworth) and Dolly Jones

Winifred W., d. 7/27/1984 in Laconia; Ira Weeks and Eliza Pickering

DRAKE,
Arthur R. C., d. 5/30/1950 at 82/6/27 in Moultonboro

Benjamin M., d. 9/20/1960 at 89 in Tamworth

Elizabeth, d. 5/25/1892 at 69/8/4 in Tamworth; housework

Nellie B., d. 6/1/1946 at 81/4/2 in Tamworth

Samuel J., d. 9/2/1895 at 73/9/4 in Tamworth; carpenter; married; b. N. Hampton; Daniel Drake (N. Hampton) and Zilah Taylor (N. Hampton)

Sumner H., d. 11/22/1893 at 44/3/1 in Tamworth; mechanic; single; b. Danvers, MA; Samuel T. Drake (Hampton) and Elizabeth A. Hyland (Hartford, CT)

DREW,
Bertha H., d. 6/6/1948 at 75/1/24 in Tamworth

Bessie F., d. 8/16/1983 in Laconia; Fred Morrison and Nellie Drew

Charles S., d. 2/8/1952 at 87/2/24 in Moultonboro

Eliza A., d. 1/27/1898 at 70/2/2 in Tamworth; widow
Etta S., d. 4/2/1889 at 25; teacher; single; b. Tamworth; John Drew (Tamworth)
Frank, d. 11/12/1942 at 58/5/3 in Tamworth
George F., d. 2/26/1921 at 0/7; bronchial pneumonia; b. Belmont; Harry H. Drew and Gladys Jeffers
Hannah J., d. 10/31/1902 at 61/1/16 in Tamworth; widow; b. Albany; William Hutchins and Lucinda Horne
Harland F., d. 4/13/1936 at 14/2/4
Hazel A., d. 10/14/2002 in Rochester; James Shaw and Eva Bean
John D., d. 9/23/1901 at 68/2/17 in Tamworth; farmer; married; b. Madison; Thomas Drew (Houlton, ME) and Martha Doe (Ossipee)
John N., d. 2/18/1938 at 76/11/4; b. Tamworth
Marilyn C., d. 3/19/1991 in N. Conway; Fred F. Canney and Roxanna Philbrick
Martha, d. 11/2/1887 at 78/3/28 in Tamworth; housekeeper; married; b. Tamworth; John Doe (Effingham) and Ester Hobbs (Newfield, ME)
William E., d. 2/9/1918 at 24; lobar pneumonia; soldier; married; b. Camp Devens, MA

DRIVER,
Sophia, d. 9/15/1908 at 68 in Tamworth; single

DRUGG,
Louise Adria, d. 3/6/1990 in Dover; Robert Henderson and Frances Lawn

DUGAS,
Florence E., d. 7/19/1974 at 61 in Conway; b. MA; residence – Tamworth

DUNHAM,
Theodore, Jr., d. 4/3/1984 in Tamworth; Theodore Dunham and Josephine Balestier

DUNN,
Richard Chaplin, d. 2/9/1920 at 36/9/17 in Tamworth; internal hemorrhage, bullet wound; married; Charles L. Dunn and Jennie Chaplin

DURRELL,
Anna, d. 3/6/1906 at 94/9/13 in Tamworth; housekeeping; widow; b. Strafford; Nathaniel Berry (Strafford) and Betsey Pitman (Strafford)
George, d. 4/8/1892 at 71/5/21 in Tamworth; farmer; b. Tamworth; Ebenezer Durrell and Betsey Edgerly
Mary E., d. 3/1/1912 at 74/11/14 in Tamworth; housewife; married; b. Meredith; Timothy Gordon (Meredith)

DWYER,
Daniel J., d. 6/8/1991 in N. Conway; Timothy Dwyer and Mary Hurley

DYER,
Stanley A., d. 5/5/2003 in Wolfeboro; Stanley Dyer and Anna Norman

DYKE,
Elizabeth M., d. 11/15/1991 in Tamworth; Daniel LaGrange and Rosiland V. Wendell

EASTMAN,
Claude P., d. 2/6/1971 at 75 in Laconia; b. NH; residence - Tamworth
Claude P., Jr., d. 11/16/1962 at 35 in Wolfeboro; b. Tamworth; residence – Tamworth
Mildred B., d. 12/23/1971 at 70 in Tamworth; b. NH; residence - Tamworth

EASTTY,
Helen Story, d. 11/1/1973 at 78 in Tamworth; b. MA; residence - Tamworth
William H., d. 5/22/1970 at 76 in Wolfeboro; b. ME; residence – Tamworth

EASTWICK,
Bertha R., d. 1/31/2001 in Wolfeboro; Chester Robinson and Grace Moody

ECHARDT,
Anatolii M., d. 2/19/1999 in Tamworth; Michalovvich Echardt and

Lydia -----

ECKER,
Mary R., d. 6/30/1983 in Wolfeboro; Ernest Thibeault and Mary Roy

EDGAR,
Elizabeth, d. 3/12/1973 at 65 in Laconia; b. MA; residence - Chocorua

EDGELL,
Anna M., d. 5/3/1963 at 88 in Cambridge, MA; residence – Cambridge, MA; buried in Tamworth

EDGERL[E]Y,
Abigail A., d. 12/27/1915 at --; bronchitis; widow; Ezekiel Dore and Abigail Clark
Armine, d. 4/23/1911 at 71/11/27 in Tamworth; housewife; widow; b. Sandwich; Samuel S. Vittum (Tamworth) and Mehitable Kenerson (Tamworth)
Daniel, d. 4/11/1899 at 68/11 in Tamworth; farmer; single; b. Tamworth; Ebenezer Edgerly (Barrington) and Abigail Cate (Tamworth)
J. C., d. 5/10/1908 at 80/1/11 in Tamworth; farmer; married; b. Tamworth; E. Edgerly (Lee) and Abagail Cate (Tamworth)
John, d. 8/6/1891 at 58/3/5 in Tamworth; farmer; married; b. Tamworth; Ebenezer Edgerly and Abigail Cate
Maude, d. 9/5/1953 at 74 in Laconia
Satchell C., d. 7/26/1933 at 68/5/19

EDWARDS,
Winifred Jane, d. 1/2/1989 in N. Conway; John Isaac Fisher and Gail Farmer

EGGLESTON,
Elva M., d. 7/13/1969 at 62 in Tamworth; b. ME; residence – Poland, ME

ELDREDGE,
Mabel Mildred, d. 1/4/1920 at 0/0/22 in Tamworth; premature birth; Raymond Eldredge (laborer) and Etta N. Eldredge

ELDRIDGE,
Andrew William, d. 4/13/1989 in Wolfeboro; Wilbur Eldridge and Cora Williams
Hazen Alpheus, d. 1/22/1993 in Wolfeboro; William Eldridge and Cora Williams
Ida J., d. 3/17/1999 in N. Conway; ----- Andrews and Nellie -----
John, d. 11/17/1928 at 54/8/7
John H., d. 4/4/1930 at 51
Lester A., d. 10/27/1973 at 69 in Tamworth; b. NH; residence - Tamworth
Marcia Evelyn, d. 7/16/1998 in Wolfeboro; Clifford Gilman and Nellie Moore
Maybelle, d. 9/15/1960 at 65 in Concord
Willie R., d. 2/21/1951 at 80/9/7 in Laconia

ELDRICK,
Irene, d. 7/21/1887 at 19/6/11 in Tamworth; housekeeper; married; b. Ossipee; Fredrick Moody (Ossipee) and Nancy Johnson (Wolfeboro)

ELIAS,
Nellie, b. 1/10/1944 at 66/8/8 in Wolfeboro
Rogy, d. 7/23/1963 at 95 in Conway; residence - Tamworth
Thomas Salem, b. 5/25/1906 at 0/9/19 in Tamworth; b. Tamworth; Rogy Elias (Syria) and Nellie Turner (London, England)

ELLERMAN,
Juanita, d. 1/10/1999 in N. Conway; Genaro Elorza and Dominga Yribat

ELLIOTT,
Albert S., d. 9/5/1971 at 65 in Laconia; b. NH; residence - Tamworth
Amanda, d. 7/21/1937 at 65/3/18
Cora M., d. 9/24/1968 at 86 in Laconia; b. NH; residence - Tamworth
Edwin J., d. 9/22/1957 at 85/1/2 in Tamworth
Elaine B., d. 7/28/1987 in Wolfeboro; Leon C. Elliott and Erdine Eldridge
Gertrude B., d. 5/18/1987 in Wolfeboro; Harry B. Berry and Elva H. Murphy
Gertrude Eleanor, d. 6/20/1997 in Concord; Edwin Elliott and Amanda Anderson

Mark Edward, d. 8/31/1974 at 15 in Laconia; b. NH; residence – Belmont

Richard J., d. 3/3/1982 in Tamworth; Edwin Elliott and Amanda Anderson

Thomas Henry, Sr., d. 3/6/1995 in Laconia; Frederick Elliott and Charlotte Guay

ELLIS,
Phillis C., d. 2/23/1931 at 15/4/4

Robert E., d. 11/4/1990 in Wolfeboro; Robert W. Ellis and Katherine M'Intyre

ELWELL,
Esther M., d. 7/11/1889 at 57/3/8; housewife; married; b. Kennebunk, ME; Benjamin Durrell (Kennebunk) and Lydia Lord (Kennebunk)

Lucie, d. 1/11/1969 at 93 in Laconia; b. NH; residence - Tamworth

EMACK,
Duncan, d. 11/19/1956 at 78/1/20 in Tamworth

EMERSON,
Gorham, d. 12/12/1902 at 83 in Tamworth; widower

Levi W., d. 6/14/1965 at 64 in Wakefield; b. Effingham; residence - Tamworth

EMERY,
Abbie M., d. --/--/1894 at 50/3/9 in Tamworth; housekeeper; married; b. Tamworth; Samuel Clough (Parsonsfield) and Mary Hawkins

James, d. 4/14/1888 at 70/3; insurance agent; married; b. Limington, ME; James Emery (Limington, ME) and Hannah Lethers (Limington, ME)

Mark B., d. 10/26/1929 at 79/3/1

Mary K., d. 1/27/1920 at 91/9/3 in Tamworth; fractured femur; widow; Merrill Perkins and Mary Kimball

Mildred B., d. 5/3/1955 at 67 in Arlington, MA

ENGLISH,
Benjamin W., Sr., d. 9/28/1986 in N. Conway; James E. English and Gertrude Worth

ERICKSON,
Sophie Claire, d. 7/8/1998 in Tamworth; Adam Jazembowski and Stella Zytowiecki

EVANS,
Almon Grover, d. 7/16/1962 at 59 in Tamworth; b. Tamworth; residence - Tamworth
Emily A., d. 4/30/1910 at 85 in Tamworth; housewife; married; Isaiah Hodsdon (Wakefield) and Susan Knight (Rochester)
Emma Idella, d. 7/13/1942 at 70/5/11 in Tamworth
Frank P., d. 7/14/1948 at 85/10/20 in Tamworth
George W., d. 1/3/1911 at 80/8/19 in Tamworth; farmer; widower; b. Tamworth; James Evans (Limerick, ME) and Rhoda Brown
Gladys C., d. 9/3/1979 in Laconia; William Corbett and Flossie Gray
Mabel Lambie, d. 2/18/1976 at 98 in Rochester; b. DC; residence - Tamworth
Walter B. K., d. 8/18/1943 at 73/4/1 in Tamworth

EVENDEN,
Marcha, d. 9/5/1978 at 73 in N. Conway; b. Russia; residence - Chocorua

EWING,
Evelyne H., d. 3/10/1999 in N. Conway

FALL,
Arthur S., d. 8/12/1949 at 71/0/2 in Tamworth

FARLANE,
Retia M., d. 12/13/1930 at 0/6/25

FARNHAM,
Eunice, d. 4/8/1904 at 63/7/15 in Tamworth; widow; b. Tamworth; George W. Moody (Ossipee) and Elizabeth Moody (Ossipee)

FARNUM,
Jane Arlene, d. 6/18/1994 in Tamworth; Tressie M. Powell and Ethelyn A. Collamore
Whipple W., d. 8/29/1976 at 64 in Wolfeboro; b. RI; residence - Tamworth

FARWELL,
Jerial, d. 11/27/1890 at 77/11/9 in Tamworth; farmer; married; b. Waterford, VT; Henry W. Farwell (Barnet, VT) and Mary Barrett (Barnet, VT)

FASTNACHT,
Virginia, d. 8/14/2002 in Tamworth; Lealand Henderson and Veronica Grace

FAULKINGHAM,
Lawrence, d. 12/13/2003 in Tamworth; Lawrence Faulkingham and Mary Starzyk

FELCH,
Catherine P., d. 9/20/1893 at 85/0/16 in Tamworth; housekeeper; widow; b. Bennington, VT; Jedediah Purdy and Sarah Fuller (VT)
Leverett, d. 11/14/1926 at 83/7

FENIMORE,
Sarah S., d. 3/28/2000 in N. Conway; John Sullivan and Helen Jordan

FERRARA,
Joseph, d. 6/7/1999 in Chocorua; Gregorio Ferrara and Vicenza Benenati

FIFFICK,
John Joseph, d. 1/12/1998 in Laconia; William Fiffick and Nellie Betz

FINLEY,
John H., Jr., d. 6/11/1995 in Exeter; John H. Finley, Sr. and Martha Boyden
Robert Lawrence, d. 4/22/1990 in Wolfeboro; John H. Finley and Martha Boyden
Sarah Barney, d. 11/28/1981 in Tamworth; Philip Bartlett and Beatrice Sturgis

FLACCUS,
Louis William, Jr., d. 1/12/1997 in Hanover; Louis William Flaccus and Laura Kimball

Ruth S., d. 2/5/1984 in Wolfeboro; Walter Shoemaker and Emma Wilson

FLACK,
Emmagene S., d. 1/7/2001 in Tamworth; Claude Stewart and Emma Nations
William E., d. 7/14/1990 in N. Conway; William P. Flack and Bertha England

FLANAGAN,
Thomas F., d. 10/15/1978 at 70 in Chocorua; b. MA; residence - Tamworth

FLEET,
Emma N., d. 9/10/1956 at 85 in Princeton, NJ

FLOYD,
Alvinza, d. 7/16/1914 at 60/3/16; traumatism; married; b. Porter, ME; Ora Floyd
Ida, d. 2/7/1895 at 28/11 in Tamworth; housekeeper; married; Richard Mason (Tamworth) and Sophronia Osgood (Tamworth)
Nettie G., d. 2/10/1980 in Wolfeboro; Aristus Grant and Elizabeth Bennett
Perley E., d. 4/11/1951 at 61/5/8 in Tamworth

FLYNN,
Daniel R., d. 6/23/1957 at 2/9/11 in Tamworth
Harry J., d. 4/22/1954 at 64 in Laconia

FOLKINS,
Olive L., d. 5/27/2002 in Laconia; Louis Puffer and Ruth Ressiguie

FOLSOM,
A. D., d. 3/25/1907 at 85/0/26 in Tamworth; post mistress; widow; b. Tamworth; Dr. R. Whipple (Wenham, MA) and Judith Dodge
John T. D., d. 8/22/1888 at 70/4/15; farmer; married; b. Tamworth; Levi F. Folsom (Tamworth) and Lydia Dodge
Samuel N., d. 10/19/1916 at 82/8/14; pneumonia; widower; b. Tamworth; Josiah Folsom

FORD,
Grace Smith, d. 8/16/1963 at 75 in Laconia; b. W. Burke, VT; residence - Tamworth

FOREST,
John, d. 5/21/1891 at -- in Tamworth; b. Tamworth; John A. Forest and Fannie Bean

FORREST,
Sarah G., d. 2/2/1907 at 82/4/20 I n Tamworth; housework; widow; b. Tamworth; W. Hayford (Tamworth) and Sophia Gannett (Tamworth)

FORRISTALL,
William, d. 1/19/1981 in Wolfeboro; George Forristall and Garaphelia Hindaugh

FORSSIUS,
Sarah Jane, d. 2/14/1922 at 70/2; b. Tamworth; Daniel Downs and Susan Johnson

FORSYTHE,
John E., d. 5/25/1977 at 71 in Tamworth; b. PA; residence – PA

FORTIER,
Albert, d. 8/13/1977 at 91 in Tamworth; b. NH; residence - Tamworth
Joseph, d. 3/30/1891 at 0/1/20 in Tamworth; b. Tamworth; Charles Fortier and Delia A. Biledan
Nellie W., d. 10/18/1970 at 79 in Laconia; b. NH; residence – Tamworth
William, d. 11/4/1976 at 56 in Milton
William M., d. 8/30/1960 at 79 in Tamworth

FOSS,
Johanna M., d. 1/25/1897 at 94/11/15 in Worcester, MA; widow; Samuel Meader

FOSTER,
Charles, d. 12/6/1985 in Tamworth
Jennie A., d. 8/2/1955 at 95/11/20 in Ossipee

FOWLER,
Andrew J., d. 11/17/2003 in Tamworth; Andrew J. Fowler and Georgiana Janvrin

FOX,
Earle K., d. 2/10/1970 at 67 in Tamworth; b. Pelham; residence - Tamworth

FRANTZ,
Wilbert Patton, d. 10/22/1990 in N. Conway; Walter Frantz and Mable Patton

FREDRICKSON,
Helen Packard, d. 6/4/1990 in N. Conway; George A. Packard and Hortence Scott

FRENCH,
Benjamin H., d. 4/22/1957 at 68/7/21 in Meredith
Luther Hamilton, d. 8/25/1963 at 45 in Tamworth; b. Everett, MA; residence – Holbrook, MA

FROMM,
Beulah M., d. 11/8/1966 at 74 in Tamworth; b. Tamworth; residence – Tamworth
Louis Woodrow, d. 4/13/1997 in Tamworth; Louis Fromm and Marie Pfund
William A., d. 8/14/1974 at 90 in Epsom; b. NJ; residence - Tamworth

FROST,
Arthur H., d. 7/25/1975 at 81 in Wolfeboro; b. NH; residence - Tamworth
Edwin M., d. 3/8/1927 at –
Marion M., d. 3/7/1983 in Laconia; John Frazee and Elizabeth Judge
William, d. 5/30/1986 in rx; Elibous Frost and Minnie Cronin

FULLER,
Bert B., d. 11/2/1947 at 66/2/16 in Tamworth
Elisha F., d. 4/2/1947 at 63/5/20 in Tamworth

FURNESS,
Edward Judah, d. 10/2/1925 at 60/8/13

GABRIEL,
Helen P., d. 6/28/2002 in Tamworth; Powell Sanuk and Alexandra ---

GAGE,
Violet Lillian, d. 6/19/1985 in N. Conway; Erastus Ellis and Amy Barter

GALLUP,
Carrie A., d. 2/14/1944 at 73/11/0 in Hartford, VT
Frank L., d. 8/31/1921 at --; congestion of the lungs; expressman; married
George W., d. 9/7/1943 at 69/11/23 in Laconia
Maria J., d. 4/7/1939 at 86/2/7; b. N. Chelmsford, MA

GALUCIA,
Harriet A., d. 8/10/1917 at 58/1/22; suppurative nephritis; housewife; married; b. Berwick, ME; John S. Homes and Harriet Horn

GANE,
Gertrude, d. 6/21/1941 at 68/11/29 in Tamworth

GANNETT,
Consider, d. 4/10/1888 at 76/0/6; farmer; married; b. Tamworth; Mathew Gannett (Bridgewater, MA) and Precilla Hayford
Faxon, d. 2/16/1897 at 89/3/25 in Tamworth; farmer; married
Maria E., d. 6/5/1929 at 90/6/21
Martha B., d. 7/14/1888 at 71/7/28; housework; widow; b. Chelsea, VT; Jonathan Brown and Sarah Blaisdell
Mary K., d. 2/17/1897 at 87/11/29 in Tamworth; housekeeper; single; Henry Remick and ----- Howard
Otis, d. 6/7/1891 at 66/0/6 in Tamworth; farmer; married

GARDNER,
Annie Drew, d. 1/8/1984 in Ossipee; George Drew and Kitty White
Edwin D., d. 11/3/1927 at 59/0/15
Etta Lunt, d. 7/26/1922 at 75; b. Lyman, ME; Albert Lunt and Sophia Hill
Raymond, d. 8/9/1981 in Wolfeboro; Luther Gardner and Mary

Bartlett
William S., d. 1/24/1920 at 83/10/19 in Tamworth; gastric carcinoma; farmer; married; John Gardner and Levine Clark

GARLAND,
Annie M., d. 12/18/1902 at 0/1/19 in Tamworth; b. Tamworth; George E. Garland (Tamworth) and Edna M. Grant (Tamworth)
Edna Mae, d. 10/9/1962 at 86 in Ossipee; b. Moultonboro; residence - Tamworth
Ellen M., d. 6/9/1911 at 52/1/13 in Tamworth; housewife; widow; b. Effingham; Phineas Hammond (Saco, ME) and Irene Hanson (Effingham)
George E., d. 2/23/1917 at 42/6/23; pulmonary phthisis; farmer; married; b. Tamworth; George D. Garland and Jane C. Ross
Hattie S., d. 8/10/1921 at 20/6/21; pulmonary tuberculosis; waitress; single; b. Tamworth; George E. Garland and Edna M. Grant
Muriel M. C., d. 3/19/1969 at 62 in Madbury; residence – Dover; buried in Tamworth

GARNETT,
Lottie May, d. 8/3/1967 at 84 in N. Conway; b. Tamworth; residence – Conway

GARRISON,
Merne, d. 3/13/1975 at 88 in Concord; b. NH; residence - Henniker

GARVIN,
Charles G., d. 7/22/1936 at 76

GASPAR,
Ralph Lewis, d. 7/4/1998 in Wolfeboro; Clayton E. Gaspar and Dorothy Clark

GASS,
Frederick A., d. 10/16/1958 at 63 in Tamworth

GAUTHIER,
Eugene H., d. 6/27/2001 in Tamworth; Harold Gauthier and Irene Lamereaux
Gary J., d. 9/21/1987 in Ctr. Ossipee; Eugene H. Gauthier and Millicent Burgess

GIBSON,
Carrie L., d. 9/5/1946 at 93/4/25 in Tamworth
Claudia Z., d. 8/17/1974 at 86 in Tamworth; b. Canada; residence – Chocorua
George A., d. 12/29/1976 at 63 in Laconia; b. MA; residence - Tamworth
Robert W., d. 10/22/1969 at 52 in Laconia; b. MA; residence - Tamworth

GIDDING,
Sadie W., d. 2/6/19155 at 71 in Conway

GIDDINGS,
son, d. 6/22/1915 at --; premature birth; b. Tamworth; Robert Giddings and Sarah Webster
child, d. 11/4/1919 at --; b. Tamworth; Robert Giddings and Sadie Webster
Robert A., d. 2/2/1931 at 66/0/1

GIGNOUX,
Agatha M., d. 10/24/1898 at 60/8/23 in Tamworth; music; widow; John B. Lasalo (Spain) and Frances C. Booth (NY)

GILE,
Mary J., d. 12/7/1892 at 46/3/7 in Tamworth; housework; b. Thetford, VT; Thomas F. Roberts and Hannah Magoon

GILL,
Clarence J., d. 1/10/1963 at 67 in Tamworth; b. Halifax, NS; residence - Tamworth

GILMAN,
infant child, d. 6/26/1912 at – in Conway; b. Conway; Sumner H. Gilman (Tamworth) and Annie Remick (Tamworth)
Ada L., d. 5/13/1930 at 61/10/20
Adeline D., d. 2/10/1902 at 58/9/4 in Tamworth; housework; married; b. Amherst, MA; Joseph C. Honey and Betsey J. Colbath
Benjamin P., d. 5/23/1898 at 81/3 in Tamworth; farmer; married; b. Brookfield; A. Hall Gilman (Brookfield) and Mary A. Pike (Wolfeboro)
Charles H., d. 3/14/1890 at 54/1/14 in Tamworth; railroading;

widower; b. Wakefield; Avery H. Gilman (Ossipee) and Sallie Savage (Wolfeboro)
Clara E., d. 10/20/1940 at 84/0/26; b. Tamworth
Edward, d. --/--/1896 at 48/8/2 in Tamworth; laborer; single; b. Tamworth; Wyatt B. Gilman (Tamworth) and Mary Eastman (St. Andrews, NB)
Ellen J., d. 3/5/1903 at 68/9/8 in Tamworth; housewife; widow; b. Barrington; James Bickford (Barrington) and Ann Arling (Barrington)
Enos P., d. 6/30/1888 at 26/5/27; married
Erwin A., d. 5/14/1931 at 72/4/14
Eva M., d. 10/3/1918 at 13/10/18; pneumonia; student; single; b. Laconia; James Gilman and Hattie Davis
George Edwin, d. 1/11/1918 at 73/7/30; pneumonia; postmaster; married; b. Tamworth; Joseph Gilman and Jane Beede
George Oliver, d. 3/18/1920 at 59/8/10 in Fryeburg, ME; pneumonia; farmer; George W. Gilman and Ellen J. Bickford
Grace A., d. 2/15/1928 at 7/2/21
Harold Ellsworth, d. 4/17/1976 at 81 in Conway; b. NH; residence - Madison
Hattie B., d. 6/12/1923 at 53/4/25; b. Tamworth; William Davis and Mary Mooney
Hazel Marion, d. 6/5/1966 at 59 in Laconia; b. Eaton; residence - Tamworth
Helen D., d. 1/3/1922 at 79/11; b. Tamworth; Wyatt B. Gilman and Mary F. Eastman
Herbert M., d. 7/19/1948 at 79/8/25 in Laconia
Howard R., d. 3/11/1957 at -- in Chocorua
James, d. 3/26/1933 at 72/2
Joseph, d. --/--/1896 at 89 in Tamworth; mechanic; widower; b. Ossipee; Hannah Huckins (Effingham)
Judith A., d. 10/17/1953 at 1 in N. Conway
Laura M., d. 12/3/1933 at 18/0/20
Lydia A., d. 8/4/1921 at 80/5/1; arterio sclerosis; widow; b. Tamworth; Joseph Lord
Margaret N., d. 12/11/1979 in N. Conway; Ezra Nickerson and Emma Perkins
Mary, d. 6/2/1912 at 96/8/16 in Tamworth; housewife; widow; b. St. Andrews, NB; David Eastman (St. Andrews, NB) and Abigail Dean
Mary, d. 7/18/1934 at --

Mary A., d. 4/8/1909 at 81/3/18 in Tamworth; widow; b. Tamworth; John Bryant (Tamworth) and Mary Chick (Effingham)

Mary J., d. 7/5/1900 at 67/8/9 in Tamworth; housework; single; b. Tamworth; Joseph Gilman (Effingham) and Jane R. Bedee (Sandwich)

Orestes A., d. 11/15/1954 at 70 in N. Conway

Orissa J., d. 11/19/1927 at 83/7/19

Patience, d. 4/10/1889 at 76/0/8; widow; b. New Durham; Edmund Tibbitts and Sarah -----

Phebe, d. 10/6/1907 at 59/11/11 in Tamworth; single; b. Tamworth; Ezra Gilman (Tamworth) and P. Tibbetts (Tamworth)

Sarah H., d. 8/21/1891 at 73 in Tamworth; housekeeper; single; b. Tamworth; David Gilman and Betsey Ayer

Sumner H., d. 3/13/1943 at 83/0/25 in Conway

GLENN,
Ralph G., d. 8/15/1954 at 69/9/26 in Tamworth

GLIDDEN,
Clain, d. 3/6/1899 at 0/0/1 in Tamworth; b. Tamworth; William Glidden and Effie Bodge

GLINES,
Persis S., d. 7/11/1934 at 0/10

GOBELLE,
Joseph A., d. 6/21/1949 at 35/0/20 in Wolfeboro

GODIN,
Cecile P., d. 9/--/1951 at 52 in Tamworth

GOLDSMITH,
John P., d. 7/22/1926 at 79/7/18

GOODALE,
Margaret A., d. 6/5/1997 in Wolfeboro; Henry Goodale and Margaret Mitchelson

GOODSON,
Mildred, d. 4/7/2003 in N. Conway; Chester Bickford and Alice Cooper

GOODWIN,
Emma L., d. 1/1/1919 at 53/1/12; housewife; married; b. Penacook; Moses H. Bean and Elizabeth Brown
Eva Louise, d. 5/14/1967 at 80 in Exeter; b. Blake Lake, Quebec; residence - Exeter
Hannah C., d. 11/13/1903 at 57/6/18 in Tamworth; housekeeper; widow; b. Acton, ME; William Hurd and Caroline Blaisdell
Harold A., d. 10/10/1970 at 70 in Tamworth; b. MA; residence – Lynn, MA
Haven K., d. 5/29/1976 at 67 in Wolfeboro
Jeremiah C., d. 7/30/1931 at 80/1/24
Julia A., d. 5/17/1905 at 81/1/28 in Somerville, MA; housekeeping; widow; b. Tamworth; Benjamin Moulton (NH) and Nancy Moulton (Tamworth)

GORDON,
Haven Earl, d. 10/21/1998 in Tamworth; Euba Ralph Gordon and Luella Ames
Louella C., d. 8/20/1975 at 67 in Ossipee; b. NH; residence - Tamworth
Maude, d. 3/28/1950 at 46 in Laconia
William, d. 11/19/1941 at 72/9/29 in Tamworth

GORHAM,
Henry W., d. 8/20/1949 at 67/0/25 in Tamworth

GOVE,
Sarah A., d. 10/29/1913 at 71/2 in Tamworth; housekeeper; widow; b. Tamworth; James Evans and Rhoda Brown

GRACE,
Carroll O., d. 8/19/2002 in Ossipee; Perley Grace and Nellie Berry
Charles E., d. 8/17/1906 at 0/0/17 in Tamworth; b. Tamworth; Ernest C. Grace (Albany) and Cora E. Smart (Tamworth)
Clara E., d. 2/8/1986 in N. Conway; Samuel Moore and Minnie Marston
Cora E., d. 4/12/1921 at 37; uteric fibroid; housewife; married; b. Tamworth; Charles E. Smart and Addie O. Berry
Eleanor M., d. 11/13/1987 in Wolfeboro; Harry Merritt and Elizabeth Delorey
Elizabeth B., d. 1/1/1905 at 80/11/15 in Tamworth; housewife;

married
Ernest C., d. 6/21/1949 at 68/2/29 in Tamworth
Florence Elizabeth, d. 2/28/1990 in Wolfeboro; Orin Eldridge and
   Elizabeth Williams
Franklin, d. 4/21/1905 at 78/7/5 in Tamworth; farmer; widower; b.
   Chatham; Thomas Grace and Priscilla Emerson
Guy Smart, d. 11/13/1998 in Wolfeboro; Ernest Charles Grace and
   Cora Smart
Howard, d. 3/30/1973 at 56 in Tamworth; b. Tamworth; residence -
   Tamworth
Lyman H., d. 3/5/1888 at 5/4; b. Tamworth; Chandler P. Grace
   (Chatham) and Abbie E. Bean (Chatham)
Nellie M., d. 8/5/1979 in ME; Orrin Berry and Elizabeth Davis
Perley C., d. 11/8/1979 in ME; Chandler Grace and Abbie Bean
Roy, d. 9/3/1994 in N. Conway; Ernest Grace and Cora Smart

GRAHM,
Rita, d. 5/6/2003 in Tamworth; Arthur Shuttleworth and Corrine
Messier

GRANT,
Aristus W., d. 10/6/1935 at 88/7/11
Harry G., d. 9/11/1956 at 77 in Tamworth

GRATZ,
Mary, d. 9/23/1981 in N. Conway; Clifford Gratz and Audrey Alford

GRAU,
Janet Ruth, d. 12/21/1998 in Wolfeboro; Melvin Greenbaum and
   Norma Brisk
John G., d. 7/30/1999 in Wolfeboro; John Grau and Helen -----

GRAVES,
Clifford R., d. 9/23/1986 in Wolfeboro; Alfred Graves and Bessie
   Whittney

GRAY,
son, d. 12/8/1920 at – in Tamworth; stillborn; Harold Gray and Bulah
   Bickford
Granville M., d. 11/8/1931 at 74/5/19
Harold M., d. 4/3/1950 at 52/2/1 in W. Ossipee

Lucy M., d. 7/12/1919 at 61/11/28; married; b. Oldtown, ME; William N. White and Harriet Lankster

GREENE,
Jean Hoag, d. 7/19/1993 in N. Conway; John H. Hoag and Isabel Cossaboom
Roscoe G., d. 2/27/1943 at 94/3/15 in N. Conway

GREENLOW,
Irma L., d. 10/26/1961 at 64 in Concord

GREENWOOD,
Edwin James, d. 6/30/1971 at 87 in Laconia; b. Gilbertville, MA; residence - Chocorua

GREGG,
Marjorie True, d. 4/20/1968 at 85 in Tamworth; b. Colorado; residence - Tamworth

GREGORY,
Mary, d. 3/16/1948 at 71/8/10 in Tamworth

GRIFFIN,
Cecile Ann, d. 3/20/1990 in N. Conway; Charles Muller and Maria Ulmschneider

GRIGG,
Elizabeth, d. 3/13/1987 in Tamworth; Thomas J. Grigg and Alberta W. Collins

GROFF,
Clara Martina, d. 4/4/1964 at 67 in Wolfeboro; b. Nebraska; residence - Tamworth

GUINEY,
Mary E., d. 9/9/1946 at 80/7/8 in Tamworth

HADDEN,
Katharine L., d. 5/30/2003 in Tamworth; Charles Loring and Katherine Page

HAINERT,
Christina, d. 9/14/1943 at 86/7/13 in Tamworth
Lorfu Eugene, d. 8/17/1936 at 49/7/4

HALBWACHS,
Marion Sylvia, d. 10/3/1996 in Wolfeboro; Thomas Shackley and Lucy Miller

HALE,
Frank G., d. 8/22/1915 at 38/11/20; automobile injury; patrolman state highway; single; b. Peabody, MA; William F. Hale and Sarah M. Emerson

HALL,
John H., d. 3/17/1908 at 70/0/28 in Tamworth; carpenter; married; b. Portland, ME; William Hall and Emma Cook

HAM,
Almira B., d. 9/16/1914 at 74/9/25; apoplexy; married; b. Peabody, MA; Justus Jones and Sophronia Wood
Frances, d. 6/13/1902 at 78/0/16
Henry E., d. 10/4/1929 at 94/1/26
Lowell, d. 5/22/1891 at 64/1/23 in Tamworth; farmer; married; b. Tamworth; Nicholas Ham and Hannah Chase
Phelena, d. --/--/1896 at 70 in Tamworth; housekeeping; single; b. Albany; James Ham and Mary -----
Sally, d. 3/21/1890 at 95/7/23 in Tamworth; housewife; widow; b. Tamworth; Alden Washburn (Bridgewater) and Sally Gannett (Bridgewater, MA)

HAMMOND,
son, d. 1/28/1918 at --; convulsions in mother; b. Tamworth; Fred M. Hammond and Gladys M. Harmon
A., d. 11/25/1908 at 63/4/20 in Tamworth; widow; b. Tamworth; Andrew Nealey and Sophia Ross
Bertha G., d. 2/3/1955 at 74 in Laconia
Edward J., d. 9/25/1971 at 65 in Tamworth; b. NH; residence - Tamworth
Edward S., d. 1/7/1963 at 91 in Ossipee; b. Ossipee; residence - Tamworth
Ethel A., d. 4/23/1915 at 35/7; cerebral apoplexy; teacher; married;

    b. Portland, ME; W. H. Parker and Lenora Paine
Florence J., d. 7/15/1965 at 84 in Rochester; b. Watertown, MA;
    residence - Tamworth
Fred L., d. 2/18/1959 at 81 in Laconia
Fred M., d. 10/8/1954 at 81 in Laconia
Gladys M., d. 1/28/1918 at 23/3/4; pregnancy; housewife; married; b.
    Tamworth; Henry Harmon and Gladys M. Harmon
Ichabod, d. 11/14/1928 at 75/2/6
Mary, d. 1/30/1895 at 44/9/2 in Tamworth; housekeeper; widow; b.
    Ossipee; J. Marston (Portsmouth) and Hannah Nickerson
    (Tamworth)
Mary, d. 3/16/1934 at 59/10
Mary E., d. 6/9/1920 at 0/0/9 in Boston, MA; multiple abscesses;
    Fred M. Hammond and Bertha Goodwin

HANSCOM,
Walter H., d. 4/17/1956 at 87 in Tamworth

HANSEN,
Linda Jean, d. 11/12/1998 in W. Ossipee; Chester Webster and
    Hazel Ames

HANSON,
Carl A., d. 7/9/1972 at 72 in Tamworth; b. MA; residence –
    Tamworth
Mona L., d. 2/11/1985 in Tamworth; John DeHaro and Elizabeth
    Cain
William Rea, d. 1/31/1997 in N. Conway; Charles Gordon Hanson
    and Florence Linton

HARDING,
Marjorie Soutter, d. 1/3/1962 at 74 in Laconia; b. Boston, MA;
    residence - Madison

HARDY,
Adeline, d. 6/5/1912 at 88/3/0 in Tamworth; housewife; widow; b.
    Tamworth; John Ames
Arthur G., d. 7/5/1906 at 22/9/10 in Tamworth; laborer; single; b.
    Tamworth; William H. Hardy (Tamworth) and Georgianna Davis
    (Effingham)
Carrie Ethel, d. 7/7/1890 at 2/10 in Tamworth; b. Tamworth; William

H. Hardy (Effingham) and Georgiana Davis (Effingham)

Edgar D., d. 5/20/1972 at 34 in Tamworth; b. NH; residence - Rochester

Edna E., d. --/--/1894 at 15/4/2 in Tamworth; at home; single; b. Tamworth; William H. Hardy (Tamworth) and Georgiana Davis (Effingham)

Mrs. William, d. 5/30/1924 at 72

Nellie F., d. 6/11/1890 at 17/11/1 in Tamworth; housework; single; b. Tamworth; William H. Hardy (Effingham) and Georgiana Davis (Effingham)

William, d. 7/4/1889 at 68; farmer; married; b. VT

William, d. 11/16/1926 at 76/6

HARKNESS,
Ana McMahon, d. 4/4/1915 at 43/9/23; cancer; married; b. Quincy, IL; Ruben W. McMahon

Stanley B., d. 6/6/1961 at 81 in Wolfeboro

HARLOW,
Barbara J., d. 7/7/2001 in Tamworth; Ronald Harlow and Marion Loud

HARMON,
Edwin, d. 10/25/1970 at 70 in Parsonsfield, ME; residence – Parsonsfield, ME; buried in Tamworth

HARRIMAN,
Eugene, d. 11/8/1913 at 69/1/28 in Tamworth; farmer; married; b. Madison; Abraham Harriman and Rebecca Forest

HARTFORD,
Phyllis M., d. 12/26/1972 at 62 in Meredith; b. ME; residence – Tamworth

HASEY,
Sarah F., d. 8/22/1889 at 64/0/8; housework; married; b. S. Berwick, ME; Benjamin Abbott (Berwick, ME) and Mary Fall (Berwick)

HASKELL,
Madelene N., d. 5/7/1970 at 59 in Laconia; b. WY; residence - Tamworth

Nelson C., d. 7/5/1952 at 85/9/21 in Tamworth

HATCH,
Ann M., d. 3/14/1911 at 85/11/14 in Tamworth; housewife; married; b. Parsonsfield, ME; Smith Marston (Hampton) and ----- Dudley (Sanbornton)
Bernard M., d. 10/29/1956 at 3 in Wolfeboro
Eliza A., d. --/--/1896 at 58 in Tamworth; housewife; married; b. Tamworth; John Bickford (Parsonsfield) and Abbie Mason (Kennebunk, ME)
George A., d. 1/17/1924 at 77
Ida M., d. 2/4/1939 at 73; b. Tamworth
Ida M, d. 12/14/1962 at 94 in Quincy, MA; b. Malden, MA; residence – Melrose, MA
Otis G., d. 6/18/1918 at --; old age; retired; widower; b. Tamworth; Newton S. Hatch and Hannah Howard

HATHAWAY,
Julia, d. 11/16/1966 at 76 in Tamworth; b. N. Tonawanda, NY; residence - Tamworth

HAYFORD,
child, d. 7/31/1934 at 0/0/1
Abner, d. 6/7/1937 at 67/5/18
Albert W., d. 12/14/1919 at 82/11/7; painter; widower; b. Tamworth; Libbeus Hayford and Lydia Huckins
Arnold D., d. 6/26/1975 at 67 in Beverly, MA; b. Chocorua; residence – Salem, MA
Arthur L., d. 10/14/1953 at 78/0/27 in Moultonboro
Catherine, d. 9/3/1926 at 51/11/5
David, d. 6/4/1903 at 76/0/22 in Tamworth; farmer; widower; b. Tamworth; Nathaniel Hayford
Elizabeth, d. 12/4/1902 at 70/1/18 in Tamworth; farmer; married; James Ames (Tamworth) and Johanna Hayford
Elizabeth, d. 4/1/1916 at 77/1/7; pneumonia; b. St. Stephens, NB
Ella M., d. 10/25/1907 at 54/6 in Tamworth; divorced; b. Tamworth; John Whiting (Limerick, ME) and Ellen Allen (Cornish, ME)
Joanna, d. 12/4/1948 at 75/11/10 in Tamworth
John Sumner, d. 6/5/1962 at 62 in Tamworth; b. Tamworth; residence – Tamworth
Josephine, d. 8/4/1975 at 61 in Concord; b. NH; residence - Concord

Lawrence, d. 2/12/1937 at 0/0/1
Lawrence D., d. 7/6/1955 at 58 in Manchester
Louise D., d. 5/30/1931 at 0/0/1
Lydia, d. 3/13/1891 at 91/8/10 in Tamworth; housewife; widow; b. Conway; ----- Hawkins
Maria M., d. 5/16/1907 at 67/7/5 in Tamworth; housewife; widow; b. ME; Gideon B. Ellis and Mary Stearns
Nora C., d. 8/19/1925 at 60/10/7
William, d. 7/6/1898 at 62/8/17 in Tamworth; farmer; married; b. Tamworth; Warren Hayford and ----- Gannett

HEALD,
Dolly C., d. 5/28/1941 at 86/10/12 in Sweden, ME

HEAMAN,
Robert I., d. 2/20/2000 in Chocorua; Robert Heaman and Margaret Grady

HECK,
William Leon, d. 7/13/1993 in Tamworth; William R. Heck and Margaret Ann Witmer

HEISLER
Percy Kent, d. 7/5/1970 at 72 in Wolfeboro; b. PA; residence - Tamworth

HEMENWAY,
Benjamin S., d. 8/13/1889 at 61/1/1; merchant; married; b. Framingham; William Hemenway (Framingham)

HENDERSON,
Edwin Dow, d. 1/12/1929 at 74/1/14
Everett Gene, d. 8/1/1967 at 59 in Tamworth; b. Tamworth; residence - Tamworth
Harry E., d. 2/17/1963 at 80 in Laconia; b. Tamworth; residence – Tamworth
Theresa, d. 8/21/1968 at 82 in Wolfeboro; residence - Tamworth

HENN,
Laverne A., d. 1/8/2000 in N. Conway; William Henn and Esther Warner

HERD,
stillborn child, d. 1/14/1887 at 0 in Tamworth; b. Tamworth; Edward Herd and Mary A. Herd

HIDDEN,
Elizabeth B., d. 11/21/1942 at 75/11/21 in Tamworth
Harriet, d. 4/26/1907 at 66/3/17 in Tamworth; farmer; single; b. Tamworth; W. P. Hidden (Tamworth) and E. Purrington (Sandwich)
Helen Bassett, d. 6/24/1964 at 70 in Tamworth; b. Tamworth; residence - Tamworth
John D., d. 9/10/1902 at 73/2/4 in Tamworth; farmer; widower; b. Tamworth; William P. Hidden (Tamworth) and Eunice Purington (Sandwich)
Julia A., d. 5/12/1951 at 84/1/13 in Cambridge, MA
Mabel B., d. 3/24/1996 in Tucson, AZ; Charlie Bray and Pearl Snide
Mary A., d. 1/30/1902 at 61/5/1 in Tamworth; married; b. Clarborne, AL; Joseph Boyden (Tamworth) and Angelina Wilson (Mobile, AL)
Mary J., d. 1/5/1901 at 84/1/12 in Tamworth; housewife; widow; b. Sandwich; John Quimby (Sandwich) and Jane Webster (Sandwich)
Samuel A., d. 10/25/1957 at 91 in Laconia
Samuel H., d. 12/27/1969 at 78 in Ossipee; b. Tamworth; residence - Tamworth
William B., d. 7/8/1924 at 86
William B., d. 4/12/1992 in Tamworth; Samuel H. Hidden and Helen Bassett
William P., d. 9/17/1895 at 96/4/9 in Tamworth; farmer; widower; b. Tamworth; Samuel Hidden (Rowley) and Elizabeth Price (Newburyport)

HIGGINS,
Harry L., d. 8/4/1953 at 23/0/11 in Tamworth

HILL,
Carlton M., d. 2/--/1930 at 63
Cordelia P., d. 9/24/1920 at 73/2/8 in Tamworth; gangrene of feet; blacksmith; married; John Chick and Sarah Hidden Clark
David A., d. 12/15/1908 at 52 in Tamworth; farmer; married; b. Dayton, ME; William W. Hill and Sarah S. Jellison

Emeline (Forrest), d. 4/20/1970 at 87 in Brockton, MA; residence – Brockton, MA; buried in Tamworth

Frank W., d. 10/7/1925 at 83/8/1

George W., d. 8/29/1890 at 39/8/3 in Tamworth; farmer; married; b. Lyman, ME; William W. Hill (Waterboro, ME) and Sarah S. Jelleson (Waterboro, ME)

Gertrude C., d. 4/3/1971 at 86 in Tamworth; b. NH; residence - Tamworth

William A., d. 12/7/1919 at 0/0/5; b. Tamworth; Charles A. Hill and Grace Cowan

William W., d. 10/17/1900 at 82/8/17 in Tamworth; farmer; widower; b. ME

HILTON,
Edward F., d. 12/7/1958 at 69 in Tamworth

Leonard R., d. 10/29/1965 at 20 in Tamworth; b. Conway; residence – Madison

HIRTLE,
Bertha A., d. 7/26/1965 at 82 in Tamworth; b. Canterbury; residence - Tamworth

HOAG,
Elizabeth A., d. 7/10/1921 at 73/4/2; epilepsy; housewife; widow; b. Tamworth; Dr. Joseph Huntress and Oriana Sargent

John H., d. 10/19/1985 in Hanover; Clarence Hoag and Anna Scattergood

Nathan, d. 2/14/1914 at 89/0/2; old age; farmer; married; b. Sandwich; John Hoag and Comfort Morrill

HOBBS,
Amanda, d. 1/6/1929 at 98/7/15

Beatrice A., d. 10/3/1943 at 7/11/23 in Laconia

Bert W., d. 6/21/1952 at 77 in Moultonboro

Celia E., d. 11/21/1956 at 48 in Laconia

Charles D., d. 5/25/1927 at --

Cora, d. 8/8/1900 at 0/2/1 in Tamworth; b. Conway; Bert W. Hobbs (Tamworth) and Harriet Swain (Albany)

David B., d. 9/21/1911 at 62/3/2 in Tamworth; farmer; married; b. Tamworth; Reuben D. Hobbs and Elmira Nickerson

Ernestine P., d. 8/8/1928 at 0/0/11

Frank O., d. 4/24/1925 at 71/6/2
Frank W., d. 7/20/1972 at 31 in Stark; b. NH; residence - Plymouth
George W., d. 12/29/1932 at 36/8/14
Gertrude E., d. 6/22/1966 at 60 in N. Conway; b. Effingham; residence – Tamworth
Grace, d. 2/1/2001 in Wolfeboro; Clyde Drinkwater and Alma Briggs
Harry Dearborn, d. 12/20/1969 at 64 in Manchester; b. NH; residence - Tamworth
Hattie F., d. 9/--/1947 at 81/10/29 in Batavia, NY
Hattie M., d. 10/14/1974 at 97 in Wolfeboro; b. NH; residence - Tamworth
Henry W., d. 9/28/1957 at 48/11/15 in Tamworth
John, d. 4/14/1912 at 49/11/23 in Tamworth; laborer; single; b. Tamworth; Reuben D. Hobbs (Ossipee) and Elmira Nickerson (Tamworth)
Leon, d. 1/16/1960 at 59 in Laconia
Lovina, d. 4/5/1928 at 76/9/30
Patience, d. 9/17/1891 at 58/3/2 in Tamworth; housewife; married; Perley B. Courier and Eliza Colamer
Reuben D., d. 10/1/1888 at 75; farmer; widower; b. Ossipee; Reuben D. Hobbs (Ossipee)
W. H., d. 5/1/1908 at 84/0/12 in Tamworth; farmer; widower; b. Ossipee; Joseph Hobbs and Dorothy Cooley
Wilbur, d. 11/7/1972 at 83 in Ossipee; b. MA; residence - Tamworth

HOBSON,
Alice, d. 7/8/1895 at 42/7/21 in Tamworth; single
Jabez H., d. 3/13/1897 at 69/11 in Tamworth; married
Olive R., d. 7/20/1898 at 68/0/4 in Tamworth; widow

HODGE,
Sabrina A., d. 4/11/1899 at 81/0/11 in Tamworth; housewife; married; b. Andover, ME; Nathaniel Abbott (Concord) and Dolly Morse

HODGKINS,
Everett, d. 5/25/1946 at 58/5/4 in Tamworth
Henry T., d. 5/17/1902 at 53/9/14 in Tamworth; teacher; married; b. Tamworth; True B. Hodgkins and Maria Hodgkins
Susan A., d. 9/6/1938 at 88/10/17; b. Ossipee

HOGAN,
Jasper B., d. 3/27/1992 in Tamworth; Daniel Hogan and Edith Bedel

HOLDEN,
Jane K., d. 10/31/1891 at 56/0/8 in Tamworth; housewife; married; b. Tamworth; Samuel Brown
Mary, d. 6/6/1919 at 96/9; married; b. Tamworth; Aaron Heard and Rhoda Webster
William H., d. 2/2/1924 at 89

HOMEYER,
William Charles, d. 11/9/1997 in N. Conway; Friedrich W. C. Homeyer and Minna L. A. Heusmann

HOOK,
Jennie E., d. 7/28/1925 at 70/11

HOOPER,
Lydia A., d. 10/25/1888 at 64/1; housework; widow; b. Tamworth; Enoch Stevenson (Tamworth) and Lydia Dow (Tamworth)

HOWARD,
John A., d. 4/6/1904 at 69/6 in Tamworth; motorman; married; b. Lovell, ME
Orman R., d. 7/31/1976 at 86 in Wolfeboro; b. ME; residence - Tamworth

HOWE,
Rebecca, d. 1/22/2002 in N. Coway; Will Howe and Elizabeth Poulson

HOYT,
Mary F., d. 9/3/1892 at 27/7/27 in Tamworth; housework; b. Milton; Stephen Nute and Mary E. Abbott

HUBBARD,
Nathaniel, d. 1/20/1892 at 71/3/3 in Tamworth; farmer; widower; b. Tamworth; Nathaniel Hubbard and Mehitable Morse
Sara A., d. 7/31/1918 at 85; cerebral hemorrhage; housewife; widow; b. Tamworth
Sarah R., d. 9/2/1904 at 84/9/2 in Tamworth; housewife; widow; b.

Tamworth; Enoch Remick (Augusta, ME) and Lucinda Edgill (Tamworth)

HUCKINS,
Ferdinand, d. 4/3/1900 at 77/11/15 in Tamworth; farmer; widower; b. Effingham; Stephen Huckins and Pauline Webber
Nancy S., d. --/--/1896 at 79/9/17 in Tamworth; housewife; married; b. Tamworth; Mark Jewell (Tamworth) and ----- (Holderness)

HUGHES,
Cornelia H., d. 10/18/1984 in Hanover; Clare Huff and Mabel Ekelman
Jesse H., d. 4/22/1977 at 19 in Hanover; b. PA; residence - Tamworth

HUMPHREY,
Denise E., d. 3/24/2001 in Tamworth; Joseph Jones and Judith Gilman

HUNT,
Ernest Leroy, d. 12/22/1998 in Tamworth; Pitman Hunt and Alice Dow

HUNTINGTON,
Minnie M., d. 10/5/1953 at 75 in Concord

HUNTON,
James Innis, d. 5/3/1976 at 27 in Chocorua; b. CA; residence - PA

HUNTOON,
Wayne A., d. 6/10/2003 in Chocorua; Lyle Huntoon and Hilda Perkins

HUNTRESS,
Amanda, d. 12/30/1911 at 81 in Tamworth; widow; b. Effingham; Robert Fulton (ME)
Eva H., d. 9/5/1952 at 78 in Tamworth
J. L., d. 4/7/1907 at 71/0/10 in Tamworth; farmer; married; b. Effingham; S. Huntress and Huldah Leavitt (Exeter)
Louisa P., d. 4/23/1910 at 70/2/11 in Tamworth; housewife; widow; b. Wakefield; Simon Blake (Wakefield) and Caroline Whiting

(Canada)
Nellie, d. 4/--/1895 at 18/0/25 in Tamworth; teacher; single; b. Tamworth; Jno. Huntress (Effingham) and Loiza Blake (Wakefield)

HURD,
William Aaron, d. 5/13/1963 at 64 in Tamworth; b. Freedom; residence - Tamworth

HUTCHINS,
Annie S., d. 10/9/1910 at 24/7/8 in Tamworth; waitress; single; b. Tamworth; William N. Hutchins (Albany) and Augusta A. Downs (Porter, ME)
Augusta, d. 4/2/1941 at 72/0/3 in Wolfeboro
Earl E., d. 9/28/1968 at 50 in Center Ossipee; residence – Center Ossipee
Elias William, d. 4/27/1971 at 85 in Concord; b. NH; residence - Tamworth
Geraldine, d. 2/10/1921 at --; stillborn; b. Tamworth; Clarence Hutchins and Ida Smith
Henry A., d. 2/4/1955 at 63/9/12 in Tamworth
Leah Christine, d. 5/11/1993 in Conway; Harold Wentworth and Stella -----
Walter C. S., d. 8/16/1955 at 58/4/16 in Tamworth
William N., d. 12/14/1928 at 71/10/1

HYNES,
Margaret, d. 7/25/1913 at 23 in Tamworth; servant

IRWIN,
Irene I., d. 10/26/1989 in Wolfeboro; Lewis Irwin and Clara McNeil
Valerie D., d. 5/7/2001 in Tamworth; Kenneth Irwin and Margaretta Heisler

JACKSON,
Elizabeth S., d. 6/13/1892 at 87/2/10 in Tamworth; housework; b. Gilmanton; Thomas Dean and Lucy Price
Emma A., d. 1/14/1947 at 91/5/29 in Tamworth
Lydia B., d. 2/23/1902 at 68/10/10 in Boston, MA; housework; married; b. Tamworth; Joseph Gilman (Ossipee) and Jane R. Beede (Sandwich)

Mary, d. 6/10/1887 at 99/3/10 in Tamworth; single
Samuel H., d. 9/17/1924 at 73

JAMES,
William, d. 8/26/1910 at 68/7/15 in Tamworth; teacher; married; b. New York, NY; Henry James (Albany, NY) and Mary Robertson (New York, NY)
William, d. 9/26/1961 at – in Tamworth

JAMIESON,
Helen Frances, d. 2/19/1966 at 80 in Conway; b. Plattsburgh, NY; residence - Tamworth

JEFFERS,
Abbie J., d. 1/13/1944 at 75/6/26 in Tamworth
Edward F., d. --/--/1896 at 71/0/22 in Tamworth; farmer; married; b. Springfield
Emaline, d. 8/9/1900 at 73/4/7 in Tamworth; housewife; widow; b. Salisbury; Benjamin Smith
Fred Laighton, d. 10/21/1933 at 73/4/18
Madeleine J., d. 12/19/1963 at 48 in Wolfeboro; b. Laconia; residence - Tamworth
Milton W., d. 6/7/1944 at 77/9/10 in Tamworth
Percy E., d. 12/6/1970 at 69 in Wolfeboro; b. NH; residence - Tamworth

JENNESS,
George, d. 7/3/1889 at 19/4/17; brakeman; single; b. VT; Stephen Jenness
Mary H., d. 10/21/1940 at 90/6/13; b. Tamworth

JENNINGS,
Alan Douglas, d. 6/4/1998 in Wolfeboro; Bernard M. Jennings and Emily Hill
Daniel E., d. 2/20/1987 in Laconia; Bernard M. Jennings and Emily Hill
Keith, d. 5/10/1954 at 0/0/1 in Wolfeboro
Thomas, d. 2/10/1990 in N. Conway; John J. Jennings and Margaret Sharkey

JOHNSON,
Betsey, d. 11/11/1889 at 72/3/19; housewife; married; Nathaniel Tuttle (Parsonsfield, ME) and Lizzie Rowlens (Parsonsfield, ME)
Cyrus K., d. 5/17/1928 at 78/7/1
Cyrus R., d. 1/8/1898 at 77/5 in Wolfeboro; farmer; widower
Edwin R., d. 12/21/1960 at 76 in Tamworth
Effie P., d. 1/13/2002 in Tamworth; Otis Bean and Elsie Brown
Elizabeth A., d. 8/26/1900 at 34/0/14 in Tamworth; housewife; married; b. Conway; Joseph Gardner (Wakefield) and Margaret Woodman (Tamworth)
Ella, d. 6/2/1897 at 43/6/18 in Tamworth; housewife; married; Alvah Moore and Lizzie Seavey (Brownfield, ME)
Ellen, d. 2/28/1953 at 93 in Moultonboro
Forrest W., d. 12/21/1971 at 53 in Wolfeboro; b. NH; residence – Tamworth
Gladys I., d. 12/27/1975 at 76 in Center Harbor
Grace, d. 3/18/1975 at 81 in Dedham, MA; residence – Dedham, MA
Irene F., d. 8/9/1958 at 66 in Tamworth
John W., d. 1/1/1937 at 78/9/23
Kenneth S., d. 9/7/1975 at 36 in Concord; b. CT; residence - Tamworth
Marshall B., d. 8/12/1990 in Wolfeboro; Harry Johnson and Alice Drake
Mary Stuart, d. 5/30/1969 at 17 in Tamworth; b. VA; residence - Tamworth
Nellie R., d. 12/12/1906 at 42/6/25 in Tamworth; housewife; married; b. Porter, ME; Orren Rogers (Porter, ME) and Betsey Merrifield (Brownfield, ME)
Newton A., d. 11/5/1926 at 84/3/3
Otis, d. 3/1/1937 at 95/0/5
Rebecca May, d. 11/4/1966 at 0/0/1-½ in Wolfeboro; b. Wolfeboro; residence – Tamworth
Rose Maire, d. 6/1/1994 in Portland, ME; Leon Hobbs and Celia -----
S. Rhoda, d. 11/8/1972 at 80 in Tamworth; b. Sandwich; residence - Tamworth
Theodore, d. 9/17/1970 at 79 in Laconia; b. MA; residence – Tamworth
Walter E., d. 9/7/1975 at 82 in Laconia; b. IL; residence - Tamworth
William H., d. 5/20/1955 at 84 in Wolfeboro

JONAH,
Althea M., d. 12/23/1971 at 72 in Wolfeboro; b. MA; residence – Tamworth
Willard E., d. 9/23/1979 in Tamworth; Archibald Jonah and Effie McCunig

JONES,
Arthur E., d. 8/2/1950 at 62/11/18 in Tamworth
Florence R., d. 8/12/1937 at 57/6/29
Nellie, d. 12/22/1946 at 86/10/26 in Tamworth
Walter V., d. 4/6/1964 at 73 in Portland, ME; residence – Tamworth

JOSEPH,
Allan J., d. 5/10/1973 at 55 in S. Tamworth; b. Boston, MA; residence – Madison

KALLIN,
Oscar E., d. 10/6/1987 in N. Conway; Oscar E. Kallin

KANE,
Carl F., d. 2/5/1975 at 58 in Chocorua; b. CT; residence - Tamworth
Linwood, d. 7/14/1930 at 12/7/7
Sarah E., d. 6/28/1962 at 65 in Farmington; residence – Ossipee; buried in Tamworth

KEITH,
Mary, d. 1/14/1981 in N. Conway; Frank Berry and Sarah Files

KELLEY,
Elizabeth, d. 9/7/1955 at 82/5/6 in Portland, ME

KELLY,
Henry B., d. 7/5/1939 at 86/3/16; b. Center Harbor
Mercy, d. 12/2/1891 at 56/1/27 in Tamworth; housewife; married; John Stockdell and Mary Smyth

KEMPTON,
Agnes J., d. 9/5/1954 at 81 in Tamworth

KENDALL,
Rebecca Kaye, d. 4/23/1983 in Tamworth; Thomas Alcenius and

Ardiss Barnes
Richard Eugene, d. 4/23/1983 in Tamworth; Edward Kendall and Carole Crippin

KENEFICK,
William M., d. 1/9/2001 in N. Conway; William Kenefick and Eva Bowden

KENERSON,
Lydia, d. 4/4/1897 at 78/7/27 in Tamworth; houskeeper; widow
Rhoda T. W., d. 12/17/1890 at 64/9/7 in Tamworth; housewife; married; b. Tamworth; Aaron Head (Kennebunk, ME) and Rhoda Webster (Kennebunk, ME)
William, d. 4/-/1895 at 59/9/19 in Tamworth; farmer; married

KENNEDY,
Angela Mitchell, d. 10/18/1975 at 87 in Tamworth; b. OH; residence - Tamworth

KENNERSON,
Sophia, d. 2/18/1931 at 94/7/28

KENNESON,
Allan S., d. 10/23/1984 in Hanover; Wesley Kenneson and Clara Stuart

KENNEY,
Elizabeth Adams, d. 9/26/1995 in Wolfeboro; Vernon Swett and Helen Eager

KENNISON,
John, d. 6/6/1929 at 71

KIERSTEAD,
George R., d. 7/4/1994 in Wolfeboro; George Kierstead and Catherine Welch

KIMBALL,
Caroline, d. 12/11/1931 at 88/8
Christene M., d. 3/22/1979 in Tamworth; Otis Bean and Elsie Brown
Isaac, d. 5/19/1887 at 72/10 in Tamworth; farmer; married; b.

Parsonsfield, ME; Joseph Kimball
Isaac N., d. 1/29/1943 at 95/3/15 in Newfields
Mary M., d. 5/3/1941 at 72/4/7 in Tamworth
Melvin N., d. 3/4/1960 at 88 in Laconia
Nancy, d. 10/7/1911 at 101/6 in Tamworth; housework; single; b.
  Parsonsfield, ME; Jonathan Kimball and Nancy Granville
Sally J., d. 2/19/1910 at 92/11/15 in Tamworth; housewife; widow; b.
  Northwood; Samuel Lawrence (Northwood) and Susan James
  (Northwood)
Samuel O., d. 8/4/1936 at 85/7/9
Sarah F., d. 12/20/1943 at 86/1/5 in Tamworth
Susan, d. 7/28/1948 at 85/8/14 in Concord
Winslow B., d. 4/7/1958 at 83 in Rochester

KING,
Arthur C., d. 9/10/1945 at 62/0/2 in Tamworth
Helen Frances, d. 2/18/1935 at 86/8/29
Leach, d. 9/7/1931 at 83/11/25
Margaret A., d. 11/17/1994 in Tamworth; Ross W. King and Mabelle
  Morse
Sadie A., d. 5/28/1930 at 9/6/28

KINGSBURY,
George D., d. 6/6/1954 at 84/7/7 in Tamworth
Grace, d. 7/16/1963 at 81 in Westmoreland; residence –
  Westmoreland; buried in Tamworth
Helen A., d. 12/27/1939 at 66/8; b. Lowell, MA
William, d. 10/5/1907 at 7/4/6 (sic) in Tamworth; clergyman; S.
  Kingsbury

KINSELLA,
Patricia N., d. 7/11/1992 in Tamworth; Charles Newcombe and
  Margaret Maltby

KJELLBERG,
Judith Priestly, d. 11/5/1997 in Lebanon; James Taggart Priestley
  and Klea Palika

KNIGHT,
Jay C., d. 12/19/1950 at 58/3/11 in Tamworth

William D., d. 10/29/1914 at 39/5/22; typhoid fever; laborer; married; b. S. Tamworth; James R. Knight and Juliette L. Clough

KNOWLTON,
Calvin C., d. 10/31/1936 at 77/8/21
Ella M., d. 2/2/1919 at 53/3/13; housewife; married; b. Sandwich; Daniel Peasley and Harriet W. Fogg
Haven C., d. 9/5/1972 at 78 in Center Harbor; b. NH; residence - Tamworth
Ida M., d. 3/27/1953 at 62 in Tamworth
Kenneth, d. 4/13/1985 in Wolfeboro; Haven Knowlton and Ida Downs
Marjorie Ellen, d. 8/23/1998 in Ossipee; Grover Griffin and Alice Ruggles
Sarah R., d. 5/25/1930 at 74/10/21
Western S., d. 1/4/1892 at 62/9/22 in Tamworth; farmer; widower; b. Poland, ME; David Knowlton and Hannah Pulsifer

KNOX,
Edward Chesley, d. 11/12/1962 at 62 in Tamworth; b. Ossipee; residence – Tamworth

KOHRS,
Rose Mary, d. 8/10/1996 in N. Conway; John Moscardini and Irene Musser

KRUIZENGA,
Leonard Samuel, d. 7/8/1997 in Wolfeboro; Samuel J. Kruizenga and Gertrude Boomsa

KUKURUZA,
Michael, d. 2/2/1981 in Tamworth; Nicholas Kukuruza and Eudokia - ----

LAFFIN,
James B., d. 1/8/1975 at 87 in Chocorua; b. Canada; residence - Tamworth
Lucy M., d. 7/8/1971 at 76 in Wolfeboro; b. NS; residence - Chocorua

LALLY,
George M., d. 4/9/1992 in Tamworth; Patrick Lally and Katherine Casey
Gertrude A., d. 7/18/1990 in N. Conway; Joseph Meany and Gertrude -----

LAMBERT,
Alfred E., Jr., d. 7/20/1993 in Laconia; Alfred E. Lambert and Alma S. Gunn

LAMONTAGNE,
Fred, d. 4/8/1924 at 82
Mrs. Fred, d. 5/25/1920 at – in Tamworth; bronchial pneumonia; married

LANE,
Elizabeth A., d. 4/2/1972 at 86 in Ossipee; b. NH; residence - Tamworth

LAPOINT,
Helen C., d. 4/1/1921 at 48/6/4; cerebral hemorrhage

LARRABEE,
child, d. 12/26/1931 at –
Albert J., d. 6/18/1937 at 76/3/26
Cora M., d. 7/5/1955 at 89/11/23 in Moultonboro
Dorothy T., d. 10/4/1966 at 59 in Tamworth; b. Tamworth; residence – Tamworth
Raymond E., d. 1/18/1973 at 68 in Wolfeboro; b. NH; residence – S. Tamworth
Raymond Lloyd, d. 5/28/1929 at 0/9/9
Sandra, d. 7/8/1980 in Wolfeboro; Donald Hutchins and Helen Keen

LARSON,
Emil Harold, d. 6/26/1975 at 72 in Tamworth; b. MA; residence - Tamworth

LARY,
Celeste A., d. 3/3/1915 at 58/2/9; chronic nephritis; married; b. Tamworth; Otis G. Hatch and Ann Marston
Charles, d. 8/7/1924 at 64

William H., d. 2/14/1943 at 89/19/19 in W. Pittsfield, ME

LAUZON,
Francis J., d. 11/2/2001 in N. Conway; George Lauzon and Leona Gagnon

LAWSON,
Marguerite E., d. 9/11/1984 in N. Conway; Artemus Smith and Jennie Jack

LAWVER,
Delores D., d. 8/13/2001 in Tamworth; Roy Parramore and Margaret Barton

LEACH,
Marjorie Louisa, d. 10/23/1923 at 0/6/15; b. Tamworth; William Leach and Alma Jeffers
Nancy B., d. 4/8/1902 at 83/2/2 in Moultonboro; housework; widow; b. Bristol, ME; Robert Little
Nathaniel H., d. 4/10/1893 at 80 in Tamworth; farmer; married; b. Moultonboro; John Leach (Sandwich) and Sarah Hill

LEARY,
Ida M., d. 5/2/1973 at 82 in Meredith; b. Roxbury, MA; residence - Tamworth
Thomas M., d. 11/11/1963 at 80 in Tamworth; b. Boston, MA; residence - Tamworth

LEAVITT,
Maurice W., d. 7/1/1947 at 29/7/17 in Tamworth
Rose C., d. 9/24/1917 at --; cerebral embolism; housekeeper; widow; b. Chatham; ----- Meader and ----- Dolf

LEBEL,
Thomas, d. 6/25/1978 at 22 in Tamworth; b. OK; residence - Londonderry

LEBLANC,
Ethel Frances, d. 2/19/1989 in Wolfeboro; Edward McLoud and Mary F. Howlett

LEBROKE,
Charles Franklin, III, d. 10/18/1997 in Tamworth; Charles F. LeBroke, Jr. and Myrtle Ilsley

LEFEBVRE,
Cecelia Mary, d. 2/15/1962 at 79 in Wolfeboro; b. Scotland; residence – Tamworth
Edward, d. 3/4/1967 at 84 in Concord; b. Haverhill, MA; residence – Tamworth

LEHAN,
James Francis, d. 8/31/1976 at 79 in Manchester; b. MA; residence – Tamworth

LEMIRE,
Kimberly, d. 3/2/1981 in Tamworth; Robert Lemire and Nancy Bastraw

LESSARD,
Pierre Luc, d. 10/7/1998 in Plymouth; Adrien Lessard and Monique Pratte

LEWIS,
Ella, d. 11/17/1917 at 65/8/24; chronic tocavitation; married; b. Portland, ME; Joshua N. Piper and Orra L. Laport

LIBBY,
Ralph Kenneth, d. 1/14/1925 at 0/6/1

LIBERTY,
James, d. 8/10/1916 at 81/3/5; epilepsy; farmer; married; b. Quebec; Peter Liberty
Miria, d. 4/27/1919 at --; widow
Rhoda, d. 1/2/1895 at 55/4/19 in Tamworth; housekeeper; married; b. Walden, VT; Lyman Weeks

LINCOLN,
Miria Louise, d. 1/12/1914 at 98/6/12; old age; widow; b. Boston, MA; Joel Prouty and Elizabeth Gates

LITCHFIELD,
Mary Emily, d. 6/8/1975 at 78 in Tucson, AZ; b. IL; residence - Tamworth

LLOYD,
Robert McAllister, d. 3/5/1997 in Chocorua; Robert McAllister Lloyd and Isabel Goodwin

LOCK,
Henrietta, d. 3/5/1964 at 85 in Tamworth; b. Effingham; residence - Tamworth

LOCKE,
Frank E., d. 12/9/1952 at 82/1/19 in Wolfeboro

LONG,
Alma Charlotte, d. 6/26/1932 at 62/11/8
Almon E., d. 11/9/1929 at 58/10/6
Jerldine T., d. 9/16/1931 at 22/9/16
Lena, d. 6/22/1939 at 51/2/1; b. Chocorua
Martha A., d. 6/22/1955 at 86 in Tamworth

LORD,
Alvah, d. 8/14/1895 at 74/4/8 in Tamworth; farmer; married; b. Ossipee; Robert Lord (Ossipee) and Nancy Goldsmith (Ossipee)
James, d. 1/4/1891 at 84/10/8 in Tamworth; farmer; single; b. Ossipee; Wentworth Lord and Sally Nay
Joseph Brackett, d. 1/1/1919 at 81/1/22; farmer; single; b. Tamworth; Joseph Lord and ----- Stanley
Julia A., d. --/--/1896 at 47 in Tamworth; housewife; married; b. Moultonboro
Lovena, d. 12/28/1889 at 73/8; housekeeper; widow; b. Beverly, MA; N. Standley (Beverly, MA) and Charity Knowlton (Beverly, MA)
Lucy J., d. 5/23/1909 at 90/9/13 in Tamworth; widow; b. Tuftonboro; ----- Leavitt (Tuftonboro) and Hannah Nay (Ossipee)

LOWD,
Marion, d. 2/15/1957 at 53 in Meredith

LOWMASTER,
Susan M., d. 4/23/1983 in Tamworth; Gerald Taylor and Deloras Anderson

LUFF,
John H., d. 11/6/1990 in Laconia; Ralph G. Luff and Eva -----

LUND,
Mathew D., d. 8/16/2001 in N. Conway; John Lund and Wendy Turgeon

LUNT,
Albert, d. 6/12/1891 at 78/5/18 in Tamworth; farmer; widower; b. Kennebunk; Rufus Lunt and Ruth Smith
Sophia, d. 3/6/1891 at 71/2/21 in Tamworth; housewife; married; b. Lyman, ME; Nathaniel Hill and Margarett Hooper

LYE,
Howard, d. 10/12/1982 in Tamworth; William Lye and Emily Snape
Madeline Isabel, d. 7/20/1993 in N. Conway; Fred L. Brooks and Jenney Gaitenby

LYMAN,
Reginald K., d. 10/16/1979 in Madison; Frank Lyman and Margaret Kenerson

LYONS,
G. Emily, d. 12/10/1985 in Wolfeboro; William Halsey

MACDONALD,
Lori Ann, d. 10/22/1959 at 0/0/4 in Laconia

MACGREGOR,
Ross Stuart, d. 11/9/2003 in Tamworth; Ross MacGregor and Ruth Magee

MACKENZIE,
Florence M., d. 1/17/1956 at 72/3/5 in Tamworth

MACKINNON,
Robert Gregory, d. 12/15/1968 at 43 in Wonalancet; b. MA; residence - Watertown

MADDOCKS,
Elizabeth H., d. 4/17/1922 at 72; b. Tamworth; David Hidden and Mary Quimby
Frank, d. 11/26/1917 at 67/8/22; apoplexy; machinist; married; b. Farmington, ME

MADUSKUIE,
Christine Faith, d. 5/27/1989 in Tamworth; Harold E. Bennett and Ruth Jones

MAGOON,
Mary A., d. 6/25/1937 at 95/2/18

MAGRUDER,
Calvert, d. 5/22/1968 at 74 in Wedgewood Nursing Home; b. Annapolis, MD; residence – Tamworth

MAHER,
Gay, d. 4/7/1980 in Wolfeboro; Henry Dalby and Dorothy Jansen

MAHLER,
William H., d. 9/16/1991 in N. Conway; William Mahler and Marie Taubert

MAHONEY,
Ida C., d. 9/18/1983 in Ossipee; Edwin Henderson and Ada Forrest
Joseph Frederick, d. 1/9/1973 at 83 in Laconia; b. NS; residence - Tamworth

MALLAR,
John L., d. 1/20/2002 in Tamworth; Nathan Mallar and Ruth Whitaker

MALLARD,
Elsa P., d. 7/22/1961 at 55 in Tamworth

MALLETT,
Edmund Eli, Jr., d. 10/4/1996 in Lebanon; Warren Mallett and Marion Halligan

MANN,
Doris W., d. 3/31/1999 in Wolfeboro; Harry Tait and Myrtile -----

MARSH,
Evelyn M., d. 8/16/1977 at 81 in Tamworth; b. VT; residence – Tamworth
Harriet Cobb, d. 1/20/1967 at 70 in N. Conway; b. Lynn, MA; residence - Tamworth
Jean Connie, d. 10/25/1998 in Wolfeboro; George Joseph Piette and Eva Beech
Mary, d. 5/15/1900 at 2 (sic) in Tamworth; housewife; married; b. Portugal
Stephen, d. 2/9/1981 in Tamworth; Stephen Marsh and Hattie Hilton

MARSHALL,
Alice L., d. 7/25/1983 in Laconia; Albert Anderson and Anna Karlson
John Lee, d. 3/3/1974 at 26 in S. Tamworth; b. ME; residence – S. Tamworth
Margaret, d. 3/7/1920 at 65 in Tamworth; valvular disease of heart; widow; ----- Palmer and Mary Woodsworth
Ruth Dean, d. 5/24/1972 at 77 in Laconia; b. NH; residence - Tamworth
William, d. 12/13/1988 in N. Conway; John Marshall and Annette Keep

MARSTON,
Clara E., d. 12/11/1899 at 44/11/9 in Tamworth; housewife; married; b. Tamworth; H. A. Remick (Tamworth) and Betsy P. Prescott (Sandwich)
Elmira, d. 4/18/1900 at 91/11/17 in Tamworth; housewife; widow; b. Sandwich; John Fellows and Miriam Jewell
Hannah D., d. 2/24/1888 at 83/4/29; housekeeper; widow; b. Sanbornton; Samuel Dudley and Mercy Thorn
Jeremiah, d. 4/--/1895 at 76/3/14 in Tamworth; farmer; widower; b. Portsmouth; J. Marston (Effingham) and Mary Hobbs (N. Hampton)

John F., d. 4/23/1907 at 56/8/12 in Tamworth; farmer; widower; b. Tamworth; W. B. Marston (Tamworth) and Elmira Fellows (Sandwich)
Mary Ellen, d. 10/17/1924 at 78
Robert A., d. 4/16/1928 at 4/9/6
Wilbur C., d. 8/16/1953 at 75 in Tamworth

MARTIN,
Almira J., d. 1/16/1918 at 86/10/12; old age; at home; widow; b. Tamworth; Jacob C. Wiggin and Mary S. Cogswell
Ida M., d. 3/10/1954 at 76 in Tamworth
John B., d. 8/4/1900 at 74/4/18 in Tamworth; landlord; married; b. Bridgton, ME; John B. Martin (Cornish, ME)
Louville Kenerson, d. 12/20/1984 in N. Conway; Lyman Martin and Ida Kenerson
Lyman L., d. 1/1/1960 at 88 in Tamworth
William, d. 3/1/1980 in N. Conway; Lyman Martin and Ida Kennerson

MASON,
Alfonso, d. 12/25/1948 at 91/8/15 in Wolfeboro
Angelina E., d. 4/19/1927 at 85/10/19
Annie L., d. 2/24/1937 at 73/2/12
Annie Q., d. 2/8/1958 at 85 in Tennessee
Arthur H., d. 9/4/1939 at 38/6/6; b. Tamworth
Arthur H., d. 2/6/1983 in S. Tamworth; Arthur Mason and Blanche Ames
Arthur L., d. 6/12/1957 at 72 in Rochester
Camilla A., d. 7/24/1931 at 15/5
Charles A., d. 10/8/1960 at 76 in Concord
Charles C., d. 11/4/1954 at 72 in Laconia
Chester L., d. 8/2/1973 at 88 in Laconia; b. NH; residence - Tamworth
Clara May, d. 4/28/1925 at 50/7/8
Edna G., d. 5/23/1986 in Wolfeboro; Ansel Cummings and Blanche Brown
Elizabeth C., d. 7/24/1971 at 87 in Newmarket; buried in Tamworth
Emily J., d. 3/18/1932 at 89/8/9
Emma J., d. 7/19/1913 at 55/9/22 in Tamworth; housewife; married; b. Porter, ME; Ira Floyd and Sarah Stanley
Ernest L., d. 8/5/1957 at 86/9/12 in Tamworth
Ernest S., d. 8/14/1932 at 72/8/12

Fred O., d. 1/11/1945 at 82/1/9 in Laconia
Harold L., d. 5/2/1994 in Wolfeboro; Chester L. Mason and Mabel G. Macphearson
Harry O., d. 9/23/1944 at 72/9/13 in Laconia
Henry M., d. 7/12/1937 at 76
Hiram D., d. 7/14/1940 at 96/9/1; b. Albany, NY
Hiram E., d. 6/28/1972 at 76 in Laconia; b. NH; residence - Tamworth
John G., d. 10/26/1892 at 53/6 in Tamworth; millman; b. Tamworth; William Mason and Nancy Mason
John L., d. 8/30/1934 at 83/9/7
Jonathan, d. 12/17/1889 at 72; farmer; married; b. Madison; David Mason (Madison) and Betsey Head (Albany)
Larkin D., d. 5/2/1903 at 82/11/17 in Tamworth; merchant; widower; b. Tamworth; Tufton Mason and Sally Gilmore
Leafy, d. 5/10/1956 at 79/10/10 in Laconia
Llewellyn G., d. 7/14/1955 at 85 in Concord
Lucetta B., d. 6/27/1914 at 72/9/5; myocarditis; widow; b. Tamworth; E. Hayford
Mabel G., d. 1/16/1967 at 74 in Tamworth; b. Milton, MA; residence - Tamworth
Mary B., d. 4/15/1889 at 80/5/2; widow; b. Buxton, ME; Thomas Bradbury (Buxton, ME) and Abigail Boothby (Buxton, ME)
Mary E., d. 12/1/1946 at 91/2/0 in Tamworth
Mary J., d. 6/15/1925 at 84/2/9
Minnie M., d. 10/27/1967 at 93 in Laconia; b. Sandwich; residence - Tamworth
N. M., d. 8/5/1908 at 60/8/15 in Tamworth; merchant; widower; b. Tamworth; Larkin D. Mason (Tamworth) and C. Staples (Lebanon, ME)
Nancy, d. 10/7/1888 at 83/6; housework; widow; b. Tamworth; Nathaniel Mason
Richard, d. 11/1/15/1905 at 72/11/16 in Tamworth; farmer; married; b. Tamworth; William Mason (Tamworth) and Nancy Mason (Tamworth)
Safrona, d. 4/26/1920 at 83/7 in Tamworth; cerebral apoplexy; widow; Moses Osgood and Betsy Chick
Sarah O., d. 2/20/1914 at 61/5/16; convulsions and cerebral apoplexy; teacher; single; b. Tamworth; Larkin D. Mason and Catherine Staples

Thomas B., d. 9/26/1897 at 53/3 in Tamworth; merchant; single; b. Tamworth; Peter G. Mason (Tamworth) and Mary Bradbury (Buxton, ME)
Victor E., d. 10/15/1898 at 1/11 in Tamworth; b. Tamworth; Ernest Mason(Tamworth) and Leafy Downs (Tamworth)
Wendy G., d. 12/4/1960 at 6 in Tamworth
William, d. 4/2/1888 at 84; farmer; married; b. Tamworth; William Mason

MATHER,
Sydney C., d. 3/31/1968 at 58 in Chocorua; b. NY; residence - Tamworth

MAYNADIER,
Mary, d. 8/20/1897 at 62 in Tamworth; housewife; married; b. Lowell, MA

McALISTER,
William, d. 4/30/1895 at 63/4 in Tamworth; laborer; single; b. Tamworth; Mahitable Foss

McAVOY,
Robert F., d. 4/13/2002 in Tamworth; Lionel McAvoy and Edith Lewis

McCABE,
Eleanor Bolles, d. 2/21/1967 at 74 in Tamworth; b. Cambridge, MA; residence - Tamworth

McCARTHEY,
Della, d. 9/1/1913 at 51 in Tamworth; servant

McCARTHY,
Richard C., d. 5/24/1976 at 30 in Tamworth; b. NH; residence - Rindge
Tillie M., d. 7/17/2000 in Wolfeboro; Nikodimus Sharinus and Tillie Lipstz

McCORMICK,
Sylvia L., d. 3/20/2001 in N. Conway; Lewis Tibbetts and Anne MacDonald

McCREARY,
Eleanor, d. 5/16/2001 in Wolfeboro; Ralph Cardinale and Theresa Winter

McDERMOTT,
Katie M., d. 8/9/1887 at 19 in Washington, DC; housekeeper; married; b. Tamworth

McFARLAND,
Bridget, d. 2/14/1922 at 66/4/10; b. Limerick, Ireland; Lawrence O'Connor

McGLONE,
John, d. 2/24/1972 at 88 in Plainfield, NJ; b. Baltimore, MD; residence – Plainfield, NJ

McGREGOR,
John, d. 6/6/1957 at 80/5/22 in Needham, MA

McGREW,
Lillian Culbertson, d. 1/23/1995 in Wolfeboro; Harry L. McGrew and Rosetta Culbertson

McINTIRE,
Harriett, d. 7/7/1925 at 92/1/19

McINTYRE,
Mae M., d. 8/7/1989 in Wolfeboro; Fred McIntyre and Mary LeBlanc

McKENNA,
Orabelle, d. 6/26/1981 in Meredith; Henry Pascoe and Philamen Dore

McKEY,
Mary J., d. 11/19/1943 at 88/9/18 in Tamworth
Richard H., d. 10/27/1956 at 68 in Laconia

McLAUGHLIN,
John D., d. 9/26/1992 in Tamworth; Patrick J. McLaughlin and Lillian Driscoll

McNEIL,
Harry, d. --/--/1896 at 37/3/11 in Tamworth; farmer; married; b. NB

McPHERSON,
Pauline L., d. 4/23/1946 at 38/9/14 in Pembroke

MEADER,
John, d. 1/12/1895 at 85/4/8 in Tamworth; laborer; married; b. Machias, ME; Isaac Hidden (Tamworth) and Thankful Moody (Machias)
Mabel B., d. 11/26/1951 at 73 in Meredith
Otis, d. 3/8/1899 at 68/8/3 in Tamworth; farmer; married; b. Sandwich; Ephraim Meader (Rochester) and Hannah Cook (Sandwich)

MEANS,
Margaret Vance Hay, d. 8/8/1999 in Tamworth; William Oscar Hay and Margaret Vance Hay

MEEKER,
Jean P., d. 4/24/1996 in N. Conway; Gilbert Peet

MELBOURNE,
Loren, d. 6/13/1998 in Tamworth; Francis Melbourne and Alice Abbott

MELVILLE,
Francis, d. 8/2/1916 at 84/7/4; heart disease; artist; b. Brooklyn, NY; Charles W. Melville and Mary Orr

MERRIAM,
Nellie S., d. 3/3/1907 at 80/11/6 in Tamworth; housework; married; b. Tamworth; H. L. Wiggin (Tamworth) and E. R. Floyd (Effingham)

MERRILL,
Lawrence J., d. 8/11/1969 at 63 in Laconia; b. VT; residence - Tamworth
Lydia M., d. 3/9/1930 at 93

MERSFELDER,
Esther Legge, d. 9/10/1990 in Tamworth; William R. Legge and Della March

MESERVE,
Arthur Percy, d. 12/7/1990 in Wolfeboro; Frank Meserve, Sr. and Margurite Emerson

MILLAR,
Frances, d. 3/22/1977 at 69 in Wolfeboro; b. MA; residence - Tamworth

MILLER,
Hattie J., d. 8/24/1892 at 24/11/7 in Tamworth; housework; b. Hyde Park; William D. F. Miller and Laura A. Seavey
Joseph H., d. 8/9/1920 at 68/1/13 in Tamworth; lobar pneumonia; sailor; married; Joseph H. Miller

MILLS,
Isaac B., d. 9/6/1940 at 84/8/29; b. Boston, MA
James C., d. 9/9/1930 at 66/5/10

MITCHELL,
Peter, d. 8/11/1915 at 69/4; cerebral apoplexy; insurance agent; widower; b. Ashland, England; Thomas Mitchell

MOIR,
Isabella, d. 9/9/1946 at 71/5/29 in Tamworth

MOLANDER,
Lois A., d. 10/7/1978 at 64 in Laconia; b. MA; residence - Tamworth

MOODY,
Atcherson, d. 1/27/1895 at 87/5/10 in Tamworth; farmer; married; b. Ossipee; Clement Moody
Dora E., d. 10/12/1899 at 27/5/16 in Tamworth; housewife; married; b. Ossipee; Joseph M. Davis (Effingham) and Louisa Hobbs (Ossipee)
Elizabeth, d. 3/26/1893 at 79/1 in Tamworth; housekeeper; married; b. Ossipee; Benjamin Moody (Ossipee) and Eunice Moody (Ossipee)

Evelyn Rose, d. 8/25/1997 in Tamworth; Eugene E. Mudgett and Eva Davis
Florence E., d. 11/6/1913 at 3/6/7 in Tamworth; b. Tamworth; Joseph A. Moody and Nettie Williams
Frank, d. 1/5/1890 at 16/8/9 in Tamworth; laborer; single; b. Tamworth; George H. Moody (Tamworth) and Mary Hobbs (Ossipee)
Frederick, d. 8/23/1914 at 88/10/7; chronic nephritis; farmer; widower; b. Ossipee; Benjamin Moody and Hannah Colby
George H., d. 5/9/1900 at 55/11/25 in Tamworth; farmer; widower; b. Tamworth; George W. Moody (Ossipee) and Elizabeth Moody (Ossipee)
George H., d. 7/12/1972 at 63 in Tamworth; b. Albany; residence - Tamworth
Gladdis B., d. 9/6/1915 at 2/7/4; gastro enteritis; b. Tamworth; Joseph Moody and Nettie Williams
John, d. 2/1/1887 at 31/6/9 in Tamworth; laborer; single; b. Tamworth; Aherson Moody (Ossipee) and ----- (Tamworth)
Joseph A., d. 12/23/1946 at 59/3/15 in Wakefield
Lavinia, d. 4/18/1913 at 86/10/22 in Tamworth; housekeeping; widow; b. Tamworth; John Lang Weeks and Judith Plummer
Lester E., d. 10/16/1952 at 69/6/10 in Conway
Levi W., d. 4/1/1938 at 85/6/6; b. Tamworth
Mary, d. 6/19/1925 at 62/1/7
Mary A., d. --/--/1894 at 45/2/11 in Tamworth; housekeeper; married; b. Ossipee; Joseph D. Hobbs (Ossipee) and Nancy Pinner (Ossipee)
Nancy, d. 2/25/1892 at 60/2/27 in Tamworth; housework; b. Wolfeboro; Stephen Johnson and Sarah Jenness
Nancy Rose, d. 4/28/1942 at 0/0/0 in Laconia
Nathaniel E., d. 10/13/1961 at 81 in Wolfeboro
Nellie, d. 4/30/1923 at 29/8/15; b. Ossipee; William Williams and Susan Welch
Robert E., d. 4/5/1994 in IL; George H. Moody and Elizabeth Hobbs
Theodore, d. 6/12/1974 at 54 in Hanover; b. NH; residence – Milton Mills

MOORE,
Abbie F., d. 4/3/1930 at 87/2
Alice M., d. 9/22/1958 at 66 in Laconia

Alvah B., d. 3/3/1905 at 82/6 in Tamworth; farmer; married; b. Parsonsfield, ME; William Moore (Parsonsfield, ME) and Hannah Huntress

Charles F., d. 7/20/1953 at 59 in Portsmouth

Edgar H., d. 3/4/1912 at 57/10/26 in Tamworth; farmer; married; b. S. Berwick, ME; Silas Moore (Newfield, ME) and Julia Harmon (Taunton, MA)

Edith R., d. 3/27/1952 at 82 in Tamworth

Eva E., d. 4/26/1972 at 76 in Tamworth; b. NH; residence – Tamworth

Fred L., d. 5/23/1919 at 58/8/10; storekeeper; widower; b. Calais, ME; William Moore and Catherine Campbell

George A., d. 10/14/1972 at 86 in Tamworth; b. NH; residence - Tamworth

Herbert Charles, d. 2/7/1969 at 76 in N. Conway; b. NH; residence - Tamworth

Herbert F., d. 7/27/1942 at 23/11/10 in Yuba Co., CA

Kenneth J., d. 11/4/1976 at 70 in Tamworth; b. NH; residence - Tamworth

Martha, d. 7/8/1912 at 63/7/13 in Tamworth; teacher; widow; b. Tamworth; David Miller (Pittsfield) and Elizabeth Stevenson (Tamworth)

Mary A., d. 10/30/1940 at 78/0/12; b. Tamworth

Minnie A., d. 3/1/1968 at 80 in Concord; b. NH; residence – Tamworth

Richard D., d. 4/19/1974 at 81 in Laconia; b. NH; residence - Chocorua

Roland S., d. 3/18/1943 at 39/7/20 in Tamworth

Samuel J., d. 1/12/1945 at 67/0/6 in Kittery, ME

Wallace Elsworth, d. 3/27/1998 in Tamworth; William D. Moore and Nellie Thurston

William E., d. 2/12/1968 at 79 in Laconia; b. NH; residence - Madison

MORRILL,
David, d. 9/12/1906 at 77/5/24 in Tamworth; manufacturer; widower; b. Candia; Theo Morrill

MORRISON,
George A., d. 1/18/1922 at 77/0/2; b. Laconia; Abraham Morrison and Susan Whipple

MOULTON,
stillborn child, d. 1/6/1927 at –
infant, d. 4/13/1928 at 0/0/1
Alonzo, d. 6/5/1911 at 76/5 in Tamworth; farmer; married; b. Albany; Daniel Moulton (Albany) and Mary Glidden (Albany)
Arthur D., d. 1/23/1980 in ME; Arthur Moulton and Emma Damrell
Arthur D., Jr., d. 6/9/1993 in N. Conway; Arthur D. Moulton, Sr. and Florence Haag
Carrie C., d. 5/27/1945 at 79/10/23 in N. Waterford, ME
Daisy E., d. 7/6/1888 at 0/1/6; b. Tamworth; Luman I. Moulton (Albany) and Carrie Davis (Tamworth)
Eliza A., d. 1/13/1892 at 83/9/25 in Tamworth; housework; widow; b. Pepperell, MA; Mary Capell
Florence Haag, d. 1/24/1998 in N. Conway; Henry F. Haag and Anna Katherine Gerlach
Frank P., d. 10/28/1917 at 74/5/27; chronic nephritis; farmer; widower; b. Sandwich; John M. Moulton and Eliza Woods
Franklin A., d. 2/10/1978 at 74 in Wolfeboro; b. NH; residence - Tamworth
George A., d. 3/1/1957 at 64 in Wolfeboro
George W., d. 4/28/1910 at 78/3/27 in Tamworth; shoemaker; widower; b. Sandwich; John M. Moulton (Moultonboro) and Eliza A. Woods (Pepperell, MA)
Gladys P., d. 8/30/1954 at 72 in Dover
Harley E., d. 7/13/1954 at 66/9/9 in Center Harbor
Hattie, d. 12/15/1895 at 28/2/5 in N. Waterford
Janet P., d. 4/21/2002 in N. Conway; Arthur Moulton and Florence Haag
Joseph, d. 5/26/1907 at 69/0/26 in Tamworth; farmer; married; b. Freedom; N. Moulton (Freedom) and E. Wallace (Epsom)
Lydia E., d. 2/22/1937 at 71/0/4
Maude L., d. 2/14/1979 in Tamworth; John Ames and Harriet Ames
Willis, d. 10/20/1949 at 80/5/1 in Tamworth

MOWRER,
Elizabeth E., d. 5/21/2002 in Chocorua; Patrick Gormley and Elizabeth Walter

MUNRO,
Marguerite, d. 11/16/1979 in Laconia; John Munro and Henrietta Drew

MYERS,
Annie C., d. 6/6/1949 at 56/0/2 in Tamworth
Eleanor Emlen, d. 12/12/1996 in Tamworth; Arthur C. Emlen and
 Marie Albertson
Howard H., d. 12/16/1978 at 86 in N. Conway; b. NY; residence -
 Tamworth

NADEAU,
Dorothy Ann, d. 12/2/1997 in N. Conway; Charles Roberts and
 Gertrude Ripley
Edmond R., d. 1/8/2002 in N. Conway; Arthur Nadeau and Anna
 Leveque

NEAL,
Leonora M., d. 1/5/1948 at 77/3/15 in Tamworth

NEALLY,
Andrew, d. 5/27/1891 at 80/3/21 in Tamworth; farmer; widower; b.
 Tamworth; Amos Neally and Ann Head

NEWMAN,
George A., d. 7/24/1957 at 11/0/17 in Tamworth

NEWSOM,
Samuel, d. 2/23/1996 in Tamworth; Samuel Newsom and Lilly
 Wilcocks
Sylvia Bowditch, d. 5/9/1989 in N. Conway; Ingersol Bowditch and
 Sylvia Scudder

NIBLOCK,
Clifton, d. 3/27/1969 at 70 in Wolfeboro; residence – Rochester;
 buried in Tamworth

NICHOLS,
George W., d. 5/1/3/1898 at 55/1/5 in Tamworth; farmer; single; b.
 Ossipee; James Nichols
James L., d. 10/1/1887 at 70/4 in Tamworth; farmer; married; b.
 Ossipee; William Nichols and Betsy Libby
Madeline, d. 6/26/1962 at 83 in Concord; b. Chicago, IL; residence –
 Tamworth

NICHOLSON,
Paul, d. 12/6/1985 in Tamworth; James Nicholson and Bertha Stanley

NICKERSON,
A. Martin, d. 11/15/1968 at 77 in Wolfeboro; b. NH; residence - Tamworth
Alonzo, d. 4/25/1925 at 92/10/20
Clarinda, d. 10/9/1910 at 90/2/9 in Tamworth; housewife; married; Eleazer Snell and Polly Danforth
Doratha, d. 3/11/1924 at 0/4
Edson S., d. 8/24/1946 at 80/5/0 in Conway
Emma M., d. 8/3/1943 at 73/3/2 in Tamworth
Erma, d. 5/11/1977 at 85 in Tamworth; b. NH; residence – Tamworth
Ezra, d. 2/11/1955 at 84 in Tamworth
George E., d. 3/4/1943 at 74/7/23 in Tamworth
George Robert, Sr., d. 1/21/1967 at 77 in Tamworth; b. Madison; residence - Tamworth
Grace H., d. 1/30/1924 at 55
Ida May, d. 6/2/1921 at 65/1/6; gastric hemorrhage
Irma J., d. 1/10/1944 at 81/0/5 in Tamworth
John H., d. 9/21/1902 at 76/2/28 in Tamworth; farmer; married; b. Tamworth
Joseph R., d. 12/28/1899 at 73/2/3 in Tamworth; farmer; widower; b. Tamworth
Lillian M., d. 9/14/1974 at 83 in Wolfeboro; b. NH; residence - Tamworth
Maude T., d. 5/8/1972 at 94 in Rochester; b. NH; residence - Tamworth
Melissa D., d. 2/17/1923 at 89/8/1; b. Albany; James Ham and Abigail Allard
Norman, d. 3/1/1987 in Hanover; Ezra Nickerson and Emma Perkins
Olaf, d. 3/20/1932 at 31/6/6
Sarah P., d. 5/28/1897 at 63/8/2 in Cambridge, MA; housewife; married
Winfield E., d. 4/14/1974 at 83 in Ossipee; b. NH; residence - Tamworth

NIXON,
James H., Jr., d. 2/17/1968 at 51 in Dr. Remick's office; b. MA; residence – Ctr. Sandwich

NORCROSS,
Arthur Z., d. 3/1/1991 in Tamworth; Elmer R. Norcross and Jennie F. Dorr

NORTON,
David D., d. 4/7/1982 in Tamworth; Edward Norton and Cora Martin

NOSS,
Frederick Boyer, d. 12/4/1967 at 66 in Laconia; b. Sendai, Japan; residence - Tamworth

NOYES,
Sylvia, d. 1/4/1992 in Tamworth; George Little and Grace DeVeber

NUTE,
Watson H., d. 8/23/1957 at 88 in Tamworth

NUTTER,
Gladys B., d. 1/1/1975 at 82 in Tamworth; b. NH; residence – Tamworth
John B., d. 7/21/1976 at 84

NYSTEDT,
Paul A., d. 9/29/1976 at 75 in Wolfeboro; b. CT; residence - Tamworth
Rosalind O., d. 6/13/1955 at 48 in Laconia

O'NEIL,
Annie J., d. 9/26/1916 at 35; unknown; nurse maid
Steven E., d. 6/13/1996 in Manchester; Walter O'Neil and Ella Space

O'SHAUNESSEY,
Charles, d. 7/24/1938 at 70/6/29; b. Ireland

OLIVER,
Sarah E. C., d. 11/15/1927 at 70

OLSON,
Carl Gustave, d. 3/24/1968 at 61 in Livermore; residence - Chocorua

OLTON,
Percy Trafford, Jr., d. 11/23/1998 in Wolfeboro; Percy Trafford Olton, Sr. and Elizabeth Theodora Matthew

OSBORNE,
Elizabeth, d. 10/1/1914 at 25/3/1; la grippe; single; b. Salem, MA; Theodore M. Osborne and S. Alice Machado

OSGOOD,
Ellen O., d. 11/17/1934 at 74/8/9
George A., d. 3/22/1899 at 2/3/14 in Tamworth; b. Tamworth; H. L. Osgood (Tamworth) and Ellen Freeman (Portsmouth)
Herman LeBert, d. 11/28/1932 at 64/6/25
Ina E., d. 1/3/1953 at 79/3/8 in Haverhill, MA
Samuel A., d. --/--/1896 at 65/6/22 in Tamworth; painter; married; b. Tamworth; Moses W. Osgood (Gilmanton) and Betsey Chick (Effingham)

OTIS,
Mary B., d. 6/10/1944 at 69/7/26; b. Tamworth

OVERSHINER,
Brenda G., d. 11/21/2000 in N. Conway; Dorothy Mathis

PAGE,
Agnes M., d. 4/22/1956 at 69 in Laconia
Arthur C., d. 7/14/1952 at 85/2/11 in Tamworth
Bertha C., d. 7/26/1912 at 55/3/6 in Tamworth; housewife; married; b. Brockton, MA; Henry Howard (Bridgewater, MA) and Mary E. Ware (Norfolk, MA)
Dorothy I., d. 11/1/1909 at 3/1/15 in Tamworth; b. Tamworth; Edgar P. Page (Lynn, MA) and Grace Davis (Tamworth)
Edgar P., d. 3/8/1960 at 79 in Laconia
Elizabeth, d. 2/18/1915 at 56; cancer of liver; housewife; married; Otis Robinson
Eva L., d. 4/2/1936 at 71/10/14
Henry T., d. 6/21/1898 at 67/3/21 in Tamworth; laborer; married; b. Gilmanton; Jabez Page (Gilmanton) and Lucy Dean (Tamworth)
Horace A., d. 5/1/1930 at 80/7/27

Howard F., d. 2/5/1975 at 85 in Ossipee; b. NH; residence - Tamworth

Lucien F., d. 6/26/1900 at 67/0/15 in Tamworth; laborer; single; b. Tamworth; Jabez Page (Gilmanton) and Susan Osgood (Gilmanton)

Lucy W., d. 9/28/1892 at 83/4/13 in Tamworth; housework; b. Gilmanton; Thomas Dean and Lucy Price

Mary A., d. 9/29/1956 at 78/9/13 in Tamworth

Mary Ann, d. 2/25/1965 at 79 in Carlisle, MA; b. Workington, England; residence - Tamworth

Moses P., d. 7/10/1936 at 76/11/10

Oliver Edwin, d. 1/23/1974 at 75 in Wolfeboro; b. NH; residence - Tamworth

Winona H., d. 7/21/1969 at 61 in N. Conway; b. NH; residence - Tamworth

PALMER,
Caroline, d. 8/20/1913 at 76 in Tamworth; widow; b. Moultonboro; Calvin Moulton and Elizabeth Reid

Evelyn G., d. 1/17/1987 in Tamworth; George Grames and Katherine Wakefield

Gertrude I., d. 10/20/1961 at 80 in Laconia

Helen, d. 6/29/1928 at 74/11/16

Herbert, d. 11/11/1935 at 34/9/7

PARKER,
Eliab, d. 7/3/1920 at 66/9 in Tamworth; interstitial nephritis; married; b. Tamworth; George K. Parker and Abigail Cook

Elizabeth Hester, d. 11/20/1988 in N. Conway; Charles E. Parker and Lena Knight

PARNELL,
David L., d. 9/1/1999 in Conway; Harold Parnell and Antonetta Ferraro

PARRIS,
Joseph O., d. 7/12/1990 in N. Conway; Pete A. Parris and Eva Comeau

Max F., d. 2/18/1978 at 70 in Hanover; b. NH; residence - Tamworth

PASCOE,
infant daughter, d. 7/24/1909 at – in Tamworth; b. Tamworth; William Pascoe (Freedom) and Josie L. Moulton (Freedom)
Francis S., d. 2/14/1955 at 79 in Concord
Josie L., d. 8/16/1953 at 75 in Tamworth
Thomas R., d. 2/17/1940 at 68/6/13; b. Freedom
William J., d. 2/13/1929 at 55/5/24

PATTERSON,
Doris A., d. 3/11/1999 in N. Conway; Joseph Truchon and Beaulie Rena

PATTISON,
William Leonard, d. 12/11/1997 in Tamworth; William L. Pattison and Gladys Stetson

PEARSON,
Carlyle L., d. 5/2/1968 at 67 in MA; residence – Chocorua
Herman W., d. 5/25/1983 in Laconia; Theodore Pearson and Carrie Smith
Ruth Lena, d. 3/5/1996 in N. Conway; Fred Barnes and Florence M. Whiting

PEASE,
Benjamin F., d. 11/10/1908 at 79/7/18 in Tamworth; farmer; married; b. Tamworth; John M. Pease (Meredith) and Betsey Whitcher (Meredith)
J. W., d. 3/18/1916 at 66/11/28; cerebral hemorrhage
Lucinda W., d. 6/5/1914 at 76/6/28; pneumonia; housekeeper; widow; b. Bolton, Canada; Simon Blake and Caroline Whitney

PEASLEE,
Charles Hoyt, d. 9/7/1996 in N. Conway; Earle C. Peaslee and Caroline Carter
Roland, d. 2/9/1958 at 57 in Tamworth

PECK,
Gloria Marion, d. 9/22/1996 in Laconia; John D. Hagen and Dorothy Ross

PENNELL,
infant, d. 2/8/1927 at –
Abbie, d. 1/12/1944 at 65/3/2 in Tamworth
Charles H., d. 5/23/1910 at 50/0/8 in Tamworth; laborer; married; b. Buxton, ME; Alexander Pennell (Buxton, ME) and Sarah Berry (Buxton, ME)

PEPPARD,
Rita Marie, d. 5/31/1998 in Tamworth; William J. Forsyth and Emma E. Sargent
Stuart W., d. 7/8/2002 in Tamworth

PERKINS,
son, d. 8/23/1915 at --; premature birth; b. Tamworth; Pike G. Perkins and Stella A. Bickford
Alice P., d. 1/6/1949 at 69/2/25 in Tamworth
Alphenia, d. 7/20/1955 at 85 in Tamworth
Alston, d. 4/30/1942 at 72 in Tamworth
Annie R., d. 9/12/1906 at 38/3/24 in Tamworth; housewife; married; b. Tamworth; Phineas Tibbetts (Effingham) and Margaret English (Guysboro, NS)
Arthur, d. 4/13/1899 at 0/9/11 in Tamworth; b. Tamworth; William Perkins (Jackson) and Elizabeth Graves (Sandwich)
Bertha E. S., d. 6/11/1955 at 84 in Rochester
Clarence A., d. 11/23/1915 at 58/8/29; chronic nephritis; farmer; married; b. Tamworth; Lorenzo D. Perkins and Sarah H. Kennerson
Elizabeth W., d. 2/18/1913 at 27/5 in Tamworth; divorced; b. Boston, MA; Levi W. Moody and Mary J. Davis
Ella M., d. 7/29/1941 at 67/7 in Ossipee
Estell B., d. 4/14/1992 in Meredith; Silas H. Bickford and Nellie Brown
Ethel A., d. 12/12/1887 at 11/4/11 in Somerville, MA; George W. Perkins
Ethel R., d. 1/1/1943 at 62/7/25 in Brookline, MA
Hiram L., d. 10/10/1916 at 67/4/27; gangrene of leg; laborer; married; b. Ossipee; Horace Perkins
James K., d. 10/11/1909 at 77/1/22 in Tamworth; farmer; widower; b. Tamworth; Merrill Perkins (Tamworth) and Mary S. Kimball (Parsonsfield, ME)

John N., d. 5/26/1902 at 71/1/25 in Tamworth; farmer; married; b.
　　Sandwich; Jonathan Perkins
Jonathan, Jr., d. 8/23/1891 at 83/11/28 in Tamworth; farmer;
　　married; b. Tamworth; Jonathan Perkins and Phebe Hunt
L. D., d. 4/24/1907 at 73/11/19 in Tamworth; farmer; married; b.
　　Tamworth; J. Perkins (Tamworth) and M. Williams (Tamworth)
Lizzie C., d. 8/30/1943 at 82/0/8 in Laconia
Mary, d. 2/17/1930 at 74
Mary A., d. 5/8/1907 at 70/1/8 in Tamworth; housewife; married; b.
　　Jackson; A. L. Eastman (Conway) and Ruth Kimball
　　(Gilmanton)
Mehitable, d. 3/27/1898 at 86/5/27 in Tamworth; widow
Pike G., d. 8/16/1917 at 83/3/7; senility carbuncle; farmer; widower;
　　b. Jackson; Thomas Perkins and Susan Burnham
Pike Gordon, d. 5/1/1975 at 80 in Tamworth; b. NH; residence –
　　Tamworth
Pike Gordon, Jr., d. 8/1/1984 in Tamworth; Pike Perkins and Estella
　　Bickford
Quincy G., d. 11/28/1950 at 76/6/25 in Moultonboro
Sarah, d. 2/11/1913 at 79/11/5 in Tamworth; housekeeping; widow;
　　b. Albany; Isaac Kenerson and Judy Fall
Susan C., d. 10/21/1891 at 78/8 in Tamworth; housewife; widow; b.
　　Jackson; Joseph Burnham and Mary Chase
Thomas, d. 3/5/1891 at 80/11/5 in Tamworth; farmer; married; b.
　　Ellsworth, ME; John Perkins and Sarah Lowe
Virginia A., d. 12/4/1960 at 8 in Tamworth
William E., d. 8/6/1920 at 56/8/27 in Tamworth; valvular heart
　　disease; farmer; married; James K. Perkins and Anna K.
　　Blaisdell
William H., d. 5/23/1934 at –

PETER,
John J., d. 3/2/2002 in Chocorua; Albert Peter and Dorothy Gurney

PETERSON,
Osler Luther, d. 1/17/1988 in Tamworth; Olaus Peterson and
　　Mathilda Johnson

PETTINGILL,
Elvira, d. 10/10/1913 at 89/6/25 in Tamworth; housekeeping; widow;
　　b. Tamworth; Samuel Pettingill and Sally Brown

Sally, d. 5/18/1892 at 98/7/15; housework

PHENIX,
Richard, d. 8/10/2001 in Wolfeboro; Spencer Phenix and Evelyn Bolles

PHILBRICK,
Stephen, d. 3/11/1931 at 81/6/18
Susanna, d. 3/7/1905 at 91/3/15 in Tamworth; housekeeping; widow; b. Northwood

PHILLIPS,
Charles E., d. 1/26/1935 at 69/7/23
Ethel Margaret, d. 11/11/1971 at 78 in Tamworth; b. Canada; residence - Tamworth
Joseph Leo, d. 10/24/1967 at 82 in Tamworth; b. Dorchester, MA; residence - Tamworth

PICKERING,
Belle L., d. 10/4/1918 at 29/10/6; la grippe; housewife; married; b. Laconia; James Gilman and Hattie Davis

PIERCE,
George Albert, d. 10/14/1936 at 84/5/23

PILLSBURY,
Enoch Freeman, d. 3/29/1923 at 86/0/25; b. Saco, ME; Samuel Pillsbury and Jane Sutherland

PINKHAM,
Bertha M., d. 11/18/1955 at 57 in Berwick, ME
Frank M., d. 4/4/1901 at 42/1/23 in Melrose, MA

PIPER,
Jennifer M., d. 6/21/1988 in Wolfeboro; Bruce Madison Piper and Patricia A. Nadeau
Orra L., d. 4/4/1902 at 92/6/5; b. Braintree, VT; ----- Laport and Polly Claflin
Pollard, d. 1/7/1927 at 16/3/1

PLANT,
Annie, d. 2/20/1903 at 17 in Tamworth; single; b. Tamworth; Joseph Plant (Canada) and Ellen Morrill (Oldtown, ME)
Joseph, d. 5/9/1919 at 76/7; farmer; b. Quebec; Elijah Plant

PLUMMER,
Charles Franklin, d. 12/6/1995 in Wolfeboro; Clarence Plummer and Luella Sturgeon

POLLARD,
Edward S., d. 6/5/1914 at 58/11/11; chronic nephritis; merchant; married; b. Tamworth; Jonathan W. Pollard and Sarah Moulton

POWELL,
Wayne, d. 11/30/1980 in Tamworth; Richard Powell and Francis Heyl

POWERS,
Bertha B., d. 1/21/1956 at 84 in Laconia
Doris Arline, d. 9/5/1970 at 62 in Bridgton, ME; buried in Tamworth
Ira Linns, d. 1/12/1942 at 73/6/13 in New Hampton

PRAY,
Harriett L., d. 6/10/1947 at 76/8/24 in Exeter
Julian, d. 7/23/1903 at 0/1 in Tamworth; b. Tamworth; Joseph Pray (Salmon Falls) and Harriet Montague (Halifax)

PRESCOTT,
James, d. 7/28/1956 at 80/1/12 in Laconia
Mary, d. 8/4/1893 at -- in Tamworth; housekeeper; married; William Foley (England) and Mercy Bradford (Missipee)

PREWITT,
Charles R., Jr., d. 8/16/1948 at 13/6 in Tamworth

PRICE,
William, d. 2/7/1911 at 91/11/3 in Tamworth; laborer; widower; b. Tamworth; John Price

PRIEST,
Ronald G., Jr., d. 4/27/1986 in Tamworth; Ronald G. Priest, Sr. and Evelyn Perkins

PRINCE,
Edward P., d. 1/11/1980 in Hanover; Herbert Prince and Ethel Abernathy
Herbert William, d. 12/18/1968 at 90 in Laconia; b. England; residence – Tamworth

PROVENZANO,
Salvatore, d. 3/29/1987 in N. Conway; Joseph Provenzano and Teresa DiBello

PURRINGTON,
Augustus E., d. 7/5/1955 at 85/1/18 in Ossipee (1956)
David A., d. 11/27/1908 at 35/4/25 in Tamworth; married; b. Tamworth; W. H. Davis (Effingham) and Mary M. Mooney (Nashua)

PURVES,
Anita P., d. 3/11/1975 at 35 in Champaign, IL

PUTNAM,
Sarah Gooll, d. 10/4/1912 at 61/6/16 in Tamworth; artist; single; b. Boston, MA; John P. Putnam (Salem, MA) and Harriet Upham (Boston, MA)

QUIMBY,
Lucy, d. 10/22/1908 at 94/3/6 in Tamworth; widow; b. Sandwich; John Fellows (Sandwich) and Meriam Jewell (Sandwich)
Lucy B., d. 11/6/1895 at 79/6 in Tamworth
Preston, d. 9/16/1901 at 48 in Danvers, MA; painter; married; b. Sandwich; Alvah Quimby (Sandwich) and Lucy Fellows (Sandwich)

QUIRON,
Philias, d. 2/2/1951 at 69/4 in Tamworth

RAABE,
Ralph Paul Max, d. 11/17/1997 in Wolfeboro; Henrich Raabe and Gertrude Lemmer
Wanda V., d. 11/19/1994 in Wolfeboro; Frank Swiader and Marya Pisiaky

RAND,
Ezekiel D., d. 6/11/1890 at 72/2 in Tamworth; farmer; married; b. Perry, ME; Aseph Rand (Pembroke) and Lucy Cushing (Pembroke, MA)
Lucy, d. -/-/1896 at 56/9/2 in Tamworth; housework

RAUNSAVILLE,
Benjamin H., d. --/--/1894 at 30 in Tamworth; journalist; single

READ,
Richard Welch, d. 7/23/1974 at 73 in Wolfeboro; b. MA; residence - Tamworth

RECORD,
Charles W., d. 10/17/2001 in N. Conway; Alden Record and Amy Campbell

REDDEN,
Mary E., d. 3/18/1999 in Lebanon; William Dickerson and Juanita Amburgey

REED,
Clara E., d. 8/16/1989 in Tamworth; Claes Enebuske and Sara Folsom

REHM,
William H., d. 5/24/2002 in Tamworth; Henry Rehm and Margaret Hoehn

REITZ,
Lizzie M., d. 8/12/1899 at 33/1/15 in Tamworth; married; Charles McNichols

REMICK,
Amanda W., d. --/--/1894 at 60/1/5 in Tamworth; housekeeper; married; b. Piermont; Stilman Tarlton (Piermont) and Harriet Webster (Piermont)
Ann J., d. 5/25/1923 at 86/9/5; b. Exeter; William Hurd and Caroline Blaisdell
Annie M., d. 5/12/1930 at 68/7/19
Betsy P., d. 3/21/1907 at 80/11/6 in Tamworth; housework; married; b. Sandwich; Asa Prescott (Sandwich) and Dolly Currier (Sandwich)
Charles H., d. 10/24/1906 at 80/8/11 in Tamworth; farmer; widower; b. Tamworth; Enoch Remick (Augusta, ME) and Lucinda Edgell (Tamworth)
Charles Haywood, d. 11/20/1912 at 51/11/25 in Tamworth; farmer; married; b. Tamworth; Levi E. Remick (Tamworth) and Harriet Beede (Tamworth)
Dexter, d. 10/27/1935 at 99/1/12
Earle, d. 2/22/1975 at 74 in Concord; b. NH; residence - Tamworth
Edwin, Dr., d. 6/5/1935 at 69/0/7
Edwin Crafts, d. 7/20/1993 in Tamworth; Edwin Remick and Emily A. Crafts
Elizabeth A., d. 6/27/1944 at 32/7/5 in Tamworth
Emily A. C., d. 4/30/1911 at 49/4/4 in Tamworth; housewife; married; b. Roxbury, MA; William A. Craft (Roxbury, MA) and Emily Daggett (Roxbury, MA)
Florence E., d. 12/2/1933 at 70/4/23
Frank, d. 6/18/1913 at 62/6/29 in Tamworth; mechanic; married; b. Tamworth; Samuel E. Remick and Hannah Hatch
Fred, d. 2/25/1958 at 88 in Laconia
George W., d. 12/28/1903 at 79/5/4 in Tamworth; carpenter; widower; b. Parsonsfield; Nathaniel Remick (Parsonsfield) and Esther Nickerson (Ossipee)
Hannah R., d. 3/8/1905 at 80/5/23 in Tamworth; housekeeping; widow; b. Tamworth; Newton S. Hatch (Tamworth) and Hannah Howard (Bridgewater, MA)
Harriet, d. 3/27/1905 at 78/0/3 in Tamworth; housekeeping; widow; b. Tamworth; Samuel S. Beede (Sandwich) and Nancy Boyden (Tamworth)
Harry H., d. 12/27/1933 at 70/10/15
Henry A., d. 5/25/1916 at 96/0/29; old age; widower; b. Tamworth; Henry Remick and Mary Howard

Herbert S., d. 1/15/1941 at 77/9/23 in Tamworth
Isabella, d. 1/10/1892 at 76/11/27 in Tamworth; housework; widow;
  b. Buxton, ME; William Paul and Isabella Thomas
James E., d. 4/3/1887 at 61/3/7 in Tamworth; farmer; married; b.
  Tamworth; James Remick (Tamworth) and Sally Edgell
  (Gardner, MA)
John, d. 6/30/1895 at 78/10/17 in Tamworth; farmer; widower; b.
  Tamworth; James Remick and Sally Edgell
Levi E., d. 7/7/1897 at 74/0/21 in Tamworth; merchant; married; b.
  Tamworth; Enoch Remick and Lucinda Edgell
Levi Wadsworth, d. 12/6/1971 at 76 in Tamworth; b. NH; residence -
  Tamworth
Lucy A., d. 9/30/1920 at 60/4/25 in Tamworth; tumor of the breast;
  farmer; widow; Edward W. Bradbury and Ester M. Yeaton
Margaret C., d. 2/27/1990 in Wolfeboro; Ansel Cummings and Rosie
  B. Brown
Marian, d. 10/30/1980 in Tamworth; Harry Miles and Ethel Edgerly
Mary K., d. 10/1?/1929 at 77/4/1
William Martin, d. 2/15/1920 at 62/7/16 in Tamworth; chronic cystitis;
  farmer; married; Henry Alvin Remick and Betsy P. Prescott
Winifred O., d. 3/7/1950 at 72 in Concord

REYCROFT,
George M., d. 2/18/1974 at 75 in Laconia; b. MA; residence -
  Chocorua

RICH,
William Coulter, d. 8/28/1965 at 76 in Laconia; b. Boston, MA;
  residence - Tamworth

RICHARDS,
Flavelle, d. 9/9/1989 in N. Conway; John E. Stewart and Ann Lee
  Knox

RICHARDSON,
Bertha M., d. 9/7/1939 at 58/1/7; b. Conway

RICKARD,
George, d. 10/6/1948 at 86/4/24 in Wolfeboro
Hanford E., d. 3/12/1961 at 56 in Manchester

RIDINGS,
Eliza, d. 3/26/1923 at 80/1/15; b. N. Chelmsford, MA; Peter Ridings and Amelia Healey

RIVERS,
Cecil G., d. 1/14/2000 in Portland, ME; George Rivers and Minnie Bumps

ROBARGE,
Bulah, d. 2/1/1914 at 1/4/0; convulsions; b. Tuftonbori; Lewis Robarge and Bessie Elliott
Irene, d. 10/22/1946 at 26/11/6 in Concord

ROBERGE,
Elizabeth A., d. 11/13/1957 at 75 in Wolfeboro

ROBERTS,
Alice Maude, d.11/8/1965 at 74 in Laconia; b. Tamworth; residence - Tamworth
Charles E., d. 3/27/2001 in Laconia; Heman Roberts and Maude Chase
Charles K., d. 7/13/1912 at 78/6/12 in Tamworth; expressman; widower; b. Tamworth; Daniel Roberts (Tamworth) and Sally Parrott (Sandwich)
Edgar J., d. 10/17/1936 at 64/9/4
Eva May, d. 10/25/1947 at 78/0/14 in Tamworth
F. M., d. 9/8/1908 at 71/1/29 in Tamworth; married; b. New Castle, ME; D. Montgomery (New Castle, ME)
George O., d. 9/9/1897 at 52/6/21 in Tamworth; farmer; married; b. Tamworth; Daniel Roberts (Ossipee) and Sally Parrott (Lynn, MA)
Hannah E., d. 1/7/1917 at 69/10/8; pneumonia; widow; b. Albany; James Emery and Mary Brown
Hannah J. N., d. 4/14/1899 at 70/0/5 in Tamworth; housewife; widow; b. Meredith; Joseph Neal (Meredith) and Lucy Dow (Meredith)
Harry C., d. 1/8/1969 at 91 in Center Harbor; b. NH; residence - Tamworth
Joseph F., d. 8/8/1888 at 63/5/5; farmer; married; b. Strafford; Joseph Roberts (Strafford) and Mary D. Donalds (Strafford)
Mary E., d. 7/14/1950 at 82 in Laconia

Thelma H., d. 6/9/1986 in Laconia; Frank Harvey and Charla Maxfield

ROBERTSON,
Charles, d. 7/13/1914 at 76/6/18; cerebral embolism; retired; married; b. Eaton; Robert Robertson and Lydia Nickerson
Eleanor, d. 10/16/1918 at 28/4/30; la grippe; at home; single; b. Tamworth; Jesse N. Robertson and Ida M. Thurston
Emma J., d. 9/3/1942 at 94/2/18 in Tamworth
Jesse N., d. 6/8/1936 at 73/5/3
Mark E., d. 4/18/1935 at 69/1/2

ROBINSON,
Addison R., d. 1/22/1940 at 94/3/9; b. Meredith
Annie F., d. 4/30/1900 at 0/5/7 in Tamworth; b. Tamworth; Henry B. Robinson (Tamworth) and Laura M. Gilman (Boston)
Bertha, d. 2/26/1913 at 32/11/27 in Tamworth; housekeeping; married; b. Tamworth; Levi W. Bunker and Hattie Ross Webber
Evelyn S., d. 4/1/1960 at 70 in Conway
Fred, d. 12/31/1895 at 0/7/15 in Tamworth; b. Tamworth; Henry B. Robinson (Tamworth) and Mary L. Wiggin (Tamworth)
Harry E., d. 6/26/1936 at 61/11/17
Henry B., d. 4/13/1954 at 87 in Concord
Henry E., d. 1/9/2003 in Laconia; Harry Robinson and Evelyn Ward
Henry W., d. 3/1/1974 at 81 in Ossipee; b. NH; residence - Tamworth
Herman L., d. 4/2/1992 in Dover; Thomas Robinson and Millie Glover
Margaret H., d. 6/8/1953 at 85/6/14 in Moultonboro
Mary, d. 4/--/1895 at 23/6/6 in Tamworth; married; b. Tamworth; Arthur E. Wiggin (Tamworth) and Mary F. Dorman
Nellie M., d. 4/3/1887 at 37/11 in Tamworth; housekeeper; married; b. Sandwich; Oscar Swazey (Laconia) and Jane Horn (Moultonboro)
Otis S., d. 12/2/1898 at 68/9/18 in Tamworth; shoemaker; married; b. Baldwin, ME; Thomas Robertson (sic) and Betsy Brewster

ROCCA,
Paul Hugo, d. 4/1/1996 in N. Conway; Paul F. Rocca and Dianne C. Norbert

ROCKSTROM,
Carl E., d. 12/1/1977 at 81 in Laconia; b. NH; residence - Tamworth

ROLLINS,
Marion B., d. 6/19/1979 at Westmoreland; William Nelson and Margery Campbell
Maurice Leon, d. 12/27/1967 at 75 in Laconia; b. Moultonboro; residence - Tamworth

ROSE,
Sally, d. 10/24/1891 at 73/0/8 in Tamworth; housewife; widow; b. Conway; William Willey and Sally Head

ROSS,
Alice M., d. 2/14/1891 at 0/7/12 in Tamworth; b. Tamworth; Onslow Ross and Hattie A. Ross
Elizabeth, d. 7/22/1898 at 76/4 in Tamworth; married; b. Albany
Elizabeth Christine, d. 11/3/1962 at 82 in Claremont; b. New London, CT; residence - Claremont
Emma G., d. 5/3/1904 at 38/1/15 in Tamworth; housewife; married; b. Albany; Jeremiah Harriman (Conway) and Mary E. Mason (Albany)
Ernest E., d. 3/31/1888 at 2/9; b. Tamworth; John W. Ross (Albany) and Hattie E. Knox (Tamworth)
Grace E., d. 12/29/1993 in N. Conway; Frank Kennett and Emma Sanborn
Harold E., d. 4/4/1978 at 86 in N. Conway; b. NH; residence - Tamworth
Harriet A., d. 10/18/1936 at 79/6
John, d. 5/11/1920 at 65 in Tamworth; chronic nephritis; farmer; married; William Ross and Sarah Willey
Kennett, d. 10/2/1985 in N. Conway; Harold Ross and Grace Kennett
Mark S., d. 3/24/1932 at 77/5/13
Onslow S., d. 2/27/1935 at 78/7/4
Paul C., d. 3/29/1900 at 85 in Tamworth; farmer; widower; b. Newfield, ME; Robert Ross (England)
Sophia, d. 12/14/1916 at 74/8/278; cerebral apoplexy; single; b. Albany; William Ross and Sally Willey

William, d. 11/20/1887 at 73/2/20 in Tamworth; farmer; married; b. Newfield, ME; Robert Ross (London, England) and Martha Rowe (Baldwin, ME)

ROUX,
Antoine J., d. 8/5/1958 at 49 in Tamworth

ROWE,
Allan, III, d. 3/2/1981 in Tamworth; Allan Rowe, Jr. and Arline Vachon
Gertrude Mary Eleanor, d. 5/10/1971 at 79 in Tamworth; b. Quebec; residence - Tamworth
Grace Aurelia, d. 3/23/1993 in Wolfeboro; Edwin Lawn and Frances Clark

ROWLAND,
Zella A., d. 1/25/1949 at 83/2/13 in Tamworth

RUNNEL[L]S,
Helen R., d. 9/17/1918 at 74/3/19; chronic Bright's disease; housewife; married; b. Tamworth; Nathaniel B. Baker and Lucretia Ten Broeck
Huldah S., d. 6/26/1906 at 86/8/23 in Tamworth; widow; b. Berwick, ME
John, Rev., d. 9/2/1887 at 70/5/21 in Tamworth; clergyman; married; b. Acton, ME; Samuel Runnells and Hannah Farnham (Acton, ME)
John Sumner, d. 7/7/1929 at 84/11/11

RUSSELL,
Harriet Bates, d. 3/2/1998 in Chocorua; Javan Mason Russell and Edith Maude Legros

RYDER,
Alton Eugene, d. 11/30/1998 in Tamworth; Perley Ryder and Gertrude Kingston
Gertrude Elizabeth, d. 8/22/1998 in Laconia; George L. Kingston and Mary Elizabeth Adams
Perley Almon, d. 7/27/1998 in Tamworth; William Ryder and Nellie Carlisle

ST. LAURENT,
Lionel J., d. 1/8/1962 at 35 in Tamworth; b. Manchester; residence – Manchester

SAGONA,
Ada Mae, d. 7/11/1968 at 75 in Edgehill Inn; b. NY; residence – Tamworth
Charles Lindsay, d. 2/21/1985 in Hanover; Charles Sagona and Mary MacKinnon

SALMONS,
Florence H., d. 5/22/1964 at 73 in Tamworth; b. Missouri; residence - Tamworth

SALVAGE,
Abbin M., d. --/--/1894 at 24/9/25 in Tamworth; housekeeper; married; b. Laconia; James Fullerton (Sandwich) and Martha J. Diamon (Loudon)

SAMPSON,
Theresa, d. 2/12/1968 at 87 in Laconia; b. NY; residence - Tamworth

SANBORN,
Alice E., d. 10/13/1936 at 54/6/20
Ellis R., d. 10/5/1918 at 24/0/20; lobar pneumonia; soldier; single; b. Hanover; John F. Sanborn and Addie Green
John F., d. 12/17/1931 at 67/8/7
John W., d. 7/8/1901 at 65/3/6 in Needham, MA; farmer; widower; b. Somersworth; Solomon Sanborn (Somersworth) and Lepha Brown (MA)
Joseph P., d. 7/20/1899 at 80/4/1 in Tamworth; farmer; widower; b. Tamworth; Daniel Sanborn (Tamworth) and Lydia Cushing (Tamworth)
Lucetta, d. 8/9/1897 at 58/5/19 in Tamworth; housewife; married; b. Tamworth; Samuel Clough
Mercy, d. 3/4/1891 at 89/0/19 in Tamworth; widow; b. Saco, ME
Olive C., d. 10/13/1897 at 75/3/8 in Tamworth; housekeeping; widow; b. Tamworth; ----- Bryer and ----- Cook
Raymond Francis, d. 10/8/1997 in Tilton; Raymond Sanborn and Marguerite Mitchell

Sarah E., d. 3/19/1905 at 84/4/16 in Tamworth; housekeeping; widow; b. Rochester; Thomas Roberts (Rochester) and Mehitable Jones

SANDERSON,
Frances A., d. 1/6/1924 at 71

SARGENT,
Alice Marguerite, d. 3/7/1990 in Wolfeboro; Austin Wiggin and Helen Porter
Edward A., d. 7/11/1994 in Tamworth; Osgood Sargent and Clara Allard
Mary E., d. 11/16/1901 at 11/16/1901 at 34/0/10 in Tamworth; housewife; married; b. Haverhill, MA; Charles E. Gould and Mary Wedgewood

SAULNIER,
Addie May, d. 8/23/1970 at 96 in Ossipee; b. NH; residence - Tamworth
John, d. 12/1/1929 at 58/11/18

SAUNDERS,
William B., d. 5/12/1956 at 56/10/29 in Tamworth

SAVARD,
Albert Joseph, d. 6/26/1965 at 77 in Tamworth; b. Quebec; residence - Tamworth
Mildred E., d. 5/17/1943 at 48/8/28 in Laconia

SAYRE,
Robert T., d. 3/9/1977 at 65 in Tamworth; b. NJ; residence - NY

SCARS,
Patricia M., d. 9/9/2000 in Wolfeboro; Paul Trundy and Ruby Phillips

SCEGGELL,
Harvey, d. 6/25/1907 at 0/2/1 in Tamworth; b. Tamworth; A. B. Sceggell (Springvale, ME) and Belle Gilman (Tamworth)

SCHANSCHIEFF,
Peter, d. 3/1/1992 in Ossipee

SCHENCK,
Abram T., d. 7/12/1900 at 66/5 in Tamworth; laborer; widower; b. Newark, NJ; Peter C. Schenck (NJ) and Rebecca Harris (NJ)
Sarah E., d. 7/1/1922 at –

SCHMIDT,
Peter Gerrit, d. 3/31/1969 at 4 in Westerly, RI; residence – RI; buried in Tamworth

SCHMITT,
Hanna N., d. 4/29/2003 in Tamworth; George Schmitt and Hazel Fazakerley

SCHOOLCRAFT,
Pearl E., d. 5/25/1901 at 0/8/4 in Tamworth; b. Tamworth; W. B. Schoolcraft (Boston, MA) and Edith M. Moulton (Albany)

SCHULTZE,
Joan B., d. 9/13/2000 in Wolfeboro; William Scruton and Mildred Stone

SCOTT,
Emma A., d. 4/21/1970 at 70 in Wolfeboro; b. MA; residence - Tamworth

SCRUTON,
Lorraine, d. 12/8/2000 in Wolfeboro; William Stone and Alice Watkins

SEAVEY,
Annie, d. 12/8/1974 at 84 in Laconia; b. England; residence - Tamworth
Harriet N., d. 8/20/1916 at 95/9/2; old age; widow; b. Jackson; Josiah Hackett and Isabel Woodis

SEELEY,
Eva Burnell, d. 12/28/1985 in Laconia; Arthur Burnell and Lea DeLorme
Milton J., d. 5/28/1943 at 51/9/2 in Wolfeboro

SEIDERS,
Gertrude H., d. 7/18/1985 in Tamworth; Robert Henry and Ava Brown

SHANNON,
Bernard, Jr., d. 12/5/1980 in N. Conway; Bernard Shannon and Carole Kennedy
Cora E., d. 9/2/1929 at 64/6/24
Grace, d. 2/18/1947 at 72/6/18 in Tamworth
Sarah E., d. 1/15/1914 at 75/7/8; senility; housewife; widow; b. Tamworth; Ebenezer E. Edgerley and Abigail Cate

SHARP,
female, d. 8/18/1912 at – in Tamworth; summer guest; married

SHARPLES,
Robert E., d. 2/25/1994 in Wolfeboro; Thomas Sharples and Gertrude I. Duffy

SHAUGHNESSY,
Mary G., d. 3/4/1978 at 73 in Wolfeboro; b. MA; residence – Tamworth

SHAW,
George Edmund, d. 12/5/1969 at 70 in Laconia; b. Peabody, MA; residence – Tamworth
Marion, d. 5/26/1984 in N. Conway; Frank Stever and Alice Goodwin

SHAYOWITZ,
Max, d. 9/1/1965 at 76 in Meredith; b. Hungary; residence - Tamworth

SHEPPARD,
Robert A., d. 9/1/2001 in Chocorua; Horace Sheppard and Beulah Weeks

SIAS,
Frances, d. 3/30/1952 at 68/9/17 in Tamworth

SIDWELL-THOMPSON,
Doris May, d. 8/9/1994 in Tamworth; Stephen Sidwell and Helen Hayden

SILVAN,
Emanuel J., d. 12/23/1935 at 67/11/18
Fannie A., d. 3/23/1933 at 75/5/17

SIMPSON,
Eleanor J., d. 5/11/1957 at 70 in Wonalancet
Norman C., d. 4/19/1951 at 73 in Tamworth

SKETCHLEY,
Shirley A., d. 8/27/2002 in Wolfeboro; Walter Graham and Jenny Harmon

SMALL,
Everett F., d. 8/17/1921 at 73/6; senility acute dementia; R. R.; widower; b. Union, ME

SMALLEY,
Helen C., d. 7/22/2000 in N. Conway; Walter Binner and Helen Pratt
Stearns Hibbard, d. 8/18/1995 in Laconia; Frank Hibbard Smalley and Elsie Lewis

SMART,
Addie E., d. 3/13/1900 at 51/9/12 in Tamworth; housewife; married; b. Tamworth; Daniel Berry and Irene Hyde (Wolfeboro)
Jacob P., d. 5/25/1887 at 77/3/13 in Tamworth; married; b. Ossipee; Winthrop Smart and ----- Heard

SMITH,
Albert W., d. 5/24/1954 at 81/10/10 in Laconia
Alice Jane, d. 3/26/1933 at 62/6/26
Allen L., d. 1/8/1917 at 88/10/6; pneumonia; farmer; widower; b. Tamworth; Simon Smith
Amy T., d. 3/23/1933 at 59/3/12
Annie Blaisdell, d. 8/26/1936 at 79/6/15
Arthur W., d. 10/27/1927 at 65/10/16
Betsey J., d. 4/8/1905 at 69/4 in Tamworth; housekeeping; widow; b. ME; Amasa Moody and Mary A. Cooley

Blanche Madeline, d. 12/1/1988 in Wolfeboro; Zemeri E. Ames and
   Ella A. Palmer
Charles C., d. 9/27/1943 at 87/7/28 in Tamworth
Curtis, d. 9/16/1914 at 4/2/12; cerebrospinal meningitis; b.
   Tamworth; Clarence Smith and Cora Forrest
Elizabeth F., d. 1/30/1948 at 93/10/18 in Tamworth
Frank, d. 5/10/1956 at 64 in Moultonboro
Gertrude, d. 12/16/1974 at 86 in Ossipee; b. Lynn, MA; residence –
   S. Tamworth
Gilbert, d. 12/9/1914 at 62/11/0; organic heart disease; farmer;
   widower; b. Tamworth; J. B. Smith and Abigail Price
Gilman A., d. 12/5/1983 in Laconia; Charles Smith and Elizabeth ----
Hattie M., d. 4/6/1931 at 56/9/2
Henry B., d. 10/29/1923 at 75/0/2; b. Tamworth; Jacob G. Smith and
   Abigail Price
Lamont C., d. 6/17/1953 at 73/8/6 in Tamworth
Marion E., d. 8/19/1994 in Tamworth; Harry L. Smith and Florence
   Bryant
Marshall E., d. 8/29/1942 at 68/11/6 in Tamworth
Miney, d. 5/30/1938 at 56/8/12; b. St. John, NB
Nellie H., d. 2/19/1954 at 77 in Laconia
Perley A., d. 3/24/1972 at 86 in Center Harbor; b. NH; residence -
   Tamworth
Ralph Binford, d. 1/21/1965 at 81 in York, ME; b. Tamworth;
   residence – Tamworth
Sarah Christine, d. 12/28/1969 at 77 in Dover; residence –
   Portsmouth; buried in Tamworth
Sarah J., d. 2/23/1920 at 87/11/3 in Tamworth; old age; farmer;
   married; William Ralston
Susan, d. 9/14/1897 at 73/10/28 in Tamworth; housekeeping; widow
Walter C., d. 5/28/1936 at 69/8/18
Wayne Scott, d. 8/6/1988 in Tamworth; Stephen W. Smith and Carol
   L. Ryan

SMULL,
Mavis L., d. 9/5/2001 in Wolfeboro; Barrow Lyons and Ann Burrows

SNELL,
Ada F., d. 8/31/1932 at 55/5/2
Willard, d. 9/7/1901 at 73/2/23 in Tamworth; laborer; single; b.
   Eaton; Eleazer Snell and Polly Danforth

SNOW,
Ella A., d. 11/6/1951 at 98/4/8 in Tamworth
Stanley Carman, d. 3/25/1987 in Chocorua; Elliot Snow and Louise Carman

SOUZA,
Alan J., d. 9/3/1983 in Tamworth; Edward Souza and Evelyn Bandarra

SPALDING,
Florence A., d. 11/21/1955 at 78 in Wolfeboro

SPAULDING,
Addison C., d. 9/20/1927 at 85/5/20
Annie M., d. 11/15/1919 at 44/9/22; housekeeper; single; b. Tamworth; Addison C. Spaulding and Ida May Felch
Eunice M., d. 1/14/1954 at 68/0/11 in Tamworth
Ida M., d. 12/9/1895 at 45/6/21 in Tamworth; housekeeper; married
Robert C., d. 4/27/1953 at 72 in Tamworth

SPAYD,
Bertha N., d. 6/14/2000 in Wolfeboro; Marti Niemi and Lempi Mackey
Frank E., Jr., d. 2/24/1993 in Manchester; Frank E. Spayd, Sr. and Irene Deforge

SPECKMAN,
Boyd H., d. 4/5/1971 at 17 in Wolfeboro; b. NH; residence - Tamworth

SPENCE[R]L[E]Y,
Clara H., d. 3/1/1914 at 29/7/17; tuberculosis of lungs; housework; widow; b. Boston, MA; Henry W. Holbrook and Minnie A. Cook
J. W., d. 10/17/1908 at 42/6/10 in Tamworth; engraver; married; b. Boston, MA; C. Spencerly and Rebecca Staples
Richard Colby, d. 7/30/1981 in Virgin Islands; Joseph Spenceley and Clare Holbrook

SPICER,
Ane A., d. 11/7/1957 at 88 in Wolfeboro

Elizabeth Sawyer, d. 1/16/1996 in Tamworth; Edmund F. Sawyer and Mary Stoddard

SPOONER,
Norman, d. 7/16/1955 at 20 in Tamworth

SPOTHOLTZ,
Frederick Edward, d. 3/25/1993 in N. Conway; Fred John Charles Spotholtz and Anna Kallman

STACY,
Gladys M., d. 12/16/1933 at 31/5
Nathan J., d. 6/14/1964 at 62 in Wolfeboro; b. Madison; residence - Tamworth

STANCHFIELD,
Lena A., d. 5/1/1934 at 60/7/20

STANDLY,
Stephen, d. 3/25/1887 at 68/7/0 in Tamworth; farmer; married; b. Wenham, MA; Nehemiah Standley and Abigail Young

STANIS,
Cindy Ann, d. 9/13/2000 in Tamworth; Gordan Evans and Marilyn Larrabee

STANLEY,
M. M., d. 7/11/1908 at 76/6/15 in Tamworth; widow; b. Madison; Caleb Jackson (Madison) and Katie Keniston

STAPLES,
George E., d. 2/11/1939 at 79/6/28; b. Tamworth
Mildred Goodwin, d. 1/21/1967 at 48 in Laconia; b. Eliot, ME; residence - Tamworth
Myron Winslow, d. 7/9/1929 at 59
Virginia B., d. 1/30/2000 in Portland, ME; Earl Bennett and Louise Harriman

STEARNS,
Aldo Mason, d. 10/5/1964 at 65 in Tamworth; b. Tamworth; residence – Tamworth

Angeline G., d. 1/24/2000 in Chocorua; Leonard Guerriero and Rosaria Serene

Marie E., d. 7/22/1977 at 83 in Laconia; b. MA; residence - Tamworth

STEELE,
Frederic L., d. 2/20/1939 at 49/3/8; b. Cincinnati, OH

Margaret, d. 9/22/1980 in Tamworth; Edward Twitchell and Elizabeth Schuster

Mary L., d. 8/21/2002 in Tamworth; Robert Lloyd and Isabelle Goodwin

STEVENS,
Esther F., d. 11/25/1972 at 67 in Wolfeboro; b. NH; residence - Tamworth

Frances, d. 7/2/2000 in Laconia; Chester Barnard and Maion Chaffee

Sadie M., d. 3/29/1953 at 82 in Tamworth

STEVENSON,
Alberta F., d. 12/3/1918 at 53/11/25; intestinal trouble; housewife; married; b. Laconia; Pike G. Perkins and Mary A. Eastman

Augusta A., d. 2/4/1923 at 93/3/11; b. Tamworth; John W. Stevenson and Martha Boyden

Charles, d. 8/23/1936 at 82/5/17

Thomas, d. --/--/1894 at 74/8 in Tamworth; miller; married; b. Tamworth; Enoch Stevenson (Tamworth)

STEWARD,
Grace Edith, d. 10/19/1993 in Tamworth; Levi McClintock and Alalia Callahan

John E., d. 7/28/1994 in Tamworth; John J. Stewart and Minnie Smith

STEWART,
John E., Jr., d. 8/26/1986 in N. Conway; Ezra D. Stewart and Leolia Stamper

STINSON,
David, d. 10/8/1887 at 67 in Tamworth; farmer; married; b. Derry

STODDARD,
Maude A., d. 6/4/1953 at 18 in Wolfeboro

STONE,
Irene L., d. 5/9/2000 in Wolfeboro; John Leso and Anna Lucca
Margaret G., d. 10/2/1953 at 88 in Tamworth
Philip William, d. 7/2/1999 in Tamworth; Lothrop Stone and Ethel Jacobs

STOREY,
William E., d. 2/7/1903 at 72/3/22 in Albany; farmer; widower; b. MA

STRASHON,
Harry, d. 2/26/1923 at 58; b. Russia; Samech Strashon and Rachel Derzen

STRAW,
Lloyd, d. 6/7/1981 in Tamworth; Albert Straw and J. Wilson

STRAWBACK,
Susie, d. 8/11/1912 at 15/11 in Tamworth; waitress; single; b. Chicago, IL

STREETER,
Charles Gray, d. 6/27/1962 at 73 in Center Harbor; b. Lancaster; residence – Tamworth
Joseph A., d. 7/14/1982 in Laconia; Charles Streeter and Sybil Potter
Lorraine Evans, d. 1/9/1998 in Tamworth; Almon G. Evans and Gladys Corbett
Minda Michelle, d. 9/19/1995 in Tamworth; William Mason and Kathleen Gregory
Richard L., d. 2/3/1994 in Laconia; Clifford R. Streeter and Lorraine Evans

STURDIVANT,
Leon H., d. 2/9/1942 at 74/10/4 in Tamworth

SULLIVAN,
Delia, d. 7/25/1913 at 26 in Tamworth; servant

George A., Jr., d. 1/8/1962 at 40 in Tamworth; b. Manchester;
    residence - Manchester
Sadie M., d. 2/8/1910 at 34/5/11 in Tamworth

SUMBERG,
Rosalie, d. 7/11/1933 at 53/4/27

SUTHERLAND,
Donald M., d. 2/19/1991 in N. Conway; George H. Sutherland and
    Ruth E. Morse
Elizabeth H., d. 5/4/2000 in Manchester; Samuel Hidden and Helen
    Bassett

SYLVIA,
Robert O., d. 5/12/2000 in N. Conway; Roger Sylvia and Ione
    Hersey

TAGGETT,
Charles W., Jr., d. 10/3/1942 at 2/7/26 in Conway

TAPLIN,
George E., d. 9/9/1928 at 19/0/2

TAPPAN,
Fred, d. 5/2/1956 at 86/3/16 in Tamworth
Henry Russell, d. 12/9/1993 in Tamworth; Fred Tappan and Abbie
    Wakefield
Ina V., d. 8/13/1957 at 76 in Laconia
Margaret V., d. 4/25/2000 in Laconia; Herbert Vittum and Alice Clark

TAYLOR,
Albert Brown, d. 1/20/1963 at 77 in Laconia; residence – Waltham,
    MA; buried in Tamworth
Alice Remick, d. 6/9/1916 at 53/3/29; heart disease and dropsy;
    married; b. Tamworth; Levi E. Remick and Harriet Beede
Geraldine, d. 2/4/1981 in Laconia; Eli Bliss and Hannah Ham
Harry C., d. 11/5/1958 at 73 in Lowell, MA
Nellie A., d. 2/1/1914 at 25/10/28; malignant disease of uterus;
    housewife; married; b. Tamworth; Samuel H. Jackson and
    Annie Purrington

TERRY,
Alfred, d. --/--/1894 at -- in Tamworth
Ernest, d. 4/19/1963 at 71 in Tamworth; b. Boston, MA; residence - Tamworth

TEWKSBURY,
Adeline, d. 7/31/1904 at 69/8/5 in rx; housewife; widow
Clayton, d. 10/9/1903 at 0/1/25 in Tamworth; b. Tamworth; W. Tewksbury (Sandwich) and Annette Barnes (Tamworth)
Eva M., d. 12/24/1949 at 69/9/23 in Rockingham
Mabel H., d. 9/2/1964 at 86 in Meredith; b. Madison; residence - Tamworth
Royal S., d. 12/3/1949 at 77/7/7 in Wolfeboro

THAYER,
John C., d. 8/21/1960 at 70 in Laconia

THOMAS,
Grace B., d. 8/17/1954 at 46/.2/14 in Wolfeboro
William J., d. 8/10/1994 in N. Conway; Henry Thomas and Mary Zehr

THOMPSON,
Alice Bemis, d. 11/17/1972 at 63 in Tamworth; b. Chestnut Hill, MA; residence - Tamworth
Arthur M., d. 9/9/1959 at 75 in Wolfeboro
Charles G., d. 5/21/1986 in Wolfeboro; William G. Thompson and Mary Huntington
Connie J., d. 10/15/1934 at 75/7
Elizabeth, d. 6/28/1994 in Laconia; Francis H. Allen and Margaret Hewins
Herbert B., d. 1/4/1944 at 80/6/6 in Tamworth
Major J., d. 1/2/1929 at 84/4/3
Maude, d. 11/17/1972 at 63 in Center Harbor; b. NH; residence – Tamworth
William, Rev., d. 11/19/1981 in Hanover; William Thompson and Mary Huntington

THORN,
Mrs. Elias, d. 5/1/1919 at 72/9/18; housewife; married; b. Madison; Timothy Gilman and Caroline Crocker

THURSTON,
Harriet Webster, d. 11/18/1975 at 87 in Conway; b. NH; residence - Conway
Howard Everett, d. 2/26/1966 at 55 in N. Conway; b. N. Fryeburg, ME; residence - Tamworth
Paris W., d. 2/1/1952 at 75 in Tamworth
Ralph Edward, d. 1/2/1963 at 63 in N. Conway; residence – Conway; buried in Tamworth

TIBBETTS,
George W., d. 9/22/1925 at 71

TIEDEMAN,
Maude, d. 1/26/1966 at 90 in Laconia; b. Cassville, Quebec; residence - Tamworth

TILTON,
Alice Lydia, d. 5/23/1914 at 49/3/25; tuberculosis; housewife; married; b. Tamworth; Otis Meader and Elizabeth Hoag
Caroline H., d. 8/22/1912 at 69/4/20 in Tamworth; housewife; widow; b. Wakefield; Simon Blake (Wakefield) and Caroline Whitney (Canada East)
Caroline T., d. 10/7/1900 at 0/3/7 in Tamworth; b. Conway; Ira B. Tilton (Tamworth) and Alice L. Meader (Tamworth)
Daniel Q., d. 1/24/1911 at 77/1/15 in Tamworth; farmer; married; b. Tamworth; Jesse Tilton (Sandwich) and Mahala Bean (Sandwich)
Elbridge Gerry, d. 11/25/1922 at 85/11/4; b. Sandwich; Samuel Tilton and Sarah Sinclair
Elizabeth J., d. 5/30/1916 at 79/0/6; gastric carcinoma; housewife; married; b. Tamworth; Charles A. Jackson and Elizabeth S. Dennett
John A., d. 11/18/1901 at 44/0/14 in Tamworth; farmer; single; b. Tamworth; William H. Tilton (Tamworth) and Mary Head (Tamworth)
Lloyd E., d. 10/16/1898 at 0/2 in Tamworth; b. Tamworth; Ira B. Tilton (Tamworth) and Alice Meader (Tamworth)
Mary E. A., d. 4/5/1916 at 80/5/20; old age; married; b. Tamworth; Daniel Head and Mary Bennett
William H., d. 6/5/1924 at 93

TITUS,
Benjamin A., d. 9/26/1910 at 64 in Tamworth; lumberman; married; b. NB; Benjamin A. Titus (NB) and Elizabeth Foster (NB)

TOBEY,
Evelyn M., d. 10/18/1926 at --

TOBIN,
Louise, d. 9/20/1910 at 37/0/8 in Tamworth; single; b. Boston, MA
Richard, d. 11/10/1953 at 75 in Conway
Stella A. S., d. 12/13/1966 at 88 in Tamworth; b. Bloomfield, NY; residence – Tamworth

TOLMAN,
Ruth Dunbar, d. 9/4/1974 at 88 in Tamworth; b. MA; residence - Chocorua

TOZZIER,
Annie, d. 10/5/1926 at 7/7/25

TRASK,
Arvilla, d. 10/25/1929 at 80/10
Elizabeth Bell, d. 4/4/1962 at 92 in Center Harbor; b. Sandwich; residence - Tamworth
Frank Wesley, d. 3/26/1929 at 59/3/8
Harold B., d. 6/16/1965 at 68 in Hartford, VT; b. Sandwich; residence – Tamworth
Robert H., d. 10/9/2001 in N. Conway; Harold Trask and Emma Moulton

TRIPP,
Dale F., d. 4/10/1986 in Tamworth; Roland Tripp and Violet Ellis
Eleanor B., d. 12/19/2003 in Manchester; Chester Bickford and Alice Cooper

TRUE,
Ann M., d. 9/21/1912 at 82/8/20 in Tamworth; housewife; widow; b. Gilmanton; Nathaniel Swasey (Gilmanton) and Hannah Griffin (Chester)

TUPPER,
Charles W., d. 12/5/1975 at 64 in Wolfeboro; b. MA; residence - Tamworth

TURNER,
Hortense M., d. 7/8/1972 at 59 in Wolfeboro; b. VT; residence - Tamworth

TWOMBLY,
Benjamin F., d. 6/1/1900 at 85/0/21 in Tamworth; farmer; widower; b. Barrington; Isaac Twombly (Madbury) and Sarah Frye (Strafford)

UNDERHILL,
George E., d. 1/21/1967 at 63 in Laconia; b. Madison; residence - Tamworth
Mary P., d. 1/30/1965 at 62 in Laconia; b. Sharon, VT; residence – Tamworth

VALCOURT,
Gertrude Louise, d. 1/25/1998 in Tamworth; Alvin Jerackas and Edna Caffrey

VALENTE,
Joseph A., Jr., d. 8/26/1968 at 20 on Rt. 16, Chocorua; b. MA; residence - Medford

VALENTINE,
Peter H., d. 7/3/1942 at 14/3/7 in Tamworth
Rita, d. 4/2/1981 in Tamworth; Paul Donnelly and Florence Clarke

VALLEY,
Alfonzo R., d. 11/14/1997 in N. Conway; Alfonzo R. Valley and Helen Berton

VARNEY,
Abby E., d. 9/14/1924 at 86
Charles, d. 11/9/1907 at 79/2/17 in Tamworth; farmer; widower; b. NY; Thomas Varney and Eunice Tabor
Charles E., d. 12/12/1954 at 18/10/20 in Tamworth
Clara E., d. 11/9/1939 at 78/4/25; b. Sandwich

Fred F., d. 3/3/1917 at 18/2/25; pulmonary tuberculosis; machinist; single; b. Tamworth; George O. Varney and Clara F. Bryer

George O., d. 12/16/1917 at 54/8/16; intestinal obstruction; farmer; married; b. W. Ossipee; Charles T. Varney and Hannah J. Hutchins

Gladys L., d. 3/28/1900 at 1/3/20 in Tamworth; b. Tamworth; George O. Varney (Ossipee) and Clara E. Bryer (Lakeport)

Loretta S., d. 3/14/1903 at 83/7/7 in Tamworth; widow; b. Center Harbor; William Paine (Center Harbor) and Mary Rogers (Center Harbor)

Nicholas H., d. 6/23/1900 at 67/0/7 in Tamworth; carpenter; married; b. Tamworth; Reuben Varney (Tamworth) and Sophia Moulton (Tamworth)

Ronald Edward, d. 1/16/1998 in Wolfeboro; Harold Varney and Viola Eldridge

VELIS,
Andrea, d. 10/5/1994 in N. Conway; Evangelo Capsambelis and Demitra -----

VILES,
Lester P., d. 4/20/1998 in Manchester; Charles Viles and Martha Shaw

VINTON,
Cora F., d. 5/5/1930 at 67/11/27
Earle B., d. 11/8/1959 at 89 in Tamworth
Edward C., d. 3/25/1933 at 89/3/2

VITTUM,
infant son, d. 11/21/1912 at 0/0/0 in Tamworth; b. Tamworth; Herbert A. Vittum (Sandwich) and Alice H. Clark (PEI)
Agnes A., d. 3/17/1977 at 81 in Madison; b. NH; residence – Tamworth
Alberta D., d. 12/17/1945 at 73/10/1 in Laconia
Alice H., d. 3/13/1960 at 78 in Tamworth
Cherolyn A., d. 9/1/1945 at 6/3/0 in Laconia
David, d. 7/25/1902 at 71/1/25 in Tamworth; laborer, b. Sandwich; Samuel Vittum (Sandwich)
Ernest F., d. 8/8/1965 at 80 in Tamworth; b. Sandwich; residence - Tamworth

Herbert A., d. 11/29/1957 at 74/8/20 in Tamworth
Jacob F., d. 8/13/1924 at 71
Kenneth F., d. 11/24/1969 at 56 in Moultonboro; buried in Tamworth
Laura I., d. 9/11/1968 at 92 in N. H. Hospital; b. MA; residence – S. Hampton
Leonard H., d. 5/11/1956 at 78/5/4 in Tamworth
Mary A., d. 12/27/1943 at 86/2/4 in Tamworth
Rita Marie, d. 5/13/1962 at 40 in Meredith; b. Newport Ctr., VT; residence - Ashland

VORIS,
Martha O., d. 10/10/1949 at 83/0/4 in Laconia

WADE,
Sarah E., d. 3/10/1940 at 79/10/24; b. Tamworth

WAKEFIELD,
Howard G., d. 6/22/1957 at 78 in Tamworth

WALDEN,
Arthur T., d. 3/26/1947 at 75/10/16 in Tamworth
Catherine S., d. 3/3/1949 at 86/3/6 in Tamworth

WALKER,
Hattie Bickford, d. 7/14/1971 at 90 in Laconia; b. NH; residence - Tamworth
Mary Louise, d. 9/6/1930 at 69/9/11
Richard E., d. 9/28/1992 in Wolfeboro; Walter E. Walker and Myrtle Page
Walter C., d. 11/29/1954 at 80/0/28 in Tamworth
Walter E., d. 6/4/1961 at 58 in Hanover

WALLACE,
Donald S., d. 3/6/1949 at 0/6/11 in Boston, MA
Donald Wilson, d. 2/14/1993 in Ossipee; Roberts S. B. Wallace and Violet J. Whyte
Evelyn M., d. 10/13/2000 in Tamworth; Robert Spaulding and Eunice Hoag
Huldah K., d. 3/18/1888 at 80/2/11; housekeeper; married; b. Tamworth; William Wallace (Sandwich) and Sally Keniston (Sandwich)

James F., d. --/--/1894 at 75 in Tamworth; farmer; widower; b.
  Sandwich; Thomas Wallace
Julia A., d. 5/26/1889 at 0/11/1; b. Tamworth; Henry Wallace
  (Westbrook) and Francis Glidden (Sandwich)

WARD,
Antoinette D., d. 1/25/1963 at 62 in Nashua; residence – Nashua;
  buried in Tamworth
Benjamin, d. 5/23/1946 at 81/0/6 in Penacook
Emelie R., d. 7/12/1941 at 71/7/20 in Tamworth
Lucille Wellinghurst, d. 11/10/1993 in Wolfeboro; Frederick L. Borsch
  and Eliza Tabor
Robert Saltonstall, d. 8/1/1995 in Wolfeboro; Robert Decourcy Ward
  and Emma Lane
William T. R., d. 6/19/1967 at 64 in Hampton; b. Lowell, MA;
  residence - Nashua

WARFEL,
Russell Lee, d. 1/19/1962 at 61 in Conway; b. Millersville, PA;
  residence – Albany

WARREN,
Diane C., d. 5/7/1991 in N. Conway; Walter Count and Marion -----
Frederick, Sr., d. 5/20/1972 at 65 in Tamworth; b. Newfoundland;
  residence – Everett, MA
Mabel F., d. 5/20/1972 at 62 in Tamworth; b. England; residence –
  Everett, MA

WASON,
Catherine L., d. 12/30/1891 at 74/4/12 in Tamworth; housewife;
  married; b. Lebanon; Nicholas Staples and Olive Ricker

WASSON,
Harry J., d. 6/2/1948 at 73/5/10 in Tamworth

WATSON,
Ellen, d. 10/31/1936 at 80/5/19
John N., d. 2/3/1945 at 81/1/8 in Portsmouth
Richard Arthur, d. 5/5/1966 at 56 in Tamworth; b. Fryeburg, ME;
  residence - Tamworth

WATT,
James Ogden, d. 8/25/1998 in Tamworth; Richard Morgan Watt and Joan Ogden

WEARE,
Donald Edmund, d. 2/13/1988 in Tamworth; Charles Weare and Bertha Jenness
Reta M., d. 12/4/2000 in Tamworth; Russell Welch and Hester Clark

WEBSTER,
Chester W., d. 2/1/1955 at 42/6/25 in Tamworth
George H., d. 11/20/1969 at 89 in Tamworth; b. Pictou, NS; residence – Tamworth
Hazel A., d. 12/14/1985 in Wolfeboro; Claude Ames and Blanche Jeffers
Horace, d. --/--/1896 at 1/8 in Tamworth; b. Tamworth; Alphene Webster (Albany) and Francena Perkins (Tamworth)
William, d. 3/5/1963 at 73 in Tamworth; b. Lee; residence – Tamworth

WEED,
Dorothy N., d. 5/4/1969 at 68 in Laconia; b. MA; residence - Tamworth

WEEKS,
Anna F., d. 1/18/1889 at 40/8/10; seamstress; single; b. Moultonboro; F. S. Weeks (Gilmanton) and Harriette E. Carter (Wakefield)
Araminta D., d. 6/6/1900 at 6 (sic) in Tamworth; housewife; widow; b. Meredith; John G. Robinson (Meredith) and Lucinda Roberts (New Hampton)
Bessie Marion, d. 10/15/1914 at 29/6/14; meningitis; single; b. Tamworth; William Weeks and Mary E. Blaisdell
Charles, d. 2/27/1942 at 54/10/15 in Tamworth
Charles A., d. --/--/1894 at 44/2/14 in Tamworth; farmer; married; b. Wakefield; Phineas J. Weeks (Wakefield) and Mercy Hayes (Tuftonboro)
Emma B., d. 1/3/1938 at 57/6/24
Lucy, d. 4/12/1971 at 79 in Laconia; b. NH; residence - Tamworth
Mary E., d. 7/12/1892 at 43/0/22 in Tamworth; housework; b. Tamworth; Zenas Blaisdell and Martha Hubbard

William, d. 4/22/1930 at 78/5/6

WEINERT,
Gertrude B., d. 9/3/1991 in Sandwich; Henning N. Borgstedt and Jennie E. Klotz

WELCH,
Agnes Louise, d. 4/13/1925 at 0/3
Austin E., d. 11/3/1986 in Manchester; James Welch and Gertrude Eldridge
Edwin P., d. 5/11/1987 in Wolfeboro; James Welch and Gertrude M. Eldridge
Francis J., d. 3/12/1971 at 55 in Wolfeboro; b. NH; residence - Tamworth
Gertrude M., d. 2/10/1966 at 73 in Wolfeboro; b. Ossipee; residence - Tamworth
James, d. 10/16/1959 at 82 in Wolfeboro
Peter A., d. 6/16/1955 at 15/9/6 in Wolfeboro
Russell, d. 9/20/1963 at 64 in Laconia; b. Ossipee; residence - Tamworth
Russell, Jr., d. 2/6/1943 at 14/1/29 in Conway

WELLINGHURST,
Jack Moreman, d. 9/29/1996 in N. Conway; George H. Wellinghurst and Lucille Borsch

WENTWORTH,
Orange, d. 12/27/1898 at 76 in Tamworth; farmer; widower

WHEELER,
Chester, d. 5/25/1993 in Tamworth; Frederick W. Wheeler and Fannie E. Price
Helen, d. 3/13/1932 at 72/7/12

WHIPPLE,
Augusta M., d. 1/9/1951 at 40/2/10 in Portland, ME
Melvin Conley, d. 1/14/1966 at 82 in Tamworth; b. Oleand, NY; residence - Tamworth
Minnie E., d. 5/8/1927 at 57/1/28
Orlando C., d. 2/10/1927 at 52/10/18

Parker C., d. 5/7/1979 in Sandwich; Melville Whipple and Dorothy Wakefield

WHITE,
Alfred P., d. 12/22/2001 in Tamworth; John White and Clara Preston
Isabelle Y., d. 4/26/1986 in Laconia; Arthur Young and Leona A. Noyes
Maria J., d. 12/5/1903 at 61 in Tamworth; housekeeper; widow; Otis Gannett
Richard A., d. 7/16/1999 in Wolfeboro; John White and Dorothy Simmons
Walter C., d. 7/14/1973 at 55 in Laconia; b. NH; residence - Tamworth
Walter LeRoy, d. 9/4/1962 at 78 in Wolfeboro; b. Phillipstown, MA; residence - Sandwich

WHITEHOUSE,
Charles W., d. 5/14/1892 at 49/8 in Tamworth; blacksmith; b. Tuftonboro; A. Whitehouse and Sarah Copp

WHITING,
daughter, d. 4/21/1919 at --; b. Tamworth; Fred H. Whiting and Ethel E. Jeffers
Almon J., d. 7/11/1913 at 53 in Tamworth; farmer; married; b. Tamworth; John Whiting and Ellen Allen
Annie H., d. 1/17/1941 at 85/4/3 in Tamworth
Arthur C., d. 5/10/1945 at 63/2/18 in Laconia
Chester F., d. 11/21/1939 at 36/6/1; b. Tamworth
Claude D., d. 8/31/1954 at 49 in Laconia
David Lyle, d. 3/15/1996 in Laconia; George R. Whiting and Hazel Mackenzie
Doris T., d. 1/19/1910 at – in Tamworth; b. Tamworth; Charles E. Whiting (Tamworth) and Jennie B. Wade (Moultonboro)
Elizabeth R., d. 2/4/1953 at 83 in Mouiltonboro
Ellen H., d. 5/22/1916 at 92/3/20; old age; widow; b. Cornish, ME; John Allen and Mary Larrabee
Ellen J., d. 9/20/1913 at 85/0/17 in Tamworth; housekeeping; widow; b. Beverly, MA; Phineas Johnson and Dolly James
Elmer, d. --/--/1894 at 11/8 in Tamworth; drowning; student; b. Tamworth; John E. Whiting (Tamworth) and Dora Wallace (Sandwich)

Frank A., d. 4/20/1943 at 85/4/12 in Laconia
Fred M., d. 5/12/1971 at 82 in Wolfeboro; residence – Center Tuftonboro; buried in Tamworth
Genevieve Alice, d. 5/17/1967 at 66 in N. Conway; b. Greenwich, CT; residence - Tamworth
George C., d. 6/29/1906 at 81/4/15 in Tamworth; farmer; married; b. Limerick, ME; John Whiting (Limerick, ME) and Martha Rankine (Limerick, ME)
George F., d. 1/7/1931 at 77/0/26
Georgia J., d. 10/5/1956 at 63/3/11 in Tamworth
Geraldine S., d. 6/19/1986 in Hanover; Wallace Nudd and Blanche LeClair
Hazel Mackenzi, d. 9/20/1995 in N. Conway; William Mackenzi and Florence Down
Howard W., d. 4/21/1974 at 71 in Hanover; b. NH; residence – S. Tamworth
Jesse E., d. 7/24/1979 in N. Conway; Charles Boothby and Ina Hayford
John, d. 6/15/1905 at 78/4/13 in Tamworth; farmer; married; b. Limerick, ME; John Whiting
John C. F., d. 10/31/1926 at 68/10/28
John Gilman, d. 5/5/1922 at 0/0/20; b. Tamworth; Fred H. Whiting and Ethel E. Jeffers
Levi F., d. 8/25/1902 at 73/3/9 in Tamworth; farmer; married; b. Tamworth; John Whiting
Lewis V., d. 5/3/1921 at 0/4/16; bronchial pneumonia; b. Meredith; Victor L. Whiting and Madeline Elliott
Lulu A., d. 4/6/1953 at 71 in Tamworth
Mabel E., d. 9/28/1909 at 2/1/10 in Tamworth; b. Tamworth; Arthur C. Whiting (Tamworth) and Fannie A. Forrest (Tamworth)
Mary A., d. 5/14/1963 at 97 in Wolfeboro; b. Tamworth; residence - Tamworth
Mary E., d. 7/22/1906 at 66/5/24 in Tamworth; housewife; widow; b. Quincy, MA; Phineas Sanborn and Ellen van Bramer (NY)
Mary E., d. 9/13/1963 at 75 in Tamworth; b. Tamworth; residence - Tamworth
Read A., d. 10/8/1905 at 3/8/14 in Georgetown, ME; b. Tamworth; Almon J. Whiting (Tamworth) and Elizabeth Palmer (Sandwich)
Robert P., d. 1/29/1970 at 64 in Tamworth; b. MA; residence - Tamworth

Roland George, d. 10/9/1965 at 58 in Tamworth; b. Tamworth; residence - Tamworth
William H., d. 10/30/1931 at 72/4/10

WHITMAN,
Donald Wilson, d. 4/19/1988 in Tamworth; Winfield A. Whitman and Elizabeth May Hill

WHITNEY,
Henry Scudder, d. 11/28/1974 at 77 in Conway; b. CT; residence - Tamworth
Julia A., d. 5/6/1916 at 64/2/17; cancer of liver; widow; b. Portsmouth; Charles H. Dennett and Julia A. Coche

WHITTEMORE,
Nathaniel, d. 9/10/1910 at 72/0/23 in Tamworth; teacher; married; b. Boston, MA; Nathaniel Whittemore (Lancaster, MA) and Mandana Ballow (Barnard, VT)

WHITTEN,
Edwin A., d. 4/6/1909 at 80/2/22 in Haverhill, MA; farmer; widower; buried in Tamworth

WHITTIER,
Thorn D., d. 10/14/1897 at 81/11/6 in Tamworth; carpenter; single; b. Tamworth

WHITTRIDGE,
Isabelle E., d. 11/30/1951 at 93 in Moultonboro

WIESNER,
Louis A., d. 9/20/2002 in Meredith; Abe Wiesner and Bertha Winner

WIGGETT,
Emelia C., d. 3/26/1949 at 52/11/29 in Tamworth

WIGGIN,
Annette, d. 6/2/1931 at 80
Arthur Elliott, d. 4/7/1913 at 71/1/15 in Tamworth; widower; b. Tamworth; Jacob C. Wiggin and Mary L. Cogswell
Charles A., d. 3/4/1943 at 78/3/12 in Ossipee

Emma R., d. 3/6/1909 at 47/5/13 in Tamworth; housewife; married; b. Effingham; Mayhew Floyd and Jane Drew (Eaton)

Frances A., d. 4/4/1915 at 71/1/15; pneumonia; housework; widow; b. Damariscotta, ME; Thomas Hutchings

Hannah O., d. 6/23/1931 at 72/1/19

Hardress L., d. 1/1/1928 at 67/3/9

Henry H., d. 5/12/1913 at 71/3 in Tamworth; laborer; single; b. Wakefield; Henry Wiggin and Hannah Emery

Jacob C., d. 6/10/1891 at 88/4/3 in Tamworth; farmer; widower; b. Wakefield; Henry Wiggin and Betsey Clark

Joseph, d. 10/--/1895 at 62/7/10 in Tamworth; farmer; married; b. Tamworth; Henry Wiggin (Wakefield)

Kate B., d. 4/28/1947 at 66/2/3 in Wolfeboro

Kenneth Earl, d. 9/18/1996 in Wolfeboro; Rosco Wiggin and Nellie Hardy

Leander F., d. 3/21/1936 at 82/2/26

Mary, d. 5/21/1893 at 82/4/16 in Tamworth; housekeeper; single; b. Dover; Andrew Wiggin and Judith Varney

Mary F., d. 9/19/1912 at 72/1/8 in Tamworth; housewife; married; b. Newington; Samuel Drown and Mehitable Pickering

Minnie E., d. 7/17/1911 at 21/0/13 in Tamworth; housewife; married; b. Tamworth; William H. Hardy (Tamworth) and Georgiana Davis (Effingham)

Nancy C., d. 10/8/1910 at 59/8 in Tamworth; housewife; married; b. Wolfeboro; Woodbury Horne (Wolfeboro) and Elizabeth Allen (Wolfeboro)

Nellie F., d. 3/26/1971 at 71 in Meredith; b. NH; residence - Tamworth

Philip D., d. 11/2/1940 at 15/3/23; b. Tamworth

Roscoe, d. 11/1/1956 at 72 in Concord

Sylvester, d. 7/6/1888 at 33/5/25; mechanic; married; b. Tamworth; Henry Wiggin, Jr. (Wakefield) and Hannah M. Emery (Kennebunk, ME)

Thomas S., d. 5/20/1899 at 51 in Tamworth; farmer; married; b. Wakefield; Henry Wiggin (Wakefield) and Hannah M. Emery (Kennebunk)

Travis Jason, d. 7/31/1988 in N. Conway; Gary W. Wiggin and Sharron Herbold

WILKESMAN,
Robert, d. 4/1/1984 in N. Conway; Charles Wilkesman and Pauline Stewart

WILKINSON,
Eileen A., d. 11/4/1994 in Tamworth; Harry O. Seymour and Mercedes Consolvo
Marion Louise, d. 3/9/1993 in Ossipee; Frank W. Trask and Elizabeth Bennett
Ralph Ernest, d. 9/5/1998 in Wolfeboro; Robert Wilkinson and Ora Meloon

WILLEY,
Cleon Tennant, d. 5/2/1973 at 66 in Laconia; b. NH; residence - Tamworth
John C., d. 12/3/1907 at 82/5 in Tamworth; farmer; married; b. Albany; William Willey (Wakefield) and Sally Head (Albany)

WILLIAMS,
infant son, d. 8/6/1909 at – in Tamworth; b. Tamworth; William H. Williams (Ossipee) and Susan Welch (Ossipee)
infant, d. 5/22/1926 at 1 hour
Allston H., d. 11/4/1923 at 19/11/14; b. Tamworth; William Williams and Susie Welch
Charles J., d. 10/10/1986 in Concord; Justus Williams and Mertle Smart
Clayton, d. 1/1/1934 at --; premature
Edith, d. 6/1/1907 at 0/10/8 in Tamworth; b. Tamworth; W. H. Williams (Ossipee) and Susie Welch (Ossipee)
Herbert Ludlow, d. 1/10/1997 in Wolfeboro; Frank Williams and Sara Jane Eldridge
John W., d. 1/20/1901 at 59/1/14 in Tamworth; carpenter; widower; b. Ossipee; Shaber Williams (Tamworth) and Lydia Welch (Tamworth)
Lilla May, d. 10/5/1993 in Wolfeboro; Charles Pennell and Addie Brown
Lydia, d. 4/15/1887 at 73/3/1 in Tamworth; housekeeper; married
Myrtie S., d. 9/14/1906 at 38 in Tamworth; housewife; married; b. Tamworth; Charles E. Smart and Addie Berry
Percy E., d. 4/17/1959 at 68 in Laconia

Perley Edward, d. 10/19/1971 at 82 in Madison; b. NH; residence - Tamworth
Ruth, d. 11/12/1898 at 60 in Tamworth; married
Walter S., d. 8/30/1913 at 3/4/24 in Tamworth; b. Tamworth; Dora Williams
Ward T., d. 8/27/1986 in Tamworth; Ward B. Williams and Judith Nickerson
William H., d. 3/12/1923 at 65/1/11; b. Ossipee; Shaber Williams and Lydia Welch

WILSON,
Annie I., d. 9/28/1960 at 79 in Conway
Bertha, d. 7/19/1918 at 88/10; old age; widow; b. Tamworth

WINSLOW,
John Arthur, d. 11/26/1995 in Manchester; George Winslow and Gertrude Heine

WOODBURY,
Caroline, d. 8/19/1921 at 69/7/24; lobar pneumonia; at home; widow; b. Beverly, MA; Ezra D. Woodbury

WOODMAN,
Albert, d. 12/6/1985 in Tamworth; Zenas Woodman and Katherine Kelly
Clarence Ronal, d. 11/7/1993 in Wolfeboro; Kenneth G. Woodman and Faye M. Saunders
Frances S., d. 11/21/1890 at 78/0/6 in Tamworth; housewife; widow; b. Tamworth; George W. Woodman and Margaret -----
Fred, d. 5/28/1909 at 53/2/6 in Tamworth; teamster; married; b. Etna, ME; J. Q. A. Woodman (Plymouth, ME) and Lydia B. Dyer (China, ME)

WOODWARD,
Edith M., d. 1/17/1970 at 70 in Tamworth; b. MA; residence – Tamworth
Forrest G., d. 3/29/2000 in Tamworth; Charles Woodward and Marion Glines

WORKS,
Lillian, d. 6/30/1984 in Tamworth; Frank Wheeler and Josephine LeBlanc

YOUNG,
Emma L., d. 8/17/1920 at 63/9/24 in Rochester; chronic bronchitis; farmer; married; Joseph Lord
Florence Ethel, d. 10/25/1973 at 90 in Peterborough; b. Hampstead; residence - Rochester
John, d. 10/27/1927 at 73/3/4
Standly, d. 5/14/1963 at 77 in Tamworth; b. Rochester; residence - Tamworth

UNKNOWN,
male, d. 7/--/1911 at –

ALBANY BIRTHS

ADAMS,
Sabrina Leigh, b. 3/3/1987

ALLARD,
Doris E., b. 4/10/1916; first; Henry Allard (chauffeur, Conway) and Esther Dow (Moultonboro)

AMES,
daughter, b. 3/24/1900; third; James H. Ames (farmer, Conway) and A. R. Marston (Brownfield, ME)
Amanda Lynn, b. 5/17/1987

AMIRAULT,
Danielle Catherine, b. 9/14/1986

ANNIS,
son, b. 12/9/1898 in Albany; second; James H. Annis (farmer, 30, Madison) and Addie R. Marston (26, Brownfield, ME)
Earl C., b. 4/17/1893 in Albany; James H. Annis (Conway) and Addie R. Marston (Brownfield, ME)

AUBIN,
stillborn daughter, b. 12/13/1909; first; Omer Aubin (laborer, Quebec, Canada) and Exilia Hartley (Berlin)
daughter, b. 12/13/1909; second; Omer Aubin (laborer, Quebec, Canada) and Exilia Hartley (Berlin)

AVIGNONE,
Ashley Marie, b. 3/10/1981 in Conway
Nicholas Anthony, b. 8/1/1985

BEALS,
Robert Drake, b. 8/19/1922; first; Charles E. Beals (Boston, MA) and Blanche D. Hammond (Albany)

BELL,
Alfred Gardner, b. 11/24/1923; ninth; Archie Bell (laborer, Westfield, MA) and Minnie Littlefield (Conway)
Basil T., b. 12/24/1915; eighth; Archie Bell (farmer) and Minnie Littlefield (Conway)
Christopher Jeremy, b. 10/21/1988

Ivan, b. 5/4/1906; second; Archie G. Bell (engineer, Westford, MA) and Minnie F. Littlefield (Conway)

Malachi Shannon, b. 1/6/2001 in N. Conway; Paul Bell and Carolann Bell

Norman V., b. 12/25/1919; eighth; Archie Bell (laborer, Westford, MA) and Minnie Littlefield (Conway)

Paula Ann, b. 11/3/1954; Robert E. Bell (NH) and Vera Virginia Varney (Rockland, ME)

BENWAY,
daughter, b. 6/19/1909; third; Edmund Benway (section foreman, Worcester, MA) and Olivine Girouard (Brookfield)

Shannon Marie, b. 4/2/1984

BERG,
Logan Joseph Raymond, b. –/–/2000; Kristopher Berg and Alicia Berg

BERNARD,
Michael William, b. 8/26/1986

BOLDUC,
son, b. 3/6/1909; seventh; Toffle Bolduc (harness maker, Canada) and Josephine Bonten (Gorham)

BOUCHER,
son, b. 5/14/1916; eighth; Ernest Boucher (lumberman, Canada) and Maggie Mixon (Russia)

BRETON,
Samantha J., b. 11/17/1987

BRETT,
Shawn Matthew, b. 4/19/1987

BROWN,
daughter, b. 12/29/1898 in Albany; tenth; Jeremiah Brown (farmer, 49, Albany) and Jane Smith (49, Porter, ME)

daughter, b. 11/10/1899; first; Frank W. Brown (laborer, Albany) and Carrie Chapman (Canada)

son, b. 6/18/1901; first; Mark W. Brown (farmer, Albany) and Martha
   Eva Mason (Albany)
son, b. 12/21/1906; fourth; Mark W. Brown (teamster, Albany) and
   Eva M. Mason (Albany)
stillborn daughter, b. 1/18/1909; first; Mamie Brown (Albany)
son, b. 1/18/1909; second; Mamie Brown (Albany)
daughter, b. 3/30/1910; fourth; Joseph Brown (section hand,
   Canada) and J. Girouard (Spencer, MA)
daughter, b. 9/26/1910; first; Ernest Brown (farmer, Albany) and
   Nina E. Rogers (Bethel, VT)
Carl Raymond, b. 8/28/1936; sixth; John L. Brown (Albany) and
   Edvia A. Thurston (Effingham)
Fordy, b. 7/3/1896 in Albany; ninth; Jerry Brown (farmer, 45, Albany)
   and Jane Smith (45, Porter, ME)
Franklin James, b. 3/24/1938; seventh; John Louville Brown
   (Albany) and Edvia Anna Thurston (Effingham)
Harold, b. 10/25/1921; first; Ford Brown (teamster, Albany) and
   Milder Willner (Russia)
Harriett, b. 5/16/1893 in Albany; J. Brown (laborer, Albany) and Jane
   Smith (Porter, ME)
Janet P., b. 6/8/1918; first; Ford Brown (teamster, Albany) and
   Minnie Hammond (Albany)
Jean Beverly, b. 11/10/1934 in Albany; fifth; John L. Brown (laborer,
   29, Albany) and Elvia Thurston (27, Effingham)
Jessie M., b. 6/18/1903; second; Mark W. Brown (laborer, Albany)
   and Eva M. Mason (Chatham)
Mabelle E., b. 12/17/1909; second; William H. Brown (blacksmith,
   Madison) and Mabelle R. Schultz (Boston, MA)
Mamie, b. 5/17/1890; Jeremiah Brown (Albany) and Jane Smith
   (Porter, ME) (1954)
Raymond, b. 6/29/1905 in Albany; third; Mark W. Brown (laborer,
   Albany) and Eva M. Mason (Albany)
Richard Wilbur, b. 11/14/1918; fifth; Mark W. Brown (farmer, Albany)
   and Eva M. Mason (Albany)
Roy, b. 10/8/1923; second; Ford Brown (teamster, Albany) and Milda
   Wilner (Russia)
William Robert, b. 6/29/1927; third; Ford Brown (teamster, Albany)
   and Milda Willner (Russia)

BRYAN,
Maggie Graves, b. 11/26/1996; Harold Bryan and Sheila Graves

BUNKER,
Audrey Alida, b. 8/27/1924; first; Frank E. Bunker (teamster, Tamworth) and Norilla R. Colbert (Quaker City)

BURGESS,
son, b. 10/11/1912; thirteenth; Edward Burgess (teamster, Canada) and Annie Tibedeau (Somersworth)
son, b. 10/26/1913; fourteenth; Edward Burgess (teamster, Canada) and Annie Thedeau (Somersworth)

BURKE,
Delia, b. 8/3/1904; Thady Burke (laborer, St. Andrews, NB) and Caroline Corneau (Ottawa, Canada)

CARRIER,
Nicholas Jacob, b. 8/12/1999; Steven Carrier and Pamela Carrier

CARRUTHERS,
Amy Elizabeth, b. 10/30/1991; Richard Carruthers (ME) and Kathy Rines (ME)

CHAMBERLIN,
Doris F., b. 6/1/1904; second; Chancy J. Chamberlin (farmer, Conway) and Mary A. Littlefield (Albany)

CHARETTE,
Curtis Lawrence, b. 8/16/1984

CHASE,
Nathan Daniel, b. 5/28/1988

CHATIANEUF,
daughter, b. 6/9/1907 in Albany; third; Joseph Chatianeuf (woodsman, Canada) and Vilaiur Moncont (Canada)

CHENEY,
infant, b. 10/21/1945; Chester J. Cheney (Wells, ME) and Gladys Eldridge (Conway)
Cecil James, b. 8/19/1941; third; Chester J. Cheney (Wells, ME) and Gladys Eldridge (Conway)

Eleanor May, b. 10/27/1934 in Albany; second; Chester J. Cheney (laborer, 35, Wells, ME) and Gladys Eldridge (30, Conway)

CLOUTMAN,
Harold J., b. 9/18/1893 in Albany; Life Cloutman (blacksmith, Conway) and Mary S. Cloutman (Albany)

COLBERT,
son, b. 7/21/1916; sixth; James H. Colbert (millman, NS) and Bessie Tuttle (Raymond)
Bessie E., b. 8/13/1920; eighth; James Colbert (millman, NB) and Bessie Tuttle (Raymond)
Ella Louise, b. 11/27/1918; seventh; James H. Colbert (lumber dealer, NS) and Bessie E. Tuttle (Raymond)

COOK,
daughter, b. 7/16/1910; first; Frank L. Cook (laborer, Ossipee) and Alice Tewksbury (Sandwich)

CRABTREE,
son, b. 8/2/1910; first; Hollis E. Crabtree (teamster, Franklin, ME) and Alice V. Moody (Tamworth)

CROTEAU,
Adam Thomas, b. 11/16/1989

DASCOLI,
Seth Ryan, b. 12/17/1986

DASCOULIAS,
Derek Charles, b. 6/4/2001 in N. Conway; David Dascoulias and Erin Dascoulias
Eva David, b. 11/24/2002 in N. Conway; David Dascoulias and Erin Dascoulias

DAWE,
John Shepard, IV, b. 7/21/1981 in Conway
Joseph James, b. 7/6/1986

DEE,
Molly, b. 12/3/1996; William Dee and Bernadette Dee

DEXTER,
Sophia Thompson, b. 1/29/1991; Stephen Dexter (MA) and Brenda Thompson (MA)

DOUGLAS,
Zachary Aaron, b. 11/22/1991; Arthur Douglas (NH) and Sandra West (IL)

DOW,
child, b. 7/16/1954; Cedric C. Dow (VT) and Mary E. Buxton (MA)

DOWNES,
Barbara B., b. 11/30/1921; first; Wilber R. Downes (farmer, Madison) and Hildergarde Schreiter (Kittery, ME)

DREW,
son, b. 9/15/1926; second; Frank Drew (laborer, Ossipee) and Bessie Morrison (Stowe, ME)
Mildred Madeline, b. 3/31/1923; first; Ralph Drew (RR section hand, Alton) and Olive Drown (Webster)

DROUIN,
Albert Joseph, Jr., b. 11/12/1936; fourth; Albert J. Drouin (Canada) and Christine M. Lyman (Albany)
Arthur Ellsworth, b. 11/28/1931 in Albany; second; Albert J. Drouin (laborer, Canada) and Christine Lyman (Albany)
Bruce Allen, b. 9/16/1943; seventh; Albert Drouin (Canada) and Christine M. Lyman (Albany)
Jennette Mae, b. 11/23/1940; sixth; Albert Drouin (Canada) and Christine M. Lyman (Albany)
Kyle Avery, b. 2/2/2002 in N. Conway; James Drouin and Anastina Drouin
Mary Annette, b. 5/5/1938; fifth; Albert J. Drouin (Canada) and Christine M. Lyman (Albany)
Richard Elbert, b. 6/10/1934 in Albany; third; Albert J. Drouin (laborer, 25, Canada) and Christine Lyman (20, Albany)
Robert Ellsworth, b. 10/23/1930 in Albany; Albert J. Drouin (laborer, Quebec, Canada) and Christine Lyman (Albany)

DROWNS,
Charles Eldin, b. 12/8/1919; second; Eldin Linwood Drowns (Bridgton, ME) and Etta Gladys Merrill (Conway)(1935)
Harriett Catherine, b. 9/15/1918; first; Eldin Linwood Drowns (Bridgton, ME) and Etta Gladys Merrill (Conway)(1935)

EALEY,
daughter, b. 4/17/1893 in Albany; Everett Ealey (farmer, Conway) and Rocksey Henderson (Eaton)
Charlie, b. 4/17/1905 in Albany; fourth; Lowell Ealey (laborer, Conway) and Mabel Whitaker (Conway)

EARLE,
Milvina, b. 3/15/1900; second; Lowell Earle (farmer, Conway) and Mary Whitaker (Conway)

EASTWOOD,
Chester Russell, b. 9/12/1985

ELDRIDGE,
Bertha May, b. 3/7/1914; fourth; Herbert Eldridge (Ossipee) and M. Littlefield (Conway)

FIELDS,
Mary Elizabeth, b. 6/12/1889; James Fields (Sherbrook, NH) and Bessie Thibodeau (Madawaska, NB) (1953)

FORD,
Daniel Webster, b. 5/20/1982 in Conway

FRICKETT,
Byron A., b. 6/17/1922; fifth; Byron Fickett (Standish, ME) and Jessie Hurd (Freedom)

GANTHIER,
son, b. 10/1/1907 in Albany; second; John Ganthier (woodsman, Canada) and Delvina White (Canada)

GAUTHIER,
daughter, b. 11/25/1908 in Albany; third; John Gauthier (trader, Canada) and Delvina White (Canada)

GAY,
Harold H., b. 12/9/1898 in Albany; third; William Gay (millman, 32, Wells, ME) and ----- (29)

GEORGE,
Emily Faith, b. 9/10/1992; Gregory George (MA) and Sandra Hammond (NY)

GILMAN,
Robert Edwin, b. 9/4/1923; fourth; Reed Gilman (laborer, Madison) and Maud Thurston (N. Shapleigh, ME)

GRACE,
Carrie E., b. 4/28/1902; fourth; F. L. Grace (farmer, Chatham) and Elizabeth Willey (Albany)
Flora M., b. 4/17/1896 in Albany; second; Frank L. Grace (laborer, 35, Chatham) and Lizzie W. Willey (25, Albany)
Lulu V., b. 11/29/1899; third; Lesley Grace (laborer, Chatham) and Elizabeth Willey (Albany)

GRANT,
Timothy Keith, b. 11/24/1983

GRAY,
Erwin N., b. 12/4/1917; second; Erwin N. Gray (laborer, Madison) and Hattie Nickerson (Tamworth)

HADAM,
Elijah J., b. 11/11/1994; John James Hadam (MA) and Diana Delany (NH)

HALE,
Rebecca Ann, b. 7/15/1983

HALEY,
Cooper Jeffrey, b. 6/7/2001 in N. Conway; Jeffrey Haley and Christine Haley
Nolan Donald, b. 1/17/2003 in N. Conway; Jeffrey Haley and Christine Haley

HALL,
Bruce Francis, b. 12/9/1953; Clyde William Hall (Fryeburg, ME) and Barbara Frances Penna (Danforth, ME)

HALLET,
John W., b. 6/1/1894; second; Hobid L. Hallet (laborer, NB) and Melvina Harriman (Conway)

HALLETT,
son, b. 1/17/1897; third; Obed E. Hallett (lumberman, NB) and Malvina Harriman (Conway)

HAM,
Nellie, b. 1/6/1904; sixth; Albert J. Ham (laborer, Fryeburg, ME) and Mary A. Thibado (Somersworth)

HAMEL,
son, b. 9/1/1908 in Albany; second; Gideon Hamel (teamster, Kingsley Falls) and Celia Gosslin (Berlin)

HAMMOND,
son, b. 5/18/1900; fourth; Frank Hammond (farmer, Albany) and Maud (Conway)
son, b. 7/9/1904; sixth; Frank O. Hammond (farmer, Albany) and Maud Ealey (Conway)
son, b. 12/26/1907 in Albany; fifth; Alfred Hammond (laborer, Albany) and Ellen Wiggin (Chatham)
son, b. 1/9/1910; ninth; Frank Hammond (farmer, Albany) and Maud Ealy (Conway)
Alfred, Jr., b. 6/7/1898 in Albany; third; Alfred Hammond (farmer, 28, Albany) and Ellen Wiggin (23, Chatham)
Brenda Mae, b. 2/13/1942; second; Victor C. Hammond (Albany) and Cora M. Grandchamp (Conway)
Frank Joseph, b. 1/9/1936; first; Victor C. Hammond (Albany) and Cora M. Grandchamp (Conway)
Hazen, b. 8/24/1902; fourth; F. O. Hammond (farmer, Albany) and Maud E. Ealy (Conway)
Mary L., b. 5/29/1903; fifth; Alfred Hammond (farmer, Albany) and Ellen Wiggin (Chatham)
Minnie V., b. 10/15/1895 in Albany; second; Frank O. Hammond (farmer, 27, Albany) and Maud E. Ealey (22, Conway)

Vera M., b. 6/27/1906; Frank Orival Hammond (Albany) and Maud Elvina Ealy (Ctr. Conway) (1953)

Willie, b. 11/14/1897; F. O. Hammond (farmer, Albany) and Maud E. Early (Conway)

Willie, b. 6/25/1908 in Albany; eighth; Frank O. Hammond (farmer, Albany) and Maud Ealy (Conway)

HANSEN,
Audrey Ann, b. 2/19/1991; Cort Hansen (NH) and Cynthia Savoia (MA)

HARTWELL,
son, b. 1/–/1920; fourth; Ed Hartwell (woodsman, NS) and Birdive (France)

HATCH,
Sumner Wells, b. 8/13/1984

HATFIELD,
Walter M., b. 10/5/1921; fifth; Ed. Hatfield (laborer, NS) and Anna E. Boudreau (Canada); residence of father - Canada; residence of mother - Albany

HIBBARD,
Helen May, b. 7/19/1923; first; Lluellin Hibbard (laborer) and Laura Nickerson (NS)

HILL,
Jackson David, b. 8/28/1999; Michael Hill and Donna Hill

HOBBS,
William H., b. 4/25/1896 in Albany; first; Bert Hobbs (laborer, 21, Tamworth) and Hattie E. Swaine (18, Albany); residence - Tamworth

HODGDON,
Charles Raymond, b. 12/26/1923; second; Raymond Hodgdon (farmer, Albany) and Bertha Jones (Eaton)

Fay Arlene, b. 12/26/1934; seventh; Raymond Hodgdon (Albany) and Bertha Jones (Eaton)

Lillian Ruth, b. 2/26/1894; Charles P. Hodgdon (Ossipee) and Abbie
  Mason (Albany) (1956)
Mary Ruth, b. 5/26/1928; second; John A. Hodgdon (farmer, Albany)
  and Josephine Smith (Lowell, MA)
Mayois B., b. 5/3/1909; John A. Hodgdon (farmer, Albany) and Angie
  B. Glidden (Effingham)
Raymond, b. 9/12/1926; fourth; Raymond Hodgdon (farmer, Albany)
  and Bertha Jones (Eaton)
Robert Edwin, b. 10/5/1929 in Albany; fifth; Ray Hodgdon (teamster,
  Albany) and Bertha Jones (Eaton)
Rupert Clifford, b. 9/12/1932 in Albany; seventh; Ray Hodgdon
  (laborer, Albany) and Bertha Jones (Eaton)
Shirley May, b. 5/18/1936; eighth; Raymond Hodgdon (Albany) and
  Bertha Jones (Eaton)
Vernon T., b. 6/12/1931 in Albany; sixth; Ray Hodgdon (farmer,
  Albany) and Bertha Jones (Eaton)

HUNTINGTON,
Ashely Marie, b. 9/9/1988

HURLEY,
Archie L., b. 7/29/1890; Thomas Hurley and Myrtle L. Sanborn
  (1954)

HUTCHINSON,
Hannah Marie, b. 5/1/1991; Clifford Hutchinson, Jr. (MA) and Diane
  Clinton (MA)

JOHNSON,
Matthew Dana, b. 9/4/1993; Dana Wayne Johnson (NH) and Nancy
  A. Wakefield (NH)
Otis Earl, b. 6/13/1894; Albert Johnson (NH) and Mary Ann
  Thibodeau (NH) (1962)

JONES,
stillborn son, b. 9/23/1924; second; Floyd Jones (lumber cutter,
  Conway) and Lula Frost (Madison)

KEEFE,
Lindsey Grace, b. 7/27/1987
Tracey Lyn, b. 12/31/1985

KIDDER,
Ashlie Marie, b. 2/6/1993; Andrew Kidder (NH) and Wendy A. Dodd (MA)

KING,
Christopher, b. 3/3/1994; Michael King (NC) and Linda Sealy (NY)
Ellen Jean, b. 3/8/1952; Francis Xavier King (Bartlett) and Fay Elaine Thurston (Fryeburg, ME)
Flora May, b. 7/28/1895 in Albany; second; John H. King (farmer, 32, NS) and Luella Cheney (19)
John O., b. –/–/1893 in Albany; John W. King (laborer, British Province) and Luilla Cheeney (Wells, ME)
Michael Peter, b. 7/19/1986
Nicholas James, b. 3/27/1991; Stephen King (NH) and Etta McDonald (NH)

KINSLOW,
infant, b. 3/14/1943; first; Weldon Kinslow (Portland) and Irma Morrill (Albany)
infant, b. 3/14/1943; second; Weldon Kinslow (Portland) and Irma Morrill (Albany)
Franklin Elliott, b. 8/21/1947; Weldon E. Kinslow (Portland, ME) and Irma Eva Morrill (Albany)

KNOWLTON,
John Buckminster, b. 7/1/1993; Bruce M. Knowlton (MA) and Lynn Rae McNutt (ME)

KNOX,
Nathaniel Emerson James, b. 6/24/1982 in Conway

LAGACE,
Mary Emma, b. 6/28/1923; fifth; Joe Lagace (woodsman, Canada) and Anna Budscoe (Canada)

LARSON,
Samuel Thomas Bird, b. 5/17/1989

LEAVITT,
Arthur William, b. 1/10/1933 in Albany; second; Harold M. Leavitt (laborer, 21, Madison) and Nora A. Bell (19, Madison)

Harold Mason, Jr., b. 2/4/1931 in Albany; first; Harold M. Leavitt (laborer, Madison) and Nora Ada Bell (Madison)
Richard Edgar, b. 1/5/1950 in N. Conway; Herbert Edgar Leavitt (truck driver, Madison) and Lillian Mildred Lyman (Albany)

LEBLAN,
son, b. 4/13/1911 in Albany; sixth; Napoleon LeBlan (log contractor, Canada) and Lublin LaFanlon (housewife, 29, Wector Mills, V. L.)

LEE,
Merian W., b. 11/10/1926; second; P. T. Lee (laborer, Manchester) and Mable Cook (Arlington, MA)

LEVESQUE,
Daniel Erney, b. 11/–/1991; Roger Levesque (ME) and Kimberly Pemberton (NH)

LYMAN,
daughter, b. 4/2/1908 in Albany; twelfth; Charles E.. Lyman (carpenter, Albany) and Mary E. Smith (Albany)
daughter, b. 12/9/1909; first; Charles Henry Lyman (box maker, Albany) and Edith Marion Goodno (Gorham)
daughter, b. 5/28/1910; thirteenth; C. E. Lyman (farmer, Albany) and Mary E. Smith (Albany)
Mildred J., b. 6/1/1905 in Albany; eleventh; Charles E. Lyman (laborer, Albany) and Mary E. Smith (Albany)

MARQUES,
Christopher Richard, b. 1/1/1985

MARSTON,
daughter, b. 3/7/1915; third; Wilbur Marston (stage driver, Brownfield, ME) and Mary Hurd (Freedom)

MARVELLI,
Edmund Peter, III, b. 12/4/1988
Kara Elizabeth, b. 8/25/1986

McCOY,
Jessie David, b. 5/3/1992; James McCoy (VT) and Kimberly Wells (CA)

McKENZIE,
Jacob Chase, b. 11/26/1987

McNALLY,
Kate, b. 7/16/1893 in Albany; Owen McNally (paving cutter, Scotland) and Eliza Parsons (Ireland)

McVICAR,
Nathaniel Sutton, b. 11/13/1983
Sarah Malka, b. 7/10/1986

MESERVE,
Robert A., b. 10/4/1926; second; Frank C. Meserve (woodsman, Freedom) and Margaret Emerson

MOODY,
son, b. 7/24/1898 in Albany; third; William Moody (farmer, 30, Ossipee) and Mabel Moore (25, Somersworth)
son, b. 12/25/1901; first; Henry B. Moody (farmer, Albany) and Mary L. Plant (Tamworth)
Charley, b. 11/20/1894; second; William Moody (stone cutter, 26, Ossipee) and Mabel Moore (19, Great Falls)
Choy, b. 11/5/1895 in Albany; first; Oscar L. Moody (blacksmith, Ossipee) and Mary E. Forrest (20, Albany)
Edward, b. 4/18/1893 in Albany; William Moody (Ossipee) and Mabel Moore
Merton, b. 1/1/1902; fifth; W. N. Moody (stone cutter, Ossipee) and Mabel Moore (Somersworth)
Myron, b. 1/1/1902; sixth; W. N. Moody (stone cutter, Ossipee) and Mabel Moore (Somersworth)
Virginia A., b. 11/10/1910; eleventh; William N. Moody (farmer, Ossipee) and Mabel G. Moore (Somersworth)
William N., Jr., b. 8/16/1912; twelfth; William N. Moody (farmer, Ossipee) and Mabel G. Moore (Somersworth)

MOORE,
David Rodrick, b. 11/12/1944; Harry J. Moore, Jr. (Albany) and Annie Louise Brooks (Freedom)
Dorothea Louise, b. 3/30/1922; first; Charles F. Moore (Albany) and Jeannette E. Moore (Tamworth)
Harry Julian, Jr., b. 5/15/1919; first; Harry J. Moore (road patrol, Albany) and Edith Nickerson (Tamworth)
Lena M., b. 10/28/1887; John Henry Moore (Springvale, ME) and Anna A. Littlefield (Albany) (1954)
Mary Evelyn, b. 9/5/1933 in N. Conway; second; Charles Franklin Moore (carpenter, 39, Madison) and Jeannette E. Moore (32, Tamworth)

MORRILL,
Clyde F., b. 10/15/1912; second; Louis F. Morrill (farmer, Nashua) and Ina B. Hammond (Albany)
Dennis Clyde, b. 7/29/1946; Clyde F. Morrill (Albany) and Almee L. White (S. Lebanon, ME)
Floyd F., b. 12/12/1910; first; Louis F. Morrill (farmer, Nashua) and Ina B. Hammond (Albany)
George Louis, b. 6/12/1915; third; Louis F. Morrill (farmer, Nashua) and Ina B. Hammond (Albany)
Gregory Lorne, b. 12/27/1946; George L. Morrill (Albany) and Ruth Celia Towle (Conway)
Irma E., b. 1/22/1921; fourth; Louis F. Morrill (laborer, Nashua) and Ina B. Hammond (Albany)

MORRISON,
Alicia Nancy, b. 9/12/1989
Sarah Margaret, b. 9/24/1986

MOULTON,
son, b. 4/13/1896 in Albany; third; Luman J. Moulton (laborer, 33, Albany) and Carrie E. Davis (25, Effingham); residence - Tamworth

MURPHY,
Caitlyn M., b. 8/27/1997; Thomas Murphy and Deborah Murphy

MUTH,
Judy, b. 11/20/1984

NEALON,
Anne Drew, b. 6/4/1982 in Conway

NELSON,
Brice Patrick, b. 3/22/1990; John Nelson, Jr. (ME) and Stacey Wilson (IA)
Joelle Katherine, b. 1/1/1982 in Conway

NICKERSON,
son, b. 9/20/1900; first; Archie Nickerson (farmer, Tamworth) and Irena J. White (Ossipee)
Charles, b. 8/26/1893 in Albany; William Nickerson (quarryman, British Province) and Lillian Littlefield (Albany)

NORCROSS,
Thomas Elmer, Jr., b. 6/19/1986

NOYES,
Gregory Paul, b. 6/9/2003 in Wolfeboro; Jonathan Noyes and Joy Noyes

OAKES,
Willie, b. 4/22/1906; first; Frank Oakes (laborer, Michigan) and Bessie A. Head (Madison)

OLSON,
Axel Paul, b. 8/18/1998 in N. Conway; Paul Olson and Wendy Olson
Ian Paul, b. 12/19/1993; Paul W. Olson (MA) and Wendy S. Magee (NH)

ORR,
Ian Randall, b. 12/30/1987

PARKER,
stillborn son, b. 3/5/1893 in Albany; Horace Parker (Bartlett) and Josie Harriman (Albany)
daughter, b. 5/24/1894; second; Horace W. Parker (farmer, 37, Bartlett) and Josephine Harriman (20, Albany)

PEARE,
Courtney Janet, b. 1/3/1991; Chris Peare (NH) and Terri Ryder (NH)

PENNELL,
Edwin Mark, b. 11/2/1922; first; Guy Pennell (Buxton, ME) and Jessie Brown (Albany)
Sarah Evelyn, b. 10/22/1924; second; Guy Pennell (teamster, Buxton, ME) and Jessie Brown (Albany)

PIPER,
son, b. 10/2/1894; second; Alonzo S. Piper (carpenter, 31, Albany) and Mary Coverley (31, Barrington)
Marion B., b. 4/15/1908 in Albany; first; Franklin P. Piper (hotel keeper, Tuftonboro) and Lucy M. Foster (Albany)
Rolland N., b. 10/6/1910; second; Frank P. Piper (farmer, Tuftonboro) and Lucy M. Foster (Albany)

QUINT,
Janice Brian, b. 2/1/1955; Theodore Hughes Quint (N. Conway) and Barbara Jean Perkins (Exeter)

RANO,
Tiffanie Celina, b. 8/4/1981 in Conway

ROBERTS,
Jennifer Elizabeth, b. 5/1/1987
Sara Jane, b. 9/23/1984

ROBITAILLE,
Brady Michael, b. 10/7/2003 in N. Conway; Kelly Robitaille and Lisa Robitaille

ROGERS,
Sloan Wayne, b. –/–/2000; Joseph Rogers and Jaime Rogers

ROWELL,
Crystal Ann, b. 3/9/1987
Kimberly Fernald, b. 9/4/1988
Kristina Marie, b. 6/6/1985

RUSHINSKI,
Aaron Walter, b. 7/11/1982 in Conway

ST. CYR,
Ethan James, b. 12/31/2001 in N. Conway; Jeffrey St. Cyr and Deborah St. Cyr

SANFORD,
Zachariah Sias, b. 11/8/1990; David S. Sanford (MA) and Lori Wiggin (NH)

SAVARY,
Allen Duane, b. 3/23/1953; Richard Allan Savary (Boston, MA) and Barbara Marilyn Toole (Waltham)
Austin, b. 4/4/1905 in Albany; first; Zantford L. Savary (carpenter, Digby, NS) and Mabel Moody (Albany)

SAWYER,
Nicole Lee, b. 8/6/1981 in Conway

SAXBY,
Dana Rae, b. 5/25/1999; Orvis J. Saxby and Donna Saxby
Orvis J., Jr., b. 3/17/1995; Orvis J. Saxby (MA) and Cynthia Wilson (MA)

SHACKFORD,
Broughton William, b. 8/27/1993; Mark W. Shackford (NH) and Andrea J. Burnell (NH)

SHANNON,
Carolyn Eliza, b. 3/14/1988
Danielle Gory, b. 5/27/1989
Daven Eugene, b. 1/14/1991; Eugene Shannon (MA) and Lee Eldridge (MA)
Emma Christina, b. 9/17/2002 in N. Conway; Christopher Shannon and Shauna Clark

SIMMONS-CORMACK,
Adria Simmons, b. 11/13/2003 in N. Conway; James Simmons and Colleen Cormack

SIROIS,
Kyle Andrew, b. 7/10/1991; Mark Sirois (ME) and Judy Levesque (ME)

SMITH,
daughter, b. 3/3/1905 in Albany; eighth; Onslow S. Smith (farmer, Albany) and Lizzie Brown (Tamworth)
daughter, b. 3/31/1909; ninth; O. S. Smith (cook, Albany) and Lizzie Brown (Tamworth)
son, b. 1/11/1910; sixth; Herbert Smith (laborer, Albany) and Susie Goodnow (Gorham)
daughter, b. 7/29/1910; tenth; Onslow S. Smith (cook, Albany) and Lizzie B. Brown (Tamworth)
son, b. 5/14/1915; fourth; Evan Smith (laborer, Albany) and Gertrude Rideout (Albany)
Arthur T., b. 1/20/1891; Onslow Shackford Smith (Albany) and Elizabeth Banks Brown (Albany) (1952)
Elizabeth Jean, b. 12/13/1992; Donald Smith, Jr. (ME) and Linda Crabtree (MA)
Evan Parish, b. 4/4/1889; Onslow Shackford Smith (Albany) and Elizabeth Banks Brown (Albany) (1952)
Everett Walter, b. 3/17/1957; Perry Everett Smith (Albany) and Mary Roselyn Avery (Acton, ME)
Isaac M., b. 1/5/1994; Billy Smith (NH) and Elissa McKenzie (NJ)
Perry Everett, b. 7/31/1933; first; Everett D. Smith (carpenter, Northwood) and Julia Avis Linscott (Brownfield, ME)
Ruth Hodgdon, b. 9/7/1913; first; Guy Smith (farmer, Conway) and Lillian Hodgdon (Albany)
Sean Henry, b. 11/21/1988
Thomas A., b. 8/29/1899; Onslow S. Smith (Albany) and Elizabeth Banks Brown (Albany) (1965)
Tyler Robert, b. 8/31/2003 in N. Conway; Paul Smith and Jaime Smith
William P., b. 9/22/1953; Perry Everett Smith (Conway) and Mary Roselyn Avery (Acton, ME)

STONE,
Helen Marie, b. 7/15/1957; Ralph Clifton Stone (Conway) and Shirley Ann Hill (Conway)

TABOR,
Jesse Scott, b. 7/28/1984

TINKHAM,
Riley Jensen, b. 10/26/2002 in N. Conway; Frederick Tinkham and Vikki Tinkham

TOWLE,
Doris Edna, b. 11/2/1954; Willie G. Towle (NH) and Eleanor Cheney (Albany)

VAN DYNE,
Jessica Marie, b. 8/18/1992; Scott Van Dyne (NH) and Renee Ferluge (NY)
Tyler P., b. 5/23/1995; Scott Van Dyne (NH) and Rene Ferluge (NH)

VARNEY,
Paul Edward, b. 5/19/1934 in Albany; third; Edward H. Varney (laborer, 35, Holyoke, MA) and Mildred L. Lyman (25, Albany); residence - Rockland, ME

VAUGHAN,
Jonathan Richard, b. 8/27/2002 in MA; Jonathan Vaughan and Paula Norton

VIZARD,
Amanda Ruth, b. 6/11/1991; Steven Vizard (MA) and Sandra Edwards (NH)
Danielle L., b. 7/16/1997; Scott Vizard and Kathleen Vizard
Jennifer M., b. 11/21/1995; Scott Vizard (MA) and Kathy Fountain (MA)
Krystina Mary, b. 10/15/1992; Scott Vizard (NH) and Kathleen Fountain (MA)

WARREN,
Andrew Patrick, b. 2/13/2002 in N. Conway; David Warren and Lisa Weaver

WATTERS,
Charles Norman, Jr., b. 8/4/1999; Charles Watters and Heather Croteau

WELCH,
Margaret E., b. 4/17/1918; first; Russell A. Welch (laborer, Ossipee) and Hester R. Clark (Alton)

WHALEN,
James David, b. 8/4/1984
Thomas Hopkins, b. 12/12/1987

WHITE,
daughter, b. 4/28/1910; fifth; Paul White (lumberman, Canada) and L. LaFountain (Norton Mills, VT)
Kimberly Jasper, b. 1/17/1985
Shavon Nicole, b. 10/6/1987

WILLENBROCK,
Amy Lauren, b. 1/11/1985
Christine Anne, b. 11/4/1986

WILLIS,
Zara Ann Deyak, b. 10/23/1986

WURTZ,
Nicole A., b. 6/13/1997; John Wurtz and Sandra Wurtz

YETTON,
Chester L., b. 4/2/1895 in Albany; first; George Yetton and Mabel Moody (19, Albany); residence - Conway

ALBANY MARRIAGES

ABBOTT,
George O. of Albany m. Carrie **Mehan** of Albany 5/17/1899 in Conway; H - 31, laborer, b. Albany, s/o James L. Abbott (Jackson) and Julia Harriman (Albany); W - housekeeper, b. Albany, d/o Thurston Smith and Hannah Smith (Albany)
James A. m. Sandra B. **Jondro** 5/15/1997

ADAMS,
Herbert A. m. Maude M. **Gilbert** 5/15/1949 in Rochester; H - 58, b. Madison, ME; W - 60, b. Derry
Stephen M. of Albany m. Kathleen S. **Christenson** of Albany 6/28/2003 in Albany

AINSWORTH,
Henry D., Jr. m. Doris R. **Kates** 8/29/1949 in Conway; H - 26, b. MA; W - 18, b. NH

ALBRECHT,
Dwight D., Jr. of NH m. Heather J. **Taylor** of NH 2/14/1998

ALLARD,
Lorenzo D. of Albany m. Edna M. **Wentworth** of Albany 3/20/1894 in Conway; H - 53, farmer, b. Conway, s/o Henry Allard (Albany) and Fannie; W - 16, housewife, b. Miland, d/o Henry Wentworth and Abbie

ANNIS,
Earl C. of Albany m. Jennie **Dale** of Albany 6/23/1915 in Tamworth; H - 22, teamster, b. Albany, s/o James H. Annis (Madison) and Addie R. Marston (Brownfield, ME); W - 19, housewife, b. Shirley, MA, d/o Pliney B. Dale and Georgiana Tucker
James H. of Albany m. Addie R. **Marston** of Brownfield, ME 3/8/1893 in Conway; H - 25, laborer, b. Conway, s/o Joseph Annis (farmer, Albany) and Martha J. Annis; W - 21, teacher, b. Brownfield, ME, d/o Joseph Martin (farmer, Brownfield, ME) and Elizabeth Annis

AVIGNONE,
Gerald A. of Albany m. Cynthia **Lourie** of Albany 10/21/1978 in Effingham

BAILEY,
Walter of Albany m. Estelle Victoria **Foss** of NJ 10/4/2000

BATCHELDER,
William H. of New York, NY m. Angeline **McKey** of Albany; H - s/o Edward Batchelder and Wilma Hemenway; W - d/o Richard H. McKey and Elizabeth Child

BEALS,
Charles E., Jr. of Albany m. Blanche D. **Hammond** of Albany 5/30/1921 in Conway; H - 24, U.S. Dist. Forest Ranger, b. Boston, MA, s/o Charles E. Beals (Stoughton, MA) and Nellie V. Drake (Stoughton, MA); W - 18, at home, b. Albany, d/o Alfred Hammond (Albany) and Ellen Wiggin (Albany)

BELL,
Paul of Albany m. Dale A. **Lane** of Albany 9/12/1970; H - s/o Robert E. Bell and Vera Varney
Paul of Albany m. Carolann **Shannon** of Albany 1/4/2001 in Conway
Robert E. of Albany m. Vera V. **Varney** of Albany 4/7/1951 in Conway; H - 20, b. NH; W - 19, b. Rockland, ME

BERRY,
Howard Ellsworth of Tamworth m. Dorothea Louise **Moore** of Albany 7/12/1941 in E. Rochester; H - 19, b. Wolfeboro; W - 19, b. Albany

BIRKBECK,
Donald Paul of Madison m. Pamela Anne **Bell** of Albany 6/18/1972; H - s/o William Birkbeck (PA) and Lillian Burke (MA); W - d/o Robert E. Bell (NH) and Vera Varney (ME)

BLOMQUIST,
Robert Stephen of Albany m. Johanna **Wilson** of Albany 6/2/1967; H - s/o Robert Carl Blomquist of Albany and Mary Alice Foody of Albany; W - d/o Joseph Sayward Wilson of Albany and Eleanor Myrtle Doherty of Albany

BOURQUE,
John P. of NH m. Hortense **Vaccianna** of NH 10/30/1993; H - 36, b. MA; W - 37, b. Jamaica

BOUTILIER,
Kenneth F. m. Debra L. **Brown** 3/12/1975; H - s/o Rosewell Boutilier and Lillian Eastman; W - d/o Arthur M. Brown and Abra Broughton

BRETON,
John P. m. Margaret E. **de Lara** 6/14/1986

BRETT,
Christopher A. m. Robin **Graves** 3/16/1985

BROWN,
Alphonso of Albany m. Minnie E. **Downs** of Tamworth 8/26/1899 in Conway; H - 20, laborer, b. Albany, s/o Jeremiah Brown (Albany) and Jane Brown (Tamworth); W - 24, housework, b. Tamworth, d/o William Kenniston (Bartlett) and Sophia (Eaton)
David C. m. Sandra L. **Beauregard** 8/27/1982
Ford of Albany m. Minnie V. **Hammond** of Albany 12/10/1917 in Conway; H - 21, teamster, b. Albany, s/o Jeremiah Brown (Ossipee) and Jane H. Smith (Porter, ME); W - 22, housework, b. Albany, d/o Frank Hammond (Albany) and Maud E. Ealey (Conway)
Ford of Albany m. Milda **Willner** of N. Conway 11/6/1920 in N. Conway; H - 24, woodsman, b. Albany, s/o Jerry Brown (Kezar Falls, ME) and Jane Smith (Ossipee); W - 25, waitress, b. Russia, d/o Andrew Willner (Dobbin, Russia) and Louise Brig (Dobbin, Russia)
Frank W. of Albany m. Carrie **Chapman** of Albany 7/20/1896 in Tamworth; H - 20, laborer, b. Tamworth, s/o Jeremiah Brown (farmer, Albany) and Jane Brown (housewife, Porter, ME); W - 19, housewife, b. Canada, d/o Theo Chapman (farmer, Canada) and Mary Chapman (housewife, Canada)
Harold of Albany m. Yvonne **Lord** of E. Hartford, CT 7/20/1941; H - 19, b. Albany; W - 18, b. Old Lyme, CT
Mark of Albany m. Eva **Mason** of Albany 4/21/1900 in Tamworth; H - 21, farmer, b. Albany, s/o Jeremiah Brown (Albany) and Jane Brown (Tamworth); W - 16, housework, b. Albany, d/o Elijah Mason and Lizzie Mason

BUCHER,
Julius Van Dyck of Peekskill, NY m. Dorothy Merrill **Hill** of Beloit, WI 8/27/1929 in Albany; H - 24, scientist, b. New York, NY, s/o John Calvin Bucher (Mechanicsville, PA) and Florence Van Dyck (Beirut, Syria); W - 22, teacher, b. Beloit, WI, d/o Charles Herbert Hill (Washington, ME) and Helen Houston (Beloit, WI)

BUNKER,
Frank E. m. Norilla R. **Colbert** 8/24/1924 in Union; H - 19, teamster, b. Tamworth, s/o Fred Bunker (Tamworth) and Elsie M. Davis (Tamworth); W - 16, housewife, b. Quaker City, NH, d/o James H. Colbert and Bessie E. Tuttle (Raymond)

BURGESS,
Lloyd John of Albany m. Gladys **Leaird** of Albany 3/4/1933 in Albany; H - 21, laborer, b. Albany, s/o Ed. Burgess (laborer, Canada) and Annie Thibadeau (housework, Somersworth); W - 35, housework, 2nd, b. Conway; Louis F. Morrill (laborer, Nashua) and Stella Smith (housework, Albany)

BUTLER,
Crawford P. m. Julia B. **McAlpine** 5/17/1980

CAMERON,
Joshua D. of Albany m. Korin G. **Knapp** of Albany 9/14/2002 in Chocorua

CAMPBELL,
Norman J. of Albany m. Mary M. **Chesley** of Albany 11/2/1994; H - 68, b. MA; W - 61, b. NH

CARTER,
James F. of Albany m. Emma **Harriman** of Albany 12/13/1900 in Albany; H - 41, farmer, b. Albany, s/o Nathaniel Carter and Betsy Carter; W - 38, housework, b. Albany, d/o Jacob Harriman and Sarah A. Harriman

CHABOT,
Gregory of Albany m. Patricia **Moran** of Albany 11/21/1992; H - 42, b. MA; W - 40, b. CT

CHASE,
G. Elmer of Albany m. Carrie B. **Littlefield** of Conway 6/1/1907 in N. Conway; H - 25, farmer, b. Lynn, MA, s/o George Chase (Lynn, MA) and Julia (Harrison, ME); W - 29, housework, b. Conway, d/o Horace Littlefield (Albany) and Helen (Conway)

CHENEY,
Alfred H. of Albany m. Louise E. **Lamper** of Albany 7/3/1951 in Conway; H - 18, b. Albany; W - 25, b. Rochester
Chester J. m. Gladys E. **Eldridge** 8/25/1923 in Conway; H - 22, woodsman, b. Wells, ME, s/o James H. Cheney (Wells, ME) and Martha Rolinsford (Wells, ME); W - 18, housewife, b. Albany, d/o Herbert Eldridge (Mountainview) and Melinda Littlefield (Conway)

CLINTON,
Norman H. m. Janice A. **Hutchinson** 11/18/1988

COLEMAN,
Curtis of Albany m. Sheri M. **O'Mara** of Albany 6/9/2001 in Moultonboro

COLLINS,
Michael of Albany m. Jodi M. **Rajotte** of Albany 4/28/2001 in N. Conway

COMINGS,
Philip m. Theresa **Reller** 8/22/1981

CORMIER,
James G. m. Claire C. **Kennerson** 10/1/1983

CROTO,
Willard Edmund of NY m. Edythe Ann **Williams** of Albany 4/21/1956 in Conway; H - 25, b. NH; W - 22, b. CT

CUNHA,
Roger of E. Taunton, MA m. Lisa **Ferreira** of E. Taunton, MA 7/5/1991; H - 29, b. MA; W - 24, b. MA

CURRIER,
Thomas O. m. Tara L. **Taylor** 6/28/1986

DANIELS,
Todd of NH m. Amayllis B. **Keyt** of NY 11/5/1993; H - 22, b. MA; W - 23, b. NY

DASCOULIAS,
David of Albany m. Erin **Moffitt** of Albany 6/17/2000

DECHAMPS,
Albert F., Jr. of CT m. Jacquelyn Anne **Hollis** of CT 4/10/1993; H - 41, b. CT; W - 44, b. CT

DEE,
William S. of NH m. Bernadette C. **Molloy** of NH 9/18/1993; H - 52, b. MA; W - 36, b. MA

DEMARINO,
Albert J. of Albany m. Beth F. **Young** of Albany 10/19/2002 in Eaton

DEMPSEY,
John Fabian of Jamaica Plain, MA m. Linda Ann **Amirault** of Albany 9/14/1968; H - s/o John R. Dempsey (deceased) and Helen Gaska of Jamaica Plain, MA; W - d/o Eugene J. Amirault of Albany and Lucy M. Pottier of Albany

DENTE,
Paul G. of Albany m. Marolyn A. **Rose** of Albany 5/1/1994; H - 49, b. MD; W - 47, b. MA

DESOUZA,
Nick m. Kathleen **Sweeney** 11/9/1996 in Albany

DICEY,
Jeffrey L. of NH m. Jill **Kenny** of NH 10/16/1993; H - 37, b. NH; W - 27, b. MA

DONALDSON,
Jeremiah K. of Albany m. Malgorzata **Kruszyn** of Sopot 9/10/2001 in Albany

DOWNS,
Wilbur R. of Albany m. Hildagarde **Shireter** of New Durham 12/4/1920 in Conway; H - 28, farmer, b. Tamworth, s/o John Downs (Hessan, Germany) and Minnie Kennison; W - 20, candy packer, b. Kittery, ME, d/o Augusta Shrieter (NS) and Jennie McLane

DRISCOLL,
John M. m. Nancy **Matthews** 11/8/1997

DROUIN,
Albert m. Christie **Lyman** of Albany 9/22/1930 in Conway; H - 22, common laborer, b. St. Theferme de Tring., s/o Archelas Drouin (St. Evaris, Conte.) and Vermique Leclaire (St. Victor de Tring); W - 22, housework, b. Albany, d/o Charles E. Lyman (Albany) and Mary Smith (Albany)
Brenton W. m. Lisa E. **Twombly** 12/7/1985
Bruce Allan of Albany m. Marie Elaine **Nelson** of N. Conway 11/23/1963 in N. Conway; H - 20, b. Albany; W - 18, b. VT

DUFRESNE,
David m. Kelly **LeRoche** 9/9/1989

EMERSLEBEN,
Otto of Brunswick, ME m. Helen **Cafferety** of Brunswick, ME 5/19/1992; H - 52, b. Germany; W - 49, b. PA

FERRIS,
Joseph G. of Albany m. Deborah L. **Knapp** of Albany 6/11/1994; H - 33, b. MA; W - 33, b. NH
Joseph G. of NH m. Laurie **Schlesinger** of NH 2/7/1998

FITZPATRICK,
Joseph M. m. Lynne R. **Cummings** 11/29/1997

FOULKE,
Richard Flaidd of PA m. Nancy **Crane** of CT 12/22/1954 in Tamworth; H - 23, b. PA; W - 21, b. Albany

GALLANT,
Joseph of Albany m. Elmina **Lavertee** of Berlin 8/18/1910 in Conway; H - 46, railroad work, b. PEI, s/o Dosithee Gallant (PEI) and Mary Casino (PEI); W - 44, housework, b. Canada, d/o Louis Lavertee (Canada) and Elmina Bailey (Canada)

GERRISH,
Lance Thad of Albany m. Mary Annette **Drouin** of Albany 8/12/1961 in Conway; H - 23, b. Merrill, ME; W - 23, b. Albany

GLAVIN,
Michael A. of MA m. Sandra L. **Wilson** of ME 11/26/1960 in N. Conway; H - 19, b. Albany; W - 20, b. Albany (Passaconaway Road)

GONZALEZ,
Roel m. Linda **Dusombe** 8/18/1989

GOULEF,
Napoleon of Albany m. Marie Adrienne **Drouin** of Albany 7/12/1932 in Conway; H - 25, laborer, b. Lake Migantic, Canada, s/o Odias Goulef (St. Bacien, Canada) and Valerie LaChance (St. Bacien, Canada); W - 18, housework, b. Lewiston, ME, d/o Archie Drouin (St. Efemme, Canada) and Veronique LeClaire (St. Victor, Canada)

GOUPIL,
Daniel of Albany m. Tammy **Larrabee** of Albany 9/28/1991; H - 27, b. NH; W - 23, b. ME

GRANT,
Keith A. m. Roxanne M. **Brown** 10/8/1983

GRIFFITH,
Joe H. m. Dianne R. **Donovan** 7/11/1987

HACHEE,
Jessie of Albany m. Delia R. **Hogan** of Albany 11/5/1895 in Rochester; H - 30, quarryman, b. NB, s/o Jestar Hachee (carpenter, NB) and Lucy Landay (housewife); W - 30, housewife, 2nd, b. Canada

HACKETT,
Thomas I. m. Amy L. **Rollnick** 6/7/1986
Thomas I. of Madison m. Cheryl J. **Brown** of Albany 8/31/2002 in Plymouth

HAMMOND,
Frank O. of Albany m. Maud E. **Ealey** 11/25/1893 in Conway; H - 25, laborer, b. Albany, s/o Phineas Hammond (farmer, Albany) and M. E. Hammond (Albany); W - 20, housewife, b. Conway, d/o Everett Ealey (laborer, Albany) and Elvinia Ealey
Victor C. of Albany m. Doris E. **Litchfield** of Conway 5/31/1969; H - s/o Frank O. Hammond (deceased) and Maude Early (deceased); W - d/o Otis M. Quint of Conway and Maude Willey (deceased)

HARRIMAN,
Ebenezer of Albany m. Maude **Hammond** of Albany 12/31/1893 in Conway; H - 26, laborer, b. Albany, s/o J. L. Harriman (farmer, Albany) and Sarah Harriman (Albany); W - 2nd

HARRIS,
James of Albany m. Susan **Burnell** of Albany 5/30/1992; H - 33, b. MA; W - 33, b. MA

HARTFORD,
Richard J. of Albany m. Christi L. **Skinner** of Conway 5/17/2001 in N. Conway

HAWES,
Vernon R. m. Pearl N. **Bacon** 12/12/1924 in Conway; H - 20, school teacher, b. Pittsburg, s/o George W. Hawes (Pittsburg) and Geneva Farnsworth (Pittsburg); W - 19, school teacher, b. Pittsburg, d/o Hiram W. Bacon (Pittsburg) and Nellie Sanborn (Pittsburg)

HEATH,
Gary P. m. Edna A. **Drouin** 7/3/1983

HENEFELD,
Louis S. m. Joan M. **Stern** 10/10/1982

HERMANCE,
Robert J. m. Audrey L. **Salo** 11/12/1980

HILLIARD,
Clarence of Albany m. Alice **Miller** of Dover 8/16/1925 in Salem; H - 21, woodsman, b. Hill, s/o Nathan Hilliard (Hill) and Mary Stone (Dover); W - 20, housework, b. Dover, d/o William Miller and Cristie McDonald

HIVELY,
Jonathon m. Jane S. **Wilcox** 7/18/1987

HOBBS,
Alpheus of Conway m. Hattie L. **Merrill** of Albany 9/2/1909 in Albany; H - 42, woodworker, b. Tamworth, s/o William H. Hobbs (Tamworth) and Urene Brown (Albany); W - 30, housework, b. Beverly, MA, d/o A. W. Montcalm (Canada) and Etta Lower (Germantown, PA)

HODGDON [see Hodsdon],
John A. of Albany m. Angie B. **Glidden** of Albany 11/25/1903 in Tamworth; H - 24, farmer, b. Albany, s/o C. P. Hodgdon (Ossipee) and Abigail Hodgdon (Albany); W - 20, housewife, b. Effingham, d/o William Glidden (Effingham) and R. A. Glidden (Effingham)
Raymond T. m. Bertha M. **Jones** 6/10/1922 in Tamworth; H - 30, b. Albany; W - 18, b. Eaton

HODSDON [see Hodgdon],
John A. of Albany m. Marguerite M. **Jones** of Eaton 4/6/1918 in Conway; H - 39, farmer, b. Albany, s/o Charles Hodgdon (Ossipee) and Abbie Mason (Albany); W - 18, housework, b. Eaton, d/o Charles Jones (Eaton) and Effie Dennett (Eaton)

HOLT,
Jeffrey T. of NH m. Theresa M. **Paquette** of NH 8/28/1993; H - 33, b. CT; W - 23, b. MA

HOWLAND,
J. Peter m. Lucy L. **Warren** 7/31/1987

HUNT,
Calvert C., Jr. m. Ann C. **Weston** 8/31/1980

HUTCHINS,
Clifford C. of Albany m. Diane F. **Clinton** of Albany 3/21/1994; H - 32, b. MA; W - 27, b. MA

INGALL,
George A. of Albany m. Luella **Moody** of Albany 6/7/1899 in Intervale; H - 22, painter, b. Hancock, VT, s/o A. E. Ingall (Brenton, VT) and Annette Ingall (Brenton, VT); W - 21, housework, b. Albany, d/o George W. Moody and Mary A. Moody (Ireland)

IRELAND,
Scott R. of Albany m. Donna L. **Lessard** of Albany 10/6/1990; H - 22, b. NH; W - 22, b. NH

JACKSON,
Jesse R. of W. Milan m. Ethel E. **Allard** of Albany 9/11/1914 in Tamworth; H - 30, laborer, b. W. Milan, s/o Reuben Jackson and Elva Hagar (W. Milan); W - 18, milliner, b. Albany, d/o Lorenzo Allard (deceased) and Eva Wentworth (Milan)

JAEGER,
Paul J. m. Tommie R. **Stivers** 12/30/1980

JOSEPHSON,
Michael A. m. Sharon E. **Croto** 10/29/1977 in Chocorua

KASPERSKI,
John of IL m. Nancy **Slazes** of IL 6/19/1995; H - 32, b. IL; W - 29, b. IL

KEEFE,
Thomas W. m. Sharon A. **Ingraham** 12/29/1984

KELLEY,
John E. m. Frances H. **White** 6/25/1949 in N. Haverhill; H - 39, b. Haverhill; W - 39, b. S. Lebanon, ME

KEYHOE,
Dewey T. of Albany m. Mildred A. **Tobin** of Albany 7/5/1951 in Conway; H - 53, b. Walpole, MA; W - 51, b. Dedham, MA

KING,
Paul m. Maura **Hogan** 8/7/1982
Richard M. m. Linda J. **Bartlett** 6/13/1980

KINSLOW,
Weldon Elliott of Conway m. Irma Eva **Morrill** of Albany 7/4/1940 in Albany; H - 21, b. Portland, ME; W - 19, b. Albany

KNOX,
Nathaniel B. of Albany m. Olive **Wright** of Albany 4/20/1915 in Conway; H - 48, painter, b. New Britain, CT, s/o Charles B. Knox (Albany) and Ann P. West (Hollis, ME); W - 34, housewife, b. Winooski, VT, d/o Loomis J. Wright (Winooski, VT) and Mary Meyers (Virgins, VT)
Russell H. of Medford, MA m. Lynn **Blomquist** of Albany 8/22/1970; H - s/o Nathaniel B. Knox and Marion V. Genthner
Stephen T. of Albany m. Sara E. **Young** of Albany 8/26/1978 in Albany

LANE,
Stephen A. of Albany m. Bertha E. **Walters** of Albany 11/23/1912 in Conway; H - 26, farmer, b. Albany, s/o Henry S. Lane and Agnes Martin; W - 21, housework, b. Warren, ME, d/o Sydney E. Butler and Annie Alice White
Timothy of Albany m. Dawn **Morin** of Albany 10/21/1995; H - 34, b. NH; W - 21, b. NH

LANOIE,
Russell Howard of Albany m. Joan **Peper** of Lexington, MA 5/22/1971; H - s/o Armand Lanoie (RI) and Anna Rousseau (RI); W - d/o Phillip Peper (Holland) and Alegonda Balte (Holland)

LAROCHELLE,
Adelard of Canada m. Eva **Martineau** of Albany 4/5/1909 in Conway; H - 23, woodsman, b. St. Claire, s/o Joe LaRochelle (Canada) and Margeret Orelle (Canada); W - 15, housework, b. Canada, d/o Frank Martineau (Canada) and Mary Martineau (Canada)

LAUZON,
Francis J. of Albany m. Mary J. **Ford** of Albany 9/16/1970; H - s/o George J. Lauzon and Leona Gagnon; W - d/o Earl W. Ford and Agnes S. Hatch

LAWRIE,
James K. of Canada m. Mara S. **Wald** of NY 9/12/1993; H - 27, b. Canada; W - 23, b. NY

LAZAREK,
Albert J. m. Patricia A. **Meehan** 8/8/1987

LEAVITT,
Arthur William of Albany m. Mary Irene **Peters** of N. Conway 6/2/1962 in Conway; H - 29, b. Albany; W - 28, b. N. Conway
John W. m. Aubrey L. **Pickering** 12/4/1976 in Tamworth

LEBLANC,
George R. of Albany m. Lisa M. **Edmunds** of Albany 9/6/2003 in Albany

LE ROYER,
Charles Phillip, III m. Marcia Grace **Salvaggio** 7/23/1977 in Albany

LEWIS,
Robert D. m. Deborah D. **Rathke** 5/8/1982
Samuel of Albany m. Lena A. **Perkins** of Albany 12/24/1900 in Tamworth; H - 28, laborer, b. Lynn, MA, s/o James S. Lewis

(Lynn, MA) and Ellen T. Lewis (Moultonboro); W - 19, housework, b. Albany, d/o Sumner Perkins (Madison) and Gusty Perkins (Ossipee)

LITTLEFIELD,
Frederick of Albany m. Luella M. **Libit** of Madison 5/12/1895 in Albany; H - 27, quarryman, b. Albany, s/o Horatio Littlefield (farmer, Albany) and Frances Littlefield (housewife, Conway); W - 18, housewife, d/o Eliphalet Libit (tool sharpener) and Amey Libit (housewife)

LOTHIAN,
Chester I. m. Ethel L. **Cresey** 5/27/1926 in Conway; H - 57, merchant, b. Truro, MA, s/o Chester H. Lothian (Truro, MA) and Maria L. Ryan (Truro, MA); W - 17, b. Gloucester, MA, d/o George Cresey (Gloucester, MA) and Lillian Thomas (Gloucester, MA)

LYMAN,
Edwin C. of Albany m. Lena E. **Smith** of Conway 8/5/1942 in Conway; H - 22, b. Berlin; W - 19, b. Fryeburg, ME
John m. Mary A. **Thibadeau** 4/30/1923 in Conway; H - 31, woodsman, b. Albany, s/o Charles E. Lyman (Albany) and Mary E. Smith (Albany); W - 49, at home, b. Somersworth, d/o John Thibadeau (Canada) and Angie Thibadeau (ME)

MALONE,
Michael G. of IL m. Caren M. **Chimick** of IL 9/5/1998

MARKO,
Anthony B. of Albany m. Mary **Melega** of N. Conway 6/13/1978 in Manchester

MASSA,
James R. m. Jean E. **Schiller** 9/8/1984

MAURA,
Edward L. m. Anne L. **Dingman** 9/22/1984

MAYHEW,
Charles E. of Albany m. Nellie G. **Kimball** of Albany 11/21/1895 in Albany; H - 26, farmer, 2nd, b. Conway, s/o James Mayhew (farmer, England) and Sarah C. Mayhew (housewife, Albany); W - 27, school teacher, b. Reading, MA, d/o Franklin Kimball (physician, Andover) and Harriet E. Kimball (housewife)

McDORMAND,
Keith F. m. Elizabeth Ann **Lloyd** 5/24/1986

McPHERSON,
Kenneth E., Jr. m. Jennifer L. **Roy** 8/9/1997

MOODY,
Henry B. of Albany m. Lucy M. **Plant** of Tamworth 9/8/1901 in Ossipee; H - 27, laborer, b. Albany, s/o George W. Moody (Albany) and Mary A. Moody (Albany); W - 19, housewife, b. Tamworth, d/o Joseph Plant (Tamworth) and Ellen Plant (Tamworth)

MOORE,
Charles T. of Albany m. Jeanette E. **Moore** of Tamworth 10/8/1919 in Tamworth; H - 25, carpenter, b. Albany, s/o William N. Moore (Great Falls) and J. Hammond (Tamworth); W - 18, housewife, b. Tamworth, d/o Edgar H. Moore (S. Berwick) and Mary A. Kenison (Tamworth)

Harry J., Jr. of Albany m. Annie L. **Brooks** of Freedom 9/5/1942 in Freedom; H - 23, b. Albany; W - 22, b. Freedom

Harry L. of Lowell, ME m. Alice **Wiggin** of Albany 5/14/1910 in Conway; H - 22, laborer, b. Lowell, ME, s/o Halis Moore (Lowell, ME) and Susan Nites (Sweden, ME); W - 20, housework, b. Chatham, d/o Isaac Wiggin (Chatham) and Celia Haley (Brownfield, ME)

Willie N. of Madison m. Josephine **Hammond** of Albany 6/20/1893 in Madison; H - 20, quarryman, b. Great Falls, s/o J. H. Moore (quarryman, Madison) and Amede Moore; W - 17, housewife, b. Tamworth, d/o J. Hammond (carpenter, Albany) and S. E. Ross (housewife, Albany)

MORRILL,
Clyde Franklin of Albany m. Almee Lois **White** of Albany 6/16/1934 in E. Rochester; H - 21, carpenter, b. Albany, s/o Louis F. Morrill (laborer, Nashua) and Ina B. Hammond (housewife, Albany); W - 22, teacher, b. Lebanon, ME, d/o Edmund John White (shoemaker, Lebanon, ME) and Annie L. Rankin (housewife, S. Berwick, ME)
Louis F. of Albany m. Ina B. **Hammond** of Albany 6/30/1910 in Tamworth; H - 38, farmer, b. Nashua, s/o George S. Morrill (Goshen) and Mary C. Bagley (Nashua); W - 19, housework, b. Albany, d/o Ichabod Hammond (Effingham) and Sarah E. Ross (Albany)

MULHERIN,
Nathan D. of Conway m. Janice C. **Knox** of Albany 9/30/1978 in Freedom

MURDOCK,
Michael m. Lori **Bowman** 6/26/1986

NELSON,
John H., Jr. of Albany m. Suzanne M. **Littlefield** of Albany 12/23/1994; H - 38, b. ME; W - 33, b. ME

NICKERSON,
Nelson of Albany m. Helen M. **Brown** of Albany 6/15/1901 in Tamworth; H - 22, laborer, b. Yarmouth, NS, s/o C. N. Nickerson (Yarmouth, NS) and Joanna Nickerson (Yarmouth, NS); W - 17, housewife, b. Albany, d/o Jerry Brown (Albany) and June Brown (Albany)

NOYES,
Jeffery A. of Conway m. Joanna T. **Gagne** of Albany 9/28/1970; H - s/o Hubert R. Noyes and Mary M. Jeffery; W - d/o Wilfred F. Gagne and Cecile T. Villeneuve
Jonathan P. of Albany m. Joy J. **Acker** of Albany 5/18/2002 in Wolfeboro

NUNN,
Stephen m. Brenda **Vladyka** 6/8/1996 in Brownfield, ME

O'CONNOR,
Dennis D. of Amherst m. Karen A. **Homa** of Amherst 8/25/1990; H - 28, b. MA; W - 28, b. CA

O'NEIL,
George C. of FL m. Nancy P. **Campbell** of Canada 7/11/1994; H - 66, b. MA; W - 51, b. Canada

OLSON,
Paul of Albany m. Wendy **McGee** of Albany 12/4/1992; H - 27, b. MA; W - 27, b. ME

PACE,
Philip of MA m. Julie **Blackwell** of MA 12/14/2000

PAINE,
Charles J. m. Sylvelin T. **Lackey** 9/14/1976 in Ctr. Ossipee

PARISEAU,
Paul m. Melodie **Lemieux** 12/21/1996 in Webster, MA

PEARE,
Chris A. of Albany m. Terri L. **Rider** of Albany 9/2/1990; H - 29, b. NH; W - 33, b. NH

PERKINS,
Jonathan of Wakefield, RI m. Lisa **Ferraro** of Wakefield, RI 5/16/1992; H - 29, b. RI; W - 29, b. RI

PIPER,
Franklin P. of Albany m. Lucy M. **Foster** of Albany 5/5/1907 in N. Conway; H - 49, hotel business, b. Tuftonboro, s/o Joshua N. Piper (Tuftonboro) and Orra L. Laport (Braintree); W - 22, housekeeper, b. Albany, d/o Joseph Foster (Canada) and Grace Harriman (Albany)

PLAICE,
Douglas of ME m. Sonja Mae **Javinen** of ME 6/5/1999

POMERLEAU,
Christopher M. m. Lisa J. **Boucher** 4/12/1997

POTTER,
Aarron S. of Albany m. Jessica M. **Martin** of Albany 6/22/2003 in Tamworth

PUTNAM,
Allan L. m. Elizabeth J. **Sanger** 11/28/1987

QUIRK,
Joseph S. m. Agnes H. **Cain** 12/26/1919 in N. Conway; H - 24, shipfitter, b. Milford, MA, s/o Thomas Quirk (Ireland) and Mary Cockran (Milford, MA); W - 19, at home, b. Charlestown, MA, d/o James J. Cain and Annie L. Murphy (Charlestown, MA)

RALPH,
Thomas of Albany m. Hope Ann **Terry** of MI 10/14/1995; H - 27, b. MA; W - 25, b. MI

RANCO,
Frederick m. Margrett **Lathrop** 6/21/1981

RENDA,
John F. of NH m. Barbara **Schamadan** of NH 8/1/1998

RICHARDSON,
Washington of Albany m. Fannie R. **Littlefield** of Albany 12/16/1894 in Albany; H - 49, stonecutter, b. Denmark, ME, s/o Lewis Richardson (Denmark, ME) and E. J.; W - 10 (sic), housewife, b. Albany, d/o Horatio Littlefield (Albany) and Frances

ROGERS,
David of Madison m. Dorothy **Hill** of Albany 8/12/1995; H - 69, b. NH; W - 58, b. NH
Frederick Dwight of Bartlett m. Donna Gail **Chesley** of Albany 8/30/1971; H - s/o Dwight Rogers (ME) and Faylene Stewart (NH); W - d/o John Chesley (NH) and Mary McLellan (NH)
Orrin K. of Albany m. Sheila A. **Harding** of Albany 3/18/1971; H - s/o Beatrice Rogers (ME); W - d/o Albert Lane (NH) and Myrtle Hobart (ME)

ROWELL,
Kimball A. m. Valeria M. **Drouin** 6/30/1984

RYAN,
Ronald P. of Albany m. Cathy A. **McKenzie** of Albany 10/26/2002 in Albany
Stephen of Albany m. Kimberly **Masterman** of Albany 3/1/1999

SANBORN,
Robert C. of Albany m. Eldesta A. **Marsters** of Conway 10/30/1965 in Moultonboro; H - 43, b. Tamworth; W - 48, b. N. Conway

SAUVAGEAU,
Michael G. of Albany m. Jennifer L. **Kronberg** of Albany 8/17/2002 in Tamworth

SEAVEY,
Roger B. m. Roberta J. **Inkell** 10/4/1986

SHACKFORD,
Joseph M., III m. Raina M. **Lance** 12/31/1997
Mark of Albany m. Andrea **Smith** of Albany 8/1/1992; H - 32, b. NH; W - 22, b. ME

SIMMONS,
James, Jr. of Albany m. Colleen L. **Cormack** of Albany 7/17/2003 in Bartlett

SMITH,
Dixie of Albany m. Laura May **Forbell** of E. Orange, NJ 8/29/1937 in Conway; H - 67, b. Albany; W - 40, b. Brooklyn, NY
Franklin m. Bonnie **Locke** 10/13/1989
George H. of Albany m. Carrie B. **Marston** of Brownfield, ME 10/2/1896 in Conway; H - 22, farmer, b. Albany, s/o Henry Smith (farmer, Albany) and Elmira Smith (housewife, Albany); W - 22, school teacher, b. Brownfield, d/o Joseph Marston (farmer, Brownfield, ME) and Lizzie Marston (housewife, Baldwin, ME)
Henry I. of Albany m. Katherine **Morris** of Waverly Hall, GA 4/9/1931 in Conway; H - 55, carpenter, 2nd, b. Machias, ME, s/o William Smith (Halifax, NS) and Emily J. Beckit (Calais, ME); W - 24, at

home, 2nd, b. Weedowee, AL, d/o Marrion Nails (Weedowee, AL) and Nora Johnson (Weedowee, AL)
Jed A. m. Fiona J. **Rotberg** 8/16/1997
Peter H. of Albany m. Lindsey N. **Tofflemoyer** of Albany 7/21/2001 in Albany
Walter of Albany m. Jennie E. **Rideout** of Albany 11/27/1907; H - 23, railroadman, b. Tamworth, s/o Alphonse Smith (Tamworth) and Anna Brown (Tamworth); W - 18, housework, b. Conway, d/o Willedon R. Rideout (NB) and Carrie (Biddeford)

STEPANAUSKAS,
Daniel A. m. Stephanie A. **Salmon** 5/19/1984

STEVENS,
George of Albany m. Grace **Day** of Albany 11/12/1907 in Conway; H - 21, laborer, b. NB, s/o Charles Stevens (NB) and Victoria (NB); W - 18, housework, b. NB, d/o Allan Day (NB) and Prudence (NB)

STROUT,
Frank F. of Reading, MA m. Ella Ervina **Bachellor** of Reading, MA 8/2/1936 in Albany; H - 78, b. Charlestown, MA; W - 70, b. N. Reading, MA

SULLIVAN,
Daniel J., III m. Donna M. **Leconte** 9/12/1981

SWANN,
Thomas J., Jr. m. Kathy L. **Weinman** 10/4/1980

SWIENTON,
John of RI m. Barbara **Huftalen** of RI 5/21/1978 in Albany

SWISHER,
John of Albany m. Deborah **Roberts** of Albany 2/16/1994; H - 31, b. MA; W - 30, b. NE

TABOR,
Stanley S. m. Doreen A. **Burke** 5/30/1980

TASKER,
Stillman P. of Albany m. Jane H. **Brown** of Albany 6/16/1914 in Albany; H - 70, paper maker, b. Tamworth, s/o Warren Tasker (Wells, ME) and Elizabeth Perkins (Porter, ME); W - 60, housework, b. Porter, ME, d/o Daniel Smith (Porter, ME) and Hannah Libby (Porter, ME)

TAYLOR,
Brian R. m. Jo-Ann **Crell** 10/18/1980

THOMAS,
David W. m. Diane C. **Harrington** 6/27/1987
Frank of Albany m. Ida **Barney** of Albany 10/24/1907 in N. Conway; H - 22, lumberman, b. Burnon, s/o Peter Thomas (Burnon) and Ida (NB); W - 16, housework, b. Burnon, d/o John Barnaby and Delphin (Montreal)

TILTON,
David J. of NH m. Nancy A. **Cushman** of NH 4/14/1993; H - 32, b. ME; W - 26, b. NH

TINKHAM,
Frederick L. of Albany m. Vikki S. **Gifford** of Albany 10/13/2001 in Effingham Falls

TOFFLEMOYER,
Douglas of Albany m. Kelly Ann **Richards** of Albany 7/24/1999

TROTT,
Frank Warren m. Esther Marion **Bickford** 7/26/1949 in Madison; H - 45, b. Biddeford, ME; W - 26, b. Wolfeboro

TUCK,
Richard G. m. Sally D. **Thibodeau** 8/16/1985

TUCKER,
Alan J. of Sharon, MA m. Donna **Goldman** of Sharon, MA 6/7/1980 in Albany Covered Bridge

TYLER,
Orrin of Albany m. Bertha E. **Butler** of Warren, ME 4/16/1909 in Tamworth; H - 40, laborer, b. Albany, s/o John F. Tyler (Albany) and Mary Jane Allard (Albany); W - 18, housework, b. Warren, ME, d/o Sydney E. Butler (Union, ME) and Annie Alice White (Appleton, ME)
Orrin J. m. Annie L. **Kane** 8/29/1915 in Conway; H - 42, laborer, b. Albany, s/o Jonathan F. Tyler (Albany) and Mary Jane Allard (Albany); W - 32, housewife, b. Charleston, M., d/o Edward Murphy (PEI) and Annie Hegan (NB)

ULMAN,
Jacob of Lynn, MA m. Alice **Newhall** of Lynn, MA 9/3/1902 in Albany; H - 28, electrician, b. Boston, MA, s/o Wilbur Ulman (Boston, MA) and Elizabeth Ulman (Boston, MA); W - 22, b. Lynn, MA, s/o Aaron Newhall (Lynn, MA) and Alice Newhall (Lowell, MA)

URTZ,
Michael P. of NY m. Cynthia A. **Clark** of NY 7/18/1998

VALLADARES,
Allan m. Leah A. **Manning** 8/29/1997

VIZARD,
Steven m. Sandra **Edwards** 10/14/1989

WALSH,
William of MA m. Stephanie **Gordon** of MA 6/10/2000

WATSON,
Donald R. m. Donna J. **Manchester** 11/5/1983

WATTERS,
Charles, Jr. of Conway m. Heather **Croteau** of Albany 9/29/2001 in Albany

WELLMAN,
George J. m. Penny B. **Brown** 1/14/1984

WEDGE,
Michael of Albany m. Lisa **Weiland** of Conway 9/23/1995; H - 23, b. NH; W - 18, b. CA

WEST,
Edward N. of Boston, MA m. Dora **Willey** of Albany 9/25/1900 in Albany; H - 31, merchant, b. Chester, s/o Nason D. West (Chester) and Sarah J. West (Chester); W - 25, housewife, b. Boston, MA, d/o Frank R. Carter

WHEELER,
David R. m. Sara A. **McKenna** 5/29/1982

WHELAN,
Daniel J. m. Susan S. **Hayes** 5/31/1980

WHIGHAM,
Jack m. Judy **Freve** 12/16/1988

WHITE,
Wayne W. m. Terry L. **Moody** 6/14/1985

WIGGIN,
Craig W. m. Peggy A. **Chute** 7/4/1985
Kenneth L., Jr. m. Linda J. **Plouff** 6/21/1980
Mark W. of Conway m. Dorothy Louise **Wilson** of Albany 5/25/1968; H - s/o Mark Wiggin of Conway and Amber Harriman of Conway; W - d/o Edward Newcomb and Rhodora Preston
Paul Ellis of Albany m. Patricia Kay **Whitman** of Raymond 9/8/1964 in Conway; H - 19, b. N. Conway; W - 18, b. Concord

WIGGINS,
George W. of Fryeburg m. Effie **Tibideau** of Albany 3/2/1901 in Conway; H - 28, mason, b. Fryeburg, ME, s/o I. Wiggins (Chatham) and Ellen Hesley (Chatham); W - 16, housewife, b. Albany, d/o John Tibideau (Albany) and Angeline Tibideau (Albany)

WILLEY,
Horatio of Albany m. ----- **Belezia** of Albany 7/16/1893 in Albany; H - 19, laborer, b. Albany, s/o G. W. Willey (laborer, Albany) and Mary Willey (housewife, Albany); W - b. Boston, MA

WILLIS,
Peter C. m. N. Kate **Deyak** 12/15/1984
Roger of Albany m. Susan **Graves** of Albany 4/22/1995; H - 31, b. AR; W - 27, b. NH

WOOD,
Richard R., Jr. of NJ m. Elizabeth Thacher **Hoag** of Northampton, MA 8/6/1954 in Albany; H - 22, b. Riverton, NJ; W - 19, b. Ardmore, PA

WRIGHT,
Loomis J. m. Margaret I. **Briley** 9/21/1928 in Conway; H - 47, machinist, 2nd, b. Burlington, VT, s/o Loomis J. Wright (Burlington, VT) and Mary Myers (Burlington, VT); W - 43, housewife, 2nd, b. NS, d/o James Wiley (NS) and Anna Langille (River John)

WYATT,
Stephen H. m. Linda R. **Calvert** 7/16/1983

Acker, Joy J. - Noyes, Jonathan P.
Allard, Ethel E. - Jackson, Jesse R.
Amirault, Linda Ann - Dempsey, John Fabian

Bachellor, Ella Ervina - Strout, Frank F.
Bacon, Pearl N. - Hawes, Vernon R.
Barney, Ida - Thomas, Frank
Bartlett, Linda J. - King, Richard M.
Beauregard, Sandra L. - Brown, David C.
Belezia, ----- - Willey, Horatio
Bell, Pamela Anne - Birkbeck, Donald Paul
Bickford, Esther Marion - Trott, Frank Warren
Blackwell, Julie - Pace, Philip
Blomquist, Lynn - Knox, Russell H.
Boucher, Lisa J. - Pomerleau, Christopher M.
Bowman, Lori - Murdock, Michael
Briley, Margaret I. (Wiley) - Wright, Loomis J.
Brooks, Annie L. - Moore, Harry J., Jr.
Brown, Cheryl J. - Hackett, Thomas I.
Brown, Debra L. - Boutilier, Kenneth F.
Brown, Helen M. - Nickerson, Nelson
Brown, Jane H. - Tasker, Stillman P.
Brown, Penny B. - Wellman, George J.
Brown, Roxanne M. - Grant, Keith A.
Burke, Doreen A. - Tabor, Stanley S.
Burnell, Susan - Harris, James
Butler, Bertha E. - Tyler, Orrin

Cafferety, Helen - Emersleben, Otto
Cain, Agnes H. - Quirk, Joseph S.
Calvert, Linda R. - Wyatt, Stephen H.
Campbell, Nancy P. - O'Neil, George C.
Chapman, Carrie - Brown, Frank W.
Chesley, Donna Gail - Rogers, Frederick Dwight
Chesley, Mary M. - Campbell, Norman J.
Chimick, Caren M. - Malone, Michael G.
Christenson, Kathleen S. - Adams, Stephen M.
Chute, Peggy A. - Wiggin, Craig W.
Clark, Cynthia A. - Urtz, Michael P.
Clinton, Diane F. - Hutchins, Clifford C.
Colbert, Norilla R. - Bunker, Frank E.

Cormack, Colleen L. - Simmons, James, Jr.
Crane, Nancy - Foulke, Richard Flaidd
Crell, Jo-Ann - Taylor, Brian R.
Cresey, Ethel L. - Lothian, Chester I.
Croteau, Heather - Watters, Charles, Jr.
Croto, Sharon E. - Josephson, Michael A.
Cummings, Lynne R. - Fitzpatrick, Joseph M.
Cushman, Nancy A. - Tilton, David J.

Dale, Jennie - Annis, Earl C.
Day, Grace - Stevens, George
de Lara, Margaret E. - Breton, John P.
Deyak, N. Kate - Willis, Peter C.
Dingman, Anne L. - Maura, Edward L.
Donovan, Dianne R. - Griffith, Joe H.
Downs, Minnie E. (Kenniston) - Brown, Alphonzo
Drouin, Edna A. - Heath, Gary P.
Drouin, Marie Adrienne - Goulef, Napoleon
Drouin, Mary A. - Gerrish, Lance Thad
Drouin, Valeria M. - Rowell, Kimball A.
Dusombe, Linda - Gonzalez, Roel

Ealey, Maude E. - Hammond, Frank O.
Edmunds, Lisa M. - Leblanc, George R.
Edwards, Sandra - Vizard, Steven
Eldridge, Gladys E. - Cheney, Chester J.

Ferraro, Lisa - Perkins, Jonathan
Ferreira, Lisa - Cunha, Roger
Forbell, Laura May - Smith, Dixie
Ford, Mary J. - Lauzon, Francis J.
Foss, Estelle Victoria - Bailey, Walter
Foster, Lucy M. - Piper, Franklin P.
Freve, Judy - Whigham, Jack

Gagne, Joanna T. - Noyes, Jeffery A.
Gifford, Vikki S. - Tinkham, Frederick L.
Gilbert, Maude M. - Adams, Herbert A.
Glidden, Angie B. - Hodgdon, John A.
Goldman, Donna - Tucker, Alan J.
Gordon, Stephanie - Walsh, William

Graves, Robin - Brett, Christopher A.
Graves, Susan - Willis, Roger

Hammond, Blanche D. - Beals, Charles E., Jr.
Hammond, Ina B. - Morrill, Louis F.
Hammond, Josephine - Moore, Willie N.
Hammond, Maude - Harriman, Ebenezer
Hammond, Minnie V. - Brown, Ford
Harding, Sheila A. (Lane) - Rogers, Orrin K.
Harriman, Emma - Carter, James F.
Harrington, Diane C. - Thomas, David W.
Hayes, Susan S. - Whelan, Daniel J.
Hill, Dorothy - Rogers, David
Hill, Dorothy Merrill - Bucher, Julius Van Dyck
Hoag, Elizabeth Thacher - Wood, Richard R., Jr.
Hogan, Delia R. - Hachee, Jessie
Hogan, Maura - King, Paul
Hollis, Jacquelyn Anne - Dechamps, Albert F., Jr.
Homa, Karen A. - O'Connor, Dennis D.
Huftalen, Barbara - Swienton, John
Hutchinson, Janice A. - Clinton, Norman H.

Ingraham, Sharon A. - Keefe, Thomas W.
Inkell, Roberta J. - Seavey, Roger B.

Javinen, Sonja Mae - Plaice, Douglas
Jondro, Sandra B. - Abbott, James A.
Jones, Bertha M. - Hodgdon, Raymond T.
Jones, Marguerite M. - Hodsdon, John A.

Kane, Annie L. - Tyler, Orrin J.
Kates, Doris R. - Ainsworth, Henry D., Jr.
Kennerson, Claire C. - Cormier, James G.
Kenny, Jill - Dicey, Jeffrey L.
Keyt, Amayllis B. - Daniels, Todd
Kimball, Nellie G. - Mayhew, Charles E.
Knapp, Deborah L. - Ferris, Joseph G.
Kanpp, Korin G. - Cameron, Joshua D.
Knox, Janice C. - Mulherin, Nathan D.
Kronberg, Jennifer L. - Sauvageau, Michael G.
Kruszyn, Malgorzata - Donaldson, Jeremiah K.

Lackey, Sylvelin T. - Paine, Charles J.
Lamper, Louise E. - Cheney, Alfred H.
Lance, Raina M. - Shackford, Joseph M., III
Lane, Dale A. - Bell, Paul
Larrabee, Tammy - Goupil, Daniel
Lathrop, Margrett - Ranco, Frederick
Lavertee, Elmina - Gallant, Joseph
Leard, Gladys (Morrill) - Burgess, Lloyd John
Leconte, Donna M. - Sullivan, Daniel J., III
Lemieux, Melodie - Pariseau, Paul
LeRoche, Kelly - Dufresne, David
Lessard, Donna L. - Ireland, Scott R.
Libit, Luella M. - Littlefield, Frederick
Litchfield, Doris E. (Quint) - Hammond, Victor C.
Littlefield, Carrie B. - Chase, G. Elmer
Littlefield, Fannie R. - Richardson, Washington
Littlefield, Suzanne M. - Nelson, John H., Jr.
Lloyd, Elizabeth Ann - McDormand, Keith F.
Locke, Bonnie - Smith, Franklin
Lord, Yvonne - Brown, Harold
Lourie, Cynthia - Avignone, Gerald A.
Lyman, Christie - Drouin, Albert

Manchester, Donna J. - Watson, Donald R.
Manning, Leah A. - Valladares, Allan
Marsters, Eldesta A. - Sanborn, Robert C.
Marston, Carrie B. - Smith, George H.
Martin, Addie R. - Annis, James H.
Martin, Jessica M. - Potter, Aarron S.
Martineau, Eva - LaRochelle, Adelard
Mason, Eva - Brown, Mark
Masterman, Kimberly - Ryan, Steven
Matthews, Nancy - Driscoll, John M.
McAlpine, Julia B. - Butler, Crawford P.
McGee, Wendy - Olson, Paul
McKenna, Sara A. - Wheeler, David R.
McKenzie, Cathy A. - Ryan, Ronald P.
McKey, Angeline - Batchelder, William H.
Meehan, Patricia A. - Lazarek, Albert J.
Mehan, Carrie (Smith) - Abbott, George O.
Melega, Mary - Marko, Anthony B.

Merrill, Hattie L. (Montcalm) - Hobbs, Alpheus
Miller, Alice - Hilliard, Clarence
Moffitt, Erin - Dascoulias, David
Molloy, Bernadette C. - Dee, William S.
Moody, Luella - Ingall, George A.
Moody, Terry L. - White, Wayne W.
Moore, Dorothea Louise - Berry, Howard Ellsworth
Moore, Jeanette E. - Moore, Charles T.
Moran, Patricia - Chabot, Gregory
Morin, Dawn - Lane, Timothy
Morrill, Irma Eva - Kinslow, Weldon Elliott
Morris, Katherine (Nails) - Smith, Henry I.

Nelson, Marie Elaine - Drouin, Bruce Allan
Newhall, Alice - Ulman, Jacob

O'Mara, Sheri M. - Coleman, Curtis

Paquette, Theresa M. - Holt, Jeffrey T.
Peper, Joan - Lanoie, Russell Howard
Perkins, Lena A. - Lewis, Samuel
Peters, Mary Irene - Leavitt, Arthur William
Pickering, Aubrey L. - Leavitt, John W.
Plant, Lucy M. - Moody, Henry B.

Plouff, Linda J. - Wiggin, Kenneth L., Jr.
Rajotte, Jodi M. - Collins, Michael
Rathke, Deborah D. - Lewis, Robert D.
Reller, Theresa - Comings, Philip
Richards, Kelly Ann - Tofflemoyer, Douglas
Rideout, Jennie E. - Smith, Walter
Rider, Terri L. - Peare, Chris A.
Roberts, Deborah - Swisher, John
Rollnick, Amy L. - Hackett, Thomas I.
Rose, Marolyn A. - Dente, Paul G.
Rotberg, Fiona J. - Smith, Jed A.
Roy, Jennifer L. - McPherson, Kenneth E., Jr.

Salo, Audrey L. - Hermance, Robert J.
Salmon, Stephanie A. - Stepanauskas, Daniel A.
Salvaggio, Marcia Grace - LeRoyer, Charles Phillip, III

Sanger, Elizabeth J. - Putnam, Allan L.
Schamadan, Barbara - Renda, John F.
Schiller, Jean E. - Massa, James R.
Schlesinger, Laurie - Ferris, Joseph G.
Shannon, Carolann - Bell, Paul
Shireter, Hildagarde - Downs, Wilbur R.
Skinner, Christi L. - Hartford, Richard J.
Slazes, Nancy - Kasperski, John
Smith, Andrea - Shackford, Mark
Smith, Lena E. - Lyman, Edwin C.
Stern, Joan M. - Henefeld, Louis S.
Stivers, Tommie R. - Jaeger, Paul J.
Sweeney, Kathleen - Desouza, Nick

Taylor, Heather J. - Albrecht, Dwight D., Jr.
Taylor, Tara L. - Currier, Thomas O.
Terry, Hope Ann - Ralph, Thomas
Thibadeau, Mary - Lyman, John
Thibodeau, Sally D. - Tuck, Richard G.
Tibideau, Effie - Wiggins, George W.
Tobin, Mildred A. - Keyhoe, Dewey T.
Tofflemoyer, Lindsey N. - Smith, Peter H.
Twombly, Lisa E. - Drouin, Brenton W.

Vaccianna, Hortense - Bourque, John P.
Varney, Vera V. - Bell, Robert E.
Vladyka, Brenda - Nunn, Stephen

Wald, Mara S. - Lawrie, James K.
Walters, Bertha E. - Lane, Stephen A.
Warren, Lucy L. - Howland, J. Peter
Weiland, Lisa - Wedge, Michael
Weinman, Kathy L. - Swann, Thomas J., Jr.
Wentworth, Edna M. - Allard, Lorenzo D.
Weston, Ann C. - Hunt, Calvert C., Jr.
White, Almee Lois - Morrill, Clyde Franklin
White, Frances H. - Kelley, John E.
Whitman, Patricia Kay - Wiggin, Paul Ellis
Wiggin, Alice - Moore, Harry L.
Wilcox, Jane S. - Hively, Jonathon
Willey, Dora - West, Edward N.

Williams, Edythe Ann - Croto, Willard Edmund
Willner, Milda - Brown, Ford
Wilson, Dorothy Louise (Newcomb) - Wiggin, Mark W.
Wilson, Johanna - Blomquist, Robert Stephen
Wilson, Sandra L. - Glavin, Michael A.
Wright, Olive - Knox, Nathaniel B.

Young, Beth F. - Demarino, Albert J.
Young, Sara E. - Knox, Stephen T.

ALBANY DEATHS

ABBOTT,
James L., d. 4/10/1910 at 63/1; farmer; married; b. Bartlett; Lewis Abbott (Conway) and Betsy Dolloff (Conway)

ALLEN,
James A., d. 7/20/1912 at 77/0/20; widower; b. Sebec, ME; Stephen A. Allen and Lizzie Thom

AMIRAULT,
Lucy, d. 5/1/1985

ANDERSEN,
Elizabeth, d. 11/26/2000 in Albany

ANDERSON,
George C., d. 9/27/2003 in Albany; George Anderson and Maude Guild

ANNIS,
Addie R., d. 12/17/1938 at 66/10/10; b. Brownfield, ME; Joseph Marston and Elizabeth Burnell
Joseph, d. 3/25/1899 at 66/3/9 in Albany; farmer; married; b. Madison; Joseph Annis (Sanford, ME) and Ellen Littlefield (Madison)
Martha J., d. 2/16/1895 at 61 in Albany; heart disease; married; b. Buckston; William Henderson (Buckston)

ARLING,
Amelia, d. 10/10/1901 at 76 in Albany; domestic; widow

AUBIN,
daughter, d. 12/13/1909 at – in Albany; stillborn; b. Albany; Omer Aubin (Quebec) and Exlia Hartley (Berlin)
daughter, d. 12/13/1909 at 0/0/1 in Albany; premature birth; b. Albany; Omer Aubin (Quebec) and Exlia Hartley (Berlin)

BACHMAN,
Standish, d. 5/15/1989

BACKES,
Harold, d. 8/–/1998 in Portland, ME

BACKMAN,
Basil, d. 8/22/1998 in N. Conway; Gustav Backman and Elsa Person

BAKER,
Deborah G., d. 5/20/1984 in Albany

BARNHART,
Michael R., d. 7/20/1986

BATSON,
Susie Florence, d. 1/25/1961 at 99; b. US; George H. Conant and Martha Bedell

BATTENLINE,
Johana M. T., d. 6/9/1954 at 68; b. Deventer, Holland; Bernard P. Aldenberg and Jessie Kluwen

BEALS,
Charles, d. 6/15/1943 at 46/10/25; b. Boston; Charles Beals and Nellie Drake
Robert Drake, d. 3/14/1923 at 0/6/23; b. Albany; Charles E. Beals, Jr. (Cambridge, MA) and Blanche Hammond (Albany)

BEAN,
Carrie Isabel, d. 10/6/1960 at 52; b. Madison; Herbert Eldridge and Malinda Littlefield
Earnest W., d. 5/3/1990 at 80; b. Lynn, MA; Eddie W. Bean and Eva Hatch
Effie E., d. 5/13/2002 in N. Conway; Arthur DeWitt and Myrtle Jones

BEAUCHEE,
Vera, d. 1/14/1916 at 0/7; b. Conway; E. Beauche (woodsman, Canada) and Maggie Mixon (Russia)

BELL,
Archibald G., d. 3/22/1946 at 74/10/6; b. Westford, MA; Hugh Bell and Anna Gardner
Minnie Foster, d. 5/17/1951 at 66; b. Conway; George Littlefield and Carrie Whitaker

BENSON,
Charles H., d. 7/28/1913 at 10/2/28; b. Providence, RI; Charles C. Benson and Sarah Needham

BERGSTROM,
Richard G., d. 11/21/2002 in N. Conway; Carl Bergstrom and Maria Strandell

BERRY,
Helen L., d. 8/8/1982

BICKFORD,
E., d. –/–/1893 at 16/9/2 in Madison; child-birth; housewife; b. Albany; Calvin Smith and Sarah E. Knox

BIGLEY,
Andrew D., d. 12/12/1937 at 64/6/28; b. Bearsville, NB; James Bigley and Jane S. Baker
Minnie E., d. 5/11/1953 at 76; b. Madison; James L. Abbott and Julia Harriman

BIRKBECK,
Jacqueline, d. 6/15/1996

BLACKEY,
Alvah, d. 11/25/1905 at 84/0/26 in Albany; farmer; married; b. Tamworth; Samuel Blackey (Alton) and Betsey Hidden (Tamworth)

BLAISDELL,
Clarence Burton, d. 10/22/1987

BLOMQUIST,
Robert C., d. 5/13/1991 at 69; b. MA; Carl Blomquist and Helen Cullinane

BOLDUC,
Irene, d. 7/27/1909 at 4/7/3 in Albany; tubercular meningitis; b. Berlin; Thomas Bolduc (Canada) and J. Bunten (Biddeford, ME)

Samuel Treffle, d. 2/10/1960 at 19; b. Grasmere; Treffle Bolduc and Helen Botting

BOTTING,
George H., d. 8/19/1939 at 26/1/2; b. Albany; Edwin Botting and Lottie Palmer

BOUCHER,
son, d. 5/5/1916 at 0/0/1; b. Albany; Ernest Boucher (Canada) and Maggie Mixon (Canada)
Anthony, d. 11/20/1988

BROWN,
daughter, d. 1/18/1909 at – in Albany; stillborn; b. Albany; Mamie Brown (Albany)
Carl R., d. 1/5/1937 at 0/4/8; b. Albany; John Brown and Edvia Thurston
Christopher M., d. 7/6/1998 in Concord; Clifford Brown and Rosemary Slez
Eva May, d. 10/27/1924 at 42/0/28; housewife; married; b. Albany; Elijah Mason (Albany) and Elizabeth Frost
James J., d. 6/16/1990 at 53; b. N. Conway; Harold Brown and Milda Wilner
M. [female], d. 5/27/1900 at 0/1/28 in Albany; b. Albany; Jerry Brown (Albany) and Jane Smith (Parsonsfield)
Mary S., d. 4/18/1919 at 83/9/21; widow; b. Sudbury, MA; ----- Dakin and Emiline Stone (Sudbury, MA)
Minnie, d. 6/1/1919 at 23/7/16; housewife; married; b. Albany; Frank Hammond (Albany) and Maude Early (Conway)
Nathan, d. 9/5/1915 at 87/5/2; farmer; widower; b. Albany; Theophilus Brown (Albany) and Annie Head (Albany)
Nellie J., d. 11/12/1910 at 0/1/16; b. Albany; Ernest C. Brown (Albany) and Nina E. Rogers (Bethel, VT)
Raymond, d. 10/8/1906 at 1/3/8; b. Albany; Mark M. Brown (Albany) and Eva M. Mason (Albany)

BURGESS,
son, d. 12/4/1913 at 0/1/4; b. Albany; Edward Burgess and Annie Tibedeau
Gladys Morrill, d. 6/28/1954 at 57; b. Conway; Louis Morrill and Stella Smith

BURTT,
George F., d. 10/22/2002 in Portland, ME; William H. Burtt, Sr. and Muriel Crosby

BYRUM,
John Frederick, d. 5/9/1970 at 36 on Piper Trail, Mt. Chocorua; Forrest Byrum and Leita; residence - Arlington, MA

CAMERON,
Yvan, d. 7/27/1970 at 20 in Passaconaway; killed by falling tree in logging woods; Gerard Cameron and Madeleine Couture; residence - Quebec

CARRIER,
Hector A., d. 10/26/2003 in Albany; John Carrier and Marie Lapierre

CATALDO,
Vincent, d. 10/6/2001 in Albany; Vincent Cataldo and Josephine Cerrana

CHACE,
Miles W., d. 9/3/1922 at 55/0/27; b. Lynn, MA; Jack Chase and Harriet Moore

CHAMBERLAIN,
Ami E., d. 9/22/1909 at 69/8/19 in Albany; cirrhosis of liver gastritis; housewife; married; b. Conway; Otis Hatch (Wells, ME) and Jane Hatch (Wells, ME)

CHAMBERS,
Mary R., d. 7/3/2002 in Albany; William Chambers and Susan Ross

CHASE,
Anna Jane, d. 10/10/1938 at 66/4/19; b. Mermaid, PEI; Donald MacEachern and Sarah Boyce
Bertha E., d. 2/28/1949 at 57 in N. Conway; b. Warren, ME; Sydney Butler and Annie Walker
Edward E., d. 5/30/1940 at 77/11/22; b. Lynn, MA; Zachariah J. Chase and Harriet L. Moore
Frank George, d. 12/8/1960 at 68; b. Albany; Henry Lane and Agnes Martin

Mary A., d. 4/8/1907 at 55/11/14 in Albany; myelitis; housework; widow; b. Farmington; Patrick Teague (Ireland) and Mary Wade (Ireland)
Rose M., d. 7/7/1919 at 75/5/19; housewife; widow; b. Albany; Lewis Ross and Menirva Rowe (Tamworth)
William C., d. 9/1/1919 at 84; farmer; widower; b. Albany; William Chase and Lucinda Hammond (Saco, ME)

CHENEY,
infant, d. 10/21/1953 at 0/0/0; b. Albany; Chester Cheney and Gladys Eldridge
Louise Littlefield, d. 10/11/1965 at 39; b. Rochester; Charles Littlefield and Ida Libby

CHESLEY,
Albert, d. 12/17/1908 at – in Albany; arteriosclerosis; laborer; married; b. Wilton; John Chesley (Wilton, ME) and Mary Crockett (Wilton, ME)
John S., d. 3/12/1991 at 63; b. NH; Edward Chesley and Della Mae Feeney

CLYNE,
Joseph A., d. 6/12/1932 at 19 in Albany; single; Flora Clyne

COLE,
Margarett A., d. 1/24/1894 at 49; cancer; housewife; married; b. NS; Manly White (NS)
William B., d. 4/20/1913 at 75/10/20; widower; b. NS

COLEMAN,
Alvin J., d. 12/9/1985
Richard J., d. 11/16/1965 at 19; b. Leominster, MA; Oscar J. Coleman and Marguerite Williams

COLLINS,
Seward B., d. 12/7/1952 at 53; b. NY; Herbert Collins and Martha Wood

COOK,
Frank L., d. 5/21/1942 at 63/5/1; James Cook and Mary Bunker

CROTEAU,
Melvin E., d. 7/5/1990 at 63; b. Boston, MA; Fredrick Croteau and Lillian Domingue
Theresa C., d. 10/10/1992 at 61; b. MA; Joseph Levesque and Claire Lawrence

CROTO,
Willard E., d. 12/12/2002 in Manchester; Napoleon Croto and Cora Crotto

CROWELL,
George W., d. 5/3/1895 at 23/10/15 in Albany; pneumonia; single; b. Barnstable; James P. Crowell (Barnstable) and Rosetta Avery

CURRIER,
Helen, d. 8/2/1907 at 34/3/30 in Albany; cancer in pelvis; housework; married; b. Gorham; Henry Goodnow (Gorham) and Kate Finnegan (Ireland)
William, d. 11/23/1908 at – in Albany; sectionman; married; b. Albany

DALTON,
Aaron, d. 4/16/1940 at 67; b. Russia; George Dalton

DEMARS,
Clara, d. 11/30/1905 at 0/7/18 in Albany; b. Albany; Angus Demars (Canada) and Louise Fortier (Canada)

DOWNS,
Grace, d. 5/11/1920 at 29/5/20; housewife; married; b. Gonic; Charles Black and Anna Nute (Wolfeboro)

DREW,
John N., d. 2/18/1938 at 76/11/4; b. Tamworth; John A. Drew and ----- Wiggin

DROUIN,
Albert J., d. 8/19/1941 at 4/9/7 in Albany; Albert J. Drouin and Christine Lyman
Albert J., d. 3/12/1993 at 82; b. Canada; Archibald Drouin and Veronica LeClerke

Christine, d. 10/22/1989
Robert E., d. 10/23/1930 at 0/1/13 in Albany; Albert J. Drouin (Quebec) and Christine Lyman (Albany)

ELDRIDGE,
Herbert, d. 12/20/1953 at 73; b. Ctr. Ossipee; Harrison Eldridge and Laura Eldridge
Malinda Littlefield, d. 12/6/1960 at 80; b. Conway; George Littlefield and Carrie Whitaker
Richard, d. 5/26/2000

ERNST,
Edward Raymond, d. 6/26/1958 at 61; b. Lackawaxen, PA; Raymond Ernst and Mary Warner

EVANS,
Harry Arthur, d. 8/12/1957 at 62; b. Rumney; Elmer Evans and Annie Wescott

EYLA,
Alvina L., d. 9/25/1901 at 1/8/1 in Albany; b. Albany; Lowell L. Eyla (Conway) and Mabel S. Eyla (Conway)
Charles S., d. 10/30/1901 at 28/4/12 in Albany; laborer; married; b. Conway; Everet W. Eyla and Alvina Snow

FLANDERS,
Lucille, d. 2/14/1999

FLINT,
Elizabeth, d. 9/24/1995 at 74; b. MA; Joseph Phelan and Marie Kirlin

FORREST,
Roxanna, d. 4/10/1896 at 58/8/10 in Albany; consumption; housewife; married; b. Westmore, VT

FORUM,
Oscar, d. 1/14/1940 at 76/10/25; b. Copenhagen, Denmark

FOSTER,
Florence, d. 8/25/1947 at 61/3/13; b. Wolfville, NS

FRENCH,
Edelweiss, d. 8/23/1982
Edward, d. 2/19/1986
Phyllis, d. 11/19/2000

FROST,
Elibeous, d. 6/20/1917 at 49/11/3; laborer; married; b. Madison; George W. Frost (NH) and Eliza Mason (NH)
Ethel Hobbs, d. 11/17/1960 at 66; b. Boston, MA; Frank Hobbs and Hattie Eastman

GAGNE,
Cecile, d. 8/17/1999
Wilfred, d. 9/6/2001 in Albany; Frank Gagne and Sohmer Osgood

GANTHIER,
daughter, d. 10/1/1907 at − in Albany; premature birth; b. Albany; John Ganthier (Canada) and Delvina White (Canada)

GAUTHIER,
Joseph, d. 12/28/1908 at − in Albany; accidental - crushed by logs; woodsman; b. Canada

GAY,
Profinda L., d. 12/25/1898 at 29/4 in Albany; septic fever; housewife; married; b. Byron, ME; Gustave Holman (Weld, ME) and Olive Brown (Tamworth)

GENESTRETI,
Gary P., d. 1/28/1994 at 51; b. NH; Bruno Genestreti and Maria Bizzocchi

GENOCK,
Edward P., d. 8/12/1985

GOODWIN,
Katherine A., d. 4/14/1940 at 61/5/29; b. Lowell, MA; Jeremiah Goodwin and Annie Macintire
Philip, d. 12/27/1911 at 43 in Albany; woodsman

GRANDCHAMP,
Calbert, d. 4/2/1909 at 62/9/24 in Albany; lobar pneumonia; section hand; widower; b. Canada

GROSS,
Konrad, d. 8/17/1959 at 1; b. Boston, MA; Rolf W. Gross and Barbara -----

GRUENBERG,
Stephen J., d. 11/26/1987

HAM,
Philene, d. 11/11/1896 at 70/3 in Tamworth; heart failure; housewife; single; b. Albany; James Ham and Nabby Allard

HAMEL,
Eddie, d. 8/15/1908 at – in Albany; ileo colitis; b. Albany; Gideon Hamel (Canada) and Celia Gosslin (Berlin)
Willie, d. 9/26/1908 at – in Albany; pneumonia; b. Albany; Gideon Hamel (Canada) and Celia Gosslin (Berlin)

HAMMOND,
son, d. 7/22/1904 at 0/0/13; pneumonia; b. Albany; Frank O. Hammond (Albany) and Maud Ealey (Conway)
Alfred, Jr., d. 11/7/1898 at 0/5/6 in Albany; convulsions; b. Albany; Alfred A. Hammond (Albany) and Ellen Wiggin (Chatham)
Alfred A., d. 2/3/1941 at 73/6/8 in Albany; Phineas Hammond and Mary Knox
Alton, d. 6/3/1908 at – in Albany; pneumonia; b. Albany; Alfred Hammond (Albany) and Ellen Wiggin (Chatham)
Clyde, d. 9/1/1909 at 7/0/7 in Albany; tubercular meningitis; b. Albany; Frank Hammond (Albany) and Maud Ealy (Conway)
Cora Maybelle, d. 1/25/1965 at 52; b. Conway; Joseph Grandchamp and Louise Eastman
Doris May, d. 3/16/1913 at 3/4/4; b. Albany; Alfred Hammond and Ellen M. Wiggin
Ellen M., d. 4/17/1953 at –; b. Albany; Isaac Wiggin and Leila Haley
Frank Orville, d. 7/16/1957 at 88; b. Albany; Phinias Hammond and Mary -----
Hazree, d. 9/24/1894 at 0/4/22; indigestion; b. Albany; Frank Hammond (Albany) and Maud Early (Conway)

Jessie, d. 5/19/1899 at 19/1 in New York; single; I. Hammond (Albany) and Sarah Ross (Albany)
Mary, d. 5/15/1897 at 55/0/17 in Albany; housewife; married; b. Albany; Barzill Knox (Conway) and Betsy Brown (Albany)
Maud, d. 6/14/1913 at 40/3; married; b. Conway; Everett Ealy and Urna Snow
Milton, d. 7/10/1909 at – in Albany; acute poliomylitis; b. Albany; Frank Hammond (Albany) and Maude Ealy (Conway)
Phineas, d. 1/22/1909 at 75/0/28 in Albany; pernicious enernia; farmer; widower; b. Saco, ME; William Hammond (Ossipee) and Mary Roberts
Sarah E., d. 3/27/1922 at 70/7/3; b. Albany; Eben Ross and Abigail Willey
Sumner W., d. 4/12/1939 at 82/6/27; b. Effingham; Phineas Hammond and Irene Hanson
Victor C., d. 2/15/1983

HARRIMAN,
Azaria, d. 12/30/1914 at 67/4/14; laborer; widower; b. Albany; Ob. Harriman and Hannah Hart
Jacob L., d. 5/4/1900 at 84/11/15 in Albany; farmer; married; William Harriman and Annie Walker

HARRIS,
Debra, d. 11/14/1991 at 28; b. ME; Ronald Guilbault, Sr. and Geraldine Snow

HATFIELD,
George Henry, d. 9/15/1923 at 3/2/12; b. Albany; Joseph E. Hatfield (Canada) and Anna E. Boudeau (Canada)
Walter M., d. 9/21/1923 at 1/11/16; b. Albany; Joseph E. Hatfield (Canada) and Anna E. Boudeau (Canada)

HAYDOCK,
Emma, d. 2/8/1895 at 38 in Albany; housewife; married; Henry Shedron (England)

HEAD,
Alvah, d. 1/23/1917 at 77/7/18; farmer; single; b. Albany; Moses Head (Burton) and Sally Allard (Burton)

Sally, d. 10/8/1895 at 86/1 in Albany; paralysis; housewife; b. Albany; David Allard (Gilmanton) and Annie Allard (Gilmanton)

HEATH,
Urban Ray, d. 8/18/1959 at 58; b. Lincoln; Clarence Heath and Nellie Cotton

HEMPEL,
Shirley S., d. 1/12/1987

HOBBS,
Hattie May, d. 3/7/1962 at 93; b. Norway, ME; John B. Hobbs and Olive S. -----

HODGDON,
Abbie, d. 8/30/1932 at 81/11/28 in Albany; Jonathon Mason (Albany) and Ruth Purrington (Sandwich)
Charles F., d. 3/11/1916 at 64/11/15; farmer; married; b. Albany; George Hodgdon (Ossipee) and Sarah Wallace (Ossipee)
Marguerite M., d. 3/20/1923 at 22/11/15; housewife; married; b. Eaton; Charles Jones (Conway) and Effie Dennett (Conway)
Oliver R., d. 9/2/1908 at – in Albany; glimoa of brain; farmer; single; b. Albany; Charles P. Hodgdon (Ossipee) and Abbie Mason (Albany)
Raymond T., d. 5/8/1938 at 45/9/29; b. Albany; Charles P. Hodgdon and Abbie Mason

HOWE,
Fred B., d. 6/21/1922 at 45/4/6; Benjamin G. Howe and Nancy Chace
John Bernard, d. 8/11/1951 at –; b. Swampscott, MA; Ernest Howe

HUNT,
Alma Chase, d. 8/7/1969 at 81; Edward E. Chase and Myra Crowell; residence - 21 Euclid Ave., Lynn, MA

HURLEY,
David, d. 1/3/1905 at 75/4/6 in Albany; farmer; b. Ireland; Thomas Hurley (Ireland) and Mary Jeffers (Ireland)

IRISH,
Nellie E., d. 1/4/1928 at 66/7/2 in Albany; housewife; married; Charles Barker (Fryeburg, ME) and Edna Barker (Fryeburg, ME)

JENNINGS,
Llewellyn Whitman, d. 6/10/1967 at 61; William Jennings; residence - 197 Carnation St., Pawtucket, RI
Lottie A., d. 2/18/1938 at 50/10/26; b. Mermaid, PEI; Donald MacEachern and Sarah Boyce

JOHNS,
Fred, d. 2/10/1912 at 27 in Albany; woodsman

JOHNSON,
Albert, d. 3/30/1935 at 63/10/18 in Conway
Dawn D., d. 7/13/1985

JONES,
son, d. 9/23/1924 at 0/0/0; b. Albany; Floyd Jones (Madison) and Lula Frost (Madison)

KEITH,
Perley, d. 8/25/1949 at 74/5/21 in Albany; b. Eaton; Edward Keith and Ellen Goldsmith

KINSLOW,
infant, d. 3/14/1943 at –; b. N. Conway; Weldon Kinslow and Irma Morrill
infant, d. 3/14/1943 at –; b. N. Conway; Weldon Kinslow and Irma Morrill

KITE,
Ethel Maud, d. 7/9/1953 at 58; b. England; James Blair and Ann Sparks

KNIGHT,
Phyllis M., d. 10/4/1978 at 62 in Albany; accident on Kancamaugus Highway; residence - Bridgton, ME

KNOX,
Harriet, d. 6/12/1900 at 75/5 in Albany; housewife; widow; b. Albany; Theo Brown (Benton) and Annie Head (Albany)
Mark, d. 10/6/1919 at 70/3/1; single; b. Albany; Joshua Knox (Albany) and Harriet Brown (Albany)
Nathaniel B., d. 6/5/1931 at 63/6/3 in Albany; married; b. New Britain, CT; Charles Knox (Albany) and Ann P. Knox (Hollis, ME)

LABLANC,
Ludivine, d. 10/3/1910 at 0/5/5; b. Albany; Paul LaBlanc (Canada) and L. LaFountain (VT)

LACIK,
Philip, d. 9/25/1914 at 26; laborer; single; b. Russia; Sam Lacik (Russia) and Polaska Delkias (Russia)

LAMPSON,
Guy E., d. 11/11/1918 at 47/7/6; Joseph Lampson

LANE,
Agnes, d. 2/20/1894 at 38; netritac; housewife; married; b. Scotland; James Martin (Scotland) and Margrett ----- (Scotland)
Henry S., d. 1/1/1894 at 48/5/4; consumption; farmer; widower; b. Albany; William Lane (Albany) and Judith Allard (Albany)
Myrtle, d. 8/2/1978 at 59 in Albany
Stephen A., d. 2/28/1949 at 62 in N. Conway; Henry Lane and Agnes Martin

LEAVITT,
Harold, d. 8/8/1989
Nora A., d. 12/4/1982

LEBLANC,
Ida, d. 3/18/1909 at 24 in Albany; pulmonary tuberculosis; single; b. Lewiston, ME; Leon LaBlanc (Canada) and A. Fonguette (Canada)

LEMIENAC,
Mark, d. 12/13/1909 at 22 in Albany; crushed by logs; teamster; single; b. St. Gervais, Canada; George Limienac (St. Anseline) and Aim Marquis (St. Gerras, Canada)

LIPPITT,
Eliphalet, d. 11/14/1921 at 69/4/2; tool sharpener; married; b. Providence, RI; Benoni Lippitt (Smithfield, RI) and Nancy Caesar (Smithfield, RI)

LISTER,
Allen Cameron Scott, d. 4/5/1954 at 72/2/8; b. Boston, MA; Thomas Lister and Margaret Lister

LITTLEFIELD,
Horatio, d. 4/1/1905 at 65/11/18 in Albany; farmer; b. Albany; Samuel Littlefield (Shapleigh, ME) and Polly Chase (Conway)
Laura A., d. 3/10/1924 at 80/6/18; housewife; married; b. Albany; Thomas Shackford (NH) and Polly Mead (Conway)
Samuel, d. 1/13/1926 at 92/11; farmer; widower; b. Albany; Samuel Littlefield (ME) and Polly Chase (Madison)

LORING,
Judith K., d. 12/24/2003 in Albany; Abraham Ash and Irene Melansen

LOVE,
Judith, d. –/–/1893 at 71; paralysis; housewife; Stephen Abbott and Mary Kennett

LYMAN,
Edwin, d. –/–/1981
Hona Blanche, d. 12/4/1976 at 76; coronary occlusion; William E. Manthorn and Bessie Grinton
John, d. 11/11/1960 at 68; b. Albany; Charles E. Lyman and Mary Smith
Mary Ann, d. 9/15/1942 at 68/8/27; John Thibodeau and Angelina Thibodeau
Owen, d. 5/6/1943 at 46/2/7; b. Portsmouth; Charles Lyman and Mary Smith

Sylvia, d. 10/19/1910 at 0/4/21; b. Albany; C. E. Lyman (Albany) and Mary E. Smith (Albany)
Urban, d. 12/26/1969 at 72; Charles E. Lyman and Mary Smith; residence - Albany
Vernon, d. 9/22/1900 at 0/2/23 in Albany; b. Albany; Charles Lyman (Albany) and Mary E. Smith (Albany)

MAILHOT,
Jason, d. 9/19/2003 in N. Conway; Ronald Mailhot and Teresa Fregin

MANUEL,
Gertrude E., d. 10/9/1913 at 0/1/16; b. Conway; Charles O. Manuel and Annie Nickerson

MARKO,
Anthony B., d. 2/21/1992 at 63; b. OH; Adam Marko and Mary Glonek

MARTINELLO,
Philip J., Jr., d. 9/5/1998 in N. Conway; Philip Martinello and Mary English

MASON,
Elijah, d. 7/5/1948 at 67/11/11 in Albany; b. Albany; Elijah Mason (Albany) and Elizabeth Frost (Madison)
Elijah L., d. 4/15/1900 at 51/6/21 in Albany; farmer; married; b. Albany; William Mason (Madison) and Sarah A. Ross (Albany)
Luella, d. 9/28/1965 at 90; b. Wells, ME; Jamaes H. Cheney and Sylvania Merton
Purley E., d. 5/6/1915 at 14/2/25; b. Albany; Elijah Mason (Albany) and Luella Cheney (Wells Beach)
Ruth, d. 12/4/1901 at 85/4/23 in Albany; housewife; widow; b. Alton; Joseph Purrington (Sandwich) and Sally Edgerly (Alton)
Sarah, d. 10/2/1903 at 74/1/20 in Albany; housewife; married; b. Albany; Robert Ross and Martha Ross
William, d. 6/6/1910 at 80/2/15; farmer; widower; b. Albany; David Mason (Madison) and Betsy Head (Albany)

MAYHEW,
James, d. 6/6/1895 at 56/8/7 in Albany; lock jaw; farmer; married; b. England; John Mayhew (England) and Mary A. Mayhew

MAYHUE,
Ida, d. 6/27/1893 at – in Albany; tuberculosis; housewife; b. Tamworth; Jane Smith

McCALLUM,
Bonnie Heather, d. 6/15/1971 at 22; accident on Kancamagus Highway; John McCallum and Gladys L. Brandes; residence - Wexford, PA

McCLAY,
John J., d. 6/27/1987
Muriel A., d. 6/27/1987

McQUESTION,
Gertrude, d. 8/15/1931 at 68 in Albany; teacher; single; b. Plymouth; Henry McQuestion (Plymouth) and Luella Smith (Bath)

MERRILL,
Fred C., d. 5/10/1909 at 59/10/10 in Albany; ac. interstitial nephritis; trapper; married; b. Parsonsfield; Clarke Merrill and Susan
Margaret M., d. 3/4/1896 at 0/6/17 in Albany; convulsions; b. Conway; William A. Merrill and Maud N. Thompson

MITCHELL,
John M., d. 10/4/1978 at 65 in Albany; accident on Kancamaugus Highway; residence - Stamford, CT

MONTCALM,
Margaret, d. 9/10/1897 at 62/5/2 in Albany; housewife; married

MOODY,
Bertha M., d. 6/6/1897 at 1/2/2 in Albany; b. Albany; William Moody (Ossipee) and Mabel Moore (Somersworth)
Charlie, d. 11/25/1894 at 0/0/5; untimely birth; b. Albany; Willie Moody (Ossipee) and Mabel Moore (Great Falls)
Choy, d. 11/14/1895 at 0/0/9 in Albany; Oscar L. Moody (Ossipee) and Mary E. Forrest (Albany)

MOORE,
Edith, d. 9/25/1983
Josephine, d. 5/15/1897 at 21/0/2 in Albany; housewife; married; b. Albany; I. Hammond (Tamworth) and Sarah A. Ross (Albany)

MORENCY,
Rene, d. 1/1/1937 at 27/1/3; b. Holyoke, MA; Frank Morency

MORRILL,
Burton Moses, d. 4/15/1954 at 73; b. N. Berwick, ME; Moses Morrill and Amy Hatch
Ina B., d. 7/11/1981
Louis F., d. 12/28/1940 at 68/3/11; b. Nashua; George Morrill and Mary Bagley
Ruth T., d. 10/14/1998 in Albany

MOULTON,
Marguerite, d. 10/19/1985
Robert H., d. 9/9/1986

MURRAY,
Joanne, d. 5/2/1985

NADWORNY,
Katherine A., d. 9/30/1992 at 72; b. MA; James Blundell and Ida MacMillan

NASON,
Phebe, d. 12/31/1895 at 86/2/7 in Albany; housewife; widow; Jerry Chadburn

NICKERSON,
Archie, d. 3/16/1927 at 61/11/24; farmer; married; b. Tamworth; Alonzo Nickerson (Tamworth) and Mellissa Ham (Albany)
Charles W., d. 10/27/1893 at 0/2/1 in Albany; consumption; b. Albany; William Nickerson and Lillian Littlefield

NORBERG,
Jeffrey E., d. 7/13/1985

O'NEIL,
Robert Newton, d. 6/29/1968 at 70; Edward O'Neil and Lavenia Hinckley; residence - 106 Lawrence St., Medford, MA

OSTWALD,
Axel, d. 11/7/1988

PEARCE,
Nelson L., d. 10/28/1965 at 68; b. Bainbridge, NY; William Pearce and Mathilda Johnson

PELSOR,
Irving, d. 8/4/1983

PHELAN,
Joseph J., d. 2/22/1985

PHELPS,
Clarence, d. 11/24/1995 at 86; b. NH; Harry Phelps and Blanche Stickney

PINGREE,
George William, d. 6/22/1958 at 68; b. Boston, MA; Henry Wood Pingree and Jennie Elizabeth MacInnes

PIPER,
Carl, d. 4/8/1895 at 0/6/6 in Albany; indigestion; b. Albany; Alonzo S. Piper (Albany) and Mary J. Caverly (Barrington)

PLUMMER,
Raymond E., Jr., d. 8/17/1994 at 40; b. NH; Raymond E. Plummer, Sr. and Bernice L. Chase

POTTER,
Harry A., d. 10/10/1936 at 8/6/2; b. Conway; John Philip Potter and Lottie Irish

PRATT,
Mabel, d. 7/30/1981

RANCO,
Margrett, d. 11/9/1999 in N. Conway; Eric Nolan and Myrtle Harriman

RANGER,
Edith L., d. 8/2/1927 at 57/10/22; at home; widow; b. Moultonboro; Luther Colby (Moultonboro) and Nancy Jane Knox (Ossipee)

REED,
Janet R., d. 12/26/1947 at 76/5/7; b. England; John Robinson and Isabel Arrowsmith

REGIN,
Jeseph, d. 12/3/1909 at 19 in Albany; crushed by logs; woodsman; single; b. Canada

RICHARDSON,
Lyle M., d. 12/4/1982

RICKER,
Wilbur, d. 12/2/1900 at – in Albany

RILEY,
Hubert John, d. 8/8/1931 at 31/2/3 in Albany; single; b. Boston, MA; Mary Ward (Ireland)

ROBERGE,
Emile, d. 1/8/1960 at 43; b. Black Lake, PQ; Joseph Roberge and Cezanie Turgeon

ROBINS,
Emma, d. 5/11/1913 at 75; married; b. PEI

ROGERS,
Eunice A., d. 8/4/1910 at 52

ROUSSEAU,
Joseph Henry Edgar, d. 10/29/1973 at 76 in Albany; coronary occlusion; Joseph Rousseau and Mary Rose Busiere; residence - Albany

RUSSELL,
Eliza M., d. 2/21/1905 at 90/2/18 in Albany; housewife; b. Conway; Daniel George (Conway) and Elizabeth Morse (Beacham, VT)
Susan M., d. 1/24/1907 at 78/11/16 in Albany; cerebral tuberculosis; housework; widow; b. Canada; ----- Sawyer and ----- Kimball

SALVAGE,
Nancy E., d. 11/28/1893 at 52/11/2 in Albany; hemorrhage; housewife; b. Albany; J. N. Piper and Martha Young

SANBORN,
A. [male], d. 3/12/1920 at 22/8/14; mechanic; single; b. Chatham; William Sanborn (Stowe, ME) and Etta M. Wiggin (Chatham)
Arthur, d. 10/19/1897 at 0/2 in Albany; b. Conway; Sarah Ryder

SARGENT,
Edward H., d. 2/25/1966 at 60; b. Northampton, MA; James H. Sargent and Mary Davis

SAVAGE,
John D., d. 11/19/1905 at 72 in Albany; cobler

SAVARD,
Phillip L., d. 12/1/1927 at 48; electric light lineman; married; b. Lake St. John, PI; Abel Savard (Canad) and Pauline LeClair (Canada)

SCALETTI,
Brian W., d. 1/29/1992 at 28; b. NH; William Scaletti and Opal Burke

SCHAUR,
Marie Elizabeth, d. 8/2/1951 at 22; b. Pittsburgh, PA; Jacob Schaur and Margaret Reiber

SCHURMAN,
David B., d. 2/22/1992 at 88; b. NH; Joseph Schurman and Annie Badger

SELUKI,
John A., d. 2/19/1915 at 29; woodsman; married; b. Russia

SENIOR,
Constance, d. 1/20/1949 at 52 in Albany; b. Providence; Holmes Winslow and Edith Ainsworth

SHAHEEN,
Joseph, Jr., d. 9/22/1990 at 22; b. Miami, FL; Joseph Saheen, Sr. (sic) and Anna M. Cobb

SHANNON,
Carole A., d. 3/24/2003 in Albany; James Kennedy and Selma Kelly

SHAW,
Emma F., d. 5/12/1914 at 43/7/21; married; Alfred B. Roots and Clara Edwards
Frank E., d. 3/21/1915 at 52/11/1; farmer; widower; b. Saugus, MA; George P. Shaw and Abra C. Clark (Rochester)

SIGMAN,
J. Henry, d. 6/17/1980; residence - Clinton, MA

SMITH,
Alfonzo, d. 5/7/1936 at 80/2/17
Almira, d. 8/14/1912 at 72/4/13; married; b. Conway; Obediah Harriman and Hannah Hart
Daniel E., d. 8/22/1896 at 84/4/29 in Albany; natural causes; farmer; widower; b. Parsonsfield, ME; David Smith and Mary -----
Esther L., d. 10/11/1974 at 83 in Albany; myocardial infarction; Wilfred S. Ball and Cora E. Crittenden; residence - Brookline, MA
Henry H., d. 10/31/1919 at 80/5/16; farmer; b. Albany; Joseph Smith (Waterborough) and Sarah Smith (Waterborough)
John Dana, d. 7/30/1984
Raymond Alpfonso, d. 10/17/1957 at 64; b. Hart's Location; Alfonso Smith and Annette Swain
Susie, d. 12/31/1909 at 34/10/6 in Albany; post-partum hemorrhage; housewife; married; b. Gorham; Henry Goodnow (Gorham) and K. Finnigan (Ireland) (see following entry)
Susie, d. 1/3/1910 at 34/10/6; housewife; married; b. Gorham; Henry Goodnow (Gorham) and K. Finnegan (Ireland) (see preceding entry)

SNODGRASS,
Arthur, d. 9/2/1986

SOULE,
William Gardner, d. 8/9/1973 at 55 on Chocorua Mtn.; coronary occlusion (sudden); William J. Soule and Gladys Garner; residence - Quechee, VT

STAPLES,
Stephen Walter, d. 11/17/1972 at 25; accident on Rte. 16, fractures of cervical spine and skull; Walter Staples and Mildred Goodwin; residence - Bellefontaine, OH

SWAN,
Henry Osgood, d. 11/29/1951 at 50; b. Woodstock, ME; Charles Henry Swan and Ida Swan

SWINSTON,
Benjamin, d. 3/18/1939 at 73/9/1; b. Wolfeboro; James Swinston and ----- Simonds

TASKER,
Elizabeth, d. 12/16/1897 at 80/1/19 in Albany; housewife; widow; b. Porter, ME; Nathaniel Perkins (Woolage, ME) and Betsy Perkins (Kennebunkport)
Jane Smith, d. 3/25/1927 at 73/10/22 in Albany; housewife; widow; Daniel Smith
Stillman P., d. 9/18/1926 at 90/8/19; married; b. Tamworth; Warren Tasker and Elizabeth Perkins (Porter, ME)

TAYLOR,
Robert, d. 5/11/1996

TEWKSBURY,
Sarah L., d. 4/24/1924 at 66/4/0; housewife; widow; b. Salem, MA; David Hurley (Ireland) and Margaretta Murphy (Ireland)

THOMPSON,
Charles Leslie, d. 3/5/1966 at 73; b. Parsonsfield, ME; Lewis R. Thompson and Lucinda Cummings
Hattie N., d. 6/14/1929 at 76/1/1 in Albany; widow; John Hartford

Leroy, d. 12/18/1952 at 80; b. Eaton; Arin Thompson

TYLER,
Jonathan F., d. 2/24/1916 at 73/6/21; farmer; widower; b. Albany; Joseph Tyler and Abigail Allard (Albany)
Susan J., d. 4/5/1914 at 65/11/10; housewife; married; b. Effingham; Phineas Hammond and Irene Hanson

WALKER,
Charles Turner, Jr., d. 10/2/1985

WALZ,
Adolph Raymond, d. 7/7/1969 at 72; Adolph F. Walz and Catherine Bissikummer; residence - Princess Anne, MD

WHITCOMB,
Madeline, d. 4/8/1982

WIGGIN,
Craig W., d. 6/16/2002 in Portsmouth; Ralph Wiggin and June Galanek
Leila F., d. 4/15/1919 at 68/8/19; housewife; widow; b. Brownfield, ME; John Haley

WILKINS,
Franklin H., d. 7/21/1932 at 63/2/1 in Albany; married; b. E. Boston, MA; Romanzo Wilkins (New Ipswich) and Adeline Munroe (Surry)

WILLEY,
Mary, d. 12/25/1906 at 66; housewife; married; b. Jackson; Jonathan Davis (Jackson) and Betsey Gray (Jackson)
Rowena, d. 7/1/1914 at 64/6/19; single; b. Albany; Samuel Willey and Esther Fletcher
Waldo P., d. 9/30/1896 at 23/0/1 in Albany; typhoid fever; quarryman; married; b. Albany; George W. Willey and Mary Davis

WILLIAMS,
Arnold, d. 10/10/1981 in Albany

WOOLLEY,
George Stanley, d. 6/22/1982 in Albany

WRIGHT,
Mary J., d. 3/3/1925 at 52/3/7; housewife; married; b. Boston, MA; Daniel Donovan (Ireland) and Julia Callahan (Ireland)

YOUNG,
Mary, d. 10/9/1997

Other Heritage Books by the author:

Alton, New Hampshire Vital Records, 1890-1997

Barnstead, New Hampshire Vital Records, 1887-2000

Barrington, New Hampshire Vital Records

Dover, New Hampshire Death Records, 1887-1937

Gilmanton, New Hampshire Vital Records, 1887-2001

Marriage Records of Dover, New Hampshire, 1835-1909

Marriage Records of Dover, New Hampshire, 1910-1937

Milton, New Hampshire Vital Records, 1888-1999

Moultonborough, New Hampshire Vital Records

New Castle, New Hampshire Vital Records, 1891-1997

New Hampshire Name Changes, 1768-1923

New Hampshire Name Changes, 1923-1947

Ossipee, New Hampshire Vital Records, 1887-2001

Rochester, New Hampshire Death Records, 1887-1951

Vital Records of Durham, New Hampshire, 1887-2002

Vital Records of Effingham and Freedom, New Hampshire, 1888-2001

Vital Records of Farmington, New Hampshire, 1887-1938

Vital Records of New Durham and Middleton, New Hampshire, 1887-1998

Vital Records of North Berwick, Maine, 1892-2002

Vital Records of Tamworth and Albany, New Hampshire, 1887-2003

Vital Records of Wakefield, New Hampshire, 1887-1998

Wolfeboro, New Hampshire Vital Records, 1887-1999

www.ingramcontent.com/pod-product-compliance
Lightning Source LLC
Chambersburg PA
CBHW051332230426
43668CB00010B/1235